OVER 23,000 COLLECTIBLES LISTED FROM AROUND THE WORLD

STAR WARS

SUPER
COLLECTOR'S
WISH BOOK

IDENTIFICATION & VALUES

Geoffrey T. Carlton

cb

COLLECTOR BOOKS
A Division of Schroeder Publishing Co., Inc.

Front cover:
Chewbacca cookie jar (Star Jars), $200.00; Episode I chess set (Really Useful), $46.00; Han Solo in Carbonite Block, loose piece from 12" figure (Kenner), $7.00; Princess Leia 1999 Portrait Edition (Hasbro), $35.00; "Star Wars Una Nueva Esperanza" board game (Montecarlo), $18.00; Yoda palm talker (Tomy), $45.00; Anakin Skywalker bank (NTD Apparel, Inc.), $18.00; Darth Vader speakerphone (American Telecommunications), $95.00; Jar Jar Binks palm talker (Tomy), $45.00; Star Wars first edition book (Ballantine), $35.00; Star Wars oil lamp (Lamplight Farms, Inc.), $122.00; C-3PO Jedicon 2001 exclusive (Hasbro), $95.00; AT-AT MicroMachines remote control (Galoob), $24.00; Darth Vader, Dagobah with 'Secret Luke' sticker (Hasbro Canada), $35.00; Stormtrooper ceramic box (Sigma), $55.00; C-3PO soap model (Cliro), $18.00; Jawa loose figure (Kenner), $8.00; Star Wars space pen, autographed, limited edition of 200 (Fisher), $70.00; Luke Skywalker loose SSP van (Kenner), $45.00; Hammerhead vintage SW 21-back vintage action figure (Kenner), $193.00; Stormtrooper vintage ROTJ action figure (Kenner), $68.00; Luke Skywalker POTF2 action figure, long saber variation (Kenner), $43.00; Ewoks toy chest (American Toy and Furniture), $125.00; Jango Fett deluxe action figure (Hasbro), $18.00; Naboo Fighter Pop-n-Fun pop-up playhouse (Worlds Apart), $54.00; Frozen Coke cups (Koolee), $10.00 ea.; Sebulba wooden chair (Pipsqueaks), $175.00.

Back cover:
Episode I chess set (Really Useful), $46.00; C-3PO mug (Sigma), $35.00; R2-D2 Transforming Action Set (Ideal), $18.00; Ewok plush toy (Applause), $75.00.

Cover design by Beth Summers
Book design by Beth Ray

COLLECTOR BOOKS
P.O. Box 3009
Paducah, Kentucky 42002-3009
www.collectorbooks.com

Copyright © 2002 Geoffrey T. Carlton

The current values in this book should be used only as a guide. They are not intended to set prices, which vary from one section of the country to another. Auction prices as well as dealer prices vary greatly and are affected by condition as well as demand. Neither the author nor the publisher assumes responsibility for any losses that might be incurred as a result of consulting this guide.

Searching For A Publisher?

We are always looking for people knowledgeable within their fields. If you feel that there is a real need for a book on your collectible subject and have a large comprehensive collection, contact Collector Books.

CONTENTS

Contents

IDENTIFICATION NUMBERS

Identification numbers used in this book are not always sequential and may not appear to have a logical basis to their origin. This guide was originally designed as a software database for Star Wars collectors, and the existing numbering system has been used and cited by individuals for everything from websites and newsletters, to dealer inventory SKUs and insurance property lists. This guide is not a one-shot publication. It will continue to grow, update, backfill, and revise as quickly as data can be accurately obtained. As it evolves, the identifying numbers should remain consistent from publication to publication.

CALCULATING SPECIFIC ITEM VALUE

The values listed are for sealed items, with packaging appearing to be in factory new condition. Items not in factory new condition will be worth less than the stated value. A condition grading scale of 1-10 (C1-C10) may be applied to any item, with 10% being taken off the value of the item for each grade its condition warrants lower than a perfect 10. An item in C8 condition would be worth 80% of the stated value. If an item is listed as "loose," the value is listed for it to be out of its packaging, in C10 condition, and with all parts and accessories included. If an item of interest is loose, C10, and complete, but not priced as "loose" in the guide, it's typically worth about 70% of the stated value. Before purchasing any item at "guide value," the buyer needs to verify that the item is in 100% flawless condition. This guide is a starting point, listing values based upon observation of current sales and other references. Any item is worth as much as it holds in value to the buyer.

TERMS OF ITEM CONDITION

There has been a recent manipulation of classic terms used to describe the condition of an item. Mint in Box (MIB) and Mint on Card (MOC) used to indicate a C10 product in C10 packaging.

Now, however, MIB and MOC indicate no more than that the item is in C10 condition and the box/packaging/card is present. Next came Mint in Sealed Box (MISB) which indicates that the packaging is still under original factory seal but speaks nothing of its condition. A box could be in C4 condition and still have its original cellophane around it. Last came Mint in Mint Box (MIMB) and Mint on Mint Card (MOMC), both indicating a C9 or better condition of packaging, still under factory seal. Be wary of sellers throwing acronyms around. They're a great way to quickly describe items to draw attention to them. Always ask specific questions before buying an item if you don't have the opportunity to inspect it first.

ORGANIZATION OF ITEMS

Instead of grouping various collectibles together into broad categories (Ceramics, Household, Paper Goods, etc.) where you have to guess where to find an item, we have all of the collectibles alphabetized by their specific group. If you want cassettes, flip to the C's. To look up a puzzle, look in the P's. It's as easy to use this book as it is to look up companies in your local yellow-paged phone directory!

REFERENCE PHOTOGRAPHS

Photographs in this guide are included solely for identification purposes and not for reproduction. It is especially important to note that they are not in scale with one another. Two completely different sized collectibles may be printed next to each other and appear in this guide to be the same size. Collectors should view each photo individually and not comparatively.

HISTORICAL DETAILS

Historical information on collectibles in this guide is limited. This guide is intended for those who already have a bookshelf of references and are in need of complete listings with current values.

SUPER COLLECTORS DON'T FEAR "THE DARK YEARS" ANY MORE

The years 1985 through 1994 were "dark years" for die-hard Star Wars collectors. After the merchandising ended from Return of the Jedi, Droids and Ewoks cartoons, and spin-off product lines (C-3PO cereal, etc.), there was a 9-year dry span where only the most enthusiastic of fans were able to keep the faith in the collecting vacuum.

From 1995 to 2000, Star Wars rose quickly to the merchandising forefront again, thanks in part to the Just Toys line of Bend 'Ems, Kenner's retooling of the Power of the Force action figure line, Dark Horse Comics, and Timothy Zahn's *Heir to the Empire* trilogy of novels.

In 1999 a massive wave of Phantom Menace products flooded the market, presenting itself in the avenues of everyday life. Sterile bandages, toothpaste, tennis shoes, toys, games, clothes, dishes, underwear, and almost every other type of item was produced with the universal black-and-red logo of Episode I.

Late 2000 saw a decline in Star Wars merchandising as overproduced lines left discounted shelf-warmers for months as collecting scavengers and scalpers picked and chose which penny-pieces to buy and hold for future value. To the faint-hearted it appeared to be the "dark years" revisited. Stores closed down their Star Wars exclusive aisles in favor of the more profitable Pokémon craze.

Super collectors weren't worried. Unlike in the late 1980s, there was the Internet supply line. Auction sites, dealer sites, collector sites, trade sites, fan sites — searching the web and the newsgroups revealed that almost any Star Wars item, regardless of vintage or scarcity, could be found!

New releases still send collectors rushing back into stores to get the latest item, but then they return to the Internet, conventions, and toy shows to continue their leisurely discovering and buying of new pieces.

Skeptics and outsiders will have you believe that the Star Wars phenomenon will recede again into nostalgia. But we on the inside are still thriving on the 25-year worldwide product base. This guide lists over 23,000 items, and die-hard collectors are still eager to find and acquire them all.

8-TRACK TAPES

RC30001   RC30002   RC30003   RC30005

20th Century Fox
RC30001 Star Wars soundtrack 8.00
RC30002 Story of Star Wars (blue plastic) 12.00
RC30003 Story of Star Wars (gray plastic) 8.00
RC30004 Story of Star Wars (white plastic) 8.00
RC30005 The Empire Strikes back 38.00

ACTION FIGURE ACCESSORIES: POTF2

P2A0001   P2A0002 front and back

Kenner
P2A0001 Binocular freeze frame viewer with 2 exclusive slides 24.00
P2A0002 Freeze frame folder / holder 14.00

ACTION FIGURE ACCESSORIES: TPM

Hasbro
P310009 Battle Bag: Sea Creatures (Angel Fish, Trigger, Soe, Opee Sea Killer) 6.00
P310010 Battle Bag: Sea Creatures (Faa, Colo Claw Fish, Grouper, Sando Aqua Monster) 6.00
P310011 Battle Bag: Swamp Creatures (Mott, Ikopi, Kaadu, Falumpaset).6.00
P310012 Battle Bag: Swamp Creatures (Nuna, Shaak, Pikobis, Fambaa).6.00
P310001 CommTech chip reader .0000.........................20.00
P310002 CommTech chip reader .0000 w/o logo sticker 24.00
P310017 CommTech chip reader .0100.........................12.00
P310018 CommTech chip reader .0100 w/o logo sticker 16.00

P310008   P310007

P310018   P310019

P310009   P310010   P310011   P310012

P310003   P310004   P310005   P310006

P310013   P310014   P310015   P310016

P310020 front and back

P310020 CommTech Chip, model 2, any - cancelled 65.00
P310007 Flash Cannon..14.00
P310019 Gungan Assault Cannon with Jar Jar Binks...............10.00
P310021 Gungan Assault Cannon with Jar Jar Binks, tri-logo packaging13.00
P310008 Gungan Catapult...10.00
P310016 Hyperdrive Repair Kit includes 5 removable panels and 4 tools..25.00
P310003 Naboo Accessories with retracting grappling hook backpack..6.00
P310015 Podracer Fuel Station, fuel dispenser shoots water..................25.00
P310013 Rappel Line Attack with rolling rappel line...........................25.00
P310004 Sith Accessories with firing backpack and 3 droid missiles 6.00
P310005 Tatooine Accessories with pull-back droid............................6.00
P310014 Tatooine Disguise Set with spring-activated attack backpack.25.00
P310006 Underwater Accessories with bubbling backpack.....................6.00

ACTION FIGURE ACCESSORIES: VINTAGE

Kenner
AVA1002 Ewok Assault Catapult, ROTJ pkg. 35.00
AVA1001 Ewok Assault Catapult, loose 15.00
AVA1004 Ewok Combat Glider, ROTJ pkg. 35.00
AVA1003 Ewok Combat Glider, loose 15.00
AVA1005 Radar Laser Cannon, ESB pkg...............................27.00
AVA1007 Radar Laser Cannon, ROTJ pkg..............................18.00
AVA1006 Radar Laser Cannon, loose 8.00
AVA1015 Survival Kit (mail-away offer) 24.00
AVA1008 Tri-Pod Laser Cannon, ESB pkg.............................27.00
AVA1010 Tri-Pod Laser Cannon, ROTJ pkg...........................17.00

AVA1002

AVA1004

AVA1005

AVA1007

AVA1008

AVA1010

AVA1011

AVA1013

AVA1009 Tri-Pod Laser Cannon, loose 8.00
AVA1011 Vehicle Maintenance Energizer, ESB pkg. 33.00
AVA1013 Vehicle Maintenance Energizer, ROTJ pkg. 18.00
AVA1012 Vehicle Maintenance Energizer, loose 12.00

Lili Ledy
AVA1019 Ewok Assault Catapult, ROTJ pkg. 145.00
AVA1018 Ewok Combat Glider, ROTJ pkg. 160.00
AVA1016 Tri-Pod Laser Cannon, ROTJ pkg. 85.00
AVA1017 Vehicle Maintenance Energizer, ROTJ pkg. 72.00

ACTION FIGURE WEAPONS AND ACCESSORIES: VINTAGE

Kenner
Numbers in brackets correspond to images on page 8.
AWA0001 2-1B medical wand (01) 4.00
AWA0003 4-LOM cloak, upholstery cloth 2.00
AWA0004 4-LOM harness, plastic 3.00
AWA0002 4-LOM pistol (21) 5.00
AWA0005 Admiral Ackbar wand (02) 3.00
AWA0006 Amanaman staff (49) 18.00
AWA0007 AT-AT Commander pistol (22) 6.00
AWA0008 AT-AT Driver rifle (31) 6.00
AWA0009 AT-ST Driver pistol (23) 4.00
AWA0010 A-Wing Pilot pistol (23) 4.00
AWA0011 Barada pike (40) 7.00
AWA0012 Ben Kenobi lightsaber 7.00
AWA0013 Bespin Security Guard pistol (22)..............................6.00
AWA0014 Bib Fortuna cloak 2.00
AWA0015 Bib Fortuna staff (36) 3.00
AWA0016 Biker Scout pistol (43) 8.00
AWA0017 Boba Fett pistol (24) 5.00
AWA0018 Bossk rifle (16) 8.00
AWA0019 B-Wing Pilot pistol (23) 4.00
AWA0020 C-3PO w/Removable Limbs plastic net 4.00

AWA0021 Chewbacca crossbow (17)......................................9.00
AWA0022 Chief Chirpa hood (56) 4.00
AWA0023 Chief Chirpa stick (47) 2.00
AWA0024 Cloud Car Pilot communicator (45) 5.00
AWA0025 Cloud Car Pilot pistol (25) 4.00
AWA0027 Darth Vader lightsaber...8.00
AWA0026 Darth Vader vinyl cape 3.00
AWA0028 Death Squad Commander pistol (24) 5.00
AWA0029 Dengar rifle (18) 7.00
AWA0079 Droopy McCool instrument (09) 5.00
AWA0080 Droopy McCool microphone......................................5.00
AWA0030 Emperor walking stick (12) 3.00
AWA0064 Emperor's Royal Guard cloth robe 3.00
AWA0031 Emperor's Royal Guard force pike (37) 4.00
AWA0032 Gamorrean Guard axe (44) 5.00
AWA0033 General Madine pointer 4.00
AWA0034 Greedo pistol (26) 5.00
AWA0035 Hammerhead pistol (24) 5.00
AWA0037 Han Solo Bespin pistol (22) 6.00
AWA0038 Han Solo Hoth pistol (26) 5.00
AWA0039 Han Solo in Carbonite block 28.00
AWA0036 Han Solo pistol (26) 5.00
AWA0040 Han Solo Trench Coat pistol (26) 5.00
AWA0041 IG-88 pistol (24) 5.00
AWA0042 IG-88 rifle (19) 7.00
AWA0043 Imperial Commander pistol (24) 5.00
AWA0044 Imperial Gunner pistol (23) 4.00
AWA0046 Imperial Stormtrooper Hoth Gear rifle (18) 7.00
AWA0045 Imperial Stormtrooper Hoth Gear vinyl apron 3.00
AWA0047 Jawa cloth cape 2.00
AWA0049 Jawa pistol (27) 9.00
AWA0048 Jawa vinyl cape 24.00
AWA0050 Klaatu palace apron...2.00
AWA0051 Klaatu palace pike (41) 4.00
AWA0052 Klaatu skiff pike (39) 6.00
AWA0054 Lando Calrissian General cloth cape 8.00
AWA0055 Lando Calrissian General pistol (28) 7.00
AWA0053 Lando Calrissian pistol (22) 6.00
AWA0056 Lando Calrissian Skiff Guard pike (41) 4.00
AWA0057 Lobot pistol (22) 6.00
AWA0058 Logray helmet 3.00
AWA0059 Logray medicine bag 2.00
AWA0060 Logray staff (48) 2.00
AWA0062 Luke Skywalker Battle Poncho cloth 15.00
AWA0063 Luke Skywalker Battle Poncho pistol (28) 7.00
AWA0065 Luke Skywalker Bespin lightsaber (yellow) (03) 7.00
AWA0066 Luke Skywalker Bespin pistol (26) 5.00
AWA0067 Luke Skywalker Hoth rifle (32) 6.00
AWA0068 Luke Skywalker Jedi cloth robe 4.00
AWA0069 Luke Skywalker Jedi lightsaber (blue) (04) 20.00
AWA0070 Luke Skywalker Jedi lightsaber (green) (05) 8.00
AWA0061 Luke Skywalker lightsaber 9.00
AWA0071 Luke Skywalker Stormtrooper Disguise helmet (55)...........15.00
AWA0072 Luke Skywalker Stormtrooper Disguise pistol (24) 5.00
AWA0073 Luke Skywalker X-Wing Pilot pistol (26) 5.00
AWA0074 Lumat bow (tan) (42) 5.00
AWA0075 Lumat hood (54) 5.00
AWA0076 Lumat pouch..5.00
AWA0077 Max Rebo keyboard (35) 9.00
AWA0081 Nien Nunb pistol (25) 4.00
AWA0082 Nikto staff (40) 7.00
AWA0083 Paploo hood (53) 8.00
AWA0084 Paploo stick (08) 5.00
AWA0087 Princess Leia Bespin pistol (29) 6.00
AWA0088 Princess Leia Boussh helmet (52) 8.00
AWA0089 Princess Leia Boussh rifle (38) 6.00
AWA0090 Princess Leia Combat Poncho cloth 5.00
AWA0091 Princess Leia Combat Poncho pistol (23) 7.00
AWA0092 Princess Leia Hoth pistol (29) 6.00
AWA0085 Princess Leia pistol (29) 6.00
AWA0086 Princess Leia vinyl cape 5.00
AWA0093 Prune Face cloth robe 4.00
AWA0094 Prune Face rifle (33) 4.00
AWA0095 R2-D2 Pop-Up Lightsaber (10).................................21.00
AWA0097 Rancor Keeper gaffi (14) 2.00
AWA0096 Rancor Keeper helmet 3.00
AWA0098 Rebel Commander rifle (32) 6.00
AWA0099 Rebel Commando rifle (34) 8.00
AWA0100 Rebel Soldier pistol (22) 6.00
AWA0101 Ree Yees rifle (13)..8.00
AWA0102 Romba hood...7.00

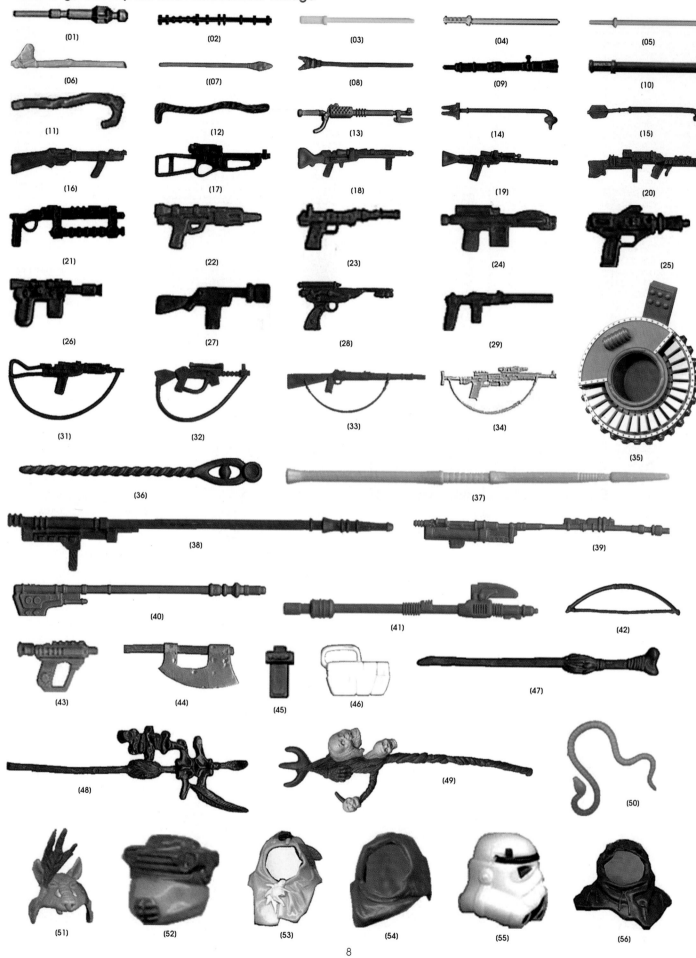

(01) (02) (03) (04) (05)

(06) ((07) (08) (09) (10)

(11) (12) (13) (14) (15)

(16) (17) (18) (19) (20)

(21) (22) (23) (24) (25)

(26) (27) (28) (29)

(31) (32) (33) (34) (35)

(36) (37)

(38) (39)

(40) (41) (42)

(43) (44) (45) (46) (47)

(48) (49) (50)

(51) (52) (53) (54) (55) (56)

AWA0103 Romba spear (07) 8.00
AWA0104 Sand People gaffi stick (15) 9.00
AWA0105 Snaggletooth pistol (26) 5.00
AWA0106 Squidhead cloth robe 2.00
AWA0107 Squidhead pistol (22) 6.00
AWA0108 Star Destroyer Commander pistol (24) 5.00
AWA0109 Stormtrooper pistol (24) 5.00
AWA0078 Sy Snootles microphone 7.00
AWA0110 Teebo helmet (51) 3.00
AWA0111 Teebo pouch 4.00
AWA0112 Teebo stick (06) 3.00
AWA0113 Tie Fighter Pilot pistol (gray) (25) 7.00
AWA0114 Ugnaught case (46) 7.00
AWA0115 Walrus Man pistol (24) 7.00
AWA0118 Warock bow (dark brown) (42) 6.00
AWA0116 Warock hood 5.00
AWA0117 Warock pouch 6.00
AWA0119 Weequay pike (41) 4.00
AWA0120 Wicket hood 7.00
AWA0121 Wicket spear (07) 8.00
AWA0122 Yak Face pike (40) 7.00
AWA0123 Yoda snake (brown) (50) 14.00
AWA0124 Yoda snake (orange) (50) 8.00
AWA0125 Yoda stick (11) 5.00
AWA0126 Zuckuss rifle (20) 9.00

P20326 Anakin Skywalker .00 with lightsaber, green card w/flashback photo 14.00
P20327 Aunt Beru .00 with service droid, green card w/flashback photo .17.00
P20328 C-3PO .00 with removable arm, green card w/flashback photo 11.00
P20356 C-3PO, Jedi-Con 2001 exclusive, ltd. to 2,000 ....95.00
P20093 Darth Vader .0000 with Imperial interrogation droid, green card w/CommTech chip 18.00
P20342 Darth Vader .0000 with Imperial interrogation droid, green card w/CommTech chip (white background chip) 12.00
P20333 Greedo .0000 with blaster, green card w/CommTech chip 9.00
P20339 Greedo .0000 with blaster, green card w/CommTech chip (white background chip) 8.00

In 2001 the Star Wars Fan Club sponsored Jedi-Con in Cologne, Germany.

Hasbro produced 2,000 C-3PO figures in limited edition packaging to commemorate the event.

Jedi-Con coordinators limited distribution of the figure to only 2 per ticket holder, and the figures were fully distributed within hours.

P20356 front and back

ACTION FIGURES: POTF2

Hasbro
P20334 Admiral Motti .0000 with Imperial blaster, green card w/CommTech chip 29.00

| P20334 | P20326 | P20327 | P20093 | P20339 | P20341 | P20340 | P20338 |

| P20336 | P20330 | P20094 | P20337 | P20001 | P20005 | P20006 | P20007 |

| P20008 | P20009 | P20010 | P20012 | P20015 | P20021 | P20023 | P20321 |

| P20109 | P20111 | P20165 | P20029 | P20030 | P20034 | P20036 | P20037 |

P20066 close-up   **P20333 close-up**

CommTech Greedo was assembled with articulation pins molded in two different colors, yellow and blue.

Although the yellow-pinned version was not difficult to find at the beginning of the figure run, the variation wasn't discovered by collectors until after most of them had already been sold.

P20066 Greedo .0000 with blaster, green card w/CommTech chip, yellow pins in knees....................................34.00

P20332 Han Solo .0000 with blaster pistol and holder, green card w/CommTech chip....................................9.00

P20341 Han Solo .0000 with blaster pistol and holder, green card w/CommTech chip (white background chip)...............8.00

P20331 Jawa and "Gonk" droid .0000, green card w/CommTech chip....................................9.00

P20054 Jawa and "Gonk" droid .0000, green card w/CommTech chip (no pegholes in feet)....................................34.00

P20081 Jawa and "Gonk" droid .0000, green card w/CommTech chip (only 1 peghole)....................................55.00

P20340 Jawa and "Gonk" droid .0000, green card w/CommTech chip (white background chip)....................................8.00

P20329 Luke Skywalker .0000 with T16 Skyhopper model, green card w/CommTech chip....................................9.00

P20338 Luke Skywalker .0000 with T16 Skyhopper model, green card w/CommTech chip (white background chip)...............8.00

P20336 Princess Leia .0000 with sporting blaster, green card w/CommTech chip....................................26.00

P20355 R2-D2 .0000 with holographic Princess Leia round foot pegs, green card w/CommTech chip....................................370.00

P20330 R2-D2 .0000 with holographic Princess Leia, green card w/CommTech chip....................................28.00

CommTech chips were originally produced with a foil/holographic background behind the character picture.

Figures produced in later runs had CommTech chips with white backgrounds.

Some figures were produced during the change-over, making them available with both styles of chip.

P20094 Stormtrooper .0000 with battle damage and blaster rifle rack, green card w/CommTech chip....................................22.00

P20343 Stormtrooper .0000 with battle damage and blaster rifle rack, green card w/CommTech chip (white background chip)...............18.00

P20337 Wuher .0000 with droid detector unit, green card w/CommTech chip....................................26.00

Kenner

P20001 2-1B Medic Droid .00 with medical diagnostic computer, col. 2, green card w/hologram....................................14.00

P20002 2-1B Medic Droid .00 with medical diagnostic computer, col. 2, green card w/picture....................................12.00

P20004 2-1B Medic Droid .01 with medical diagnostic computer, col. 2, green card w/hologram, new bubble....................................10.00

P20003 2-1B Medic Droid .01 with medical diagnostic computer, col. 2, green card w/hologram, old bubble....................................12.00

P20005 4-LOM .00 with blaster pistol and blaster rifle, col. 2, green card w/hologram....................................16.00

P20006 8D8 .00 with droid branding device, col. 2, green card w/freeze frame....................................12.00

P20007 Admiral Ackbar .00 with comlink wrist blaster, col. 2, green card w/hologram....................................10.00

P20008 Admiral Ackbar .01 with comlink wrist blaster, col. 2, green card w/freeze frame....................................12.00

P20009 ASP-7 Droid .00 with spaceport supply rods, col. 2, green card w/hologram....................................11.00

P20010 AT-AT Driver .00 with Imperial issue blaster, col. 3, green card w/freeze frame, Fan Club exclusive....................................27.00

P20012 AT-ST Driver .00 with blaster rifle and pistol, col. 2, green card w/hologram....................................14.00

P20011 AT-ST Driver .00 with blaster rifle and pistol, col. 2, green card w/picture....................................15.00

P20013 AT-ST Driver .02 with blaster rifle and pistol, col. 3, green card w/hologram, old bubble....................................9.00

P20014 AT-ST Driver .02 with blaster rifle and pistol, col. 3, green card w/hologram....................................7.00

P20015 AT-ST Driver .03 with blaster rifle and pistol, col. 3, green card w/freeze frame....................................89.00

P20017 Ben (Obi-Wan) Kenobi .00 with lightsaber and removable cloak, orange card w/picture (long saber; close-up photo; brown belt)....................................56.00

P20016 Ben (Obi-Wan) Kenobi .00 with lightsaber and removable cloak, orange card w/picture (long saber; close-up photo; gold belt)....................................62.00

P20321 Ben (Obi-Wan) Kenobi .00 with lightsaber, green card w/flashback photo....................................10.00

P20020 Ben (Obi-Wan) Kenobi .01 with lightsaber and removable cloak, orange card w/hologram (short saber)....................................18.00

P20018 Ben (Obi-Wan) Kenobi .01 with lightsaber and removable cloak, orange card w/picture (long saber)....................................60.00

P20021 Ben (Obi-Wan) Kenobi .01 with lightsaber and removable cloak, orange card w/picture (short saber; brown belt)....................................16.00

P20019 Ben (Obi-Wan) Kenobi .01 with lightsaber and removable cloak, orange card w/picture (short saber; gold belt)....................................18.00

P20023 Ben (Obi-Wan) Kenobi .02 with lightsaber and removable cloak, col. 1, green card w/hologram, new bubble (short saber)....................................8.00

P20022 Ben (Obi-Wan) Kenobi .02 with lightsaber and removable cloak, col. 1, green card w/hologram, old bubble (short saber)....................................12.00

P20024 Ben (Obi-Wan) Kenobi .02 with lightsaber and removable cloak, col. 1, green card w/picture, new bubble (short saber)....................................8.00

P20109 Bespin Han Solo .00 with heavy assault rifle and blaster, col. 1, green card w/hologram....................................7.00

P20110 Bespin Han Solo .00 with heavy assault rifle and blaster, col. 1, green card w/picture....................................7.00

P20111 Bespin Han Solo .01 with heavy assault rifle and blaster pistol, col. 1, green card w/freeze frame....................................24.00

P20112 Bespin Han Solo .02 with heavy assault rifle and blaster pistol, col. 1, green card w/freeze frame....................................9.00

P20165 Bespin Luke Skywalker .00 with lightsaber and blaster pistol, col. 1, green card w/freeze frame....................................34.00

P20166 Bespin Luke Skywalker .01 with lightsaber and blaster pistol, col. 1, green card w/freeze frame....................................11.00

P20027 Bib Fortuna .00 with hold-out blaster, col. 1, green card w/hologram....................................16.00

P20029 Bib Fortuna .01 with hold-out blaster, col. 2, green card w/hologram, new bubble....................................10.00

P20028 Bib Fortuna .01 with hold-out blaster, col. 2, green card w/hologram, old bubble....................................12.00

P20030 Biggs Darklighter .00 with blaster pistol, col. 2, green card w/freeze frame....................................20.00

P20031 Boba Fett .00 with sawed-off blaster rifle and jet pack, orange card w/picture (half circles on hands; "Empire" on bio)....................................93.00

P20032 Boba Fett .01 with sawed-off blaster rifle and jet pack, orange card w/picture (half circles on hands; "Empire" on bio)....................................73.00

P20034 Boba Fett .01 with sawed-off blaster rifle and jet pack, orange card w/picture....................................19.00

P20033 Boba Fett .01 with sawed-off blaster rifle and jet pack, orange card w/picture (no circle on one hand)....................................325.00

P20055 Boba Fett .01 with sawed-off blaster rifle and jet pack, orange card w/picture (no circles or chest emblem)....................................725.00

P20035 Boba Fett .02 with sawed-off blaster rifle and jet pack, col. 1, green card w/hologram....................................34.00

P20036 Boba Fett .03 with sawed-off blaster rifle and jet pack, col. 3, green card w/hologram....................................28.00

P20350 Boba Fett .03 with sawed-off blaster rifle and jet pack, col. 3, green card w/picture....................................28.00

P20037 Boba Fett .04 with sawed-off blaster rifle and jet pack, col. 3, green card w/freeze frame ("Imprisioned" on slide)....................................48.00

P20040 Bossk .00 with blaster rifle and pistol, col. 2, green card w/hologram, new bubble....................................7.00

P20039 Bossk .00 with blaster rifle and pistol, col. 2, green card w/hologram, old bubble....................................15.00

P20038 Bossk .00 with blaster rifle and pistol, col. 2, green card w/picture....................................14.00

P20042 Bossk .01 with blaster rifle and pistol, col. 2, green card w/hologram, new bubble....................................13.00

P20041 Bossk .01 with blaster rifle and pistol, col. 2, green card w/hologram, old bubble....................................14.00

P20046 C-3PO .00 with realistic metalized body and cargo net, col. 1, green card w/freeze frame 12.00
P20043 C-3PO .00 with realistic metalized body, orange card w/picture 14.00
P20045 C-3PO .01 with realistic metalized body, col. 1, green card w/hologram, new bubble 16.00
P20044 C-3PO .01 with realistic metalized body, col. 1, green card w/hologram, old bubble 18.00
P20103 Captain Piett .00 with blaster pistol and baton, col. 3, green card w/freeze frame 72.00
P20047 Captain Piett .00 with blaster rifle and pistol, col. 3, green card w/freeze frame 25.00

Capatin Piett's accessories were originally labeled "Blaster Rifle and Pistol." Toward the end of the run, the sticker was changed to a more accurate "Blaster Pistol and Baton."

Because this change was made so late in production, there are significantly fewer figures with the corrected sticker.

P20047 close-up   **P20103 close-up**

P20048 Chewbacca .00 with bowcaster and heavy blaster rifle, orange card w/picture 17.00
P20318 Chewbacca .00 with bowcaster rifle, green card w/flashback photo 10.00
P20050 Chewbacca .01 with bowcaster and heavy blaster rifle, col. 1, green card w/hologram, new bubble 8.00
P20049 Chewbacca .01 with bowcaster and heavy blaster rifle, col. 1, green card w/hologram, old bubble 9.00
P20051 Chewbacca .01 with bowcaster and heavy blaster rifle, col. 1, green card w/picture, new bubble.....................8.00
P20053 Chewbacca as Boushh's Bounty .00 with bowcaster, col. 1, green card w/freeze frame 20.00
P20052 Chewbacca in bounty hunter disguise .00 with vibro axe and heavy blaster rifle, purple card w/hologram 14.00
P20056 Clone Emperor Palpatine .02 from Dark Empire comics, col. 2, green card w/EU picture 23.00
P20323 Dark Trooper .01 from Dark Forces video game, col. 2, green card w/EU picture 30.00
P20058 Darth Vader .00 with lightsaber and removable cape, orange card w/picture (long saber) 35.00
P20057 Darth Vader .00 with lightsaber and removable cape, orange card w/picture (short saber / long tray) 48.00
P20059 Darth Vader .00 with lightsaber and removable cape, orange card w/picture (short saber) 16.00
P20060 Darth Vader .00 with lightsaber and removable cape, orange card w/picture (tiny saber) 18.00
P20320 Darth Vader .00 with lightsaber, green card w/flashback photo16.00
P20061 Darth Vader .01 with lightsaber and removable cape, col. 1, green card w/hologram 17.00
P20063 Darth Vader .02 with lightsaber and removable cape, col. 3, green card w/hologram, new bubble 9.00
P20064 Darth Vader .02 with lightsaber and removable cape, col. 3, green card w/hologram, new bubble (Shadows of the Empire 2-pack pose) 190.00

The SOTE pose Darth Vader has two very distinguishing characteristics. There are depressions in the bubble to accommodate the feet, and the lightsaber is raised in the bubble due to the up-flip of Vader's cape.

The SOTE Vader was produced as a Collection 3, .02 figure, which is the same designation as the regular Vader.

P20063 close-up   **P20064 close-up**

P20062 Darth Vader .02 with lightsaber and removable cape, col. 3, green card w/hologram, old bubble 11.00

P20354 Darth Vader .02 with lightsaber and removable cape, col. 3, green card w/picture, new bubble 12.00
P20065 Darth Vader .03 with lightsaber and removable cape, col. 3, green card w/freeze frame 26.00
P20068 Darth Vader with removable helmet .00 and lightsaber, col. 3, green card w/freeze frame (1 blue and 1 red button on chestplate)............42.00
P20067 Darth Vader with removable helmet .00 and lightsaber, col. 3, green card w/freeze frame (2 blue buttons on chestplate)............46.00
P20069 Dash Rendar .00 with heavy blaster pack, purple card w/hologram 19.00
P20313 Death Star Droid .00 with Mouse Droid, col. 2, green card w/freeze frame, Fan Club exclusive 28.00
P20070 Death Star Gunner .00 with radiation suit and blaster pistol, col. 1, orange card w/picture 25.00
P20072 Death Star Gunner .01 with Imperial blaster and assault rifle, col. 1, green card w/hologram 12.00
P20071 Death Star Gunner .01 with Imperial blaster and assault rifle, col. 1, green card w/picture 14.00
P20074 Death Star Gunner .02 with Imperial blaster and assault rifle, col. 3, green card w/hologram, new bubble 10.00
P20073 Death Star Gunner .02 with Imperial blaster and assault rifle, col. 3, green card w/hologram, old bubble 12.00
P20075 Death Star Trooper .00 with blaster rifle, col. 3, green card w/freeze frame 28.00
P20076 Dengar .00 with blaster rifle, col. 2, green card w/hologram 16.00
P20314 Emperor Palpatine .00 with Force lightning, green card w/flashback photo 16.00
P20077 Emperor Palpatine .00 with walking stick, col. 1, green card w/hologram 14.00
P20079 Emperor Palpatine .01 with walking stick, col. 3, green card w/hologram, new bubble 7.00
P20078 Emperor Palpatine .01 with walking stick, col. 3, green card w/hologram, old bubble 8.00
P20352 Emperor Palpatine .01 with walking stick, col. 3, green card w/picture, new bubble 8.00
P20080 Emperor Palpatine .02 with walking stick, col. 3, green card w/freeze frame 8.00
P20082 Emperor's Royal Guard .00 with force pike, col. 3, green card w/hologram 18.00
P20348 Emperor's Royal Guard .00 with force pike, col. 3, green card w/picture 16.00
P20083 Emperor's Royal Guard .01 with force pike, col. 3, green card w/freeze frame 26.00
P20084 Endor Rebel Soldier .00 with survival backpack and blaster rifle, col. 1, green card w/freeze frame 21.00
P20085 Endor Rebel Soldier .01 with survival backpack and blaster rifle, col. 1, green card w/freeze frame 7.00
P20086 EV-9D9 .00 with datapad, col. 2, green card w/hologram 12.00
P20087 EV-9D9 .01 with datapad, col. 2, green card w/freeze frame 17.00
P20088 Ewoks:Wicket & Logray .00 staff, medicine pouch and spear, col. 2, green card w/freeze frame 22.00
P20089 Gamorrean Guard .00 with vibro axe, col. 2, green card w/hologram 10.00
P20090 Gamorrean Guard .01 with vibro axe, col. 2, green card w/freeze frame 17.00
P20091 Garindan (Long Snoot) .00 with hold-out pistol .00 col. 3, green card w/hologram 9.00
P20351 Garindan (Long Snoot) .00 with hold-out pistol .00 col. 3, green card w/picture 7.00
P20092 Garindan .01 with hold-out pistol, col. 3, green card w/freeze frame 26.00
P20095 Grand Admiral Thrawn .02 from Heir To The Empire novel, col. 2, green card w/EU picture..............................26.00
P20096 Grand Moff Tarkin .00 with Imperial issue blaster rifle and pistol, col. 2, green card w/hologram 36.00
P20098 Grand Moff Tarkin .01 with Imperial issue blaster rifle and pistol, col. 3, green card w/hologram 8.00
P20097 Grand Moff Tarkin .01 with Imperial issue blaster rifle and pistol, col. 3, green card w/picture 8.00
P20099 Grand Moff Tarkin .02 with Imperial blaster rifle and pistol, col. 3, green card w/freeze frame 14.00
P20100 Greedo .00 with Rodarian blaster rifle, col. 1, orange card w/picture 24.00
P20102 Greedo .01 with blaster pistol, col. 1, green card w/hologram...10.00
P20101 Greedo .01 with blaster pistol, col. 1, green card w/picture 10.00
P20104 Han Solo .00 with heavy assault rifle and blaster, orange card w/picture 16.00
P20106 Han Solo .01 with heavy assault rifle and blaster, col. 1, green card w/hologram, new bubble 8.00
P20105 Han Solo .01 with heavy assault rifle and blaster, col. 1, green card w/hologram, old bubble 12.00

P20039

P20043

P20044

P20047

P20048

P20051

P20318

P20046

P20053

P20052

P20056

P20323

P20059

P20063

P20065

P20320

P20068

P20069

P20313

P20070

P20071

P20075

P20076

P20077

P20080

P20314

P20082

P20083

P20084

P20086

P20087

P20088

P20089

P20090

P20091

P20092

P20095

P20098

P20099

P20100

P20107 Han Solo .01 with heavy assault rifle and blaster, col. 1, green card w/picture, new bubble 8.00
P20108 Han Solo .02 with blaster pistol, col. 1, green card w/freeze frame .18.00
P20113 Han Solo in carbonite .00 with carbonite freezing chamber, orange card w/picture 18.00
P20115 Han Solo in carbonite .01 block, orange card w/picture 12.00

P20117 Han Solo in carbonite .02 with carbonite block, col. 2, green card w/hologram, new bubble...................................8.00
P20116 Han Solo in carbonite .02 with carbonite block, col. 2, green card w/hologram, old bubble...................................10.00
P20118 Han Solo in carbonite .03 with carbonite block, col. 1, green card w/hologram 8.00

P20102   P20113   P20117   P20120   P20123   P20125   P20344   P20130

P20104   P20106   P20108   P20132   P20136   P20138   P20139   P20140

P20142   P20197   P20201   P20310   P20145   P20154   P20157   P20150

P20147   P20148   P20237   P20239   P20158   P20162   P20164   P20168

P20170   P20171   P20177   P20180   P20181   P20184   P20187   P20192

Action Figures: POTF2

P20113

P20115

The carbonite frozen Han originally stated that it came with a "Carbonite Freezing Chamber."

Kenner quickly corrected its description of the accessory to a "Carbonite block."

P20119 Han Solo in carbonite .03 with carbonite block, col. 1, green card w/picture...8.00
P20120 Han Solo in carbonite .04 with carbonite block, col. 1, green card w/freeze frame...22.00
P20121 Han Solo in carbonite .05 with carbonite block, col. 1, green card w/freeze frame...10.00
P20123 Han Solo in Endor gear .00 with blaster pistol, col. 1, green card w/hologram, new bubble.....................................10.00
P20122 Han Solo in Endor gear .00 with blaster pistol, col. 1, green card w/hologram, old bubble.....................................14.00
P20124 Han Solo in Endor gear .00 with blaster pistol, col. 1, green card w/picture, new bubble.......................................10.00
P20125 Han Solo in Endor gear .00 with blaster pistol, col. 1, green card w/picture, new bubble (brown pants).................18.00
P20127 Han Solo in Endor gear .01 with blaster pistol, col. 1, green card w/freeze frame (gun in pkg.)...........................14.00
P20126 Han Solo in Endor gear .01 with blaster pistol, col. 1, green card w/freeze frame (gun on side)...........................15.00
P20344 Han Solo in Endor gear .02 with blaster pistol, col. 1, green card w/freeze frame...10.00
P20130 Han Solo in Hoth gear .00 with blaster pistol and assault rifle, orange card w/picture (closed right hand)..............28.00
P20128 Han Solo in Hoth gear .00 with blaster pistol and assault rifle, orange card w/picture (open right hand; blue visor)....14.00
P20129 Han Solo in Hoth gear .00 with blaster pistol and assault rifle, orange card w/picture (open right hand; white visor).....30.00

P20128 close-up

P20130 close-up

In the original release, Hoth Han's right hand was sculpted wide open, preventing him from being able to hold either of his accessories.

A quick re-sculpt fixed the problem and gave super collectors another variation to search out.

P20132 Hoth Rebel Soldier .00 with survival backpack and blaster rifle, col. 2, green card w/hologram...............................12.00
P20131 Hoth Rebel Soldier .00 with survival backpack and blaster rifle, col. 2, green card w/picture.................................12.00
P20134 Hoth Rebel Soldier .01 with survival backpack and blaster rifle, col. 1, green card w/hologram, new bubble.............8.00
P20133 Hoth Rebel Soldier .01 with survival backpack and blaster rifle, col. 1, green card w/hologram, old bubble............12.00
P20135 Hoth Rebel Soldier .02 with survival backpack and blaster rifle, col. 1, green card w/freeze frame.....................24.00
P20136 Hoth Rebel Soldier .03 with survival backpack and blaster rifle, col. 1, green card w/freeze frame.......................7.00
P20138 Imperial Sentinel .01 from Dark Empire comics, col. 2, green card w/EU picture...24.00
P20139 Ishi Tib .00 with blaster rifle, col. 3, green card w/freeze frame ...25.00
P20140 Jawas .00 with glowing eyes and ionization blasters, col. 2, orange card w/picture...27.00
P20142 Jawas .01 with glowing eyes and blaster pistols, col. 2, green card w/hologram...16.00
P20141 Jawas .01 with glowing eyes and blaster pistols, col. 2, green card w/picture...14.00

P20143 Jawas .02 with glowing eyes and blaster pistols, col. 2, green card w/hologram, old bubble.....................................16.00
P20144 Jawas .02 with glowing eyes and blaster pistols, col. 2, green card w/hologram..14.00
P20197 Jedi Knight Luke Skywalker .00 with lightsaber and removable cloak, orange card w/picture (black vest)..................16.00
P20195 Jedi Knight Luke Skywalker .00 with lightsaber and removable cloak, orange card w/picture (tan vest; "innie" saber)....74.00
P20196 Jedi Knight Luke Skywalker .00 with lightsaber and removable cloak, orange card w/picture (tan vest; "outie" saber)....78.00
P20200 Jedi Knight Luke Skywalker .01 with lightsaber and removable cloak, col. 2, green card w/hologram........................27.00
P20199 Jedi Knight Luke Skywalker .01 with lightsaber and removable cloak, col. 2, green card w/picture...........................25.00
P20202 Jedi Knight Luke Skywalker .02 with lightsaber and removable cloak, col. 1, green card w/picture.............................9.00
P20201 Jedi Knight Luke Skywalker .02, with lightsaber and removable cloak, col. 1, green card w/hologram..........................9.00
P20310 Kyle Katarn .02 from Dark Forces video game, col. 2, green card w/EU picture...26.00
P20145 Lak Sivrak .00 with blaster pistol and vibro blade, col. 2, green card w/freeze frame...22.00
P20146 Lak Sivrak .01 with blaster pistol and vibro blade, col. 2, green card w/freeze frame...18.00
P20147 Lando Calrissian .00 with heavy rifle and blaster pistol, orange card w/picture...9.00
P20148 Lando Calrissian .01 with heavy rifle and blaster pistol, col. 1, green card w/hologram (wholesale club ESB 3-pack)....51.00
P20153 Lando Calrissian .00 as skiff guard with skiff guard force pike, col. 1, green card w/hologram (silver circle)..............10.00
P20155 Lando Calrissian .00 as skiff guard with skiff guard force pike, col. 1, green card w/hologram, new bubble (gold circle)....11.00
P20154 Lando Calrissian .00 as skiff guard with skiff guard force pike, col. 1, green card w/hologram, old bubble (gold circle)....12.00
P20156 Lando Calrissian .01 as skiff guard with skiff guard force pike, col. 1, green card w/freeze frame..........................23.00
P20157 Lando Calrissian .02 as skiff guard with skiff guard force pike, col. 1, green card w/freeze frame...........................9.00
P20149 Lando Calrissian .00 in General's gear with blaster pistol, col. 1, green card w/freeze frame (1 sticker on bubble)......19.00
P20150 Lando Calrissian .00 in General's gear with blaster pistol, col. 1, green card w/freeze frame (2 stickers on bubble)....23.00
P20151 Lando Calrissian .01 in General's gear with blaster pistol, col. 1, green card w/freeze frame (1 sticker on bubble).......9.00
P20152 Lando Calrissian .01 in General's gear with blaster pistol, col. 1, green card w/freeze frame (2 stickers on bubble).....9.00
P20237 Leia in Boushh disguise .00 blaster rifle and bounty hunter helmet, purple card w/hologram.............................12.00
P20238 Leia in Boushh disguise .02 with blaster rifle and bounty hunter helmet, col. 1, green card w/hologram, new bubble (wholesale club ROTJ 3-pack).......................................24.00
P20239 Leia in Boushh disguise .02 with blaster rifle and bounty hunter helmet, col. 1, green card w/hologram, old bubble........18.00
P20240 Leia in Boushh disguise .02 with blaster rifle and bounty hunter helmet, col. 1, green card w/picture, old bubble 17.00
P20158 Lobot .00 with blaster pistol and transmitter, col. 1, green card w/freeze frame..10.00
P20159 Luke Skywalker .00 with grappling hook blaster and lightsaber, orange card w/picture (long saber; with eyebrows)............40.00
P20160 Luke Skywalker .00 with grappling hook blaster and lightsaber, orange card w/picture (long saber; without eyebrows)........43.00
P20162 Luke Skywalker .00 with grappling hook blaster and lightsaber, orange card w/picture (short saber)..........................16.00
P20161 Luke Skywalker .00 with grappling hook blaster and lightsaber, orange card w/picture (short saber; long tray)............235.00
P20164 Luke Skywalker .01 from Dark Empire comics, col. 2, green card w/EU picture...22.00
P20167 Luke Skywalker in ceremonial outfit .00 with medal of valor and blaster pistol, col. 2, green card w/hologram..............40.00
P20170 Luke Skywalker in ceremonial outfit .01 with blaster pistol, col. 1, green card w/freeze frame................................12.00
P20168 Luke Skywalker in ceremonial outfit .01 with medal of valor and blaster pistol, col. 1, green card w/hologram..............9.00
P20169 Luke Skywalker in ceremonial outfit .01 with medal of valor and blaster pistol, col. 1, green card w/picture................9.00
P20171 Luke Skywalker in Dagobah fatigues .00 with lightsaber and blaster pistol, orange card w/picture (long saber)...........32.00
P20173 Luke Skywalker in Dagobah fatigues .00 with lightsaber and blaster pistol, orange card w/picture (short saber)..........14.00
P20172 Luke Skywalker in Dagobah fatigues .00 with lightsaber and blaster pistol, orange card w/picture (short saber; long tray) 32.00

P20174 Luke Skywalker in Dagobah fatigues .00 with lightsaber and blaster pistol, orange card w/picture (tiny saber) 16.00
P20175 Luke Skywalker in Dagobah fatigues .00 with lightsaber and blaster pistol, orange card w/picture, new bubble (wholesale club ESB 3-pack)...27.00
P20177 Luke Skywalker in Hoth gear .00 with blaster pistol and lightsaber, col. 2, green card w/hologram 15.00
P20176 Luke Skywalker in Hoth gear .00 with blaster pistol and lightsaber, col. 2, green card w/picture 13.00
P20179 Luke Skywalker in Hoth gear .01 with blaster pistol and lightsaber, col. 1, green card w/hologram, new bubble....................10.00
P20178 Luke Skywalker in Hoth gear .01 with blaster pistol and lightsaber, col. 1, green card w/hologram, old bubble....................12.00
P20180 Luke Skywalker in Imperial disguise .00 with taser staff weapon, purple card w/hologram 21.00
P20181 Luke Skywalker in Stormtrooper disguise .00 with Imperial issue blaster, col. 2, orange card w/picture 35.00
P20183 Luke Skywalker in Stormtrooper disguise .01 with Imperial issue blaster, col. 2, green card w/hologram 16.00
P20182 Luke Skywalker in Stormtrooper disguise .01 with Imperial issue blaster, col. 2, green card w/picture 16.00
P20185 Luke Skywalker in Stormtrooper disguise .02 with Imperial issue blaster, col. 1, green card w/hologram, new bubble....................10.00
P20184 Luke Skywalker in Stormtrooper disguise .02 with Imperial issue blaster, col. 1, green card w/hologram, old bubble....................12.00
P20186 Luke Skywalker in Stormtrooper disguise .02 with Imperial issue blaster, col. 1, green card w/hologram, new bubble....................10.00
P20187 Luke Skywalker in Stormtrooper disguise .03 with Imperial blaster, col. 1, green card w/freeze frame....................26.00
P20188 Luke Skywalker in Stormtrooper disguise .04 with Imperial blaster, col. 1, green card w/freeze frame....................12.00
P20189 Luke Skywalker in X-wing fighter pilot gear .00 with lightsaber and blaster pistol, orange card w/picture (long saber)....................28.00
P20190 Luke Skywalker in X-wing fighter pilot gear .01 with lightsaber and blaster pistol, orange card w/picture (long saber)....................25.00
P20192 Luke Skywalker in X-wing fighter pilot gear .01 with lightsaber and blaster pistol, orange card w/picture (short saber)....................15.00
P20191 Luke Skywalker in X-wing fighter pilot gear .01 with lightsaber and blaster pistol, orange card w/picture (short saber; long tray)....................26.00
P20194 Luke Skywalker in X-wing fighter pilot gear .02 with lightsaber and blaster pistol, col. 1, green card w/hologram, new bubble....................15.00

P20193 Luke Skywalker in X-wing fighter pilot gear .02 with lightsaber and blaster pistol, col. 1, green card w/hologram, old bubble....................18.00
P20198 Luke Skywalker Jedi Knight .00 Theater Edition .00, green card w/Special Logo 115.00
P20203 Luke Skywalker with blast shield helmet .00 and lightsaber, col. 1, green card w/freeze frame....................14.00
P20319 Luke Skywalker with blaster rifle .00 and electrobinoculars, green card w/flashback photo....................8.00
P20204 Malakili (Rancor Keeper) .00 with long-handled vibro-blade, col. 2, green card w/hologram 10.00
P20205 Malakili (Rancor Keeper) .01 with long-handled vibro-blade, col. 2, green card w/freeze frame....................14.00
P20209 Mara Jade .03 from *Heir to the Empire* novel, col. 2, green card w/EU picture....................26.00
P20210 Momaw Nadon "Hammerhead" .00 with double-barreled blaster rifle, col. 2, orange card w/picture....................22.00
P20212 Momaw Nadon "Hammerhead" .01 with double-barreled blaster rifle, col. 2, green card w/hologram....................14.00
P20211 Momaw Nadon "Hammerhead" .01 with double-barreled blaster rifle, col. 2, green card w/picture....................14.00
P20213 Mon Mothma .00 with baton, col. 1, green card w/freeze frame 14.00
P20214 Nien Nunb .00 with blaster pistol and blaster rifle, col. 2, green card w/hologram....................9.00
P20215 Nien Nunb .01 with blaster pistol and rifle, col. 2, green card w/freeze frame....................18.00
P20025 Obi-Wan (Ben) Kenobi .03 with lightsaber, col. 1, green card w/freeze frame (short saber)....................27.00
P20026 Obi-Wan (Ben) Kenobi .04 with lightsaber, col. 1, green card w/freeze frame (short saber)....................19.00
P20216 Orrimaarko (Prune Face) .00 with blaster rifle, col. 1, green card w/freeze frame....................12.00
P20218 Ponda Baba .00 with blaster pistol and rifle, col. 2, green card w/hologram (black beard)....................42.00
P20217 Ponda Baba .00 with blaster pistol and rifle, col. 2, green card w/hologram (gray beard)....................56.00
P20220 Ponda Baba .01 with blaster pistol and rifle, col. 3, green card w/hologram (black beard)....................8.00
P20219 Ponda Baba .01 with blaster pistol and rifle, col. 3, green card w/hologram (gray beard)....................24.00

P20194   P20198   P20203   P20319   P20204   P20205   P20209   P20210

P20212   P20213   P20214   P20215   P20026   P20216   P20220   P20221

P20222   P20317   P20236   P20244   P20224   P20228   P20230   P20231

P20353 Ponda Baba .01 with blaster pistol and rifle, col. 3, green card w/picture (black beard) 8.00

P20221 Pote Snitkin .00 with force pike and blaster pistol, col. 3, green card w/freeze frame, Fan Club exclusive 16.00

P20222 Prince Xizor .00 with energy blade shields, purple card w/hologram 9.00

P20317 Princess Leia .00 in ceremonial dress with medal of honor, green card w/flashback photo 8.00

P20236 Princess Leia .03 from Dark Empire comics, col. 2, green card w/EU picture 24.00

P20244 Princess Leia Organa .00 with blaster rifle and long-barreled pistol, col. 1, green card w/freeze frame....................16.00

P20224 Princess Leia Organa .00 with laser pistol and assault rifle, orange card w/picture (2 bands on belt) 17.00

P20223 Princess Leia Organa .00 with laser pistol and assault rifle, orange card w/picture (3 bands on belt) 21.00

P20226 Princess Leia Organa .01 with laser pistol and assault rifle, col. 1, green card w/hologram, new bubble (2 bands on belt) 10.00

P20227 Princess Leia Organa .01 with laser pistol and assault rifle, col. 1, green card w/hologram, new bubble (3 bands on belt) 11.00

P20225 Princess Leia Organa .01 with laser pistol and assault rifle, col. 1, green card w/hologram, old bubble.........................13.00

P20228 Princess Leia Organa .01 with laser pistol and assault rifle, col. 1, green card w/picture, new bubble (3 bands on belt) 11.00

P20229 Princess Leia Organa as Jabba's prisoner .00, col. 1, green card w/hologram 10.00

P20230 Princess Leia Organa as Jabba's prisoner .00, col. 1, green card w/picture...11.00

P20231 Princess Leia Organa as Jabba's prisoner .01, col. 1, green card w/freeze frame...18.00

P20232 Princess Leia Organa as Jabba's prisoner .02, col. 1, green card w/freeze frame...12.00

P20241 Princess Leia Organa in Ewok celebration outfit .00, col. 1, green card w/freeze frame 22.00

P20242 Princess Leia Organa in Ewok celebration outfit .01, col. 1, green card w/freeze frame 9.00

P20243 Princess Leia Organa in Hoth gear .00 with blaster pistol, col. 3, green card w/freeze frame, Fan Club exclusive 31.00

P20246 R2-D2 .00 with light-pipe eye port and retractable leg, orange card w/picture..18.00

P20248 R2-D2 .01 with light-pipe eye port and retractable leg, col. 1, green card w/hologram, new bubble 20.00

P20247 R2-D2 .01 with light-pipe eye port and retractable leg, col. 1, green card w/hologram, old bubble 24.00

The lightsaber was originally mounted on the right with R2-D2 flat against the card.

Kenner decided to rotate the figure into an 'action pose' which included repositioning the lightsaber.

P20315 close-up

P20316 close-up

P20315 R2-D2 .00 with launching lightsaber, green card w/flashback photo (lightsaber on left side of bubble)............................10.00

P20316 R2-D2 .00 with launching lightsaber, green card w/flashback photo (lightsaber on right side of bubble)..........................117.00

P20249 R2-D2 .00 with spring-loaded pop-up scanner; remote action, retractable scomp link; grasper arm; circular saw, col. 1, green card w/freeze frame ("Death Star Trash Compactor" on FF slide).............14.00

P20325 R2-D2 .00 with spring-loaded pop-up scanner; remote action, retractable scomp link; grasper arm; circular saw, col. 1, green card w/freeze frame ("Imperial Trash Compactor" on FF slide).................68.00

P20311 R5-D4 .00 with concealed missile launcher, col. 2, orange card w/picture (no warning) 20.00

P20250 R5-D4 .00 with concealed missile launcher, col. 2, orange card w/picture (warning sticker) 22.00

P20253 R5-D4 .01 with concealed missile launcher, col. 2, green card w/hologram (no warning; hooked firing pin) 22.00

P20258 R5-D4 .01 with concealed missile launcher, col. 2, green card w/hologram (printed warning; hooked firing pin) 8.00

P20256 R5-D4 .01 with concealed missile launcher, col. 2, green card w/hologram (warning sticker; hooked firing pin) 14.00

P20252 R5-D4 .01 with concealed missile launcher, col. 2, green card w/picture (no warning; hooked firing pin) 22.00

P20241

P20243

P20246

P20248

P20316

P20249

P20250

P20251

P20261

P20262

P20265

P20266

P20267

P20273

P20274

P20277

P20278

P20312

P20279

P20282

P20283

P20269

P20286

P20287

P20251 R5-D4 .01 with concealed missile launcher, col. 2, green card w/picture (no warning; straight firing pin)................................24.00
P20257 R5-D4 .01 with concealed missile launcher, col. 2, green card w/picture (printed warning; hooked firing pin)................................8.00
P20255 R5-D4 .01 with concealed missile launcher, col. 2, green card w/picture (warning sticker; hooked firing pin)................................10.00
P20254 R5-D4 .01 with concealed missile launcher, col. 2, green card w/picture (warning sticker; straight firing pin)................................20.00
P20260 Rebel Fleet Trooper .00 with blaster pistol and rifle, col. 2, green card w/hologram................................34.00
P20263 Rebel Fleet Trooper .01 with blaster pistol and rifle, col. 1, green card w/freeze frame (.01 is stickered on back)................................18.00
P20262 Rebel Fleet Trooper .01 with blaster pistol and rifle, col. 1, green card w/freeze frame (.01 is stickered on back; FF error)................................18.00
P20261 Rebel Fleet Trooper .01 with blaster pistol and rifle, col. 1, green card w/hologram................................11.00
P20264 Rebel Fleet Trooper .02 with blaster pistol and rifle, col. 1, green card w/freeze frame................................15.00
P20265 Ree-Yees .00 with blaster pistols, col. 3, green card w/freeze frame................................28.00
P20266 Saelt-Marae (Yak face) .00 with battle staff, col. 2, green card w/hologram................................10.00
P20267 Saelt-Marae (Yak face) .01 with battle staff, col. 2, green card w/freeze frame................................16.00
P20271 Sandtrooper .01 with heavy blaster rifle, col. 1, green card w/hologram................................16.00
P20270 Sandtrooper .01 with heavy blaster rifle, col. 1, green card w/picture................................16.00
P20273 Sandtrooper .02 with heavy blaster rifle, col. 3, green card w/hologram, new bubble................................8.00
P20274 Sandtrooper .03 with concussion grenade cannon, col. 3, green card w/freeze frame................................147.00
P20345 Scanner Crew Technician, from Millennium Falcon carry case, yellow insert cardback................................16.00
P20277 Snowtrooper .00 with Imperial issue blaster rifle, col. 3, green card w/hologram................................8.00
P20275 Snowtrooper .00 with Imperial issue blaster rifle, col. 3, green card w/picture................................12.00
P20278 Snowtrooper .01 with Imperial blaster rifle, col. 3, green card w/freeze frame................................10.00

P20312 Spacetrooper .03 from *Heir to the Empire* novel, col. 2, green card w/EU picture................................19.00
P20280 Stormtrooper .00 with blaster rifle and heavy infantry cannon, orange card w/hologram................................31.00
P20279 Stormtrooper .00 with blaster rifle and heavy infantry cannon, orange card w/picture................................22.00
P20282 Stormtrooper .01 with blaster rifle and heavy infantry cannon, col. 3, green card w/hologram, new bubble................................15.00
P20281 Stormtrooper .01 with blaster rifle and heavy infantry cannon, col. 3, green card w/hologram, old bubble................................12.00
P20349 Stormtrooper .01 with blaster rifle and heavy infantry cannon, col. 3, green card w/picture, new bubble................................16.00
P20283 Stormtrooper .02 with blaster rifle and heavy infantry cannon, col. 3, green card w/freeze frame................................18.00
P20269 Tatooine Stormtrooper .00 with concussion grenade cannon, col. 1, orange card w/picture................................46.00
P20284 Tie Fighter Pilot .00 with Imperial blaster pistol and rifle, orange card w/picture (warning sticker)................................28.00
P20285 Tie Fighter Pilot .01 with Imperial blaster pistol and rifle, orange card w/picture (warning is printed)................................12.00
P20286 Tie Fighter Pilot .02 with Imperial blaster pistol and rifle, orange card w/picture................................11.00
P20287 Tie Fighter Pilot .03 with Imperial blaster pistol and rifle, col. 2, green card w/hologram................................12.00
P20289 Tie Fighter Pilot .04 with Imperial blaster pistol and rifle, col. 3, green card w/hologram, new bubble................................12.00
P20288 Tie Fighter Pilot .04 with Imperial blaster pistol and rifle, col. 3, green card w/hologram, old bubble................................14.00
P20290 Tie Fighter Pilot .05 with Imperial blaster pistol and rifle, col. 3, green card w/freeze frame................................71.00
P20292 Tusken Raider .00 with gaderffii stick battle club, col. 2, orange card w/picture................................26.00
P20291 Tusken Raider .00 with gaderffii stick battle club, col. 2, orange card w/picture (left hand closed)................................65.00
P20295 Tusken Raider .01 with gaderffii stick, col. 2, green card w/hologram................................14.00
P20294 Tusken Raider .01 with gaderffii stick, col. 2, green card w/picture................................12.00
P20293 Tusken Raider .01 with gaderffii stick, col. 2, green card w/picture (left hand closed)................................38.00

| P20290 | P20291 | P20295 | P20297 | P20299 | P20304 | P20322 | P20309 |

| P20456 | P20454 | P20452 | P20455 | P20453 | P20357 | P20358 | P20359 |

| P20360 | P20361 | P20362 | P20363 | P20364 | P20407 | P20365 | P20366 |

Action Figures: POTF2

P20296 Tusken Raider .02 with gaderffii stick, col. 2, green card w/hologram, new bubble (wholesale club SW 3-pack)..................17.00
P20297 Ugnaughts .00 with tool-kit, col. 2, green card w/freeze frame ..12.00
P20347 Wedge Antilles, corrected helmet, from Millennium Falcon carry case, yellow insert cardback 14.00
P20346 Wedge Antilles, original helmet, from Millennium Falcon carry case, yellow insert cardback 12.00
P20298 Weequay Skiff Guard .00 with force pike and blaster rifle, col. 2, green card w/hologram..................31.00
P20299 Weequay Skiff Guard .01 with force pike and blaster rifle, col. 3, green card w/hologram..................8.00
P20300 Weequay Skiff Guard .02 with force pike and blaster rifle, col. 3, green card w/freeze frame..................390.00
P20322 Yoda .00 with cane and boiling pot, green card w/flashback photo 16.00
P20303 Yoda .00 with Jedi trainer backpack and gimer stick, orange card w/hologram 34.00
P20302 Yoda .00 with Jedi trainer backpack and gimer stick, orange card w/picture..................18.00
P20304 Yoda .01 with Jedi trainer backpack and gimer stick, orange card w/picture..................14.00
P20306 Yoda .02 with Jedi trainer backpack and gimer stick, col. 2, green card w/hologram..................12.00
P20305 Yoda .02 with Jedi trainer backpack and gimer stick, col. 2, green card w/picture..................12.00
P20308 Yoda .03 with Jedi trainer backpack and gimer stick, col. 1, green card w/hologram, new bubble 10.00
P20307 Yoda .03 with Jedi trainer backpack and gimer stick, col. 1, green card w/hologram, old bubble 10.00
P20309 Zuckuss .00 with heavy assault blaster rifle, col. 3, green card w/freeze frame..................24.00

Hasbro (Canada)

P20456 Darth Vader with Interrogation Droid, green card w/CommTech chip..................18.00
P20454 Greedo, green card w/CommTech chip 9.00
P20452 Han Solo, green card w/CommTech chip..................8.00
P20455 Jawa with "Gonk" Droid, green card w/CommTech chip 8.00
P20453 Luke Skywalker with T16 Model, green card w/CommTech chip .8.00
P20457 Stormtrooper with Rifle Rack, green card w/CommTech chip ...18.00

Kenner (Canada)

P20357 2-1B, green card w/hologram 12.00
P20358 4-LOM, green card w/hologram 16.00
P20435 8D8, green card w/freeze frame 12.00
P20359 Admiral Ackbar, green card w/hologram 10.00
P20450 Anakin Skywalker with lightsaber, green card w/flashback photo 14.00
P20360 ASP-7 Droid, green card w/hologram 11.00
P20361 AT-ST Driver, green card w/freeze frame 58.00
P20362 AT-ST Driver, green card w/hologram 11.00
P20449 Aunt Beru with Service Droid, green card w/flashback photo....17.00
P20441 Ben (Obi-Wan) Kenobi with lightsaber, green card w/flashback photo 10.00
P20363 Ben Kenobi, orange card w/picture..................18.00
P20364 Bib Fortuna, green card w/hologram 16.00
P20430 Biggs Darklighter, green card w/freeze frame 20.00
P20365 Boba Fett, green card w/freeze frame ("Imprisoned" on FF slide)..................29.00
P20407 Boba Fett, orange card w/picture 18.00
P20366 Bossk, green card w/hologram 14.00
P20433 C-3PO / Removable Limbs, green card w/freeze frame 12.00
P20451 C-3PO with Removable Arm, green card w/flashback photo....11.00
P20367 C-3PO, square orange card w/picture 20.00
P20436 Chewbacca / Snoova, purple card w/hologram 14.00
P20444 Chewbacca with Bowcaster Rifle, green card w/flashback photo 11.00
P20368 Chewbacca, square orange card w/picture 20.00
P20442 Darth Vader with Lightsaber, green card w/flashback photo 16.00
P20411 Darth Vader, green card w/hologram 11.00
P20369 Darth Vader, square orange card w/picture 20.00
P20437 Dash Rendar, purple card w/hologram 19.00
P20370 Death Star Gunner, green card w/hologram 12.00
P20371 Dengar, green card w/hologram 16.00
P20443 Emperor Palpatine with Force Lightning, green card w/flashback photo 16.00
P20372 Emperor Palpatine, green card w/hologram 8.00
P20460 Emperor's Royal Guard, green card w/freeze frame 26.00
P20373 Emperor's Royal Guard, green card w/hologram 18.00
P20427 Endor Rebel Soldier, green card w/freeze frame 8.00
P20374 EV-9D9, green card w/hologram 12.00

P20367 P20436 P20444 P20368 P20369 P20437 P20370 P20371

P20372 P20373 P20460 P20374 P20429 P20375 P20376 P20377

P20378 P20379 P20380 P20381 P20428 P20405 P20409 P20415

P20429 Ewok 2-Pack (Wicket/Logray), green card w/freeze frame 22.00
P20424 Gamorrean Guard, green card w/freeze frame 17.00
P20375 Gamorrean Guard, green card w/hologram...................................9.00
P20376 Garindan, green card w/hologram...7.00
P20377 Grand Moff Tarkin, green card w/hologram..................................8.00
P20378 Greedo, green card w/hologram..10.00
P20423 Han Solo in Bespin gear, green card w/hologram.......................7.00
P20419 Han Solo in Carbonite, orange card w/picture...........................12.00
P20406 Han Solo in Endor Gear, green card w/hologram.....................10.00
P20414 Han Solo in Hoth Gear, orange card w/picture..........................14.00
P20379 Han Solo, square orange card w/picture....................................20.00
P20380 Hoth Rebel Soldier, green card w/hologram...............................8.00
P20381 Jawas, green card w/hologram, includes insert 15.00
P20428 Lak Sivrak, green card w/freeze frame 18.00
P20426 Lando Calrissian as General, green card w/hologram...............9.00
P20382 Lando Calrissian in Skiff Disguise, green card w/hologram.......9.00
P20405 Lando Calrissian, orange card w/picture.....................................9.00
P20409 Lobot, green card w/freeze frame 10.00
P20425 Luke Skywalker in Bespin Gear, green card w/freeze frame 11.00
P20383 Luke Skywalker in Ceremonial Attire, green card w/freeze frame ..9.00
P20415 Luke Skywalker in Dagobah Fatigues, orange card w/picture ...14.00
P20421 Luke Skywalker in Hoth Gear, green card w/hologram 10.00
P20438 Luke Skywalker in Imperial Disguise, purple card w/hologram....21.00
P20384 Luke Skywalker in Stormtrooper Disguise, green card w/holo-gram 10.00
P20385 Luke Skywalker Jedi Knight, green card w/hologram 9.00
P20420 Luke Skywalker Jedi Knight, orange card w/THX insert...............20.00
P20445 Luke Skywalker with Blaster Rifle, green card w/flashback photo ...8.00
P20431 Luke Skywalker with Blastshield Helmet, green card w/freeze frame..14.00
P20386 Luke Skywalker, square orange card w/picture...........................20.00
P20413 Luke Skywalker, X-Wing Pilot, orange card w/picture 15.00
P20387 Malakili, green card w/hologram..10.00
P20388 Momaw Nadon, green card w/hologram....................................14.00
P20410 MonMothma, green card w/freeze frame 14.00
P20389 Nien Nunb, green card w/hologram...9.00
P20390 Ponda Baba, green card w/hologram..9.00
P20439 Prince Xizor, purple card w/hologram...9.00
P20458 Princess Leia as Jabba's Prisoner, green card w/freeze frame and insert..15.00

P20391 Princess Leia as Jabba's Prisoner, green card w/hologram 10.00
P20440 Princess Leia in Boushh Disguise, purple card w/hologram 12.00
P20446 Princess Leia in Ceremonial Dress, green card w/flashback photo8.00
P20392 Princess Leia in Ewok Celebration Dress, green card w/freeze frame 9.00
P20432 Princess Leia Organa (New Likeness), green card w/freeze frame 16.00
P20393 Princess Leia Organa, square orange card w/picture 20.00
P20408 R2-D2 w/scanner/comp link/grasp arm/saw, green card w/freeze frame 9.00
P20447 R2-D2 with Launching Lightsaber, green card w/flashback photo..10.00
P20394 R2-D2, square orange card w/picture...20.00
P20395 R5-D4, green card w/hologram, includes insert 9.00
P20422 Rebel Fleet Trooper, green card w/hologram...........................11.00
P20396 Saelt-Marae, green card w/hologram.......................................10.00
P20397 Sandtrooper, green card w/hologram.......................................16.00
P20459 Snowtrooper, green card w/freeze frame 10.00
P20398 Snowtrooper, green card w/hologram..8.00
P20412 Stormtrooper, green card w/hologram.....................................12.00
P20400 Stormtrooper, square orange card w/picture............................20.00
P20461 Tie Fighter Pilot, green card w/freeze frame...........................55.00
P20418 Tie Fighter Pilot, green card w/hologram.................................12.00
P20417 Tie Fighter Pilot, orange card w/picture, new bubble...............18.00
P20416 Tie Fighter Pilot, orange card w/picture, old bubble.................14.00
P20401 Tusken Raider, green card w/hologram.....................................14.00
P20434 Ugnaughts (2-pack), green card w/freeze frame 12.00
P20402 Weequay, green card w/freeze frame, includes insert................45.00
P20403 Weequay, green card w/hologram 8.00
P20448 Yoda with Cane and Boiling Pot, green card w/flashback photo .16.00
P20404 Yoda, orange card w/picture..18.00

Kenner (Italy)

P20480 Ben Kenobi, orange card w/picture (long saber)......................56.00
P20481 Ben Kenobi, orange card w/picture (short saber).....................16.00
P20462 Boba Fett, orange card w/picture...21.00
P20463 Bossk, green card w/picture..16.00
P20464 C1-P8 (R2-D2), orange card w/picture.......................................20.00
P20490 Chewbacca / Snoova, orange card w/hologram.........................16.00
P20465 Chewbacca, orange card w/picture...19.00
P20466 D-3PO (C-3PO), orange card w/picture 14.00

P20410   P20389   P20390   P20458   P20440   P20446   P20392   P20432

P20393   P20408   P20394   P20395   P20396   P20397   P20398   P20459

P20412   P20417   P20461   P20401   P20434   P20402   P20403   P20404

Action Figures: POTF2

P20467 Darth Vader, orange card w/picture (long saber) 37.00
P20468 Darth Vader, orange card w/picture (short saber) 18.00
P20491 Dash Rendar, orange card w/hologram 21.00
P20469 Death Star Gunner, green card w/picture 14.00
P20470 Emperor Palpatine, green card w/picture 9.00
P20471 Greedo, green card w/picture 12.00
P20474 Han Solo in Carbonite, green card w/picture 10.00
P20475 Han Solo in Endor Gear, green card w/picture 12.00
P20473 Han Solo in Hoth Gear, orange card w/picture 16.00
P20472 Han Solo, orange card w/picture 18.00
P20478 Luke Skywalker in Dagobah Fatigues, orange card w/picture ..16.00
P20477 Luke Skywalker in Hoth Gear, green card w/picture 23.00
P20492 Luke Skywalker in Imperial Disguise, orange card w/hologram ..17.00
P20479 Luke Skywalker in X-wing Fighter Pilot Gear, orange card w/picture..16.00
P20476 Luke Skywalker, orange card w/picture 14.00
P20482 Ponda Baba, green card w/picture 10.00
P20493 Prince Xizor, orange card w/hologram 11.00
P20484 Princess Leia in Boushh Disguise, green card w/picture 20.00
P20483 Princess Leia Organa, orange card w/picture 19.00
P20485 Sandtrooper, green card w/picture 10.00
P20486 Stormtrooper, orange card w/picture 24.00
P20487 Tie Fighter Pilot, orange card w/picture 13.00
P20488 Tusken Raider, green card w/picture 14.00
P20489 Yoda, orange card w/picture 16.00

Kenner (Japan)

Figures were released in U.S. packaging with a Japanese sticker placed over the card. With the exception of the green tinted C-3PO, add $2.00 to U.S. figure value.

P20494 C-3PO, green card w/picture, green tinted plastic 17.00

Kenner (UK)

P20495 4-LOM, green card w/tri-language w/o tri-logo 17.00
P20496 Admiral Ackbar, green card w/tri-language w/o tri-logo 14.00
P20497 Bib Fortuna, green card w/tri-language w/o tri-logo 11.00
P20501 Boba Fett, orange card w/THX insert 24.00
P20498 Boba Fett, orange card, new bubble 22.00
P20499 Boba Fett, orange card, new bubble (sticker on bar code) 23.00
P20500 Boba Fett, orange card, old bubble 23.00

P20502 Bossk, green card 9.00
P20503 Bossk, green card, new bubble 8.00
P20506 C-3PO, orange card THX 22.00
P20504 C-3PO, orange card, new bubble 14.00
P20505 C-3PO, orange card, old bubble 14.00
P20507 Chewbacca / Snoova, orange card w/hologram, limited to 5,000...30.00
P20510 Chewbacca, orange card w/THX insert 24.00
P20508 Chewbacca, orange card, new bubble 14.00
P20509 Chewbacca, orange card, old bubble 14.00
P20515 Darth Vader, orange card w/THX insert (short saber)...............20.00
P20511 Darth Vader, orange card, new bubble (short saber w/sticker on bar code) 16.00
P20512 Darth Vader, orange card, new bubble (short saber) 14.00
P20513 Darth Vader, orange card, old bubble (long saber) 18.00
P20514 Darth Vader, orange card, old bubble (short saber) 14.00
P20516 Dash Rendar, orange card w/hologram, limited to 5,000 ....30.00
P20517 Death Star Gunner, green card 12.00
P20518 Emperor Palpatine, green card, new bubble 12.00
P20519 Emperor Palpatine, green card, new bubble (sticker on bar code) 12.00
P20520 Emperor Palpatine, green card, old bubble 12.00
P20521 Emperor's Royal Guard, green card w/tri-language w/o tri-logo .13.00
P20522 Endor Rebel Soldier, green card w/tri-language w/o tri-logo 10.00
P20523 Ewok 2-pack (Wicket/Logray), green card w/tri-language w/o tri-logo 18.00
P20524 Gamorrean Guard, green card w/tri-language w/o tri-logo 12.00
P20525 Grand Moff Tarkin, green card w/tri-language w/o tri-logo 12.00
P20526 Greedo, green card 12.00
P20527 Han Solo in Bespin Gear, green card w/tri-language w/o tri-logo 12.00
P20528 Han Solo in Carbonite, green card, new bubble 12.00
P20529 Han Solo in Carbonite, green card, old bubble 12.00
P20530 Han Solo in Endor Gear, green card, new bubble (blue pants) .12.00
P20531 Han Solo in Endor Gear, green card, new bubble (brown pants)..17.00
P20532 Han Solo in Endor Gear, green card, old bubble (blue pants) ...12.00
P20533 Han Solo in Hoth Gear, orange card 12.00
P20534 Han Solo, orange card 14.00
P20535 Han Solo, orange card w/THX insert 20.00
P20536 Hoth Rebel Soldier, green card 12.00
P20537 Jawas, green card w/tri-language w/o tri-logo 17.00

P20476

P20482

P20493

P20485

P20486

P20487

P20488

P20489

P20538 Lando Calrissian in Skiff Disguise, green card 10.00
P20539 Lando Calrissian, orange card 12.00
P20540 Lando Calrissian, orange card w/THX insert....................23.00
P20541 Luke Skywalker in Bespin Gear, green card w/tri-language w/o tri-logo..34.00
P20542 Luke Skywalker in Dagobah Fatigues, orange card (short saber) .15.00
P20543 Luke Skywalker in Hoth Gear, green card, new bubble (short saber) ..12.00
P20544 Luke Skywalker in Hoth Gear, green card, old bubble (short saber) 12.00
P20545 Luke Skywalker in Imperial Disguise, orange card w/hologram, limited to 5,000...33.00
P20546 Luke Skywalker in Stormtrooper Disguise, green card 14.00
P20550 Luke Skywalker in X-Wing Fighter Pilot Gear, orange card w/THX insert (long saber) 24.00
P20547 Luke Skywalker in X-Wing Fighter Pilot Gear, orange card, new bubble (short saber) 14.00
P20548 Luke Skywalker in X-Wing Fighter Pilot Gear, orange card, old bubble (long saber) 18.00
P20549 Luke Skywalker in X-Wing Fighter Pilot Gear, orange card, old bubble (short saber) 14.00
P20551 Luke Skywalker Jedi Knight, green card (short saber) 13.00
P20582 Luke Skywalker Jedi Knight, green card, new bubble (short saber)..15.00
P20583 Luke Skywalker, green card w/flashback photo 8.00
P20552 Luke Skywalker, orange card (long saber) 18.00
P20553 Luke Skywalker, orange card (short saber) 14.00
P20554 Luke Skywalker, orange card w/THX insert (long saber)...............24.00
P20555 Momaw Nadon (Hammerhead), green card w/tri-language w/o tri-logo..12.00

P20556 Obi-Wan Kenobi, orange card (long saber)..........................18.00
P20557 Obi-Wan Kenobi, orange card (short saber) 14.00
P20558 Obi-Wan Kenobi, orange card w/THX insert 24.00
P20559 Ponda Baba, green card 13.00
P20560 Prince Xizor, orange card w/hologram, limited to 5,000 ....29.00
P20561 Princess Leia as Jabba's Prisoner, green card......................19.00
P20562 Princess Leia in Boushh Disguise, green card 14.00
P20566 Princess Leia Organa, orange card w/THX insert 23.00
P20563 Princess Leia Organa, orange card, new bubble (2 belt rings) .14.00
P20564 Princess Leia Organa, orange card, old bubble (2 belt rings) 14.00
P20565 Princess Leia Organa, orange card, old bubble (3 belt rings) 16.00
P20584 R2-D2 with launching lightsaber, green card w/flashback photo .14.00
P20567 R2-D2, orange card...14.00
P20568 R2-D2, orange card w/THX insert 22.00
P20569 Rebel Fleet Trooper, green card 10.00
P20570 Sandtrooper, green card, new bubble 12.00
P20571 Sandtrooper, green card, new bubble (sticker on bar code) 12.00
P20572 Sandtrooper, green card, old bubble 12.00
P20573 Snowtrooper, green card w/tri-language w/o tri-logo.................12.00
P20574 Stormtrooper, orange card 15.00
P20575 Stormtrooper, orange card w/THX insert 28.00
P20576 Tie Fighter Pilot, orange card 12.00
P20577 Tusken Raider, green card 12.00
P20578 Tusken Raider, green card w/hologram 15.00
P20579 Weequay Skiff Guard, green card w/tri-language w/o tri-logo..22.00
P20580 Yoda, orange card, new bubble 14.00
P20581 Yoda, orange card, old bubble 15.00

P20500   P20502   P20507   P20510   P20513   P20516   P20520   P20522

P20523   P20529   P20532   P20534   P20533   P20539   P20541   P20542

P20545   P20548   P20550   P20551   P20553   P20556   P20559   P20560

P20562   P20564   P20567   P20569   P20572   P20574   P20576   P20581

ACTION FIGURES: POTF2, UNLICENSED

BAG0001   BAG0002   BAG0003

BAG0004   BAG0005   BAG0006   BAG0007

Galaxy Empire

Figures are approximately 6" in height.

BAG0153   BAG0008   BAG0148   BAG0149

BAG0001 Boba Fett 12.00
BAG0002 Chewbacca / Snoova 6.00
BAG0003 Chewbacca 9.00
BAG0004 Darth Vader 9.00
BAG0005 Han Solo 9.00
BAG0006 Luke Jedi 9.00
BAG0007 Stormtrooper 9.00

Galaxy Heroes

BAG0153 Darth Vader mask with Vader figure, approx 5" 4.00

Space Power Warrior

BAG0008 Darth Vader black or white armor, approx 8" 26.00

Star Force

Toys feature "pull back" action.
BAG0148 Millennium Falcon 8.00
BAG0149 X-Wing Fighter 8.00

Star Warrio

SOTE AT-ST Driver card.
BAG0010 Ben Kenobi 5.00
BAG0011 C-3PO 5.00
BAG0012 Chewbacca 5.00
BAG0013 Darth Vader 5.00
BAG0014 Han Solo 5.00
BAG0015 Luke Imperial Disguise 5.00
BAG0016 Luke Skywalker 5.00
BAG0017 Princess Leia 5.00
BAG0018 Princess Leia/Boushh 5.00
BAG0019 R2-D2 ....5.00
BAG0020 Stormtrooper 5.00
BAG0021 Yoda 7.00

SOTE Stormtrooper card.
BAG0022 Biker Scout 34.00
BAG0023 Deluxe Han 8.00
BAG0024 Deluxe Luke 8.00
BAG0025 Han Solo in Carbonite 14.00
BAG0152 Luke 10.00
BAG0026 Luke Jedi 10.00
BAG0027 Stormtrooper 12.00
BAG0028 Swoop Rider 10.00
BAG0029 Tie Fighter Pilot 5.00

Vs. 2-Pack

2-packs. Figures are approximately 5" in height.
BAG0030 Boba Fett vs. Luke in Imperial Guard Disguise 32.00
BAG0031 Dash Rendar vs. Carbonite Han 16.00
BAG0032 Lando vs. Momaw Nadon 19.00
BAG0033 Leia / Boushh vs. Hoth Han 16.00
BAG0034 Prince Xizor vs. Jedi Luke 16.00

2-Packs on POTF2 hanger cards.
BAG0035 C-3PO and Darth Vader with alien ship 24.00
BAG0036 C-3PO and R2-D2 with alien ship 30.00
BAG0037 C-3PO and Stormtrooper with alien ship 24.00
BAG0038 C-3PO and Yoda with alien ship 28.00
BAG0039 Darth Vader and C-3PO driving a Landspeeder 18.00
BAG0040 Darth Vader and Dagobah Luke with alien ship 14.00
BAG0041 Darth Vader and Stormtrooper with a Sport Skiff 21.00
BAG0042 Darth Vader and Stormtrooper, each driving a Sport Skiff 12.00
BAG0151 Two Sport Skiffs on a hanger card 11.00
BAG0043 Stormtroopers resembling Applause PVC figures on a Darth Vader card 15.00

AT-ST Driver oversized card. Figures are approximately 5" in height.
BAG0044 AT-ST Driver 8.00
BAG0045 Hoth Luke 8.00
BAG0046 Hoth Rebel Soldier 8.00
BAG0047 Imperial Gunner 9.00

C-3PO card.
BAG0048 Chewbacca 5.00
BAG0049 Darth Vader 5.00
BAG0050 Dash Rendar 5.00
BAG0051 Han Solo 5.00
BAG0052 Han Solo in Hoth Gear 5.00
BAG0053 Obi-Wan Kenobi 5.00
BAG0054 Princess Leia 5.00
BAG0055 R2-D2 ....11.00
BAG0056 Stormtrooper 5.00
BAG0057 Tie Fighter Pilot 5.00
BAG0058 Yoda 5.00

Chewbacca card. Figures are approximately 5" in height.
BAG0150 Bespin Luke 11.00
BAG0059 Lando as Skiff Guard 9.00

Deluxe Han Solo card.
BAG0062 Deluxe Han 5.00

BAG0010   BAG0011   BAG0012   BAG0013

BAG0014   BAG0015   BAG0016   BAG0017   BAG0018   BAG0019   BAG0020   BAG0021

BAG0063 Deluxe Luke 5.00
BAG0064 Deluxe Stormtrooper 5.00
BAG0065 Speeder Bike and Scout 16.00
BAG0066 Swoop Bike and Rider 5.00

Deluxe Stormtrooper card.
BAG0067 Deluxe Han 5.00
BAG0068 Deluxe Luke 5.00
BAG0069 Swoop Bike Rider 14.00

Endor Han card.
BAG0070 C-3PO 5.00
BAG0071 R2-D2 ....6.00
BAG0072 Yoda 6.00

Luke Dagobah card.
BAG0076 Boba Fett 15.00
BAG0077 C-3PO 5.00
BAG0078 Chewbacca 5.00
BAG0079 Darth Vader 5.00
BAG0080 Han Solo 5.00
BAG0081 Hoth Han 5.00
BAG0082 Lando 5.00
BAG0083 Luke, Dagobah 5.00
BAG0084 Luke Skywalker 7.00
BAG0085 Luke, X-Wing Pilot 6.00
BAG0086 R2-D2 ....5.00
BAG0087 Yoda 7.00

Jedi Luke oversized card. Figures are approximately 5" in height.
BAG0088 Snoova 8.00
BAG0089 Dash Rendar 8.00
BAG0090 Han Carbonite 8.00
BAG0091 Han Hoth 8.00
BAG0092 Lando 8.00
BAG0093 Luke, Jedi 8.00
BAG0094 Momaw Nadon 8.00
BAG0095 Tie Pilot 8.00
BAG0096 Yoda 8.00

Jedi Luke card.
BAG0097 C-3PO 5.00
BAG0098 Chewbacca 5.00
BAG0099 Han Solo (brown belt) 5.00
BAG0100 Han Solo (silver belt) 5.00
BAG0101 Leia / Boushh 5.00
BAG0102 Luke Imperial Guard Disguise 9.00
BAG0103 Luke Skywalker 7.00
BAG0104 Obi-Wan Kenobi 5.00
BAG0105 Princess Leia (red belt) 5.00
BAG0106 Princess Leia (white belt) 5.00
BAG0107 R2-D2 ....6.00
BAG0108 Stormtrooper 5.00
BAG0109 Yoda 5.00

Luke Skywalker card.
BAG0110 Ben Kenobi 5.00

BAG0111 Boba Fett 15.00
BAG0112 C-3PO 5.00
BAG0113 Chewbacca 5.00
BAG0114 Darth Vader 5.00
BAG0115 Han Hoth 5.00
BAG0116 Han Solo 5.00
BAG0117 Luke Skywalker 7.00
BAG0118 Luke X-Wing Pilot 6.00
BAG0119 R2-D2 ....5.00
BAG0120 Stormtrooper 5.00
BAG0121 Yoda 5.00

Luke in Stormtrooper Disguise card.
BAG0122 2-1B 5.00
BAG0123 AT-ST Driver 5.00
BAG0124 Ben Kenobi 5.00
BAG0125 Bossk 5.00
BAG0126 Darth Vader 5.00
BAG0127 Darth Vader bendy 12.00
BAG0128 Greedo 6.00
BAG0129 Han Solo bendy 12.00
BAG0130 Hoth Rebel Soldier 5.00
BAG0131 Imperial Gunner 6.00
BAG0132 Jawas 5.00
BAG0133 Leia / Boushh 5.00
BAG0134 Luke Hoth 5.00
BAG0135 Luke Skywalker 5.00
BAG0136 Luke Stormtrooper 5.00
BAG0137 R5-D4 ....7.00
BAG0138 Sandtrooper 5.00
BAG0139 Stormtrooper 5.00
BAG0140 Tusken Raider 5.00

Sandtrooper oversized card. Figures are approximately 5" in height.
BAG0141 Luke Stormtrooper 8.00
BAG0142 Stormtrooper 8.00

Loose figures, any color, approximately 2" in height.
BAG0073 C-3PO 5.00
BAG0074 Darth Vader.......................................3.00
BAG0075 Luke Skywalker 3.00

Figures are approximately 11" in height.
BAG0061 Darth Vader.......................................28.00

BAG0073 **BAG0074** **BAG0075**

BAG0030 **BAG0045** **BAG0129** **BAG0141** **BAG0061** **BAG0145** **BAG0146** **BAG0147**

BAG0054 **BAG0121** **BAG0128** **BAG0097** **BAG0098** **BAG0104** **BAG0105** **BAG0107**

Action Figures: POTF2, Unlicensed

BAG0060 Darth Vader, Thunderforce 35.00
BAG0145 Stormtrooper 31.00
BAG0144 Stormtrooper, Thunderforce 18.00
BAG0146 AT-AT Driver on "Plastic Toys" header card 22.00
BAG0143 Stormtrooper driving an alien sled on a Star Wars header card .17.00
BAG0147 X-Wing similar to Galoob Micromachine with 2 micro-pilots and
    three 2" figures: Luke, C-3PO, and Vader 27.00

P2S1006 front and back   P2S1011 (back)

P2S1003   P2S1005   P2S1010

P2S1002   P2S1004   P2S1008

ACTION FIGURES: POTF2 DELUXE

Kenner
P2S1001 Boba Fett w/Wing-Blast Rocketpack .00 ....24.00
P2S1002 Boba Fett w/Wing-Blast Rocketpack .01 ....12.00
P2S1009 Crowd Control Stormtrooper .00 ....24.00
P2S1010 Crowd Control Stormtrooper .01 ....12.00
P2S1003 Han Solo with Smuggler Flight Pack .00 ....8.00
P2S1004 Hoth Rebel Soldier with Radar Laser Gun .00....................8.00
P2S1006 Imperial Probe Droid .00; Orange Back 35.00
P2S1007 Imperial Probe Droid .01 ....14.00
P2S1011 Imperial Probe Droid .02 ....12.00
P2S1005 Luke Skywalker .00 ....18.00
P2S1008 Snowtrooper with E-Web Heavy Repeating Blaster .00 ....8.00

Kenner (Canada)
P2S1013 Boba Fett w/Wing-Blast Rocketpack 14.00
P2S1017 Crowd Control Stormtrooper 14.00
P2S1014 Han Solo w/Smuggler Flight Pack 9.00
P2S1016 Hoth Rebel Soldier with Radar Laser Gun 9.00
P2S1018 Imperial Probe Droid 16.00
P2S1012 Luke Skywalker w/Desert Sport Skiff................................20.00
P2S1015 Snowtrooper with E-Web Heavy Repeating Blaster 9.00

Kenner (Italy)
P2S1020 Hoth Rebel Soldier with Radar Laser Gun 15.00
P2S1019 Snowtrooper with E-Web Heavy Repeating Blaster 15.00

Kenner (UK)
P2S1022 Boba Fett w/Wing-Blast Rocketpack 15.00
P2S1023 Han Solo w/Smuggler Flight Pack 9.00

P2S2M002   P22M003   P22M004

P2S1025 Hoth Rebel Soldier with Radar Laser Gun 9.00
P2S1021 Luke Skywalker w/Desert Sport Skiff 24.00
P2S1024 Snowtrooper with E-Web Heavy Repeating Blaster 9.00

ACTION FIGURES: POTF2 ELECTRONIC FX

Kenner
P2S2001 Ben Kenobi .00 ....10.00
P2S2002 Darth Vader .00 ....10.00
P2S2003 Darth Vader .00; signed by David Prowse for Previews ...35.00
P2S2004 Emperor Palpatine .00 ....12.00
P2S2013 Emperor Palpatine .01 ....10.00
P2S2005 Luke Skywalker .00 ....10.00
P2S2006 R2-D2 .00 ....24.00
P2S2007 R2-D2 .01 ....12.00
P2S2008 R2-D2 .02 ....10.00

Kenner (UK)
P2S2010 Ben (Obi-Wan) Kenobi w/Glowing Lightsaber and Remote Dueling
    Action 12.00
P2S2011 Darth Vader w/Glowing Lightsaber and Remote Dueling
    Action 12.00
P2S2013 Luke Skywalker w/Glowing Lightsaber and Remote Dueling
    Action 12.00
P2S2012 R2-D2 w/Light-Up Radar Eye, authentic sounds and remote
    action 16.00

ACTION FIGURES: POTF2 GUNNER STATION

Kenner
P2S3001 Darth Vader 10.00
P2S3002 Han Solo...8.00
P2S3003 Luke Skywalker 8.00

ACTION FIGURES: POTF2 MAX REBO BAND 2-PACKS

Kenner
P22M001 Barquin D'an and Droopy McCool .00..............................27.00
P22M002 Barquin D'an and Droopy McCool .01..............................22.00
P22M003 Joh Yowza and Sy Snootles .00 ....22.00
P22M004 Max Rebo and Bodonawieedo .00 ....35.00

P2S2001   P2S2002   P2S2004   P2S2005   P2S2008   P2S3001   P2S3002   P2S3003

P2S4001

P2S4002

P2S4003

P2S4005

P2S4006

P2S4007

P2S4008

P2S4009

P2S4010

ACTION FIGURES: POTF2 MILLENNIUM MINTED COIN

Kenner

P2S4002 Bespin Han Solo .00 ....14.00
P2S4001 Bespin Han Solo .00; words behind coin 24.00
P2S4003 C-3PO .00 ....15.00
P2S4005 Chewbacca .00 ....14.00
P2S4004 Chewbacca .00; words behind coin 24.00
P2S4006 Emperor Palpatine .00 ....10.00
P2S4007 Endor Leia .00 ....24.00
P2S4010 Endor Leia .01 ....12.00
P2S4008 Endor Luke .00 ....24.00

P2S4011 Endor Luke .01 ....12.00
P2S4010 Snowtrooper .00 ....14.00
P2S4009 Snowtrooper .00; words behind coin 24.00

ACTION FIGURES: POTF2 MULTI-PACKS

Hasbro

P2M0017 Cantina Aliens; Labria, Nabrun Leids, Takeel 26.00
P2M0020 Jabba's Skiff Guards; Klaatu, Barada, Nikto 35.00
P2M0018 Jedi Spirits; Anakin, Yoda, Obi-Wan 21.00
P2M0019 Rebel Pilots; Ten Numb, Wedge Antilles, Arvel Crynyd.............38.00

Kenner

P2M0025 10-pack: Mos Eisley Cantina pop-up with ten carded action figures, Toys R Us, Japan exclusive 139.00
P2M0024 3-Pack: Boba Fett, Darth Vader, Stormtrooper, 1997 Hong Kong commemorative 28.00
P2M0023 3-Pack: C-3PO, Luke Skywalker, Princess Leia, 1997 Hong Kong commemorative 28.00
P2M0001 Cantina Showdown; Ben Kenobi, Dr. Evazan, Ponda Baba .00 ..27.00
P2M0014 Classic 4-pack; Chewbacca, Darth Vader, Han Solo, Luke Skywalker 46.00
P2M0013 Collectors Pack ANH: Stormtrooper Luke, Tusken Raider, Ben Kenobi 42.00
P2M0011 Collectors Pack ESB: Dagobah Luke, Lando Calrissian, Tie Fighter Pilot 75.00
P2M0012 Collectors Pack ROTJ: Jedi Luke, AT-ST Driver, Leia as Boushh .40.00
P2M0002 Collectors Pack: Han Solo, Chewbacca, Lando Calrissian 30.00
P2M0003 Collectors Pack: Luke Skywalker, Ben Kenobi, Darth Vader....32.00
P2M0004 Collectors Pack: R2-D2, C-3PO, Stormtrooper 36.00
P2M0005 Death Star Escape; Han and Luke in Stormtrooper Disguises, and Chewbacca .00 ....45.00
P2M0006 Death Star Escape; Han and Luke in Stormtrooper Disguises, and Chewbacca .01 ....35.00
P2M0007 Final Jedi Duel; Emperor Palpatine, Luke Skywalker, Darth Vader .00 ....22.00
P2M0016 Final Jedi Duel; Emperor Palpatine, Luke Skywalker, Darth Vader .01 ....18.00
P2M0008 Jabba's Dancers; Rystall, Greeta, Lyn Me .00 ....26.00
P2M0021 Kabe and Muftak .00, Fan Club exclusive 35.00
P2M0015 Mynock Hunt; Han Solo, Chewbacca, Princess Leia, Mynock Creature .00...40.00
P2M0026 Mynock Hunt; Han Solo, Chewbacca, Princess Leia, Mynock Creature, tri-logo 50.00
P2M0022 Oola and Salacious Crumb .00, Fan Club exclusive 24.00
P2M0009 Purchase of the Droids; Luke Skywalker, Uncle Owen, C-3PO .00 ....95.00
P2M0010 Purchase of the Droids; Luke Skywalker, Uncle Owen, C-3PO .01....22.00

P2M0017

P2M0020

P2M0018

P2M0019

P2M0001

P2M0005

P2M0007

P2M0008

P2M0015

P2M0009

P2M0014

P2M0021

P2M0022

ACTION FIGURES: POTF2 PHILADELPHIA TOY EXPO

Kenner

P2S6001 Bib Fortuna..65.00
P2S6002 Boba Fett 75.00
P2S6003 Chewbacca...75.00
P2S6004 R2-D2 ....75.00

ACTION FIGURES: POTF2 PRINCESS COLLECTION

P22P001   P22P003   P22P005   P22P007

Kenner

P22P001 Princess Leia and Han Solo .00 ....28.00
P22P002 Princess Leia and Han Solo .01 ....10.00
P22P003 Princess Leia and Luke Skywalker .00.................28.00
P22P004 Princess Leia and Luke Skywalker .01.................10.00
P22P005 Princess Leia and R2-D2 .00..................................28.00
P22P006 Princess Leia and R2-D2 .01..................................14.00
P22P007 Princess Leia and Wicket the Ewok .00................30.00
P22P008 Princess Leia and Wicket the Ewok .01................16.00

ACTION FIGURES: POTF2 SOTE 2-PACKS

P22S001   P22S002

Kenner

P22S001 Boba Fett vs. IG-88 .00...32.00
P22S002 Prince Xizor vs. Darth Vader .00 ....24.00

ACTION FIGURES: POTF2 SPECIAL OFFER

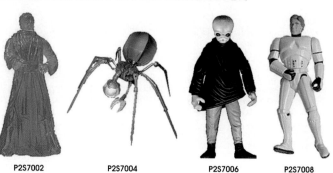

P2S7002   P2S7004   P2S7006   P2S7008

Kenner

P2S7002 Ben Kenobi (Spirit); "made in" sticker 16.00
P2S7001 Ben Kenobi (Spirit); "made" sticker 16.00
P2S7003 Ben Kenobi (Spirit); printed warning 14.00
P2S7004 B'Omarr Monk...17.00
P2S7006 Cantina Band Member; printed warning 18.00
P2S7005 Cantina Band Member; warning sticker 20.00
P2S7008 Han Solo in Stormtrooper Disguise; no tabs inside of helmet 30.00
P2S7007 Han Solo in Stormtrooper Disguise; tabs inside helmet 35.00

P2S7009   P2S7010   P2S7011   P2S7012

Kenner (UK)

P2S7009 Obi-Wan Kenobi spirit, ltd. to 40,000, UK 35.00

Spirit figures speculated to have originated from Japan. Although similar in size, they are
not from the same molds as those distributed in Hasbro's Cinema Scene.

P2S7010 Anakin Skywalker spirit 65.00
P2S7011 Ben Kenobi spirit...50.00
P2S7012 Yoda spirit 85.00

P2M0013   P2M0011   P2M0012

P2M0002   P2M0003   P2M0004

ACTION FIGURES: POTJ, CLASSIC

Hasbro

PJ0004 Ben (Obi-Wan) Kenobi Jedi Knight .0100, col. 1, w/force file 0000 ...9.00
PJ0030 Bespin Guard Cloud City Security .0400, col. 2, w/force file 0000 .9.00
PJ0011 Boba Fett .0100, 300th figure, misprinted box 35.00
PJ0029 Boba Fett .0200, 300th figure 15.00
PJ0001 Chewbacca Dejarik Champion .0000, col. 2, w/force file 0000 ..28.00
PJ0012 Chewbacca Dejarik Champion .0000, col. 2, w/force file 0100 ....9.00
PJ0013 Chewbacca Dejarik Champion .0100, col. 2, w/force file 0000 ....9.00
PJ0016 Chewbacca Millennium Falcon Mechanic .0300, col. 1, w/force file
    0000 ....9.00
PJ0002 Darth Vader Dagobah .0100, col. 1, w/force file 0000 ....9.00
PJ0034 Darth Vader Emperors Wrath .0400, col. 1, w/force file 0000 ....9.00
PJ0031 Ellors Madak .0400, col. 2, w/force file 0000 ....9.00
PJ0007 Han Solo Bespin Capture .0100, col. 1, w/force file 0000............9.00
PJ0035 Han Solo Death Star Escape .0400, col. 1, w/force file 0000 ....9.00
PJ0019 IG-88 Bounty Hunter .0100, col. 2, w/force file 0000, closed right
    claw 9.00
PJ0008 IG-88 Bounty Hunter .0100, col. 2, w/force file 0000, open right
    claw 22.00
PJ0020 IG-88 Bounty Hunter .0300, col. 2, w/force file 0000, closed right
    claw 9.00
PJ0003 Jek Porkins .0000, col. 2, w/force file 0000 ....9.00
PJ0014 Jek Porkins .0100, col. 2, w/force file 0000 ....9.00
PJ0018 Jek Porkins .0300, col. 2, w/force file 0000 ....9.00
PJ0009 K-3PO Echo Base Protocol Droid .0100, col. 2, w/force file 0000 ...9.00
PJ0032 Ketwol .0400, col. 2, w/force file 0000 ....9.00

PJ0022 Lando Calrissian Bespin Capture .0400, col. 2, w/force file 0000...9.00
PJ0015 Leia Organa Bespin Escape .0300, col. 1, w/force file 0000...........9.00
PJ0005 Leia Organa General .0000, col. 1, w/force file 0000.....................9.00
PJ0017 Leia Organa General .0100, col. 1, w/force file 0000.....................9.00
PJ0036 Luke Skywalker X-Wing Pilot .0400, col. 1, w/force file 0000..........9.00
PJ0010 Mon Calamari Officer .0100, col. 2, w/force file 0000 ....9.00
PJ0021 R2-Q5 Imperal Astromech Droid .0400, col. 2, w/force file 0000 -
    "Imperial" misspelled 9.00
PJ0025 Sandtrooper Tatooine Patrol .0400, col. 1, with force file 0000 ......9.00
PJ0006 Scout Trooper Imperial Patrol .0100, col. 1, w/force file 0000........11.00
PJ0033 Scout Trooper Imperial Patrol .0400, col. 1, w/force file 0000, dirty
    boots and blaster damage 9.00
PJ0028 Tessek .0400, col. 2, w/force file 0000 ....9.00

Hasbro (Canada)

PJ0023 Ben (Obi-Wan) Kenobi Jedi Knight, bi-language w/force file 9.00
PJ0027 Darth Vader Dagobah, bi-language w/force file 9.00
PJ0024 Darth Vader Dagobah, tri-logo w/force file 0000, secret Luke
    sticker..35.00
PJ0026 Scout Trooper Imperial Patrol, tri-logo w/force file 0000 ....9.00

ACTION FIGURES: POTJ, TPM

Hasbro

PJ10005 Anakin Skywalker Mechanic .0000, col. 1, w/force file 0000......10.00
PJ10017 Anakin Skywalker Mechanic .0100, col. 1, w/force file 0100........8.00
PJ10028 Aurra Sing Bounty Hunter .0300, col. 1, w/force file 0000............12.00

PJ0004

PJ0030

PJ0011

PJ0029

PJ0001

PJ0016

PJ0002

PJ0034

PJ0031

PJ0007

PJ0035

PJ0008

PJ0003

PJ0009

PJ0032

PJ0022

PJ0015

PJ0005

PJ0036

PJ0010

PJ0021

PJ0025

PJ0006

PJ0033

PJ0028

.0000 back close-up

.0100 back close-up

.0300 back close-up

.0400 back close-up

PJ0023

PJ0024

PJ0026

Action Figures: POTJ, TPM

PJ10015 Battle Droid Boomer Damage .0100, col. 1, w/force file 0000 .....8.00
PJ10001 Battle Droid Security .0000, col. 2, w/force file 0000 ....8.00
PJ10018 Battle Droid Security .0100, col. 2, w/force file 0000 ....8.00
PJ10006 Boss Nass Gungan Sacred Place .0000, col. 2, w/force file 0000.8.00
PJ10002 Coruscant Guard .0000, col. 2, w/force file 0000 ....8.00
PJ10019 Coruscant Guard .0100, col. 2, w/force file 0100 ....8.00
PJ10040 Coruscant Guard .0300, col. 2, w/force file 0100 ....7.00
PJ10007 Darth Maul Final Duel .0000, col. 1, w/force file 0000 ....8.00
PJ10020 Darth Maul Final Duel .0000, col. 1, w/force file 0000, sticker on
   front 8.00
PJ10021 Darth Maul Final Duel .0100, col. 1, w/force file 0000, sticker on
   front 8.00
PJ10032 Darth Maul Sith Apprentice .0300, col. 1, w/force file 0000........12.00
PJ10008 Fode and Beed Podrace Announcer .0100, col. 2, w/force file
   0000 ....8.00
PJ10009 Gungan Warrior .0000, col. 2, w/force file 0000 ....18.00
PJ10022 Gungan Warrior .0100, col. 2, w/force file 0000 ....8.00
PJ10041 Jar Jar Binks Tatooine .0400, col. 2, w/force file 0000 ....9.00
PJ10003 Mas Amedda .0000, col. 2, w/force file 0100 ....8.00
PJ10023 Mas Amedda .0100, col. 2, w/force file 0100 ....8.00
PJ10033 Mas Amedda .0300, col. 2, w/force file 0100 ....7.00
PJ10039 Mas Amedda .0400, col. 2, w/force file 0100 ....7.00
PJ10043 Obi-Wan Kenobi Cold Weather Gear .0400, col. 1, w/force file
   0000 ....9.00
PJ10010 Obi-Wan Kenobi Jedi .0000, col. 1, w/force file 0100 ....8.00
PJ10024 Obi-Wan Kenobi Jedi .0100, col. 1, w/force file 0100 ....8.00
PJ10043 Obi-Wan Kenobi Jedi Training Gear .0400, col. 1, w/force file
   0000 ....9.00
PJ10016 Plo Koon Jedi Master .0100, col. 2, w/force file 0000 ....18.00
PJ10031 Plo Koon Jedi Master .0300, col. 2, w/force file 0000 ....12.00
PJ10035 Plo Koon Jedi Master .0400, col. 2, w/force file 0000 ....7.00
PJ10029 Queen Amidala Theed Invasion .0100, col. 2, w/force file 000012.00
PJ10038 Queen Amidala Theed Invasion .0300, col. 2, w/force file 0000..7.00
PJ10044 Qui-Gon Jinn Jedi Training Gear .0400, col. 1, w/force file 0000 .9.00
PJ10011 Qui-Gon Jinn Mos Espa Disguise .0000, col. 1, w/force file 0100..8.00
PJ10025 Qui-Gon Jinn Mos Espa Disguise .0100, col. 1, w/force file 0100..8.00
PJ10012 R2-D2 Naboo Escape .0000, col. 1, w/force file 0000 ....8.00
PJ10026 R2-D2 Naboo Escape .0100, col. 1, w/force file 0000 ....8.00
PJ10045 Sabe Queen's Decoy .0400, col. 2, w/force file 0000 ....9.00
PJ10030 Saesee Tiin Jedi Master .0100, col. 2, w/force file 0000 ....12.00

PJ10036 Saesee Tiin Jedi Master .0400, col. 2, w/force file 0000 ....7.00
PJ10014 Sebulba Boonta Eve Challenge .0100, col. 2, w/force file 0000 ..9.00
PJ10050 Shmi Skywalker .0400, col. 2, w/force file 0000 ....9.00
PJ10004 Tusken Raider Desert Sniper .0000, col. 2, w/force file 0000 ....8.00
PJ10027 Tusken Raider Desert Sniper .0100, col. 2, w/force file 0000 ....8.00
PJ10034 Tusken Raider Desert Sniper .0300, col. 2, w/force file 0000 ....7.00
PJ10037 Tusken Raider Desert Sniper .0400, col. 2, w/force file 0000 ....7.00

Hasbro (Canada)

PJ20001

PJM0001

PJ10049 Aurra Sing Bounty Hunter, tri-logo w/force file 0000 ....9.00
PJ10046 Darth Maul, bi-language w/force file 7.00
PJ10047 Obi-Wan Kenobi, bi-language w/force file 7.00
PJ10048 Qui-Gon Jinn, bi-language w/force file 7.00

ACTION FIGURES: POTJ, 2-PACKS

Hasbro
PJ20001 Masters of the Dark Side, Darth Maul and Darth Vader 42.00

ACTION FIGURES: POTJ, MULTI-PACKS

Hasbro
PJM0001 Figure 4-Pack 846480640, Internet e-tailer offer.........................24.00

| PJ10005 | PJ10028 | PJ10015 | PJ10001 | PJ10006 | PJ10002 | PJ10020 | PJ10032 |

| PJ10008 | PJ10009 | PJ10041 | PJ10003 | PJ10043 | PJ10042 | PJ10016 | PJ10029 |

| PJ10044 | PJ10011 | PJ10012 | PJ10045 | PJ10030 | PJ10014 | PJ10050 | PJ10004 |

ACTION FIGURES: POTJ, SCREEN SCENE DELUXE

Hasbro

SSD0002   SSD0003

SSD0001 Amanaman with Salacious Crumb and bounty 18.00
SSD0002 Luke Skywalker in Bacta tank...18.00
SSD0003 Princess Leia, Jabba's Barge 18.00

ACTION FIGURES: TPM

Hasbro

P30020 Adi Gallia with lightsaber .0000, col. 3 ....6.00
P30073 Anakin Skywalker (Naboo Pilot) with flight simulator .0000, col.1 ..6.00
P30021 Anakin Skywalker (Naboo) with comlink unit .0000 col. 1 ....8.00
P30002 Anakin Skywalker (Tatooine) with backpack and grease gun .00, col. 1 (no Innovision logo, blue backpack) 6.00
P30019 Anakin Skywalker (Tatooine) with backpack and grease gun .00, col. 1 (no Innovision logo, brown backpack) 28.00
P30058 Anakin Skywalker (Tatooine) with backpack and grease gun .0100, col. 1 ....7.00
P30022 Battle Droid with blaster rifle (Clean) .00, col. 1 (no Innovision logo)...12.00
P30052 Battle Droid with blaster rifle (Clean) .0100, col. 1 (no Innovision logo)...7.00
P30059 Battle Droid with blaster rifle (Clean) .0200, col. 1 ....6.00
P30003 Battle Droid with blaster rifle (Dirty) .00, col. 1 (no Innovision logo)...12.00
P30056 Battle Droid with blaster rifle (Dirty) .0100, col. 1 (no Innovision logo)...7.00
P30060 Battle Droid with blaster rifle (Dirty) .0200, col. 1 ....6.00
P30023 Battle Droid with blaster rifle (Shot) .00, col. 1 (no Innovision logo)...12.00
P30053 Battle Droid with blaster rifle (Shot) .0100, col. 1 (no Innovision logo)...7.00
P30054 Battle Droid with blaster rifle (Shot) .0200, col. 1 ....6.00
P30024 Battle Droid with blaster rifle (Sliced) .00, col. 1 (no Innovision logo)...12.00
P30055 Battle Droid with blaster rifle (Sliced) .0100, col. 1 (no Innovision logo).7.00
P30061 Battle Droid with blaster rifle (Sliced) .0200, col. 1 ....6.00
P30045 Boss Nass with Gungan staff .0000, col. 3 ....8.00
P30103 Boss Nass with Gungan staff .0100, col. 3 ....6.00
P30010 C-3PO .00, col. 2 (no Innovision logo)......................................8.00

P30062 C-3PO .0100, col. 2...6.00
P30025 Captain Panaka with blaster rifle and pistol .0000, col. 2 ....12.00
P30015 Captain Panaka with blaster rifle and pistol .0000, col. 2 (sticker corrects CommTech lines)...11.00
P30095 Captain Panaka with blaster rifle and pistol .0100, col. 2 ....6.00
P30026 Captain Tarpals with electropole .0100, col. 3 ....6.00
P30016 Chancellor Valorum with ceremonial staff, .00, col. 3.................8.00
P30047 Chancellor Valorum with ceremonial staff, .0000, col. 3 (printed warning)..12.00
P30048 Chancellor Valorum with ceremonial staff, .0000, col. 3 (sticker over printed warning)..8.00
P30093 Darth Maul (Jedi Duel) with double-bladed lightsaber .00, col. 1 (new sculpt, no Innovision logo)...16.00
P30004 Darth Maul (Jedi Duel) with double-bladed lightsaber .00, col. 1 (original sculpt, no Innovision logo)...14.00
P30017 Darth Maul (Jedi Duel) with double-bladed lightsaber .0000, col. 1 ....15.00
P30082 Darth Maul (Jedi Duel) w/double-bladed lightsaber .0000, col. 1 (white background chip)...11.00
P30051 Darth Maul (Jedi Duel) with double-bladed lightsaber .0100, col. 1 ....8.00
P30094 Darth Maul (Jedi Duel) with double-bladed lightsaber .0100, col. 1 (new sculpt)..6.00
P30075 Darth Maul (Sith Lord) with lightsaber with removable blade .0000, col. 1 ....7.00
P30027 Darth Maul (Tatooine) with cloak and lightsaber .0000, col. 1 ......8.00
P30091 Darth Maul (Tatooine) with cloak and lightsaber .0100, col. 1 (white background chip)...11.00
P30072 Darth Sidious (holograph) .0000, col. 2 ....10.00
P30011 Darth Sidious .00, col. 2 (no Innovision logo)..............................9.00
P30064 Darth Sidious .0100, col. 2..6.00
P30078 Destroyer Droid (battle damaged) .0000, col. 1 ....14.00
P30028 Destroyer Droid .0000, col. 2...8.00
P30057 Gasgano with Pit Droid .0100, col. 3 ....8.00
P30014 Gasgano with Pit Droid .0200, col. 3 ....6.00
P30084 Jar Jar Binks (Naboo swamp) with fish .0000, col. 1 ....24.00
P30005 Jar Jar Binks with Gungan battle staff .00, col. 1 (no Innovision logo)..12.00
P30041 Jar Jar Binks with Gungan battle staff .0100, col. 1 (no Innovision logo)..9.00
P30042 Jar Jar Binks with Gungan battle staff .0200, col. 1 ....7.00
P30049 Ki-Adi-Mundi with lightsaber .0000, col. 3 ....9.00
P30105 Ki-Adi-Mundi with lightsaber .0100, col. 3 ....6.00
P30044 Mace Windu with lightsaber and Jedi cloak .0000, col. 3 (no Innovision logo)...15.00
P30018 Mace Windu with lightsaber and Jedi cloak .0100, col. 3..............8.00
P30083 Mace Windu with lightsaber and Jedi cloak .0100, col. 3 (white background chip)...6.00
P30071 Naboo Royal Guard with laser pistol and helmet .0000, col. 2....12.00
P30030 Naboo Royal Security with blaster pistol and rifle .0000, col. 2......8.00
P30031 Nute Gunray .0000, col. 2 ....8.00
P30006 Obi-Wan Kenobi (Jedi Duel) with lightsaber .00, col. 1 (no Innovision logo)..10.00
P30043 Obi-Wan Kenobi (Jedi Duel) with lightsaber .0100, col. 1 ....7.00
P30074 Obi-Wan Kenobi (Jedi Knight) with lightsaber and commlink .0000, col. 1 ....8.00

P30020   P30073   P30021   P30002   P30022   P30045   P30010   P30095

P30026   P30047   P30017   P30075   P30027   P30072   P30011   P30078

P30028   P30057   P30083   P30071   P30030   P30084   P30041   P30049

P30032 Obi-Wan Kenobi (Naboo) with lightsaber and handle .0000, col. 1 ....10.00
P30096 Obi-Wan Kenobi (Naboo) with lightsaber and handle .0100, col. 1 ....7.00
P30033 Ody Mandrell with Otoga 222 pit droid .0000, col. 3 .....9.00
P30097 Ody Mandrell with Otoga 222 pit droid .0100, col. 3 .....6.00
P30101 Ody Mandrell with Otoga 222 pit droid .0100, col. 3 (white background chip) 7.00
P30034 OOM-9 with blaster and binoculars .0000, col. 3...........8.00
P30069 OOM-9 with blaster and binoculars .0000, col. 3 (binoculars mounted in bubble) 36.00
P30092 OOM-9 with blaster and binoculars .0000, col. 3 (white background chip) 10.00
P30007 Padme Naberrie with pod race view screen .00, col. 1 (no Innovision logo) 8.00
P30046 Padme Naberrie with pod race view screen .0100, col. 1 ....6.00
P30086 Pit Droids (2-pack) .0000, col. 2 ....14.00
P30085 Queen Amidala (Battle) with ascension gun .0100, col. 2 ....24.00
P30035 Queen Amidala (Coruscant) .0100, col. 1 ....9.00
P30008 Queen Amidala (Naboo) with blaster pistols .00, col. 1 (no Innovision logo) 9.00
P30065 Queen Amidala (Naboo) with blaster pistols .0100, col. 1 .0100 col. 1 ....6.00
P30009 Qui-Gon Jinn (Jedi Duel) with lightsaber .00, col. 1 (no Innovision logo) 9.00
P30066 Qui-Gon Jinn (Jedi Duel) with lightsaber .0100, col. 1 ....6.00
P30080 Qui-Gon Jinn (Jedi Master) with lightsaber and comlink .0000, col. 1 ....7.00
P30102 Qui-Gon Jinn (Naboo) with lightsaber and handle .0100, col. 1...7.00
P30077 R2-B1 Astromech Droid with power harness .0000, col. 3 ....16.00
P30099 R2-B1 Astromech Droid with power harness .0100, col. 3 ....12.00
P30037 R2-D2 with booster rockets .0000, col. 2 ....6.00
P30100 R2-D2 with booster rockets .0000, col. 2, small bubble 9.00
P30012 Ric Olie with helmet and Naboo blaster .00, col. 2 (no Innovision logo) 9.00
P30050 Ric Olie with helmet and Naboo blaster .0100, col. 2...................6.00
P30070 Ric Olie with helmet and Naboo blaster .0100, col. 2 (closed hand) 18.00
P30038 Rune Haako .0000, col. 2...6.00
P30013 Senator Palpatine with Senate cam droid .00, col. 2 (no Innovision logo) 9.00
P30067 Senator Palpatine with Senate cam droid .0100, col. 2 ....6.00

P30087 Sio Bibble with blaster pistol .0000, col. 2 ....24.00
P30076 TC-14 protocol droid with serving tray .0000, col. 3.......16.00
P30098 TC-14 protocol droid with serving tray .0100, col. 3.......10.00
P30014 Watto with datapad .00, col. 2 (no Innovision logo) 9.00
P30068 Watto with datapad .0100, col. 2 ....7.00
P30040 Yoda with Jedi Council chair .0000, col. 2 ....19.00
P30039 Yoda with Jedi Council chair .0000, col. 2 (missing EPI logo)..........8.00

Kenner
P30001 Mace Windu (mail-away premium)...................................14.00

To receive this figure, collectors had to purchase six individual POTF2 figures between 10/01/98-12/31/98, then mail in dated receipts, the proof-of-purchase from each figure, and $2.99.

P30001 front and back

Hasbro (Canada)
P30118 Anakin Skywalker (Tatooine) .00 col. 1 (no Innovision logo, blue backpack) 6.00
P30117 Anakin Skywalker (Tatooine) .00 col. 1 (no Innovision logo, brown backpack) 28.00
P30119 Anakin Skywalker (Tatooine) .0100 col. 1 ....7.00
P30127 Battle Droid (Clean) .00 col. 1 (no Innovision logo)......12.00
P30128 Battle Droid (Clean) .0100 col. 1 ....7.00
P30110 Battle Droid (Dirty) .00 col. 1 (no Innovision logo).......12.00
P30129 Battle Droid (Dirty) .0100 col. 1 ....7.00
P30130 Battle Droid (Shot) .00 col. 1 (no Innovision logo).........12.00
P30131 Battle Droid (Shot) .0100 col. 1 ....7.00
P30132 Battle Droid (Sliced) .00 col. 1 (no Innovision logo).......12.00
P30133 Battle Droid (Sliced) .0100 col. 1 ....7.00

P30031   P30043   P30096   P30097   P30069   P30092   P30007   P30086

P30085   P30035   P30008   P30009   P30080   P30102   P30077   P30100

P30147 Boss Nass .0000 col. 3 ....7.00
P30142 C-3PO .00 col. 2 (no Innovision logo) 8.00
P30143 C-3PO .0100 col. 2 ....6.00
P30136 Chancellor Valorum .00 col. 3 ....8.00
P30145 Chancellor Valorum .0100 col. 3 ....12.00
P30111 Darth Maul (Jedi Duel) .00 col. 1 (no Innovision logo) 14.00
P30112 Darth Maul (Jedi Duel) .0100 col. 1 ....8.00
P30138 Darth Sidious .00 col. 2 (no Innovision logo) 9.00
P30139 Darth Sidious .0100 col. 2 ....6.00
P30109 Gasgano and Pit Droid .00 col. 3 ....7.00
P30124 Jar Jar Binks .00 col. 1 (no Innovision logo).....12.00
P30125 Jar Jar Binks .0100 col. 1 (no Innovision logo)....9.00
P30126 Jar Jar Binks .0200 col. 1 ....7.00
P30146 Ki-Adi-Mundi .0000 col. 3 ....8.00
P30120 Mace Windu .0000 col. 3 (no Innovision logo) ...15.00
P30144 Mace Windu .0100 col. 3 ....8.00
P30113 Obi-Wan Kenobi (Jedi Duel) .00 col. 1 (no Innovision logo).........7.00
P30114 Obi-Wan Kenobi (Jedi Duel) .0100 col. 1 ....8.00
P30106 Padme Naberrie .00 col. 1 ....8.00
P30121 Padme Naberrie .0100 col. 1 ....6.00
P30122 Queen Amidala (Naboo) .00 col. 1 (no Innovision logo) 9.00
P30123 Queen Amidala (Naboo) .0100 col. 1 ....6.00
P30107 Queen Amidala .00 col. 1 ....9.00
P30115 Qui-Gon Jinn (Jedi Duel) .00 col. 1 (no Innovision logo)........9.00
P30116 Qui-Gon Jinn (Jedi Duel) .0100 col. 1 ....6.00
P30134 Ric Olie .00 col. 2 (no Innovision logo) 6.00
P30135 Ric Olie .0100 col. 2 ....6.00
P30108 Senator Palpatine .00 col. 2 ....9.00
P30137 Senator Palpatine .0100 col. 2 ....6.00
P30140 Watto .00 col. 2 (no Innovision logo) 9.00
P30141 Watto .0100 col. 2 ....7.00

Hasbro (UK)

P30149 Adi Gallia...8.00
P30148 Anakin Skywalker...................................9.00
P30184 Anakin Skywalker (Naboo pilot).............9.00
P30150 Anakin Skywalker (Naboo)....................9.00
P30151 Battle Droid (Clean)...............................9.00
P30152 Battle Droid (Dirty)................................9.00
P30153 Battle Droid (Shot)................................9.00
P30154 Battle Droid (Sliced).............................9.00
P30155 Boss Nass..9.00
P30156 C-3PO..8.00
P30157 Captain Tarpals..................................10.00
P30158 Chancellor Valorum............................11.00
P30190 Darth Dark Sidious (Hologram).............14.00
P30159 Darth Maul..9.00
P30185 Darth Maul (Sith Lord).........................10.00
P30160 Darth Maul (Tatooine)...........................9.00
P30161 Darth Sidious..9.00
P30162 Destroyer Droid....................................9.00
P30163 Destroyer Droid Battle Damaged...........15.00
P30164 Gasgano and Pit Droid..........................9.00
P30165 Jar Jar Binks..8.00

P30166 Jar Jar Binks (Naboo Swamp)................25.00
P30167 Ki-Adi-Mundi..8.00
P30188 Naboo Royal Guard..............................13.00
P30168 Nute Gunray...7.00
P30169 Obi-Wan Kenobi.....................................9.00
P30186 Obi-Wan Kenobi (Jedi Knight)................9.00
P30170 Obi-Wan Kenobi (Naboo).......................9.00
P30171 OOM-9..9.00
P30172 Padme Naberrie......................................9.00
P30189 Pit Droids...16.00
P30173 Queen Amidala......................................10.00
P30174 Queen Amidala (Coruscant)..................10.00
P30175 Qui-Gon Jinn..9.00
P30176 Qui-Gon Jinn (Jedi Master).....................9.00
P30177 Qui-Gon Jinn (Naboo)............................9.00
P30178 R2-D2 w/Booster Rockets......................10.00
P30179 Ric Olie..9.00
P30180 Rune Haako..10.00
P30181 Senator Palpatine...................................9.00
P30187 Sio Bibble...17.00
P30182 Watto..8.00
P30183 Yoda w/Jedi Council Chair......................9.00

ACTION FIGURES: TPM, UNLICENSED

2-pack on Darth Maul 'Space Wars' card.
BAF0001 Darth Maul and Ric Olie.....................20.00
BAF0002 Darth Sidious and C-3PO....................20.00
BAF0003 Senator Palpatine and Mace Windu......20.00

C-3PO card with fake CommTech chip.
BAF0004 C-3PO...7.00
BAF0005 Darth Sidious.....................................7.00
BAF0006 Ric Olie...7.00
BAF0007 Senator Palpatine...............................7.00
BAF0008 Watto..7.00

Darth Maul card with full-card bubble. Figures are approximately 8" in height.
BAF0010 Anakin Skywalker 8.00

BAF0005   BAF0006   BAF0007   BAF0008

P30012   P30038   P30013   P30087   P30076   P30014   P30039   P30040

BAF0001   BAF0002   BAF0003   BAF0009   BAF0010   BAF0011   BAF0012   BAF0013

Action Figures: TPM, Unlicensed

BAF0011 Darth Maul 12.00
BAF0012 Jar Jar Binks 9.00
BAF0009 Obi-Wan Kenobi 8.00
BAF0013 Qui-Gon Jinn 8.00

Darth Maul card. Figures are approximately 6" in height.
BAF0014 Anakin Skywalker 8.00
BAF0015 C-3PO 8.00
BAF0016 Darth Maul 12.00
BAF0017 Obi-Wan Kenobi 8.00
BAF0018 Queen Amidala 8.00
BAF0019 Qui-Gon Jinn 8.00
BAF0020 Darth Maul on Anakin Skywalker card, fake CommTech chip ..9.00
BAF0021 Darth Maul on Darth Maul card, fake CommTech chip 6.00

Queen Amidala card, no CommTech chip attached.
BAF0022 Anakin Skywalker 7.00
BAF0023 Battle Droid (gold) 20.00
BAF0024 Boss Nass 9.00
BAF0025 C-3PO 7.00
BAF0026 Chancellor Valorum 7.00
BAF0027 Darth Maul 9.00
BAF0028 Gasgano and Pit Droid 10.00
BAF0037 Jar Jar Binks 7.00
BAF0029 Ki-Adi-Mundi 7.00
BAF0030 Mace Windu 7.00
BAF0031 Obi-Wan Kenobi 7.00
BAF0032 Padme 7.00
BAF0038 Queen Amidala 7.00
BAF0033 Qui-Gon Jinn 7.00
BAF0034 Ric Olie 7.00
BAF0035 Senator Palpatine 7.00
BAF0036 Watto 7.00
BAF0040 Darth Maul, bagged with header card 8.00
BAF0039 Yoda, bagged with header card 9.00

ACTION FIGURES: TPM 2-PACK

Hasbro
P3L0001 Any 2 Figures (only dist. through wholesale clubs) 22.00

P3L0003 CommTech plus any figure (only dist. through wholesale
    clubs) 25.00
P3L0002 Darth Maul vs. Obi-Wan Kenobi.......................24.00

ACTION FIGURES: TPM 2-PACK BONUS

P3L0001 Sample   P3L0002

Hasbro
Bonus 2-pack. Each figure includes one bonus (unpainted) Battle Droid.
P3T0029 Anakin Skywalker (Naboo) col. 1 ....18.00
P3T0006 Anakin Skywalker col. 1 ....12.00
P3T0007 Battle Droid (Clean) col. 1 ....16.00
P3T0008 Battle Droid (Dirty) col. 1 ....14.00
P3T0009 Battle Droid (Shot) col. 1 ....16.00
P3T0010 Battle Droid (Sliced) col. 1 ....16.00
P3T0003 C-3PO col. 2 ....12.00
P3T0043 Capt. Panaka col. 2 ....79.00
P3T0016 Darth Maul (Jedi Duel) col. 1 ....20.00
P3T0022 Darth Maul (Jedi Duel, resculpted face) col. 1 ....18.00
P3T0025 Darth Maul (Tatooine) Battle Droid col. 1 ....20.00
P3T0002 Darth Sidious col. 2 ....16.00
P3T0011 Destroyer Droid col. 2 ....15.00
P3T0018 Jar Jar Binks col. 1 ....14.00

BAF0014   BAF0015   BAF0016   BAF0017   BAF0018   BAF0019   BAF0020   BAF0021

BAF0022   BAF0023   BAF0027   BAF0037   BAF0031   BAF0032   BAF0038   BAF0033

P3T0006   P3T0007   P3T0008   P3T0009   P3T0003   P3T0016   P3T0025   P3T0002

P3T0044 Naboo Royal Security col. 2 ....79.00
P3T0001 Nute Gunray col. 2 ....12.00
P3T0013 Obi-Wan Kenobi (Jedi Duel) col. 1 ....12.00
P3T0024 Obi-Wan Kenobi (Naboo) col. 1 ....16.00
P3T0014 Padme Newberrie col. 1 ....12.00
P3T0023 Queen Amidala (Coruscant) col. 1 ....14.00
P3T0004 Queen Amidala col. 1 ....12.00
P3T0005 Qui-Gon Jinn (Jedi Duel) col. 1 ....12.00
P3T0028 Qui-Gon Jinn (Naboo) col. 1 ....17.00
P3T0020 R2-D2 col. 2 ....14.00
P3T0017 Ric Olie col. 2 ....12.00
P3T0015 Rune Haako col. 2 ....12.00
P3T0012 Senator Palpatine col. 2 ....12.00
P3T0019 Watto col. 2 ....12.00
P3T0021 Yoda col. 2 ....18.00

Bonus 2-pack. Each figure includes one bonus Pit Droid. Three Pit Droid variations available.

P3T0035 Anakin Skywalker w/brown pit droid col. 1 ....25.00
P3T0036 Anakin Skywalker w/cream pit droid col. 1 ....25.00
P3T0037 Anakin Skywalker w/tan pit droid 25.00
P3T0038 Darth Maul w/brown pit droid col. 1 ....25.00
P3T0039 Darth Maul w/cream pit droid col. 1 ....25.00
P3T0040 Darth Maul w/tan pit droid col. 1 ....25.00
P3T0032 Obi-Wan Kenobi w/brown pit droid col. 1 ....25.00
P3T0033 Obi-Wan Kenobi w/cream pit droid col. 1 ....25.00
P3T0034 Obi-Wan Kenobi w/tan pit droid col. 1 ....25.00
P3T0042 Darth Sidious w/brown pit droid col. 2 ....65.00
P3T0041 Darth Sidious w/cream pit droid col. 2 ....65.00
P3T0026 Darth Sidious w/tan pit droid col. 2 ....65.00
P3T0027 Naboo Royal Guard w/brown pit droid col. 2 ....65.00
P3T0030 Naboo Royal Guard w/cream pit droid col. 2 ....65.00
P3T0031 Naboo Royal Guard w/tan pit droid col. 2 ....65.00

P3T0042	P3T0041	P3T0026	P3T0027	P3T0030	P3T0031
P3T0023	P3T0004	P3T0021	P3T0032	P3T0039	P3T0040
P3T0011	P3T0018	P3T0001	P3T0013	P3T0024	P3T0014
P3T0005	P3T0020	P3T0017	P3T0015	P3T0012	P3T0019
P3T0033	P3T0034	P3T0035	P3T0036	P3T0037	P3T0038

Action Figures: TPM Cinema Scenes

P3M0001   P3M0002   P3M0005

ACTION FIGURES: TPM CINEMA SCENES

Hasbro
CommTech chip included with each Cinema Scene.
P3M0002 Mos Espa Encounter 24.00
P3M0004 Mos Espa Encounter (white background chip)...........24.00
P3M0001 Tatooine Showdown 28.00
P3M0003 Tatooine Showdown (white background chip) 28.00
P3M0005 Watto's Box (white background chip) 45.00

ACTION FIGURES: TPM DELUXE

P3Z0001   P3Z0002   P3Z0003

Hasbro
P3Z0001 Darth Maul...8.00
P3Z0002 Obi-Wan Kenobi 8.00
P3Z0003 Qui-Gon Jinn 8.00

ACTION FIGURES: TPM MINI

P3D0007   P3D0006   P3D0005

P3D0002   P3D0008   P3D0004

P3D0003   P3D0001   P3D card back

Hasbro
Figures are approximately 2" in height.
P3D0007 Anakin Skywalker 12.00
P3D0006 Battle Droid 13.00
P3D0005 Darth Maul 15.00
P3D0002 Jar Jar Binks 13.00
P3D0008 Obi-Wan Kenobi 12.00
P3D0004 Padme Naberrie 12.00
P3D0003 Queen Amidala 12.00
P3D0001 Qui-Gon Jinn 13.00

ACTION FIGURES: TPM, LIGHT-UP

Hasbro
P340001 Darth Maul as Holograph with holoprojector 18.00
P340002 Qui-Gon Jinn as Holograph with holoprojector............21.00

ACTION FIGURES: TPM, TROPHY

Hasbro
P390001 Darth Maul with Sith Infiltrator 15.00

ACTION FIGURES: VINTAGE

AV0463   AV0464   AV0467   AV0469

Glasslite
AV0463 C-3PO 95.00
AV0464 Chewbacca 115.00
AV0465 Guerreiro Imperial 125.00
AV0466 Han Solo 112.00
AV0467 Luke Skywalker 114.00
AV0468 Princess Leia 122.00
AV0469 R2-D2 ....125.00

Habert
AV0485 Chewbacca 95.00
AV0486 Darth Vader 112.00
AV0487 R2-D2 (C1P8)...75.00

Kenner

AV0001 2-1B ESB pkg. 82.00
AV0003 2-1B ROTJ pkg. 52.00
AV0002 2-1B, loose 14.00
AV0005 4-LOM ESB pkg. 195.00
AV0007 4-LOM ROTJ pkg. 49.00
AV0455 4-LOM mailer bag, sealed 35.00
AV0006 4-LOM, loose 24.00
AV0010 8D8 ROTJ pkg. 47.00
AV0009 8D8, loose 10.00
AV0013 Admiral Ackbar ROTJ pkg. 39.00
AV0447 Admiral Ackbar mailer bag, sealed 21.00
AV0012 Admiral Ackbar, loose 10.00
AV0016 Amanaman, POTF pkg. 295.00
AV0015 Amanaman, loose 95.00
AV0019 Anakin Skywalker POTF pkg. 1,875.00
AV0448 Anakin Skywalker mailer bag, sealed 40.00
AV0018 Anakin Skywalker, loose 24.00
AV0021 AT-AT Commander ESB pkg. 75.00
AV0023 AT-AT Commander ROTJ pkg. 49.00
AV0022 AT-AT Commander, loose 12.00
AV0025 AT-AT Driver ESB pkg. 79.00
AV0028 AT-AT Driver ROTJ pkg. 44.00
AV0027 AT-AT Driver POTF pkg. 552.00
AV0026 AT-AT Driver, loose 12.00
AV0032 AT-ST Driver ROTJ pkg. 41.00
AV0031 AT-ST Driver POTF pkg. 65.00
AV0030 AT-ST Driver, loose 8.00
AV0035 A-Wing Pilot, POTF pkg. 151.00
AV0034 A-Wing Pilot, loose 40.00
AV0038 Barada, POTF pkg. 111.00
AV0037 Barada, loose 35.00
AV0040 Ben Kenobi (gray hair) 12-SW pkg. 310.00
AV0041 Ben Kenobi (gray hair) 21-SW pkg. 175.00
AV0042 Ben Kenobi (gray hair) ESB pkg. 110.00
AV0045 Ben Kenobi (gray hair) ROTJ pkg. 55.00
AV0044 Ben Kenobi (gray hair) POTF pkg. 105.00
AV0043 Ben Kenobi (gray hair) loose 26.00
AV0047 Ben Kenobi (white hair) 12-SW pkg. 325.00
AV0048 Ben Kenobi (white hair) 21-SW pkg. 165.00
AV0049 Ben Kenobi (white hair) ESB pkg. 115.00
AV0052 Ben Kenobi (white hair) ROTJ pkg. 55.00
AV0051 Ben Kenobi (white hair) POTF pkg. 115.00
AV0050 Ben Kenobi (white hair) loose 24.00
AV0054 Bespin Security Guard (black) ESB pkg. 60.00
AV0056 Bespin Security Guard (black) ROTJ pkg. 54.00
AV0055 Bespin Security Guard (black) loose 12.00
AV0058 Bespin Security Guard (white) ESB pkg. 66.00
AV0060 Bespin Security Guard (white) ROTJ pkg. 44.00
AV0059 Bespin Security Guard (white) loose 10.00
AV0063 Bib Fortuna ROTJ pkg. 35.00
AV0062 Bib Fortuna, loose 10.00
AV0389 Biker Scout ROTJ pkg. 45.00
AV0388 Biker Scout, POTF pkg. 89.00
AV0387 Biker Scout, loose 14.00
AV0065 Boba Fett 21-SW pkg. 425.00
AV0066 Boba Fett ESB pkg. 425.00
AV0069 Boba Fett ROTJ pkg. (desert scene) 335.00
AV0070 Boba Fett ROTJ pkg. (fireball) 365.00
AV0446 Boba Fett, loose (mail-away packaging) 375.00
AV0449 Boba Fett mailer bag, sealed 105.00
AV0067 Boba Fett loose 45.00
AV0072 Bossk ESB pkg. 135.00
AV0074 Bossk ROTJ pkg. 65.00
AV0450 Bossk mailer bag, sealed 33.00
AV0073 Bossk loose 23.00
AV0078 B-Wing Pilot ROTJ pkg. 37.00
AV0077 B-Wing Pilot, POTF pkg. 42.00
AV0076 B-Wing Pilot loose 8.00
AV0080 C-3PO 12-SW pkg. 255.00
AV0081 C-3PO 21-SW pkg. 125.00
AV0082 C-3PO ESB pkg. 92.00
AV0083 C-3PO loose 18.00
AV0086 C-3PO w/Removable Limbs ESB pkg. 90.00
AV0089 C-3PO w/Removable Limbs ROTJ pkg. 47.00
AV0088 C-3PO w/Removable Limbs, POTF pkg. 85.00
AV0087 C-3PO w/Removable Limbs loose 12.00
AV0092 Chewbacca 12-SW pkg. 300.00
AV0093 Chewbacca 21-SW pkg. 200.00
AV0094 Chewbacca ESB pkg. 110.00
AV0097 Chewbacca ROTJ pkg. 45.00

AV0488 Chewbacca ROTJ pkg., Endor photo 50.00
AV0096 Chewbacca, POTF pkg. 135.00
AV0091 Chewbacca (green crossbow) loose 55.00
AV0095 Chewbacca, loose 17.00
AV0100 Chief Chirpa ROTJ pkg. 35.00
AV0099 Chief Chirpa, loose 11.00
AV0102 Cloud Car Pilot ESB pkg. 85.00
AV0104 Cloud Car Pilot ROTJ pkg. 45.00
AV0103 Cloud Car Pilot loose 22.00
AV0106 Darth Vader 12-SW pkg. 350.00
AV0107 Darth Vader 21-SW pkg. 235.00
AV0108 Darth Vader ESB pkg. 98.00
AV0445 Darth Vader ROTJ pkg. (lightsaber drawn) 70.00
AV0111 Darth Vader ROTJ pkg. (pointing) 65.00
AV0110 Darth Vader, POTF pkg. 130.00
AV0109 Darth Vader, loose 30.00
AV0113 Death Squad Commander 12-SW pkg. 285.00
AV0114 Death Squad Commander 21-SW pkg. 166.00
AV0115 Death Squad Commander ESB pkg. 110.00
AV0116 Death Squad Commander loose 32.00
AV0119 Death Star Droid 21-SW pkg. 175.00
AV0120 Death Star Droid ESB pkg. 145.00
AV0122 Death Star Droid ROTJ pkg. 80.00
AV0121 Death Star Droid, loose 19.00
AV0124 Dengar ESB pkg. 71.00
AV0126 Dengar ROTJ pkg. 47.00
AV0125 Dengar, loose 19.00
AV0130 Emperor ROTJ pkg. 25.00
AV0129 Emperor POTF pkg. 80.00
AV0451 Emperor mailer bag, sealed 40.00
AV0128 Emperor, loose 14.00
AV0133 Emperor's Royal Guard ROTJ pkg. 55.00
AV0132 Emperor's Royal Guard loose 14.00
AV0136 EV-9D9, POTF pkg. 179.00
AV0135 EV-9D9, loose 46.00
AV0138 FX-7 ESB pkg. 65.00
AV0140 FX-7 ROTJ pkg. 48.00
AV0139 FX-7, loose 9.00
AV0144 Gamorrean Guard ROTJ pkg. 37.00
AV0143 Gamorrean Guard POTF pkg. 233.00
AV0142 Gamorrean Guard loose 13.00
AV0147 General Madine ROTJ pkg. 45.00
AV0146 General Madine, loose 10.00
AV0149 Greedo 21-SW pkg. 168.00
AV0150 Greedo ESB pkg. 125.00
AV0152 Greedo ROTJ pkg. 66.00
AV0151 Greedo, loose 18.00
AV0154 Hammerhead 21-SW pkg. 193.00
AV0155 Hammerhead ESB pkg. 135.00
AV0157 Hammerhead ROTJ pkg. 72.00
AV0156 Hammerhead, loose 17.00

AV0001   AV0003   AV0005   AV0007

AV0010   AV0013   AV0016   AV0019

Action Figures: Vintage

AV0159 Han Solo (large head) 12-SW pkg.	680.00	AV0178 Han Solo in Carbonite, POTF pkg.	282.00
AV0160 Han Solo (large head) 21-SW pkg.	520.00	AV0177 Han Solo in Carbonite, loose	95.00
AV0161 Han Solo (large head) ESB pkg.	257.00	AV0182 Han Solo Trench Coat ROTJ pkg.	47.00
AV0461 Han Solo (large head) ROTJ pkg. (Death Star)	172.00	AV0181 Han Solo Trench Coat, POTF pkg.	390.00
AV0163 Han Solo (large head) ROTJ pkg. (Mos Eisley)	182.00	AV0180 Han Solo Trench Coat, loose	15.00
AV0162 Han Solo (large head) loose	43.00	AV0184 IG-88 ESB pkg.	154.00
AV0165 Han Solo (small head) 12-SW pkg.	670.00	AV0186 IG-88 ROTJ pkg.	77.00
AV0167 Han Solo (small head) ESB pkg.	315.00	AV0185 IG-88, loose	26.00
AV0168 Han Solo (small head) loose	35.00	AV0188 Imperial Commander ESB pkg.	64.00
AV0169 Han Solo Bespin ESB pkg.	149.00	AV0190 Imperial Commander ROTJ pkg.	36.00
AV0171 Han Solo Bespin ROTJ pkg.	99.00	AV0189 Imperial Commander, loose	10.00
AV0170 Han Solo Bespin, loose	22.00	AV0193 Imperial Dignitary POTF pkg.	131.00
AV0173 Han Solo Hoth Battle Gear ESB pkg.	114.00	AV0192 Imperial Dignitary loose	34.00
AV0175 Han Solo Hoth Battle Gear ROTJ pkg.	75.00	AV0196 Imperial Gunner POTF pkg.	178.00
AV0174 Han Solo Hoth Battle Gear, loose	15.00	AV0195 Imperial Gunner loose	65.00

AV0021   AV0023   AV0025   AV0028   AV0027   AV0032   AV0031   AV0035

AV0038   AV0041   AV0042   AV0045   AV0047   AV0052   AV0051   AV0054

AV0056   AV0058   AV0060   AV0063   AV0389   AV0388   AV0065   AV0066

AV0069   AV0070   AV0072   AV0074   AV0078   AV0077   AV0080   AV0082

AV0198 Imperial Stormtrooper in Hoth Weather Gear ESB pkg. 88.00
AV0200 Imperial Stormtrooper in Hoth Weather Gear ROTJ pkg. 52.00
AV0199 Imperial Stormtrooper in Hoth Weather Gear, loose 21.00
AV0202 Jawa 12-SW pkg., plastic cape 2,750.00
AV0204 Jawa 12-SW pkg. 263.00
AV0205 Jawa 21-SW pkg. 185.00
AV0206 Jawa ESB pkg. 110.00

AV0208 Jawa POTF pkg. 125.00
AV0209 Jawa ROTJ pkg. 67.00
AV0203 Jawa loose, plastic cape 85.00
AV0207 Jawa, loose 27.00
AV0212 Klaatu (Palace Outfit) ROTJ pkg. 44.00
AV0211 Klaatu (Palace Outfit) loose..10.00
AV0215 Klaatu (Skiff Outfit) ROTJ pkg. 44.00

| AV0086 | AV0089 | AV0088 | AV0092 | AV0094 | AV0097 | AV0488 | AV0096 |

| AV0100 | AV0102 | AV0104 | AV0106 | AV0108 | AV0445 | AV0111 | AV0110 |

| AV0113 | AV0115 | AV0119 | AV0120 | AV0122 | AV0124 | AV0126 | AV0130 |

| AV0129 | AV0133 | AV0136 | AV0138 | AV0140 | AV0144 | AV0143 | AV0147 |

| AV0149 | AV0150 | AV0152 | AV0154 | AV0155 | AV0157 | AV0160 | AV0165 |

Action Figures: Vintage

AV0161	AV0163	AV0461	AV0169	AV0171	AV0173	AV0175	AV0178
AV0182	AV0181	AV0184	AV0186	AV0188	AV0190	AV0193	AV0196
AV0198	AV0200	AV0202	AV0204	AV0206	AV0208	AV0209	AV0212
AV0215	AV0220	AV0222	AV0217	AV0225	AV0228	AV0230	AV0232
AV0235	AV0238	AV0239	AV0242	AV0251	AV0254	AV0253	AV0256

AV0254 Luke Skywalker Bespin Fatigues (blonde) ESB pkg. (looking) 160.00
AV0255 Luke Skywalker Bespin Fatigues (blonde) loose 35.00
AV0253 Luke Skywalker Bespin Fatigues (blonde hair) ESB pkg. (walking)...210.00
AV0256 Luke Skywalker Bespin Fatigues (blonde hair) ROTJ pkg. (looking)...95.00
AV0259 Luke Skywalker Bespin Fatigues (brown hair) ESB pkg. (looking) 120.00
AV0258 Luke Skywalker Bespin Fatigues (brown hair) ESB pkg. (walking) 175.00
AV0261 Luke Skywalker Bespin Fatigues (brown hair) ROTJ pkg. (looking) ..110.00
AV0260 Luke Skywalker Bespin Fatigues (brown hair) loose....................20.00
AV0263 Luke Skywalker Hoth Battle Gear ESB pkg. 96.00
AV0265 Luke Skywalker Hoth Battle Gear ROTJ pkg. 42.00
AV0264 Luke Skywalker Hoth Battle Gear, loose 18.00
AV0268 Luke Skywalker Jedi (blue lightsaber) ROTJ pkg.....................175.00
AV0267 Luke Skywalker Jedi (blue lightsaber) loose 59.00
AV0272 Luke Skywalker Jedi (green lightsaber) ROTJ pkg. 100.00
AV0271 Luke Skywalker Jedi (green lightsaber) POTF pkg. 244.00
AV0270 Luke Skywalker Jedi (green lightsaber) loose 28.00
AV0275 Luke Skywalker Stormtrooper Disguise, POTF pkg. 480.00
AV0274 Luke Skywalker Stormtrooper Disguise loose 145.00
AV0277 Luke Skywalker X-Wing Pilot 21-SW pkg. 180.00
AV0278 Luke Skywalker X-Wing Pilot ESB pkg. 133.00
AV0281 Luke Skywalker X-Wing Pilot ROTJ pkg. 65.00
AV0280 Luke Skywalker X-Wing Pilot POTF pkg. 117.00
AV0279 Luke Skywalker X-Wing Pilot, loose 20.00

AV0285 Lumat ROTJ pkg...49.00
AV0284 Lumat POTF pkg...55.00
AV0283 Lumat, loose...18.00
AV0290 Nien Nunb ROTJ pkg..33.00
AV0453 Nien Nunb, mailer bag, sealed 19.00
AV0289 Nien Nunb, loose 8.00
AV0294 Nikto ROTJ pkg...40.00
AV0293 Nikto POTF pkg...575.00
AV0292 Nikto, loose...11.00
AV0298 Paploo ROTJ pkg...48.00
AV0297 Paploo POTF pkg...46.00
AV0296 Paploo, loose..15.00
AV0300 Power Droid 21-SW pkg...170.00
AV0301 Power Droid ESB pkg..115.00
AV0303 Power Droid ROTJ pkg..69.00
AV0302 Power Droid, loose...25.00
AV0305 Princess Leia, 12-SW pkg...425.00
AV0306 Princess Leia 21-SW pkg..265.00
AV0307 Princess Leia ESB pkg...289.00
AV0309 Princess Leia ROTJ pkg..465.00
AV0308 Princess Leia, loose..34.00
AV0311 Princess Leia Bespin (crew neck) ESB pkg. (front view) 170.00
AV0313 Princess Leia Bespin (crew neck) ROTJ pkg. (front view).............89.00

AV0259   AV0261   AV0263   AV0265   AV0268   AV0272   AV0271   AV0275

AV0277   AV0278   AV0281   AV0280   AV0285   AV0284   AV0290   AV0294

AV0293   AV0298   AV0297   AV0300   AV0301   AV0303   AV0305   AV0307

AV0309   AV0311   AV0318   AV0320   AV0324   AV0328   AV0327   AV0330

Action Figures: Vintage

AV0312 Princess Leia Bespin (crew neck) loose 28.00
AV0318 Princess Leia Bespin (turtleneck) ESB pkg. (front view) 185.00
AV0317 Princess Leia Bespin (turtleneck) ESB pkg. (profile)...................170.00
AV0320 Princess Leia Bespin (turtleneck) ROTJ pkg. (front view)............89.00
AV0319 Princess Leia Bespin (turtleneck) loose 36.00
AV0324 Princess Leia Boushh Disguise ROTJ pkg. 61.00
AV0452 Princess Leia Boushh Disguise, mailer bag, sealed...................27.00
AV0323 Princess Leia Boushh Disguise, loose 18.00
AV0328 Princess Leia Combat Poncho ROTJ pkg. 59.00
AV0327 Princess Leia Combat Poncho POTF pkg. 121.00
AV0326 Princess Leia Combat Poncho, loose 21.00
AV0330 Princess Leia Hoth ESB pkg. 160.00
AV0332 Princess Leia Hoth ROTJ pkg. 93.00
AV0331 Princess Leia Hoth, loose 26.00
AV0335 Pruneface ROTJ pkg. 36.00
AV0454 Pruneface. mailer bag, sealed...................27.00
AV0334 Pruneface, loose 14.00
AV0337 R2-D2 12-SW pkg. 245.00
AV0338 R2-D2 21-SW pkg. 150.00
AV0339 R2-D2 ESB pkg. 85.00
AV0340 R2-D2, loose...................18.00
AV0344 R2-D2 Pop-Up Lightsaber, POTF pkg. 213.00
AV0343 R2-D2 Pop-Up Lightsaber, loose 64.00
AV0346 R2-D2 w/Sensorscope ESB pkg...................78.00
AV0348 R2-D2 w/Sensorscope ROTJ pkg. 52.00
AV0456 R2-D2 w/Sensorscope, mailer bag, sealed 20.00

AV0347 R2-D2 w/Sensorscope, loose...................12.00
AV0350 R5-D4 21-SW pkg. 135.00
AV0351 R5-D4 ESB pkg. 160.00
AV0353 R5-D4 ROTJ pkg. 73.00
AV0352 R5-D4, loose...................28.00
AV0356 Rancor Keeper ROTJ pkg. 34.00
AV0355 Rancor Keeper, loose 11.00
AV0358 Rebel Commander ESB pkg. 71.00
AV0360 Rebel Commander ROTJ pkg. 37.00
AV0359 Rebel Commander loose 11.00
AV0363 Rebel Commando ROTJ pkg. 31.00
AV0362 Rebel Commando, loose 10.00
AV0365 Rebel Soldier ESB pkg. 77.00
AV0367 Rebel Soldier ROTJ pkg. 44.00
AV0366 Rebel Soldier, loose 15.00
AV0370 Ree-Yees ROTJ pkg. 34.00
AV0369 Ree-Yees loose 12.00
AV0373 Romba POTF pkg. 58.00
AV0372 Romba, loose 22.00
AV0375 Sandpeople 12-SW pkg. 265.00
AV0376 Sandpeople 21-SW pkg. 152.00
AV0377 Sandpeople ESB pkg. 99.00
AV0378 Sandpeople, loose 22.00
AV0382 Snaggletooth 21-SW pkg. 185.00
AV0383 Snaggletooth ESB pkg. 136.00
AV0385 Snaggletooth ROTJ pkg. 59.00

 AV0332
 AV0335
 AV0337
 AV0339
 AV0344
 AV0346
 AV0348
 AV0350

 AV0351
 AV0353
 AV0356
 AV0358
 AV0360
 AV0363
 AV0365
 AV0367

 AV0370
 AV0373
 AV0376
 AV0377
 AV0382
 AV0383
 AV0391
 AV0459

 AV0393
 AV0395
 AV0398
 AV0397
 AV0402
 AV0401
 AV0404
 AV0406

AV0379

AV0408

AV0410

AV0412

AV0413

AV0415

AV0418

AV0421

AV0425

AV0424

AV0427

AV0431

AV0434

AV0433

AV0440

AV0442

AV0384 Snaggletooth, loose 16.00
AV0381 Snaggletooth (blue body) loose 190.00
AV0391 Squidhead ROTJ pkg. 40.00
AV0390 Squidhead, loose 11.00
AV0459 Star Destroyer Commander ESB pkg. 135.00
AV0460 Star Destroyer Commander ROTJ pkg. 60.00
AV0393 Stormtrooper 12-SW pkg. 283.00
AV0394 Stormtrooper 21-SW pkg. 177.00
AV0395 Stormtrooper ESB pkg. 95.00
AV0398 Stormtrooper ROTJ pkg. 68.00
AV0397 Stormtrooper POTF pkg. 276.00
AV0396 Stormtrooper, loose 20.00
AV0288 Sy Snootles and the Max Rebo Band (3-piece) ROTJ pkg. 150.00
AV0287 Sy Snootles and the Max Rebo Band (3-piece) loose 65.00
AV0402 Teebo ROTJ pkg. 51.00
AV0401 Teebo POTF pkg. 183.00
AV0400 Teebo, loose 13.00
AV0404 Tie Fighter Pilot ESB pkg. 90.00
AV0406 Tie Fighter Pilot ROTJ pkg. 64.00
AV0405 Tie Fighter Pilot, loose 18.00
AV0379 Tusken Raider ROTJ pkg. 74.00
AV0408 Ugnaught ESB pkg. 46.00
AV0410 Ugnaught ROTJ pkg. 39.00
AV0409 Ugnaught, loose 12.00
AV0412 Walrus Man 21-SW pkg. 158.00
AV0413 Walrus Man ESB pkg. 135.00
AV0415 Walrus Man ROTJ pkg. 68.00
AV0414 Walrus Man, loose 18.00
AV0418 Warok POTF pkg. 74.00
AV0417 Warok, loose 26.00
AV0421 Weequay ROTJ pkg. 31.00
AV0420 Weequay, loose 10.00
AV0425 Wicket Warrick ROTJ pkg. 50.00
AV0424 Wicket Warrick POTF pkg. 186.00
AV0423 Wicket Warrick, loose 16.00
AV0427 Yak Face (weapon included), POTF pkg. 2,179.00
AV0428 Yak Face (weapon not included) POTF pkg. 1,995.00
AV0429 Yak Face, loose 160.00
AV0431 Yoda (brown snake) ESB pkg. 277.00
AV0434 Yoda (brown snake) ROTJ pkg. 90.00
AV0433 Yoda (brown snake) POTF pkg. 463.00
AV0432 Yoda (brown snake) loose 26.00

AV0436 Yoda (orange snake) ESB pkg. 135.00
AV0437 Yoda (orange snake) loose 33.00
AV0440 Zuckuss ESB pkg. 95.00
AV0442 Zuckuss ROTJ pkg. 56.00
AV0441 Zuckuss, loose 18.00

Kenner (Canada)

Empire Strikes Back card, Sears Canada exclusive.
AV0509 Ben Kenobi (gray hair) ESB pkg. 550.00
AV0510 Dengar 480.00
AV0511 General Veers 3,500.00
AV0512 Han Solo (Cloud City Outfit) 500.00
AV0513 Lobot (Lando's Aid) 480.00
AV0514 Luke Skywalker (Hoth Outfit) 500.00
AV0515 R2-D2 with Parascope 535.00
AV0516 Ugnaught 450.00

Kenner (UK)

Figures in tri-logo packaging.
AV0004 2-1B 85.00
AV0008 4-LOM 45.00
AV0011 8D8 ....95.00
AV0014 Admiral Ackbar 38.00
AV0017 Amanaman 175.00
AV0020 Anakin Skywalker 160.00
AV0024 AT-AT Commander 42.00
AV0029 AT-AT Driver 96.00
AV0033 AT-ST Driver 31.00
AV0036 A-Wing Pilot 110.00
AV0039 Barada 69.00
AV0046 Ben Kenobi (gray hair) 65.00
AV0053 Ben Kenobi (white hair) 65.00
AV0057 Bespin Security Guard (black) 32.00
AV0061 Bespin Security Guard (white) 32.00
AV0064 Bib Fortuna 35.00
AV0458 Boba Fett, loose (sky blue instead of gray) 170.00
AV0068 Boba Fett, loose 65.00
AV0071 Boba Fett 635.00
AV0457 Boba Fett (sky blue instead of gray) 1,275.00
AV0075 Bossk 71.00
AV0079 B-Wing Pilot 28.00
AV0090 C-3PO w/Removable Limbs 40.00

AV0510

AV0511

Produced for Kenner in Canada by Irwin Toys, these figures in Sears exclusive packaging were simply vacuum sealed onto logo header cards.

The most sought after of this series is the AT-AT Commander, who is identified on the card as "General Veers."

AV0512

AV0513

AV0514

AV0515

AV0516

Action Figures: Vintage

AV0004 AV0011 AV0014 AV0017 AV0020 AV0024 AV0029 AV0033

AV0036 AV0039 AV0053 AV0064 AV0071 AV0075 AV0079 AV0090

AV0098 AV0112 AV0123 AV0127 AV0131 AV0134 AV0137 AV0141

AV0145 AV0148 AV0164 AV0172 AV0176 AV0179 AV0183 AV0187

AV0191 AV0194 AV0197 AV0201 AV0213 AV0216 AV0226 AV0229

AV0243 Luke Skywalker (blonde hair) 200.00
AV0247 Luke Skywalker (brown hair).............................245.00
AV0252 Luke Skywalker Battle Poncho 101.00
AV0257 Luke Skywalker Bespin Fatigues (blonde hair) (looking) 105.00
AV0262 Luke Skywalker Bespin Fatigues (brown hair) (looking) 135.00
AV0266 Luke Skywalker Hoth Battle Gear 34.00
AV0269 Luke Skywalker Jedi (blue lightsaber) 210.00
AV0273 Luke Skywalker Jedi (green lightsaber) 130.00
AV0276 Luke Skywalker Stormtrooper Disguise 250.00
AV0282 Luke Skywalker X-Wing Pilot 125.00
AV0286 Lumat 31.00
AV0507 Max Rebo Band (3-piece) 118.00
AV0291 Nien Nunb 74.00
AV0295 Nikto 25.00
AV0299 Paploo 66.00
AV0304 Power Droid...60.00

AV0316 Princess Leia Bespin (crew neck) (front view)..........92.00
AV0314 Princess Leia Bespin (crew neck) (profile) 99.00
AV0322 Princess Leia Bespin (turtleneck) (front view)........177.00
AV0321 Princess Leia Bespin (turtleneck) (profile) 121.00
AV0325 Princess Leia Boushh Disguise.........................188.00
AV0329 Princess Leia Combat Poncho 38.00
AV0333 Princess Leia Hoth.....................................54.00
AV0310 Princess Leia 187.00
AV0336 Pruneface..32.00
AV0345 R2-D2 Pop-Up Lightsaber...............................166.00
AV0349 R2-D2 w/Sensorscope 30.00
AV0354 R5-D4 ....80.00
AV0357 Rancor Keeper 49.00
AV0361 Rebel Commander 30.00
AV0364 Rebel Commando 30.00
AV0368 Rebel Soldier 30.00

| AV0223 | AV0233 | AV0236 | AV0252 | AV0262 | AV0269 | AV0273 | AV0276 |

| AV0282 | AV0286 | AV0507 | AV0291 | AV0295 | AV0299 | AV0325 |

| AV0329 | AV0333 | AV0310 | AV0336 | AV0345 | AV0349 | AV0354 | AV0361 |

| AV0364 | AV0368 | AV0371 | AV0374 | AV0392 | AV0399 | AV0403 | AV0407 |

| AV0380 | AV0411 | AV0419 | AV0422 | AV0426 | AV0430 | AV0435 | AV0443 |

Action Figures: Vintage

AV0371 Ree-Yees 30.00
AV0374 Romba 39.00
AV0386 Snaggletooth 73.00
AV0392 Squidhead 30.00
AV0399 Stormtrooper 85.00
AV0403 Teebo 27.00
AV0407 Tie Fighter Pilot 105.00
AV0380 Tusken Raider 75.00
AV0411 Ugnaught 30.00
AV0416 Walrus Man 84.00
AV0419 Warok 80.00
AV0422 Weequay 30.00
AV0426 Wicket Warrick 23.00
AV0430 Yak Face 482.00
AV0435 Yoda (brown snake) 73.00
AV0439 Yoda (orange snake) 117.00
AV0443 Zuckuss 34.00

| AV0517 | AV0525 | AV0519 | AV0531 |

| AV0520 | AV0501 | AV0523 | AV0503 |

Lili Ledy

AV0517 Admiral Ackbar, ROTJ pkg. 195.00
AV0518 AT-ST Driver, ROTJ pkg. 235.00
AV0529 Bib Fortuna, ROTJ pkg. 185.00
AV0519 Biker Scout, ROTJ pkg. 175.00
AV0525 Boba Fett, ROTJ pkg. 415.00
AV0524 C-3PO, ROTJ pkg. 155.00
AV0504 Chewbacca, ROTJ pkg. 230.00
AV0528 Cloud Car Pilot, ROTJ pkg. 130.00
AV0531 Emperor's Royal Guard, ROTJ pkg. 164.00
AV0527 Han Solo, Bespin, ROTJ pkg. 135.00
AV0520 Imperial Commander, ROTJ pkg. 125.00
AV0501 Jawa (cloth cape), ROTJ pkg. 202.00
AV0502 Klaatu (palace outfit), ROTJ pkg. 189.00
AV0523 Lumat, ROTJ pkg. 160.00
AV0521 Nien Numb, ROTJ pkg. 165.00
AV0508 Princess Leia Boushh Disguise, ROTJ pkg. 140.00
AV0530 Squidhead, ROTJ pkg. 150.00
AV0522 Star Destroyer Commander, ROTJ pkg. 175.00
AV0503 Tie Fighter Pilot, ROTJ pkg. 255.00

Meccano

AV0505 Death Squad Commander 272.00
AV0506 Princess Leia 290.00

Palitoy

AV0489 C-3PO 210.00
AV0490 Darth Vader 220.00
AV0491 Death Star Droid 165.00
AV0492 Greedo 182.00
AV0493 Han Solo 435.00
AV0494 Power Droid 124.00
AV0495 R2-D2 .... 215.00
AV0496 Sand People 137.00
AV0497 Snaggletooth 114.00
AV0498 Stormtrooper 162.00

| AV0470 | AV0472 | AV0473 | AV0476 | AV0477 |

| AV0478 | AV0480 | AV0481 | AV0482 | AV0483 |

Popy

AV0470 S 1 Boba Fett 265.00
AV0471 S 2 Darth Vader 180.00
AV0472 S 3 R2-D2 .... 165.00
AV0473 S 4 C-3PO 165.00
AV0474 S 5 Luke Skywalker, Bespin 97.00
AV0475 S 6 Han Solo, Hoth 92.00
AV0476 S 7 Chewbacca 175.00
AV0477 S 8 Luke Skywalker, Tatooine 205.00
AV0478 S 9 Han Solo 175.00
AV0479 S10 Imperial Snowtrooper 96.00
AV0480 S11 Death Star Droid 114.00
AV0481 S12 Luke Skywalker, Hoth 92.00
AV0482 S13 Luke Skywalker, X-Wing Pilot 95.00
AV0483 S14 R5-D4 .... 90.00
AV0484 S15 Stormtrooper 117.00

ACTION FIGURES: VINTAGE MULTI-PACKS

Kenner

AVM0021 2-Pack; ROTJ (random figures) 85.00
AVM0022 3-Pack mail-away premium 85.00
AVM0001 3-Pack: 2-1B, Princess Leia (Hoth Outfit), Rebel Commander 530.00
AVM0002 3-Pack: Admiral Ackbar, Chief Chirpa, Princess Leia (Boushh Disguise) 455.00
AVM0003 3-Pack: AT-AT Driver, Dengar, Imperial Commander 610.00
AVM0004 3-Pack: AT-AT Driver, Tie Fighter Pilot, Zuckuss 530.00
AVM0015 3-Pack: Ben Kenobi, Han Solo, Luke Skywalker X-Wing Pilot .. 480.00
AVM0005 3-Pack: Ben Kenobi, Han Solo, Princess Leia Organa 300.00
AVM0006 3-Pack: Bespin Security Guard, Lando Calrissian, Luke Skywalker (Bespin Fatigues) 560.00
AVM0007 3-Pack: Bib Fortuna, Biker Scout, Imperial Royal Guard 455.00
AVM0016 3-Pack: Boba Fett, Sand People, Snaggletooth 550.00
AVM0008 3-Pack: Bossk, IG-88, (Hoth) Stormtrooper 625.00
AVM0009 3-Pack: C-3PO, Chewbacca, R2-D2 .... 350.00
AVM0010 3-Pack: C-3PO, Cloud Car Pilot, Ugnaught 485.00
AVM0011 3-Pack: Darth Vader, Death Squad Commander, Stormtrooper 800.00
AVM0017 3-Pack: Death Star Droid, Power Droid, R5-D4 .... 450.00

AVM0021 Samples

AVM0012 3-Pack: FX-7, Han Solo (Hoth Outfit), Rebel Commander......550.00
AVM0018 3-Pack: Greedo, Hammerhead, Walrus Man.........................510.00
AVM0013 3-Pack: Han Solo (Bespin Outfit), Lobot, Ugnaught 530.00
AVM0014 3-Pack: Luke Skywalker (Hoth Outfit), Princess Leia (Hoth Outfit), R2-D2 (Sensorscope)......................................660.00
AVM0019 6-Pack: AT-AT Driver, Darth Vader, IG-88, Rebel Soldier, (Hoth) Stormtrooper, Yoda 765.00
AVM0020 6-Pack: C-3PO, Darth Vader, Han Solo (Hoth Outfit), R2-D2 (Sensorscope), Rebel Soldier, (Hoth) Stormtrooper 670.00

Parker Bros.
AVM0023 Any 2 figures plus vehicle 790.00
AVM0024 Any 2 figures plus accessory 685.00

ACTION FIGURES: VINTAGE, DROIDS

Glasslite
AVS1025 R2-D2 ....145.00

Kenner
AVS1001 A-Wing Pilot 187.00
AVS1013 A-Wing Pilot, loose 35.00
AVS1002 Boba Fett 1,085.00
AVS1014 Boba Fett, loose 95.00
AVS1003 C-3PO 112.00
AVS1015 C-3PO, loose 28.00
AVS1004 Jann Tosh 31.00

AVM0019 AVM0020 AVM0023 sample AVM0024 sample

AVM0001 AVM0002 AVM0003 AVM0004 AVM0015 AVM0005

AVM0006 AVM0007 AVM0016 AVM0008 AVM0009 AVM0010

AVM0011 AVM0017 AVM0012 AVM0018 AVM0013 AVM0014

Action Figures: Vintage, Droids

AVS1016 Jann Tosh, loose..8.00
AVS1005 Jord Dusat..30.00
AVS1017 Jord Dusat, loose..8.00
AVS1006 Kea Moll..32.00
AVS1018 Kea Moll, loose..8.00
AVS1007 Kez-Iban...30.00
AVS1019 Kez-Iban, loose...8.00
AVS1008 R2-D2...125.00
AVS1020 R2-D2, loose...30.00
AVS1009 Sise Fromm..105.00
AVS1021 Sise Fromm, loose...35.00
AVS1010 Thall Joben..30.00
AVS1022 Thall Joben, loose..8.00
AVS1011 Tig Fromm...74.00
AVS1023 Tig Fromm, loose...22.00
AVS1012 Uncle Gundy..28.00
AVS1024 Uncle Gundy, loose..8.00
AVS1026 Vlix (non-US)..4,500.00
AVS1027 Vlix (non-US), loose.......................................380.00

ACTION FIGURES: VINTAGE, EWOKS

Kenner
AVS2001 Dulok Scout...26.00
AVS2007 Dulok Scout, loose...8.00
AVS2002 Dulok Shaman...26.00
AVS2008 Dulok Shaman, loose.......................................8.00
AVS2003 King Gorneesh...26.00
AVS2009 King Gorneesh, loose.......................................8.00
AVS2004 Lady Ugrah Gorneesh.......................................28.00
AVS2010 Lady Ugrah Gorneesh, loose...........................8.00
AVS2005 Logray..26.00
AVS2011 Logray, loose...8.00
AVS2006 Wicket...30.00
AVS2012 Wicket, loose...10.00

AVS1001 AVS1002 AVS1003 AVS1004

AVS1005 AVS1006 AVS1007 AVS1008

BAH0001 BAH0002 BAH0003 BAH0004

BAH0005 BAH0006 BAH0009 BAH0010

ACTION FIGURES: VINTAGE, UNLICENSED

Uzay
BAH0001 AT Driver...275.00
BAH0002 Blue Stars...314.00
BAH0003 C-3PO...275.00
BAH0004 Chewbacca..280.00
BAH0005 Darth Vader..330.00
BAH0006 Imperial Gunner...250.00
BAH0007 MLC-3 Mini Rig...325.00
BAH0008 MTV-7 Mini Rig...325.00
BAH0009 Royal Guard..290.00
BAH0010 Stormtrooper..310.00

2-Pack on ROTJ hanger card. Figures are approximately 4" in height.
BAH0011 C-3PO and Darth Vader....................................48.00
BAH0012 C-3PO and R2-D2...51.00
BAH0013 Chewbacca and Darth Vader...........................45.00

BAH0018 BAH0022

Figures from Hungary.
BAH0015 Biker Scout..265.00
BAH0016 Boba Fett..265.00
BAH0017 C-3PO...235.00
BAH0018 Chewbacca..235.00
BAH0019 Darth Vader..235.00
BAH0020 Han Solo...235.00
BAH0021 Luke Skywalker..235.00
BAH0022 Princess Leia...235.00
BAH0023 Snowtrooper...235.00
BAH0024 Wicket...235.00

ACTION VALUE PACK

Spectra Star
AVQ0001 Star Wars kite, frisbee, and yo-yo...................17.00

AVS1009 AVS1010 AVS1011 AVS1012 AVS2001 AVS2002 AVS2005 AVS2006

ADDRESS BOOKS

PPA0001   PPA0002

Antioch
PPA0001 Cover art from "The Glove of Darth Vader" 5.00

Day Runner
Character telephone books.
PPA0004 Jar Jar Binks 7.00
PPA0007 Jar Jar Binks, 6-ring binder 12.00
PPA0002 Queen Amidala...7.00
PPA0005 Queen Amidala, 6-ring binder 12.00
PPA0003 Qui-Gon Jinn...7.00
PPA0006 Qui-Gon Jinn, 6-ring binder 12.00

PPA0008   PPA0009   PPA0010

PPA0011 Episode I Address Book and Notepad 6.00
PPA0010 Adventures, EPI 5.00
PPA0008 Heroes, EPI 5.00
PPA0009 Jedi Battles, EPI 5.00

ADVERTISING/DISPLAYS

Agfa
AD0005 Poster: free frisbee or yo-yo w/film purchase 11.00

At-A Glance
AD0029 Hexagonal dump w/double-corrugated die-cut header for
     posters..11.00

Avon
AD0057 Relive the magic, Jedi Knights tin card set 2.00

Burger King
AD0069 Counter display for ROTJ glasses..94.00
AD0012 Counter display for ROTJ glasses, Vader-shaped 47.00
AD0014 Translite display for ROTJ glasses..54.00

Butterfly Originals
AD0066 Pencil Top Eraser counter display..12.00
AD0064 ROTJ pen display, cardboard box with die-cut header, 36 count
     pens..8.00
AD0068 Vending machine header, pencil toppers, and paper protec-
     tors..18.00

Clarks
AD0010 Handbill flyer advertising Clarks shoe line 26.00
AD0011 Handbill flyer with Clarks shoe line prices 7.00
AD0013 Order form for Clarks shoe line...11.00

Coca-Cola
AD0007 "Match Star Wars Pairs And You Could Win A Cash Prize" bottlecap
     game promotion..24.00

Colgate
AD0027 Colgate SW:EPI retail toothbrush cardboard display 14.00

Deka
AD0021 Flyer for plastic merchandise 11.00

Factors, Etc.
AD0062 Pendant and necklace countertop display rack, Darth Vader.85.00
AD0058 Pendant and necklace countertop display rack, rotating 33.00

Forbidden Zone
AD0019 Forbidden Zone poster promoting SW Exhibition 9/10-9/30/98 ..28.00

H.E. Harris and Company
AD0030 Display bin and 2-piece header for stamp collecting set 64.00

Kenner
AD0067 "The Force" Lightsaber 12-saber retail display 38.00
AD0023 4-Sided overstock concealer with velcro 38.00
AD0061 Paper stock cover: "Star Wars Is Here" 44.00
AD0022 Toy advertisement (magazine), full-page glossy, 1979 ....6.00

Kentucky Fried Chicken
AD0042 8-piece meal/flying topper menu topper (straight bottom,
     shaped top) outdoor advertising, made of corrugated plasticized card-
     board 26.00
AD0044 Cup toppers vertical sign outdoor advertising, made of corrugated
     plasticized cardboard..17.00
AD0024 EP1 pre-release maketing plan 77.00
AD0043 Jar Jar/kid's meal toys, vertical sign outdoor advertising, made of
     corrugated plasticized cardboard...24.00

Lays
AD0006 Can You Resist framed game cards, promotional 45.00

Lego
AD0073 Enter The Lego Galactic Challenge Building Contest, padded
     poster..16.00
AD0053 Star Wars Galactic Challenge building contest, official entry
     form..1.00

Lucasarts
AD0003 Jedi Power Battles, Coming in April standee 35.00

MPC
AD0018 MPC plastic model squadron promotes ROTJ model ships,
     newsprint from comic books 4.00

Natural Balance
AD0071 Floor display, Luke, Leia, Chewbacca, Wicket, Yoda, R2-D2 .....43.00

Parker Bros.
AD0016 ROTJ game cartridge advertisement, glossy from publication 1.00

Pepsi Cola
AD0017 Episode I 3-D wall hanger..16.00

Pez Candy, Inc.
AD0020 Advertising sticker, Europe 7.00
AD0028 Handbill flyer advertising Pez line of candy dispensers 1.00
AD0008 Star Wars fun and games dispenser, cardboard dump with header
     card 10.00
AD0009 Star Wars fun and games dispenser, header card only 6.00

Pizza Hut
AD0050 "Collect Them All!" (toys) 4"x6" plasticized card for table-top
     display 2.00
AD0052 "Don't Leave Coruscant Without Them." two-sided counter
     standee (6 toys / cup toppers)..35.00
AD0051 "Take A Piece Of Coruscant Home." (cup toppers) 4"x6" plasticized
     card for table-top display 2.00
AD0049 Building-shaped header card, "Welcome to Coruscant, Your Sen-
     ate box is being prepared" 69.00
AD0002 Kids Pack with mini-transforming playsets 3.00
AD0059 Micromachine heads, one-sheet flyer 8.00

Rarities Mint
AD0001 Silver and gold coins flyer...12.00

Rawcliffe
AD0054 Counter sign: "Coming to this store May 3, 1999" 4.00

Advertising/Displays

Star Jars
AD0070 Advertising flyer, one-sheet, color, 8½"x11" 4.00

Topps
AD0074 1977 One-sheet flyer, "Topps Introduces 15 cent Star Wars Movie Photo Cards!" 24.00

Toys R Us
AD0060 Naboo Sweepstakes hanging poster 3.00

Wells
AD0015 Battle Droid ice-pop counter display 8.00

AD0005

AD0057

AD0069

AD0012

AD0014

AD0066

AD0064

AD0068

AD0010

AD0011

AD0013

AD0007

AD0027

AD0022

AD0021

AD0062

AD0058

AD0024

AD0067

Yves Saint Laurent
AD0004 One Love, Queen Amidala cover 13.00

ANIMATION CELS

Royal Animation Art
Limited edition cel reproductions.
AF0008 Droids: Battle Cruiser 85.00
AF0007 Droids: Best Friends...85.00

AF0009 Droids: Boba Fett: Bounty Hunter 85.00
AF0010 Droids: Stranded...85.00
AF0011 Ewoks: Celebration 85.00
AF0012 Ewoks: The Big Hug...85.00
AF0005 "The Great Heap" feature with background, any...................225.00
AF0006 "The Great Heap" feature w/o background, any.....................175.00
AF0001 Droids series with background, any.....................................225.00
AF0002 Droids series without background, any................................175.00
AF0003 Ewoks series with background, any....................................225.00
AF0004 Ewoks series without background, any 175.00

AD0006

AD0073

AD0018

AD0004

AD0071 top and front

AD0016

AD0020

AD0017

AD0028

AD0009

AD0050

AD0051

AD0059

AD0054

AD0070

AD0074

AD0060

AD0015

ANSWERING MACHINES

AMS0001

Tiger Electronics
AMS0001 Royal Naboo Starship answering machine 50.00

APRONS

Barco
Pizza Hut Episode I employee aprons.
APR0001 Dark Maul 24.00
APR0002 Anakin 16.00
APR0003 Queen Amidala 21.00

ARCADE GAMES

NA0004 NA0001 NA0002 NA0005

Atari
NA0003 Empire Strikes Back...1,100.00
NA0004 Return of the Jedi...1,000.00
NA0001 Star Wars...1,800.00
NA0002 Star Wars, sit-down case..2,250.00

Sega
NA0005 Star Wars Trilogy 4,725.00

ART

2N Enterprise
ART0007 Lacquer L.E.D. (Lite Edition Decor) Series: X-Wing computer game
    artwork...47.00

Authentic Images
Matted and framed, limited to 5,000.
ART0008 Darth Vader and Luke in shaft 95.00
ART0009 Luke and Yoda 95.00
ART0010 At Last We Will Have Revenge, neon poster 315.00

ART KITS

FK0004 FK0003

FK0002 FK0001

Hasbro
FK0004 R2-D2 Art Center...14.00
FK0003 Star Wars Ultimate Art Kit...9.00

Rose Art Industries
FK0002 Activity Case, ANH 10.00
FK0001 Star Wars Fun Kit with stickers, pens, scissors...........................8.00

ART: PORTFOLIOS

Aardvark-Vanaheim Press
PPD0005 Star Wars: A Collection of Ten Prints, unlicensed, approx 250 pro-
    duced..145.00

Ballantine
Artwork by Ralph McQuarrie.
PPD0002 Star Wars 45.00
PPD0003 Empire Strikes Back 25.00
PPD0004 Return of the Jedi 25.00

PPD0001 PPD0006

 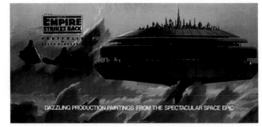 

PPD0002 PPD0003 PPD0004

Chronicle Books
PPD0001 The Art of Ralph McQuarrie (art box)............................30.00

Classico
PPD0006 Star Wars...18.00
PPD0007 Star Wars Episode I: The Phantom Menace 40.00
PPD0008 Star Wars Episode I: The Phantom Menace, deluxe...............379.00

ART: PRINTS

Gifted Images Publishing
AH0001 Darth Vader by Ken Steacy, 23½"x30", limited to 500...............475.00

Icarus
Mounted in silver plastic frame.
AH0003 Boba Fett..24.00
AH0004 C-3PO and R2-D2...24.00
AH0005 Chewbacca...24.00
AH0006 Darth Vader...24.00
AH0002 Luke Skywalker..24.00
AH0007 Yoda..24.00

Star Struck
AH0008 X-Wing Fighters and Death Star II by Michael David Ward, limited to 3,000...225.00

Willetts Design
Signed, numbered, with film clip. Limited to 2,500. 18"x12". By Ralph McQuarrie.
AH0010 Cloud City of Bespin..179.00
AH0021 Darth Vader's Arrival...179.00
AH0020 Death Star Main Reactor...179.00
AH0017 Jabba the Hutt..179.00
AH0014 Luke and Darth Vader Duel...179.00
AH0011 Millennium Falcon...179.00
AH0015 Rebel Attack on Death Star..179.00
AH0013 Rebel Celebration...179.00
AH0016 Rebel Patrol of Echo Base...179.00
AH0019 Speeder Bike Chase..179.00
AH0009 The Battle of Hoth..179.00
AH0012 The Cantina on Mos Eisley...179.00
AH0018 The Rancor Pit..179.00

AH0010   AH0020   AH0017

AH0014   AH0011   AH0015

AH0013   AH0016   AH0019

AH0009   AH0012   AH0018

AK0005   AK0024   AK0007

AK0025   AK0010   AK0013

AK0016   AK0019   AK0023

ART: PRINTS, CHROME

Zanart
Prints are 11"x14" and matted.
AK0001 AT-ATs...12.00
AK0002 Bounty Hunters..12.00
AK0003 B-Wing..12.00
AK0004 B-Wing, blueprint style...12.00
AK0005 C-3PO and R2-D2...12.00
AK0024 Dark Forces cover art...12.00
AK0007 Darth Vader, art..12.00
AK0006 Darth Vader...12.00
AK0008 Darth Vader...12.00
AK0025 Empire Strikes Back, international art.................................12.00
AK0009 Empire Strikes Back...12.00
AK0010 Empire Strikes Back, video box art....................................12.00
AK0011 Escape from Hoth..12.00
AK0012 Prince Xizor..12.00
AK0013 Return of the Jedi..12.00
AK0014 Return of the Jedi..12.00
AK0015 Shadows of the Empire...12.00
AK0016 Space Battle..12.00
AK0017 Star Destroyer..12.00
AK0018 Star Destroyer, blueprint style.......................................12.00
AK0019 Star Wars...12.00
AK0020 Star Wars, video box art..12.00
AK0021 Stormtrooper, trilogy art...12.00
AK0022 X-Wing, blueprint style...12.00
AK0023 Yoda, trilogy art style...12.00

AUTOGRAPHS

Celebrity Autographs
ATG0001 Ahmed Best, 8"x10" photo..60.00
ATG0002 Ahmed Best, adds value to item..55.00
ATG0003 Anthony Daniels, 8"x10" photo...40.00
ATG0004 Anthony Daniels, adds value to item...................................25.00
ATG0005 Bill Hookins, 8"x10" photo..15.00
ATG0006 Bill Hookins, adds value to item......................................10.00
ATG0007 Billy Dee Williams, 8"x10" photo......................................50.00
ATG0008 Billy Dee Williams, adds value to item................................30.00
ATG0009 Caroline Blakistan, 8"x10" photo......................................30.00

Autographs

ATG0010 Caroline Blakistan, adds value to item.................18.00
ATG0011 Carrie Fisher, 8"x10" photo.................75.00
ATG0012 Carrie Fisher, adds value to item.................60.00
ATG0013 David Prowse, 8"x10" photo.................40.00
ATG0014 David Prowse, adds value to item.................25.00
ATG0015 Ewan McGregor, 8"x10" photo.................65.00
ATG0016 Ewan McGregor, adds value to item.................40.00
ATG0017 Femi Taylor, 8"x10" photo.................25.00
ATG0018 Femi Taylor, adds value to item.................15.00
ATG0019 Garrick Hagon, 8"x10" photo.................25.00
ATG0020 Garrick Hagon, adds value to item.................20.00
ATG0021 Gary Kurtz, 8"x10" photo.................50.00
ATG0022 Gary Kurtz, adds value to item.................25.00
ATG0023 George Lucas, 8"x10" photo.................130.00
ATG0024 George Lucas, adds value to item.................85.00
ATG0025 Harrison Ford, 8"x10" photo.................125.00
ATG0026 Harrison Ford, adds value to item.................100.00
ATG0027 Ian MaDiarmid, 8"x10" photo.................70.00
ATG0028 Ian MaDiarmid, adds value to item.................55.00
ATG0029 Jake Lloyd, 8"x10" photo.................40.00
ATG0030 Jake Lloyd, adds value to item.................35.00
ATG0031 James Earl Jones, 8"x10" photo.................60.00
ATG0032 James Earl Jones, adds value to item.................45.00
ATG0033 Jeremy Bulloch, 8"x10" photo.................45.00
ATG0087 Jerome Blake, adds value to item.................25.00
ATG0088 Jerome Blake, 8"x10" photo.................10.00
ATG0034 Jeremy Bulloch, adds value to item.................35.00
ATG0035 John Hollis, 8"x10" photo.................25.00
ATG0036 John Hollis, adds value to item.................20.00
ATG0037 John Morton, 8"x10" photo.................15.00
ATG0038 John Morton, adds value to item.................10.00
ATG0039 Kenneth Colley, 8"x10" photo.................20.00
ATG0040 Kenneth Colley, adds value to item.................15.00
ATG0041 Kenny Baker, 8"x10" photo.................40.00
ATG0042 Kenny Baker, adds value to item.................35.00
ATG0043 Liam Neeson, 8"x10" photo.................65.00
ATG0044 Liam Neeson, adds value to item.................40.00
ATG0045 Marie De'Argon, 8"x10" photo.................15.00
ATG0046 Marie De'Argon, adds value to item.................10.00
ATG0047 Mark Hamill, 8"x10" photo.................75.00
ATG0048 Mark Hamill, adds value to item.................45.00
ATG0049 Melissa Kurtz, 8"x10" photo.................15.00
ATG0050 Melissa Kurtz, adds value to item.................10.00
ATG0051 Mercedes Ngoh, 8"x10" photo.................20.00
ATG0052 Mercedes Ngoh, adds value to item.................15.00
ATG0053 Michael Carter, 8"x10" photo.................25.00
ATG0054 Michael Carter, adds value to item.................15.00
ATG0055 Michael Edmonds, 8"x10" photo.................45.00
ATG0056 Michael Edmonds, adds value to item.................35.00
ATG0057 Michael Sheard, 8"x10" photo.................20.00
ATG0058 Michael Sheard, adds value to item.................15.00
ATG0059 Mike Quinn, 8"x10" photo.................20.00
ATG0060 Mike Quinn, adds value to item.................15.00
ATG0061 Natalie Portman, 8"x10" photo.................65.00
ATG0062 Natalie Portman, adds value to item.................35.00
ATG0063 Peter Cushing, 8"x10" photo.................260.00
ATG0064 Peter Cushing, adds value to item.................55.00
ATG0065 Peter Mayhew, 8"x10" photo.................55.00
ATG0066 Peter Mayhew, adds value to item.................35.00
ATG0067 Phil Brown, 8"x10" photo.................20.00
ATG0068 Phil Brown, adds value to item.................15.00
ATG0083 Ray Park, 8"x10" photo.................35.00
ATG0084 Ray Park, adds value to item.................15.00
ATG0069 Richard LaParmontier, 8"x10" photo.................25.00
ATG0070 Richard LaParmontier, adds value to item.................20.00
ATG0071 Rick McCallum, 8"x10" photo.................25.00
ATG0072 Rick McCallum, adds value to item.................15.00
ATG0085 Samuel L. Jackson, 8"x10" photo.................140.00
ATG0086 Samuel L. Jackson, adds value to item.................45.00
ATG0073 Shannon Baksa, 8"x10" photo.................40.00
ATG0074 Shannon Baksa, adds value to item.................35.00
ATG0075 Shelagh Fraser, 8"x10" photo.................55.00
ATG0076 Shelagh Fraser, adds value to item.................45.00
ATG0085 Silas Carson, 8"x10" photo.................20.00
ATG0086 Silas Carson, adds value to item.................10.00
ATG0077 Sir Alec Guinness, 8"x10" photo.................95.00
ATG0078 Sir Alec Guinness, adds value to item.................60.00
ATG0079 Tiffany Kurtz, 8"x10" photo.................15.00
ATG0080 Tiffany Kurtz, adds value to item.................10.00
ATG0081 Timothy Zahn, adds value to item.................25.00
ATG0082 Warwick Davis, 8"x10" photo.................35.00

ATG0083 Warwick Davis, adds value to item.................30.00

BACKPACKS / CARRYBAGS

LB0007   LB0014   LB0049

Adam Joseph Industries
LB0001 AT-AT and Speederbikes.................25.00
LB0002 C-3PO and R2-D2, bookbag.................20.00
LB0003 C-3PO and R2-D2, reversed design.................20.00
LB0004 C-3PO and R2-D2, tear-shaped.................25.00
LB0049 Darth Vader and Emperor's Royal Guards, backpack.................30.00
LB0007 Darth Vader and Emperor's Royal Guards, bookbag.................25.00
LB0010 ROTJ cast.................25.00
LB0011 Wicket the Ewok, bookbag.................20.00
LB0012 Wicket the Ewok, reversed design.................20.00
LB0013 Wicket the Ewok, tear-shaped.................25.00
LB0014 Yoda, bookbag.................20.00
LB0015 Yoda, reversed design.................20.00
LB0016 Yoda, tear-shaped.................25.00

Calego International
LB0046 Brown, hard-sided with CD wallet.................18.00

Disney / MGM
LB0044 Star Tours with logo.................22.00

Factors, Etc.
LB0009 "May The Force Be With You".................20.00
LB0005 Chewbacca.................25.00
LB0006 Chewbacca and Han Solo.................25.00
LB0008 Darth Vader and Stormtroopers.................25.00

Fan Club
LB0045 Episode I canvas carry bag with handles and over-shoulder strap.................35.00

Giftware International
LB0065 C-3PO, 16"x12".................18.00
LB0066 Darth Maul, 16"x12".................18.00
LB0067 Ewok, 15"x10".................24.00
LB0068 Jar Jar Binks, 24"x18".................24.00
LB0047 R2-D2 character backpack, 20"x8"x14".................39.00
LB0048 Yoda character backpack, 21"x4"x8".................39.00

LB0046   LB0047   LB0048   LB0065

LB0067   LB0066   LB0068

Pyramid

LB0060 Anakin Skywalker in pod racer gear with checkerboard, vinyl ...12.00
LB0055 Anakin Skywalker in pod racer gear, canvas 12.00
LB0059 Anakin Skywalker in pod racer gear, vinyl...12.00
LB0017 Boba Fett, Dark Side collection, nylon with embossed rubber art-
work 16.00
LB0021 Boba Fett, Destroyer collection, vinyl with metallic trim and inset art-
work 16.00
LB0025 Boba Fett, Hi-Tech collection, nylon with all-over artwork...........16.00
LB0029 Boba Fett, Imperial collection, nylon with rubber patch 16.00
LB0034 Boba Fett, Star Class collection, vinyl with inset artwork.............16.00
LB0038 Boba Fett, Zoom collection, vinyl with all-over artwork 16.00
LB0035 C-3PO, Star Class collection, vinyl with inset artwork 16.00
LB0051 Darth Maul art 7.00
LB0056 Darth Maul bust, canvas..12.00
LB0057 Darth Maul full-body, canvas..12.00
LB0069 Darth Maul shoulderbag...12.00
LB0042 Darth Vader / Tie Fighter, Interactive collection, lights and battle
sounds 19.00
LB0032 Darth Vader / Tie Fighter, Pilot collection, vinyl with schematic art-
work 16.00
LB0018 Darth Vader, Dark Side collection, nylon with embossed rubber art-
work 16.00
LB0022 Darth Vader, Destroyer collection, vinyl with metallic trim and inset
artwork...16.00
LB0026 Darth Vader, Hi-Tech collection, nylon with all-over artwork.......16.00
LB0030 Darth Vader, Imperial collection, nylon with rubber patch 16.00
LB0041 Darth Vader, Interactive collection, breathing sound..................19.00
LB0036 Darth Vader, Star Class collection, vinyl with inset artwork 16.00
LB0039 Darth Vader, Zoom collection, vinyl with all-over artwork............16.00
LB0050 Episode I canvas carry bag with handles and over-shoulder strap,
black or blue...16.00
LB0062 Jar Jar Binks, vinyl...12.00
LB0052 Jedi vs. Sith art 7.00
LB0058 Jedi, vinyl 12.00
LB0043 Luke Skywalker / X-Wing Fighter, Interactive collection, lights and
battle sounds...19.00

LB0033 Luke Skywalker / X-Wing Fighter, Pilot collection, vinyl with schematic
artwork...16.00
LB0019 Luke Skywalker, Dark Side collection, nylon with embossed rubber
artwork...16.00
LB0023 Luke Skywalker, Destroyer collection, vinyl with metallic trim and
inset artwork...16.00
LB0040 Luke Skywalker, Zoom collection, vinyl with all-over artwork 16.00
LB0053 Pod racing art 7.00
LB0054 Queen Amidala 18.00
LB0064 Queen Amidala, mini..8.00
LB0063 Starfighters flip action, vinyl 15.00
LB0061 Starfighters, vinyl...12.00
LB0020 Stormtrooper, Dark Side collection, nylon with embossed rubber art-
work 16.00
LB0024 Stormtrooper, Destroyer collection, vinyl with metallic trim and inset
artwork...16.00
LB0027 Stormtrooper, Hi-Tech collection, nylon with all-over artwork......16.00
LB0031 Stormtrooper, Imperial collection, nylon with rubber patch 16.00
LB0037 Stormtrooper, Star Class collection, vinyl with inset artwork 16.00
LB0028 Yoda, Hi-Tech collection, nylon with all-over artwork 16.00

Scholastic

LB0071 Star Wars Junior sign-up premium...14.00
LB0070 Imperial black, Darth Vader embossed rubber flap 14.00

BADGES

Fan Club

ACC0013 #1 Imperial / Mara Jade collectible badge similar size, shape,
design as celebration passes 4.00
ACC0014 #2 Rebel / Jek Porkins collectible badge similar size, design
as celebration passes 4.00
ACC0015 #3 Bounty Hunter / Aurra Sing collectible badge similar size,
shape, design as celebration passes 4.00
ACC0016 #4 Tatooine / Wuher the bartender collectible badge similar size,
shape, design as celebration passes 6.00

LB0060 LB0055/LB0059 LB0051 LB0056 LB0057 LB0069 LB0032 LB0022

LB0030 LB0036 LB0039 LB0050 LB0062 LB0052 LB0058 LB0054

LB0064   LB0063   LB0061   LB0024   LB0037   LB0071   LB0070
closed and flipped

Badges

ACC0001   ACC0002   ACC0003   ACC0004   ACC0005/ACC0006 front and back   ACC0007   ACC0008

ACC0009   ACC0010   ACC0011/ACC0012   ACC0028   ACC0013   ACC0014   ACC0015   ACC0016

ACC0030   ACC0029   ACC0027 front and back

ACC0030 #5 Imperial / Darth Vader collectible badge similar size, shape, design as celebration passes 4.00
ACC0029 #6 Jedi Council / Mace Windu collectible badge similar size, shape, design as celebration passes 4.00
ACC0010 SW Celebration pass replica: All access Sebulba "Star Wars Insider - Limited Edition" printed on back 6.00
ACC0007 SW Celebration pass replica: Backstage Pit Droid "Star Wars Insider - Limited Edition" printed on back 8.00
ACC0006 SW Celebration pass replica: Exhibitors Jar Jar (autographed by Ahmed Best) "Star Wars Insider - Limited Edition" printed on back 50.00
ACC0005 SW Celebration pass replica: Exhibitors Jar Jar "Star Wars Insider - Limited Edition" printed on back 6.00
ACC0001 SW Celebration pass replica: Friday Obi-Wan Kenobi "Star Wars Insider - Limited Edition" printed on back 6.00
ACC0002 SW Celebration pass replica: Saturday Qui-Gon Jinn "Star Wars Insider - Limited Edition" printed on back 6.00
ACC0012 SW Celebration pass replica: Staff C-3PO (autographed by Anthony Daniels) "Star Wars Insider - Limited Edition" printed on back 44.00
ACC0011 SW Celebration pass replica: Staff C-3PO "Star Wars Insider - Limited Edition" printed on back 6.00
ACC0003 SW Celebration pass replica: Sunday Anakin Skywalker "Star Wars Insider - Limited Edition" printed on back 6.00
ACC0004 SW Celebration pass replica: Three-Day Darth Maul "Star Wars Insider - Limited Edition" printed on back 6.00
ACC0009 SW Celebration pass replica: VIP guest Queen Amidala "Star Wars Insider - Limited Edition" printed on back...................23.00
ACC0008 SW Celebration pass replica: Volunteer battle droid "Star Wars Insider - Limited Edition" printed on back 6.00

Kay Bee Toys
ACC0028 EPI Premiere Weekend Commemorative Badge, May 19-23, 1999 ....8.00

Marin County
ACC0027 Marin County Star Wars summit, 1996 ....7.00

Star Wars Celebration, 1999
ACC0025 All access Sebulba...133.00
ACC0022 Backstage Pit Droid 35.00
ACC0021 Exhibitors Jar Jar 25.00
ACC0017 Friday Obi-Wan Kenobi 12.00
ACC0018 Saturday Qui-Gon Jinn 8.00
ACC0026 Staff C-3PO 82.00
ACC0019 Sunday Anakin Skywalker 8.00
ACC0020 Three-Day Darth Maul 10.00
ACC0024 VIP guest Queen Amidala 68.00
ACC0023 Volunteer Battle Droid 30.00

BAGS: PARTY

PFA0002   PFA0003   PFA0004

Drawing Board
PFA0001 Darth Vader and Luke Duel, 8-pack 8.00
PFA0002 Ewoks, 8-pack 8.00

Party Express
PFA0004 Darth Maul with Jedi vs. Sith scene in background, 8-pack........5.00
PFA0003 Millennium Falcon flees Death Star, 8-pack 8.00

BALANCING TOYS
Galoob

BTY0001

BTY0001 X-Wing vs. Tie Fighter, Fan Club exclusive....................................12.00

BALLOONS

PFB0015

PFB0016

PFB0024

PFB0023

PFB0015

PFB0016

PFB0018

Anagram International
PFB0023 "Happy Birthday" R2-D2 and C-3PO 5.00
PFB0017 "Happy Birthday Young Jedi," mylar 4.00
PFB0015 Anakin Skywalker in pod racer, mylar 4.00
PFB0019 Darth Maul head on plastic stick 5.00
PFB0016 Darth Maul, mylar 4.00
PFB0014 Darth Vader / Millennium Falcon, "Happy Birthday," mylar 4.00
PFB0013 Darth Vader / Millennium Falcon, mylar 4.00
PFB0020 Jar Jar Binks head on plastic stick 5.00
PFB0018 Jar Jar Binks, mylar..4.00
PFB0021 Naboo fighter on plastic stick 5.00
PFB0024 Naboo Space Battle 5.00
PFB0022 R2-D2 on plastic stick.....................................5.00

Ariel
PFB0006 AT-AT assorted colors 5.00
PFB0007 C-3PO assorted colors 5.00
PFB0008 Chewbacca assorted colors 5.00
PFB0009 Darth Vader assorted colors 5.00
PFB0010 Millennium Falcon assorted colors....................5.00
PFB0011 R2-D2 assorted colors 5.00
PFB0012 Stormtrooper assorted colors 5.00

PFB0005

Drawing Board
PFB0001 ESB, 10-pack assorted 8.00
PFB0002 ROTJ 5-pack, assorted 8.00
PFB0003 ROTJ 6-pack, assorted Ewoks....................10.00
PFB0004 ROTJ punch balloons, 4-pack assorted 10.00
PFB0005 ROTJ, 10-pack assorted 8.00

BALLS

SBB0001

Tapper Candies
SBB0001 Super Bounce balls, 4-pack...........................4.00

BANDAGES

BND0001

BND0002

BND0003

BND0004

BND0006

BND0005

Curad
Boxes of 30 sterile bandages.
BND0001 C-3PO 8.00
BND0003 EPI: Anakin Skywalker, collector's edition 8.00
BND0004 EPI: Darth Maul, collector's edition..................8.00
BND0002 EPI: Jar Jar Binks..9.00
BND0006 EPI: Jar Jar Binks box, collector's edition 8.00
BND0005 EPI: Queen Amidala, collector's edition 8.00

BANKS

PEB0016

PEB0013

PEB0004

PEB0009

PEB0014

PEB0011

Adam Joseph Industries
PEB0004 Darth Vader 45.00
PEB0009 Emperor's Royal Guard 45.00
PEB0011 Gamorrean Guard, Canadian exclusive 125.00
PEB0013 Princess Kneesaa 15.00
PEB0014 R2-D2..25.00
PEB0016 Wicket 15.00

Applause
PEB0026 Darth Maul on Sith Speeder 8.00
PEB0025 Jar Jar Binks...8.00

PEB0025

PEB0026

Banks

Commonwealth Savings
PEB0029 R2-D2, figural 35.00
PEB0034 Darth Vader 35.00

Kinnerton Confectionery
PEB0032 R2-D2 ....7.00

Merir
PEB0021 Return of the Jedi coin sorter 85.00

Metal Box Ltd.
Lithographed tin boxes.

PEB0010   PEB0018 front and back

PEB0006 Darth Vader with combination dials 30.00
PEB0010 ESB, octagonal 18.00
PEB0018 Yoda with combination dials 30.00

NTD Apparel Inc.
Plastic busts, contain Episode I T-shirt.

PEB0031   PEB0033

PEB0033 Anakin Skywalker 18.00
PEB0031 Darth Maul 18.00

Pepsi Cola

PEB0030 front and back

PEB0030 EPI Soda Can R2-D2 No. 7 with slit top, Pepsi Cola premium 6.00

Roman Ceramics

PEB0002   PEB0005   PEB0015

PEB0002 C-3PO ceramic...75.00
PEB0005 Darth Vader ceramic.................................90.00
PEB0015 R2-D2 ceramic 45.00

Sigma

PEB0003   PEB0007   PEB0017

PEB0003 Chewbacca 30.00
PEB0007 Darth Vader 125.00
PEB0012 Jabba the Hutt 27.00
PEB0017 Yoda 40.00

Thinkway

PEB0019   PEB0020   PEB0001   PEB0008

PEB0024   PEB0022   PEB0023

PEB0027   PEB0028

PEB0019 C-3PO 17.00
PEB0001 C-3PO and R2-D2 talking electronic 12.00
PEB0022 Darth Maul, electronic, interacts with Obi-Wan Kenobi and Qui-Gon Jinn 32.00
PEB0020 Darth Vader 18.00
PEB0008 Darth Vader talking electronic 12.00
PEB0023 Obi-Wan Kenobi, electronic, interacts with Darth Maul and Qui-Gon Jinn 32.00
PEB0024 Qui-Gon Jinn, electronic, interacts with Obi-Wan Kenobi and Darth Maul 32.00
PEB0028 Darth Maul ceramic.....................................26.00
PEB0027 Darth Vader ceramic....................................14.00

BANNERS

PFC0003

PFC0002

Drawing Board
PFC0001 ESB Birthday 12.00

Party Express
PFC0003 Happy Birthday 4.00

Unique
PFC0002 Jedi vs. Sith...6.00

BARRETTES

JBA0001

JBA0002

JBA0003

Factors, Etc.
JBA0001 C-3PO 14.00
JBA0002 Darth Vader 14.00
JBA0003 R2-D2 ....14.00

BATH MATS

RUG0001

Jay Franco and Sons
RUG0001 Naboo Space Battle, nylon 20"x30" 14.00

BATHROBES

Wilker Bros.
ABR0002 "May The Force Be With You" 20.00
ABR0001 Darth Vader 30.00

BATHROOM SETS

Jay Franco and Sons
BTH0001 Toothbrush holder, soap dish, tumbler, all featuring space battle
 scenes..16.00

BTH0001

BEACHPADS

Bibb Co.
CBZ0001 SW: Galaxy design...18.00

BEDCOVERS

CBE0014

Bibb Co.
CBE0001 ESB: Boba Fett 25.00
CBE0002 ESB: Boba Fett (J.C. Penney)....................................25.00
CBE0003 ESB: Darth Vader and Yoda 25.00
CBE0004 ESB: Darth's Den 25.00
CBE0005 ESB: Ice Planet 25.00
CBE0006 ESB: Lord Vader 25.00
CBE0007 ESB: Lord Vader's Chamber 25.00
CBE0008 ESB: Yoda 25.00
CBE0009 ROTJ: Jabba the Hutt, Ewoks, etc. 25.00
CBE0010 ROTJ: logos from all 3 films 25.00
CBE0011 ROTJ: Luke and Darth Vader Duel, AT-ST, etc. 25.00
CBE0012 ROTJ: Star Wars Saga 25.00
CBE0013 SW: Aztec Gold 25.00
CBE0014 SW: Galaxy 25.00
CBE0015 SW: Jedi Knights 25.00
CBE0016 SW: Lord Vader 25.00
CBE0017 SW: Space Fantasy...25.00

BEDSKIRTS

BSK0001 Spaceships design, 39"x75" 15.00

BELT BUCKLES

Leather Shop
BB0013 C-3PO and R2-D2 ....24.00
BB0014 Darth Vader 24.00
BB0001 Darth Vader, oval with name on either side of helmet 30.00
BB0002 Darth Vader, oval with name under helmet.....................30.00
BB0019 May The Force Be With You 24.00
BB0015 R2-D2 ....24.00
BB0004 Star Wars logo 30.00
BB0005 X-Wing fighter with Star Wars logo 30.00

Lee Co.
BB0012 C-3PO and R2-D2, enameled rectangle..........................16.00
BB0006 Darth Vader, oval 23.00
BB0009 Darth Vader, oval enameled 16.00
BB0011 Empire Strikes Back logo, enameled..............................16.00
BB0007 Jabba the Hutt, rectangle 23.00
BB0010 Jabba the Hutt, rectangle enameled..............................16.00
BB0017 Return of the Jedi logo, enameled.................................16.00

Belt Buckles

BB0013 BB0014 BB0004

BB0001 BB0002 BB0005

BB0012 BB0006 BB0007

BB0016 BB0011 BB0017

BB0016 Star Wars logo, enameled.............................26.00
BB0008 Yoda, circle...23.00
BB0018 Yoda, circle enameled................................16.00

BELT PACKS

Disney / MGM
BD0025 Star Tours with logo 11.00

Pyramid

BD0026 BD0027

BD0026 Anakin Skywalker, TPM 4.00
BD0001 Boba Fett, Dark Side collection, nylon with embossed rubber art-
work 12.00
BD0005 Boba Fett, Destroyer collection, vinyl with metallic trim and inset art-
work 12.00
BD0009 Boba Fett, Hi-Tech collection, nylon with all-over artwork...........12.00
BD0013 Boba Fett, Imperial collection, nylon with rubber patch 12.00
BD0018 Boba Fett, Star Class collection, vinyl with inset artwork............12.00
BD0022 Boba Fett, Zoom collection, vinyl with all-over artwork.............12.00
BD0019 C-3PO, Star Class collection, vinyl with inset artwork 12.00
BD0016 Darth Vader / Tie Fighter, Pilot collection, vinyl with schematic art-
work 12.00
BD0002 Darth Vader, Dark Side collection, nylon with embossed rubber art-
work 12.00
BD0006 Darth Vader, Destroyer collection, vinyl with metallic trim and inset
artwork..12.00
BD0010 Darth Vader, Hi-Tech collection, nylon with all-over artwork 12.00
BD0014 Darth Vader, Imperial collection, nylon with rubber patch 12.00
BD0020 Darth Vader, Star Class collection, vinyl with inset artwork 12.00
BD0023 Darth Vader, Zoom collection, vinyl with all-over artwork.........12.00
BD0027 Jedi, TPM 4.00
BD0017 Luke Skywalker / X-Wing Fighter, Pilot collection, vinyl with schemat-
ic artwork 12.00
BD0003 Luke Skywalker, Dark Side collection, nylon with embossed rubber
artwork..12.00
BD0007 Luke Skywalker, Destroyer collection, vinyl with metallic trim and
inset artwork..12.00
BD0024 Luke Skywalker, Zoom collection, vinyl with all-over artwork 12.00

BD0004 Stormtrooper, Dark Side collection, nylon with embossed rubber art-
work 12.00
BD0008 Stormtrooper, Destroyer collection, vinyl with metallic trim and inset
artwork..12.00
BD0011 Stormtrooper, Hi-Tech collection, nylon with all-over artwork...12.00
BD0015 Stormtrooper, Imperial collection, nylon with rubber patch 12.00
BD0021 Stormtrooper, Star Class collection, vinyl with inset artwork........12.00
BD0012 Yoda, Hi-Tech collection, nylon with all-over artwork 12.00

BD0028

BD0028 Sith Lord...11.00

BELTS

Lee Co.
AB0001 Fabric: Dancing Ewoks, Wicket sticker on buckle.........................8.00
AB0002 Fabric: Droids, pewter buckle w/cartoon R2-D2, C-3PO and Land-
speeder 12.00
AB0027 Fabric: ROTJ w/stitched logo and brass logo buckle....................8.00
AB0003 Fabric: SW and ROTJ printed, enamel Darth Vader buckle 10.00
AB0004 Fabric: SW and ROTJ printed, round brass Jabba the Hutt
buckle 8.00
AB0005 Fabric: SW and ROTJ printed, round brass Wicket buckle 8.00
AB0006 Fabric: w/stitched logo and SW enamel buckle 15.00
AB0007 Fabric: w/stitched logo and SW sticker on buckle 10.00
AB0026 Vinyl: w/screened art of Darth Vader, Luke, Leia, Droids, and SW
logo 20.00

The Leather Shop

AB0023

AB0002

AB0027

AB0004

AB0026

AB0018

AB0008 C-3PO and R2-D2 on enameled brass buckle, boxed................18.00
AB0009 C-3PO and R2-D2 on enameled brass buckle, hanging tag 15.00
AB0010 Darth Vader on enameled brass buckle, boxed..........................18.00
AB0011 Darth Vader on enameled brass buckle, hanging tag 15.00
AB0012 Droids, screened logo and droids in landspeeder 10.00
AB0013 Droids, space emblems and 3D droid busts on brass buckle.....15.00
AB0014 Droids, space emblems and 3D droid busts on pewter buckle..16.00
AB0015 ESB Darth Vader 3D bust on enameled brass buckle 15.00
AB0016 ESB logo on enameled brass buckle 10.00
AB0017 ESB Yoda 3D on round brass buckle 16.00
AB0018 Han and Chewbacca, Droids and Luke, Leia and Darth Vader ..20.00
AB0019 Obi-Wan and Darth Vader pattern 20.00
AB0025 Oval Darth Vader buckle 15.00
AB0020 ROTJ circular portraits and logo screened on belt....................12.00
AB0021 ROTJ embossed w/logo on rectangular enameled brass buckle..14.00
AB0022 ROTJ Jabba the Hutt 3D on rectangular brass buckle.................16.00
AB0023 Star Wars logo on enameled brass buckle, boxed 18.00
AB0024 Star Wars logo on enameled brass buckle, hanging tag 15.00

BEND-EMS

Just Toys

TYB0036 4-Piece gift set: Admiral Ackbar, Bib Fortuna, Boba Fett, Wicket, brass collectors coin, with bonus trading card 16.00
TYB0001 4-Piece gift set: C-3PO, Darth Vader, R2-D2, Stormtrooper........12.00
TYB0002 4-Piece gift set: C-3PO, Darth Vader, R2-D2, Stormtrooper, with bonus trading card...16.00
TYB0003 4-Piece gift set: C-3PO, Han, Leia, Obi-Wan, with bonus trading card 12.00
TYB0004 4-Piece gift set: Chewbacca, Stormtrooper, Wicket, Yoda.......12.00
TYB0005 4-Piece gift set: Chewbacca, Stormtrooper, Wicket, Yoda, with bonus trading card...16.00
TYB0038 4-Piece gift set: Darth Vader, Emperor, Luke Skywalker, R2-D2, with bonus trading card 18.00
TYB0006 8-Piece gift set: Darth Vader, Luke, C-3PO, Emperor, Stormtrooper, R2-D2, Leia, Wicket 24.00

TYB0033 8-Piece gift set: Darth Vader, Luke, C-3PO, R2-D2, Obi-Wan, Stormtrooper, Leia, Wicket...24.00
TYB0034 8-Piece gift set: Darth Vader, Luke, C-3PO, Yoda, Stormtrooper, R2-D2, Leia, Wicket..24.00
TYB0035 10-Piece gift set: Ackbar, Bib Fortuna, Chewbacca, Darth Vader, Royal Guard, Han, Leia, Luke, R2-D2, Stormtrooper, brass collectors coin, with bonus trading card 28.00
TYB0030 Admiral Ackbar, with bonus trading card 8.00
TYB0007 Bib Fortuna, with bonus trading card 10.00
TYB0040 Boba Fett, with bonus trading card 22.00
TYB0008 C-3PO...8.00
TYB0009 C-3PO, with bonus trading card 7.00
TYB0010 Chewbacca...8.00
TYB0011 Chewbacca, with bonus trading card 8.00
TYB0012 Darth Vader...11.00
TYB0013 Darth Vader, with bonus trading card 11.00
TYB0014 Emperor, with bonus trading card...................................17.00
TYB0031 Emperor's Royal Guard, with bonus trading card 14.00
TYB0041 Gamorrean Guard, with bonus trading card........................15.00
TYB0015 Han Solo, with bonus trading card 22.00
TYB0037 Lando Calrissian, with bonus trading card 4.00
TYB0016 Luke Skywalker 11.00
TYB0017 Luke Skywalker, with bonus trading card 7.00
TYB0039 Luke Skywalker, X-Wing Pilot, with bonus trading card 17.00
TYB0018 Obi-Wan Kenobi...11.00
TYB0019 Obi-Wan Kenobi, with bonus trading card...........................9.00
TYB0020 Princess Leia..17.00
TYB0021 Princess Leia, with bonus trading card 12.00
TYB0022 R2-D2..11.00
TYB0023 R2-D2, with bonus trading card 5.00
TYB0024 Stormtrooper..9.00
TYB0025 Stormtrooper, with bonus trading card..............................11.00
TYB0032 Tusken Raider, with bonus trading card.............................13.00
TYB0026 Wicket the Ewok 12.00
TYB0027 Wicket the Ewok, with bonus trading card...........................16.00
TYB0028 Yoda...11.00
TYB0029 Yoda, with bonus trading card 9.00

TYB0035

TYB0036

TYB0001

TYB0002

TYB0007

TYB0040

TYB0009

TYB0011

TYB0013

TYB0041

TYB0015

TYB0037

TYB0017

TYB0019

TYB0021

TYB0023

TYB0025

TYB0029

Bicycles

BICYCLES

Dynacraft
B0006 Darth Maul, boys 16" 70.00
B0007 Queen Amidala, girls 12" 60.00

Huffy
B0001 Baba Ewok, Baga, and Princess Kneesaa first bike, girls 135.00
B0002 C-3PO and R2-D2 first bike, boys 225.00
B0003 Princess Kneesa high rise, girls...175.00
B0005 X-Wing first bike, boys/girls...185.00

Kenner

B0004

B0004 Speeder Bike pedal vehicle 860.00

BINDERS

SUB0002　　SUB0003　　SUB0010　　SUB0022

SUB0018　　SUB0019　　SUB0020　　SUB0021

Grand Toys
SUB0018 Obi-Wan Kenobi...10.00
SUB0019 Queen Amidala...12.00

Impact, Inc.
SUB0012 Anakin Skywalker..4.00
SUB0020 Anakin, Jar Jar / Tatooine 4.00
SUB0021 Darth Maul, Darth Sidious / Jedi vs. Sith 4.00
SUB0013 Jar Jar 4.00
SUB0014 Queen Amidala..4.00
SUB0015 Qui-Gon Jinn 4.00
SUB0016 R2-D2 / C-3PO...4.00
SUB0017 Sith Lord 4.00

Letraset
SUB0025 X-Wing pursues Tie Fighter over Death Star....................19.00

Mead
SUB0002 Ben Kenobi, Han Solo, Luke Skywalker, Princess Leia.......24.00
SUB0003 C-3PO and R2-D2..25.00
SUB0005 Chewbacca, Han Solo, and Star Destroyer.....................24.00
SUB0006 Darth Vader 24.00
SUB0010 Darth Vader, blue zippered...12.00
SUB0011 Darth Vader, gray zippered...12.00

Merlin Publishing International Ltd.
SUB0023 Empire Strikes Back, 2-ring 9.00

Stuart Hall
SUB0001 2-1B, Bounty Hunters, Probot, Ugnaught 15.00
SUB0004 C-3PO and R2-D2 ....15.00
SUB0007 Darth Vader and Stormtroopers....................................15.00
SUB0008 Luke on Dagobah 15.00
SUB0009 Yoda 15.00

Topps
SUB0024 Star Wars Finest 44.00
SUB0022 Star Wars Widevision, includes Widevision promo card 46.00

BINOCULARS

BIN0001

Tiger Electronics
BIN0001 Darth Maul binoculars with listening device................................38.00

BLANKETS

CBL0018　　　CBL0019　　　CBL0020

The Northwest
Multi-layered woven jacquard blanket/throws.
CBL0018 Anakin Skywalker and pod racer 28.00
CBL0019 Darth Maul and SW logo...35.00
CBL0022 Darth Maul...20.00
CBL0021 Episode I...28.00
CBL0027 Jar Jar..20.00
CBL0028 Jar Jar Binks..20.00
CBL0026 Jedi...20.00
CBL0023 Jedi vs. Sith..20.00
CBL0024 Naboo fighters 20.00
CBL0020 Naboo space battle..28.00
CBL0029 R2-D2...20.00
CBL0025 Star Wars fighters...20.00
CBL0030 The Dark Side..20.00

Bibb Co.
CBL0001 ESB: Boba Fett..30.00
CBL0004 ESB: Ice Planet 15.00
CBL0005 ESB: Lord Vader 25.00
CBL0006 ESB: Lord Vader's Chamber 25.00
CBL0007 ESB: Spectre 15.00
CBL0008 ESB: Yoda 30.00
CBL0009 ROTJ: Jabba the Hutt, Ewoks, etc. 20.00
CBL0010 ROTJ: logos from all 3 films 20.00
CBL0011 ROTJ: Luke and Darth Vader duel, AT-ST, etc....................................20.00
CBL0013 SW: Aztec Gold 15.00
CBL0014 SW: Galaxy 20.00
CBL0015 SW: Jedi Knights 20.00
CBL0016 SW: Lord Vader..20.00
CBL0017 SW: Space Fantasy 15.00

BLOWOUTS: PARTY

PFD0006   PFD0004

Drawing Board
PFD0001 Darth Vader, 4-pack...10.00
PFD0002 Darth Vader, 4-pack red top bag 8.00
PFD0003 Ewoks, 4-pack...8.00

Party Express
PFD0004 Jedi and Sith silhouettes, 8-pack.............................3.00
PFD0006 X-Wing vs. Tie Fighter, 8-pack 4.00

BLUEPRINTS

PPB0001

Ballantine
PPB0001 Blueprints, 15 in plastic pouch 24.00

BOARD GAMES

Avalon Hill
NB0041 The Queen's Gambit...60.00

EG
NB0036 Star Wars The Game (Escape from Death Star)..........20.00

Gamma Two
NB0039 Star Wars 55.00

Hasbro
NB0026 Battle for Naboo 3D action game................................20.00
NB0031 Galactic Battle, Episode I, electronic..........................35.00
NB0032 Jar Jar Binks 3-D adventure game..............................15.00
NB0027 Lightsaber Duel battle game......................................20.00
NB0030 Simon space battle game...34.00
NB0028 Star Wars Monopoly, Episode I edition........................35.00

Kenner
NB0001 Adventures of R2-D2..25.00
NB0006 Destroy Death Star..35.00
NB0007 Escape from Death Star...20.00
NB0010 Hoth Ice Planet adventure 30.00
NB0018 Yoda the Jedi Master...75.00

Milton Bradley
NB0034 Fighting Figures, Darth Vader vs. Luke Skywalker........16.00

Montecarlo
NB0025 "Star Wars El Imperio Contra Ataca" (Star Wars).........24.00
NB0024 "Star Wars Una Nueva Esperanza" (Empire Strikes Back) 18.00

Parker Bros.
NB0003 Battle at Sarlacc's Pit...35.00
NB0005 Death Star Assault...15.00
NB0009 Escape the Death Star action figure game 40.00
NB0011 Star Wars 30.00
NB0012 Star Wars Monopoly, classic trilogy edition..................28.00
NB0013 Star Wars Monopoly, collectors edition.........................55.00
NB0035 Star Wars The Game (Escape from Death Star)............17.00
NB0014 Star Wars video board game.......................................25.00
NB0015 The Ewoks save the trees...15.00

NB0039

NB0001

NB0017

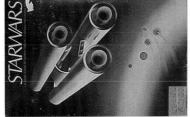

NB0011

NB0010

NB0018

NB0036

NB0007

NB0035

Board Games

NB0016 Trivial Pursuit, Star Wars edition 55.00
NB0017 Wicket the Ewok 20.00

Scholastic
NB0033 Star Wars EPI: Adventures, Darth Maul case 8.00
NB0022 Star Wars Missions..16.00

Tiger Electronics
NB0029 Escape from Naboo 18.00
NB0023 Galactic Battle, electronic 43.00

Toltoys
NB0040 Star Wars The Game (Escape from Death Star)...........17.00

Uzay
NB0037 "Yildiz Savaslari" (Star Wars)..27.00

Waddington
NB0038 Star Wars Monopoly, Episode I edition 34.00

West End Games
NB0002 Assault on Hoth 30.00
NB0004 Battle for Endor...30.00
NB0008 Escape from the Death Star 26.00
NB0020 Lightsaber dueling pack 10.00
NB0019 Star Warriors, starfighter combat 25.00
NB0021 Starfighter battle book 10.00

NB0037

NB0025

NB0024

NB0006

NB0003

NB0014

NB0005

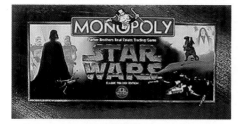

NB0012

NB0013

NB0023

NB0034

NB0009

NB0016

NB0029

NB0033

NB0027

NB0032

NB0031

NB0026

NB0028

NB0038

NB0030

NB0002

NB0004

NB0008

NB0020

BODY WASH

BW0001   BW0002   BW0003   BW0004

Minnetonka
BW0003 Darth Maul bottle with sculpted character cap............................6.00
BW0001 Darth Vader bottle with sculpted character cap............................6.00
BW0002 Stormtrooper bottle with sculpted character cap..........................6.00
BW0004 Pod racer game on container 17.00

BOOK COVERS

PPE0001 front and back   PPE0003

Butterfly Originals
PPE0001 Jabba the Hutt and Speeder Bikes...14.00

Factors, Etc.
PPE0002 Original Fan Club logo...6.00

Impact, Inc.
PPE0003 Episode I, 4-pack 7.00

BOOKCASES

FUB0001

American Toy and Furniture Co.
FUB0001 Return of the Jedi bookcase 130.00

BOOKENDS

HOB0001 front and side

Sigma
HOB0001 Chewbacca and Darth Vader bookends...............................225.00

BOOKLISTS

PPF0001 back and front   PPF0002 back and front   PPF0003

Booklists

Bantam Books
PPF0001 1996 Darth Vader / Shadows of the Empire 3.00
PPF0002 1997 "The Adventure Continues" / Lightsaber 3.00

Del Rey
PPF0003 The Time Line 3.00

BOOKMARKS

A.H. Prismatic
BKM0042 B-Wing, Millennium Falcon, Tie Fighter 5.00
BKM0043 Millennium Falcon, Darth Vader, Star Destroyer 5.00
BKM0044 X-Wing Fighter, Tie Interceptor, AT-AT 5.00

American Library Association
BKM0048 Darth Vader, Conquer the Information Universe 4.00

Antioch
BKM0053 Anakin Skywalker w/tassel 4.00
BKM0027 Ben Kenobi, w/tassel 4.00
BKM0017 Boba Fett, diecut 4.00
BKM0018 C-3PO, diecut 4.00
BKM0028 C-3PO, w/tassel 4.00
BKM0019 Chewbacca, diecut 3.00
BKM0029 Chewbacca, w/tassel 4.00
BKM0054 Darth Maul w/tassel 4.00
BKM0052 Darth Maul, diecut 4.00
BKM0020 Darth Vader, diecut 4.00
BKM0030 Darth Vader, w/tassel 4.00
BKM0021 Han Solo, diecut 4.00
BKM0047 Han Solo, w/tassel 4.00
BKM0059 Jar Jar Binks, diecut 4.00
BKM0022 Jawa, diecut 4.00
BKM0031 Lando Calrissian, w/tassel 4.00
BKM0032 Luke Skywalker, w/tassel 4.00
BKM0060 Mos Eisley Cantina, w/tassel 4.00
BKM0055 Obi-Wan Kenobi w/tassel 4.00
BKM0033 Princess Leia Organa, w/tassel 4.00
BKM0051 Queen Amidala, diecut 4.00
BKM0056 Qui-Gon Jinn w/tassel 4.00
BKM0023 R2-D2, diecut 4.00
BKM0057 Rune Haako, diecut 4.00
BKM0034 Rystall, w/tassel 6.00
BKM0058 Sebulba, diecut 4.00
BKM0035 Special Edition, w/tassel 4.00
BKM0024 Stormtrooper, diecut 3.00
BKM0036 The Courtship of Princess Leia, w/tassel 4.00
BKM0037 The Crystal Star, w/tassel 4.00
BKM0038 The Glove of Darth Vader, w/tassel 4.00
BKM0039 The Lost City of the Jedi, w/tassel 4.00
BKM0040 Truce at Bakura, w/tassel 4.00
BKM0025 Tusken Raider, diecut 4.00
BKM0026 Yoda, diecut 4.00
BKM0041 Zorba the Hutt's Revenge, w/tassel 4.00

Dark Horse Comics
BKM0049 "May The Horse Be With You" 3.00

Fantasma
BKM0045 Darth Vader 3D 3.00
BKM0046 Darth Vader and Luke Skywalker 3D 3.00

Random House
BKM0001 #01 Luke Skywalker 4.00
BKM0002 #02 Darth Vader 4.00
BKM0003 #03 Princess Leia (Boushh) 4.00
BKM0004 #04 R2-D2 .... 5.00
BKM0005 #05 C-3PO 5.00
BKM0006 #06 Lando Calrissian 4.00
BKM0007 #07 Chewbacca 4.00
BKM0008 #08 Yoda 5.00
BKM0009 #09 Ben Kenobi 4.00
BKM0010 #10 Han Solo 4.00
BKM0011 #11 Boba Fett 5.00
BKM0012 #12 Wicket the Ewok 4.00
BKM0013 #13 Emperor's Royal Guard 4.00
BKM0014 #14 Stormtrooper 4.00
BKM0015 #15 Jabba the Hutt 4.00
BKM0016 #16 Admiral Ackbar 4.00

Smithsonian Institute
BKM0050 Darth Vader, Yoda, Luke, promotes "The Magic of Myth" display, with plastic case 6.00

BKM0036 BKM0037 BKM0038 BKM0042 BKM0048 BKM0049 BKM0046 BKM0050

BKM0017 BKM0018 BKM0020 BKM0022 BKM0023 BKM0025 BKM0026 BKM0060 BKM0053 BKM0028 BKM0054 BKM0055 BKM0056 BKM0052 front/back

BKM0027 BKM0030 BKM0047 BKM0031 BKM0032 BKM0033 BKM0034 BKM0040 BKM0041 BKM0059 front and back BKM0051 front and back BM0057 front and back BKM0058 front and back

BKM0001 BKM0002 BKM0003 BKM0004 BKM0005 BKM0006 BKM0007 BKM0008

BKM0009 BKM0010 BKM0011 BKM0012 BKM0013 BKM0014 BKM0015 BKM0016

Antioch
PPG0002 C-3PO and R2-D2 ....8.00
PPG0003 Dark Empire, 10 pack on hanger card 6.00
PPG0007 Dark Empire, 30 pack boxed 9.00
PPG0008 Darth Vader, Boba Fett, Luke in X-Wing gear, 3 of each 5.00

Random House
PPG0001 C-3PO and R2-D2 ....10.00
PPG0004 Darth Vader 10.00
PPG0005 Wicket the Ewok 10.00
PPG0006 Yoda 10.00

BOOKS: ACTIVITY

Ballantine
BKA0021 The Star Wars Iron-On Transfer Book 25.00

DK Publishing
BKA0040 Ultimate Star Wars Episode I sticker book 8.00
BKA0041 Ultimate Star Wars sticker book..8.00

Fun Works
BKA0031 Millennium Falcon Punch-Out book..8.00

Golden Books
BKA0032 A More Wretched Hive, The Mos Eisley Cantina scratch and
    sniff 12.00
BKA0045 Royal Rescue, galactic search 11.00
BKA0016 Tell-a-Story stickerbook...4.00
BKA0019 The Rebel Alliance vs. The Imperial Forces 4.00
BKA0022 The Training of a Jedi Knight 4.00

Random House
BKA0002 Artoo Detoo's Activity book 7.00
BKA0003 Chewbacca's Activity book 7.00
BKA0030 Darth Vader's Activity book 7.00
BKA0004 Dot-to-Dot Fun, ROTJ 4.00
BKA0018 Empire Strikes Back mix or match storybook 15.00
BKA0046 Episode I Mask Punch-Out Book 8.00
BKA0033 Episode I Micro Vehicle Punch-Outs 4.00
BKA0044 Episode I Posters to Color, mail-in premium...............................12.00

BOOKPLATES

PPG0003

PPG0007

PPG0008

BKA0002

BKA0003

BKA0030

BKA0006

BKA0015

BKA0020

BKA0007 BKA0004 BKA0008 BKA0009 BKA0023 BKA0026 BKA0025 BKA0018

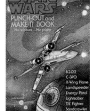
BKA0005

BKA0024

BKA0021

BKA0011

BKA0012

BKA0013

Books: Activity

BKB0019

BKB0020

BKB0021

BKB0012

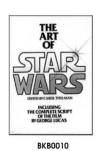
BKB0010

BKB0015

BKB0016

BKB0022

BKB0023

BKB0024

BKB0025

BKB0002

BKB0026

BKB0027

BKB0029

BKB0028

BKB0006

BKB0008

BKA0016

BKA0022

BKA0032

BKA0041

BKA0040

BKA0001

BKA0010

BKA0035

BKA0033

BKA0031

BKA0038

BKA0043

BKA0037

BKA0042

BKA0025 Word Puzzle Book, ROTJ 4.00
BKA0026 Yoda's Activity Book...................................9.00

Sandylion
BKA0039 My Sticker Tote, includes over 100 stickers.....................7.00

Scholastic
BKA0001 Anakin's Activity Magazine 2.00
BKA0010 Obi-Wan's Activity Magazine 2.00

BOOKS: ART

Ballantine
BKB0019 The Art of Return of The Jedi, 1994 cover, trade paperback 18.00
BKB0020 The Art of Return of The Jedi, 1997 Special Edition section, trade paperback.......................................20.00
BKB0018 The Art of Return of The Jedi, hardcover.....................60.00
BKB0021 The Art of Return of The Jedi, trade paperback.......................25.00
BKB0011 The Art of Star Wars, 1994 cover, trade paperback...................18.00
BKB0012 The Art of Star Wars, 1997 Special Edition section, trade paperback.......................................20.00
BKB0010 The Art of Star Wars, hardcover......................50.00
BKB0013 The Art of Star Wars, trade paperback......................25.00
BKB0015 The Art of The Empire Strikes Back, 1994 cover, trade paperback.......................................18.00
BKB0016 The Art of The Empire Strikes Back, 1997 Special Edition section, trade paperback......................20.00
BKB0014 The Art of The Empire Strikes Back, hardcover......................60.00
BKB0017 The Art of The Empire Strikes Back, trade paperback.................25.00
BKB0024 The Empire Strikes Back Sketchbook......................12.00
BKB0022 The Illustrated Star Wars Universe 40.00
BKB0025 The Return of the Jedi Sketchbook......................12.00

BKB0023 The Star Wars Sketchbook.......................12.00

Benford Books
BKB0001 The Art of Dave Dorman, numbered and signed, hardcover...80.00
BKB0002 The Art of Dave Dorman, trade paperback...............25.00

Chronicle Books
BKB0028 Episode I: 20 Lithographic Reproductions by Doug Chiang......55.00

Del Rey
BKB0029 Art of Star Wars: Episode I, TPM.......................23.00
BKB0026 The Art of the Brothers Hildebrandt......................25.00
BKB0027 The Art of The Phantom Menace, trade paperback.................29.00

Topps
BKB0006 The Art of Star Wars Galaxy.......................20.00
BKB0007 The Art of Star Wars Galaxy II, foil cover, trade paperback 25.00
BKB0008 The Art of Star Wars Galaxy II, trade paperback.....................20.00
BKB0005 The Art of Star Wars Galaxy, QVC exclusive w/card sheet........25.00

Underwood-Miller Inc.
BKB0009 The Art of Star Wars Galaxy, limited edition (bound and boxed) 175.00

BOOKS: AUDIO, CASSETTE

Bantam Books
ABK0021 Before the Storm 15.00
ABK0022 Children of the Jedi 14.00
ABK0032 Courtship of Princess Leia 18.00
ABK0008 Crystal Star 14.00
ABK0023 Dark Apprentice 15.00

AKB0001 AKB0037 AKB0002 AKB0042 AKB0011 AKB0012 AKB0015 AKB0007

AKB0016 AKB0017 AKB0033 AKB0025 AKB0027 AKB0004 AKB0030 AKB0038 AKB0018

AKB0034 AKB0036 AKB0013 AKB0035 AKB0014 AKB0020 AKB0005 AKB0010 AKB0043

Books: Audio, Cassette

ABK0001 Dark Empire 12.00
ABK0037 Dark Empire II 16.00
ABK0002 Dark Empire trilogy in Millennium Falcon collector's box..........46.00
ABK0009 Dark Force Rising...14.00
ABK0024 Dark Saber...15.00
ABK0042 Han Solo Omnibus : The Paradise Snare, the Hutt Gambit, Rebel
  Dawn 30.00
ABK0011 Heir to the Empire 15.00
ABK0012 Hutt Gambit..16.00
ABK0015 Jedi Academy Omnibus..24.00
ABK0007 Jedi Search..14.00
ABK0016 Last Command..14.00
ABK0017 Mandalorean Armor...14.00
ABK0026 Nightlily, the Lovers' Tale...12.00
ABK0033 Paradise Snare...18.00
ABK0025 Planet of Twilight...18.00
ABK0027 Rogue Planet..25.00
ABK0004 Shadows of the Empire...18.00
ABK0028 Shield of Lies..18.00
ABK0029 Showdown at Centerpoint..18.00
ABK0030 Slave Ship...18.00
ABK0031 Specter of the Past...18.00
ABK0006 Star Wars sampler, 6 stories...8.00
ABK0038 Star Wars: Episode I...40.00
ABK0018 The New Rebellion..14.00
ABK0003 The Phantom Menace, unabridged..................................17.00
ABK0034 Thrawn Omnibus...30.00
ABK0040 Truce at Bakura...17.00
ABK0041 Tyrant's Test..17.00
ABK0036 X-Wing 05: Wraith Squadron..18.00
ABK0013 X-Wing 06: Iron Fist..14.00
ABK0035 X-Wing 07: Solo Command...18.00
ABK0014 X-Wing 08: Isard's Revenge..15.00
ABK0039 X-Wing 09: Starfighters of Adumar...................................18.00

Del Rey
ABK0005 Vector Prime...18.00

Griffin
ABK0019 The Science of Star Wars, unabridged..............................25.00

Highbridge Company
ABK0020 Soldier for the Empire 15.00

Random House
ABK0043 Agents of Chaos 1 : Hero's Trial 18.00
ABK0044 Agents of Chaos 2 : Jedi Eclipse......................................18.00
ABK0045 Balance Point...18.00
ABK0010 Dark Tide I: Onslaught 16.00

BOOKS: AUDIO, CD

Bantam Books
ABC0008 Nightlily, the Lovers' Tale...14.00
ABC0004 Rogue Planet..30.00
ABC0002 Shadows of the Empire 20.00
ABC0001 Star Wars: Episode I...28.00

Penguin Audiobooks
ABC0003 Crimson Empire 24.00
ABC0005 Dark Forces : The Collector's Trilogy 50.00

Random House
ABC0007 Star Wars: Episode I, unabridged......................................40.00
ABC0006 Star Wars: Episode I, unabridged limited edition boxed set...160.00

BOOKS: COLORING

Golden Books
BKC0027 A Galaxy of Creatures, Characters, and Droids.................5.00
BKC0001 An Ewok Adventure 4.00
BKC0010 Galactic Adventures 2.00
BKC0011 Heroes and Villains 2.00
BKC0033 Invisible Forces 9.00
BKC0026 Join the Jedi 4.00
BKC0015 Mark and See Magic 8.00
BKC0017 Posters to Color 6.00

Kenner
BKC0003 C-3PO and Chewbacca, ESB...7.00
BKC0002 C-3PO and Luke, SW...15.00
BKC0004 Chewbacca, SW..15.00
BKC0005 Chewbacca and Luke, SW...15.00
BKC0023 Chewbacca and Princess Leia, ESB................................7.00
BKC0006 Chewbacca, Han, Lando, and Princess Leia, ESB 7.00

BKC0006   BKC0023   BKC0022   BKC0012   BKC0014   BKC0016   BKC0008   BKC0034

BKC0027   BKC0001   BKC0010   BKC0011 front and back   BKC0033   BKC0026   BKC0028

BKC0035   BKC0030   BKC0029   BKC0032   BKC0036   BKC0031   BKC0037   BKC0038

BKC0007 Darth Vader and Stormtroopers, ESB 7.00
BKC0012 Lando, ROTJ 5.00
BKC0024 Lando as Skiff Guard, ROTJ 5.00
BKC0013 Luke, ESB 7.00
BKC0014 Luke with lightsaber, ROTJ 5.00
BKC0016 Max Rebo band, ROTJ 5.00
BKC0018 R2-D2, ESB 7.00
BKC0019 R2-D2, SW 15.00
BKC0021 Wicket and Kneesaa, ROTJ 5.00
BKC0020 Wicket the Ewok, ROTJ 5.00
BKC0025 Wicket, Kneesaa, and Logray, ROTJ 6.00
BKC0009 Wicket's World 7.00
BKC0022 Yoda, ESB 7.00

Oral-B
BKC0008 Dental Health Adventure Book...........................12.00

Random House
BKC0028 Battles To Color, TPM 4.00
BKC0035 Droids, Creatures, and Vehicles 3.00
BKC0030 EP1 Anakin's Adventures To Color 3.00
BKC0029 EP1 Heroes and Villains 3.00
BKC0032 EP1 Jedi Missions 3.00
BKC0036 Giant Coloring Fun 12.00
BKC0031 Jar Jar's Coloring Fun.................................3.00
BKC0037 Jedi Knights and Heroes 4.00
BKC0038 Podracer! 4.00
BKC0040 Queen Amidala 4.00
BKC0039 The Phantom Menace...................................4.00
BKC0034 The Droid Colouring Book of the Future.................19.00

BOOKS: COOKING

Chronicle Books
BKX0003 Star Wars Cookbook II, Darth Malt and More Galactic
Recipes 17.00

BKX0001 Star Wars Cookbook, Wookie Cookies and other Galactic
Recipes 28.00

Enterprise Incidents
BKX0002 The Alien Cook 16.00

BOOKS: EDUCATIONAL

Golden Books
BKE0035 Han Solo's Rescue from Jabba the Hutt, math grades 2-3..........7.00
BKE0028 Luke Skywalker's Battle with Darth Vader, reading grades 2-3 ...7.00
BKE0027 Princess Leia's Escape from the Death Star, spelling grades 2-3.7.00
BKE0026 Super Shape Book: Chewbacca the Wookie.....................5.00
BKE0025 Super Shape Book: Han Solo.................................5.00
BKE0016 Super Shape Book: Luke Skywalker, Jedi Knight................6.00
BKE0017 Super Shape Book: Princess Leia.............................5.00
BKE0018 Super Shape Book: R2-D2 and C-3PO, Droid Duo.....................5.00

Pendulum Press
BKE0014 Remedial Reading multimedia kit 135.00

Random House
BKE0001 ABC Readiness...5.00
BKE0002 Addition and Subtraction Workbook 5.00
BKE0003 Attack on Reading: Comprehension 1 ....20.00
BKE0004 Attack on Reading: Comprehension 2 ....20.00
BKE0005 Attack on Reading: Study Skills 20.00
BKE0006 Attack on Reading: Teacher's Guide 25.00
BKE0007 Attack on Reading: Word Study 20.00
BKE0008 C-3PO's Book About Robots 12.00
BKE0009 Early Numbers Workbook 5.00
BKE0010 Ewok: ABC Fun 10.00
BKE0011 Ewok: Learn-to-Read.......................................10.00
BKE0012 Multiplication Workbook.....................................5.00
BKE0013 Reading and Writing Workbook 5.00
BKE0015 Spelling Workbook...5.00

BKX0001

BKX0003

BKX0002

BKE0008

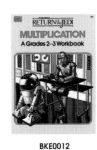
BKE0012

BKE0013

BKE0020

BKE0021

BKE0025

BKE0016

BKE0017

BKE0018

BKE0028

BKE0027

BKE0035

BKE0029

BKE0030

BKE0031

BKE0033

Books: Educational

BKE0029 SW Learning Fun Book Grade 1 Simple Adding and Subtracting ..5.00
BKE0030 SW Learning Fun Book Kindergarten Learning Word Sounds 5.00
BKE0034 SW Learning Fun Book Preschool - Kindergarten Counting Numbers 1-20 ....5.00
BKE0033 SW Learning Fun Book Preschool - Kindergarten Learning Shapes 5.00
BKE0031 SW Learning Fun Book Preschool - Kindergarten Writing Letters A to Z 5.00
BKE0032 SW Learning Fun Book Preschool - Kindergarten Writing Numbers 1 to 10 ....5.00
BKE0019 The Star Wars Book About Flight 12.00
BKE0020 The Star Wars Question and Answer Book About Computers, soft-cover 12.00
BKE0021 The Star Wars Question and Answer Book About Space, hard-cover..20.00

Scholastic
BKE0022 The Star Wars Question and Answer Book About Space, soft-cover..14.00

BOOKS: GALAXY OF FEAR

Bantam Books
BKH0001 01 Eaten Alive................................8.00
BKH0002 02 City of the Dead 8.00
BKH0003 03 Planet Plague 8.00
BKH0004 04 The Nightmare Machine 8.00
BKH0005 05 The Ghost of the Jedi 8.00
BKH0006 06 Army of Terror 8.00
BKH0007 07 The Brain Spiders 8.00
BKH0008 08 The Swarm 8.00
BKH0009 09 Spore 8.00
BKH0010 10 The Doomsday Ship 8.00
BKH0011 11 Clones 8.00
BKH0012 12 Hunger................................8.00

BOOKS: GAME GUIDES

BradyGames Strategy Guides
BKF0012 Tie Fighter: Authorized Strategy Guide 10.00

Infotainment World Books
BKF0004 Rebel Assault II: Official Player's Guide................................12.00

Lucas Arts
BKF0001 Dark Forces: Official Player's Guide 18.00

Nintendo
BKF0026 Episode I: Pod Racer, Official Nintendo Player's Guide 15.00

Prima Publishing
BKF0025 EPI: The Phantom Menace 15.00
BKF0021 Episode I: Pod Racer 15.00
BKF0024 Gungan Frontier................................18.00
BKF0023 Jedi Power Battles 15.00
BKF0019 Masters of Teras Kasi................................15.00
BKF0005 Rebel Assault: The Official Insider's Guide................................14.00
BKF0020 Star Wars: Force Commander 16.00
BKF0022 X-Wing Alliance................................15.00
BKF0017 Battle Masters Guide 8.00
BKF0002 Defender of the Empire: Secrets and Solutions................................10.00
BKF0003 Jedi Knight Strategy Guide 14.00
BKF0018 Secrets of Shadows of the Empire 12.00
BKF0006 Shadows of the Empire: Strategy Guide 16.00
BKF0007 Star Wars Nintendo Hint Book (Special Offer) 15.00
BKF0008 Super Empire Strikes Back Official Secrets 10.00
BKF0009 Super ROTJ Official Game Secrets 10.00
BKF0010 Super Star Wars Official Game Secrets................................12.00
BKF0011 Tie Fighter Collector's CD-ROM 12.00
BKF0013 Tie Fighter: The Official Strategy Guide................................12.00
BKF0014 X-Wing Collector's CD-ROM: The Official Strategy Guide.........15.00
BKF0015 X-Wing vs. Tie Fighter Strategy Guide................................18.00

BKH0001   BKH0002   BKH0003   BKH0004   BKF0001   BKF0025   BKF0021   BKF0024

  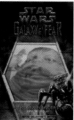     

BKH0005   BKH0006   BKH0007   BKH0008   BKF0023   BKF0019   BKF0020   BKF0022

BKH0009   BKH0010   BKH0011   BKH0012   BKF0003   BKF0018   BKF0006   BKF0013

BKF0016 X-Wing: The Official Strategy Guide 12.00

BOOKS: GRAPHIC NOVELS

BGN0001

BGN0002

BGN0003

Dark Horse Comics
BGN0001 Dark Forces: Jedi Knight................................25.00
BGN0002 Dark Forces: Rebel Agent 25.00
BGN0003 Dark Forces: Soldier For the Empire 28.00

BOOKS: GUIDES

Antique Trader Books
BKG0027 Galaxy's Greatest Star Wars Collectibles....................25.00

Back Bay Books
BKG0045 Unauthorized SW Companion: The Complete Guide to the SW Galaxy 18.00

Ballantine
BKG0001 A Guide to the Star Wars Universe 12.00
BKG0002 A Guide to the Star Wars Universe, 2nd ed................18.00
BKG0060 A Guide to the Star Wars Universe, 3rd ed. 15.00

Beckett
BKG0052 Collectibles from a galaxy far, far away 20.00
BKG0053 Everything you need to know about Collecting Star Wars.......20.00

Chronicle Books
BKG0019 Anakin Skywalker, The Story of Darth Vader, includes 13" collectible doll figure 75.00
BKG0050 Aurra Sing Masterpiece Edition 135.00
BKG0056 C-3PO: Tales of the Golden Droid.........................55.00
BKG0054 The Action Figure Archive 30.00

Collector's Guide
BKG0063 Irwin Toys the Canadian Star Wars Connection.......................27.00

DK Publishing
BKG0061 Inside the Worlds of Star Wars Episode I 22.00
BKG0021 SW: Incredible Cross-Sections 35.00
BKG0020 SW: The Visual Dictionary 35.00
BKG0029 TPM: Cross Sections 22.00
BKG0046 TPM: Cross Sections, inside metal box with combination lock, 500 produced for promotion.............................360.00
BKG0030 TPM: The Visual Dictionary 17.00

Henderson Publishing
BKG0047 Funfax Mission 1: Star Wars 5.00
BKG0048 Funfax Mission 2: Empire Strikes Back 5.00
BKG0049 Funfax Mission 3: Return of the Jedi 5.00
BKG0032 Microfax #01: Darth Vader...................................2.00
BKG0033 Microfax #02: C-3PO and R2-D2.............................2.00
BKG0034 Microfax #03: Galactic Empire..............................2.00
BKG0035 Microfax #04: Jabba the Hutt and Bounty Hunters.......2.00
BKG0036 Microfax #05: Princess Leia................................2.00
BKG0037 Microfax #06: Luke Skywalker 2.00
BKG0038 Microfax #07: Millennium Falcon 2.00
BKG0039 Microfax #08: Obi-Wan Kenobi.............................2.00
BKG0040 Microfax #09: Han Solo and Chewbacca 2.00
BKG0041 Microfax #10: Imperial Fleet...............................2.00

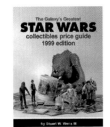
BKG0027

BKG0022

BKG0002

BKG0060

BKG0052

BKG0053

BKG0054

BKG0019

BKG0056

BKG0050

BKG0061

BKG0021

BKG0020

BKG0029

BKG0030

BKG0044

BKG0028

BKG0062

BKG0031

BKG0017

Books: Guides

BKG0042 Microfax #11: Rebel Fleet 2.00
BKG0043 Microfax #12: Rebel Alliance 2.00
BKG0044 Microfax Mini-Binder 5.00
BKG0028 Star Wars Data File 18.00

Krause Publications
BKG0062 Star Wars Collector's Pocket Companion......................12.00

Little, Brown
BKG0022 The Unauthorized Star Wars Compendium : The Complete Guide to the Movies, Comic Books, Novels, and More 20.00

Random House
BKG0031 EPI:TPM Scrapbook...12.00
BKG0017 House of Collectibles Price Guide to Star Wars Collectibles.....14.00
BKG0059 Secrets of the Sith Movie Scrapbook 7.00

Reeds
BKG0066 Darth Vader mini-book 4.00
BKG0065 Han Solo mini-book 4.00

Running Press
BKG0026 Star Wars Collectibles : A Pocket Guide.......................7.00
BKG0057 Tie Fighter: A Pocket Manual 6.00
BKG0055 Who's Who : A Pocket Guide to the Characters of the Phantom Menace 6.00
BKG0058 X-Wing: A Pocket Manual 6.00

Schiffer Publishing
BKG0018 Collecting SW Toys 1977–1997: An Unauthorized Practical Guide 30.00

Scholastic
BKG0004 The Complete Star Wars Trilogy Scrapbook.....................10.00
BKG0024 The Star Wars Trilogy Scrapbook: The Galactic Empire 8.00
BKG0023 The Star Wars Trilogy Scrapbook: Rebel Alliance 8.00

Tomart
BKG0013 Tomart's Price Guide to Worldwide Star Wars Collectibles.......30.00
BKG0016 Tomart's Price Guide to Worldwide Star Wars Collectibles, 2nd edition 30.00
BKG0014 All About the Star Wars..37.00
BKG0006 Essential Guide to Characters 16.00
BKG0005 Essential Guide to Characters, condensed 8.00
BKG0007 Essential Guide to Droids 18.00
BKG0008 Essential Guide to Planets & Moons 18.00
BKG0010 Essential Guide to Vehicles & Vessels 16.00
BKG0009 Essential Guide to Vehicles & Vessels, condensed 8.00
BKG0011 Essential Guide to Weapons and Technology 18.00
BKG0015 Force of Star Wars 36.00
BKG0067 Kiddie Meal Collectibles, Darth Maul cover 16.00
BKG0003 Star Wars Encyclopedia 50.00
BKG0012 World of Star Wars 12.00

BOOKS: JEDI APPRENTICE

Scholastic
BKD0001 01 The Rising Force 5.00
BKD0002 02 The Dark Rival...5.00
BKD0003 03 The Hidden Past 5.00
BKD0004 04 The Mark of the Crown 5.00
BKD0005 05 The Defenders of the Dead 5.00
BKD0006 06 The Uncertain Path 5.00
BKD0007 07 The Captive Temple 5.00
BKD0008 08 The Day of Reckoning...5.00

BKG0059

BKG0026

BKG0057

BKG0025

BKG0058

BKG0018

BKG0004

BKG0024

BKG0023

BKG0013

BKG0015

BKG0003

BKG0006

BKG0007

BKG0008

BKG0010

BKG0011

BKD0001

BKD0002

BKD0003

BKD0004

BKD0005

BKD0006

BKD0007

BKD0008

BKJ0001 BKJ0002 BKJ0003 BKJ0004 BKJ0005 BKJ0006 BKV0001 BKV0002

BKV0003 BKV0004 BKV0005 MB0006 BKZ0005 BKZ0024 BKZ0019 BKZ0013

BKD0009 09 The Fight for Truth.................................5.00
BKD0010 10 The Shattered Peace 5.00
BKD0011 11 The Deadly Hunter 5.00
BKD0012 12 The Evil Experiment 5.00
BKD0013 13 The Dangerous Rescue 5.00
BKD0013 14 The Ties That Bind 5.00
BKD0050 Special Edition: Deceptions........................7.00

BOOKS: JUNIOR JEDI KNIGHTS

Boulevard
BKJ0001 01 The Golden Globe.................................8.00
BKJ0002 02 Lyric's World 6.00
BKJ0003 03 Promises 6.00
BKJ0004 04 Anakin's Quest 6.00
BKJ0005 05 Vader's Fortress 6.00
BKJ0006 06 Kenobi's Blade 6.00

BOOKS: MAKE YOUR OWN ADVENTURE

Bantam Books
BKV0004 Empire Strikes Back 6.00

BKV0005 Return of the Jedi 6.00
BKV0003 Star Wars 6.00

West End Games
BKV0001 Jedi's Honor 12.00
BKV0002 Scoundrel's Luck 12.00

BOOKS: MUSIC

Fox Fanfare Music
MB0001 Star Wars...15.00
MB0002 Star Wars Picture Book.............................15.00
MB0003 Star Wars Saga Book................................24.00
MB0004 The Empire Strikes Back 12.00

Warner Bros. Publications
MB0011 Music from the Star Wars Trilogy for Flute 10.00
MB0007 Phantom Menace Clarinet Songbook with CD 12.00
MB0008 Phantom Menace Tenor Sax Songbook with CD 12.00
MB0009 Phantom Menace Trumpet Songbook with CD.......12.00
MB0005 Selections from Star Wars for Guitar...............15.00
MB0010 Music from ROTJ and 20 movie gems, for trumpet 6.00
MB0006 Star Wars plus 12 giant pop chart winners 4.00

BKZ0001 BKZ0002 BKZ0016 BKZ0017

BKZ0003 BKZ0009 BKZ0022 BKZ0007 BKZ0036 BKZ0031 BKZ0033 BKZ0037

BOOKS: NON-FICTION

Abrams
BKZ0023 George Lucas The Creative Impulse: Lucasfilm's First Twenty Years 40.00
BKZ0006 George Lucas: The Creative Impulse.....................35.00
BKZ0005 George Lucas: The Creative Impulse, 2nd edition 35.00
BKZ0024 Monsters and Aliens from George Lucas......................25.00

Ballantine
BKZ0019 Making of Return of the Jedi................................16.00
BKZ0020 Once Upon A Galaxy, The Making of Empire Strikes Back.........22.00
BKZ0021 Star Wars, Star Trek, and 21st Century Christians...........................26.00

Bantam Books
BKZ0013 The Magic of Myth, hardcover 35.00
BKZ0014 The Magic of Myth, trade paperback 24.00

CG Publishing
BKZ0038 Irwin Toys: The Canadian Star Wars Connection 17.00

Chronicle Books
BKZ0001 Aliens and Creatures (postcard book) 16.00
BKZ0002 Behind the Scenes (postcard book) 16.00
BKZ0003 From Star Wars to Indiana Jones: The Best of Lucasfilm Archives, hardcover 45.00
BKZ0004 From Star Wars to Indiana Jones: The Best of Lucasfilm Archives, trade paperback 25.00
BKZ0009 Star Wars Chronicles...........................175.00
BKZ0017 Star Wars Scrapbook: The Essential Collection 35.00
BKZ0010 Star Wars: From Concept to Screen to Collectible, hardcover .35.00
BKZ0011 Star Wars: From Concept to Screen to Collectible, paperback25.00
BKZ0016 The Toys (postcard book) 16.00

Citadel
BKZ0022 Empire Building: The Remarkable Real Life Story of SW 16.00

Del Rey
BKZ0007 Industrial Light and Magic: Into the Digital Realm......................65.00

BKZ0008 Industrial Light and Magic: The Art of Special Effects 75.00

DK Publishing
BKZ0026 Classic Gift Pack (Visual Dict., Cross-Sections, Ultimate Sticker book, Power of Myth book, calendar) 65.00
BKZ0027 EP1 Gift Pack (Visual Dict., Cross-Sections, Ultimate Sticker book, Power of Myth book, Calendar) 65.00
BKZ0025 The Power of Myth..14.00

Facts on Demand
BKZ0036 The Incredible Internet Guide to Star Wars................................12.00

Fictioneer Books, Ltd.
BKZ0028 David Anthony Kraft's Comics Interview Super Special: SW 18.00

Franklin Watts
BKZ0034 George Lucas : Creator of Star Wars.......................7.00
BKZ0035 George Lucas : Creator of Star Wars, hardcover.............16.00

Griffin
BKZ0031 The Science of Star Wars, hardcover.......................22.00
BKZ0032 The Science of Star Wars, paperback 15.00

Hobby Japan
BKZ0033 The Modeling of Star Wars................................19.00

Lucas Books
BKZ0037 Making of Episode I: The Phantom Menace 40.00

Random House
BKZ0018 Star Wars, The Making of the Movie, step-up...............12.00

Samuel French Trade
BKZ0029 Skywalking: The Life and Films of George Lucas.............15.00
BKZ0030 Skywalking: The Life and Films of George Lucas; updated edition 1997..17.00

Starlog
BKZ0012 Starlog Salutes Star Wars, 10th Anniversary souvenir program...15.00

BKN0060

BKN0061

BKN0063

BKN0105

BKN0061

BKN0077

BKN0074

BKN0077

BKN0077 reprinted

BKN0047

BKN0045

BKN0048

BKN0104

BKN0104 reprinted

BKN0057

BKN0057 reprinted

BKN0021

BKN0024

BKN0024 reprinted

BKN0019

BKN0019 reprinted

BKN0078

BKN0078 reprinted

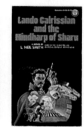
BKN0037

Trafalgar Square
BKZ0039 The Power of the Force, The Spirituality of the Star Wars films....15.00

BOOKS: NOVELS

Ballantine
BKN0127 Balance Point, hardcover 24.00
BKN0075 Empire Strikes Back, hardcover....................................16.00
BKN0076 Empire Strikes Back, illustrated edition, paperback..................10.00
BKN0077 Empire Strikes Back, paperback....................................6.00
BKN0074 Empire Strikes Back, Trilogy art on cover, hardcover 12.00
BKN0078 Han Solo Adventures, paperback compilation...........................8.00
BKN0018 Han Solo and the Lost Legacy, hardcover.............................15.00
BKN0019 Han Solo and the Lost Legacy, paperback.............................6.00
BKN0020 Han Solo at Star's End, hardcover..................................15.00
BKN0021 Han Solo at Star's End, paperback..................................6.00
BKN0022 Han Solo paperback boxed set......................................24.00
BKN0023 Han Solo's Revenge, hardcover.....................................15.00
BKN0024 Han Solo's Revenge, paperback.....................................6.00
BKN0079 Lando Calrissian Adventures, paperback compilation.............8.00
BKN0034 Lando Calrissian and the Flamewind of Oseon, hardcover......35.00
BKN0035 Lando Calrissian and the Flamewind of Oseon, paperback......6.00
BKN0036 Lando Calrissian and the Mindharp of Sharu, hardcover 35.00
BKN0037 Lando Calrissian and the Mindharp of Sharu, paperback..........6.00
BKN0038 Lando Calrissian and the Starcave of Thonboka, hardcover....35.00
BKN0039 Lando Calrissian and the Starcave of Thonboka, paperback....6.00
BKN0046 Return of the Jedi, hardcover......................................20.00
BKN0047 Return of the Jedi, illustrated edition, paperback.....................10.00

BKN0048 Return of the Jedi, paperback 6.00
BKN0045 Return of the Jedi, Trilogy art on cover, hardcover...................12.00
BKN0056 Splinter of the Mind's Eye, hardcover 15.00
BKN0057 Splinter of the Mind's Eye, paperback.............................6.00
BKN0061 Star Wars novelization by George Lucas.............................6.00
BKN0060 Star Wars novelization by George Lucas, 1st edition: 1976 (concept cover)..35.00
BKN0063 Star Wars novelization by George Lucas, hardcover.................15.00
BKN0064 Star Wars novelization by George Lucas, hardcover w/gold dust jacket...80.00
BKN0062 Star Wars novelization by George Lucas, hardcover: 1976.......12.00
BKN0104 Star Wars Trilogy 12.00
BKN0088 Star Wars Trilogy, paperback boxed set 28.00
BKN0105 Star Wars, Trilogy art on cover, hardcover 12.00

Bantam Books
BKN0001 Ambush at Corellia..7.00
BKN0103 Ambush at Corellia, signed 34.00
BKN0002 Assault on Selonia...7.00
BKN0003 Before the Storm..8.00
BKN0004 Black Fleet Crisis Trilogy, hardcover compilation....................21.00
BKN0107 Bounty Hunter Wars: 01 Mandalorian Armor..........................7.00
BKN0108 Bounty Hunter Wars: 02 Slave Ship....................................7.00
BKN0121 Bounty Hunter Wars: 03 Hard Merchandise............................7.00
BKN0005 Champions of the Force..6.00
BKN0006 Children of the Jedi, book club edition, hardcover...................12.00
BKN0007 Children of the Jedi, hardcover..25.00
BKN0008 Children of the Jedi, paperback..6.00
BKN0009 Corellian Trilogy, hardcover compilation 16.00

BKN0039

BKN0079

BKN0027

BKN0014

BKN0082

BKN0033

BKN0011

BKN0005

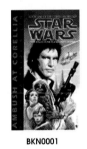
BKN0001

BKN0002

BKN0053

BKN0009

BKN0092

BKN0008

BKN0030

BKN0073

BKN0028

BKN0040

BKN0044

BKN0051

BKN0017

BKN0070

BKN0085

BKN0043

BKN0003

BKN0052

BKN0094

BKN0124

BKN0067

BKN0107

BKN0108

BKN0121

Books: Novels

BKN0106

BKN0065

BKN0066

BKN0055

BKN0095

BKN0098

BKN0101

BKN0100

BKN0099

BKN0102

BKN0097

BKN0109

BKN0122

BKN0126

BKN0116

BKN0119

BKN0128

BKN0127

BKN0110

BKN0111

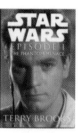
BKN0112

BKN0113

BKN0125

BKN0118

BKN0010 Corellian Trilogy, paperback boxed set 24.00
BKN0068 Courtship of Princess Leia, book club edition, hardcover 10.00
BKN0069 Courtship of Princess Leia, hardcover 25.00
BKN0070 Courtship of Princess Leia, paperback 6.00
BKN0071 Crystal Star, book club edition, hardcover 10.00
BKN0072 Crystal Star, hardcover 25.00
BKN0073 Crystal Star, paperback 6.00
BKN0011 Dark Apprentice 6.00
BKN0013 Dark Force Rising, hardcover 24.00
BKN0014 Dark Force Rising, paperback 8.00
BKN0012 Dark Force Rising, signed and numbered, hardcover w/slip
    cover 175.00
BKN0015 Darksaber, book club edition, hardcover 12.00
BKN0016 Darksaber, hardcover 20.00
BKN0017 Darksaber, paperback 5.00
BKN0026 Heir to the Empire, hardcover 25.00
BKN0027 Heir to the Empire, paperback 8.00
BKN0025 Heir to the Empire, signed and numbered, hardcover w/slip-
    cover 175.00
BKN0028 Hutt Gambit 7.00
BKN0029 I, Jedi, hardcover 25.00
BKN0030 I, Jedi, paperback 7.00
BKN0031 Jedi Acadamy Trilogy, hardcover compilation 14.00
BKN0032 Jedi Acadamy Trilogy, paperback boxed set 20.00
BKN0033 Jedi Search 6.00
BKN0081 Last Command, hardcover 24.00
BKN0082 Last Command, paperback 8.00
BKN0080 Last Command, signed and numbered, hardcover w/slipcover...175.00
BKN0083 New Rebellion, book club edition, hardcover 12.00
BKN0084 New Rebellion, hardcover 22.00
BKN0085 New Rebellion, paperback 6.00
BKN0040 Paradise Snare 8.00
BKN0041 Planet of Twilight, hardcover 20.00
BKN0043 Planet of Twilight, paperback 4.00
BKN0044 Rebel Dawn 7.00
BKN0049 Shadows of the Empire, book club edition, hardcover 15.00
BKN0050 Shadows of the Empire, hardcover 23.00
BKN0051 Shadows of the Empire, paperback 17.00
BKN0052 Shield of Lies 8.00

BKN0053 Showdown at Centerpoint 7.00
BKN0054 Specter of the Past, hardcover 28.00
BKN0055 Specter of the Past, paperback 9.00
BKN0113 Star Wars: Episode I TPM, hardcover, Anakin Skywalker Cover ...25.00
BKN0110 Star Wars: Episode I TPM, hardcover, Darth Maul Cover 25.00
BKN0112 Star Wars: Episode I TPM, hardcover, Obi-Wan Kenobi Cover ...25.00
BKN0111 Star Wars: Episode I TPM, hardcover, Queen Amidala Cover ..25.00
BKN0065 Tales from Jabba's Palace 8.00
BKN0066 Tales from Mos Eisley Cantina 8.00
BKN0106 Tales from the Empire 9.00
BKN0124 Tales from the New Republic 6.00
BKN0067 Tales of the Bounty Hunters 8.00
BKN0093 Thrawn Trilogy, paperback boxed set 32.00
BKN0090 Truce at Bakura, book club edition, hardcover 10.00
BKN0091 Truce at Bakura, hardcover 25.00
BKN0092 Truce at Bakura, paperback 6.00
BKN0094 Tyrant's Test 8.00
BKN0095 Vision of the Future, hardcover 28.00
BKN0096 Vision of the Future, paperback 9.00
BKN0098 X-Wing: Rogue Squadron 6.00
BKN0101 X-Wing: Wedge's Gamble 6.00
BKN0100 X-Wing: The Krytos Trap 6.00
BKN0099 X-Wing: The Bacta War 6.00
BKN0102 X-Wing: Wraith Squadron 8.00
BKN0097 X-Wing: Iron Fist 7.00
BKN0109 X-Wing: Solo Command 8.00
BKN0122 X-Wing: Isard's Revenge 7.00
BKN0126 X-Wing: Starfighters of Adumar 7.00

Cimino
BKN0114 The SW Diaries, 84-page paperback with CD-ROM 25.00

Del Rey
BKN0128 Agents of Chaos 1 : Hero's Trial 8.00
BKN0129 Agents of Chaos 2 : Jedi Eclipse 8.00
BKN0133 Cloak of Deception, hardcover 26.00
BKN0130 Darth Maul: Shadow Hunter, hardcover 26.00
BKN0131 Edge of Victory I: Conquest 8.00
BKN0132 Edge of Victory II: Rebirth 8.00

BKN0123 Star Wars: Episode I TPM, paperback 6.00
BKN0117 Vector Prime, hardcover 22.00
BKN0116 Vector Prime, paperback 8.00

G.K. Hall and Co.
BKN0115 Specter of the Past, large print 26.00

Random House
BKN0119 Dark Tide I: Onslaught 8.00
BKN0120 Dark Tide II: Ruin 8.00
BKN0118 Rogue Planet, hardcover 26.00
BKN0089 Star Wars Trilogy, paperback compilation 8.00

Scholastic
BKN0125 The Phantom Menace Collector's Edition, foil slipcase 12.00
BKN0058 Star Wars Chronology, hardcover 30.00
BKN0059 Star Wars Chronology, trade paperback 16.00
BKN0087 Star Wars Trilogy Omnibus Edition 10.00
BKN0086 Star Wars Trilogy Omnibus Edition, 10th anniversary edition......15.00

BOOKS: POP-UP/ACTION/FLAP

Collins
BKO0022 Star Wars Pop-Up 18.00

Dark Horse Comics
BKO0003 Battle of the Bounty Hunters Pop-Up 26.00

Fun Works
BKO0007 Heroes in Hiding 6.00
BKO0012 Return of the Jedi, flip 4.00
BKO0001 Star Wars, flip 4.00
BKO0002 Star Wars, shimmer 8.00
BKO0018 The Empire Strikes Back, flip 4.00

Little, Brown
BKO0004 Death Star Pop-Up 15.00
BKO0008 Jabba's Palace Pop-Up 20.00

BKO0009 Millennium Falcon Pop-Up 18.00
BKO0010 Mos Eisley Cantina Pop-Up 20.00
BKO0014 Rebel Alliance Ships of the Fleet 12.00
BKO0021 The Galactic Empire, Ships of the Fleet 12.00

Random House
BKO0026 Anakin Skywalker 8.00
BKO0025 EP1 Great Big Flap Book 14.00
BKO0005 Han Solo's Rescue, hardcover 8.00
BKO0006 Han Solo's Rescue, softcover 14.00
BKO0027 Jar Jar Binks 8.00
BKO0011 Return of the Jedi Pop-Up 18.00
BKO0013 Star Wars Lift the Flap 12.00
BKO0015 Star Wars Pop-Up 16.00
BKO0016 The Empire Strikes Back Panorama 23.00
BKO0017 The Empire Strikes Back Pop-Up 16.00
BKO0019 The Ewoks Save The Day, hardcover 8.00
BKO0020 The Ewoks Save The Day, softcover 12.00

BOOKS: POSTER
Scholastic

BKP0001   BKP0003   BKP0004

BKP0001 Star Wars pull-out posters 6.00
BKP0004 Empire Strikes Back pull-out posters 6.00
BKP0003 Return of the Jedi pull-out posters 6.00

BKO0003   BKO0012   BKO0002   BKO0004   BKO0008   BKO0009

BKO0010   BKO0014   BKO0021   BKO0011   BKO0015   BKO0025

BKO0017   BKO0016   BKO0019   BKO0013   BKO0026   BKO0027

BOOKS: SCIENCE ADVENTURES

Scholastic
BSA0001 Emergency in Escape Pod Four 5.00
BSA0003 Emergency in Escape Pod Four (pages 45-46 missing, pages 55-56
   appear twice) 7.00
BSA0002 Journey Across Planet-X 5.00

BOOKS: STAR WARS ADVENTURES, TPM

Scholastic
BKI0001 #01 Search for the Lost Jedi 4.00
BKI0002 #01 Search for the Lost Jedi Game Book 3.00
BKI0003 #02 The Bartokk Assassins 4.00
BKI0004 #02 The Bartokk Assassins Game Book 3.00
BKI0005 #03 The Fury of Darth Maul 4.00
BKI0006 #03 The Fury of Darth Maul Game Book 3.00
BKI0007 #04 Jedi Emergency 4.00
BKI0008 #04 Jedi Emergency Game Book 3.00
BKI0009 #05 The Ghostling Children 4.00
BKI0010 #05 The Ghostling Children Game Book 3.00
BKI0011 #06 The Hunt for Anakin Skywalker 4.00
BKI0012 #06 The Hunt for Anakin Skywalker Game Book 3.00
BKI0013 #07 Capture Arawynne 4.00
BKI0014 #07 Capture Arawynne Game Book 3.00
BKI0015 #08 Deep Trouble 4.00
BKI0016 #08 Deep Trouble Game Book 3.00
BKI0017 #09 Rescue in the Core 4.00
BKI0018 #09 Rescue in the Core Game Book 3.00
BKI0019 #10 The Festival of Warriors 4.00
BKI0020 #10 The Festival of Warriors Game Book 3.00
BKI0021 #11 Pirates From Beyond the Sea 4.00
BKI0022 #11 Pirates From Beyond the Sea Game Book 3.00
BKI0023 #12 The Bongo Rally 4.00
BKI0024 #12 The Bongo Rally Game Book 3.00

BOOKS: STORY

Ballantine
BKS0054 Star Wars Album...32.00
BKS0016 Star Wars Storybook, hardcover 12.00

BSA0001   BSA0002   BKI0001   BKI0002

BKI0003   BKI0005   BKI0007   BKI0009

Chronicle Books
BKS0029 Empire Strikes Back, mini hardcover..8.00
BKS0010 Return of the Jedi, mini hardcover..8.00
BKS0001 Star Wars, mini hardcover..8.00

BKS0001   BKS0029   BKS0010

BKS0086   BKS0072   BKS0073   BKS0074   BKS0009   BKS0068

BKS0075   BKS0060   BKS0057   BKS0061   BKS0056   BKS0066

BKS0064   BKS0063   BKS0067   BKS0065   BKS0047   BKS0028

BKS0082

BKS0003

BKS0004

BKS0077

BKS0078

BKS0007

BKS0042

BKS0014

BKS0015

BKS0011

BKS0026

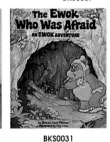
BKS0027

BKS0031

BKS0032

BKS0034

BKS0035

BKS0036

BKS0037

BKS0038

BKS0039

BKS0055

BKS0043

BKS0045

BKS0046

BKS0070

BKS0071

BKS0069

BKS0079

BKS0080

BKS0081

BKS0017 hardcover

BKS0017 softcover

BKS0030 hardcover

BKS0030 softcover

BKS0012 hardcover

BKS0086 The Phantom Menace, mini hardcover 8.00
BKS0087 The Queen's Amulet 14.00

Collins
BKS0048 Star Wars Storybook, with dust jacket 27.00

Fun Works
BKS0072 Darth Vader's Mission: The Search for the Secret Plans, toy bound
  into spine 8.00
BKS0073 Han Solo's Rescue Mission, toy bound into spine 8.00
BKS0074 Luke Skywalker's Race Against Time, toy bound into spine 8.00
BKS0009 R2-D2's Mission: A Little Heroes Journey, toy bound into spine 8.00

Futura
BKS0049 Return of the Jedi, "Special Junior Edition" 14.00

Golden Books
BKS0068 A Droid's Tale soundstory...24.00

BKS0012 softcover

BKS0084

BKS0083

BKS0060 A New Hope...5.00
BKS0057 A New Hope (with tattoos)..5.00
BKS0056 Adventure in Beggar's Canyon...5.00
BKS0061 Empire Strikes Back..5.00
BKS0058 Empire Strikes Back (with tattoos)...5.00
BKS0066 Escape from Jabba's Palace 5.00

Books: Story

BKS0064 Journey to Mos Eisley 5.00
BKS0063 Pilots and Spacecraft (glow in dark pages) 5.00
BKS0062 Return of the Jedi 5.00
BKS0059 Return of the Jedi (with tattoos) 5.00
BKS0067 SW: The Greatest Battles, includes 3D glasses 6.00
BKS0065 The Hoth Adventure 5.00

Keibunsha
BKS0053 Return of the Jedi picture book w/dust jacket 24.00

Marvel Comics
BKS0075 World of Fire, Star Wars 2 ....12.00

Publications International
Play-a-sound book with effects.
BKS0088 Episode I 14.00
BKS0089 Episode I, R2-D2 ....8.00
BKS0047 Star Wars 11.00

Random House
BKS0013 Droid Dilemma 12.00
BKS0051 Droids 10.00
BKS0028 Empire Strikes Back Storybook, hardcover 12.00
BKS0085 Empire Strikes Back, classic 7.00
BKS0076 EP1 TPM Movie Storybook 8.00
BKS0003 Escape from the Monster Ship 16.00
BKS0004 Fuzzy as an Ewok 10.00
BKS0005 How the Ewoks Saved the Trees, hardcover 15.00
BKS0006 How the Ewoks Saved the Trees, softcover 8.00
BKS0077 I am a Droid, includes foil stickers 5.00
BKS0078 I am a Jedi, includes foil stickers 5.00
BKS0093 I am a Pilot, includes foil stickers 5.00
BKS0092 I am a Queen, includes foil stickers 5.00
BKS0007 Luke's Fate 5.00
BKS0008 Luke's Fate, "Brand New" on cover 6.00
BKS0091 Luke's Fate, brown cover 6.00
BKS0011 Return of the Jedi Storybook, hardcover 12.00
BKS0052 School Days, Ewoks 12.00
BKS0014 Shiny as a Droid 10.00
BKS0015 Star Wars Storybook Trilogy 10 year anniversary 12.00
BKS0050 Star Wars Storybook, hardcover 12.00
BKS0019 Step-Up Movie Adventure, Return of the Jedi 12.00
BKS0020 Step-Up Movie Adventure, Return of the Jedi, 1995 ...5.00
BKS0021 Step-Up Movie Adventure, Star Wars 10.00
BKS0022 Step-Up Movie Adventure, Star Wars, 1995 ....5.00
BKS0023 Step-Up Movie Adventure, Empire Strikes Back 12.00
BKS0024 Step-Up Movie Adventure, Empire Strikes Back, 1995 ...5.00
BKS0025 The Adventures of R2-D2 and C-3PO 12.00
BKS0026 The Adventures of Teebo 25.00
BKS0027 The Baby Ewoks' Picnic Surprise 4.00
BKS0031 The Ewok Who Was Afraid 12.00
BKS0032 The Ewoks and the Lost Children 12.00
BKS0033 The Ewoks' Hang-Gliding Adventure 4.00
BKS0034 The Ewoks Join the Fight 5.00
BKS0035 The Lost Prince 20.00
BKS0036 The Maverick Moon 4.00
BKS0037 The Mystery of the Rebellious Robot 4.00
BKS0038 The Pirates of Tarnoonga 20.00
BKS0039 The Red Ghost 6.00
BKS0040 The Ring, The Witch, and the Crystal 6.00
BKS0041 The Shadow Stone 8.00
BKS0055 The White Witch - A Droid Adventure 14.00
BKS0042 The Wookie Storybook 12.00
BKS0043 Three Cheers for Kneesaa 4.00
BKS0044 Wicket and the Dandelion Warriors 8.00
BKS0045 Wicket Finds a Way 4.00
BKS0046 Wicket Goes Fishing 8.00

Scholastic
BKS0030 Empire Strikes Back, softcover 8.00
BKS0082 Episode I: The Phantom Menace 7.00
BKS0079 Journal: Anakin Skywalker 5.00
BKS0069 Journal: Captive to Evil by Princess Leia 5.00
BKS0080 Journal: Darth Maul 6.00
BKS0070 Journal: Hero for Hire by Han Solo 5.00
BKS0081 Journal: Queen Amidala 6.00
BKS0071 Journal: Fight for Justice by Luke Skywalker 5.00
BKS0012 Return of the Jedi Storybook, softcover 8.00
BKS0084 Star Wars Junior: Obi-Wan's Bongo Adventure 2.00
BKS0083 Star Wars Junior: Podrace! 2.00
BKS0017 Star Wars Storybook, softcover 8.00

BKS0018 Star Wars Treasury, all 3 softcover in a slipcase 28.00
BKS0002 Beyond the Stars, Tales of Adventure in Time and Space 7.00
BKS0090 Ewoks Annual 16.00

BOOKS: TECHNICAL

BKT0003   BKT0006   BKT0007   BKT0008

Starlog
BKT0001 Star Wars Technical Journal, hardcover 35.00
BKT0004 Starlog Technical Journal Vol. 1: Tatooine 10.00
BKT0002 Starlog Technical Journal Vol. 1: Tatooine, foil cover 15.00
BKT0003 Starlog Technical Journal Vol. 1: Tatooine, special edition insert .12.00
BKT0006 Starlog Technical Journal Vol. 2: Imperial Forces 10.00
BKT0005 Starlog Technical Journal Vol. 2: Imperial Forces, special edition insert 12.00
BKT0008 Starlog Technical Journal Vol. 3: Rebel Forces 10.00
BKT0007 Starlog Technical Journal Vol. 3: Rebel Forces, special edition insert 12.00

BOOKS: TRIVIA

Ballantine
BKU0005 425 Questions and Answers about Star Wars and The Empire Strikes Back 18.00
BKU0001 Diplomatic Corps Extrance Exam 12.00

   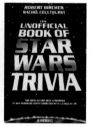

BKU0001   BKU0003   BKU0009   BKU0007

BKU0003 I'd Just as soon Kiss a Wookiee: The Quotable Star Wars 4.00
BKU0002 I'd Just as soon Kiss a Wookiee: The Quotable Star Wars, condensed 2.00
BKU0004 The Jedi Master's Quizbook (black cover) 6.00
BKU0009 The Jedi Master's Quizbook (blue cover) 8.00

Carol Publishing
BKU0008 The Jedi Academy Entrance Exam: Tantalizing Trivia from the Star Wars Trilogy 12.00

Kensington
BKU0006 Ultimate Unauthorized Star Wars Trilogy Challenge 12.00

Summersdale Publishing
BKU0007 The Unofficial Book of Star Wars Trivia 17.00
BKU0010 From The Blob to Star Wars - The Science Fiction Movie Quiz Book 4.00

BOOKS: YOUNG JEDI KNIGHTS

Berkley
BKQ0001 01 Heirs to the Force 7.00
BKQ0002 02 Shadow Acadamy 7.00
BKQ0003 03 The Lost Ones 7.00
BKQ0004 04 Lightsabers 7.00
BKQ0005 05 Darkest Knight 7.00
BKQ0006 06 Jedi Under Seige 7.00

BOOKS: YOUNG READER

Bantam Books

Barnes and Noble

Bullseye Books

BKQ0001   BKQ0002   BKQ0003   BKQ0004   BKQ0005   BKQ0006   BKQ0007   BKQ0008

BKQ0009   BKQ0010   BKQ0011   BKQ0012   BKQ0013   BKQ0014   BKY0002   BKY0004

BKY0006   BKY0008   BKY0010   BKY0012   BKY0018   BKY0022   BKY0023   BKY0024

BKY0034   BKY0037   BKY0033   BKY0031   BKY0038   BKY0036   BKY0035

Books: Young Reader

Del Rey
BKY0054 Marvel Comics Illustrated Version of Star Wars.............................6.00

Random House
BKY0032 Anakin to the Rescue 5.00
BKY0034 Anakin's Fate 5.00
BKY0037 Anakin's Pit Droid 4.00
BKY0036 Anakin's Race for Freedom 4.00
BKY0033 Dangers of the Core 5.00
BKY0055 Darth Maul's Revenge 5.00
BKY0031 Jar Jar's Mistake 5.00
BKY0038 Queen in Disguise...5.00
BKY0035 Watch Out Jar Jar!..4.00

Scholastic

| BKY0019 | BKY0021 | BKY0040 | BKY0042 |

Star Wars Missions game books.
BKY0019 01: Assault on Yavin Four 3.00
BKY0020 02: Escape from Thyferra 3.00
BKY0021 03: Attack on Delrakkin 3.00
BKY0039 04: Destroy the Liquidator 4.00
BKY0040 05: The Hunt for Han Solo...4.00
BKY0041 06: The Search for Grubba the Hutt 4.00
BKY0042 07: Ithorian Invasion 4.00
BKY0043 08: Togorian Trap 4.00
BKY0044 09: Revolt of the Battle Droids...4.00
BKY0045 10: Showdown in Mos Eisley 4.00
BKY0046 11: Bounty Hunters vs. Battle Droids................................4.00
BKY0047 12: The Vactooine Disaster 4.00
BKY0048 13: Prisoner of the Nikto Pirates 4.00
BKY0049 14: The Monsters of Dweem 4.00

BKY0050 15: Voyage to the Underworld 4.00
BKY0051 16: Imperial Jailbreak 4.00
BKY0052 17: Darth Vader's Return 4.00
BKY0053 18: Rogue Squadron to the Rescue 4.00

Sphere
Young reader editions.
BKY0017 Empire Strikes Back...17.00
BKY0016 Star Wars..23.00

BOOTS

SHB0003 Darth Maul, attacking 8.00
SHB0006 Darth Maul, face 8.00
SHB0005 Darth Vader 8.00
SHB0001 Darth Vader, vinyl 45.00
SHB0002 Ewoks, vinyl...45.00
SHB0004 Podracing 8.00

BOP BAGS

| YB0002 | YB0004 | YB0003 | YB0005 |

Intex Recreation Corp.
YB0005 Darth Maul bop bag...12.00

Kenner
Bop bags
YB0001 Chewbacca 58.00
YB0002 Darth Vader 58.00
YB0003 Jawa 85.00
YB0004 R2-D2...65.00

BCJ0001 BCJ0002 BCJ0003 BCJ0005 BCJ0006 BCJ0007 BCJ0009 BCJ0010 BCJ0012 BCJ0013 BCJ0015 BCJ0016 BCJ0017

BCJ0018 BCJ0019 BCJ0020 BCJ0021 BCJ0023 BCJ0024 BCJ0025 BCJ0027 BCJ0028 BCJ0030 BCJ0031 BCJ0032 BCJ0033

BCJ0034 BCJ0035 BCJ0036 BCJ0037 BCJ0039 BCJ0040 BCJ0042 BCJ0043 BCJ0045 BCJ0046 BCJ0047 BCJ0050 BCJ0051

BCJ0004 BCJ0008 BCJ0011 BCJ0014 BCJ0022 BCJ0026 BCJ0029 BCJ0038 BCJ0041 BCJ0044 BCJ0049 BCJ0052

BOTTLE CAP ACCESSORIES

PRB0001

Pepsi Cola
PRB0001 Stage to hold EPI bottle caps mail-in premium, Japan exclusive.135.00

BOTTLE CAPS

Coca-Cola
BTL0001 Coca-Cola bottle caps featuring Star Wars characters 3.00

BOTTLE CAPS, JAPAN

Pepsi Cola
BCJ0053 Concealment bag for bottle cap figure 4.00
BCJ0001 Anakin Skywalker 3.00
BCJ0002 Anakin Skywalker podracer gear 3.00
BCJ0003 Anakin Skywalker podracer gear, head..4.00
BCJ0004 Anakin Skywalker podracer gear, head with moveable arms .15.00
BCJ0005 Battle Droid..3.00
BCJ0006 Boss Nass 3.00
BCJ0007 Boss Nass, head..4.00
BCJ0008 Boss Nass, head with moveable arms 15.00
BCJ0009 C-3PO..3.00
BCJ0010 Captain Tarpals, head 4.00
BCJ0011 Captain Tarpals, head with moveable arms..15.00
BCJ0012 Chancellor Velorum 3.00
BCJ0013 Darth Maul, head 4.00
BCJ0014 Darth Maul, head with moveable arms..15.00
BCJ0015 Darth Maul, Jedi duel..3.00
BCJ0016 Darth Maul, Tatooine..3.00

BCJ0017 Darth Sidious..3.00
BCJ0018 Darth Vader..4.00
BCJ0019 Darth Vader, head..4.00
BCJ0020 Jar Jar Binks 3.00
BCJ0021 Jar Jar Binks, head 5.00
BCJ0022 Jar Jar Binks, head with moveable arms 15.00
BCJ0023 Ki Adi Mundy 3.00
BCJ0024 Mace Windu..3.00
BCJ0025 Mace Windu, head..4.00
BCJ0026 Mace Windu, head with moveable arms 15.00
BCJ0027 Nute Gunray 3.00
BCJ0028 Nute Gunray, head..5.00
BCJ0029 Nute Gunray, head with moveable arms 15.00
BCJ0030 Obi-Wan Kenobi Jedi duel 3.00
BCJ0031 Obi-Wan Kenobi Tatooine 3.00
BCJ0032 Padme 3.00
BCJ0033 Princess Leia as Jabba's Prisoner 2.00
BCJ0034 Queen Amidala battle dress 3.00
BCJ0035 Queen Amidala Coruscant 3.00
BCJ0036 Queen Amidala Naboo 3.00
BCJ0037 Queen Amidala, head..4.00
BCJ0038 Queen Amidala, head with moveable arms 15.00
BCJ0039 Qui-Gon Jinn 3.00
BCJ0040 R2-D2 ....12.00
BCJ0041 R2-D2 with moveable arms..24.00
BCJ0042 Sebulba 3.00
BCJ0043 Sebulba, head 5.00
BCJ0044 Sebulba, head with moveable arms 15.00
BCJ0045 Senator Palpatine 3.00
BCJ0046 Tusken Raider 2.00
BCJ0047 Watto 3.00
BCJ0048 Watto, head 4.00
BCJ0049 Watto, head with moveable arms 15.00
BCJ0050 Yoda..3.00
BCJ0051 Yoda, head 12.00
BCJ0052 Yoda, head with moveable arms................................15.00

BOTTLE CAPS, MEXICO

Pepsi Cola
BTC0001 Clario 01 Jar Jar Sonriendo 1.00
BTC0002 Clario 02 R2-D2 ....1.00
BTC0003 Clario 03 Jar Jar Sacando La Lengua 1.00
BTC0004 Clario 04 Boss Nass En Su Trono 1.00
BTC0005 Clario 05 C-3PO..1.00

BTL0001 with sample inserts   BTC0001   BTC0002   BTC0003   BTC0004   BTC0005   BTC0006   BTC0007

BTC0008   BTC0009   BTC0010   BTC0011   BTC0012   BTC0013   BTC0014   BTC0015   BTC0016   BTC0017

BTC0018   BTC0019   BTC0020   BTC0021   BTC0022   BTC0023   BTC0024   BTC0025   BTC0026   BTC0027

BTC0028   BTC0029   BTC0030   BTC0031   BTC0032   BTC0033   BTC0034   BTC0035   BTC0036   BTC0037

Bottle Caps, Mexico

BTC0006 Clario 06 Anakin Skywalker 1.00
BTC0007 Clario 07 Qui-Gon 1.00
BTC0008 Clario 08 R2-D2 ....1.00
BTC0009 Clario 09 Jar Jar 1.00
BTC0010 Clario 10 Mace Windu 1.00
BTC0011 Clario 11 Boss Nass 1.00
BTC0012 Clario 12 Reina Amidala 1.00
BTC0013 Clario 13 Obi-Wan 1.00
BTC0014 Clario 14 Captain Panaka 1.00
BTC0015 Clario 15 Anakin Skywalker 1.00
BTC0016 Clario 16 Padme (handmaiden) 1.00
BTC0017 Clario 17 Reina Amidala 1.00
BTC0018 Clario 18 Padme (Tatooine) 1.00
BTC0019 Clario 19 Qui-Gon En Batalla 1.00
BTC0020 Clario 20 Shmi Y Qui-Gon 1.00
BTC0021 Clario 21 C-3PO Y R2-D2 ....1.00
BTC0022 Clario 22 Qui-Gon Y Jar Jar 1.00
BTC0023 Clario Yoda 1 (facing right) 3.00
BTC0024 Clario Yoda 2 (facing left) 3.00
BTC0025 Lado 01 Androide De Batalla 1.00
BTC0026 Lado 02 Watto 1.00
BTC0027 Lado 03 Darth Sidious Y Darth Maul 1.00
BTC0028 Lado 04 Watto 1.00
BTC0029 Lado 05 Darth Sidious 1.00
BTC0030 Lado 06 Sebulba 1.00
BTC0031 Lado 07 Nute Gunray Y Rune Haako 1.00
BTC0032 Lado 08 Qui-Gon Y Darth Maul 1.00
BTC0033 Lado 09 Senador Palpatine 1.00
BTC0034 Lado 10 Darth Maul Y Obi-Wan 1.00
BTC0035 Lado Darth Maul 1 (face only, Tatooine) 3.00
BTC0036 Lado Darth Maul 3 (face only, Jedi duel) 3.00
BTC0037 Lado Darth Maul 3 (lightsaber drawn) 3.00

Lenticular motion caps.
BTC0038 01 Jar Jar Sonriendo 1.00
BTC0039 02 R2-D2 ....1.00
BTC0040 03 Jar Jar Sacando La Lengua 1.00
BTC0041 04 Boss Nass En Su Trono 1.00
BTC0042 05 C-3PO 1.00
BTC0043 06 Anakin Skywalker 1.00
BTC0044 07 Qui-Gon 1.00
BTC0045 08 R2-D2 ....1.00
BTC0046 09 Jar Jar 1.00
BTC0047 10 Mace Windu 1.00
BTC0048 11 Boss Nass 1.00
BTC0049 12 Reina Amidala 1.00
BTC0050 13 Obi-Wan 1.00
BTC0051 14 Captain Panaka 1.00

BTC0052 15 Anakin Skywalker 1.00
BTC0053 16 Padme (handmaiden) 1.00
BTC0054 17 Reina Amidala 1.00
BTC0055 18 Padme (Tatooine) 1.00
BTC0056 19 Qui-Gon En Batalla 1.00
BTC0057 20 Shmi Y Qui-Gon 1.00
BTC0058 21 C-3PO Y R2-D2 ....1.00
BTC0059 22 Qui-Gon Y Jar Jar 1.00
BTC0060 23 Yoda 1 (facing right) 1.00
BTC0061 24 Yoda 2 (facing left) 1.00
BTC0062 25 Androide De Batalla 1.00
BTC0063 26 Watto 1.00
BTC0064 27 Darth Sidious Y Darth Maul 1.00
BTC0065 28 Watto 1.00
BTC0066 29 Darth Sidious 1.00
BTC0067 30 Sebulba 1.00
BTC0068 31 Nute Gunray Y Rune Haako 1.00
BTC0069 32 Qui-Gon Y Darth Maul 1.00
BTC0070 33 Senador Palpatine 1.00
BTC0071 34 Darth Maul Y Obi-Wan 1.00
BTC0072 35 Darth Maul 1 (face only, Tatooine) 1.00
BTC0073 36 Darth Maul 3 (face only, Jedi duel) 1.00
BTC0074 37 Darth Maul 3 (lightsaber drawn) 1.00

BOTTLE TOPPERS

BTT0001

Pepsi Cola
BTT0001 C-3PO, Musical with movement, Japan exclusive 25.00

BTC0038 BTC0039 BTC0040 BTC0041 BTC0042 BTC0043 BTC0044 BTC0045 BTC0046 BTC0047

BTC0048 BTC0049 BTC0050 BTC0051 BTC0052 BTC0053 BTC0054 BTC0055 BTC0056 BTC0057

BTC0058 BTC0059 BTC0060 BTC0061 BTC0062 BTC0063 BTC0064 BTC0065 BTC0066 BTC0067

BTC0068 BTC0069 BTC0070 BTC0071 BTC0072 BTC0073 BTC0074

BOWLS

Deka
DIB0004 Empire Strikes Back 14 oz. 12.00
DIB0005 Empire Strikes Back 20 oz. 12.00
DIB0006 Return of the Jedi 14 oz. 12.00
DIB0007 Return of the Jedi 20 oz. 12.00
DIB0001 Star Wars 14 oz. 15.00
DIB0002 Star Wars 16 oz. 15.00
DIB0003 Star Wars 20 oz. 15.00

Zak Designs
DIB0008 Pod Racer, white with scene in bottom and black rim................4.00

BOXES PLASTIC

3D Arts
Hologram foil on lid, 2" square.
BOX0010 C-3PO and R2-D2 ....7.00
BOX0011 Darth Vader 7.00
BOX0012 Millennium Falcon 7.00
BOX0013 X-Wing Fighter 7.00

A.H. Prismatic
Hologram foil on lid, 2" square.
BOX0001 AT-AT 7.00
BOX0002 B-Wing 7.00
BOX0003 Darth Vader 7.00
BOX0004 Darth Vader's Tie Fighter 7.00
BOX0005 Imperial Cruiser 7.00
BOX0006 Millennium Falcon 7.00
BOX0007 Millennium Falcon w/SW logo 7.00
BOX0008 Tie Interceptor 7.00
BOX0009 X-Wing Fighter 7.00

BRACELETS

JBR0007

Disney / MGM
JBR0007 Star Tours admission band, opening day 6.00

Factors, Etc.
JBR0001 C-3PO, gold finished head 14.00
JBR0003 Darth Vader, black painted head 14.00
JBR0004 R2-D2, unfinished metal 14.00
JBR0005 Stormtrooper, white painted head 14.00
JBR0006 X-Wing, unfinished metal 14.00

BUBBLE BATH

TOB0010   TOB0013

Addis
TOB0008 Ben Kenobi 32.00
TOB0009 C-3PO..32.00

TOB0010 Chewbacca...32.00
TOB0011 Darth Vader..32.00
TOB0012 Gamorrean Guard 32.00
TOB0013 Han Solo..32.00
TOB0015 Princess Leia 32.00

Grosvenor

TOB0017   TOB0023

TOB0017 Galactic Bath Foam 16.00
TOB0023 Gungan Bongo 12.00

Minnetonka

TOB0018   TOB0019   TOB0020   TOB0021   TOB0022

TOB0022 Darth Vader with foil label...3.00
TOB0020 Gungan Sub with Tub Fizzers 6.00
TOB0019 Jar Jar Binks bottle with sculpted character cap 5.00
TOB0021 Jar Jar Binks with foil label...3.00
TOB0018 Yoda bottle with sculpted character cap 5.00

Omni Cosmetics

TOB0006   TOB0007   TOB0016

TOB0003   TOB0014   TOB0005   TOB0002

TOB0001 Battle Scene "refuling station" 8.00
TOB0002 Chewbacca figural bottle...12.00
TOB0003 Darth Vader figural bottle...12.00
TOB0004 Jabba the Hutt figural bottle 12.00
TOB0014 Luke Skywalker 18.00
TOB0005 Princess Leia figural bottle 12.00
TOB0016 R2-D2 ....18.00
TOB0006 Wicket the Ewok figural bottle 12.00

Bubble Bath

| BBB0001 | BBB0003 | BBB0005 | BBB0007 | BBB0008 | BBB0010 | BBB0012 | BBB0013 |

| BBB0015 | BBB0016 | BBB0017 | BB30001 | BB30002 | BB30003 | BB30004 | BB30005 | BB30006 |

TOB0007 Yoda figural bottle..12.00

BUDDIES

Kenner
BBB0001 C-3PO 8.00
BBB0002 Chewbacca, black bandolier.............................8.00
BBB0003 Chewbacca, brown bandolier 22.00
BBB0005 Figrin D'An 10.00
BBB0007 Jabba the Hutt 8.00
BBB0008 Jawa..9.00
BBB0010 Max Rebo 8.00
BBB0012 R2-D2..10.00
BBB0013 Salacious Crumb 10.00
BBB0015 Wampa..10.00
BBB0016 Wicket the Ewok 9.00
BBB0017 Yoda 15.00

BUDDIES: TPM

Hasbro
BB30001 Darth Maul 21.00
BB30005 JarJar Binks 15.00
BB30003 Obi-Wan Kenobi 15.00
BB30002 Padme Naberrie 15.00
BB30004 Qui-Gon Jinn 15.00
BB30006 Watto 21.00

BUMPER STICKERS

Creation Entertainment
BS0001 10th Anniversary bumper sticker.........................8.00

Fantasma
BS0002 Star Wars logo on Holographic foil 5.00

BUTTONS

20th Century Fox
BT0095 Darth Maul, "Ask me how to reserve." 10.00
BT0093 EPI: "The One To Own On Video" promotional...............5.00

A.H. Prismatic
BT0073 AT-AT hologram..4.00
BT0074 B-Wing hologram 4.00
BT0075 C-3PO and R2-D2 hologram, 2nd series..............4.00
BT0076 Darth Vader hologram..4.00
BT0077 Darth Vader hologram, 2nd series.......................4.00
BT0078 Darth Vader's Tie Fighter hologram 5.00
BT0079 Imperial Cruiser hologram....................................4.00
BT0080 Millennium Falcon hologram 4.00
BT0081 Millennium Falcon hologram, 2nd series..............4.00
BT0082 Millennium Falcon w/SW logo, hologram 4.00
BT0083 Tie Interceptor hologram......................................4.00
BT0084 X-Wing Fighter hologram 4.00

Adam Joseph Industries
BT0045 Baby Ewok 8.00
BT0012 Baby Ewoks..3.00

BT0046 Chewbacca...5.00
BT0047 Darth Vader...5.00
BT0048 Emperor's Royal Guard 5.00
BT0014 Ewok Daydreaming 3.00
BT0015 Ewok Flying Glider 3.00
BT0016 Ewok Lessons 3.00
BT0017 Ewok Village in Snow 3.00
BT0013 Ewok with Basket on Head 3.00
BT0049 Gamorrean Guard 5.00
BT0050 Heroes on Endor..5.00
BT0051 Jabba the Hutt 5.00
BT0018 Kneesaa and Wicket Feed Baga.........................3.00
BT0052 Max Rebo 5.00
BT0019 Princess Kneesaa 3.00
BT0053 R2-D2 and C-3PO 5.00
BT0055 Revenge art..6.00
BT0056 Revenge Logo 12.00
BT0054 ROTJ Logo 5.00
BT0020 Wicket and R2-D2 ....3.00
BT0021 Wicket on a Vine 3.00
BT0022 Wicket Tells a Story 3.00
BT0023 Wicket the Ewok..3.00
BT0057 Yoda 6.00

| BT0015 | BT0020 | BT0022 | BT0023 |

| BT0046 | BT0048 | BT0049 | BT0050 |

| BT0051 | BT0052 | BT0054 | BT0057 |

Burger King
BT0039 "Ask Me For Your ROTJ Glasses" 12.00

Coca-Cola
BT0092 Things Go Better. 18.00

BT0097 Y A Rien Comme Un Coke...24.00

Disney / MGM
BT0087 Star Tours and Disney-MGM logos.........................4.00
BT0089 Star Tours and Disney-MGM logos with C-3PO and R2-D2............6.00
BT0090 Star Tours Flight Test Team.................................17.00
BT0088 Star Tours logo with C-3PO and R2-D2.................5.00
BT0086 Star Tours logo, 3" glow-in-dark..........................6.00
BT0094 Star Wars Weekends - May 2000 ....8.00

DK Publishing
BT0099 Ask me about the Star Wars EPI books. 5.00

Factors, Etc.
BT0067 "May The Force Be With You" 6.00
BT0072 "May The Force Be With You" 5.00

BT0068 "May The Force Be With You" w/Kenner logo...............................20.00
BT0058 Ben (Obi-Wan) Kenobi 6.00
BT0006 Boba Fett 8.00
BT0059 C-3PO 6.00
BT0007 C-3PO and R2-D2 ....7.00
BT0008 Chewbacca 7.00
BT0061 Darh Vader (photo)...6.00
BT0062 Darth Vadar Lives (misspelled)..............................10.00
BT0009 Darth Vader 7.00
BT0063 Darth Vader mirrored keychain..............................8.00
BT0064 Darth Vader mirrored necklace..............................8.00
BT0065 Han Solo and Chewbacca 6.00
BT0010 Luke Skywalker 7.00
BT0069 Princess Leia..6.00
BT0070 R2-D2 ....6.00
BT0071 R2-D2 and C-3PO w/logo 10.00

BT0095   BT0093   BT0056   BT0097   BT0092   BT0090   BT0088

BT0067   BT0058   BT0059   BT0008   BT0061   BT0062   BT0065   BT0010   BT0069   BT0070   BT0071

BT0026   BT0028   BT0029   BT0030   BT0032   BT0033   BT0034

BT0031   BT0024   BT0035   BT0036   BT0037   BT0027   BT0038

BT0094   BT0099   BT0072   BT0001   BT0040   BT0100

BT0003   BT0041   BT0098   BT0096   BT0091   BT0044

Buttons

BT0011 Yoda...8.00

Fan Club
BT0025 Bantha, "Rebel Recruiter".....................10.00
BT0026 Ben Kenobi...8.00
BT0028 Chewbacca...8.00
BT0029 Darth Vader..8.00
BT0030 George Lucas..8.00
BT0032 Han Solo...8.00
BT0033 Jawa...8.00
BT0034 Luke..8.00
BT0031 Moff Tarkin..8.00
BT0024 Official Member....................................10.00
BT0035 Princess Leia...8.00
BT0036 R2-D2...8.00
BT0037 Stormtrooper...8.00
BT0027 Threepio..8.00
BT0038 Tusken Raider..8.00

Kenner
BT0102 The Kenner Star Wars Convention, 2" round.....................34.00

Kenner (POTF)
BT0085 Biker Scout...15.00

Skywalkers
BT0103 Don't Give In To The Dark Side.............11.00

BT0001 C-3PO and R2-D2, Tenth Anniversary.............6.00
BT0101 Continue the Adventure on Video...........6.00
BT0002 Darth Vader, Tenth Anniversary.............6.00
BT0040 Droids: On Video Now............................8.00
BT0003 First 10 Years, pewter.........................25.00
BT0100 Happy EMPIRE Day...............................12.00
BT0042 Ice Capades and Ewoks w/light-up eyes, 2¼".....8.00
BT0041 Ice Capades and Ewoks, 3½"................5.00
BT0004 Leia and Luke, Tenth Anniversary..........6.00
BT0043 Special Edition Trilogy...........................7.00
BT0098 Star Wars Books On Sale Now.................3.00
BT0096 Star Wars Sandpeople............................9.00
BT0091 Star Wars: First Ten Years.......................6.00
BT0005 Star Wars: The First Ten Years.................8.00
BT0044 Trilogy Video Re-Release Aug 29.............7.00

CAKE PANS

BP0001

BP0002

BP0005

BP0003

BP0004

Wilton
BP0001 Boba Fett..35.00
BP0002 C-3PO..20.00
BP0005 Darth Vader Decorating Kit.................25.00
BP0003 Darth Vader.....................................25.00
BP0006 R2-D2 Decorating Kit........................25.00
BP0004 R2-D2..20.00

CAKE TOPS

BR0002

BR0003

Decopac
BR0004 Jar Jar Binks..4.00
BR0005 Watto...9.00

Wilton
BR0001 C-3PO and R2-D2 Cake Put-Ons, Empire Strikes Back.....10.00
BR0002 C-3PO and R2-D2 Cake Tops, Star Wars.....10.00
BR0003 Darth Vader and Stormtrooper Cake Tops.....10.00

CALCULATORS

Tiger Electronics

CC0001 closed and open

CC0001 A-Wing solar calculator, 3 sound FX.....................18.00

CALENDARS

20th Century Fox
PPC0027 1999 Fox Movie Release desktop calendar.....16.00

Abrams
PPC0007 1991 Lucasfilm...................................8.00

Andrews and McNeel
PPC0011 1995 Trilogy 3D................................11.00

Antioch
PPC0009 1995 Trilogy....................................10.00

Ballantine
PPC0001 1978 Star Wars.................................16.00
PPC0002 1979 Star Wars.................................15.00
PPC0003 1980 Star Wars.................................18.00
PPC0004 1981 Empire Strikes Back...................12.00
PPC0020 1984 Return of the Jedi......................16.00

Bay Street Publishing
PPC0032 1999 Darth Vader Reveals Anakin Skywalker.....11.00

Cedco
PPC0006 1990 Trilogy....................................14.00
PPC0008 1991 Trilogy....................................16.00
PPC0013 1996 Wide Image..............................14.00
PPC0033 1997 Art of Star Wars........................11.00
PPC0034 1997 Star Wars 20th Anniversary.........14.00
PPC0017 1998 Art of Star Wars: Classic Characters.....16.00
PPC0018 1998 Trilogy Special Edition, Han and Jabba on cover.....8.00
PPC0021 1999 Darth Vader Reveals Anakin Skywalker.....14.00
PPC0022 1999 Empire Strikes Back...................14.00
PPC0035 1999 May The Force Be With You..........8.00

PPC0023 1999 Star Wars...14.00
PPC0024 1999 Star Wars Trilogy 11.00
PPC0025 1999 Weapons and Technology 15.00
PPC0026 1999 Wisdom of Star Wars 12.00
PPC0055 2001 Star Wars flip animation trivia box calendar, Tie Fighters ...8.00
PPC0063 2001 Star Wars flip animation trivia box calendar, X-Wings 8.00

Chronicle Books
PPC0014 1997 Vehicles with blueprints 16.00

Day Runner
11"x17" laminated wipe-off 1-month blank wall calendar.
PPC0044 Darth Maul 7.00
PPC0049 Jar Jar Binks, horizontal 7.00
PPC0050 Jar Jar Binks, vertical 7.00
PPC0045 Jedi..7.00
PPC0041 Naboo fighters 7.00
PPC0043 Obi-Wan Kenobi 7.00
PPC0046 Queen Amidala 7.00
PPC0042 Qui-Gon Jinn 7.00
PPC0047 Watto, horizontal 7.00
PPC0048 Watto, vertical 7.00

24"x35" laminated, 2-sided sheet.
PPC0036 Jar Jar Binks 6.00
PPC0037 Naboo Fighter 6.00
PPC0038 Obi-Wan Kenobi 6.00
PPC0039 Podrace 6.00
PPC0040 Queen Amidala 6.00

Golden Turtle Press
PPC0016 1997 20th Anniversary Collector's Edition........8.00
PPC0028 1999 Darth Maul 18-month mini wall calendar.........5.00
PPC0031 1999 EP1 20-month hanging wall calendar 18.00
PPC0029 1999 Jar Jar Binks 18-month mini wall calendar 5.00
PPC0030 1999 Queen Amidala 18-month mini wall calendar........5.00
PPC0065 2000 366 day trivia box calendar w/flip animation, podracer
 cover 5.00
PPC0066 2000 52 week engagement calendar................12.00
PPC0068 2000 Han Solo cover 5.00
PPC0069 2000 Mos Eisley Cantina Regulars 14.00
PPC0067 2000 Yoda cover 5.00
PPC0058 2001 Bounty Hunters 7.00
PPC0057 2001 Heroes 7.00
PPC0056 2001 Jedi Forces 14.00
PPC0061 2001 Podrace 14.00
PPC0060 2001 Vehicles 7.00
PPC0059 2001 Villains 7.00

Hallmark
PPC0012 1996 Star Wars..8.00

Ink Group
PPC0064 1999 day-to-day calendar 7.00

PPC0051 1998 day-to-day calendar 8.00
PPC0062 2000 day-to-day calendar 8.00

Landmark
PPC0010 1995 Trilogy 6.00

Random House
PPC0005 1984 Return Of The Jedi w/Ewok Stickers 16.00

Shooting Star Press
PPC0015 1997 20th Anniversary 10.00

Slow Dazzle Worldwide
PPC0052 1999 Empire Strikes Back 5.00
PPC0053 1999 Return of the Jedi 5.00
PPC0054 1999 Star Wars 5.00

Thomas Foreman and Sons
PPC0019 1982 Star Wars / Empire Strikes Back 18.00

CALLING CARDS: TELEPHONE

Globalcall
TPC0054 $10 Star Wars: Episode I collage 7.00

GTI

TPC0001   TPC0058   TPC0059

TPC0058 $5 Luke Skywalker in Landspeeder 8.00
TPC0059 $5 Speeder Bike Trooper 8.00
TPC0001 $5 Yoda 8.00
TPC0002 $10 ANH Ben 15.00
TPC0003 $10 ANH ceremony.....................................15.00
TPC0004 $10 AT-AT 15.00
TPC0005 $10 A-Wing 15.00
TPC0006 $10 B-Wings 15.00
TPC0007 $10 Darth Vader at Cloud City....................15.00
TPC0008 $10 Emperor..15.00
TPC0009 $10 Han and Chewbacca..........................15.00
TPC0010 $10 Jabba and Bib Fortuna 15.00
TPC0011 $10 Luke and Yoda.....................................15.00
TPC0012 $10 Millennium Falcon 15.00
TPC0013 $10 Ties and X-Wing Fighters......................15.00
TPC0014 $20 ceremonial droids................................18.00

PPC0027   PPC0001   PPC00020   PPC0006   PPC0008

PPC0018   PPC0021   PPC0022   PPC0023   PPC0024   PPC0025

Calling Cards: Telephone

TPC0015 $20 ceremonial Leia 18.00
TPC0016 $20 Rebels on Hoth 18.00
TPC0017 $20 ROTJ ceremony 18.00
TPC0018 $20 ROTJ duel 18.00
TPC0019 $20 Tie bomber 18.00

Intelcom
50 Units - ANH, 3D.
TPC0021 Desert C-3PO and Luke 4.00
TPC0022 Jawas 4.00
TPC0023 Leia and Luke 4.00
TPC0024 Lightsaber duel 4.00
TPC0025 Vader choking rebel 4.00
TPC0026 X-wings 4.00

50 Units - ESB, 3D.
TPC0027 AT-AT 4.00
TPC0028 Chewie and Leia 4.00
TPC0029 Finale scene...4.00

50 Units - ROTJ, 3D.
TPC0030 AT-AT 4.00
TPC0031 Boushh and frozen Han 4.00
TPC0032 B-wings 4.00
TPC0033 Death Star & star destroyer...4.00

50 Units - TPM, 3D.
TPC0034 Naboo fighter 4.00

TPC0035 Royal Starship 4.00

100 Units - ANH, 3D.
TPC0036 Han promo shot 7.00
TPC0037 R2-D2 ....7.00
TPC0038 Stormtrooper promo shot..7.00

100 Units - ESB, 3D.
TPC0039 Fett 7.00
TPC0040 Yoda 7.00

100 Units - TPM, 3D.
TPC0041 Anakin 7.00
TPC0050 Battle Droid / Federation Tanks 7.00
TPC0051 Darth Maul / Tatooine Lightsaber Battle 7.00
TPC0042 Jar Jar 7.00
TPC0043 Obi-Wan Kenobi 7.00
TPC0052 Queen Amidala 7.00
TPC0044 Qui-Gon Jinn..7.00
TPC0053 Watto 7.00

200 Units, 3D.
TPC0045 ESB intl video artwork 8.00
TPC0046 TPM characters 8.00

Matav
TPC0073 Anakin Skywalker 11.00
TPC0074 Obi-Wan Kenobi 11.00

TPC0022

TPC0024

TPC0025

TPC0026

TPC0028

TPC0032

TPC0033

TPC0034

TPC0035

TPC0036

TPC0038

TPC0039

TPC0041

TPC0050

TPC0051

TPC0042

TPC0043

TPC0052

TPC0044

TPC0053

TPC0076 Queen Amidala 14.00
TPC0075 Qui-Gon Jinn...11.00

Mitsubushi

TPC0054   TPC0045   TPC0046   TPC0048

TPC0047   TPC0049   TPC0056   TPC0057   TPC0020

TPC0060 C-3PO and R2-D2 ....12.00

Singapore Telecom
TPC0048 Jar Jar Binks..6.00
TPC0047 Obi-Wan Kenobi 6.00
TPC0049 Watto..6.00

Swift Communications International
TPC0077 01 Millennium Falcon over Mos Eisley 14.00
TPC0078 02 Millennium Falcon over Bespin 14.00
TPC0079 03 Millennium Falcon over Death Star II 14.00
TPC0080 04 X-Wings in formation 14.00
TPC0081 05 Heroes on Hoth......................................14.00
TPC0082 06 Yoda in hut 14.00
TPC0083 07 Princess Leia, Yavin celebration...............14.00
TPC0084 08 Cloud City welcome 14.00
TPC0085 09 Emperor's throne room 14.00
TPC0086 10 Heroes in 3863827 ....14.00
TPC0087 11 Chewbacca saves R2 from power outlet.....14.00
TPC0088 12 Logray 14.00
TPC0089 13 Obi-Wan and Vader duel.........................14.00
TPC0090 14 X-Wing and medical frigate 14.00
TPC0091 15 Millennium Falcon docked 14.00
TPC0092 16 Ben's hut: "Help me Obi-Wan Kenobi..." ...14.00
TPC0093 17 Preparing Han for carbon freeze 14.00
TPC0094 18 Battle above Death Star II........................14.00
TPC0095 19 Ronto in Mos Eisley 14.00
TPC0096 20 Cloud City residents...............................14.00
TPC0097 21 Shuttle landing on Death Star II................14.00
TPC0098 22 Luke, Han, and Chewbacca, Yavin ceremony ...14.00
TPC0099 23 Cloud cars outside Leia's window 14.00
TPC0100 24 Bib Fortuna and Boushh 14.00
TPC0101 25 Cantina patron reports disturbance 14.00
TPC0102 26 Millennium Falcon lands on Cloud City......14.00
TPC0103 27 Emperor in his throne room 14.00
TPC0104 28 Jabba and Han in Mos Eisley 14.00
TPC0105 29 Wampa's meal disturbed 14.00
TPC0106 30 Imperial welcome 14.00

Teleca
TPC0056 ANH movie poster art 9.00
TPC0057 C-3PO and R2-D2 ....8.00

Telefonica
TPC0068 Anakin Skywalker 5.00
TPC0069 Battle Droid..5.00
TPC0070 C-3PO 5.00
TPC0071 Jedi Knights..5.00
TPC0072 Naboo Fighter 5.00
TPC0061 Anakin Skywalker 5.00
TPC0062 C-3PO and R2-D2.......................................5.00
TPC0063 Darth Maul 5.00
TPC0064 Jar Jar Binks...5.00
TPC0065 Queen Amidala 5.00
TPC0066 Qui-Gon Jinn...5.00

TPC0020 ROTJ Chewbacca 6.00
TPC0055 Star Wars SE, promotion for pre-ordering videos......6.00
TPC0067 Yoda 5.00

CAMERAS

CAM0001   CAM0001 detail   CAM0002 detail

Tiger Electronics
CAM0002 Picture Plus Image Camera, Darth Maul w/background, 'droid' misspelled.............35.00
CAM0001 Picture Plus Image Camera, Darth Maul w/o background 25.00

CAN HOLDERS

CH0001   CH0002   CH0003

Pepsi Cola
CH0001 Battle Droid mail-in premium, Japan exclusive 65.00
CH0002 C-3PO mail-in premium, Japan exclusive 95.00
CH0003 R2-D2 mail-in premium, Japan exclusive 95.00

CANDLES

BC0004   BC0001   BC0002   BC0003 front and back

Unique
BC0004 Round Candle, SW:EPI with classic logo 5.00

Wilton
BC0001 Chewbacca Cake Candle...................................7.00
BC0002 Darth Vader Cake Candle...................................7.00
BC0003 R2-D2 Cake Candle 7.00

CANDLESTICK HOLDERS

Sigma
HOA0001 Yoda candlestick holder, ceramic.........65.00

HOA001

Candy Molds

CANDY MOLDS

BM0001   BM0005 header   BM0005

Wilton
BM0001 Boba Fett, Darth Vader, Stormtrooper 12.00
BM0002 C-3PO, Chewbacca, Darth Vader, R2-D2, Stormtrooper, Ewok, Yoda lollipop..25.00
BM0003 Chewbacca, C-3PO, R2-D2, Yoda 12.00
BM0004 R2-D2, large 10.00
BM0005 Two mold sheets featuring Darth Vader, R2-D2, Chewbacca, C-3PO, Yoda, Stormtrooper 27.00

CAPS

B/W Character Merchandising
AC0001 ESB black and silver 18.00
AC0002 ESB black and silver (visor) 10.00

Chase Authentics

AC0043 front and sides

AC0043 Nascar Jeff Gordon, Space Battle 24.00

Dixie/Northern Inc.
AC0003 Mesh w/characters and ESB logo..15.00

Factors
AC0006 SW Fan Club, navy w/embroidered logo, stars on bill 30.00

Fan Club
AC0031 Episode I black cap with silver embroidered logo and elastic strap 14.00
AC0030 Episode I bucket hat with embroidered silver logo 14.00

Fresh Caps Ltd.

AC0039 front and back

AC0034 "Star Wars Celebration" embroidered on back cap, slide buckle..43.00
AC0032 3-D plastic Vader head on cap bill 14.00
AC0033 Glitter X-Wing..7.00
AC0035 Stormtrooper, "Freeze you Rebel scum" black cap with THX-style character on front, quotation on back..8.00
AC0036 Stormtrooper, "Freeze you Rebel scum" black cap with THX-style character on front, quotation on front..8.00
AC0037 SW EP1 logo, dark green cap, slide buckle 10.00
AC0038 SW EP1 logo, olive green cap, slide buckle................................10.00
AC0039 Vader, "Never underestimate the Dark Side" black cap with THX-style character on front, quotation on back......................................8.00
AC0040 Vader, "Never underestimate the Dark Side" black cap with THX-style character on front, quotation on front..8.00

AC0041 Yoda, "May the force be with you" black cap with THX-style character on front, quotation on back..8.00
AC0042 Yoda, "May the force be with you" black cap with THX-style character on front, quotation on front...8.00

Grossman Cap
AC0009 C-3PO, knit 10.00
AC0010 Chewbacca, knit 15.00
AC0011 Gamorrean Guard, knit 10.00
AC0012 Paploo (Ewok), knit 10.00
AC0023 R2-D2, knit 10.00
AC0013 ROTJ logo, knit 10.00
AC0014 Wicket (Ewok), knit 10.00

Hi-C
AC0015 ROTJ Hi-C premium cap 25.00

Kellogg's
AC0016 Kellogg's "C-3PO's The Force" 50.00

Lucasarts
AC0017 X-Wing embroidered logo, knit 23.00

Sales Corp. of America
AC0018 Admiral Ackbar 9.00
AC0019 Darth Vader and Royal Guards 12.00
AC0020 Gamorrean Guard 10.00
AC0021 Jabba the Hutt 10.00
AC0022 Luke and Darth Vader Duel..12.00
AC0024 ROTJ logo 10.00

Thinking Cap
AC0025 ESB logo..10.00
AC0026 Imperial w/metal rank insignia 24.00
AC0027 SW Rebel Forces 18.00
AC0028 Yoda ears..25.00
AC0044 10th Anniversary 14.00
AC0007 Mesh w/battle scene and SW logo 35.00
AC0008 Mesh w/ESB logo 10.00
AC0029 Star Wars logo with trimmed bill..18.00
AC0004 SW Fan Club 20.00
AC0005 SW Fan Club, black w/embroidered logo patch 18.00

CAPS, TPM
Applause

ACI0002   ACI0003   ACI0005

ACI0006   ACI0007   ACI0008

ACI0003 Darth Maul baseball cap 7.00
ACI0002 Darth Maul bucket hat with red band 10.00
ACI0005 Jar Jar Binks baseball cap 7.00
ACI0006 Podracer baseball cap, featuring Anakin Skywalker 7.00
ACI0008 R2-D2 baseball cap 7.00
ACI0004 Star Wars logo, Episode I 7.00
ACI0007 Star Wars logo, Episode I bucket hat 8.00

CARD ALBUMS

Burger King
CA0003 4-Page album for Super Scene stickers....................................12.00

CA0001   CA0002   CA0003   CA0004

DinaMics
CA0001 DinaMics sticker album 11.00

General Mills
CA0005 Wallet for holding 3¼"x4½" cards, brown with gold border and Star Wars logo. Holds 18 cereal premium cards 15.00

Topps
CA0006 Return of the Jedi Sticker Album, 25 cents 8.00
CA0002 Star Wars Galaxy card album 27.00

Walkers
CA0004 Tazo Collector's Force Pack 7.00

CARD GAMES

Decipher
NC0012 Empire Strikes Back 2 player intro. game 15.00
NC0007 Episode I Customizable Card Game, 160 cards in 4 decks plus rules........................14.00
NC0010 First Anthology Collectible Card Game (CCG) with 6 preview cards........................19.00
NC0011 Official Tournament Sealed Deck........................43.00
NC0008 Young Jedi Collectible Card Game (CCG) 40 Card Sample Pack 'Not For Sale' 5.00

Hasbro
NC0009 Clash of the Lightsabers w/mini-pewter Qui-Gon Jinn and Darth Maul........................8.00

Nick Trost
NC0005 Star Wars Card Trick........................12.00

Parker Bros.

NC0007   NC0011   NC0003

NC0004   NC0009

NC0001 Ewoks: Favorite Five 8.00
NC0002 Ewoks: Paw Pals........................8.00
NC0003 Ewoks: Say "Cheese"........................8.00
NC0004 Return of the Jedi: Play for Power........................15.00

CARDS: 24K GOLD

Authentic Images
Cards are in acrylic holder inside leatherette jewel gift box; 1,997 produced of each ANH card.
1,000 produced of each ESB and ROTJ card.
PMC0006 ANH: Ben Kenobi 85.00
PMC0005 ANH: Darth Vader 85.00
PMC0002 ANH: Han and Jabba 85.00
PMC0003 ANH: Leia and Vader 85.00
PMC0004 ANH: Luke training 85.00
PMC0007 ESB: Boba Fett 85.00
PMC0008 ESB: Darth Vader in shaft 85.00
PMC0010 ESB: Emperor Palpatine 85.00
PMC0009 ESB: Luke loses his hand 85.00
PMC0011 ESB: Yoda 85.00
PMC0015 ROTJ: Darth Vader unmasked 85.00
PMC0013 ROTJ: Droids 85.00
PMC0012 ROTJ: Jabba's court 85.00
PMC0016 ROTJ: Jedi spirits 85.00
PMC0014 ROTJ: Luke vs. Boba Fett........................85.00
PMC0001 Trilogy Movie Poster design, 24k gold ingot image, 5000 produced........................170.00

Score Board

PMC0018   PMC0019   PMC0021

PMC0022 cover and cards

Cards are 23k gold, and only 10,000 of each set were produced.
PMC0018 Bounty Hunters........................40.00
PMC0019 Darth Vader 40.00
PMC0020 Millennium Falcon 40.00
PMC0021 Shadows of the Empire........................40.00
PMC0022 SW Trilogy Movie Posters........................89.00

CARDS: 3D, TPM

Topps
TE30001 01 The Phantom Alliance 1.00
TE30002 02 To Trap a Jedi 1.00
TE30003 03 Besieged by Battle Droids 1.00
TE30004 04 Destroyer Droid Challenge 1.00
TE30005 05 Escaping the Neimoidians 1.00
TE30006 06 Planet Naboo Invaded 1.00
TE30007 07 Refuge In a Water World 1.00
TE30008 08 "How Rude!" 1.00
TE30009 09 Facing Boss Nass 1.00
TE30010 10 Target: Planet Naboo 1.00
TE30011 11 Warcraft Closing In 1.00
TE30012 12 Rescuing Queen Amidala 1.00
TE30013 13 Valiant R2-D2 ....1.00
TE30014 14 The Sith Apprentice........................1.00
TE30015 15 Encountering Anakin 1.00
TE30016 16 Day of the Podrace 1.00
TE30017 17 High-Speed Thrills 1.00
TE30018 18 Treacherous Dug 1.00
TE30019 19 The Fast and the Furious 1.00
TE30020 20 Racing Across Tatooine 1.00

Cards: 3D, TPM

TE30021 21 The Home Stretch....1.00
TE30022 22 Maul's Quarry....1.00
TE30023 23 Decision at Coruscant....1.00
TE30024 24 Facing the Jedi Council....1.00
TE30025 25 The Galactic Senate....1.00
TE30026 26 Amidala's Gamble....1.00
TE30027 27 A Prophecy Fulfilled?....1.00
TE30028 28 Counterattack....1.00
TE30029 29 Face-Off With Maul....1.00
TE30030 30 Adversaries....1.00
TE30031 31 Regal Battlefield....1.00
TE30032 32 Reclaiming the Palace....1.00
TE30033 33 Gungans Go to War....1.00
TE30034 34 Trade Federation Offensive....1.00
TE30035 35 The Reluctant Hero....1.00
TE30036 36 Implacable Foes....1.00
TE30037 37 In the Generator Complex....1.00
TE30038 38 Fury of the Sith....1.00
TE30039 39 The Fate of Qui-Gon Jinn....1.00
TE30040 40 Starpilot Anakin....1.00
TE30041 41 Skywalker's First Battle....1.00
TE30042 42 The Enemy Within....1.00
TE30043 43 Vanquishing Darth Maul....1.00
TE30044 44 Naboo Liberated....1.00
TE30045 45 Yoda's Warning....1.00
TE30046 46 A Pause for Peace....1.00
TE30047 Destroyer Droids Raise Their Shields, multi-motion chase card.....7.00
TE30048 Obi-Wan and Darth Maul Battle, multi-motion chase card.........7.00
TE30049 P1 Naboo Hangar Scene - Obi-Wan and Qui-Gon, promo card ..8.00

CARDS: 3DI

Topps

DI30001 001 Star Wars: A New Hope....1.00
DI30002 002 Pursuit in Space!....1.00
DI30003 003 Droids in the Crossfire!....1.00
DI30004 004 A Princess Strikes Back!....1.00
DI30005 005 Release of the Escape Pod!....1.00
DI30006 006 Toward Tatooine!....1.00
DI30007 007 Jawas in Hiding!....1.00
DI30008 008 Enter Luke Skywalker!....1.00
DI30009 009 The Leia Hologram!....1.00
DI30010 010 Spotting the Sand People!....1.00
DI30011 011 Attacked by Tusken Raiders!....1.00
DI30012 012 Rescued by Ben Kenobi!....1.00

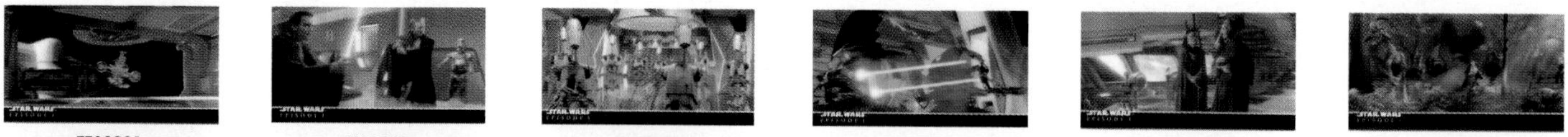

TE30001 TE30002 TE30003 TE30004 TE30005 TE30006

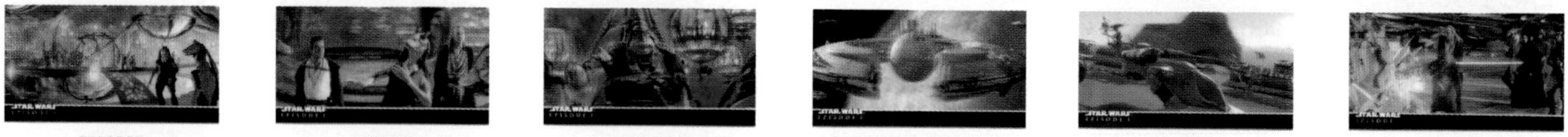

TE30007 TE30008 TE30009 TE30010 TE30011 TE30012

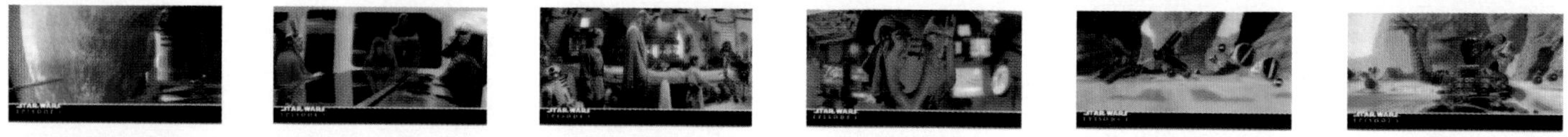

TE30013 TE30014 TE30015 TE30016 TE30017 TE30018

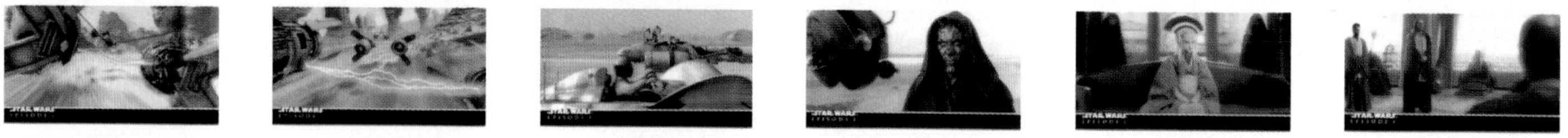

TE30019 TE30020 TE30021 TE30022 TE30023 TE30024

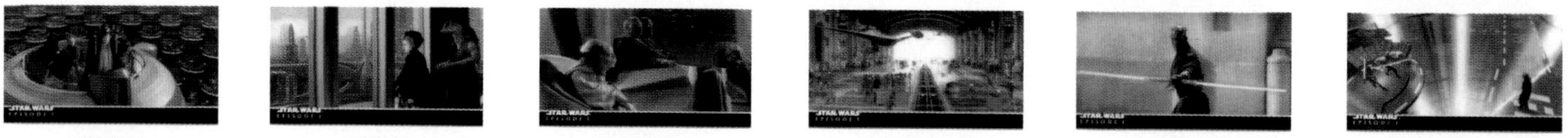

TE30025 TE30026 TE30027 TE30028 TE30029 TE30030

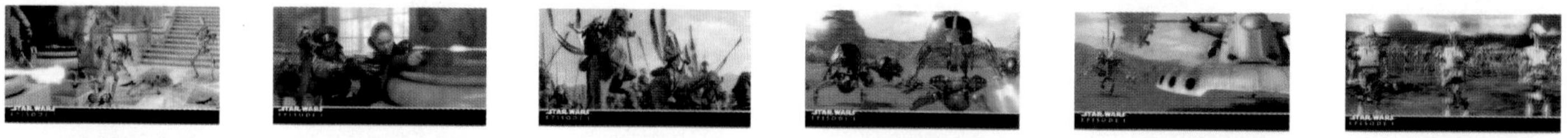

TE30031 TE30032 TE30033 TE30034 TE30035 TE30036

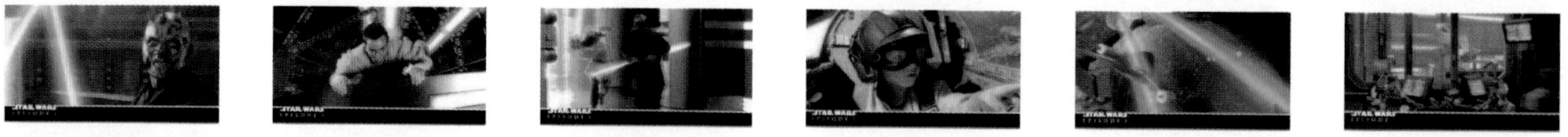

TE30037 TE30038 TE30039 TE30040 TE30041 TE30042

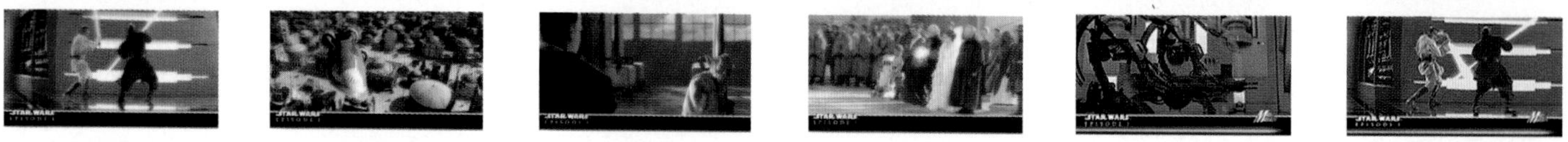

TE30043 TE30044 TE30045 TE30046 TE30047 TE30048

DI30001   DI30002   DI30003   DI30004   DI30005   DI30006

DI30007   DI30008   DI30009   DI30010   DI30011   DI30012

DI30013   DI30014   DI30015   DI30016   DI30017   DI30018

DI30019   DI30020   DI30021   DI30022   DI30023   DI30024

DI30025   DI30026   DI30027   DI30028   DI30029   DI30030

DI30031   DI30032   DI30033   DI30034   DI30035   DI30036

DI30037   DI30038   DI30039   DI30040   DI30041   DI30042

DI30043   DI30044   DI30045   DI30046   DI30047   DI30048

DI30049   DI30050   DI30051   DI30052   DI30053   DI30054

DI30055   DI30056   DI30057   DI30058   DI30059   DI30060

DI30061   DI30062   DI30063   DI30065   DI30067   DI30068

Cards: 3 Di

DI30013 013 A Message for Help! 1.00
DI30014 014 Power of the Dark Side! 1.00
DI30015 015 Fate of the Lars Homestead! 1.00
DI30016 016 Cantina Denizens! 1.00
DI30017 017 Meet Han and Chewie! 1.00
DI30018 018 Alerting the Sandtroopers! 1.00
DI30019 019 Preparing for Space Travel! 1.00
DI30020 020 Escape from Tatooine! 1.00
DI30021 021 Han Solo in Command! 1.00
DI30022 022 Jumping Into Hyperspace! 1.00
DI30023 023 Target: Alderaan! 1.00
DI30024 024 Laser of Destruction! 1.00
DI30025 025 Leia's Ordeal! 1.00
DI30026 026 Destruction of a Planet! 1.00
DI30027 027 Lightsaber Practice! 1.00
DI30028 028 Approaching the Death Star! 1.00
DI30029 029 Drawn into Danger! 1.00
DI30030 030 Heroes in Hiding! 1.00
DI30031 031 Accessing Imperial Data! 1.00
DI30032 032 Luke's Rescue Plan! 1.00
DI30033 033 A "Captured" Chewbacca! 1.00
DI30034 034 Han Solo's Bluff! 1.00
DI30035 035 Trapped in the Alcove! 1.00
DI30036 036 Trash compactor peril! 1.00
DI30037 037 The power generator trench! 1.00
DI30038 038 Shoot-Out in the Shaft! 1.00
DI30039 039 Swinging to Safety! 1.00
DI30040 040 When Jedi Clash! 1.00
DI30041 041 "Run, Luke! Run!" 1.00
DI30042 042 Escaping the Death Star! 1.00
DI30043 043 "I Can't Believe He's Gone!" 1.00
DI30044 044 Skirmish in Space! 1.00
DI30045 045 "Got Him! I Got Him!" 1.00
DI30046 046 Destination: Yavin! 1.00
DI30047 047 The Rebel Hideout! 1.00
DI30048 048 Briefing the Rebels! 1.00
DI30049 049 X-Wings Away! 1.00
DI30050 050 Assault on the Death Star! 1.00
DI30051 051 Monitoring the Battle! 1.00
DI30052 052 Vader in the Trench! 1.00
DI30053 053 "Targets Coming Up!" 1.00
DI30054 054 Artoo Hanging On! 1.00
DI30055 055 Blasted by Vader! 1.00
DI30056 056 Luke Uses the Force! 1.00
DI30057 057 Surprise Attack! 1.00
DI30058 058 Vader's Final Stand! 1.00
DI30059 059 Solo to the Rescue! 1.00
DI30060 060 Death Star Departure! 1.00
DI30061 061 The Victorious Rebels! 1.00
DI30062 062 Honored for Their Bravery! 1.00
DI30063 063 Heroes of the Rebellion! 1.00
DI30064 1m MultiMotion Exploding Death Star 6.00
DI30065 3Di 1 Vader and troops, promo card 5.00
DI30066 3Di 2 Artwork - Vader, promo card 5.00
DI30067 ESB P1 Empire Strikes Back, promo card ..5.00
DI30068 Wrapper, 3di cards 2.00

CARDS: ACTION MASTERS

OA0006   OA0007   OA0008   OA0011   OA0012   OA0013

Kenner

OA0001 509218-01 Darth Vader (reaching out to Luke) 1.00
OA0002 509221-01 Luke Skywalker (duel with Vader) 1.00
OA0003 509223-01 C-3PO (in control room) 1.00
OA0004 509225-01 R2-D2 (in Cloud City) 1.00
OA0005 509227-01 Stormtrooper (2 troopers firing weapons) 1.00
OA0006 509996-00 Darth Vader (from carbon chamber) 1.00
OA0007 509997-00 Stormtrooper (3 troopers firing weapons) 1.00
OA0008 509998-00 Boba Fett (ESB scene) 1.00
OA0009 511819-00 Princess Leia Organa (Star Wars scene) 1.00
OA0010 511820-00 Obi-Wan Kenobi (Star Wars) 1.00
OA0011 511821-00 Han Solo (SW scene) 1.00

OA0012 515859-00 Chewbacca (close-up) 1.00
OA0013 515860-00 Luke Skywalker (ESB scene) 1.00
OA0014 515861-00 C-3PO (entering cantina) 1.00
OA0015 515862-00 R2-D2 (on Dagobah) 1.00
OA0016 523290 .00 Han Solo (same scene as first card with different coloring) 1.00
OA0017 523291 .00 Chewbacca (close-up) 1.00
OA0018 523292 .00 Stormtrooper (3 troopers) 1.00
OA0019 523293 .00 Boba Fett (ESB scene) 1.00
OA0020 523294 .00 Darth Vader (in carbon chamber) 1.00
OA0021 523295 .00 Luke Skywalker (ESB scene) 1.00
OA0022 523296 .00 Princess Leia Organa (SW scene) 1.00
OA0023 523297 .00 Obi-Wan Kenobi (publicity shot) 1.00
OA0024 523298 .00 R2-D2 (cloud city) 1.00
OA0025 523299 .00 C-3PO (entering cantina) 1.00

CARDS: ANH

Topps
OVP0001 001 Luke Skywalker 1.35
OVP0002 002 See-Threepio and Artoo-Detoo 1.35
OVP0003 003 The Little Droid, Artoo-Deetoo 1.35
OVP0004 004 Space Pirate Han Solo 1.35
OVP0005 005 Princess Leia Organa 1.35
OVP0006 006 Ben (Obi-Wan) Kenobi 1.35
OVP0007 007 The Villainous Darth Vader 1.35
OVP0008 008 Grand Moff Tarkin 1.35
OVP0009 009 Rebels Defend Their Starship! 1.35
OVP0010 010 Princess Leia - Captured! 1.35
OVP0011 011 Artoo is Imprisoned by the Jawas 1.35
OVP0012 012 The Droids are Reunited! 1.35
OVP0013 013 A Sale on Droids 1.35
OVP0014 014 Luke Checks Out His New Droid 1.35
OVP0015 015 Artoo-Detoo is Left Behind! 1.35
OVP0016 016 Jawas of Tatooine 1.35
OVP0017 017 Lord Vader Threatens Princess Leia! 1.35
OVP0018 018 Artoo-Detoo is Missing! 1.35
OVP0019 019 Searching for the Little Droid 1.35
OVP0020 020 Hunted by the Sandpeople! 1.35
OVP0021 021 The Tusken Raiders 1.35
OVP0022 022 Rescued by Ben Kenobi 1.35
OVP0023 023 See-Threepio is Injured! 1.35
OVP0024 024 Stormtroopers Seek the Droids! 1.35
OVP0025 025 Luke Rushes to his Loved Ones 1.35
OVP0026 026 A Horrified Luke Sees His Family Killed ..1.35
OVP0027 027 Some Repairs for See-Threepio 1.35
OVP0028 028 Luke Agrees to Join Ben Kenobi 1.35
OVP0029 029 Stopped by Stormtroopers 1.35
OVP0030 030 Han in the Millennium Falcon 1.35
OVP0031 031 Sighting the Death Star 1.35
OVP0032 032 Lord Vader's Guards 1.35
OVP0033 033 The Droids in the Control Room 1.35
OVP0034 034 See-Threepio Diverts the Guards 1.35
OVP0035 035 Luke and Han as Stormtroopers 1.35
OVP0036 036 Blast of the Laser Rifle! 1.35
OVP0037 037 Cornered in the Labyrinth 1.35
OVP0038 038 Luke and Han in the Refuse Room 1.35
OVP0039 039 Steel Walls Close in on Our Heroes! 1.35
OVP0040 040 Droids Rescue Their Masters! 1.35
OVP0041 041 Facing the Deadly Chasm 1.35
OVP0042 042 Stormtroopers Attack! 1.35
OVP0043 043 Luke Prepares to Swing Across the Chasm ...1.35
OVP0044 044 Han and Chewie Shoot it Out! 1.35
OVP0045 045 The Light Saber 1.35
OVP0046 046 A Desperate Moment for Ben 1.35
OVP0047 047 Luke Prepares for the Battle 1.35
OVP0048 048 Artoo-Detoo is Loaded Aboard 1.35
OVP0049 049 The Rebels Monitor the Raid 1.35
OVP0050 050 Rebel Leaders Wonder About Their Fate! ..1.35
OVP0051 051 See-Threepio and Princess Leia 1.35
OVP0052 052 Who Will Win the Final Star War? 1.35
OVP0053 053 Battle in Outer Space! 1.35
OVP0054 054 The Victors Receive Their Reward 1.35
OVP0055 055 Han, Chewie, and Luke 1.35
OVP0056 056 A Day of Rejoicing 1.35
OVP0057 057 Mark Hamill as Luke Skywalker 1.35
OVP0058 058 Harrison Ford as Han Solo 1.35
OVP0059 059 Alec Guinness as Ben Kenobi 1.35
OVP0060 060 Peter Cushing as Grand Moff Tarkin 1.35
OVP0061 061 Mark Hamill in Control Room 1.35

OVP0001 OVP0002 OVP0003 OVP0004 OVP0005 OVP0006 OVP0007 OVP0008 OVP0009 OVP0010 OVP0011
OVP0012 OVP0013 OVP0014 OVP0015 OVP0016 OVP0017 OVP0018 OVP0019 OVP0020 OVP0021 OVP0022
OVP0023 OVP0024 OVP0025 OVP0026 OVP0027 OVP0028 OVP0029 OVP0030 OVP0031 OVP0032 OVP0033
OVP0034 OVP0035 OVP0036 OVP0037 OVP0038 OVP0039 OVP0040 OVP0041 OVP0042 OVP0043 OVP0044
OVP0045 OVP0046 OVP0047 OVP0048 OVP0049 OVP0050 OVP0051 OVP0052 OVP0053 OVP0054 OVP0055
OVP0056 OVP0057 OVP0058 OVP0059 OVP0060 OVP0061 OVP0062 OVP0063 OVP0064 OVP0065 OVP0066
OVP0067 OVP0068 OVP0069 OVP0070 OVP0071 OVP0072 OVP0073 OVP0074 OVP0075 OVP0076 OVP0077

Cards: ANH

OVP0078	OVP0079	OVP0080	OVP0081	OVP0082	OVP0083	OVP0084	OVP0085	OVP0086	OVP0087	OVP0088
OVP0089	OVP0090	OVP0091	OVP0092	OVP0093	OVP0094	OVP0095	OVP0096	OVP0097	OVP0098	OVP0099
OVP0100	OVP0101	OVP0102	OVP0103	OVP0104	OVP0105	OVP0106	OVP0107	OVP0108	OVP0109	OVP0110
OVP0111	OVP0112	OVP0113	OVP0114	OVP0115	OVP0116	OVP0117	OVP0118	OVP0119	OVP0120	OVP0121
OVP0122	OVP0123	OVP0124	OVP0125	OVP0126	OVP0127	OVP0128	OVP0129	OVP0130	OVP0131	OVP0132
OVP0133	OVP0134	OVP0135	OVP0136	OVP0137	OVP0138	OVP0139	OVP0140	OVP0141	OVP0142	OVP0143
OVP0144	OVP0145	OVP0146	OVP0147	OVP0148	OVP0149	OVP0150	OVP0151	OVP0152	OVP0153	OVP0154

OVP0155	OVP0156	OVP0157	OVP0158	OVP0159	OVP0160	OVP0161	OVP0162	OVP0163	OVP0164	OVP0165
OVP0166	OVP0167	OVP0168	OVP0169	OVP0170	OVP0171	OVP0172	OVP0173	OVP0174	OVP0175	OVP0176
OVP0177	OVP0178	OVP0179	OVP0180	OVP0181	OVP0182	OVP0183	OVP0184	OVP0185	OVP0186	OVP0187
OVP0188	OVP0189	OVP0190	OVP0191	OVP0192	OVP0193	OVP0194	OVP0195	OVP0196	OVP0197	OVP0198
OVP0199	OVP0200	OVP0201	OVP0202	OVP0203	OVP0204	OVP0205	OVP0206	OVP0207	OVP0208	OVP0209
OVP0210	OVP0211	OVP0212	OVP0213	OVP0214	OVP0215	OVP0216	OVP0217	OVP0218	OVP0219	OVP0220

OVP0232	OVP0233	OVP0234	OVP0235	OVP0236	OVP0237	OVP0238	OVP0239	OVP0241	OVP0242	OVP0243
OVP0244	OVP0245	OVP0246	OVP0247	OVP0248	OVP0249	OVP0250	OVP0251	OVP0252	OVP0253	OVP0254
OVP0255	OVP0256	OVP0257	OVP0258	OVP0259	OVP0260	OVP0261	OVP0262	OVP0263	OVP0264	OVP0265
OVP0266	OVP0267	OVP0268	OVP0269	OVP0270	OVP0271	OVP0272	OVP0273	OVP0274	OVP0275	OVP0276
OVP0277	OVP0278	OVP0279	OVP0280	OVP0281	OVP0282	OVP0283	OVP0284	OVP0285	OVP0286	OVP0287
OVP0288	OVP0289	OVP0290	OVP0291	OVP0292	OVP0293	OVP0294	OVP0295	OVP0296	OVP0297	OVP0298

OVP0310	OVP0311	OVP0312	OVP0313	OVP0314	OVP0315	OVP0316	OVP0317	OVP0318	OVP0319	OVP0320
OVP0321	OVP0322	OVP0323	OVP0324	OVP0325	OVP0326	OVP0327	OVP0328	OVP0329	OVP0330	OVP0331
OVP0332	OVP0333	OVP0334	OVP0335	OVP0336	OVP0337	OVP0338	OVP0339	OVP0340	OVP0341	OVP0342
OVP0343	OVP0344	OVP0345	OVP0346	OVP0347	OVP0348	OVP0349	OVP0350	OVP0351	OVP0352	OVP0353
OVP0354	OVP0355	OVP0356	OVP0357	OVP0358	OVP0359	OVP0360	OVP0361	OVP0362	OVP0363	OVP0364
OVP0365	OVP0366	OVP0367	OVP0368	OVP0369	OVP0370	OVP0371	OVP0372	OVP0373	OVP0374	OVP0375
OVP0376	OVP0377	OVP0378	OVP0379	OVP0380	OVP0381	OVP0382	OVP0383	OVP0384	OVP0385	OVP0386

Cards: ANH

OVP0376 Sticker 45 A Crucial Moment for Luke Skywalker 1.75
OVP0377 Sticker 46 Chewie Gets Riled!...1.75
OVP0378 Sticker 47 Threepio and Artoo..1.75
OVP0379 Sticker 48 Various Droids Collected by the Jawas.....................1.75
OVP0380 Sticker 49 Luke, Star Warrior!..1.75
OVP0381 Sticker 50 Director George Lucas and Greedo 1.75
OVP0382 Sticker 51 Technicians Ready C-3PO for the Cameras 1.75
OVP0383 Sticker 52 The Jawas Ready Their New Merchandise 1.75
OVP0384 Sticker 53 Directing the Cantina Creatures..............................1.75
OVP0385 Sticker 54 Leia Wishes Luke Good Luck!................................1.75
OVP0386 Sticker 55 A Touch-up For Chewbacca!.................................1.75

CARDS: BEND-EMS

Just Toys

OB0001 A Vader (#4)...3.00
OB0002 AA ESB Concept Poster Art (#195)...............................3.00
OB0003 B C-3PO (#11)...3.00
OB0004 BB Poster Concept (#167)..3.00
OB0005 C R2-D2 (#12)...3.00
OB0006 D Snowtroopers (#137)..3.00
OB0007 E Yoda (#10)...3.00
OB0008 F Chewbacca (#8)...3.00
OB0009 G Luke Skywalker (#3)...3.00
OB0010 H Obi-Wan "Ben" Kenobi (#6).....................................3.00
OB0011 I Han Solo (#7)...3.00
OB0012 J Leia (#5)...3.00
OB0013 K The Emperor (#14)..3.00
OB0014 L Ewoks (#129)...3.00
OB0015 M Boba Fett (#13)...3.00
OB0016 N Death Star Trench (#16)..3.00
OB0017 O Death Star (#16)..3.00
OB0018 P Lando (#9)...3.00
OB0019 Q Vader (#71)..3.00
OB0020 R Luke X-Wing (#87)...3.00
OB0021 S Ackbar (#98)...3.00
OB0022 T Sand People (#110)...3.00
OB0023 U Royal Guard (#112)..3.00
OB0024 V Gamorrean (#118)..3.00
OB0025 W Bib Fortuna (#121)...3.00
OB0026 X Luke and Vader (#241)...3.00
OB0027 Y ESB Lunchbox Art (#202)...3.00
OB0028 Z Luke and Leia Swinging (#264).....................................3.00

CARDS: CERAMIC

OVV0001 front and back   OVV0002   OVV0003

Score Board

Cards limited to 5,000 of each.
OVV0001 Star Wars...35.00
OVV0002 Empire Strikes Back...35.00
OVV0003 Return of the Jedi...35.00

The Hamilton Collection

OVV0004   OVV0005   OVV0006   OVV0007

OVV0008   OVV0009   OVV0010   OVV0011

OVV0011 A Daring Escape...18.00
OVV0004 Capture of Leia's Ship..18.00
OVV0005 Good vs Evil...18.00

CDC0001   CDC0002   CDC0003   CDC0004   CDC0005   CDC0006   CDC0007   CDC0008   CDC0009   CDC0010

CDC0011   CDC0012   CDC0013   CDC0014   CDC0015   CDC0016   CDC0017   CDC0018   CDC0019   CDC0020

CDC0021   CDC0022   CDC0023   CDC0024   CDC0025   CDC0026   CDC0027   CDC0028   CDC0029   CDC0030

OVV0006 Leia in Detention 18.00
OVV0007 Leia's Rescue 18.00
OVV0008 Luke Skywalker 18.00
OVV0009 Millennium Falcon Cockpit 18.00
OVV0010 Obi-Wan and Luke 18.00

CARDS: CHILE

Lider
CDC0001 01 Anakin Skywalker 1.00
CDC0002 02 Obi Wan Kenobi 1.00
CDC0003 03 Qui-Gon Jinn 1.00
CDC0004 04 Reina Amidala 1.00
CDC0005 05 Jar Jar 1.00
CDC0006 06 C-3PO 1.00
CDC0007 07 R2-D2 ....1.00
CDC0008 08 Darth Maul 1.00
CDC0009 09 Battle Droid 1.00
CDC0010 10 Watto 1.00
CDC0011 11 Sebulba 1.00
CDC0012 12 Battle Droid 1.00
CDC0013 13 Anakin Skywalker 1.00
CDC0014 14 Darth Maul 1.00
CDC0015 15 Reina Amidala 1.00
CDC0016 16 Obi Wan Kenobi 1.00
CDC0017 17 Jar Jar 1.00
CDC0018 18 Balla Espacial 1.00
CDC0019 19 Amidala 1.00
CDC0020 20 Podrace Scene 1.00
CDC0021 21 Anakin's Podracer 1.00
CDC0022 22 Trade Federation Starfighter 1.00
CDC0023 23 Qui-Gon duels Darth Maul 1.00
CDC0024 24 Naboo Fighter 1.00
CDC0025 25 Obi Wan and Qui-Gon 1.00
CDC0026 26 Final Duel 1.00
CDC0027 27 Royal Starship 1.00
CDC0028 28 Darth Maul 1.00
CDC0029 29 Yoda, Qui-Gon, and Obi-Wan 1.00
CDC0030 30 Anakin and Shmi 1.00

CARDS: CHROME ARCHIVES

Topps
OTC0001 01 Darth Vader Strangles A Rebel! 1.00
OTC0002 02 A Message From Princess Leia! 1.00
OTC0003 03 Princess Leia - Captured! 1.00

OTC0004 04 The Escape Pod is Jettisoned! 1.00
OTC0005 05 The Droids on Tatooine 1.00
OTC0006 06 Stormtroopers Seek The Droids 1.00
OTC0007 07 Luke Checks Out His New Droid 1.00
OTC0008 08 The Tusken Raiders 1.00
OTC0009 09 Ben Kenobi Rescues Luke! 1.00
OTC0010 10 Interrogated By Stormtroopers! 1.00
OTC0011 11 Han Solo Cornered by Greedo! 1.00
OTC0012 12 Distracted by Solo's Assault 1.00
OTC0013 13 The Millennium Falcon Speeds Through Space! 1.00
OTC0014 14 Lord Vader Threatens Princess Leia! 1.00
OTC0015 15 Sighting the Death Star 1.00
OTC0016 16 Deadly Blasters! 1.00
OTC0017 17 Planning An Escape! 1.00
OTC0018 18 Stormtroopers Attack! 1.00
OTC0019 19 Carrie Fisher and Mark Hamill 1.00
OTC0020 20 Han and Chewie Shoot It Out! 1.00
OTC0021 21 Ben With the Lightsaber! 1.00
OTC0022 22 The Lightsaber 1.00
OTC0023 23 Han in the Millennium Falcon 1.00
OTC0024 24 Luke Prepares for the Battle 1.00
OTC0025 25 Who Will Win the Final Star War? 1.00
OTC0026 26 Preparing For the Raid! 1.00
OTC0027 27 The Empire Strikes Back! 1.00
OTC0028 28 Battle in Outer Space! 1.00
OTC0029 29 Spectacular Battle! 1.00
OTC0030 30 The Honored Heroes! 1.00
OTC0031 31 Luke Astride His Tauntaun 1.00
OTC0032 32 Rejuvenation Chamber 1.00
OTC0033 33 Imperial Spy 1.00
OTC0034 34 The Snow Walkers 1.00
OTC0035 35 Rebel Snowspeeders Zero In! 1.00
OTC0036 36 Vader and His Snowtroopers 1.00
OTC0037 37 Emergency Blast Off! 1.00
OTC0038 38 Battle of the Star Destroyer 1.00
OTC0039 39 Canyons of Death! 1.00
OTC0040 40 Misty World of Dagobah 1.00
OTC0041 41 "Welcome, Young Luke!" 1.00
OTC0042 42 Journey Through the Swamp 1.00

OTC0001 OTC0002 OTC0003 OTC0004 OTC0005

OTC0006 OTC0007 OTC0008 OTC0009 OTC0010 OTC0011 OTC0012 OTC0013 OTC0014 OTC0015 OTC0016

OTC0017 OTC0018 OTC0019 OTC0020 OTC0021 OTC0022 OTC0023 OTC0024 OTC0025 OTC0026 OTC0027

OTC0028 OTC0029 OTC0030 OTC0031 OTC0032 OTC0033 OTC0034 OTC0035 OTC0036 OTC0037 OTC0038

OTC0039 OTC0040 OTC0041 OTC0042 OTC0043 OTC0044 OTC0045 OTC0046 OTC0047 OTC0048 OTC0049

Cards: Chrome Archives

OTC0043 43 "Use the Force, Luke" 1.00
OTC0044 44 Luke Battles... Himself? 1.00
OTC0045 45 The Bounty Hunters 1.00
OTC0046 46 Star Lovers 1.00
OTC0047 47 The Landing 1.00
OTC0048 48 Enter Lando Calrissian 1.00
OTC0049 49 Han's Torment 1.00
OTC0050 50 The Prize of Boba Fett 1.00
OTC0051 51 His Day of Triumph 1.00
OTC0052 52 The Fate of Han Solo 1.00
OTC0053 53 Boba's Special Delivery 1.00
OTC0054 54 The Search for Vader 1.00
OTC0055 55 The Confrontation 1.00
OTC0056 56 The Force and the Fury 1.00
OTC0057 57 "Embrace The Dark Side!" 1.00
OTC0058 58 "Hate Me, Luke! Destroy Me!" 1.00
OTC0059 59 Luke's Last Stand 1.00
OTC0060 60 Toward Tomorrow 1.00
OTC0061 61 The New Death Star 1.00
OTC0062 62 Intergalactic Gangster 1.00
OTC0063 63 Han Solo's Plight 1.00
OTC0064 64 The Princess Enslaved 1.00
OTC0065 65 The Young Jedi 1.00
OTC0066 66 The Dreaded Rancor 1.00
OTC0067 67 Toward the Sarlacc Pit 1.00
OTC0068 68 Jabba the Hutt's New Dancing Girl 1.00
OTC0069 69 Boba Fett Attacks! 1.00
OTC0070 70 The Raging Battle 1.00
OTC0071 71 Swing to Safety 1.00
OTC0072 72 The Deciders 1.00
OTC0073 73 Yoda, The Jedi Master 1.00
OTC0074 74 A Word With Ben Kenobi 1.00
OTC0075 75 Droids on the Move 1.00
OTC0076 76 Captured! 1.00
OTC0077 77 All Hail See-Threepio! 1.00
OTC0078 78 Unexpected Allies 1.00
OTC0079 79 Luke Skywalker's Destiny 1.00
OTC0080 80 Imperial Biker Scout 1.00
OTC0081 81 Ready for Action! 1.00
OTC0082 82 Artoo-Deetoo - Hit! 1.00
OTC0083 83 Chewbacca Triumphant 1.00
OTC0084 84 Facing the Emperor 1.00
OTC0085 85 The Emperor's Offer 1.00

OTC0086 86 Darth Vader is Down! 1.00
OTC0087 87 The Death Star Raid 1.00
OTC0088 88 Admiral Ackbar 1.00
OTC0089 89 Within the Death Star 1.00
OTC0090 90 The Triumphant Trio / Checklist 1.00
OTC0091 C1 May the Force be with you! 6.00
OTC0092 C2 Dave Prowse as Darth Vader 6.00
OTC0093 C3 Harrison Ford as Han Solo 6.00
OTC0094 C4 Liberated Princess! 4.00
OTC0095 D1 Darth Vader 4.25
OTC0096 D2 Luke Skywalker 4.25
OTC0097 D3 Princess Leia 4.25
OTC0098 D4 Han Solo 4.25
OTC0099 D5 Chewbacca 4.25
OTC0100 D6 Ben (Obi-Wan) Kenobi 4.25
OTC0101 D7 See-Threepio 4.25
OTC0102 D8 Artoo-Detoo 4.25
OTC0103 D9 The Tusken Raider 4.25
OTC0104 P1 "Hate Me, Luke! Destroy Me!" 3.00
OTC0105 P2 "Welcome, Young Luke!" 3.00

CARDS: DINAMICS

DinaMics

OC0001 001 No description available 1.00
OC0002 002 Vader Enters the Rebel Ship 1.00
OC0003 003 No description available 1.00
OC0004 004 Escape Pod Away 1.00
OC0005 005 R2 ....1.00
OC0006 006 R2 carried by Jawas 1.00
OC0007 007 No description available 1.00
OC0008 008 No description available 1.00
OC0009 009 Luke and C-3PO 1.00
OC0010 010 C-3PO and Luke 1.00
OC0011 011 Tusken Raider 1.00
OC0012 012 Luke and Obi help C-3PO 1.00
OC0013 013 Watching the Leia Holo 1.00
OC0014 014 C-3PO sketch 1.00
OC0015 015 Obi-Wan 1.00
OC0016 016 No description available 1.00
OC0017 017 Entering Mos Eisley 1.00
OC0018 018 Obi-Wan and Luke 1.00

OTC0050 OTC0051 OTC0052 OTC0053 OTC0054 OTC0055 OTC0056 OTC0057 OTC0058 OTC0059 OTC0060

OTC0061 OTC0062 OTC0063 OTC0064 OTC0065 OTC0066 OTC0067 OTC0068 OTC0069 OTC0070 OTC0071

OTC0072 OTC0073 OTC0074 OTC0075 OTC0076 OTC0077 OTC0078 OTC0079 OTC0080 OTC0081 OTC0082

OTC0083 OTC0084 OTC0085 OTC0086 OTC0087 OTC0088 OTC0089 OTC0090 OTC0091 OTC0092 OTC0093

OTC0094 OTC0095 OTC0096 OTC0097 OTC0098 OTC0099 OTC0100 OTC0101 OTC0102 OTC0103 OTC0104

OC0019 019 1/2 - Han and Chewbacca 1.00
OC0020 020 1/2 - Luke and Obi-Wan 1.00
OC0021 021 Han and Jabba 1.00
OC0022 022 No description available 1.00
OC0023 023 Tarkin and Vader 1.00
OC0024 024 Death Star Gunner 1.00
OC0025 025 No description available 1.00
OC0026 026 Falcon Interior Scene 1.00
OC0027 027 Death Star Docking Bay 1.00
OC0028 028 R2 and C-3PO on Death Star 1.00
OC0029 029 R2 sketch 1.00
OC0030 030 No description available 1.00
OC0031 031 Han, Luke, and Leia 1.00
OC0032 032 Luke and Leia 1.00
OC0033 033 Obi-Wan at tractor beam 1.00
OC0034 034 No description available 1.00
OC0035 035 Stormtroopers 1.00
OC0036 036 The Falcon 1.00
OC0037 037 No description available 1.00
OC0038 038 X-Wing hangar scene 1.00
OC0039 039 The Battle Board 1.00
OC0040 040 No description available 1.00
OC0041 041 Ties in Death Star chasm 1.00
OC0043 043 Ceremony scene 1.00
OC0044 044 Chewbacca sketch 1.00
OC0045 045 Luke on Tauntaun 1.00
OC0046 046 Wampa (SE Scene) 1.00
OC0047 047 Leia in Hoth Hangar 1.00
OC0048 048 No description available 1.00
OC0049 049 Han finds Luke on Hoth 1.00
OC0050 050 Luke in Bacta 1.00
OC0051 051 No description available 1.00
OC0052 052 Probot 1.00
OC0053 053 No description available 1.00
OC0054 054 Rebel soldier Hoth 1.00
OC0055 055 Hoth hangar scene 1.00
OC0056 056 AT-AT art scene 1.00
OC0057 057 Hoth battle 1.00
OC0058 058 Probot sketch 1.00
OC0059 059 No description available 1.00
OC0060 060 Run to the Falcon 1.00
OC0061 061 No description available 1.00
OC0062 062 No description available 1.00
OC0063 063 No description available 1.00
OC0064 064 Luke and Yoda 1.00
OC0065 065 Luke and Yoda in hut 1.00
OC0066 066 Luke Sketch 1.00
OC0067 067 1/2 - Luke and Yoda 1.00
OC0068 068 1/2 - Yoda on Luke's back 1.00
OC0069 069 Luke and X-wing on Dagobah 1.00
OC0070 070 No description available 1.00
OC0071 071 No description available 1.00
OC0072 072 No description available 1.00
OC0073 073 Yoda sketch 1.00
OC0074 074 Double cross at Cloud City 1.00
OC0075 075 No description available 1.00
OC0076 076 Han readied for freezing 1.00
OC0077 077 Han frozen 1.00
OC0078 078 Vader, Boba Fett, and Lando 1.00
OC0079 079 No description available 1.00
OC0080 080 Luke 1.00
OC0081 081 Lando Sketch 1.00
OC0082 082 Darth Vader 1.00
OC0083 083 No description available 1.00
OC0084 084 Join me... ....1.00
OC0085 085 Luke hangs out (Cloud City) 1.00
OC0086 086 No description available 1.00
OC0087 087 Looking out on the galaxy 1.00
OC0088 088 Leia Sketch 1.00
OC0089 089 No description available 1.00
OC0090 090 Jabba and Bib 1.00
OC0091 091 C-3PO and R2 before Jabba 1.00
OC0092 092 Chewbacca and Boushh 1.00
OC0093 093 Boushh and frozen Han 1.00
OC0094 094 No description available 1.00
OC0095 095 Wicket Sketch 1.00
OC0096 096 No description available 1.00
OC0097 097 Leia prisoner and Jabba 1.00
OC0098 098 No description available 1.00
OC0099 099 Luke at Jabba's 1.00
OC0100 100 Lando as Guard 1.00

OC0101 101 Luke with bone (rancor pit) 1.00
OC0102 102 No description available 1.00
OC0103 103 Rancor 1.00
OC0104 104 Han and Luke 1.00
OC0105 105 No description available 1.00
OC0106 106 Luke on Skiff 1.00
OC0107 107 No description available 1.00
OC0108 108 Boba Fett 1.00
OC0109 109 No description available 1.00
OC0110 110 No description available 1.00
OC0111 111 No description available 1.00
OC0112 112 No description available 1.00
OC0113 113 Emperor 1.00
OC0114 114 Caught in a net 1.00
OC0115 115 The Divine 3PO 1.00
OC0116 116 No description available 1.00
OC0117 117 No description available 1.00
OC0118 118 Battle on Endor 1.00
OC0119 119 Ewoks on the Run 1.00
OC0120 120 Luke and Vader 1.00
OC0121 121 No description available 1.00
OC0122 122 The Emperor sketch 1.00
OC0123 123 No description available 1.00
OC0124 124 1/2 scene Vader duel 1.00
OC0125 125 No description available 1.00
OC0126 126 1/2 scene Nien Nunb 1.00
OC0127 127 No description available 1.00
OC0128 128 No description available 1.00
OC0129 129 Emperor's Lightning 1.00
OC0130 130 Admiral Ackbar 1.00
OC0131 131 No description available 1.00
OC0132 132 Falcon 1.00
OC0133 133 Tie Bomber 1.00
OC0134 134 Falcon 1.00
OC0135 135 No description available 1.00
OC0136 136 Speeder 1.00
OC0137 137 Sandcrawler 1.00
OC0138 138 Star Destroyer 1.00
OC0139 139 X-Wing 1.00
OC0140 140 Shuttle 1.00
OC0141 141 Medical Frigate 1.00
OC0142 142 Y-Wing 1.00
OC0143 143 Sail Barge 1.00
OC0144 144 Skiff 1.00
OC0145 145 Tie Interceptor 1.00
OC0146 146 Leia's Ship 1.00
OC0147 147 No description available 1.00
OC0148 148 AT-ATs artwork 1.00
OC0149 149 A-Wing 1.00
OC0150 150 Cloud Cars artwork 1.00
OC0151 151 Tie 1.00
OC0152 152 Slave I 1.00
OC0153 153 Scout Trooper 1.00
OC0154 154 AT-ST 1.00
OC0155 155 Patrolling Mos Eisley 1.00
OC0156 156 same scene SE 1.00
OC0157 157 Droids in Mos Eisley 1.00
OC0158 158 same scene SE 1.00
OC0159 159 pulling away from checkpoint 1.00
OC0160 160 No description available 1.00
OC0161 161 entering Mos Eisley 1.00
OC0162 162 same scene but with Ronto 1.00
OC0163 163 Searching the Desert 1.00
OC0164 164 Dewbacks on patrol 1.00
OC0165 165 Lars Homestead 1.00
OC0166 166 No description available 1.00
OC0167 167 Landspeeder 1.00
OC0168 168 Same Scene; New Effects 1.00

CARDS: ESB

Scanlens
OVQ0001 001 Title Card - Darth and Troopers (A Scanlens Picture Card Series) 1.20
OVQ0002 002 Star File: Luke Skywalker 1.20
OVQ0003 003 Star File: Princess Leia 1.20
OVQ0004 004 Star File: Han Solo 1.20
OVQ0005 005 Star File: Chewbacca 1.20
OVQ0006 006 Star File: See-Threepio 1.20
OVQ0007 007 Star File: Artoo-Deeto 1.20

Cards: ESB

OVQ0133	OVQ0134	OVQ0135	OVQ0136	OVQ0137	OVQ0138	OVQ0139	OVQ0140	OVQ0141	OVQ0142	OVQ0143	OVQ0144
OVQ0145	OVQ0146	OVQ0147	OVQ0148	OVQ0149	OVQ0150	OVQ0151	OVQ0152	OVQ0153	OVQ0154	OVQ0155	OVQ0156
OVQ0157	OVQ0158	OVQ0159	OVQ0160	OVQ0161	OVQ0162	OVQ0163	OVQ0164	OVQ0165	OVQ0166	OVQ0167	OVQ0168
OVQ0169	OVQ0170	OVQ0171	OVQ0172	OVQ0173	OVQ0174	OVQ0175	OVQ0176	OVQ0177	OVQ0178	OVQ0179	OVQ0180
OVQ0181	OVQ0182	OVQ0183	OVQ0184	OVQ0185	OVQ0186	OVQ0187	OVQ0188	OVQ0189	OVQ0190	OVQ0191	OVQ0192

Cards: ESB

OVQ0193 OVQ0194 OVQ0195 OVQ0196 OVQ0197 OVQ0198 OVQ0199 OVQ0200 OVQ0201 OVQ0202 OVQ0203 OVQ0204

OVQ0205 OVQ0206 OVQ0207 OVQ0208 OVQ0209 OVQ0210 OVQ0211 OVQ0212 OVQ0213 OVQ0214 OVQ0215 OVQ0216

OVQ0217 OVQ0218 OVQ0219 OVQ0220 OVQ0221 OVQ0222 OVQ0223 OVQ0224 OVQ0225 OVQ0226 OVQ0227 OVQ0228

OVQ0229 OVQ0230 OVQ0231 OVQ0232 OVQ0233 OVQ0234 OVQ0235 OVQ0236 OVQ0237 OVQ0238 OVQ0239 OVQ0240

OVQ0241 OVQ0242 OVQ0243 OVQ0244 OVQ0245 OVQ0246 OVQ0247 OVQ0248 OVQ0249 OVQ0250 OVQ0251 OVQ0252

OVQ0253 OVQ0254 OVQ0255 OVQ0256 OVQ0257 OVQ0258 OVQ0259 OVQ0260 OVQ0261 OVQ0262 OVQ0263 OVQ0264

OVQ0298 OVQ0299 OVQ0300 OVQ0301 OVQ0302 OVQ0303 OVQ0304 OVQ0305 OVQ0306 OVQ0307 OVQ0308

OVQ0309 OVQ0310 OVQ0311 OVQ0312 OVQ0313 OVQ0314 OVQ0315 OVQ0316 OVQ0317 OVQ0318 OVQ0319

OVQ0320 OVQ0321 OVQ0322 OVQ0323 OVQ0324 OVQ0325 OVQ0326 OVQ0327 OVQ0328 OVQ0329 OVQ0330

OVQ0331 OVQ0332 OVQ0333 OVQ0334 OVQ0335 OVQ0336 OVQ0337 OVQ0338 OVQ0339 OVQ0340 OVQ0341

OVQ0342 OVQ0343 OVQ0344 OVQ0345 OVQ0346 OVQ0347 OVQ0348 OVQ0349 OVQ0350 OVQ0351 OVQ0352

OVQ0353 OVQ0354 OVQ0355 OVQ0356 OVQ0357 OVQ0358 OVQ0359 OVQ0360 OVQ0361 OVQ0362 OVQ0363

Cards: ESB

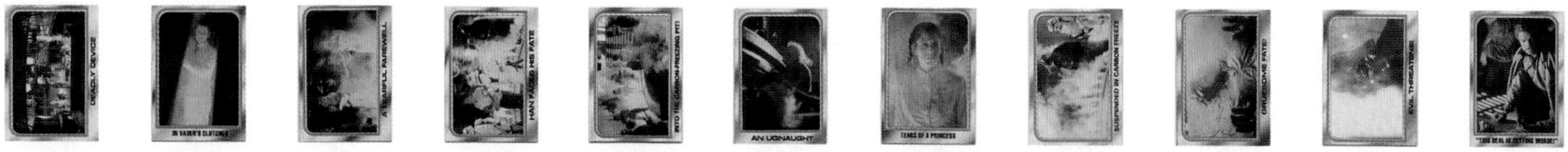

OVQ0364

OVQ0365

OVQ0366

OVQ0367

OVQ0368

OVQ0369

OVQ0370

OVQ0371

OVQ0372

OVQ0373

OVQ0374

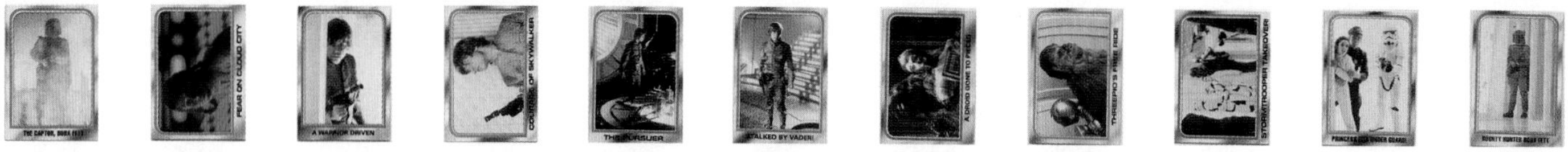

OVQ0375

OVQ0376

OVQ0377

OVQ0378

OVQ0379

OVQ0380

OVQ0381

OVQ0382

OVQ0383

OVQ0384

OVQ0385

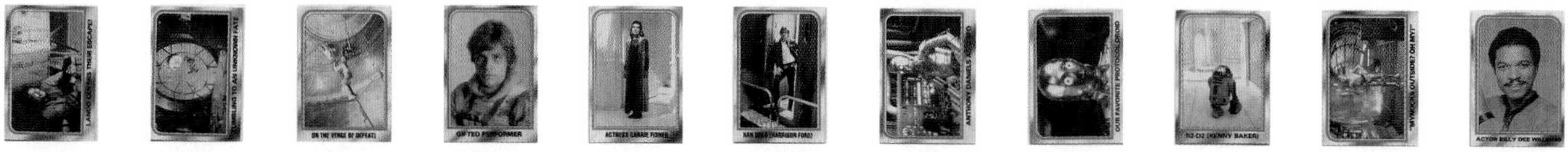

OVQ0386

OVQ0387

OVQ0388

OVQ0389

OVQ0390

OVQ0391

OVQ0392

OVQ0393

OVQ0394

OVQ0395

OVQ0396

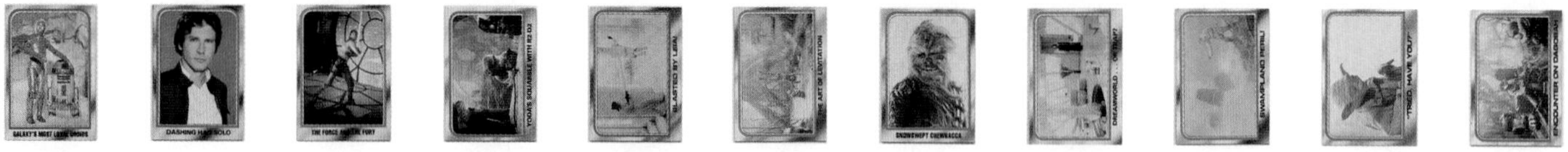

OVQ0397

OVQ0398

OVQ0399

OVQ0400

OVQ0401

OVQ0402

OVQ0403

OVQ0404

OVQ0405

OVQ0406

OVQ0407

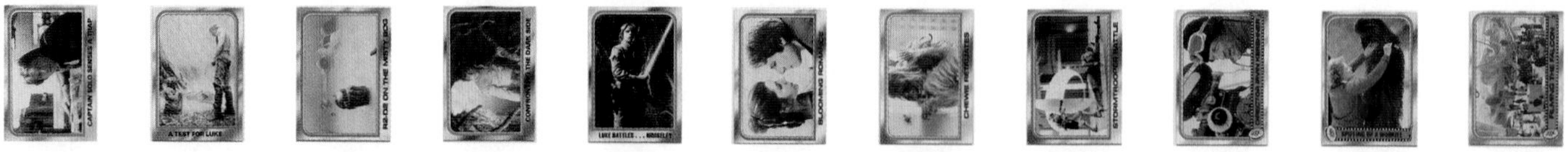

OVQ0408

OVQ0409

OVQ0410

OVQ0411

OVQ0412

OVQ0413

OVQ0414

OVQ0415

OVQ0416

OVQ0417

OVQ0418

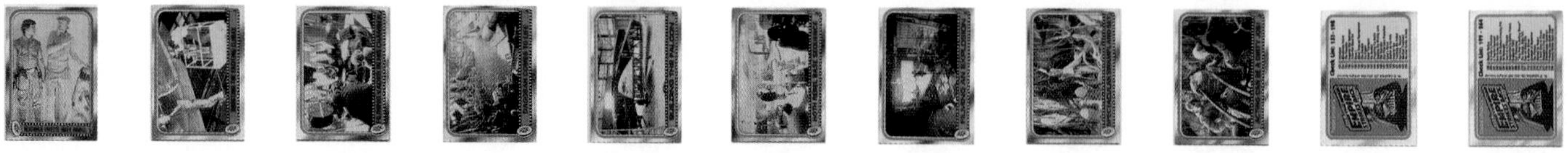

OVQ0419

OVQ0420

OVQ0421

OVQ0422

OVQ0423

OVQ0424

OVQ0425

OVQ0426

OVQ0427

OVQ0428

OVQ0429

OVQ0540 342 Cloud City Reactor Shaft 0.60
OVQ0541 343 Yoda's Home 0.60
OVQ0542 344 Escape from Bespin 0.60
OVQ0543 345 Deadly Stompers 0.60
OVQ0544 346 Snow Walker Model 0.60
OVQ0545 347 Of Helmets and Costumes..0.60
OVQ0546 348 Filming the Star Destroyer 0.60
OVQ0547 349 Millennium Falcon Miniature 0.60
OVQ0548 350 Launching an X-Wing 0.60
OVQ0549 351 Model Star Destroyer 0.60
OVQ0550 352 Checklist - 265-352 ....0.60
OVQ0573 Rack-Pack of 3 wax packs 12.00
OVQ0265 Sticker 01 F O 1.25
OVQ0266 Sticker 02 R I 1.25
OVQ0267 Sticker 03 A E 1.25
OVQ0268 Sticker 04 B X 1.25
OVQ0269 Sticker 05 U I 1.25
OVQ0270 Sticker 06 W U 1.25
OVQ0271 Sticker 07 M N 1.25
OVQ0272 Sticker 08 C D 1.25
OVQ0273 Sticker 09 O U 1.25

OVQ0274 Sticker 10 H E 1.25
OVQ0275 Sticker 11 E O 1.25
OVQ0276 Sticker 12 Y U 1.25
OVQ0277 Sticker 13 A K 1.25
OVQ0278 Sticker 14 A V 1.25
OVQ0279 Sticker 15 E S 1.25
OVQ0280 Sticker 16 Q L 1.25
OVQ0281 Sticker 17 A I 1.25
OVQ0282 Sticker 18 I O 1.25
OVQ0283 Sticker 19 Z T 1.25
OVQ0284 Sticker 20 G J 1.25
OVQ0285 Sticker 21 E I 1.25
OVQ0286 Sticker 22 A P 1.25
OVQ0287 Sticker 23 C-3PO / Darth Vader / Luke 1.25
OVQ0288 Sticker 24 C-3PO 1.25
OVQ0289 Sticker 25 Luke and Yoda / Han and Tauntaun 1.25
OVQ0290 Sticker 26 Stormtrooper / Boba Fett 1.25
OVQ0291 Sticker 27 Luke and Yoda 1.25
OVQ0292 Sticker 28 2-1B / Bossk / Lobot 1.25
OVQ0293 Sticker 29 Chewbacca / Han / Leia / Luke 1.25
OVQ0294 Sticker 30 Boba Fett...1.25

OVQ0463	OVQ0464	OVQ0465	OVQ0466	OVQ0467	OVQ0468	OVQ0469	OVQ0470	OVQ0471	OVQ0472	OVQ0473
OVQ0474	OVQ0475	OVQ0476	OVQ0477	OVQ0478	OVQ0479	OVQ0480	OVQ0481	OVQ0482	OVQ0483	OVQ0484
OVQ0485	OVQ0486	OVQ0487	OVQ0488	OVQ0489	OVQ0490	OVQ0491	OVQ0492	OVQ0493	OVQ0494	OVQ0495
OVQ0496	OVQ0497	OVQ0498	OVQ0499	OVQ0500	OVQ0501	OVQ0502	OVQ0503	OVQ0504	OVQ0505	OVQ0506
OVQ0507	OVQ0508	OVQ0509	OVQ0510	OVQ0511	OVQ0512	OVQ0513	OVQ0514	OVQ0515	OVQ0516	OVQ0517
OVQ0518	OVQ0519	OVQ0520	OVQ0521	OVQ0522	OVQ0523	OVQ0524	OVQ0525	OVQ0526	OVQ0527	OVQ0528
OVQ0529	OVQ0530	OVQ0531	OVQ0532	OVQ0533	OVQ0534	OVQ0535	OVQ0536	OVQ0537	OVQ0538	OVQ0539
OVQ0540	OVQ0541	OVQ0542	OVQ0543	OVQ0544	OVQ0545	OVQ0546	OVQ0547	OVQ0548	OVQ0549	OVQ0550

Cards: ESB

OVQ0295 Sticker 31 Stormtrooper / IG-88 ....1.25
OVQ0296 Sticker 32 C-3PO / Lando / R2-D2 ....1.25
OVQ0297 Sticker 33 Darth Vader 1.25
OVQ0430 Sticker 34 F O 1.25
OVQ0431 Sticker 35 R I 1.25
OVQ0432 Sticker 36 A E 1.25
OVQ0433 Sticker 37 B X 1.25
OVQ0434 Sticker 38 U I 1.25
OVQ0435 Sticker 39 W U 1.25
OVQ0436 Sticker 40 M N 1.25
OVQ0437 Sticker 41 C D 1.25
OVQ0438 Sticker 42 O U 1.25
OVQ0439 Sticker 43 H E 1.25
OVQ0440 Sticker 44 E O 1.25
OVQ0441 Sticker 45 Y U 1.25
OVQ0442 Sticker 46 A K 1.25
OVQ0443 Sticker 47 A V 1.25
OVQ0444 Sticker 48 E S 1.25
OVQ0445 Sticker 49 Q L 1.25
OVQ0446 Sticker 50 A I 1.25
OVQ0447 Sticker 51 I O 1.25
OVQ0448 Sticker 52 Z T 1.25
OVQ0449 Sticker 53 G J 1.25
OVQ0450 Sticker 54 E I 1.25
OVQ0451 Sticker 55 A P 1.25
OVQ0452 Sticker 56 Darth Vader 1.25
OVQ0453 Sticker 57 Boba Fett 1.25
OVQ0454 Sticker 58 Probot 1.25
OVQ0455 Sticker 59 Luke Skywalker 1.25
OVQ0456 Sticker 60 Princess Leia 1.25
OVQ0457 Sticker 61 Han Solo 1.25
OVQ0458 Sticker 62 Lando Calrissian 1.25
OVQ0459 Sticker 63 Chewbacca 1.25
OVQ0460 Sticker 64 R2-D2 ....1.25
OVQ0461 Sticker 65 C-3PO 1.25
OVQ0462 Sticker 66 Yoda 1.25
OVQ0551 Sticker 67 F O 1.00
OVQ0552 Sticker 68 R I 1.00
OVQ0553 Sticker 69 A E 1.00
OVQ0554 Sticker 70 B X 1.00
OVQ0555 Sticker 71 U I 1.00
OVQ0556 Sticker 72 W U 1.00
OVQ0557 Sticker 73 M N 1.00
OVQ0558 Sticker 74 C D 1.00
OVQ0559 Sticker 75 O U 1.00
OVQ0560 Sticker 76 H E 1.00
OVQ0561 Sticker 77 E O 1.00
OVQ0562 Sticker 78 Y U 1.00
OVQ0563 Sticker 79 A K 1.00
OVQ0564 Sticker 80 A V 1.00

OVQ0565 Sticker 81 E S 1.00
OVQ0566 Sticker 82 Q L 1.00
OVQ0567 Sticker 83 A I 1.00
OVQ0568 Sticker 84 I O 1.00
OVQ0569 Sticker 85 Z T 1.00
OVQ0570 Sticker 86 G J 1.00
OVQ0571 Sticker 87 E I 1.00
OVQ0572 Sticker 88 A P 1.00

CARDS: ESB GIANT PHOTO

Topps

OOA0031 01 Darth Vader 1.75
OOA0032 02 Lando Calrissian 1.75
OOA0033 03 Chewbacca 1.75
OOA0034 04 Leia and Han Embrace 1.75
OOA0035 05 Vader and Luke Duel 1.75
OOA0036 06 Vader and Boba Fett 1.75
OOA0037 07 Han and C-3PO 1.75
OOA0038 08 Yoda and Luke Train 1.75
OOA0039 09 In the Cockpit of the Falcon 1.75
OOA0040 10 Leia and Chewbacca 1.75
OOA0041 11 Bounty Hunters 1.75
OOA0042 12 Yoda 1.75
OOA0043 13 Luke on Tauntaun 1.75
OOA0044 14 Into the Asteroid Field 1.75
OOA0045 15 AT-ATs in Battle 1.75
OOA0046 16 Darth Reaches Out 1.75
OOA0047 17 Yoda 1.75
OOA0048 18 Falcon and Star Destroyers 1.75
OOA0049 19 Tauntaun 1.75
OOA0050 20 X-Wing Near Dagobah 1.75
OOA0051 21 Looking Out on the Galaxy 1.75
OOA0052 22 Snowspeeders Attack 1.75
OOA0053 23 Darth Vader 1.75
OOA0054 24 Han Solo 1.75
OOA0055 25 Stormtrooper 1.75
OOA0056 26 Luke 1.75
OOA0057 27 Luke and Yoda 1.75
OOA0058 28 Droids on Hoth 1.75
OOA0059 29 Yoda 1.75
OOA0060 30 Cast Photo 1.75
OOA0061 Wrapper 3.00

CARDS: EVOLUTIONS

Topps
BCE0001 01 4-LOM 1.00

OOA0031

OOA0032

OOA0033

OOA0034

OOA0035

OOA0036

OOA0037

OOA0038

OOA0039

OOA0040

OOA0041

OOA0042

OOA0043

OOA0044

OOA0045

BCE0002 02 Adi Gallia...1.00
BCE0003 03 Admiral Ackbar.......................................1.00
BCE0004 04 Admiral Piett..1.00
BCE0005 05 Anakin Skywalker....................................1.00
BCE0006 06 Aurra Sing...1.00
BCE0007 07 Ben Quadrinaros......................................1.00
BCE0008 08 Beru Lars..1.00
BCE0009 09 Bib Fortuna...1.00
BCE0010 10 Biggs Darklighter......................................1.00
BCE0011 11 Boba Fett..1.00
BCE0012 12 Boss Nass..1.00
BCE0013 13 Bossk..1.00
BCE0014 14 C-3PO...1.00
BCE0015 15 Captain Needa...1.00
BCE0016 16 Captain Panaka..1.00
BCE0017 17 Captain Tarpals..1.00
BCE0018 18 Chancellor Valorum....................................1.00
BCE0019 19 Chewbacca..1.00
BCE0020 20 Darth Maul..1.00
BCE0021 21 Darth Vader...1.00
BCE0022 22 Dengar..1.00
BCE0023 23 Depa Billaba...1.00
BCE0024 24 Eeth Koth...1.00
BCE0025 25 Even Piell...1.00
BCE0026 26 Figrin D'an..1.00
BCE0027 27 Fode and Beed..1.00
BCE0028 28 General Carlist Rieekan................................1.00
BCE0029 29 General Crix Madine....................................1.00
BCE0030 30 General Jan Dodonna...................................1.00
BCE0031 31 General Maximillian Veers..............................1.00
BCE0032 32 Grand Moff Tarkin......................................1.00
BCE0033 33 Greedo..1.00
BCE0034 34 Han Solo..1.00
BCE0035 35 IG-88...1.00
BCE0036 36 Jabba the Hutt..1.00
BCE0037 37 Jar Jar Binks..1.00
BCE0038 38 Jawa..1.00
BCE0039 39 Ki-Adi-Mundi..1.00
BCE0040 40 Klaatu...1.00
BCE0041 41 Lak Sivrak...1.00
BCE0042 42 Lando Calrissian.......................................1.00
BCE0043 43 Lobot...1.00
BCE0044 44 Logray..1.00
BCE0045 45 Luke Skywalker..1.00
BCE0046 46 Mace Windu..1.00
BCE0047 47 Max Rebo..1.00
BCE0048 48 Moff Jerjerrod...1.00
BCE0049 49 Momaw Nadon..1.00
BCE0050 50 Mon Mothma...1.00
BCE0051 51 Muftak..1.00
BCE0052 52 Nien Nunb...1.00
BCE0053 53 Nute Gunray...1.00
BCE0054 54 Obi-Wan Kenobi.......................................1.00
BCE0055 55 Oola..1.00
BCE0056 56 OOM-9...1.00
BCE0057 57 Oppo Rancisis...1.00
BCE0058 58 Owen Lars...1.00
BCE0059 59 Padme Amidala...1.00
BCE0060 60 Plo Koon..1.00
BCE0061 61 Ponda Baba..1.00
BCE0062 62 Princess Leia..1.00
BCE0063 63 Qui-Gon Jinn..1.00
BCE0064 64 R2-D2...1.00
BCE0065 65 R5-D4...1.00
BCE0066 66 Rancor..1.00
BCE0067 67 Ric Olie...1.00
BCE0068 68 Royal Guard..1.00
BCE0069 69 Rune Haako..1.00
BCE0070 70 Saesee Tiin..1.00
BCE0071 71 Salacious Crumb..1.00
BCE0072 72 Sebulba...1.00
BCE0073 73 Senator Palpatine......................................1.00
BCE0074 74 Shmi Skywalker..1.00
BCE0075 75 Sio Bibble...1.00
BCE0076 76 Stormtrooper..1.00
BCE0077 77 Sy Snootles..1.00
BCE0078 78 Tessek..1.00
BCE0079 79 Tusken Raider..1.00
BCE0080 80 Wald..1.00
BCE0081 81 Wampa..1.00
BCE0082 82 Watto...1.00

BCE0083 83 Wedge Antilles...1.00
BCE0084 84 Wicket..1.00
BCE0085 85 Wuhrer..1.00
BCE0086 86 Yaddle..1.00
BCE0087 87 Yarael Poof..1.00
BCE0088 88 Yoda..1.00
BCE0089 89 Zuckuss...1.00
BCE0090 90 Zutton..1.00
BCE0091 C1 Anakin and Shmi checklist..............................3.00
BCE0092 C2 Luke and Darth Vader checklist.........................3.00
BCE0093 C3 Luke and Leia checklist................................3.00

Autographed insert cards. Number indicates total number of cards signed.
BCE0094 Admiral Ackbar / Tim Rose, 1,000.............................35.00
BCE0095 Admiral Ozzel / Michael Sheard, 1,000........................35.00
BCE0096 Admiral Piett / Kenneth Colley, 1,000.........................35.00
BCE0097 Aurra Sing / Michonne Bourriague, 1,000......................45.00
BCE0098 Boba Fett / Jeremy Bulloch, 1,000............................75.00
BCE0099 C-3PO / Anthony Daniels, 100.............................1,200.00
BCE0100 Captain Needa / Michael Culver, 1,000........................35.00
BCE0101 Chewbacca / Peter Mayhew, 400............................200.00
BCE0115 Darth Vader / James Earl Jones, 1000.........................75.00
BCE0102 General Crix Madine / Dermot Crowley, 1,000..................35.00
BCE0103 Greedo / Paul Blake, 1,000..................................35.00
BCE0104 Lando Calrissian / Billy Dee Williams, 300...................425.00
BCE0105 Lyn Me / Dalyn Chew, 1,000.................................30.00
BCE0106 Moff Jerjerrod / Michael Pennington, 1,000....................35.00
BCE0107 Mon Mothma / Caroline Blakiston, 1,000.......................30.00
BCE0108 Nien Nunb / Mike Quinn, 1,000..............................30.00
BCE0109 Oola / Femi Taylor, 1,000...................................40.00
BCE0110 Owen Lars / Phil Brown, 1,000...............................45.00
BCE0111 Princess Leia Organa / Carrie Fisher, 100..................1,200.00
BCE0112 R2-D2 / Kenny Baker, 1,000.................................60.00
BCE0113 Rystall / Mercedes Ngoh, 1,000..............................45.00
BCE0114 Senator Palpatine / Ian McDiarmid, 400......................250.00
BCE0116 Sebulba / Lewis MacLeod, 1,000.............................45.00
BCE0117 Watto / Andrew Secombe, 1,000..............................45.00
BCE0118 Wicket W. Warrick / Warwick Davis, 1,000....................40.00

Evolution insert cards. Set A and Set B.
BCE0119 Anakin Skywalker (A)..2.00
BCE0120 Anakin Skywalker (B)..3.00
BCE0121 Beru Lars (A)..3.00
BCE0122 C-3PO (A)..2.00
BCE0123 C-3PO (B)..3.00
BCE0124 Han Solo (A)..2.00
BCE0125 Han Solo (B)..3.00
BCE0126 Lando Calrissian (A)..2.00
BCE0127 Lando Calrissian (B)..3.00
BCE0128 Luke Skywalker (A)...2.00
BCE0129 Luke Skywalker (B)...3.00
BCE0130 Obi-Wan Kenobi (A)...2.00
BCE0131 Obi-Wan Kenobi (B)...3.00
BCE0132 Owen Lars (A)..3.00

BCE0133 Padme Amidala (A) 2.00
BCE0134 Padme Amidala (B) 3.00
BCE0135 Princess Leia (A) 2.00
BCE0136 Princess Leia (B) 3.00
BCE0137 Qui-Gon Jinn (A) 3.00
BCE0138 Yoda (A) 3.00

Promotional cards.
BCE0139 P1 Obi-Wan Kenobi, TPM 4.00
BCE0140 P2 Obi-Wan Kenobi, ANH 4.00
BCE0141 P3 Nien Nunb, Alphacon exclusive autographed and numbered, limited to 250 ....75.00
BCE0142 P3 Nien Nunb, Alphacon excl., ltd. to 5,000 ....24.00
BCE0138 P4 Darth Vader, "Connections" conv. excl. 10.00

CARDS: FANCLUB

PRF0001 front and back

PRF0002 front and back

PRF0003 front and back

PRF0004 front and back

PRF0005 front and back

PRF0006 front and back

Skywalkers
PRF0007 Membership 11.00
PRF0001 Chewbacca 8.00
PRF0002 Darth Vader 8.00
PRF0003 Han Solo 8.00
PRF0005 Luke Skywalker 8.00
PRF0004 Princess Leia Organa 8.00
PRF0006 Yoda 8.00

CARDS: FRENCH

Biscuiterie Nantaise
OD0137 Admiral Ackbar 2.00
OD0127 Aldorande 2.00
OD0146 Admiral 2.00
OD0152 Bib Fortuna 2.00
OD0150 Boba Fett 2.00
OD0138 Chewbacca 2.00
OD0143 Chief Chirpa 2.00

OD0137

OD0127

OD0146

OD0152

OD0150

OD0138

OD0145 Dark Vador 2.00
OD0147 Empereur 2.00
OD0128 Endor 2.00
OD0126 Etoile Noir 2.00
OD0151 Garde de Gamorre 2.00
OD0148 Garde Royal 2.00
OD0130 Hoth 2.00
OD0149 Jabba the Hutt 2.00
OD0139 Lando Calrissian 2.00
OD0135 Luc Skywalker 2.00
OD0153 Motorangers 2.00
OD0136 Obi-Wan Kenobi 2.00
OD0142 Paploo 2.00
OD0132 Princesse Leia 2.00
OD0141 R2-D2 ....2.00
OD0131 Sabre Laser 2.00
OD0155 Soldat es Neiges 2.00
OD0154 Soldat Imperial 2.00
OD0129 Tatouine 2.00
OD0144 Wicket 2.00
OD0133 Yann Solo 2.00
OD0134 Yoda 2.00
OD0140 Z-6P0 ....2.00

Merlin Publishing Internat'l Ltd.
OD0001 001 Star Destroyer-Vaisseau Imperial 2.00
OD0002 002 R2-D2 et C-3PO 2.00
OD0003 003 Forces Rebelles 2.00
OD0004 004 Dark Vador 2.00
OD0005 005 C-3PO 2.00
OD0006 006 Sandcrawler - Char des Sables 2.00
OD0007 007 Troupes d'assaut sur Dewback 2.00
OD0008 008 Luke Skywalker et Owen Lars 2.00
OD0009 009 Luke, C-3PO et R2-D2 ....2.00
OD0010 010 Tusken Raider 2.00
OD0011 011 Luke Skywalker et son sabre laser 2.00
OD0012 012 L'Etoile de la Mort et le Star Destroyer 2.00
OD0013 013 Landspeeder dans Mos Eisley 2.00
OD0014 014 Luke, Bet et C-3PO avec les Troupes d'assaut 2.00
OD0015 015 Yan Solo et Chewbacca 2.00
OD0016 016 Yan Solo avec Jabba le Forestier 2.00
OD0017 017 Le Faucon Millenium 2.00
OD0018 018 La princesse Leia avec le Grand Moff Tarkin 2.00
OD0019 019 L'interieur du Faucon Millenium 2.00
OD0020 020 La baie d'arrimage de l'Etoile de la Mort 2.00
OD0021 021 Luke, Yan et C-3PO 2.00
OD0022 022 Yan Solo et la princesse Leia 2.00
OD0023 023 Ben Kenobi 2.00
OD0024 024 Le Faucon Millenium 2.00
OD0025 025 Le Faucon Millenium approche Yavin 4 ....2.00
OD0026 026 Yan Solo avec Luke Skywalker 2.00
OD0027 027 X-wing fighters 2.00
OD0028 028 X-wing fighters et Tie fighter 2.00
OD0029 029 Y-wing fighters dans la fente de l'Etoile de la Mort 2.00
OD0030 030 Dark Vador / Interieur du Tie fighter 2.00
OD0031 031 Princesse Leia et C-3PO 2.00
OD0032 032 Luke Skywalker / Interieur X-wing 2.00
OD0033 033 La porte de sortie de l'Etoile de la Mort 2.00
OD0034 034 Luke, Leia et Yan 2.00
OD0035 035 Le clin d'ceil de Yan Solo 2.00
OD0036 036 Droid de detection imperial 2.00
OD0037 037 Luke Skywalker dans le repaire de Wampa 2.00
OD0038 038 Yan Solo avec le commandeant Rebelle 2.00
OD0039 039 Yan Solo fait des signes au snowspeeder 2.00
OD0040 040 Yan Solo tire sur le droid de detection 2.00

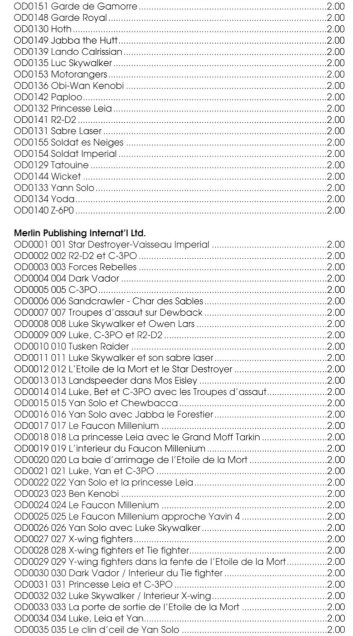

OD0143

OD0145

OD0147

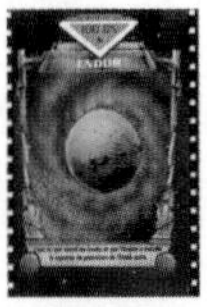
OD0128

OD0126

OD0151

OD0148

OD0130

OD0149

OD0139

OD0135

OD0153

OD0136

OD0142

OD0132

OD0141

OD0131

OD0155

OD0154

OD0129

OD0144

OD0133

OD0134

OD0140

OD0001 OD0002 OD0003 OD0004 OD0005 OD0006 OD0007 OD0008 OD0009

OD0010 OD0011 OD0012 OD0013 OD0014 OD0015 OD0016 OD0017 OD0018

OD0019 OD0020 OD0021 OD0022 OD0023 OD0024 OD0025 OD0026 OD0027

OD0028 OD0029 OD0030 OD0031 OD0032 OD0033 OD0034 OD0035 OD0036

OD0037 OD0038 OD0039 OD0040 OD0041 OD0042 OD0043 OD0044 OD0045

OD0046 OD0047 OD0048 OD0049 OD0050 OD0051 OD0052 OD0053 OD0054

OD0055 OD0056 OD0057 OD0058 OD0059 OD0060 OD0061 OD0062 OD0063

Cards: French

OJ0001 back and front OJ0002 OJ0003 OJ0004 OJ0005 OJ0006 OJ0007 OJ0008 OJ0009 OJ0010 OJ0011

OJ0012 OJ0013 OJ0014 OJ0016 OJ0017 OJ0018 OJ0019 OJ0020 OJ0021 OJ0022 OJ0023 OJ0024

OJ0025 OJ0026 OJ0027 OJ0028 OJ0029 OJ0030

CARDS: GAMESA

Sonrics

OD0064 OD0065 OD0066 OD0067 OD0068 OD0069 OD0070 OD0071 OD0072

OD0073 OD0074 OD0075 OD0076 OD0077 OD0078 OD0079 OD0080 OD0081

OD0082 OD0083 OD0084 OD0085 OD0086 OD0087 OD0088 OD0089 OD0090

OD0091 OD0092 OD0093 OD0094 OD0095 OD0096 OD0097 OD0098 OD0099

OD0100 OD0101 OD0102 OD0103 OD0104 OD0105 OD0106 OD0107 OD0108

OD0109 OD0110 OD0111 OD0112 OD0113 OD0114 OD0115 OD0116 OD0117

OD0118 OD0119 OD0120 OD0121 OD0122 OD0123 OD0124 OD0125

OJ0015 15 Bib Fortuna..1.75
OJ0016 16 Jabba the Hutt...1.75
OJ0017 17 Emperador Palpatine...............................1.75
OJ0018 18 Gamorrean Guard...................................1.75
OJ0019 19 Rancor...1.75
OJ0020 20 Boba Fett..1.75
OJ0021 21 R2-D2..1.75
OJ0022 22 Lando Calrissian......................................1.75
OJ0023 23 Han Solo..1.75
OJ0024 24 Princess Leia...1.75
OJ0025 25 Darth Vader...1.75
OJ0026 26 Tusken Raider..1.75
OJ0027 27 Jawa...1.75
OJ0028 28 C-3PO..1.75
OJ0029 29 Salacious Crumb......................................1.75
OJ0030 30 Ben (Obi-Wan) Kenobi..............................1.75

CARDS: GERMAN

Merlin Publishing Internat'l Ltd.
OK0001 001 Imperialer Sternenzerstorer......................1.35
OK0002 002 R2-D2 und C-3PO..................................1.35
OK0003 003 Rebellentruppen.....................................1.35
OK0004 004 Darth Vader..1.35
OK0005 005 C-3PO...1.35
OK0006 006 Sandraupenschlepper..............................1.35
OK0007 007 Sandsoldet auf Reitechse.........................1.35
OK0008 008 Luke Skywalker und Owen Lars..................1.35
OK0009 009 Luke, C-3PO und R2-D2............................1.35
OK0010 010 Tuskenrauber...1.35
OK0011 011 Luke Skywalker mit Laserschwart................1.35
OK0012 012 Todesstern und Sternenzerstorer.................1.35
OK0013 013 Landgleiter in Mos Eisley..........................1.35
OK0014 014 Luke, Ben und C-3PO mit Sturmsoldaten.......1.35
OK0015 015 Han Solo und Chewbacca.........................1.35
OK0016 016 Han Solo mit Jabba dem Hutten..................1.35
OK0017 017 Der Millennium Falke.................................1.35
OK0018 018 Prinzessin Leia mit Gouverneur Tarkin...........1.35
OK0019 019 Der Millennium Falke / innen......................1.35
OK0020 020 Anlegestelle des Todesstern.......................1.35
OK0021 021 Luke, Han und C-3PO...............................1.35
OK0022 022 Han Solo und Prinzessin Leia.....................1.35
OK0023 023 Ben Kenobi...1.35
OK0024 024 Der Millennium Falke.................................1.35
OK0025 025 Der Millennium Falke beim Anflug von Yavin 4.....1.35
OK0026 026 Han Solo mit Luke Skywalker......................1.35
OK0027 027 X-Flugeljager...1.35
OK0028 028 X-Flugeljager und Tie -Jager......................1.35
OK0029 029 Y-Flugeljager im Graben des Todesstern......1.35
OK0030 030 Darth Vader / Tie -Jager............................1.35
OK0031 031 Prinzessin Leia und C-3PO.........................1.35
OK0032 032 Luke Skywalker / X-Flugeljager...................1.35
OK0033 033 Abluftoffnung des Todesstern.....................1.35
OK0034 034 Luke, Leia und Han...................................1.35
OK0035 035 Han Solo zwinkert.....................................1.35
OK0036 036 Imperialer Sondendroide............................1.35
OK0037 037 Luke Skywaker in der Wampa-Hohle (same error as UK).......1.35
OK0038 038 Han Solo mit dem Rebellenkommandeur (actually Luke 37) 1.35
OK0039 039 Han Solo winkt Schneegleiter......................1.35
OK0040 040 Han Solo feuert auf Sondendroiden..............1.35
OK0041 041 Darth Vader mit General Veers......................1.35
OK0042 042 Luke Skywalker..1.35
OK0043 043 Schneegleiter / AT-AT-Beine........................1.35
OK0044 044 Der Millennium Falke beim Verlassen der Basis........1.35
OK0045 045 Der Falke fliegt in ein Asteroidenfeld ein..........1.35
OK0046 046 Explodierander Tie -Jager.............................1.35
OK0047 047 Yoda...1.35
OK0048 048 Luke und Yoda...1.35
OK0049 049 Millennium Falke und Sternenzerstorer............1.35
OK0050 050 Der Falke auf dem Sternenzerstorer..............1.35
OK0051 051 Im Cockpit des Millennium Falke....................1.35
OK0052 052 Ankunft der Rebellen in Bespin......................1.35
OK0053 053 Darth Vader foltert Han Solo.........................1.35
OK0054 054 Lukes X-Flugeljager beim Anflug auf Cloud City.....1.35
OK0055 055 Han Solo / Kohlenstoff-Gefrierkammer.............1.35
OK0056 056 Luke und Darth Vader beim Duell....................1.35
OK0057 057 Slave 1 verlasst Cloud City...........................1.35
OK0058 058 Darth Vader...1.35
OK0059 059 Luke Skywalker..1.35
OK0060 060 Luke Skywalker / Reaktorschacht....................1.35

OK0061 061 Luke und Vader beim Duell / Reaktorschacht.......1.35
OK0062 062 Darth Vader streckt Luke die Hand hin...........1.35
OK0063 063 Luke Skywalker..1.35
OK0064 064 Der Millennium Falke und Cloud City..............1.35
OK0065 065 R-D2 repariert C-3PO..................................1.35
OK0066 066 Luke / Frachtraum des Millennium Falken..........1.35
OK0067 067 Leia / Cockpit des Millennium Falken...............1.35
OK0068 068 Luke Skywalkers kunstliche Hand.....................1.35
OK0069 069 R2-D2 mit C-3PO.......................................1.35
OK0070 070 Luke, Leia, R2-D2 und C-3PO.........................1.35
OK0071 071 Fahre verlasst Sternenzerstorer.......................1.35
OK0072 072 Darth Vader mit Gouverneur Jerjerod...............1.35
OK0073 073 Jabbas Palast...1.35
OK0074 074 Jabba der Hutte...1.35
OK0075 075 Boushh der Kopfgeldjager.............................1.35
OK0076 076 Han Solos Karbonithulle platzt.......................1.35
OK0077 077 Luke mit Bib Fortuna...................................1.35
OK0078 078 Luke Skywalker im Griff des Rancor.................1.35
OK0079 079 Luke, Han und Chewbacca............................1.35
OK0080 080 Luke Skywalker..1.35
OK0081 081 Boba Fett...1.35
OK0082 082 Han Solo halt Lando....................................1.35
OK0083 083 C-3PO und Salacious Crumb...........................1.35
OK0084 084 Luke und Leia auf Jabbas Wustenschiff............1.35
OK0085 085 Imperator Palpatine....................................1.35
OK0086 086 Yoda unterweist Luke..................................1.35
OK0087 087 Mon Mothma und Admiral Ackbar....................1.35
OK0088 088 Raumfahre Tydirium / Cockpit.........................1.35
OK0089 089 Luke und Leia auf Speedbike..........................1.35
OK0090 090 Luke im Zweikampf mit Kundschafter................1.35
OK0091 091 Luke, Han und Chewie sind umzingelt................1.35
OK0092 092 Luke und Leia im Ewok-Dorf............................1.35
OK0093 093 Die Rebellenflotte.......................................1.35
OK0094 094 Vader und Luke vor dem Imperator...................1.35
OK0095 095 Ackbar beobachtet die Rebellenflotte................1.35
OK0096 096 Kampf uber dem Todesstern............................1.35
OK0097 097 Han bringt dem Sprengstoff an.........................1.35
OK0098 098 Der Todesstern feuert auf die Rebellen..............1.35
OK0099 099 Laserschwerter traffen aufeinander...................1.35
OK0100 100 Darth Vader ist besiegt................................1.35
OK0101 101 Der Imperator / Thronsaal.............................1.35
OK0102 102 Millennium Falken im Todesstern.....................1.35
OK0103 103 Anakin Skywalker.......................................1.35
OK0104 104 Der Todesstern explodiert............................1.35
OK0105 105 Anakin, Ben und Yoda.................................1.35
OK0106 106 Luke Skywalker...1.35
OK0107 107 Han Solo...1.35
OK0108 108 Leia Organa..1.35
OK0109 109 Obi-Wan Kenobi..1.35
OK0110 110 Chewbacca...1.35
OK0111 111 C-3PO...1.35
OK0112 112 R2-D2..1.35
OK0113 113 Darth Vader...1.35
OK0114 114 Yoda...1.35
OK0115 115 Boba Fett...1.35
OK0116 116 X-Flugeljager..1.35
OK0117 117 Todesstern...1.35
OK0118 118 Sandraupenschlepper....................................1.35
OK0119 119 Millennium Falke..1.35
OK0120 120 Tie -Jager...1.35
OK0121 121 Imperiale Raumfahre....................................1.35
OK0122 122 AT-AT..1.35
OK0123 123 Sternenzerstorer..1.35
OK0124 124 Darth Vaders Tie-Jager................................1.35
OK0125 125 Checkliste..1.35

CARDS: GIANT MOVIE PIN-UPS

Topps
VCB0001 Card #5: Star Wars...6.00
VCB0002 Card #8: The Empire Strikes Back........................6.00

CARDS: GREEK

LHA0201 front/back   LHA0044   LHA0058

Cards: Greek

LHA0062 163 Han and C-3PO in Hoth debris.................................1.50
LHA0063 164 Han in carbonite...1.50
LHA0064 165 X-Wing vs. Tie at Death Star..................................1.50
LHA0065 166 Darth chokes Captain Antilles................................1.50
LHA0066 167 Falcon under guard...1.50
LHA0067 168 Leia leans on Chewie...1.50
LHA0068 169 Preparing the snowspeeder...................................1.50
LHA0069 170 Preparing an X-Wing...1.50
LHA0070 171 Death star gunner...1.50
LHA0071 172 Chewie...1.50
LHA0072 173 Hoth commander..1.50
LHA0073 174 Sketch of Luke falling out window............................1.50
LHA0074 175 Jawas...1.50
LHA0075 176 C-3PO and R2 in Tatooine workshed.........................1.50
LHA0076 177 The Hoth trenches...1.50
LHA0077 178 Hoth battle ground..1.50
LHA0078 179 Hoth hangar..1.50
LHA0079 180 No description available.......................................1.50
LHA0080 181 Obi-Wan disables tractor beam..............................1.50
LHA0081 182 Hoth command center in disrepair..........................1.50
LHA0082 183 Hoth battle...1.50
LHA0083 184 Escaping a damaged snowspeeder.........................1.50
LHA0084 185 The Falcon..1.50
LHA0085 186 X-Wings...1.50
LHA0086 187 Trapped in a snowspeeder...................................1.50
LHA0087 188 Stormtroopers..1.50
LHA0088 189 Darth on Hoth..1.50
LHA0089 190 Luke and R2 on Cloud City...................................1.50
LHA0090 191 R2 and C-3PO...1.50
LHA0091 192 Star Trek character...1.50
LHA0092 193 AT-ATs...1.50
LHA0093 194 Sketch of snowspeeder downing an AT-AT..................1.50
LHA0094 195 Preparing to freeze Han......................................1.50
LHA0095 196 C-3PO and R2 on Tatooine...................................1.50
LHA0096 197 Hoth medical center..1.50
LHA0097 198 Captain Kirk...1.50
LHA0098 199 R2 in Tatooine canyon..1.50
LHA0099 200 No description available.......................................1.50
LHA0201 Unopened Packet of cards..12.00

CARDS: ITALIAN

Merlin Publishing Internat'l Ltd.
OL0001 001 Star Destroyer imperiale..2.00
OL0002 002 C1-P8 e D-3B0...2.00
OL0003 003 Forze Ribelli..2.00
OL0004 004 Darth Vader..2.00
OL0005 005 D-3B0...2.00
OL0006 006 Cingolato Jawa..2.00
OL0007 007 Assaltatore in sella al Dewback...............................2.00
OL0008 008 Luke Skywalker e Owen Lars..................................2.00
OL0009 009 Luke, D-3B0 e C1-P8...2.00
OL0010 010 Predone Tusken...2.00
OL0011 011 Luke Skywalker con la spada laser............................2.00
OL0012 012 La Morte Nera e la Star Destroyer............................2.00
OL0013 013 Il landspeeder a Mos Eisley....................................2.00
OL0014 014 Luke, Ben e D-3B0 con gli assaltatori.........................2.00
OL0015 015 Han Sole e Chewbacca...2.00
OL0016 016 Han Solo e Jabba de Hutt......................................2.00
OL0017 017 Il Millennium Falcon...2.00
OL0018 018 La principessa Leia con il Gran Moff Tarkin...................2.00
OL0019 019 Interno del Millennium Falcon..................................2.00
OL0020 020 L'hangar della Morte Nera.....................................2.00
OL0021 021 Luke, Han e D-3B0...2.00
OL0022 022 Han Solo e la principessa Leia.................................2.00
OL0023 023 Ben Kenobi...2.00
OL0024 024 Il Millennium Falcon...2.00
OL0025 025 Il Millennium Falcon si avvicina a Yavin 4....................2.00
OL0026 026 Han Solo con Luke Skywalker.................................2.00
OL0027 027 I caccia Ala-X..2.00
OL0028 028 I caccia Ala-X e I caccia Tie....................................2.00
OL0029 029 I caccia Alaa-Y nel canalone della Morte Nera................2.00
OL0030 030 Darth Vader / interno del caccia Tie..........................2.00
OL0031 031 La principessa Leia e D-3B0....................................2.00
OL0032 032 Luke Skywalker / interno dell'Ala-X...........................2.00
OL0033 033 La luce di scarico termico della Morte Nera..................2.00
OL0034 034 La sala del trano del tempio Massassi.........................2.00
OL0035 035 Han Solo che ammicca..2.00
OL0036 036 La robosonda imperiale...2.00
OL0037 037 Luke Skywalker nella tana del wampa (same error as UK)....2.00

OL0038 038 Han Solo con un commandante ribelle (37)...................2.00
OL0039 039 Han Solo saluta uno snowspeeder...........................2.00
OL0040 040 Han Solo spara alla robosonda................................2.00
OL0041 041 Darth Vader con il general Veers..............................2.00
OL0042 042 Luke Skywalker..2.00
OL0043 043 Snowspeeder / le gambe di un Camminatore................2.00
OL0044 044 Il Millennium Falcon lascia la base ribelle....................2.00
OL0045 045 Il Falcon entra in un campo di asteroidi......................2.00
OL0046 046 Il caccia Tie esplode..2.00
OL0047 047 Yoda..2.00
OL0048 048 Luke e Yoda...2.00
OL0049 049 Il Millennium Falcon e lo Star Destroyer.....................2.00
OL0050 050 Il Falcon attaccato allo Star Destroyer.......................2.00
OL0051 051 L'interno del Millennium Falcon...............................2.00
OL0052 052 I Ribelli arrivano a Bespin.....................................2.00
OL0053 053 Darth Vader tortura Han Solo.................................2.00
OL0054 054 L'Ala-X di Luke si avvicina a Cloud City......................2.00
OL0055 055 Han Solo / La camera di congelamento al carbonio..........2.00
OL0056 056 Il duello di Luke e Darth Vader...............................2.00
OL0057 057 Lo Slave I lascia Cloud City....................................2.00
OL0058 058 Darth Vader...2.00
OL0059 059 Luke Skywalker..2.00
OL0060 060 Luke Skywalker / Il pozzo del reattore.......................2.00
OL0061 061 Luke e Vader duellano / il pozzo del reattore................2.00
OL0062 062 Darth Vader incita Luke a seguirio...........................2.00
OL0063 063 Luke Skywalker..2.00
OL0064 064 Il Millennium Falcon e Cloud City.............................2.00
OL0065 065 C1-P8 ripara D-3B0...2.00
OL0066 066 Luke / la stiva del Millennium Falcon.........................2.00
OL0067 067 Leia / la cabina del Millennium Falcon........................2.00
OL0068 068 La mano bionica di Luke Skywalker...........................2.00
OL0069 069 C1-P8 e D-3B0...2.00
OL0070 070 Luke, Leia, C1-P8 e D-3B0.....................................2.00
OL0071 071 La navetta lascia lo Star Destroyer...........................2.00
OL0072 072 Darth Vader con il Gran Moff Jerjerrod.......................2.00
OL0073 073 Il palazzo di Jabba...2.00
OL0074 074 Jabbe de' Hutt..2.00
OL0075 075 Boushh, il cacciatore di taglie................................2.00
OL0076 076 Han Solo liberato dalla carbonite.............................2.00
OL0077 077 Luke con Bib Fortuna...2.00
OL0078 078 No description available...2.00
OL0079 079 Luke, Han e Chewbacca..2.00
OL0080 080 Luke Skywalker..2.00
OL0081 081 Boba Fett..2.00
OL0082 082 Han Solo cerca di raggiungere Lando........................2.00
OL0083 083 D-3B0 a Salacious Crumb......................................2.00
OL0084 084 Luke e Leia sul Galeone a Vela di Jabba.....................2.00
OL0085 085 L'Imperatore Galattico...2.00
OL0086 086 Yoda istruisce Luke..2.00
OL0087 087 Mon Mothma e l'Ammiraglio Ackbar.........................2.00
OL0088 088 La navetta Tydirium / la cabina di pilotaggio.................2.00
OL0089 089 Luke e Leia sulla speeder bike................................2.00
OL0090 090 Luke affronta un esploratore imperiale.......................2.00
OL0091 091 Luke, Han e Chewie circondati................................2.00
OL0092 092 Luke e Leia al villaggio Ewok.................................2.00
OL0093 093 La flotta ribelle...2.00
OL0094 094 Vader e Luke davanti all'Imperatore.........................2.00
OL0095 095 Ackbar osserva la flotta ribelle..............................2.00
OL0096 096 La battaglia intorno alla Morte Nera.........................2.00
OL0097 097 Han piazza della cariche esplosive...........................2.00
OL0098 098 La Morte Nera spara ai ribelli.................................2.00
OL0099 099 Scontro di spade laser...2.00
OL0100 100 Darth Vader viene sconfitto...................................2.00
OL0101 101 L'Imperatore / la sala del trono..............................2.00
OL0102 102 Millennium Falcon / interno della Morte Nera...............2.00
OL0103 103 Anakin Skywalker...2.00
OL0104 104 La Morte nera esplode...2.00
OL0105 105 Anakin, Ben e Yoda..2.00
OL0106 106 Luke Skywalker..2.00
OL0107 107 Han Solo...2.00
OL0108 108 Leia Organa..2.00
OL0109 109 Obi-Wan Kenobi...2.00
OL0110 110 Chewbacca...2.00
OL0111 111 D-3B0...2.00
OL0112 112 C1-P8...2.00
OL0113 113 Darth Vader..2.00
OL0114 114 Yoda..2.00
OL0115 115 Boba Fett..2.00
OL0116 116 Caccia Ala-X...2.00
OL0117 117 Morte Nera..2.00
OL0118 118 Cingolato Jawa...2.00

Cards: Italian

CARDS: JAPANESE

Topps

JPC0079 **JPC0080**

CARDS: MASTERVISION

Topps

OO0001 OO0002 OO0003 OO0004 OO0005 OO0006 OO0007 OO0008 OO0009 OO0010

OO0011 OO0012 OO0013 OO0014 OO0015 OO0016 OO0017 OO0018 OO0019 OO0020

OO0025 25 Ray Lago: In the Cave..2.00
OO0026 26 Ralph McQuarrie: Concept Art 2.00
OO0027 27 Bill Schmidt: Lando 2.00
OO0028 28 Ralph McQuarrie: Vader - Luke Battle 2.00
OO0029 29 Miran Kim: Luke 2.00
OO0030 30 Ralph McQuarrie: Cloud City Scene 2.00
OO0031 31 Frank Brunner: Rancor...2.00
OO0032 32 Ralph McQuarrie: Jabba's Palace 2.00
OO0033 33 Gene Lemery: Luke and Gamorreans 2.00
OO0034 34 Ralph McQuarrie: Skiff Scene 2.00
OO0035 35 Ken Barr: Characters 2.00
OO0036 36 Michael Whelan: Yoda Writes.....................................2.00
OO0037 Promo: AT-AT fires on Tauntaun rider, concept art 2.00
OO0038 Promo: Bounty Hunters 2.00
OO0039 Promo: SW Finest 2.00
OO0040 Promo: Vader and Emperor watch over Coruscant 2.00

CARDS: MISC.

Comic Images
CR10004 Card #29 of the "Lost Worlds by William Stout" set features Luke, his Tauntaun, and a fleet of Twin Pod Cloud Cars on Hoth; artwork for a Varese Sarabond record album of 1980.....................................9.00

Packaging Parodies
CR10019 Bar Wars parody 3.00

Runnin Bare QSL Cards

CR10006   CR10007   CR10010   CR10011   CR10012

CR10014   CR10015   CR10016   CR10017   CR10018

Flat-finished, 3"x5" cards.
CR10006 Story of SW: 01, Story of Star Wars title card 1.50
CR10007 Story of SW: 02, R2-D2 and C-3PO aboard cruiser 1.50
CR10008 Story of SW: 03, No description available 1.50
CR10008 Story of SW: 04, No description available 1.50
CR10010 Story of SW: 05, Darth Vader strangles cruiser Captain 1.50
CR10011 Story of SW: 06, Leia faces Vader aboard cruiser 1.50
CR10012 Story of SW: 07, Stormtrooper and Vader aboard cruiser 1.50
CR10013 Story of SW: 08, R2-D2 and C-3PO separate on Tatooine 1.50
CR10014 Story of SW: 09, Jawa captures R2-D2 ....1.50
CR10015 Story of SW: 10, C-3PO and R2-D2 reunited 1.50
CR10016 Story of SW: 11, Jawas prepare droids for inspection 1.50
CR10017 Story of SW: 12, Uncle Owen inspects C-3PO....................1.50
CR10018 Story of SW: 13, Uncle Owen's inspection continues 1.50

Sci-Fi Expo and Toy Show

CR10001 front and back   CR10002

CR10001 P1 Garrick Hagon (Biggs Darklighter)...12.00
CR10002 P2 Peter Mayhew (Chewbacca) 12.00

Topps
CR10003 Gummy Award card, limited to 1,000....................................23.00
CR10005 Married with Children Star Wars parody............................6.00

CARDS: MOVIE SHOTS

Movie Shots (Belgium)
OE0001 01 Vader Confronts Leia 1.60
OE0002 02 Jawas 1.60
OE0003 03 Sandtroopers and Dewback 1.60
OE0004 04 Luke Inspects R5-D4..1.60
OE0005 05 R2 and C-3PO 1.60
OE0006 06 R2 Hiding in the Cliffs 1.60
OE0007 07 Tusken Raider 1.60
OE0008 08 Awards Ceremony 1.60
OE0009 09 Luke on Tauntaun 1.60
OE0010 10 C-3PO and Hoth Droid 1.60
OE0011 11 AT-ATs 1.60
OE0012 12 X-Wing Approaches Dagobah 1.60
OE0013 13 Yoda 1.60
OE0014 14 Luke, Leia, and Droids Watch the Galaxy 1.60
OE0015 15 Jabba 1.60
OE0016 16 Vader Inspects the Troops 1.60
OE0017 17 Yoda 1.60
OE0018 18 Logray 1.60
OE0019 19 Vader and Luke Duel 1.60
OE0020 20 Nien Nunb and Lando in Falcon 1.60
OE0021 21 Purchasing the Droids 1.60
OE0022 22 The Cockpit of the Millennium Falcon 1.60
OE0023 23 C-3PO and Luke 1.60
OE0024 24 Luke and Leia Prepare to Swing 1.60
OE0025 25 Obi-Wan and Vader Duel 1.60
OE0026 26 Han and Chewbacca 1.60
OE0027 27 X-Wings Near Yavin 1.60
OE0028 28 Wampa 1.60
OE0029 29 Chewbacca in Hoth Hangar 1.60
OE0030 30 Han on Hoth 1.60
OE0031 31 Luke Gets Out of Snowspeeder 1.60
OE0032 32 Yoda and Luke Train 1.60
OE0033 33 Cloud City Landing Platform 1.60
OE0034 34 C-3PO 1.60
OE0035 35 Han Prepares to be Frozen 1.60
OE0036 36 Frozen Han 1.60
OE0037 37 C-3PO on Chewbacca's Back 1.60
OE0038 38 Leia, Chewbacca, and Droids 1.60
OE0039 39 Droids Approach Jabba's Palace 1.60
OE0040 40 R2 and C-3PO at Jabba's Door....................................1.60

OO0021   OO0022   OO0023   OO0024   OO0025   OO0026   OO0027   OO0028   OO0029   OO0030

OO0031   OO0032   OO0033   OO0034   OO0035   OO0036   OO0037   OO0038   OO0039   OO0040

Cards: Movie Shots

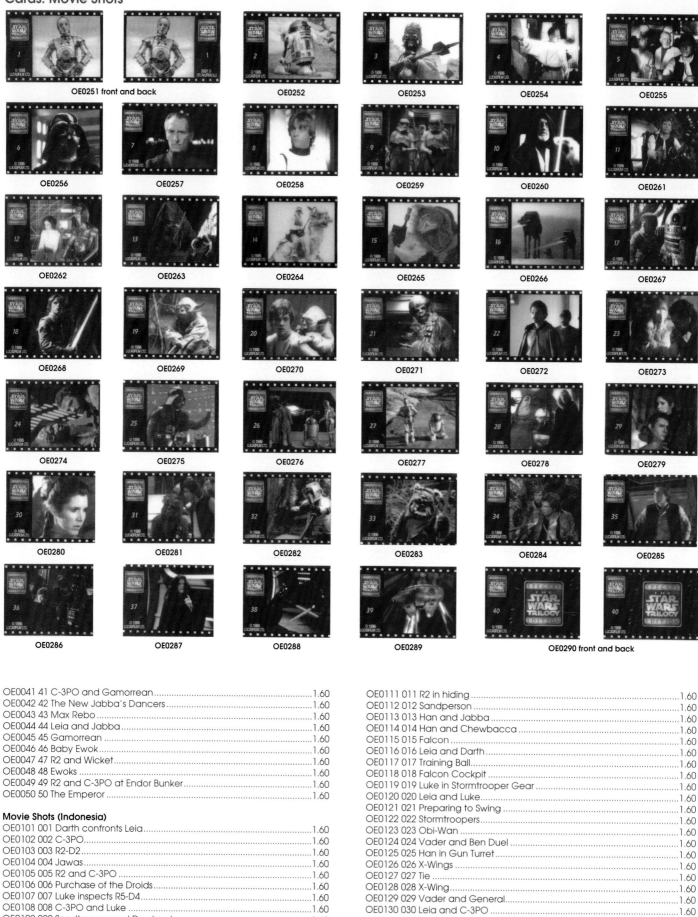

OE0251 front and back OE0252 OE0253 OE0254 OE0255

OE0256 OE0257 OE0258 OE0259 OE0260 OE0261

OE0262 OE0263 OE0264 OE0265 OE0266 OE0267

OE0268 OE0269 OE0270 OE0271 OE0272 OE0273

OE0274 OE0275 OE0276 OE0277 OE0278 OE0279

OE0280 OE0281 OE0282 OE0283 OE0284 OE0285

OE0286 OE0287 OE0288 OE0289 OE0290 front and back

OE0041 41 C-3PO and Gamorrean...1.60
OE0042 42 The New Jabba's Dancers 1.60
OE0043 43 Max Rebo 1.60
OE0044 44 Leia and Jabba 1.60
OE0045 45 Gamorrean 1.60
OE0046 46 Baby Ewok 1.60
OE0047 47 R2 and Wicket 1.60
OE0048 48 Ewoks 1.60
OE0049 49 R2 and C-3PO at Endor Bunker 1.60
OE0050 50 The Emperor 1.60

Movie Shots (Indonesia)
OE0101 001 Darth confronts Leia...1.60
OE0102 002 C-3PO 1.60
OE0103 003 R2-D2 ....1.60
OE0104 004 Jawas 1.60
OE0105 005 R2 and C-3PO 1.60
OE0106 006 Purchase of the Droids...1.60
OE0107 007 Luke inspects R5-D4..1.60
OE0108 008 C-3PO and Luke...1.60
OE0109 009 Sandtrooper and Dewback...1.60
OE0110 010 Luke and Lightsaber..1.60

OE0111 011 R2 in hiding 1.60
OE0112 012 Sandperson 1.60
OE0113 013 Han and Jabba 1.60
OE0114 014 Han and Chewbacca 1.60
OE0115 015 Falcon 1.60
OE0116 016 Leia and Darth...1.60
OE0117 017 Training Ball..1.60
OE0118 018 Falcon Cockpit 1.60
OE0119 019 Luke in Stormtrooper Gear 1.60
OE0120 020 Leia and Luke..1.60
OE0121 021 Preparing to Swing 1.60
OE0122 022 Stormtroopers..1.60
OE0123 023 Obi-Wan 1.60
OE0124 024 Vader and Ben Duel 1.60
OE0125 025 Han in Gun Turret 1.60
OE0126 026 X-Wings 1.60
OE0127 027 Tie 1.60
OE0128 028 X-Wing 1.60
OE0129 029 Vader and General..1.60
OE0130 030 Leia and C-3PO...1.60
OE0131 031 Vader's Tie in trench 1.60
OE0132 032 Tarkin...1.60

OE0133 033 Luke Skywalker 1.60
OE0134 034 Awards Ceremony 1.60
OE0135 035 Luke on Tauntaun Closeup 1.60
OE0136 036 Luke on Tauntaun 1.60
OE0137 037 Wampa (SE) 1.60
OE0138 038 Chewbacca in Hoth Hangar 1.60
OE0139 039 C-3PO and Hoth Droid 1.60
OE0140 040 Luke in Bacta 1.60
OE0141 041 Probot 1.60
OE0142 042 Han on Hoth 1.60
OE0143 043 Darth 1.60
OE0144 044 AT-ATs 1.60
OE0145 045 Hoth Battle Trench 1.60
OE0146 046 AT-ATs 1.60
OE0147 047 Luke Skywalker 1.60
OE0148 048 Snowtroopers 1.60
OE0149 049 X-Wing and Dagobah 1.60
OE0150 050 Luke and R2 1.60
OE0151 051 Yoda 1.60
OE0152 052 Luke in Cave 1.60
OE0153 053 Yoda 1.60
OE0154 054 Luke and Yoda 1.60
OE0155 055 Chewbacca 1.60
OE0156 056 Leia makes repairs 1.60
OE0157 057 Falcon at Cloud City 1.60
OE0158 058 Lando and others 1.60
OE0159 059 Lando and Leia 1.60
OE0160 060 C-3PO and Chewbacca 1.60
OE0161 061 Han prepares for freezing 1.60
OE0162 062 Frozen Han 1.60
OE0163 063 Luke 1.60
OE0164 064 Vader reaches out 1.60
OE0165 065 C-3PO and Chewbacca 1.60
OE0166 066 Escaping Cloud City 1.60
OE0167 067 Luke, Leia and Droids 1.60
OE0168 068 Vader 1.60
OE0169 069 C-3PO and R2 1.60
OE0170 070 At Jabba's Door 1.60
OE0171 071 C-3PO and Gamorrean 1.60
OE0172 072 Jabba 1.60
OE0173 073 Han and Leia 1.60
OE0174 074 Lando and Leia 1.60
OE0175 075 Jabba 1.60
OE0176 076 Max Rebo 1.60
OE0177 077 Gamorrean Guard 1.60
OE0178 078 Gamorrean Guard 1.60
OE0179 079 Leia 1.60
OE0180 080 Han and Chewbacca 1.60
OE0181 081 Darth Vader 1.60
OE0182 082 Yoda 1.60
OE0183 083 Imperial Biker Scout 1.60
OE0184 084 Wicket 1.60
OE0185 085 Han and Ewoks 1.60
OE0186 086 Logray 1.60
OE0187 087 Baby Ewok 1.60
OE0188 088 Wicket and R2 1.60
OE0189 089 Luke and Vader 1.60
OE0190 090 Emperor 1.60
OE0191 091 Luke and Vader Duel 1.60
OE0192 092 Luke 1.60
OE0193 093 Y-Wing Pilot 1.60
OE0194 094 Nien Nunb and Lando 1.60
OE0195 095 Han and Leia 1.60
OE0196 096 Leia, Han and Stormtroopers 1.60
OE0197 097 Ewoks 1.60
OE0198 098 R2 and C-3PO at Bunker 1.60
OE0199 099 AT-ST 1.60
OE0200 100 Millennium Falcon 1.60

Movie Shots (Mexico)

OE0251 01 C-3PO 1.00
OE0252 02 R2-D2 1.00
OE0253 03 Tusken Raider 1.00
OE0254 04 Luke in Ben's hut 1.00
OE0255 05 Luke, Ben, and Han in Falcon cockpit 1.00
OE0256 06 Darth Vader 1.00
OE0257 07 Grand Moff Tarkin 1.00
OE0258 08 Luke in Stormtrooper disguise 1.00
OE0259 09 Stormtroopers 1.00
OE0260 10 Obi-Wan Kenobi 1.00
OE0261 11 Han Solo 1.00
OE0262 12 Princess Leia and C-3PO in Yavin war room 1.00
OE0263 13 Vader and wingman in Death Star trench 1.00
OE0264 14 Luke on Tauntaun 1.00
OE0265 15 Han on Hoth 1.00
OE0266 16 AT-AT attack 1.00
OE0267 17 Luke and R2-D2 on Dagobah 1.00
OE0268 18 Luke in Dagobah cave 1.00
OE0269 19 Yoda 1.00
OE0270 20 Luke and Yoda 1.00
OE0271 21 Chewbacca 1.00
OE0272 22 Lando Calrissian 1.00
OE0273 23 Leia and Lando 1.00
OE0274 24 Lando and carbon-frozen Han 1.00
OE0275 25 Vader on Bespin gantry 1.00
OE0276 26 Luke, Leia, R2-D2, C3PO 1.00
OE0277 27 C-3PO and R2-D2 on Tatooine 1.00
OE0278 28 Jabba and Bib Fortuna 1.00
OE0279 29 Leia and Han in Jabba's palace 1.00
OE0280 30 Princess Leia 1.00
OE0281 31 Han and Chewbacca 1.00
OE0282 32 Imperial Scout trooper 1.00
OE0283 33 Wicket the Ewok 1.00
OE0284 34 Ewoks capture the heroes 1.00
OE0285 35 Han in Endor bunker 1.00
OE0286 36 Vader and Luke 1.00
OE0287 37 Emperor Palpatine 1.00
OE0288 38 Vader and Luke duel 1.00
OE0289 39 Falcon inside second Death Star 1.00
OE0290 40 Special Edition logo 1.00

Movie Shots (Netherlands)

OE0051 01 Vader and Leia 1.60
OE0052 02 Jawas 1.60
OE0053 03 Stormtroopers and Dewback 1.60
OE0054 04 Looking at the Droids 1.60
OE0055 05 Luke inspects R5D4 1.60
OE0056 06 R2 and C-3PO 1.60
OE0057 07 R2 in Hiding 1.60
OE0058 08 Tusken Raider 1.60
OE0059 09 Millennium Falcon Cockpit 1.60
OE0060 10 Luke and C-3PO 1.60
OE0061 11 Luke and Leia 1.60
OE0062 12 Vader and Ben Duel 1.60
OE0063 13 Han and Chewbacca 1.60
OE0064 14 X-Wing Formation 1.60
OE0065 15 Awards Ceremony 1.60
OE0066 16 Luke on Tauntaun 1.60
OE0067 17 Wampa 1.60
OE0068 18 Chewbacca in Hoth Hangar 1.60
OE0069 19 C-3PO and Hoth Droid 1.60
OE0070 20 Han on Hoth w/Blaster 1.60
OE0071 21 AT-ATs 1.60
OE0072 22 Luke / Snowspeeder 1.60
OE0073 23 X-Wing Approaches Dagobah 1.60
OE0074 24 Yoda 1.60
OE0075 25 Luke and Yoda 1.60
OE0076 26 Arriving at Cloud City 1.60
OE0077 27 Chewbacca and Most of C-3PO 1.60
OE0078 28 Han Being Readied for Carbon Freezing 1.60
OE0079 29 A Frozen Han 1.60
OE0080 30 Chewbacca w/C-3PO 1.60
OE0081 31 Leia, Droids, and Chewbacca at Cloud City 1.60
OE0082 32 Watching the Galaxy 1.60
OE0083 33 Droids Approaching Jabba's Palace 1.60
OE0084 34 Jabba 1.60
OE0085 35 Droids at the Door 1.60
OE0086 36 C-3PO and Gamorrean 1.60
OE0087 37 The New Dancers 1.60
OE0088 38 Max Rebo 1.60
OE0089 39 Jabba and Leia 1.60
OE0090 40 Gamorrean Guard 1.60
OE0091 41 Darth Vader 1.60
OE0092 42 Yoda 1.60
OE0093 43 Ewoks 1.60
OE0094 44 Baby Ewok 1.60
OE0095 45 R2 and Wicket 1.60
OE0096 46 Ewoks 1.60
OE0097 47 R2 and C-3PO 1.60
OE0098 48 The Emperor 1.60
OE0099 49 Luke and Vader Duel 1.60
OE0100 50 Lando and Nien Nub on Falcon 1.60

Cards: Movie Shots

Movie Shots (Spain)

OE0201 01 Vader and Leia 1.60
OE0202 02 Jawas 1.60
OE0203 03 Stormtroopers and Dewback 1.60
OE0204 04 Looking at the Droids 1.60
OE0205 05 Luke inspects R5D4 ....1.60
OE0206 06 R2 and C-3PO 1.60
OE0207 07 R2 in Hiding 1.60
OE0208 08 Tusken Raider 1.60
OE0209 09 Millennium Falcon Cockpit 1.60
OE0210 10 Luke and C-3PO 1.60
OE0211 11 Luke and Leia 1.60
OE0212 12 Vader and Ben Duel 1.60
OE0213 13 Han and Chewbacca 1.60
OE0214 14 X-Wing Formation 1.60
OE0215 15 Awards Ceremony 1.60
OE0216 16 Luke on Tauntaun 1.60
OE0217 17 Wampa 1.60
OE0218 18 Chewbacca in Hoth Hangar 1.60
OE0219 19 C-3PO and Hoth Droid 1.60
OE0220 20 Han on Hoth w/Blaster 1.60
OE0221 21 AT-ATs 1.60
OE0222 22 Luke / Snowspeeder 1.60
OE0223 23 X-Wing Approaches Dagobah 1.60
OE0224 24 Yoda 1.60
OE0225 25 Luke and Yoda 1.60
OE0226 26 Arriving at Cloud City 1.60
OE0227 27 Chewbacca and Most of C-3PO 1.60
OE0228 28 Han Being Readied for Carbon Freezing 1.60
OE0229 29 A Frozen Han 1.60
OE0230 30 Chewbacca w/C-3PO 1.60
OE0231 31 Leia, Droids and Chewbacca at Cloud City 1.60
OE0232 32 Watching the Galaxy 1.60
OE0233 33 Droids Approaching Jabba's Palace 1.60
OE0234 34 Jabba 1.60
OE0235 35 Droids at the Door 1.60
OE0236 36 C-3PO and Gamorrean 1.60
OE0237 37 The New Dancers 1.60
OE0238 38 Max Rebo 1.60
OE0239 39 Jabba and Leia 1.60
OE0240 40 Gamorrean Guard 1.60
OE0241 41 Darth Vader 1.60
OE0242 42 Yoda 1.60
OE0243 43 Ewoks 1.60
OE0244 44 Baby Ewok 1.60
OE0245 45 R2 and Wicket 1.60
OE0246 46 Ewoks 1.60

OE0247 47 R2 and C-3PO 1.60
OE0248 48 The Emperor 1.60
OE0249 49 Luke and Vader Duel 1.60
OE0250 50 Lando and Nien Nub on Falcon 1.60

CARDS: MOVIE SHOTS, TPM

Pelis

CME0001 01 Watto 1.00
CME0002 02 Obi-Wan on Queen's starship 1.00
CME0003 03 Jar Jar in custody 1.00
CME0004 04 Gungan submarine 1.00
CME0005 05 Anakin in podracer 1.00
CME0006 06 Darth Maul and Obi-Wan duel 1.00
CME0007 07 Watto and Qui-Gon 1.00
CME0008 08 The Jedi at Trade Federation window 1.00
CME0009 09 Godzilla-like Sea Monster 1.00
CME0010 10 Yoda 1.00
CME0011 11 Sebulba 1.00
CME0012 12 R2-D2 ....1.00
CME0013 13 Jar Jar gets zapped 1.00
CME0014 14 Captain Tarpals 1.00
CME0015 15 Anakin in podracer 1.00
CME0016 16 Jar Jar on Queen's starship 1.00
CME0017 17 Opee sea monster 1.00
CME0018 18 C-3PO 1.00
CME0019 19 Neimoidians 1.00
CME0020 20 Anakin in Naboo fighter 1.00
CME0021 21 Obi-Wan and Qui-Gon in Gungan City 1.00
CME0022 22 Darth Maul in hologram 1.00
CME0023 23 Queen Amidala (black outfit) 1.00
CME0024 24 Naboo's capital 1.00
CME0025 25 Boss Nass at ruined temple 1.00
CME0026 26 Darth Maul on Tattooine 1.00
CME0027 27 Qui-Gon Jinn 1.00
CME0028 28 Jar Jar and Amidala kneel before Boss Nass 1.00
CME0029 29 Queen's starship in hologram 1.00
CME0030 30 Jabba the Hutt 1.00
CME0031 31 Sebulba confronts Jar Jar 1.00
CME0032 32 Podracer 1.00
CME0033 33 Jedi and Maul duel 1.00
CME0034 34 Jar Jar and Anakin 1.00
CME0035 35 Qui-Gon Jinn on Tattooine 1.00
CME0036 36 Gungans emerge from the mist 1.00
CME0037 37 Battle Droid Commander 1.00
CME0038 38 Battle Droids 1.00

CME0001   CME0002   CME0003   CME0004   CME0005   CME0006   CME0007   CME0008

CME0009   CME0010   CME0011   CME0012   CME0013   CME0014   CME0015   CME0016

CME0017   CME0018   CME0019   CME0020   CME0021   CME0022   CME0023   CME0024

CME0025   CME0026   CME0027   CME0028   CME0029   CME0030   CME0031   CME0032

CME0033   CME0034   CME0035   CME0036   CME0037   CME0038   CME0039   CME0040

CME0039 39 Jar Jar and Obi-Wan meet 1.00
CME0040 40 Maul on Sith speeder 1.00

CARDS: PILOT LICENSES

| OVZ0001 | OVZ0002 | OVZ0003 | OVZ0004 | OVZ0005 |

OVZ0001 Chewbacca 8.00
OVZ0003 Darth Vader 8.00
OVZ0002 Han Solo 8.00
OVZ0004 Luke Skywalker 8.00
OVZ0005 Obi-Wan Kenobi 8.00

CARDS: PREMIUMS

PRM0001 sheets 1, 2, 3

Burger King

PRM0001 6-Card sheet, uncut...................................8.00
PRM0002 Battle of the Lightsabers............................1.30
PRM0003 Cantina Denizens...................................1.30
PRM0004 Captured by the Jawas.............................1.30
PRM0005 Chase Through the Asteroids.....................1.30
PRM0006 Darth Vader and Boba Fett.......................1.30
PRM0007 Droids Inside the Rebel Base.....................1.30
PRM0008 Flight of the Millennium Falcon..................1.30
PRM0009 Han and Chewie Mean Business..................1.30
PRM0010 Han Solo in Action..................................1.30
PRM0011 Imperial Stormtrooper..............................1.30
PRM0012 Jawas of Tatooine...................................1.30
PRM0013 Jedi Warrior Ben Kenobi..........................1.30
PRM0014 Luke Disguised as a Stormtrooper..............1.30
PRM0015 Luke Instructed by Yoda...........................1.30
PRM0016 Luke's Training.......................................1.30
PRM0017 One of the Sandpeople.............................1.30
PRM0018 Princess Leia Organa...............................1.30
PRM0019 Pursued by the Empire.............................1.30
PRM0020 R2-D2 and C-3PO...................................1.30
PRM0021 Raid on the Death Star.............................1.30
PRM0022 Search for the Droids...............................1.30
PRM0023 Seduced by the Dark Side.........................1.30
PRM0024 Snowswept Chewbacca............................1.30
PRM0025 Space Adventurer Han Solo.......................1.30

PRM0026 Star Pilots Prepare for Battle.......................1.30
PRM0027 Star Pilots Prepare for Battle.......................1.30
PRM0028 Stormtrooper Attack..................................1.30
PRM0029 The Bounty Hunters.................................1.30
PRM0030 The Dark Lord of the Sith...........................1.30
PRM0031 The Dashing Han Solo...............................1.30
PRM0032 The Defenders of Freedom.........................1.30
PRM0033 The Imperial Snow Walkers........................1.30
PRM0034 The Wonderful Droid, R2-D2........................1.30
PRM0035 Weird Cantina Patrons..............................1.30
PRM0036 Yoda on Dagobah....................................1.30
PRM0037 Yoda, the Jedi Master...............................1.30

Confection Concepts

PRM0038 ANH 01 Luke's landspeeder on the plains of Tatooine 1.00
PRM0039 ANH 02 Vader enters the blockade runner 1.00
PRM0040 ANH 03 Leia gives Death Star plans to R2 ....1.00
PRM0041 ANH 04 No description available 1.00
PRM0042 ANH 05 Jawas with R2 ....1.00
PRM0043 ANH 06 The Jawa's sandcrawler. 1.00
PRM0044 ANH 07 Luke inspects the droids for sale 1.00
PRM0045 ANH 08 Artoo with C-3PO 1.00
PRM0046 ANH 09 Luke plays with model skyhopper 1.00
PRM0047 ANH 10 R2-D2 is found by Luke and C-3PO in a rock canyon ...1.00
PRM0048 ANH 11 Sandtrooper riding a dewback 1.00
PRM0049 ANH 12 Sandtroopers scan the Tatooine desert 1.00
PRM0050 ANH 13 Threepio "I don't think I can make it. You go on, Master Luke. There's no sense in you risking yourself on my account. I'm done for." 1.00
PRM0051 ANH 14 The recorded image of the beautiful Rebel Princess Leia is projected from Artoo's face. 1.00
PRM0052 ANH 15 Imperial sandtrooper with probe droid 1.00
PRM0053 ANH 16 Overlooking Mos Eisley spaceport 1.00
PRM0054 ANH 17 Luke's landspeeder approaches Mos Eisley 1.00
PRM0055 ANH 18 Luke, Ben, R2-D2, and C-3PO arrive at Mos Eisley ..1.00
PRM0056 ANH 19 The main street of Mos Eisley 1.00
PRM0057 ANH 20 Luke's landspeeder is stopped by sandtroopers ...1.00
PRM0058 ANH 21 R2 and C-3PO watch as sandtroopers question locals.1.00
PRM0059 ANH 22 A swoop startles a ronto 1.00
PRM0060 ANH 23 ASP droid on front of Rebel transport 1.00
PRM0061 ANH 24 Patrons inside a cantina at Mos Eisley 1.00
PRM0062 ANH 25 Ben and Luke talk to Han 1.00
PRM0063 ANH 26 Docking Bay 94................................1.00
PRM0064 ANH 27 Jabba confronts Han Solo 1.00
PRM0065 ANH 28 Interior of the Falcon's cockpit..................1.00
PRM0066 ANH 29 Princess Leia watches the destruction of Alderaan 1.00
PRM0067 ANH 30 Obi-Wan feels a disturbance in the force.........1.00
PRM0068 ANH 31 Luke in stormtrooper disguise 1.00
PRM0069 ANH 32 Princess Leia in her cell 1.00

| PRM0088 | PRM0089 | PRM0090 | PRM0091 | PRM0092 | PRM0093 |

| PRM0094 | PRM0095 | PRM0096 | PRM0097 | PRM0098 | PRM0099 | PRM0100 | PRM0101 | PRM0102 | PRM0103 | PRM0104 | PRM0105 | PRM0106 |

| PRM0107 | PRM0108 | PRM0109 | PRM0110 | PRM0111 | PRM0112 | PRM0113 | PRM0114 | PRM0115 | PRM0116 | PRM0117 | PRM0118 | PRM0119 |

| PRM0120 | PRM0121 | PRM0122 | PRM0123 | PRM0124 | PRM0125 | PRM0126 | PRM0127 | PRM0128 | PRM0129 | PRM0130 | PRM0131 | PRM0132 |

Cards: Premiums

PRM0070 ANH 33 R2-D2 and C-3PO aboard blockade runner 1.00
PRM0071 ANH 34 Han and Luke scan the garbage room of the Death Star for a way out 1.00
PRM0072 ANH 35 Princess Leia returns laserfire to the stormtroopers as Luke works with a thin nylon cable from his trooper utility belt. 1.00
PRM0073 ANH 36 Luke, Han, Chewbacca, and Leia in a hallway outside the Death Star garbage room. 1.00
PRM0074 ANH 37 No description available...1.00
PRM0075 ANH 38 In the hallway of the Death Star ... Darth Vader and Ben Kenobi continue their powerful lightsaber duel. 1.00
PRM0076 ANH 39 "The Force is what gives the Jedi his power. . ." 1.00
PRM0077 ANH 40 Han Solo and Chewbacca fend off stormtroopers.......1.00
PRM0078 ANH 41 Yavin Sentry 1.00
PRM0079 ANH 42 R2 is hoisted into Luke's X-Wing 1.00
PRM0080 ANH 43 Luke and R2 head into battle...................................1.00
PRM0081 ANH 44 Princess Leia listens to the battle 1.00
PRM0082 ANH 45 X-Wing fighters fly in formation past Yavin.....................1.00
PRM0083 ANH 46 Rebel X-Wing fighter and Imperial Tie fighter in the shadow of the Death Star. 1.00
PRM0084 ANH 47 Darth Vader is escorted by two Imperial Tie fighters. 1.00
PRM0085 ANH 48 No description available...1.00
PRM0086 ANH 49 Rebel awards ceremony...1.00
PRM0087 ANH 50 Princess Leia presents the awards..............................1.00
PRM0088 ESB 01 Luke on Tauntaun notices something in the sky.............0.85
PRM0089 ESB 02 C-3PO and R2-D2 head to the main hangar deck of the rebel base 0.85
PRM0090 ESB 03 The wampa eats a meal...0.85
PRM0091 ESB 04 Princess Leia and C-3PO anxiously wait for a signal from Han 0.85
PRM0092 ESB 05 Han Solo braves the hostile landscape of Hoth searching for Luke 0.85
PRM0093 ESB 06 Han attempts to revive Luke..0.85
PRM0094 ESB 07 Luke receives medical attention 0.85
PRM0095 ESB 08 Leia and 2-1B oversee Luke's recovery...........................0.85
PRM0096 ESB 09 Han Solo targets an Imperial probe droid 0.85
PRM0097 ESB 10 An Imperial probe droid is destroyed by Han Solo............0.85
PRM0098 ESB 11 The rebel fortification receives irreparable damage 0.85
PRM0099 ESB 12 General Rieekan monitors the computer screens of the command center 0.85
PRM0100 ESB 13 Snowspeeders attempt to defend the rebel base 0.85
PRM0101 ESB 14 Luke scrambles from his crippled snowspeeder.............0.85
PRM0102 ESB 15 Darth Vader searches the now destroyed rebel base.......0.85
PRM0103 ESB 16 Luke's X-Wing speeds towards the planet Dagobah....0.85
PRM0104 ESB 17 Luke cautiously surveys the planet Dagobah 0.85
PRM0105 ESB 18 R2-D2 is ejected from the murky swamp by a bog beast..0.85
PRM0106 ESB 19 Luke discusses his search for a great warrior 0.85
PRM0107 ESB 20 Yoda's small home radiates a small glow......................0.85
PRM0108 ESB 21 Luke is pleasantly surprised by the meal of rootleaf........0.85
PRM0109 ESB 22 Under training from Yoda, Luke pushes deeper into the tree cave 0.85
PRM0110 ESB 23 Yoda's deceptive features conceal his Jedi abilities.......0.85
PRM0111 ESB 24 With guidance from Yoda, Luke explores the Force 0.85
PRM0112 ESB 25 Yoda instructs Luke during physical training...................0.85
PRM0113 ESB 26 Luke, sensing his friends are in danger, leaves Dagobah0.85
PRM0114 ESB 27 The Millennium Falcon evades attack from the Imperial forces...0.85
PRM0115 ESB 28 Han Solo repairs the Falcon yet again 0.85
PRM0116 ESB 29 Imperial Tie fighters pursue the Falcon 0.85
PRM0117 ESB 30 C-3PO interrupts an intimate moment 0.85
PRM0118 ESB 31 Darth Vader briefs the bounty hunters 0.85
PRM0119 ESB 32 IG-88 and Boba Fett prepare to track the Falcon 0.85
PRM0120 ESB 33 New shots of the Falcon and cloud cars 0.85
PRM0121 ESB 34 Visitors to Cloud City 0.85
PRM0122 ESB 35 Lando Calrissian welcomes everyone to Cloud City.......0.85
PRM0123 ESB 36 Betrayed by Lando, Han finds himself face to face with Darth Vader 0.85
PRM0124 ESB 37 Han is tortured 0.85
PRM0125 ESB 38 Chewbacca reassembles C-3PO 0.85
PRM0126 ESB 39 A coffin-like, carbon-frozen Han Solo 0.85
PRM0127 ESB 40 Lando checks to see that Han is in perfect hibernation .0.85
PRM0128 ESB 41 Princess Leia warns Luke of Darth's trap 0.85
PRM0129 ESB 42 Lightsaber in hand, Luke battles with Darth Vader..........0.85
PRM0130 ESB 43 Luke confronts Vader..0.85
PRM0131 ESB 44 Darth beckons Luke to the Dark Side 0.85
PRM0132 ESB 45 Luke awaits rescue, clinging to the weather vane 0.85

Doritos
3D Motion Discs.
PRM0133 01-Darth Vader and Grand Moff Tarkin 1.25
PRM0134 02-Princess Leia 1.25

PRM0135 03-Luke with Blastshield Helmet...1.25
PRM0136 04-Ben Kenobi...1.25
PRM0137 05-Luke and Leia Swinging 1.25
PRM0138 06-Stormtroopers..1.25
PRM0139 07-Obi-Wan Kenobi..1.25
PRM0140 08-Tie Fighter...1.25
PRM0141 09-Lobot..1.25
PRM0142 10-Wicket the Ewok..1.25
PRM0143 11-Han Solo..1.25
PRM0144 12-AT-ST..1.25
PRM0145 13-Emperor and Luke..1.25
PRM0146 14-Lando Calrissian..1.25
PRM0147 15-Exploding Tie Fighter..1.25
PRM0148 16-B-Wing Pilot..1.25
PRM0149 17-Princess Leia and R2-D2 ....1.25
PRM0150 18-Boba Fett and Luke on Bespin...1.25
PRM0151 19-Luke (X-Wing) and Han Solo..1.25
PRM0152 20-Wedge...1.25

Doritos/Chee-tos
3D Motion Cards.

PRM0153   PRM0154   PRM0155   PRM0156

PRM0157   PRM0158   PRM0159   PRM0160

PRM0153 01-Falcon Cockpit 1.25
PRM0154 02-Lightsaber Duel 1.25
PRM0155 03-X-Wing Fighter 1.25
PRM0156 04-Space Battle...1.25
PRM0157 05-Imperial Shuttle...1.25
PRM0158 06-Han Solo...1.25
PRM0159 Bonus: Leia and C-3PO 1.25
PRM0160 Bonus: Luke and Boba Fett...1.25

General Mills

PRM0161   PRM0162   PRM0170

PRM0171   PRM0173   PRM0174

PRM0176 front and back   PRM0177

Cards 1-6 yellow, 7-12 blue, 13-18 red bordered.
PRM0161 01 Rebels...2.00
PRM0162 02 Artoo-Detoo 2.00
PRM0163 03 Obi-Wan Kenobi and Darth Vader......................................2.00
PRM0164 04 R2-D2 and C-3PO 2.00
PRM0165 05 Han Solo and Chewbacca 2.00
PRM0166 06 See-Threepio and Luke 2.00
PRM0167 07 Sandperson...2.00

PRM0168 08 Ben Kenobi and Luke 2.00
PRM0169 09 X-wing fighter and Tie fighter...............................2.00
PRM0170 10 Luke Skywalker 2.00
PRM0171 11 Han Solo 2.00
PRM0172 12 Luke Skywalker 2.00
PRM0173 13 Princess Leia..2.00
PRM0174 14 Rebel Squadron 2.00
PRM0175 15 Darth Vader 2.00
PRM0176 16 Stormtroopers 2.00
PRM0177 17 Jawas 2.00
PRM0178 18 Princess Leia and C-3PO 2.00

Kellogg
PRM0179 AT-ATs on Hoth...2.00
PRM0180 Boba Fett 2.00
PRM0181 C-3PO 2.00
PRM0182 Chewbacca 2.00
PRM0183 Darth Vader 2.00
PRM0184 Emperor Palpatine 2.00
PRM0185 Han in Carbonite 2.00
PRM0186 Jabba the Hutt 2.00
PRM0187 Lando Calrissian 2.00
PRM0188 Leia as Jabba Prisoner 2.00
PRM0189 Luke 2.00
PRM0190 Obi-Wan Kenobi 2.00
PRM0191 R2-D2 ....2.00
PRM0192 Shuttle Tyderium Cockpit 2.00
PRM0193 SOTE Artwork (Black Sun Emblem) 2.00
PRM0194 SOTE Artwork (Leia and Boba Fett).............................2.00
PRM0195 SOTE Artwork (Novel Cover) 2.00
PRM0196 SOTE Artwork (Prince Xizor) 2.00
PRM0197 X-Wings in Space 2.00

Quality Bakers

PRM0208 | PRM0209 | PRM0210 | PRM0211 | PRM0212
PRM0213 | PRM0214 | PRM0215 | PRM0216 | PRM0217

PRM0208 01 R2-D2 ....1.15
PRM0209 02 Han Solo 1.15
PRM0210 03 Princess Leia..1.15
PRM0211 04 Chewbacca 1.15
PRM0212 05 Darth Vader 1.15
PRM0213 06 Boba Fett 1.15
PRM0214 07 C-3PO 1.15
PRM0215 08 Obi-Wan Kenobi 1.15
PRM0216 09 Yoda 1.15
PRM0217 10 Luke Skywalker 1.15

Sonrics
PRM0218 01 Scout Walker..1.80
PRM0219 02 Bantha..1.80
PRM0220 03 Biker Scout 1.80
PRM0221 04 Boba Fett 1.80
PRM0222 05 Gamorrean Guard 1.80
PRM0223 06 Probe Droid..1.80
PRM0224 07 Lobot 1.80
PRM0225 08 No description available..1.80
PRM0226 09 Luke Skywalker 1.80
PRM0227 10 Jawa 1.80
PRM0228 11 C-3PO 1.80
PRM0229 12 R2-D2 - C-3PO 1.80
PRM0230 13 R2-D2 ....1.80

PRM0231 14 R5-D4 ....1.80
PRM0232 15 Sand People 1.80
PRM0233 16 Storm Trooper 1.80
PRM0234 17 Ugnaught 1.80
PRM0235 18 Yoda 1.80
PRM0236 19 No description available..1.80
PRM0237 20 Storm Trooper 1.80
PRM0238 21 Boba Fett 1.80
PRM0239 22 Chewbacca 1.80
PRM0240 23 Darth Vader 1.80
PRM0241 24 Star Destroyer 1.80
PRM0242 25 No description available..1.80
PRM0243 26 No description available..1.80
PRM0244 27 B-Wing Fighter 1.80
PRM0245 28 No description available..1.80
PRM0246 29 Tie Fighter 1.80
PRM0247 30 Transbordador Imperial (shuttle) 1.80
PRM0248 Hoth 1 cutaway scene Hoth..4.00
PRM0249 Hoth 2 cutaway scene Hoth..3.00
PRM0250 Hoth 3 cutaway scene Hoth..3.00
PRM0251 Sarlacc 1 cutaway scene Sarlacc................................4.00
PRM0252 Sarlacc 2 cutaway scene Sarlacc................................3.00
PRM0253 Sarlacc 3 cutaway scene Sarlacc................................3.00

Topps
PRM0254 01 Darth Vader 1.50
PRM0255 02 Han and Chewbacca 1.50
PRM0256 03 Yoda 1.50
PRM0257 04 Luke in Gun Turret 1.50
PRM0258 05 Boba Fett 1.50
PRM0259 06 R2-D2 ....1.50
PRM0260 07 Obi-Wan Kenobi 1.50
PRM0261 08 C-3PO 1.50
PRM0262 09 Princess Leia..1.50
PRM0263 10 Admiral Ackbar 1.50

Wonder Bread

PRM0265 | PRM0266 | PRM0267 | PRM0268
PRM0269 | PRM0270 | PRM0271 | PRM0272
PRM0273 | PRM0274 | PRM0275 | PRM0276
PRM0277 | PRM0278 | PRM0279 | PRM0280

Cards: Premiums

PRM0265 01 Luke Skywalker 2.00
PRM0266 02 Ben (Obi-Wan) Kenobi 2.00
PRM0267 03 Princess Leia Organa 2.00
PRM0268 04 Han Solo 2.00
PRM0269 05 Darth Vader...2.00
PRM0270 06 Grand Moff Tarkin 2.00
PRM0271 07 See-Threepio 2.00
PRM0272 08 Artoo-Deetoo 2.00
PRM0273 09 Chewbacca 2.00
PRM0274 10 Jawas 2.00
PRM0275 11 Tusken Raiders 2.00
PRM0276 12 Stormtroopers 2.00
PRM0277 13 Millennium Falcon 2.00
PRM0278 14 Star Destroyer..2.00
PRM0279 15 X-Wing 2.00
PRM0280 16 Tie - Vader's Ship..2.00

York

PRM0281   PRM0283   PRM0282

PRM0284   PRM0285   PRM0286

PRM0281 2-1B Medic Droid...4.00
PRM0282 C-3PO and Princess Leia 4.00
PRM0283 C-3PO and R2-D2 ....4.00
PRM0284 Chewbacca 4.00
PRM0285 Darth Vader 4.00
PRM0286 Luke in X-Wing Gear, Dagobah Swamp 4.00

CARDS: ROLE PLAYING

West End Games

LHB0001 1X-2A, SW Lords of the Expanse.............................0.50
LHB0002 Absorb/Dissipate Energy, SW Introd. Adv. game 0.50
LHB0003 Adana Vermor, SW Tapani Sec. Inst. Adv. book 0.50
LHB0004 Affect Mind, SW Introd. Adv. game 0.50
LHB0005 Aldine Brigade Soldiers, SW Tapani Sec. Inst. Adv. book....0.50
LHB0006 Annora Calandra, SW Lords of the Expanse 0.50
LHB0007 Aratech REPSUB, SW Tapani Sec. Inst. Adv. book.......0.50
LHB0008 Armored Repulsorlift Transport, SW Introd. Adv. game...............0.50
LHB0009 AT-AT Walker, SW Introd. Adv. game 0.50
LHB0010 AT-ST Walker, SW Introd. Adv. game 0.50
LHB0011 Automap, SW Inst. Adv. book 0.50
LHB0012 A-Wing Fighter, SW Introd. Adv. game 0.50
LHB0013 B'aerlak Beasts, SW Inst. Adv. book........................0.50
LHB0014 Bantha, SW Introd. Adv. game 0.50
LHB0015 Barloz-class Medium Freighter, SW Stock Ships book....0.50
LHB0016 Battz, SW Inst. Adv. book.......................................0.50
LHB0017 Biker Scout Patrol, SW Inst. Adv. book......................0.50
LHB0018 Boe Vixe, SW Inst. Adv. book..................................0.50
LHB0019 Bounty Hunter, SW Introd. Adv. game 0.50
LHB0020 Brak Dunell, SW Lords of the Expanse 0.50
LHB0021 B-Wing Fighter, SW Introd. Adv. game 0.50
LHB0022 Captain Brixus Aidine, SW Tapani Sec. Inst. Adv. book....0.50
LHB0023 Captain Lin Nunsk, SW Lords of the Expanse 0.50
LHB0024 Captain Nils Wender, SW Tapani Sec. Inst. Adv. book ...0.50
LHB0025 Colonel Deers, SW Introd. Adv. game 0.50
LHB0026 Colonel Pertarn (drawn image), SW Introd. Adv. game...0.50
LHB0027 Colonel Raibat, SW Tapani Sec. Inst. Adv. book 0.50
LHB0028 COMPFORCE Assault Troopers, SW Inst. Adv. book.....0.50
LHB0029 Concentration, SW Introd. Adv. game 0.50
LHB0030 Container Ship, SW Tapani Sec. Inst. Adv. book..........0.50

LHB0031 Control Pain, SW Introd. Adv. game 0.50
LHB0032 Corellian Corvette, SW Introd. Adv. game 0.50
LHB0033 Corellian HT-2200 Frighter, SW Stock Ships book 0.50
LHB0034 Corellian XS-800 Light Freighter, SW Stock Ships book...0.50
LHB0035 Corellian YT-1300 Freighter, SW Introd. Adv. game......0.50
LHB0036 Crimson Slug, SW Tapani Sec. Inst. Adv. book 0.50
LHB0037 Dantaree, SW Introd. Adv. game 0.50
LHB0038 DepotSec Troops, SW Inst. Adv. book.......................0.50
LHB0039 Dewback, SW Introd. Adv. game 0.50
LHB0040 Dr. Arkeld, SW Lords of the Expanse 0.50
LHB0041 Edan Tiger (Snowcat), SW Introd. Adv. game 0.50
LHB0042 F'ej D'aw, SW Inst. Adv. book 0.50
LHB0043 Floating Fortress, SW Inst. Adv. book.......................0.50
LHB0044 Gamorrean Guard, SW Introd. Adv. game 0.50
LHB0045 Gennan Var, SW Inst. Adv. book 0.50
LHB0046 Hamar-Chaktak, SW Tapani Sec. Inst. Adv. book 0.50
LHB0047 Hamar's Mercenaries, SW Tapani Sec. Inst. Adv. book...0.50
LHB0048 Heavy Assault Starfighter, SW Inst. Adv. book...........0.50
LHB0049 Hibernation Trance, SW Introd. Adv. game 0.50
LHB0050 House Barnaba Guard, SW Tapani Sec. Inst. Adv. book...0.50
LHB0051 House Mecetti Agent, SW Tapani Sec. Inst. Adv. book...0.50
LHB0052 House Pelagia Agent, SW Tapani Sec. Inst. Adv. book...0.50
LHB0053 Hyrotil Crescent-class Transport, SW Stock Ships book...0.50
LHB0054 Identification Card, SW Inst. Adv. book 0.50
LHB0055 Imperial Army Trooper, SW Introd. Adv. game 0.50
LHB0056 Imperial Heavy Repulsortank, SW Introd. Adv. game....0.50
LHB0057 Imperial Lambda Shuttle, SW Introd. Adv. game 0.50
LHB0058 Imperial Navy Trooper, SW Tapani Sec. Inst. Adv. book...0.50
LHB0059 Imperial Officer, SW Introd. Adv. game......................0.50
LHB0060 Imperial Patrol Landspeeder, SW Introd. Adv. game....0.50
LHB0061 Imperial Scout Trooper, SW Introd. Adv. game 0.50
LHB0062 Imperial Star Destroyer, SW Introd. Adv. game...........0.50
LHB0063 Imperial Storm Commandos, SW Inst. Adv. book 0.50
LHB0064 Imperial Stormtrooper, SW Introd. Adv. game 0.50
LHB0065 Imperial Supply Depot, SW Inst. Adv. book...............0.50
LHB0066 JAN Commando, SW Tapani Sec. Inst. Adv. book.......0.50
LHB0067 JAN Terrorist, SW Lords of the Expanse 0.50
LHB0068 Janna Pallask, SW Tapani Sec. Inst. Adv. book..........0.50
LHB0069 Janos Marsh, SW Tapani Sec. Inst. Adv. book...........0.50
LHB0070 Jawa Trader, SW Introd. Adv. game 0.50
LHB0071 Jorus Kai, SW Introd. Adv. game 0.50
LHB0072 K4 Security Droid, SW Tapani Sec. Inst. Adv. book 0.50
LHB0073 Kala Kevv, SW Inst. Adv. book 0.50
LHB0074 Kijo Mnuue, SW Lords of the Expanse 0.50
LHB0075 Lady Brigta Hejaran, SW Tapani Sec. Inst. Adv. book...0.50
LHB0076 Landspeeder, SW Introd. Adv. game 0.50
LHB0077 Lantillian Short Hauler, SW Stock Ships book 0.50
LHB0078 Leona Makk, SW Inst. Adv. book 0.50
LHB0079 Life Detection, SW Introd. Adv. game 0.50
LHB0080 Lightsaber Combat, SW Introd. Adv. game 0.50
LHB0081 Locux Hyen, SW Introd. Adv. game 0.50
LHB0082 Lord Alec Lamere, SW Lords of the Expanse 0.50
LHB0083 Lord Vaskel Savill, SW Lords of the Expanse 0.50
LHB0084 Magnify Senses, SW Introd. Adv. game 0.50
LHB0085 Major General Tessala Corvae, SW Lords of the Expanse 0.50
LHB0086 Manta-class Assault Starfighter, SW Lords of the Expanse...0.50
LHB0087 Melchi, SW Lords of the Expanse 0.50
LHB0088 Mobquet Corona, SW Inst. Adv. book.......................0.50
LHB0089 Mon Calamari Scout, SW Introd. Adv. game 0.50
LHB0090 Mon Calamari Star Cruiser, SW Introd. Adv. game 0.50
LHB0091 Nawnam the Hutt, SW Inst. Adv. book.......................0.50
LHB0092 Nebulon-B Frigate, SW Introd. Adv. game 0.50
LHB0093 Nikal Kam, SW Inst. Adv. book 0.50
LHB0094 Nova-Drive 3-Z Light Freighter, SW Stock Ships book...0.50
LHB0095 Pershon, SW Tapani Sec. Inst. Adv. book...................0.50
LHB0096 Pirate Corvette, SW Inst. Adv. book 0.50
LHB0097 Pirate Y-Tie Ugly 0.50
LHB0098 Probe Droid, SW Introd. Adv. game 0.50
LHB0099 Protocol Droid, SW Introd. Adv. game 0.50
LHB0100 R2 Astromech Droid, SW Introd. Adv. game 0.50
LHB0101 R2-C9, SW Inst. Adv. book 0.50
LHB0102 R2-D6, SW Inst. Adv. book 0.50
LHB0103 Rebel Alliance Combat Landspeeder, SW Inst. Adv. book...0.50
LHB0104 Rebel Alliance Soldier, SW Introd. Adv. game 0.50
LHB0105 Regul Staganac, SW Tapani Sec. Inst. Adv. book........0.50
LHB0106 Rodian Bounty Hunter, SW Introd. Adv. game 0.50
LHB0107 Rodian Karstag, SW Lords of the Expanse 0.50
LHB0108 Salvaged Y-Wing Fighter, SW Introd. Adv. game 0.50
LHB0109 Scruts, SW Introd. Adv. game 0.50
LHB0110 Sense Force, SW Introd. Adv. game...........................0.50
LHB0111 Shela Jalahafi, SW Introd. Adv. game 0.50

LHB0112 Ship’s Operating License, SW Stock Ships book ... 0.50
LHB0113 Sir Ajax Wennel, SW Tapani Sec. Inst. Adv. book ... 0.50
LHB0114 Sir Tazur Pheron, SW Tapani Sec. Inst. Adv. book ... 0.50
LHB0115 Sir Trevas Jotane, SW Tapani Sec. Inst. Adv. book ... 0.50
LHB0116 Skiff, SW Introd. Adv. game ... 0.50
LHB0117 Solar Flare, SW Lords of the Expanse ... 0.50
LHB0118 Spaceport Guard, SW Tapani Sec. Inst. Adv. book ... 0.50
LHB0119 Speeder Bike, SW Introd. Adv. game ... 0.50
LHB0120 Spin-blade, SW Tapani Sec. Inst. Adv. book ... 0.50
LHB0121 Standard Stormtrooper, SW Inst. Adv. book ... 0.50
LHB0122 Starfield ZH-25 Questor, SW Stock Ships book ... 0.50
LHB0123 Starlight Light Freighter, SW Stock Ships book ... 0.50
LHB0124 Stock DeepWater Light Freighter, SW Stock Ships book ... 0.50
LHB0125 Stock Kazellis Light Freighter, SW Stock Ships book ... 0.50
LHB0126 Stock Starwind Yacht, SW Stock Ships book ... 0.50
LHB0127 Stock Surronian L19 Freighter, SW Stock Ships book ... 0.50
LHB0128 Stocke YT-2400 Transport, SW Stock Ships book ... 0.50
LHB0129 Sullustan Smuggler, SW Introd. Adv. game ... 0.50
LHB0130 Surveillance Droid, SW Tapani Sec. Inst. Adv. book ... 0.50
LHB0131 Suwantek Systems TL-1800, SW Stock Ships book ... 0.50
LHB0132 Tapani Frigate, SW Lords of the Expanse ... 0.50
LHB0133 Tapani Guardsman, SW Lords of the Expanse ... 0.50
LHB0134 Tauntaun, SW Introd. Adv. game ... 0.50
LHB0135 Telekinesis, SW Introd. Adv. game ... 0.50
LHB0136 Teles Jalahafi, SW Introd. Adv. game ... 0.50
LHB0137 The Bright Seekers, SW Tapani Sec. Inst. Adv. book ... 0.50
LHB0138 The Knife’s Edge, SW Tapani Sec. Inst. Adv. book ... 0.50
LHB0139 The Nal Hutta Jewel, SW Inst. Adv. book ... 0.50
LHB0140 Themion Hejaran, SW Tapani Sec. Inst. Adv. book ... 0.50
LHB0141 Tie Bomber, SW Inst. Adv. book ... 0.50
LHB0142 Tie Bomber, SW Introd. Adv. game ... 0.50
LHB0143 Tie Fighter, SW Introd. Adv. game ... 0.50
LHB0144 Tie Interceptor, SW Introd. Adv. game ... 0.50
LHB0145 Trel Modetto, SW Tapani Sec. Inst. Adv. book ... 0.50
LHB0146 Tusken Raider, SW Introd. Adv. game ... 0.50
LHB0147 Twi’lek Merchant, SW Introd. Adv. game ... 0.50
LHB0148 Valka, SW Tapani Sec. Inst. Adv. book ... 0.50
LHB0149 Vee Naaq, SW Inst. Adv. book ... 0.50
LHB0150 Vindicator, SW Introd. Adv. game ... 0.50
LHB0151 Viv, SW Introd. Adv. game ... 0.50
LHB0152 Voxen Tass, SW Inst. Adv. book ... 0.50
LHB0153 Wookie Outlaw, SW Introd. Adv. game ... 0.50
LHB0154 Xishel, SW Inst. Adv. book ... 0.50
LHB0155 X-Wing Fighter, SW Introd. Adv. game ... 0.50
LHB0156 Y-Wing Fighter, SW Introd. Adv. game ... 0.50
LHB0157 Z-10 Seeker, SW Stock Ships book ... 0.50
LHB0158 Z-95 Headhunter, SW Inst. Adv. book ... 0.50
LHB0159 Zarfeen, SW Inst. Adv. book ... 0.50
LHB0160 Zobberan Hounds, SW Inst. Adv. book ... 0.50

CARDS: ROTJ

Monty Factories

OVR0001 001 Desert Skiff Above the Sarlacc Pit ... 1.00
OVR0002 002 Darth Vader (posed picture) ... 1.00
OVR0003 003 Luke Skywalker ... 1.00
OVR0004 004 Wicket the Ewok (posed picture) ... 1.00
OVR0005 005 Biker Scout ... 1.00
OVR0006 006 Leia and Wicket Share a Log ... 1.00
OVR0007 007 Luke on Ewok Village Walkway ... 1.00
OVR0008 008 Han Solo (posed picture) on Endor ... 1.00
OVR0009 009 Jabba’s Palace Flute Player ... 1.00
OVR0010 010 Jabba’s Palace Singer ... 1.00
OVR0011 011 Jabba the Hutt ... 1.00
OVR0012 012 C-3PO ... 1.00
OVR0013 013 C-3PO and Logray ... 1.00
OVR0014 014 Emperor and Royal Guards ... 1.00
OVR0015 015 Gamorreans and Other Palace Aliens ... 1.00
OVR0016 016 Wicket and R2-D2 ... 1.00
OVR0017 017 Weequay Guard Falling Into Sarlacc ... 1.00
OVR0018 018 Battle on the Desert Skiff ... 1.00
OVR0019 019 Yoda ... 1.00
OVR0020 020 R2 and C-3PO Walk to Jabba’s Palace ... 1.00
OVR0021 021 Jabba and Bib Fortuna ... 1.00
OVR0022 022 Chief Chirpa ... 1.00
OVR0023 023 Ackbar at the Bridge ... 1.00
OVR0024 024 Boushh Approaches Frozen Han ... 1.00
OVR0025 025 Leia in Ewok Village ... 1.00
OVR0026 026 Jawas ... 1.00
OVR0027 027 Wicket ... 1.00
OVR0028 028 Han Solo (posed picture) ... 1.00
OVR0029 029 Wicket (close up) ... 1.00
OVR0030 030 Luke With Saber ... 1.00
OVR0031 031 The Falcon ... 1.00
OVR0032 032 Jabba’s Singer ... 1.00
OVR0033 033 Jedi Luke Enters the Palace ... 1.00
OVR0034 034 Logray ... 1.00
OVR0035 035 Inside the Shuttle Cockpit (fly casual) ... 1.00
OVR0036 036 C-3PO Tells a Story ... 1.00
OVR0037 037 Baby Ewok ... 1.00
OVR0038 038 Battle on Endor ... 1.00
OVR0039 039 Captured Han Solo ... 1.00
OVR0040 040 Bib Fortuna ... 1.00
OVR0041 041 Max Rebo ... 1.00
OVR0042 042 Max Rebo and Band ... 1.00
OVR0043 043 Lando and Nien Nunb ... 1.00
OVR0044 044 Max and Band (different view) ... 1.00
OVR0045 045 Desert Sail Barge ... 1.00
OVR0046 046 Disguised Lando and Leia ... 1.00
OVR0047 047 Luke Takes Aim ... 1.00
OVR0048 048 Jabba ... 1.00
OVR0049 049 Yak Face ... 1.00
OVR0050 050 R2 and C-3PO at Jabba’s Door ... 1.00
OVR0051 051 Leia ... 1.00
OVR0052 052 C-3PO ... 1.00
OVR0053 053 Lando Fights a Skiff Guard ... 1.00
OVR0054 054 Luke and Leia Prepare to Swing ... 1.00
OVR0055 055 Lando ... 1.00
OVR0056 056 Luke with Saber on Endor (posed) ... 1.00
OVR0057 057 Han with Blaster at Bunker ... 1.00
OVR0058 058 Emperor ... 1.00
OVR0059 059 Boba Fett ... 1.00
OVR0060 060 Ewoks ... 1.00
OVR0061 061 Boba Fett and Other Palace Dwellers ... 1.00
OVR0062 062 Emperor and Royal Guards ... 1.00
OVR0063 063 Scout Trooper Arrests Leia ... 1.00
OVR0064 064 Ewok ... 1.00
OVR0065 065 Vader and Royal Guards ... 1.00
OVR0066 066 Jabba’s Palace Denizens (posed shot) ... 1.00
OVR0067 067 A Captured Chewbacca ... 1.00
OVR0068 068 Palace Denizens (including Fett) ... 1.00
OVR0069 069 Ewoks ... 1.00
OVR0070 070 Dangling From the Skiff ... 1.00
OVR0071 071 Jabba ... 1.00
OVR0072 072 AT-ST Firing ... 1.00
OVR0073 073 On the Skiff ... 1.00
OVR0074 074 Vader and Luke Duel ... 1.00
OVR0075 075 Han, Leia, and Luke on Endor (posed) ... 1.00
OVR0076 076 Vader ... 1.00
OVR0077 077 Wicket, R2, and C-3PO (posed) ... 1.00
OVR0078 078 Gamorrean ... 1.00
OVR0079 079 Ewok ... 1.00
OVR0080 080 Salacious Crumb ... 1.00
OVR0081 081 Luke ... 1.00
OVR0082 082 Poster Art ... 1.00
OVR0083 083 Chewbacca ... 1.00
OVR0084 084 Cast on Endor (posed) ... 1.00
OVR0085 085 Jabba with Oola and Crumb ... 1.00
OVR0086 086 Luke on Stairs of Throne Room ... 1.00
OVR0087 087 Luke and Vader Face Off Across Emperor’s Throne ... 1.00
OVR0088 088 Jabba ... 1.00
OVR0089 089 Ackbar and Other Mon Calamari ... 1.00
OVR0090 090 Briefing ... 1.00
OVR0091 091 Gamorrean on a Barge ... 1.00
OVR0092 092 Scout Arrests Leia ... 1.00

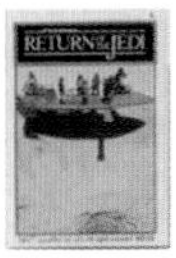
OVR0001

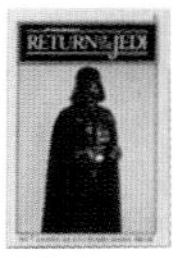
OVR0002

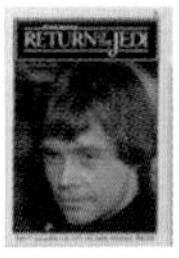
OVR0003

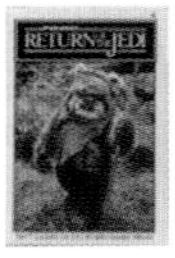
OVR0004

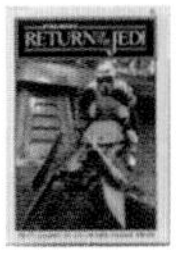
OVR0005

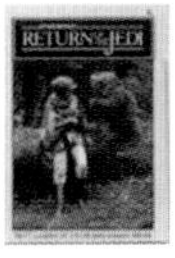
OVR0006

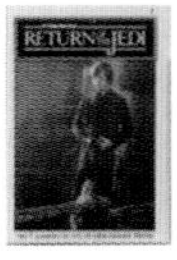
OVR0007

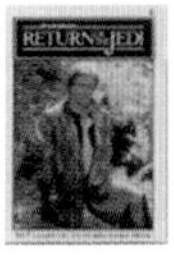
OVR0008

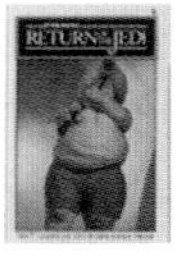
OVR0009

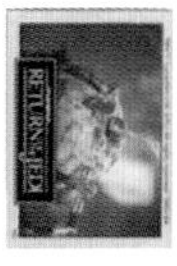
OVR0010

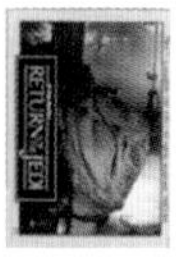
OVR0011

Cards: ROTJ

OVR0012　OVR0013　OVR0014　OVR0015　OVR0016　OVR0017　OVR0018　OVR0019　OVR0020　OVR0021　OVR0022

OVR0023　OVR0024　OVR0025　OVR0026　OVR0027　OVR0028　OVR0029　OVR0030　OVR0031　OVR0032　OVR0033

OVR0034　OVR0035　OVR0036　OVR0037　OVR0038　OVR0039　OVR0040　OVR0041　OVR0042　OVR0043　OVR0044

OVR0045　OVR0046　OVR0047　OVR0048　OVR0049　OVR0050　OVR0051　OVR0052　OVR0053　OVR0054　OVR0055

OVR0056　OVR0057　OVR0058　OVR0059　OVR0060　OVR0061　OVR0062　OVR0063　OVR0064　OVR0065　OVR0066

OVR0067　OVR0068　OVR0069　OVR0070　OVR0071　OVR0072　OVR0073　OVR0074　OVR0075　OVR0076　OVR0077

OVR0078　OVR0079　OVR0080　OVR0081　OVR0082　OVR0083　OVR0084　OVR0085　OVR0086　OVR0087　OVR0088

OVR0089　OVR0090　OVR0091　OVR0092　OVR0093　OVR0094　OVR0095　OVR0097　OVR0098　OVR0099　OVR0100

OVR0101 · OVR0102 · OVR0103 · OVR0104 · OVR0105 · OVR0106

OVR0107 · OVR0108 · OVR0109 · OVR0110 · OVR0111 · OVR0112 · OVR0113 · OVR0114 · OVR0115 · OVR0116 · OVR0117

OVR0118 · OVR0119 · OVR0120 · OVR0121 · OVR0122 · OVR0123 · OVR0124 · OVR0125 · OVR0126 · OVR0127 · OVR0128

OVR0129 · OVR0130 · OVR0131 · OVR0132 · OVR0133 · OVR0134 · OVR0135 · OVR0136 · OVR0137 · OVR0138 · OVR0139

OVR0140 · OVR0141 · OVR0142 · OVR0143 · OVR0144 · OVR0145 · OVR0146 · OVR0147 · OVR0148 · OVR0149 · OVR0150

OVR0151 · OVR0152 · OVR0153 · OVR0154 · OVR0155 · OVR0156 · OVR0157 · OVR0158 · OVR0159 · OVR0160 · OVR0161

OVR0162 · OVR0163 · OVR0164 · OVR0165 · OVR0166 · OVR0167 · OVR0168 · OVR0169 · OVR0170 · OVR0171 · OVR0172

Cards: ROTJ

OVR0173 OVR0174 OVR0175 OVR0176 OVR0177

OVR0178 OVR0179 OVR0180 OVR0181 OVR0182 OVR0183 OVR0184 OVR0185 OVR0186 OVR0187 OVR0188

OVR0189 OVR0190 OVR0191 OVR0192 OVR0193 OVR0194 OVR0195 OVR0196 OVR0197 OVR0198 OVR0199

OVR0200 OVR0201 OVR0202 OVR0203 OVR0204 OVR0205 OVR0206 OVR0207 OVR0208 OVR0209 OVR0210

OVR0211 OVR0212 OVR0213 OVR0214 OVR0215 OVR0216 OVR0217 OVR0218 OVR0219 OVR0220 OVR0221

OVR0222 OVR0223 OVR0224 OVR0225 OVR0226 OVR0227 OVR0228 OVR0229 OVR0230 OVR0231 OVR0232

OVR0266 OVR0267 OVR0268 OVR0269 OVR0270 OVR0271 OVR0272 OVR0273 OVR0274 OVR0275 OVR0276
OVR0277 OVR0278 OVR0279 OVR0280 OVR0281 OVR0282 OVR0283 OVR0284 OVR0285 OVR0286 OVR0287
OVR0288 OVR0289 OVR0290 OVR0291 OVR0292 OVR0293 OVR0294 OVR0295 OVR0296 OVR0297 OVR0298
OVR0299 OVR0300 OVR0301 OVR0302 OVR0303 OVR0304 OVR0305 OVR0306 OVR0307 OVR0308 OVR0309
OVR0310 OVR0311 OVR0312 OVR0313 OVR0314 OVR0315 OVR0316 OVR0317 OVR0318 OVR0319 OVR0320
OVR0321 OVR0322 OVR0323 OVR0324 OVR0325 OVR0326 OVR0327 OVR0328 OVR0329 OVR0330 OVR0331
OVR0332 OVR0333 OVR0334 OVR0335 OVR0336 OVR0337 OVR0338 OVR0339 OVR0340 OVR0341 OVR0342
OVR0343 OVR0344 OVR0345 OVR0346 OVR0347 OVR0348 OVR0349 OVR0350 OVR0351 OVR0352 OVR0353

Cards: ROTJ

OVR0354 Rack-Pack of 45 movie cards 12.00
OVR0233 Sticker 01 Yoda 1.25
OVR0234 Sticker 02 Ewok Medicine Man 1.25
OVR0235 Sticker 03 Horn Player 1.25
OVR0236 Sticker 04 Jabba 1.25
OVR0237 Sticker 05 Cantina Alien 1.25
OVR0238 Sticker 06 Admiral Ackbar 1.25
OVR0239 Sticker 07 Boushh 1.25
OVR0240 Sticker 08 Han Solo 1.25
OVR0241 Sticker 09 Leia 1.25
OVR0242 Sticker 10 Luke 1.25
OVR0243 Sticker 11 Han Solo 1.25
OVR0244 Sticker 12 C-3PO 1.25
OVR0245 Sticker 13 Chewbacca 1.25
OVR0246 Sticker 14 Band Singer 1.25
OVR0247 Sticker 15 Baby Ewok 1.25
OVR0248 Sticker 16 Nien Nunb 1.25
OVR0249 Sticker 17 Lando Calrissian 1.25
OVR0250 Sticker 18 R2-D2 ....1.25
OVR0251 Sticker 19 Obi-Wan Kenobi 1.25
OVR0252 Sticker 20 Luke Skywalker 1.25
OVR0253 Sticker 21 Luke 1.25
OVR0254 Sticker 22 Gamorrean Guard 1.25
OVR0255 Sticker 23 Salacious Crumb 1.25
OVR0256 Sticker 24 Wicket 1.25
OVR0257 Sticker 25 Boba Fett 1.25
OVR0258 Sticker 26 Ewok 1.25
OVR0259 Sticker 27 Jabba 1.25
OVR0260 Sticker 28 Lando in Skiff Disguise 1.25
OVR0261 Sticker 29 Max Rebo 1.25
OVR0262 Sticker 30 Leia on Endor 1.25
OVR0263 Sticker 31 Leia 1.25
OVR0264 Sticker 32 Han Solo 1.25
OVR0265 Sticker 33 Biker Scout 1.25

CARDS: SIGNING

OAS0007   OAS0005   OAS0006   OAS0003   OAS cardback

Dark Horse Comics
Values are for unsigned cards.
OAS0001 Dark Force Rising..9.00
OAS0007 Star Wars Darth Maul 6.00
OAS0005 Star Wars Tales...6.00
OAS0006 Star Wars Twilight...6.00
OAS0002 Tales of the Jedi: The Fall of the Sith Empire 6.00
OAS0003 The Protocol Offensive 8.00

Disney / MGM

OAS0004   OAS0008 signed

5"x7", May 2000. Values are for unsigned cards.
See Autographs category to add signature value.
OAS0004 Carrie Fisher 8.00
OAS0008 Kenny Baker 6.00

CARDS: SOTE

Topps
ON0001 001 Xizor is Lurking 1.00
ON0002 002 Leia's Recurring Nightmare 1.00
ON0003 003 Luke Feels the Dark Side 1.00
ON0004 004 Leia Defends Herself 1.00
ON0005 005 Reunion on Tatooine 1.00

ON0006 006 Xizor Greets Vader...1.00
ON0007 007 Xizor's Dirty Handiwork 1.00
ON0008 008 Ferreting Out a Traitor 1.00
ON0009 009 Beautiful... and Lethal 1.00
ON0010 010 Xizor Summons Jabba 1.00
ON0011 011 Leia Meets Dash Rendar 1.00
ON0012 012 Vader Stays Sharp 1.00
ON0013 013 Xizor Relishes the Good Life 1.00
ON0014 014 Fancy Flying 1.00
ON0015 015 Luke Scores a Tie 1.00
ON0016 016 "Help Me, Obi-Wan..." 1.00
ON0017 017 Boba Fett Escapes From Gall 1.00
ON0018 018 Narrow Escape...1.00
ON0019 019 Dealing With Dash 1.00
ON0020 020 Vader Grows Wary of Xizor 1.00
ON0021 021 Xizor Wants it All 1.00
ON0022 022 The Emperor Insists 1.00
ON0023 023 It'th Greedo'th Uncle 1.00
ON0024 024 The Waiting Game..1.00
ON0025 025 Luke Hones His Lightsaber Skills......................1.00
ON0026 026 Swoop Troop Attack 1.00
ON0027 027 Luke Axes a Swooper 1.00
ON0028 028 Good Ol' Beggar's Canyon 1.00
ON0029 029 Vader Destroys the Rebel Base 1.00
ON0030 030 Guri Does Xizor's Dirty Work 1.00
ON0031 031 Luke and Dash's Bothan Mission 1.00
ON0032 032 Dash's Persuasive Charm 1.00
ON0033 033 Attack on the Suprosa 1.00
ON0034 034 Leia Meets Guri 1.00
ON0035 035 Luke and Melan are Ambushed 1.00
ON0036 036 Luke's Taken Prisoner 1.00
ON0037 037 Guri Turns the Tables 1.00
ON0038 038 Boarding Guri's Stinger 1.00
ON0039 039 Chewbacca in Disguise 1.00
ON0040 040 Leia and Chewbacca Go Underground...........1.00
ON0041 041 Leia Visits Spero's Plant Shop 1.00
ON0042 042 Vader Seethes Over Luke's Escape 1.00
ON0043 043 Leia Arrives at Xizor's Palace 1.00
ON0044 044 Leia Finally Meets Xizor 1.00
ON0045 045 Leia is Smitten 1.00
ON0046 046 Vader Senses His Son 1.00
ON0047 047 Leia Prepares for Xizor 1.00
ON0048 048 Hyperspace... at Last! 1.00
ON0049 049 Xizor Prepares for Leia 1.00
ON0050 050 The Kiss 1.00
ON0051 051 Take That Xizor 1.00
ON0052 052 Xizor Sharpens his Claws 1.00
ON0053 053 Dash Does it Again 1.00
ON0054 054 Luke Becomes One With the Force 1.00
ON0055 055 Xizor's Troubled World 1.00
ON0056 056 Vader Uncovers Xizor's Secret Past 1.00
ON0057 057 Same Beast, Different Sewer 1.00
ON0058 058 Dash Fires the Guide 1.00
ON0059 059 Artoo and Threepio Helm the Falcon...............1.00
ON0060 060 Luke Blocks Xizor's Fire 1.00
ON0061 061 Will Xizor Call Luke's Bluff?..............................1.00
ON0062 062 Five Minutes Until Impact 1.00
ON0063 063 Guri Goes Toe-to-Toe With Luke......................1.00
ON0064 064 Xizor Narrowly Escapes 1.00
ON0065 065 Xizor's Castle Blows Up 1.00
ON0066 066 Battle Over Coruscant Part I............................1.00
ON0067 067 Battle Over Coruscant Part II...........................1.00
ON0068 068 Battle Over Coruscant Part III..........................1.00
ON0069 069 Good Riddance, Xizor!.....................................1.00
ON0070 070 Watch Out, Dash! 1.00
ON0071 071 Dash's Secret Getaway 1.00
ON0072 072 Luke Plans Han's Rescue 1.00
ON0073 073 Luke Skywalker 1.00
ON0074 074 Leia and Chewbacca 1.00
ON0075 075 Lando Calrissian 1.00
ON0076 076 R2-D2 and C-3PO 1.00
ON0077 077 Dash and Leebo 1.00
ON0078 078 Xizor 1.00
ON0079 079 Guri 1.00
ON0080 080 Darth Vader...1.00
ON0081 081 Jix and Big Gizz 1.00
ON0082 082 Boba Fett 1.00
ON0083 083 Millennium Falcon 1.00
ON0084 084 Outrider 1.00
ON0085 085 Virago 1.00
ON0086 086 Stinger 1.00

ON0087 087 Swoop 1.00
ON0088 088 Slave I 1.00
ON0089 089 Slave I in Battle 1.00
ON0090 090 Boba Fett 1.00
ON0091 091 Fett in Battle 1.00
ON0092 092 Fett and 4-Lom 1.00
ON0093 093 4-Lom 1.00
ON0094 094 Jabba's Palace 1.00
ON0095 095 AT-AT Under Attack 1.00
ON0096 096 Dash 1.00
ON0097 097 Dash on the Run 1.00
ON0098 098 Dash in Battle 1.00
ON0099 099 Ord Mantell Hovertram 1.00
ON0100 100 IG-88 ....1.00
ON0110 Premium: Autographed card only available via mail-in redemption. 8.00
ON0109 Reservation Coupon 1.15
ON0106 SOTE 6 Guri (Fan #18) 2.00
ON0101 SOTE1 Prince Xizor (SW Galaxy Magazine #7) 2.00
ON0102 SOTE2 Darth Vader (Advance Comics #93) 2.00
ON0103 SOTE3 Luke Skywalker (SW Finest Boxes) 3.25
ON0104 SOTE4 Dash Rendar (SW Galaxy Magazine #8) ..2.00
ON0105 SOTE5 Boba Fett (E3 Convention / QVC) 4.50
ON0107 SOTE7 C-3PO and R2-D2 (Collect 11/96 or San Diego ComicCon) 3.25
ON0108 SOTE7 C-3PO and R2-D2 (Collect 11/96 or San Diego ComicCon) Signed 6.50

CARDS: STAR WARS GALAXY MAGAZINE

Topps
OP0005 C1 Cover Art Issue #8 ....4.00
OP0006 C2 Cover Art Issue #9 ....4.00
OP0007 C3 Cover Art Issue #10 ....4.00
OP0008 C4 Cover Art Issue #11 ....4.00
OP0001 SWGM1 Cloud Cars 4.00
OP0002 SWGM2 Lambda Shuttle Over Coruscant.......4.00
OP0003 SWGM3 AT-AT and Snowspeeder 4.00
OP0004 SWGM4 Luke on Dagobah 4.00

CARDS: SW FINEST

Topps
OBA0001 01 Title Card...1.00
OBA0002 02 Luke Skywalker 1.00
OBA0003 03 Princess Leia 1.00
OBA0004 04 Mon Mothma 1.00
OBA0005 05 Admiral Ackbar..1.00
OBA0006 06 Jan Dodonna..1.00

OBA0007 07 Han Solo..1.00
OBA0008 08 Chewbacca...1.00
OBA0009 09 Lando Calrissian 1.00
OBA0010 10 Crix Madine..1.00
OBA0011 11 Garm Bel Iblis..1.00
OBA0012 12 Borsk Fey'lya..1.00
OBA0013 13 Wedge Antilles 1.00
OBA0014 14 Biggs Darklighter 1.00
OBA0015 15 Nien Nunb 1.00
OBA0016 16 Winter 1.00
OBA0017 17 Wicket W. Warrick 1.00
OBA0018 18 Qwi Xux 1.00
OBA0019 19 Emperor Palpatine 1.00
OBA0020 20 Darth Vader..1.00
OBA0021 21 Moff Tarkin 1.00
OBA0022 22 Joruus C'Baoth 1.00
OBA0023 23 Admiral Thrawn 1.00
OBA0024 24 Gilad Pellaeon 1.00
OBA0025 25 Admiral Piett 1.00
OBA0026 26 Admiral Daala 1.00
OBA0027 27 General Veers 1.00
OBA0028 28 Emperor's Royal Guard 1.00
OBA0029 29 Death Star Gunners 1.00
OBA0030 30 Stormtroopers 1.00
OBA0031 31 Tie Fighter Pilots 1.00
OBA0032 32 AT-AT Walker Pilots 1.00
OBA0033 33 Biker Scouts 1.00
OBA0034 34 Boba Fett 1.00
OBA0035 35 Dengar 1.00
OBA0036 36 Bossk 1.00
OBA0037 37 Obi-Wan Kenobi 1.00
OBA0038 38 Yoda 1.00
OBA0039 39 Callista 1.00
OBA0040 40 Jacen Solo 1.00
OBA0041 41 Anakin Solo 1.00
OBA0042 42 Jaina Solo 1.00
OBA0043 43 Kyp Durron 1.00
OBA0044 44 Kirani Ti 1.00
OBA0045 45 Tionne 1.00
OBA0046 46 Mara Jade 1.00
OBA0047 47 Talon Karrde 1.00
OBA0048 48 Salla Zend 1.00
OBA0049 49 Zuckuss 1.00
OBA0050 50 Lobot 1.00
OBA0051 51 Gallandro 1.00
OBA0052 52 Moruth Doole 1.00
OBA0053 53 Garindan 1.00
OBA0054 54 Lady Valarian 1.00
OBA0055 55 Tusken Raiders 1.00
OBA0056 56 Bantha 1.00
OBA0057 57 Jawa 1.00

OBA0001	OBA0002	OBA0003	OBA0004	OBA0005	OBA0006	OBA0007	OBA0008	OBA0009	OBA0010	OBA0011
OBA0012	OBA0013	OBA0014	OBA0015	OBA0016	OBA0017	OBA0018	OBA0019	OBA0020	OBA0021	OBA0022
OBA0023	OBA0024	OBA0025	OBA0026	OBA0027	OBA0028	OBA0029	OBA0030	OBA0031	OBA0032	OBA0033
OBA0034	OBA0035	OBA0036	OBA0037	OBA0038	OBA0039	OBA0040	OBA0041	OBA0042	OBA0043	OBA0044

OBA0058 58 Ugnaught..1.00
OBA0059 59 Noghri...1.00
OBA0060 60 Ssi-Ruuk...1.00
OBA0061 61 Wampa..1.00
OBA0062 62 Tauntaun...1.00
OBA0063 63 Sarlacc..1.00
OBA0064 64 Greedo..1.00
OBA0065 65 Cantina Band...1.00
OBA0066 66 Labria...1.00
OBA0067 67 Dr. Evazan..1.00
OBA0068 68 Ponda Baba...1.00
OBA0069 69 Feltipern Trevagg...1.00
OBA0070 70 Kabe and Muftak...1.00
OBA0071 71 Momaw Nadon..1.00
OBA0072 72 Wuher and Chalmun.......................................1.00
OBA0073 73 Jabba The Hutt..1.00
OBA0074 74 Bib Fortuna..1.00
OBA0075 75 Salacious Crumb..1.00
OBA0076 76 Max Rebo Band..1.00
OBA0077 77 Oola..1.00
OBA0078 78 Rancor..1.00
OBA0079 79 Gamorrean Guard..1.00
OBA0080 80 Weequay..1.00
OBA0081 81 Tessek...1.00
OBA0082 82 C-3PO...1.00
OBA0083 83 R2-D2...1.00
OBA0084 84 2-1B..1.00
OBA0085 85 R5-D4..1.00
OBA0086 86 4-LOM...1.00
OBA0087 87 Blue Max and Bullux..1.00
OBA0088 88 EV-9D9..1.00
OBA0089 89 IG-88...1.00
OBA0090 90 Probot / Checklist...1.00
OBA0095 F1 Darth Vader..4.00
OBA0096 F2 Luke Skywalker...4.00
OBA0097 F3 Obi-Wan Kenobi..4.00
OBA0098 F4 Jaina Solo..4.00
OBA0099 F5 Princess Leia and Anakin Solo.........................4.00
OBA0100 F6 Jacen Solo...4.00
OBA0091 Matrix 1 Han Solo and Chewbacca 8.00
OBA0092 Matrix 2 C-3PO and R2-D2.................................8.00
OBA0093 Matrix 3 Emperor Palpatine................................8.00
OBA0094 Matrix 4 Boba Fett...8.00
OBA0104 Oversized Card - Montage from Card 1 (Hobby Retailers).......5.00
OBA0105 Oversized Refractor Card - Montage from Card 1 (Hobby Retail-
ers)..5.00
OBA0101 SWF1 Boba Fett (SW Galaxy Magazine #6) 4.50
OBA0102 SWF2 Darth Vader (SW Galaxy Magazine #7).........4.50
OBA0103 SWF3 Luke on Tauntaun (Non-Sports Update v.7 n.3 / Sales
Force) 4.50

CARDS: SW GALAXY 1

Topps

OGX0147 #0 Darth Vader - Box Art (Millennium Falcon Factory Set / Just Toys
Offer) 9.00
OGX0001 001 Title Card...1.00
OGX0002 002 George Lucas Art Montage...........................1.00
OGX0003 003 Luke Skywalker..1.00
OGX0004 004 Darth Vader..1.00
OGX0005 005 Leia Organa...1.00
OGX0006 006 Obi-Wan "Ben" Kenobi 1.00
OGX0007 007 Han Solo..1.00
OGX0008 008 Chewbacca...1.00
OGX0009 009 Lando Calrissian...1.00
OGX0010 010 Yoda...1.00
OGX0011 011 C-3PO..1.00
OGX0012 012 R2-D2..1.00
OGX0013 013 Boba Fett..1.00
OGX0014 014 Emperor..1.00
OGX0015 015 Ralph McQuarrie...1.00
OGX0016 016 The Death Star Trench..................................1.00
OGX0017 017 Ron Cobb...1.00
OGX0018 018 Hammerhead...1.00
OGX0019 019 "Typical Wookie Family"................................1.00
OGX0020 020 Holiday Special..1.00
OGX0021 021 Too-Onebee..1.00
OGX0022 022 AT-AT..1.00
OGX0023 023 Yoda (Johnston)..1.00
OGX0024 024 A Space Slug..1.00
OGX0025 025 IG-88...1.00
OGX0026 026 The Death Star...1.00
OGX0027 027 Jabba The Hutt..1.00
OGX0028 028 Costume Design...1.00
OGX0029 029 Princess Leia...1.00
OGX0030 030 Original Sketches..1.00
OGX0031 031 Lando (Rodis-Jamero)....................................1.00
OGX0032 032 Yoda as Gremlin...1.00
OGX0033 033 Bad Hair Day?...1.00
OGX0034 034 The Rancor..1.00
OGX0035 035 Jabba's Menagerie.......................................1.00
OGX0036 036 Gamorrean Guards..1.00
OGX0037 037 Bib Fortuna...1.00
OGX0038 038 Creature Collaboration...................................1.00
OGX0039 039 Princess Leia's Hair.......................................1.00
OGX0040 040 Ewoks..1.00
OGX0041 041 Leia as a Pin-Up..1.00
OGX0042 042 Droid Torture Chamber..................................1.00
OGX0043 043 The Max Rebo Band......................................1.00
OGX0044 044 Luke's Confrontation....................................1.00
OGX0045 045 The Speeder Bike Chase................................1.00

OBA0045 OBA0046 OBA0047 OBA0048 OBA0049 OBA0050 OBA0051 OBA0052 OBA0053 OBA0054 OBA0055

OBA0056 OBA0057 OBA0058 OBA0059 OBA0060 OBA0061 OBA0062 OBA0063 OBA0064 OBA0065 OBA0066

OBA0067 OBA0068 OBA0069 OBA0070 OBA0071 OBA0072 OBA0073 OBA0074 OBA0075 OBA0076 OBA0077

OBA0078 OBA0079 OBA0080 OBA0081 OBA0082 OBA0083 OBA0084 OBA0085 OBA0086 OBA0087 OBA0088

OGX0001 OGX0002 OGX0003 OGX0004 OGX0005 OGX0006 OGX0007 OGX0008 OGX0009 OGX0010 OGX0011

OGX0012 OGX0013 OGX0014 OGX0015 OGX0016 OGX0017 OGX0018 OGX0019 OGX0020 OGX0021 OGX0022

OGX0023 OGX0024 OGX0025 OGX0026 OGX0027 OGX0028 OGX0029 OGX0030 OGX0031 OGX0032 OGX0033

OGX0034 OGX0035 OGX0036 OGX0037 OGX0038 OGX0039 OGX0040 OGX0041 OGX0042 OGX0043 OGX0044

OGX0045 OGX0046 OGX0047 OGX0048 OGX0049 OGX0050 OGX0051 OGX0052 OGX0053 OGX0054 OGX0055

OGX0056 OGX0057 OGX0058 OGX0059 OGX0060 OGX0061 OGX0062 OGX0063 OGX0064 OGX0065 OGX0066

OGX0067 OGX0068 OGX0069 OGX0070 OGX0071 OGX0072 OGX0073 OGX0074 OGX0075 OGX0076 OGX0077

OGX0100 100 Gil Kane (B) 1.00
OGX0101 101 Cam Kennedy 1.00
OGX0102 102 Dale Keown 1.00
OGX0103 103 Karl Kesel 1.00
OGX0104 104 Sam Keith (A) 1.00
OGX0105 105 Sam Keith (B) 1.00
OGX0106 106 David Lapham 1.00
OGX0107 107 Mike Lemos 1.00
OGX0108 108 Estoban Maroto 1.00
OGX0109 109 Cynthia Martin 1.00
OGX0110 110 Michael Mignola 1.00
OGX0111 111 Moebius 1.00
OGX0112 112 Jerome Moore 1.00
OGX0113 113 Jon J. Muth 1.00
OGX0114 114 Mark Nelson 1.00
OGX0115 115 Earl Norem 1.00
OGX0116 116 Allen Nunis 1.00
OGX0117 117 Jason Palmer 1.00
OGX0118 118 George Perez 1.00
OGX0119 119 George Pratt 1.00
OGX0120 120 Joe Quesada 1.00
OGX0121 121 P. Craig Russell 1.00
OGX0122 122 Mark Shultz 1.00
OGX0123 123 Bill Seinkiewicz 1.00
OGX0124 124 Walter Simonson 1.00
OGX0125 125 Ken Steacy 1.00
OGX0126 126 Brian Stelfreeze (A) 1.00
OGX0127 127 Brian Stelfreeze (B) 1.00
OGX0128 128 Dale Stevens 1.00
OGX0129 129 William Stout 1.00
OGX0130 130 Greg Theakston 1.00
OGX0131 131 Angelo Torres 1.00
OGX0132 132 Jim Valentino 1.00
OGX0133 133 John Van Fleet 1.00
OGX0134 134 Charles Vess 1.00
OGX0135 135 Russell Walks 1.00
OGX0136 136 Al Williamson (A) 1.00
OGX0137 137 Al Williamson (B) 1.00
OGX0138 138 Thomas Wm. Yeates II 1.00
OGX0139 139 Bruce Zick 1.00
OGX0140 140 Checklist 1.00
OGX0152 6"x8" Sam Keith and Walt Simonson, Previews 2/93 and Heroes World Scoreboard 2/93 .... 4.00
OGX0153 Boba Fett and Dengar (Dark Horse Comics Classic SW #8) 4.00
OGX0141 c1 Darth Vader 3.40
OGX0142 c2 Han Solo 3.40
OGX0143 c3 Luke and R2 .... 3.40
OGX0144 c4 Chewie and C-3PO 3.40
OGX0145 c5 Obi-Wan and Yoda 3.40
OGX0146 c6 Leia 3.40
OGX0151 Jabba and Crumb (Non-Sports Update v.4, n.2 / Starlog 191) 4.00
OGX0148 Princess Leia/Artist Checklist (Non-Sports Update v.4,n.2 / Conventions) 7.00
OGX0149 Stormtrooper on Dewback (Conventions) 7.00
OGX0154 Truce at Bakura Cover Art (Waldenbooks w/Novel Purchase) 5.50
OGX0150 Uncut Sheet of Cards (Advance Comics #52) 5.00

CARDS: SW GALAXY II

Topps

OGY0144 #00 Darth Vader on Bridge (QVC "SWG1" Sheetlet / SWG2 Factory Set) 18.00
OGY0001 141 Series title card 1.00
OGY0002 142 Ralph McQuarrie 1.00
OGY0003 143 A Giant Swamp Slug 1.00
OGY0004 144 Imperial Walkers 1.00
OGY0005 145 High Over Bespin 1.00

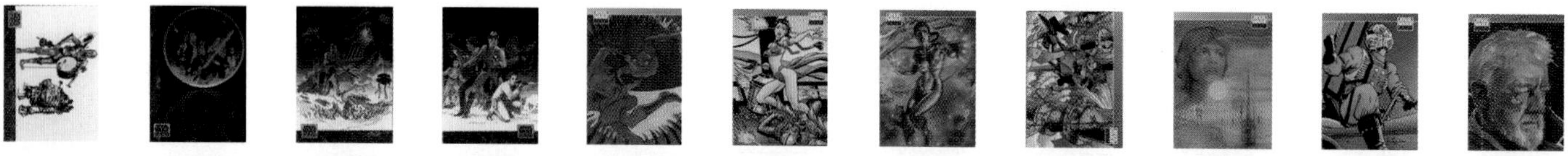

OGX0078 OGX0079 OGX0080 OGX0081 OGX0082 OGX0083 OGX0084 OGX0085 OGX0086 OGX0087 OGX0088

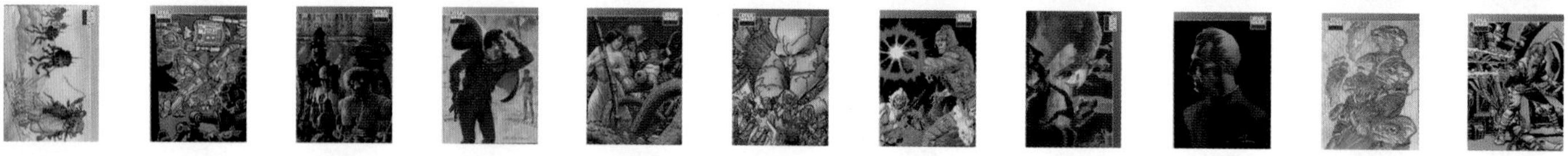

OGX0089 OGX0090 OGX0091 OGX0092 OGX0093 OGX0094 OGX0095 OGX0096 OGX0097 OGX0098 OGX0099

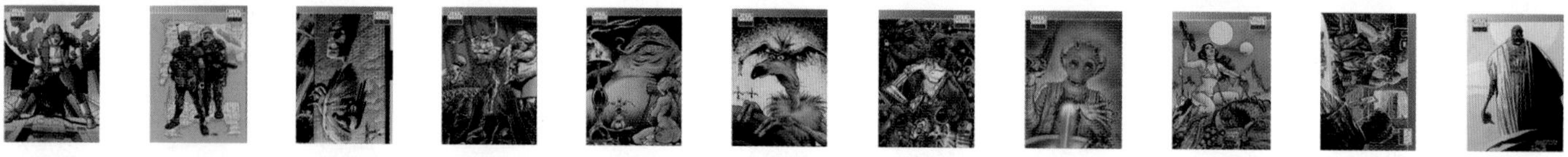

OGX0100 OGX0101 OGX0102 OGX0103 OGX0104 OGX0105 OGX0106 OGX0107 OGX0108 OGX0109 OGX0110

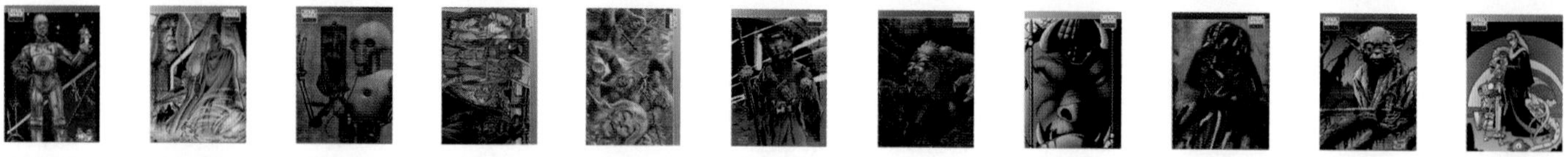

OGX0111 OGX0112 OGX0113 OGX0114 OGX0115 OGX0116 OGX0117 OGX0118 OGX0119 OGX0120 OGX0121

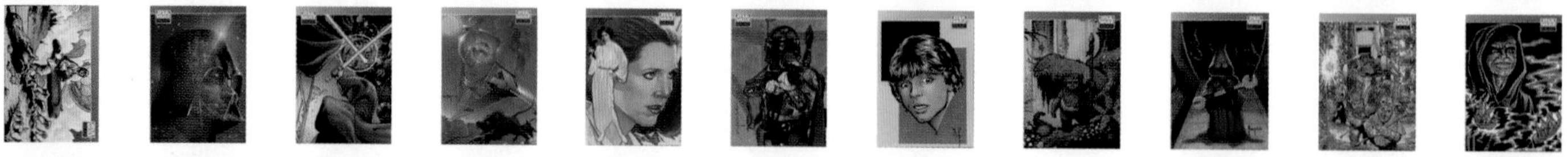

OGX0122 OGX0123 OGX0124 OGX0125 OGX0126 OGX0127 OGX0128 OGX0129 OGX0130 OGX0131 OGX0132

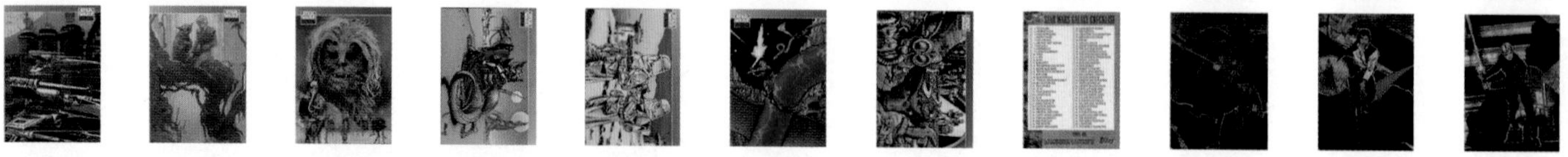

OGX0133 OGX0134 OGX0135 OGX0136 OGX0137 OGX0138 OGX0139 OGX0140 OGX0141 OGX0142 OGX0143

OGY0001 OGY0002 OGY0003 OGY0004 OGY0005 OGY0006 OGY0007 OGY0008 OGY0009 OGY0010 OGY0011

OGY0012 OGY0013 OGY0014 OGY0015 OGY0016 OGY0017 OGY0018 OGY0019 OGY0020 OGY0021 OGY0022

OGY0023 OGY0024 OGY0025 OGY0026 OGY0027 OGY0028 OGY0029 OGY0030 OGY0031 OGY0032 OGY0033

OGY0034 OGY0035 OGY0036 OGY0037 OGY0038 OGY0039 OGY0040 OGY0041 OGY0042 OGY0043 OGY0044

OGY0045 OGY0046 OGY0047 OGY0048 OGY0049 OGY0050 OGY0051 OGY0052 OGY0053 OGY0054 OGY0055

OGY0056 OGY0057 OGY0058 OGY0059 OGY0060 OGY0061 OGY0062 OGY0063 OGY0064 OGY0065 OGY0066

OGY0067 OGY0068 OGY0069 OGY0070 OGY0071 OGY0072 OGY0073 OGY0074 OGY0075 OGY0076 OGY0077

Cards: SW Galaxy II

OGY0078 OGY0079 OGY0080 OGY0081 OGY0082 OGY0083 OGY0084 OGY0085 OGY0086 OGY0087 OGY0088

OGY0089 OGY0090 OGY0091 OGY0092 OGY0093 OGY0094 OGY0095 OGY0096 OGY0097 OGY0098 OGY0099

OGY0100 OGY0101 OGY0102 OGY0103 OGY0104 OGY0105 OGY0106 OGY0107 OGY0108 OGY0109 OGY0110

OGY0111 OGY0112 OGY0113 OGY0114 OGY0115 OGY0116 OGY0117 OGY0118 OGY0119 OGY0120 OGY0121

OGY0122 OGY0123 OGY0124 OGY0125 OGY0126 OGY0127 OGY0128 OGY0129 OGY0130 OGY0131 OGY0132

OGY0133 OGY0134 OGY0135 OGY0142 OGY0143 OGY0146 OGY0147 OGY0148 OGY0149 OGY0150 OGY0151

OGY0130 270 Jill Thompson...1.00
OGY0131 271 Tim Truman...1.00
OGY0132 272 Keith Tucker...1.00
OGY0133 273 Jeff Watts..1.00
OGY0134 274 Mike Zeck...1.00
OGY0135 275 Checklist..1.00
OGY0145 5"x7" Rancor / AT-ATs (Previews v.4,n.2).............6.00
OGY0136 c07 Tarkin...3.00
OGY0137 c08 Stormtroopers...3.00
OGY0138 c09 Emperor...3.00
OGY0139 c10 Boba Fett...4.00
OGY0140 c11 Jabba..3.00
OGY0141 c12 Oola..3.00
OGY0143 Evil Ewoks (Triton Comic Cards and Collectibles #2) 4.00
OGY0146 P1 Rancor (Advance Comics 2/93 and Conventions)..........4.00
OGY0147 P2 Luke Builds Lightsaber (Non-Sports Update v.5, n.2)........4.00
OGY0148 P3 Yodas (Not Available to the Public) 2,300.00
OGY0149 P4 Jawas and C-3PO (Millennium Falcon Factory Set) 4.00
OGY0150 P5 Chewbacca at Holochess (Cards Illustrated #6).........4.00
OGY0151 P6 Boba Fett (Hero Magazine #12).....................5.00
OGY0142 Sandpeople (Star Wars #20 / Just Toys Offer)........4.00
OGY0152 SWB1 Grand Moff Tarkin (Galaxy Card Binder)........7.00

CARDS: SW GALAXY III

Topps

OGZ0117 #000 Zorba's Revenge (SW Galaxy Magazine #4) 4.00
OGZ0001 276 Title Card 1.00
OGZ0002 277 The Glove of Darth Vader...........................1.00
OGZ0003 278 The Lost City of the Jedi 1.00
OGZ0004 279 Mission from Mount Yoda 1.00
OGZ0005 280 The Truce at Bakura..................................1.00
OGZ0006 281 The Courtship of Princess Leia 1.00
OGZ0007 282 The Crystal Star...1.00
OGZ0008 283 Ambush at Corellia....................................1.00
OGZ0009 284 Assault at Selonia..1.00
OGZ0010 285 Showdown at Centerpoint.......................1.00
OGZ0011 286 Children of the Jedi.....................................1.00
OGZ0012 287 "We Don't Do Weddings": The Band's Tale ...1.00
OGZ0013 288 C-3PO "Thinker" 1.00
OGZ0014 289 C-3PO Birthday 1.00
OGZ0015 290 Luke and Starfighters 1.00
OGZ0016 291 C-3PO and R2-D2......................................1.00
OGZ0017 292 Cantina Poster..1.00
OGZ0018 293 Bounty Hunters..1.00
OGZ0019 294 C-3PO Robot Book 1.00
OGZ0020 295 Luke With Gang 1.00
OGZ0021 296 Marvel Comic..1.00
OGZ0022 297 The Ewok Adventure...................................1.00
OGZ0023 298 Cindel and Ewok 1.00

OGZ0024 299 Wicket Finds a Way 1.00
OGZ0025 300 Lando Montage 1.00
OGZ0026 301 Boba Fett Cloud City....................................1.00
OGZ0027 302 C-3PO Director..1.00
OGZ0028 303 Mos Eisley Cantina.....................................1.00
OGZ0029 304 Mos Eisley at Dark 1.00
OGZ0030 305 Christmas Card 1.00
OGZ0031 306 Magistrates of the Empire...........................1.00
OGZ0032 307 Grand Moff Tarkin.......................................1.00
OGZ0033 308 Han and Chewie Fight Boba Fett.................1.00
OGZ0034 309 The Tatooine Years 1.00
OGZ0035 310 The Four Jedi 1.00
OGZ0036 311 The Reluctant Jedi 1.00
OGZ0037 312 Nick Choles 1.00
OGZ0038 313 David Deitrick...1.00
OGZ0039 314 Gary Gianni 1.00
OGZ0040 315 Courtney Skinner 1.00
OGZ0041 316 Lou Harrison 1.00
OGZ0042 317 Les Dorscheid...1.00
OGZ0043 318 Brian Ashmore 1.00
OGZ0044 319 Hector Gomez 1.00
OGZ0045 320 Jae Lee...1.00
OGZ0046 321 Arthur Adams 1.00
OGZ0047 322 Dave Dorman 1.00
OGZ0048 323 Dave Dorman 1.00
OGZ0049 324 Hugh Fleming 1.00
OGZ0050 325 Hugh Fleming 1.00
OGZ0051 326 Kilian Plunkett 1.00
OGZ0052 327 June Brigman 1.00
OGZ0053 328 Dave Dorman 1.00
OGZ0054 329 Mark Harrison 1.00
OGZ0055 330 The Call to Adventure 1.00
OGZ0056 331 Supernatural Aid 1.00
OGZ0057 332 The Road of Trials 1.00
OGZ0058 333 The Ultimate Boon 1.00
OGZ0059 334 Joseph Campbell / George Lucas...................1.00
OGZ0060 335 The Force 1.00
OGZ0061 336 Leia 1.00
OGZ0062 337 Han Solo..1.00
OGZ0063 338 Skywalker / Vader.......................................1.00
OGZ0064 339 Kelly Freas 1.00
OGZ0065 340 Gene Colan 1.00
OGZ0066 341 Mitch O'Connell 1.00
OGZ0067 342 Mike Avon Deming 1.00
OGZ0068 343 Tim Eldred 1.00
OGZ0069 344 Cathleen Thole 1.00
OGZ0070 345 Don Punchatz 1.00
OGZ0071 346 John Pound 1.00
OGZ0072 347 Rick Buckler 1.00
OGZ0073 348 Scott Neely 1.00
OGZ0074 349 Joann Daley..1.00

OGZ0001	OGZ0002	OGZ0003	OGZ0004	OGZ0005	OGZ0006	OGZ0007	OGZ0008	OGZ0009	OGZ0010	OGZ0011
OGZ0012	OGZ0013	OGZ0014	OGZ0015	OGZ0016	OGZ0017	OGZ0018	OGZ0019	OGZ0020	OGZ0021	OGZ0022
OGZ0023	OGZ0024	OGZ0025	OGZ0026	OGZ0027	OGZ0028	OGZ0029	OGZ0030	OGZ0031	OGZ0032	OGZ0033
OGZ0034	OGZ0035	OGZ0036	OGZ0037	OGZ0038	OGZ0039	OGZ0040	OGZ0041	OGZ0042	OGZ0043	OGZ0044

OGZ0075 350 Jack Davis 1.00
OGZ0076 351 Mark "Crash" McCreery 1.00
OGZ0077 352 Mike Smithson 1.00
OGZ0078 353 John Eaves 1.00
OGZ0079 354 Clark Schaffer 1.00
OGZ0080 355 Will Vinton Studios 1.00
OGZ0081 356 Gahan Wilson 1.00
OGZ0082 357 Steve Reiss 1.00
OGZ0083 358 Mark Harrison 1.00
OGZ0084 359 Campbell / Garner 1.00
OGZ0085 360 Vince Locke 1.00
OGZ0086 361 John K. Snyder 1.00
OGZ0087 362 Therese Nielson 1.00
OGZ0088 363 Chris Moeller 1.00
OGZ0089 364 John Paul Leon 1.00
OGZ0090 365 Checklist 1.00
OGZ0116 5"x7" AT-ATs and Zorba's Revenge (Previews v.5, n.9) 4.00
OGZ0115 Boba Fett (SW Galaxy 2 Factory Set) 4.00
OGZ0109 c13 Lando 3.00
OGZ0110 c14 Millennium Falcon 4.00
OGZ0111 c15 Ewoks 4.00
OGZ0112 c16 Jawa 4.00
OGZ0113 c17 Tusken Raiders 4.00
OGZ0114 c18 Three Ghost Jedi 3.00
OGZ0103 E1 Boba Fett 3.00
OGZ0104 E2 Bossk 3.00
OGZ0105 E3 4-Lom 3.00
OGZ0106 E4 IG-88 ....3.00
OGZ0107 E5 Zuckuss 3.00
OGZ0108 E6 Dengar 3.00
OGZ0091 L01 Dark Forces Display Art 3.00
OGZ0092 L02 Dark Forces Ad Art 3.00
OGZ0093 L03 Dark Trooper 3.00
OGZ0094 L04 Keith Carter 3.00
OGZ0095 L05 Tie Fighter 3.00
OGZ0096 L06 Defender of the Empire 3.00
OGZ0097 L07 Keith Carter 3.00
OGZ0098 L08 X-Wing 3.00
OGZ0099 L09 The Farlander Papers 3.00
OGZ0100 L10 Keith Carter 3.00
OGZ0101 L11 Rebel Assault 3.00
OGZ0102 L12 Keith Carter 3.00
OGZ0118 P2 Snowtroopers (Conventions) 3.00
OGZ0119 P3 Darth Vader on Hoth (Non-Sports Update v.6, n.4) 3.00
OGZ0120 P4 Luke in Dream State (Combo Magazine #7) 3.00
OGZ0121 P5 Snowspeeder and AT-AT (Advance Comics #83) 3.00
OGZ0122 P6 SW Galaxy Magazine #5 Cover (SW Galaxy Magazine #5) ..3.00
OGZ0123 P7 Princess Leia with Twins (Wizard #52) 3.00
OGZ0124 P8 Darth Vader and Boba Fett (Cards Illustrated #25) 3.00

OLA0105 031 Luke and C-3PO 1.50
OLA0106 077 The Mighty Chewbacca 1.50
OLA0107 078 R2-D2 and C-3PO 1.50
OLA0001 201 AS T-5 (probe droid) 1.50
OLA0002 202 Luke Skywalker 1.50
OLA0003 203 Klaatu, Boba Fett 1.50
OLA0004 204 Emperor 1.50
OLA0005 205 Stormtrooper 1.50
OLA0006 206 Yoda, Luke Skywalker 1.50
OLA0007 207 C-3PO, Ewoks 1.50
OLA0008 208 Luke Skywalker 1.50
OLA0009 209 Luke Skywalker (Cloud City) 1.50
OLA0010 210 Darth Vader, Stormtrooper 1.50
OLA0011 211 R2-D2, C-3PO 1.50
OLA0012 212 Darth Vader (with Fett on Cloud City) 1.50
OLA0013 213 R2-D2, Wicket W. Warrick 1.50
OLA0014 214 C-3PO, Luke Skywalker 1.50
OLA0015 215 Stjarnornas Krig (Cantina Aliens) 1.50
OLA0016 216 Prinsessan Leia 1.50
OLA0017 217 Ben Kenobi 1.50
OLA0018 218 Stjarnornas Krig (Interior of Falcon cockpit) 1.50
OLA0019 219 Boba Fett 1.50
OLA0020 220 Stjarnornas Krig (Falcon cockpit - ESB) 1.50
OLA0021 221 Darth Vader 1.50
OLA0022 222 Luke Skywalker (on Tauntaun) 1.50
OLA0023 223 Stjarnornas Krig (Star Destroyer) 1.50
OLA0024 224 Darth Vader (Cloud City) 1.50
OLA0025 225 Darth Vader m.fl. (addressing the bounty hunters) 1.50
OLA0026 226 C-3PO, Han Solo, Leia 1.50
OLA0027 227 Stjarnornas Krig (Leia, Vader, and Tarkin) 1.50
OLA0028 228 Stjarnornas Krig (awards ceremony) 1.50
OLA0029 229 Luke Skywalker (on Tatooine) 1.50
OLA0030 230 Darth Vader (dueling Ben) 1.50
OLA0031 231 Han Solo 1.50
OLA0032 232 Stjarnornas Krig (Star Destroyer) 1.50
OLA0033 233 Chewbacca samt Han Solo 1.50
OLA0034 234 Luke Skywalker (in landspeeder) 1.50
OLA0035 235 Luke, Leia och Han Solo 1.50
OLA0036 236 C-3PO m.fl. (running to the Falcon - ESB) 1.50
OLA0037 237 Leia och R2-D2 ....1.50
OLA0038 238 Stormtrooper (Snowtrooper) 1.50
OLA0039 239 AT-AT 1.50
OLA0040 240 C-3PO 1.50
OLA0041 241 Luke Skywalker 1.50
OLA0042 242 Han Solo (sketch) 1.50
OLA0043 243 Admiral Ackbar (sketch) 1.50
OLA0044 244 Han Solo (actually a sketch of Lando in skiff gear!) 1.50

OGZ0045	OGZ0046	OGZ0047	OGZ0048	OGZ0049	OGZ0050	OGZ0051	OGZ0052	OGZ0053	OGZ0054	OGZ0055
OGZ0056	OGZ0057	OGZ0058	OGZ0059	OGZ0060	OGZ0061	OGZ0062	OGZ0063	OGZ0064	OGZ0065	OGZ0066
OGZ0067	OGZ0068	OGZ0069	OGZ0070	OGZ0071	OGZ0072	OGZ0073	OGZ0074	OGZ0075	OGZ0076	OGZ0077
OGZ0078	OGZ0079	OGZ0080	OGZ0081	OGZ0082	OGZ0083	OGZ0084	OGZ0085	OGZ0086	OGZ0087	OGZ0088

OLA0045 245 Klattuu (sketch) 1.50
OLA0046 246 Prinsessan Leia (sketch in Boussh gear) 1.50
OLA0047 247 Skiff (sketch) 1.50
OLA0048 248 Admiral Ackbar 1.50
OLA0049 249 Paploo (sketch) 1.50
OLA0050 250 Baby Ewoks (sketch) 1.50
OLA0051 251 Stjarnornas Krig (cast promotional photo on Hoth) 1.50
OLA0052 252 Jawa 1.50
OLA0053 253 Sy Snootle (sketch) 1.50
OLA0054 254 Emperors guard (sketch) 1.50
OLA0055 255 Wicket W. Warrick (sketch) 1.50
OLA0056 256 Biker Scout (sketch) 1.50
OLA0057 257 Wicket W. Warrick 1.50
OLA0058 258 Emperors guard 1.50
OLA0059 259 AT-ST (sketch) 1.50
OLA0060 260 Shuttle Tydirium (sketch) 1.50
OLA0061 261 C-3PO 1.50
OLA0062 262 No description available 1.50
OLA0063 263 Yoda, The Jedi Master 1.50
OLA0064 264 C-3PO, R2-D2 (on Endor) 1.50
OLA0065 265 C-3PO, Prinsessan Leia 1.50
OLA0066 266 No description available 1.50
OLA0067 267 Prinsessan Leia 1.50
OLA0068 268 The Emperor (sketch)..1.50
OLA0069 269 Lando Calrissian m.fl. (actually Han, Chewie and Leia at the
   rebel briefing) 1.50
OLA0070 270 The Sail Barge (sketch) 1.50
OLA0071 271 Lando Calrissian 1.50
OLA0072 272 Leia och Luke 1.50
OLA0073 273 Luke Skywalker, Han Solo 1.50
OLA0074 274 Luke Skywalker 1.50
OLA0075 275 R2-D2 samt C-3PO 1.50
OLA0076 276 Jabba the Hutt (sketch) 1.50
OLA0077 277 Gamorrean Guard (sketch)..1.50
OLA0078 278 Bib Fortuna (sketch) 1.50
OLA0079 301 Stjarnornas Krig (Falcon) 1.50
OLA0080 302 Sy Snootles 1.50
OLA0081 303 Han Solo 1.50
OLA0082 304 Stjarnornas Krig (B-Wing) 1.50
OLA0083 305 Stjarnornas Krig (Endor) 1.50
OLA0084 306 Bib Fortuna 1.50
OLA0085 307 Luke, Leia, Han Solo 1.50
OLA0086 308 Prinsessan Leia (in Slave attire) 1.50
OLA0087 309 Gamorrean Guard 1.50
OLA0088 310 Jabba The Hutt...1.50
OLA0089 311 C-3PO 1.50
OLA0090 312 Lando Calrissian 1.50
OLA0091 313 The Sail Barge 1.50
OLA0092 314 Sy Snootles 1.50
OLA0093 315 C-3PO 1.50
OLA0094 316 Lando Calrissian 1.50

OLA0095 317 The Skiff..1.50
OLA0096 318 Baby Ewok 1.50
OLA0097 319 Paploo 1.50
OLA0098 320 Luke Skywalker 1.50
OLA0099 321 Wicket W. Warrick 1.50
OLA0100 322 Rancor 1.50
OLA0101 323 Mon Calamari 1.50
OLA0102 324 Ewok 1.50
OLA0103 325 Ewok (Chief Chirpa)..1.50
OLA0104 326 Ewoks 1.50

CARDS: THAILAND
Pepsi Cola

CTP0001   CTP0002   CTP0003   CTP0004   All 4 cardbacks

CTP0001 A New Hope 5.00
CTP0002 Empire Strikes Back 5.00
CTP0003 Return of the Jedi..5.00
CTP0004 Star Wars Special Edition logo 5.00
CTP0005 The set of 4 ....20.00

CARDS: TIN, ANH

Metallic Images
CTS0001 01 Luke Skywalker..2.00

CTS0001   CTS0002   CTS0003   CTS0004   CTS0005

CTS0006   CTS0007   CTS0008   CTS0009   CTS0010

OLA0105 OLA0106 OLA0107 OLA0001 OLA0002 OLA0003 OLA0004 OLA0005 OLA0006 OLA0007 OLA0008

OLA0009 OLA0010 OLA0011 OLA0012 OLA0013 OLA0014 OLA0015 OLA0016 OLA0017 OLA0018 OLA0019

OLA0020 OLA0021 OLA0022 OLA0023 OLA0024 OLA0025 OLA0026 OLA0027 OLA0028 OLA0029 OLA0030

OLA0031 OLA0032 OLA0033 OLA0034 OLA0035 OLA0036 OLA0037 OLA0038 OLA0039 OLA0040 OLA0041

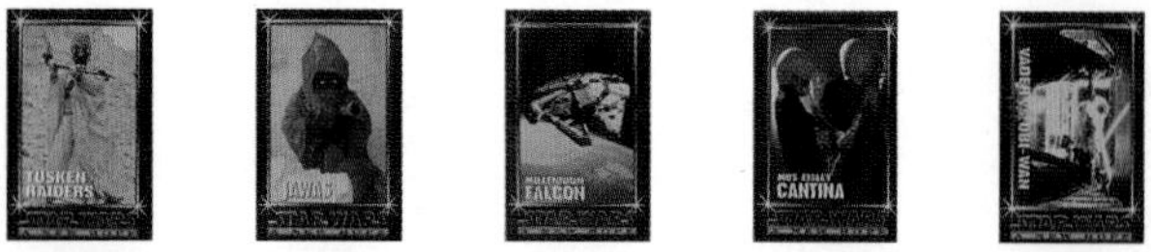

CTS0011 CTS0012 CTS0013 CTS0014 CTS0015

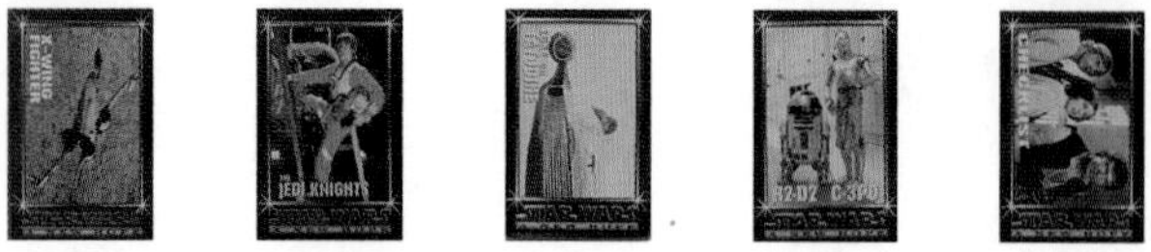

CTS0016 CTS0017 CTS0018 CTS0019 CTS0020

CTS0002 02 Darth Vader 2.00
CTS0003 03 C-3PO 2.00
CTS0004 04 Princess Leia 2.00
CTS0005 05 Han Solo 2.00
CTS0006 06 R2-D2 .... 2.00
CTS0007 07 Obi-Wan Kenobi 2.00
CTS0008 08 Chewbacca 2.00
CTS0009 09 Stormtroopers 2.00
CTS0010 10 Grand Moff Tarkin 2.00
CTS0011 11 Tusken Raiders 2.00
CTS0012 12 Jawas 2.00
CTS0013 13 Millennium Falcon 2.00
CTS0014 14 Mos Eisley Cantina 2.00
CTS0015 15 Vader vs. Obi-Wan 2.00
CTS0016 16 X-Wing Fighter 2.00
CTS0017 17 Jedi Knights 2.00
CTS0018 18 Luke on Tatooine 2.00
CTS0019 19 C-3PO and R2-D2 .... 2.00
CTS0020 20 Checklist 2.00
CTS0021 P1 ANH Poster Art Style "A" 15.00
CTS0022 Set of 20 in collector's tin 44.00

CARDS: TIN, BOUNTY HUNTERS

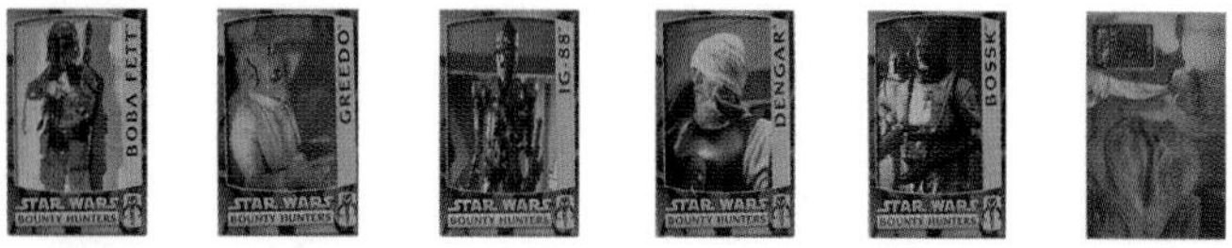

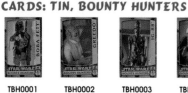

TBH0001 TBH0002 TBH0003 TBH0004 TBH0005 TBH0006

Metallic Images

TBH0001 1 Boba Fett 2.00
TBH0002 2 Greedo 2.00
TBH0003 3 IG-88 .... 2.00
TBH0004 4 Dengar 2.00
TBH0005 5 Bossk 2.00
TBH0006 Han Solo and Jabba the Hutt SW:SE 2.00
TBH0007 Set of 6 in collector's tin 17.00

CARDS: TIN, DARK EMPIRE

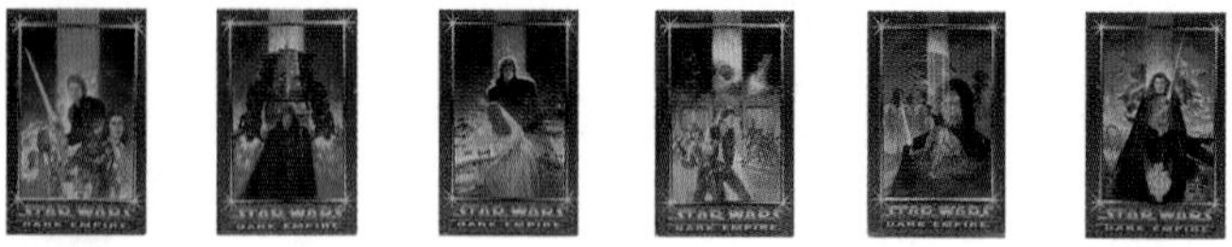

OF0001 OF0002 OF0003 OF0004 OF0005 OF0006

Metallic Images

OF0001 Issue 1: The Destiny of a Jedi 5.00
OF0002 Issue 2: Devastator of Worlds 5.00
OF0003 Issue 3: The Battle for Calamari 5.00
OF0004 Issue 4: Confrontation on the Smuggler's Moon 5.00
OF0005 Issue 5: Emperor Reborn 5.00
OF0006 Issue 6: The Fate of a Galaxy 5.00
OF0007 Set of 6 in collector's tin 34.00

CARDS: TIN, DARK EMPIRE II

Metallic Images

OF20001 Issue 1: Operation Shadow Hand 5.00
OF20002 Issue 2: Duel on Nar Shadda 5.00

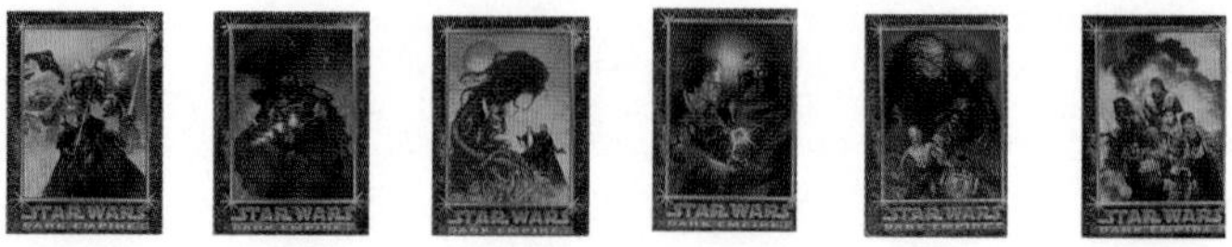

OF20001 OF20002 OF20003 OF20004 OF20005 OF20006

OF20003 Issue 3: World of the Ancient Sith 5.00
OF20004 Issue 4: Battle on Byss 5.00
OF20005 Issue 5: The Galaxy Weapon 5.00
OF20006 Issue 6: Hand of Darkness 5.00
OF20007 Set of 6 in collector's tin 34.00

CARDS: TIN, ESB

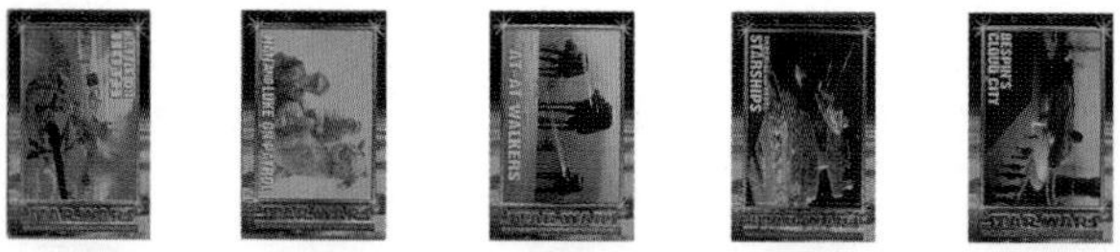

OG0001 OG0002 OG0003 OG0004 OG0005

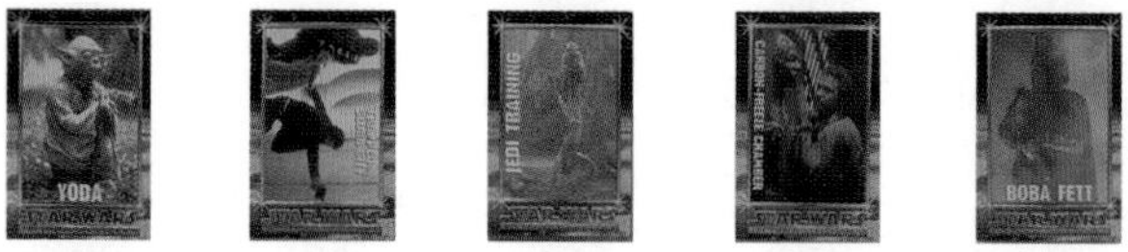

OG0006 OG0007 OG0008 OG0009 OG0010

OG0011 OG0012 OG0013 OG0014 OG0015

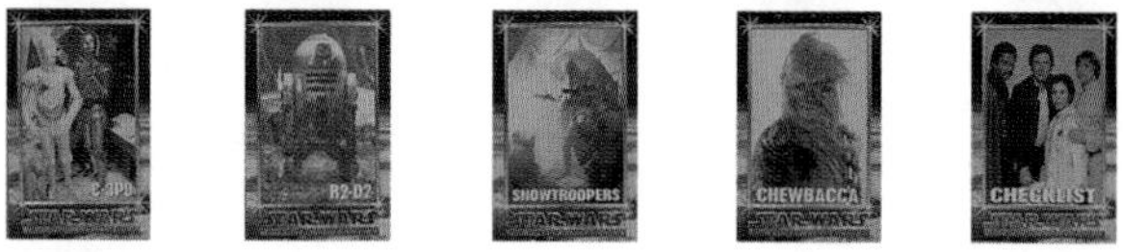

OG0016 OG0017 OG0018 OG0019 OG0020

Metallic Images

OG0001 21 Battle on Hoth 3.00
OG0002 22 Han and Luke on Patrol 3.00
OG0003 23 AT-AT Walkers 3.00
OG0004 24 Imperial and Rebel Starships 3.00
OG0005 25 Bespin's Cloud City 3.00
OG0006 26 Yoda 3.00
OG0007 27 Trapped on Cloud City 3.00
OG0008 28 Jedi Training 3.00
OG0009 29 Carbon Freeze Chamber 3.00
OG0010 30 Boba Fett 3.00
OG0011 31 Lando Calrissian 3.00
OG0012 32 Luke Battles Vader 3.00
OG0013 33 Darth Vader 3.00
OG0014 34 Luke Skywalker 3.00
OG0015 35 Princess Leia 3.00
OG0016 36 C-3PO 3.00
OG0017 37 R2-D2 .... 3.00
OG0018 38 Snowtroopers 3.00
OG0019 39 Chewbacca 3.00
OG0020 40 Checklist (cast photo) 3.00
OG0021 Set of 20 in collector's tin 62.00

CARDS: TIN, JEDI KNIGHTS

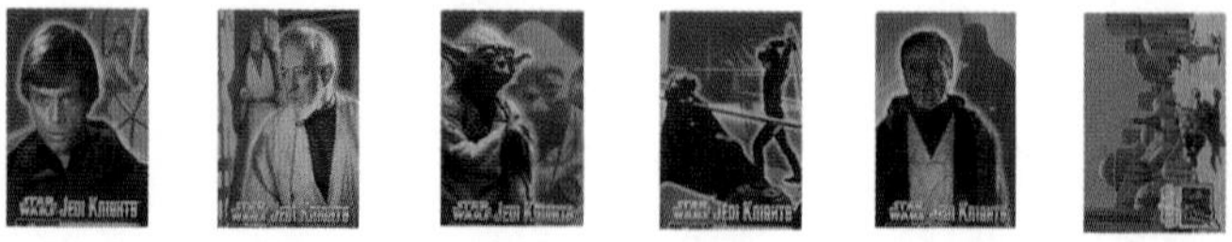

OM0001 OM0002 OM0003 OM0004 OM0005 OM0006

Metallic Impressions

OM0001 1 Luke Skywalker 4.00

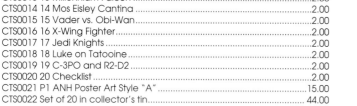

OM0002 2 Obi-Wan Kenobi..4.00
OM0003 3 Jedi Master Yoda 4.00
OM0004 4 Luke vs. Vader 4.00
OM0005 5 Anakin Skywalker 4.00
OM0006 6 Mos Eisley Spaceport (SE) 3.00
OM0007 Set of 6 in collector's tin 25.00

CARDS: TIN, RALPH MCQUARRIE ART

OM10001 OM10002 OM10003 OM10004 OM10005 OM10006 OM10007

OM10008 OM10009 OM10010 OM10011 OM10012 OM10013 OM10014

OM10015 OM10016 OM10017 OM10018 OM10019 OM10020

Metallic Impressions
OM10001 01 Star Wars Poster Concept / Character Sketches...................3.00
OM10002 02 C-3PO and R2-D2 / The Star Wars 3.00
OM10003 03 Faceoff / Poster Concept - Luke and Leia 3.00
OM10004 04 Darth Vader and Luke's Lightsaber Duel / Poster Concept - Full
Cast...3.00
OM10005 05 Imperial Stormtrooper with Lightsaber / Paperback Cover..3.00
OM10006 06 Escaping the Jawa Sandcrawler / Tusken Raiders 3.00
OM10007 07 Luke and the Twin Suns of Tatooine / Falcon in Docking Bay -
Early Concept..3.00
OM10008 08 Falcon in a City in the Clouds Hangar / Watching from the
Death Star 3.00
OM10009 09 Death Star Interior / Luke and Leia in Death Star Reactor
Core 3.00
OM10010 10 Y-Wing Fighters - Early Concept / The Main Throne Room,
Rebel Base on Yavin Four..................................3.00
OM10011 11 Imperial Walkers Attack Tauntaun Rider / Rebel Soldiers in the
Ice Trenches..
OM10012 12 Millennium Falcon Escapes Space Slug / Star Destroyers 3.00
OM10013 13 Luke and Yoda / Rendezvous with Destiny...............3.00
OM10014 14 Tie Fighter Approaches a City in the Clouds / Darth Vader
Awaits ....
OM10015 15 Confrontation in the Carbon-Freezing Chamber / Luke and
Leia 3.00
OM10016 16 The Droids Seek Jabba / In the Custody of a Gamorrean
Guard 3.00
OM10017 17 Luke in Jabba's Lair / Above the Sarlacc Pit........................3.00
OM10018 18 Rebels Plot Attack / Speeder Bike Chase 3.00
OM10019 19 Dark Lord's Arrival / Duel of the Jedi 3.00
OM10020 20 Emperor's Throne Room / Luke Attacked by the Emperor ...3.00
OM10021 Set of 20 in collector's tin 65.00

CARDS: TIN, ROTJ

OZ0001 OZ0002 OZ0003 OZ0004 OZ0005 OZ0006 OZ0007

OZ0008 OZ0009 OZ0010 OZ0011 OZ0012 OZ0013 OZ0014

OZ0015 OZ0016 OZ0017 OZ0018 OZ0019 OZ0020

Metallic Images
OZ0001 41 Death Star Reborn 3.00
OZ0002 42 In Jabba's Clutches 3.00
OZ0003 43 Cloaked Calrissian 3.00
OZ0004 44 Droid Dilemma 3.00
OZ0005 45 Max Rebo Band 3.00
OZ0006 46 Han Is Rescued 3.00
OZ0007 47 The Rancor Pit 3.00
OZ0008 48 Aboard A Skiff 3.00
OZ0009 49 The Escape Begins 3.00
OZ0010 50 Luke And Leia Escape 3.00
OZ0011 51 Ackbar In Command 3.00
OZ0012 52 Wily Wicket 3.00
OZ0013 53 Imperial Scout 3.00
OZ0014 54 Welcome To Endor 3.00
OZ0015 55 Battle Of Endor 3.00
OZ0016 56 Lord Vader Commands 3.00
OZ0017 57 Emperor's Trap 3.00
OZ0018 58 On Target..3.00
OZ0019 59 Final Battle 3.00
OZ0020 60 Checklist (Millennium Falcon Above Death Star II) 3.00
OZ0022 P3 ROTJ Poster Art..16.00
OZ0021 Set of 20 in collector's tin 62.00

CARDS: TIN, SOTE

ONE0001 ONE0002 ONE0003 ONE0004 ONE0005 ONE0006

Metallic Impressions
ONE0001 Issue 1: Art Montage of Major Characters.....................2.80
ONE0002 Issue 2: Boba Fett on Gall.....................................2.80
ONE0003 Issue 3: Luke Attacked on Tatooine 2.80
ONE0004 Issue 4: Leia and Chewie Disguised..........................2.80
ONE0005 Issue 5: Luke's Escape 2.80
ONE0006 Issue 6: Art Montage: Xizor....................................2.80
ONE0007 Set of 6 in collector's tin 20.00

CARDS: TOP TRUMPS

OTT0001 – OTT0004

Waddington
32 cards in deck. Only 4 show Star Wars designs.
OTT0002 Combat Craft (Star Destroyer) 4.00
OTT0003 Fighter Ship (X-Wing)...4.00
OTT0004 Outter Spacecraft (Tie Fighter)...............................4.00
OTT0001 Space Colonies (Death Star) 4.00

CARDS: TPM

Bluebird
Set of 30 large cards.

Cards: TPM

CRD0093 01 Anakin Skywalker 1.50
CRD0094 02 Obi-Wan Kenobi 1.50
CRD0095 03 Qui-Gon Jinn 1.50
CRD0096 04 Queen Amidala 1.50
CRD0097 05 Darth Maul 1.50
CRD0098 06 Padme 1.50
CRD0099 07 Jar Jar Binks 1.50
CRD0100 08 C-3PO 1.50
CRD0101 09 R2-D2 ....1.50
CRD0102 10 Watto 1.50
CRD0103 11 Mos Espa 1.50
CRD0104 12 Qui-Gon and Watto 1.50
CRD0105 13 Anakin's Podracer 1.50
CRD0106 14 Energy Binders (Jar Jar has trouble) 1.50
CRD0107 15 Podrace 1.50
CRD0108 16 Podrace 1.50
CRD0109 17 Sebulba 1.50
CRD0110 18 Desert Duel 1.50
CRD0111 19 Lightsaber Battle 1.50
CRD0112 20 Sith Lord (Darth Maul) 1.50
CRD0113 21 Master Yoda 1.50
CRD0114 22 Jedi vs. Sith 1.50
CRD0115 23 Gungan Sub 1.50
CRD0116 24 Gungans 1.50
CRD0117 25 Trade Federation Assault 1.50
CRD0118 26 Battle of Naboo (droid and tank).................................1.50
CRD0119 27 Ready for Combat 1.50
CRD0120 28 Battle Droids 1.50
CRD0121 29 Space Battle Over Naboo 1.50
CRD0122 30 Naboo Pilot 1.50

Set of 36 cards. 1-18 are medium, 19-36 are mini.
CRD0123 01 Boss Nass 1.00
CRD0124 02 C-3PO 1.00
CRD0125 03 Jar Jar Binks 1.00
CRD0126 04 R2-D2 ....1.00
CRD0127 05 Anakin Skywalker 1.00

CRD0093	CRD0094	CRD0095	CRD0096	CRD0097	CRD0098
CRD0099	CRD0100	CRD0101	CRD0102	CRD0103	CRD0104
CRD0105	CRD0106	CRD0107	CRD0108	CRD0109	CRD0110
CRD0111	CRD0112	CRD0113	CRD0114	CRD0115	CRD0116
CRD0117	CRD0118	CRD0119	CRD0120	CRD0121	CRD0122

CRD0128 06 Queen Amidala 1.00
CRD0129 07 Qui-Gon Jinn 1.00
CRD0130 08 Mace Windu 1.00
CRD0131 09 Obi-Wan Kenobi 1.00
CRD0132 10 Battle Droid 1.00
CRD0133 11 Sebulba 1.00

CRD0134 12 Darth Sidious 1.00
CRD0135 13 Nute Gunray 1.00
CRD0136 14 Rune Haako 1.00
CRD0137 15 Trade Federation Droid Starfighter 1.00
CRD0138 16 Trade Federation Tank 1.00
CRD0139 17 Darth Maul 1.00
CRD0140 18 Watto 1.00
CRD0141 19 Sio Bibble 1.00
CRD0142 20 Gungans on Kaadu 1.00
CRD0143 21 Naboo Starfighter 1.00
CRD0144 22 Jedi Temple 1.00
CRD0145 23 Royal Starship 1.00
CRD0146 24 Obi-Wan Kenobi 1.00
CRD0147 25 R2-D2 ....1.00
CRD0148 26 Anakin 1.00
CRD0149 27 Boss Nass 1.00
CRD0150 28 Bib Fortuna 1.00
CRD0151 29 Darth Maul 1.00
CRD0152 30 Darth Sidious 1.00
CRD0153 31 Battle Droid on STAP 1.00
CRD0154 32 Sebulba 1.00
CRD0155 33 Droid Control Ship 1.00
CRD0156 34 Trade Federation Landing Ship 1.00
CRD0157 35 Battle Droid 1.00
CRD0158 36 Jabba the Hutt 1.00

Frito-Lay

CRD0003	CRD0004	CRD0005	CRD0006	CRD0007	CRD0008
CRD0009	CRD0010	CRD0011	CRD0012	CRD0013	CRD0014

CRD0003 Anakin / Helping 1.00
CRD0004 Darth Maul / Pursuit 1.00
CRD0005 Darth Sidious / Domination 1.00
CRD0006 Jar Jar / Appetite 1.00
CRD0007 Nute and Rune / Cowardice 1.00
CRD0008 Obi-Wan / Honor 1.00
CRD0009 Padme / Curiosity 1.00
CRD0010 Queen Amidala / Duty 1.00
CRD0011 Qui-Gon / Instincts 1.00
CRD0012 R2-D2 / Bravery 1.00
CRD0013 Sebulba / Cheating 1.00
CRD0014 Watto / Chance 1.00

iKon

CRD0020 01 Padme 0.50
CRD0021 02 C-3PO 0.50
CRD0022 03 R2-D2 ....0.50
CRD0023 04 Watto 0.50
CRD0024 05 Mos Espa 0.50
CRD0025 06 Qui-Gon and Watto 0.50
CRD0026 07 Anakin's Podracer 0.50
CRD0027 08 Energy Binders 0.50
CRD0028 09 Podrace 0.50
CRD0029 10 Podrace 0.50
CRD0030 11 Sebulba 0.50
CRD0031 12 Darth Maul 0.50
CRD0032 13 Lightsaber Battle 0.50
CRD0033 14 Sith Lord 0.50
CRD0034 15 Master Yoda 0.50
CRD0035 16 Jedi vs. Sith 0.50
CRD0036 17 Gungan Sub 0.50
CRD0037 18 Gungans 0.50
CRD0038 19 Trade Federation Assault 0.50
CRD0039 20 Battle of Naboo 0.50
CRD0040 21 Ready for Combat 0.50
CRD0041 22 Battle Droids 0.50
CRD0042 23 Space Battle over Naboo 0.50
CRD0043 24 Naboo Pilot 0.50

CRD0044 25 Boss Nass 0.50
CRD0045 26 C-3PO 0.50
CRD0046 27 Jar Jar Binks 0.50
CRD0047 28 R2-D2 ....0.50
CRD0048 29 Anakin Skywalker 0.50
CRD0049 30 Queen Amidala 0.50
CRD0050 31 Qui-Gon Jinn 0.50
CRD0051 32 Mace Windu 0.50
CRD0052 33 Obi-Wan Kenobi 0.50
CRD0053 34 Battle Droid 0.50
CRD0054 35 Sebulba 0.50
CRD0055 36 Darth Sidious 0.50
CRD0056 37 Nute Gunray 0.50
CRD0057 38 Rune Haako 0.50
CRD0058 39 Trade Federation Droid Starfighter 0.50
CRD0059 40 Trade Federation Tank 0.50
CRD0060 41 Desert Duel 0.50
CRD0061 42 Watto 0.50
CRD0062 43 Sio Bibble 0.50
CRD0063 44 Gungans on Kaadu 0.50
CRD0064 45 Naboo Starfighter 0.50
CRD0065 46 Jedi Temple 0.50
CRD0066 47 Royal Starship 0.50
CRD0067 48 Obi-Wan Kenobi 0.50
CRD0068 49 R2-D2 ....0.50
CRD0069 50 Anakin Skywalker 0.50
CRD0070 51 Boss Nass 0.50
CRD0071 52 Trade Federation Landing Ship 0.50
CRD0072 53 Darth Maul 0.50
CRD0073 54 Darth Sidious 0.50
CRD0074 55 Battle Droid on STAP 0.50
CRD0075 56 Sebulba 0.50
CRD0076 57 Droid Control Ship 0.50
CRD0077 58 Bib Fortuna 0.50
CRD0078 59 Battle Droid 0.50
CRD0079 60 Jabba the Hutt 0.50
CRD0080 61 Checklist 0.50

Kentucky Fried Chicken

CRD0255	CRD0256	CRD0257	CRD0258	CRD0259	CRD0260	CRD0261
CRD0262	CRD0263	CRD0264	CRD0015	CRD0016	CRD0017	CRD0018
CRD0019	CRD0265	CRD0266	CRD0267	CRD0268	CRD0269	CRD0270
CRD0271	CRD0272	CRD0273	CRD0274	CRD0275	CRD0276	CRD0277
CRD0278	CRD0279	CRD0280	CRD0281	CRD0282	CRD0283	CRD0284

CRD0255 01 Qui-Gon Jinn 1.20
CRD0256 02 Jar Jar Binks 1.20
CRD0257 03 Queen Amidala 1.20
CRD0258 04 Obi-Wan Kenobi 1.20
CRD0259 05 Mace Windu 1.20

CRD0260 06 Destroyer Droid 1.20
CRD0261 07 Sebulba 1.20
CRD0262 08 Darth Maul 1.20
CRD0263 09 Watto 1.20
CRD0264 10 Anakin Skywalker 1.20
CRD0015 Darth Maul 1.75
CRD0016 Jar Jar Binks 1.75
CRD0017 Obi-Wan Kenobi 1.75
CRD0019 Queen Amidala 1.75
CRD0018 Qui-Gon 1.75

Kentucky Fried Chicken (UK)
CRD0265 01 Qui-Gon Jinn 1.00
CRD0266 02 R2-D2 ....1.00
CRD0267 03 Jar Jar Binks 1.00
CRD0268 04 Queen Amidala 1.00
CRD0269 05 Shmi Skywalker 1.00
CRD0270 06 Obi-Wan Kenobi 1.00
CRD0271 07 Senator Palpatine 1.00
CRD0272 08 Mace Windu 1.00
CRD0273 09 Destroyer Droid 1.00
CRD0274 10 Jabba the Hutt 1.00
CRD0275 11 Sebulba 1.00
CRD0276 12 Yoda 1.00
CRD0277 13 Darth Maul 1.00
CRD0278 14 C-3PO 1.00
CRD0279 15 Watto 1.00
CRD0280 16 Padme 1.00
CRD0281 17 Battle Droid 1.00
CRD0282 18 Nute Gunray 1.00
CRD0283 19 Darth Sidious 1.00
CRD0284 20 Anakin Skywalker 1.00

Pepsi Cola
CRD0159 01 Anakin Skywalker 1.00
CRD0160 02 Sebulba 1.00
CRD0161 03 Qui-Gon Jinn 1.00
CRD0162 04 Watto 1.00
CRD0163 05 Jabba the Hutt 1.00
CRD0164 06 Senator Palpatine 1.00
CRD0165 07 R2-D2 ....1.00
CRD0166 08 Darth Sidious 1.00
CRD0167 09 Darth Maul 1.00
CRD0168 10 Jar Jar Binks 1.00
CRD0169 11 Mace Windu 1.00
CRD0170 12 Obi-Wan Kenobi 1.00
CRD0171 13 Captain Panaka 1.00
CRD0172 14 Rune Haako 1.00
CRD0173 15 Ric Olie 1.00
CRD0174 16 Destroyer Droid 1.00
CRD0175 17 Queen Amidala 1.00
CRD0176 18 Padme Naberrie 1.00
CRD0177 19 Shmi Skywalker 1.00
CRD0178 20 Battle Droid 1.00
CRD0179 21 Chancellor Velorum 1.00
CRD0180 22 C-3PO 1.00
CRD0181 23 Nute Gunray 1.00
CRD0182 24 Boss Nass 1.00
CRD0183 Collector Card Game Booklet.......................2.00

Pepsi Cola (Australia)
3" circular carton cut-outs.
CRD0081 Anakin Skywalker 0.50
CRD0082 C-3PO 0.50
CRD0083 Darth Maul 0.50
CRD0084 Jabba the Hutt 0.50
CRD0085 Jar Jar Binks 0.50
CRD0086 Obi-Wan Kenobi 0.50
CRD0087 Queen Amidala 0.50
CRD0088 Qui-Gon Jinn 0.50
CRD0089 R2-D2 ....0.50
CRD0090 Sebulba 0.50
CRD0091 Watto 0.50
CRD0092 Yoda 0.50

Pepsi Cola (Germany)
CRD0210 01 Anakin Skywalker (podrace gear)..............1.00
CRD0211 02 Anakin Skywalker 1.00
CRD0212 03 Shmi Skywalker 1.00
CRD0213 04 Queen Amidala (red) 1.00
CRD0214 05 Queen Amidala (white)...........................1.00

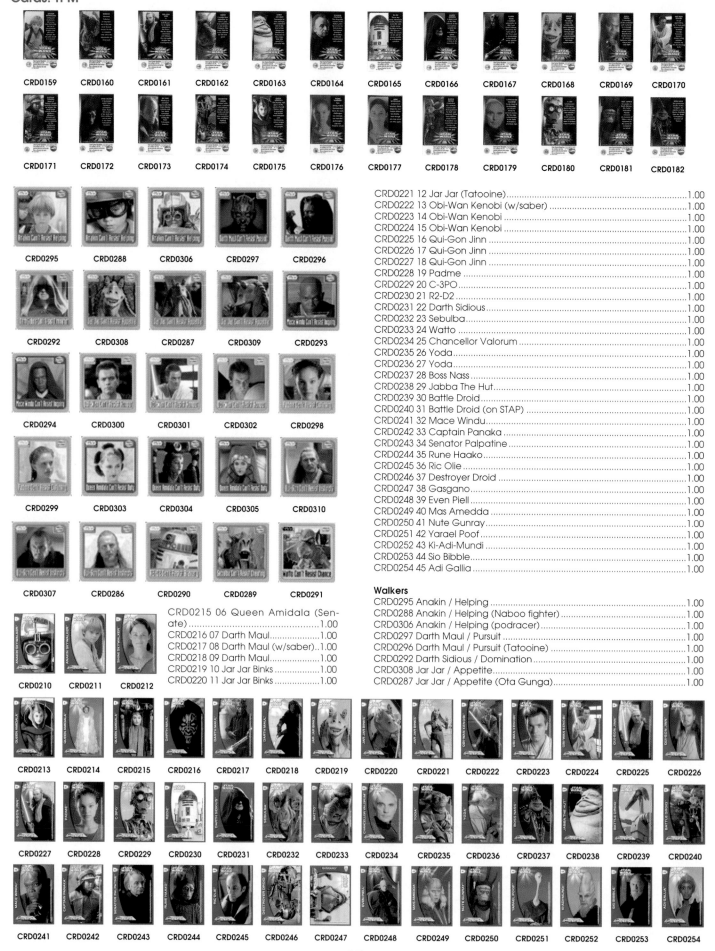

CRD0159 CRD0160 CRD0161 CRD0162 CRD0163 CRD0164 CRD0165 CRD0166 CRD0167 CRD0168 CRD0169 CRD0170

CRD0171 CRD0172 CRD0173 CRD0174 CRD0175 CRD0176 CRD0177 CRD0178 CRD0179 CRD0180 CRD0181 CRD0182

CRD0295 CRD0288 CRD0306 CRD0297 CRD0296

CRD0292 CRD0308 CRD0287 CRD0309 CRD0293

CRD0294 CRD0300 CRD0301 CRD0302 CRD0298

CRD0299 CRD0303 CRD0304 CRD0305 CRD0310

CRD0307 CRD0286 CRD0290 CRD0289 CRD0291

CRD0210 CRD0211 CRD0212

CRD0215 06 Queen Amidala (Senate) 1.00
CRD0216 07 Darth Maul....................1.00
CRD0217 08 Darth Maul (w/saber)..1.00
CRD0218 09 Darth Maul....................1.00
CRD0219 10 Jar Jar Binks 1.00
CRD0220 11 Jar Jar Binks 1.00

CRD0221 12 Jar Jar (Tatooine)..1.00
CRD0222 13 Obi-Wan Kenobi (w/saber) 1.00
CRD0223 14 Obi-Wan Kenobi 1.00
CRD0224 15 Obi-Wan Kenobi 1.00
CRD0225 16 Qui-Gon Jinn 1.00
CRD0226 17 Qui-Gon Jinn 1.00
CRD0227 18 Qui-Gon Jinn 1.00
CRD0228 19 Padme 1.00
CRD0229 20 C-3PO 1.00
CRD0230 21 R2-D2 ....1.00
CRD0231 22 Darth Sidious 1.00
CRD0232 23 Sebulba 1.00
CRD0233 24 Watto 1.00
CRD0234 25 Chancellor Valorum 1.00
CRD0235 26 Yoda...1.00
CRD0236 27 Yoda...1.00
CRD0237 28 Boss Nass 1.00
CRD0238 29 Jabba The Hut 1.00
CRD0239 30 Battle Droid 1.00
CRD0240 31 Battle Droid (on STAP) 1.00
CRD0241 32 Mace Windu 1.00
CRD0242 33 Captain Panaka 1.00
CRD0243 34 Senator Palpatine 1.00
CRD0244 35 Rune Haako 1.00
CRD0245 36 Ric Olie 1.00
CRD0246 37 Destroyer Droid 1.00
CRD0247 38 Gasgano 1.00
CRD0248 39 Even Piell 1.00
CRD0249 40 Mas Amedda 1.00
CRD0250 41 Nute Gunray 1.00
CRD0251 42 Yarael Poof 1.00
CRD0252 43 Ki-Adi-Mundi 1.00
CRD0253 44 Sio Bibble 1.00
CRD0254 45 Adi Gallia 1.00

Walkers
CRD0295 Anakin / Helping 1.00
CRD0288 Anakin / Helping (Naboo fighter) 1.00
CRD0306 Anakin / Helping (podracer) 1.00
CRD0297 Darth Maul / Pursuit 1.00
CRD0296 Darth Maul / Pursuit (Tatooine) 1.00
CRD0292 Darth Sidious / Domination 1.00
CRD0308 Jar Jar / Appetite...1.00
CRD0287 Jar Jar / Appetite (Ota Gunga)..................................1.00

CRD0213 CRD0214 CRD0215 CRD0216 CRD0217 CRD0218 CRD0219 CRD0220 CRD0221 CRD0222 CRD0223 CRD0224 CRD0225 CRD0226

CRD0227 CRD0228 CRD0229 CRD0230 CRD0231 CRD0232 CRD0233 CRD0234 CRD0235 CRD0236 CRD0237 CRD0238 CRD0239 CRD0240

CRD0241 CRD0242 CRD0243 CRD0244 CRD0245 CRD0246 CRD0247 CRD0248 CRD0249 CRD0250 CRD0251 CRD0252 CRD0253 CRD0254

CRD0309 Jar Jar / Appetite (Tatooine)........................1.00
CRD0293 Mace Windu / Inquiry...............................1.00
CRD0294 Mace Windu / Inquiry (hooded).....................1.00
CRD0300 Obi-Wan / Honor...................................1.00
CRD0301 Obi-Wan / Honor (Jedi duel).......................1.00
CRD0302 Obi-Wan / Honor (Queen's starship)................1.00
CRD0298 Padme / Curiosity.................................1.00
CRD0299 Padme / Curiosity (Tatooine)......................1.00
CRD0303 Queen Amidala / Duty (celebration)................1.00
CRD0304 Queen Amidala / Duty (Coruscant)..................1.00
CRD0305 Queen Amidala / Duty (Naboo)......................1.00
CRD0310 Qui-Gon / Instincts (Jedi duel)...................1.00
CRD0307 Qui-Gon / Instincts (Queen's starship)............1.00
CRD0286 Qui-Gon / Instincts (Tatooine)....................1.00
CRD0290 R2-D2 / Bravery...................................1.00
CRD0289 Sebulba / Cheating................................1.00
CRD0291 Watto / Chance....................................1.00

CARDS: TV WEEK

OH0001   OH0002   OH0003   OH0004

TV Week
OH0001 1 Darth Vader......................................3.50
OH0002 2 Luke and Leia....................................3.50
OH0003 3 C-3PO and R2-D2..................................3.50
OH0004 4 Han and Chewbacca................................3.50

CARDS: UK

Merlin Publishing Internat'l Ltd.
OCU0001 001 Imperial Star Destroyer 1.60
OCU0002 002 R2-D2 and C-3PO...............................1.60
OCU0003 003 Rebel Forces..................................1.60
OCU0004 004 Darth Vader...................................1.60
OCU0005 005 C-3PO...1.60
OCU0006 006 Sandcrawler...................................1.60
OCU0007 007 Stormtrooper on Dewback.......................1.60
OCU0008 008 Luke Skywalker and Owen Lars..................1.60
OCU0009 009 Luke, C-3PO, and R2-D2........................1.60
OCU0010 010 Tusken Raider.................................1.60
OCU0011 011 Luke Skywalker with Lightsaber 1.60
OCU0012 012 Death Star and Star Destroyer.................1.60
OCU0013 013 Landspeeder in Mos Eisley.....................1.60
OCU0014 014 Luke, Ben, and C-3PO with Stormtroopers.......1.60
OCU0015 015 Han Solo and Chewbacca........................1.60
OCU0016 016 Han Solo with Jabba the Hutt..................1.60
OCU0017 017 The Millenniun Falcon 1.60
OCU0018 018 Princess Leia with Grand Moff Tarkin..........1.60
OCU0019 019 Millennium Falcon Interior....................1.60
OCU0020 020 Death Star Docking Bay........................1.60
OCU0021 021 Luke, Han, and C-3PO..........................1.60
OCU0022 022 Han Solo and Princess Leia 1.60
OCU0023 023 Ben Kenobi....................................1.60
OCU0024 024 Millennium Falcon.............................1.60
OCU0025 025 Millennium Falcon approaching Yavin 1.60
OCU0026 026 Han Solo with Luke Skywalker..................1.60
OCU0027 027 X-Wing fighters...............................1.60
OCU0028 028 X-Wing fighter and Tie fighter................1.60
OCU0029 029 Y-Wing fighter and Tie fighter................1.60
OCU0030 030 Darth Vader / Tie fighter interior............1.60
OCU0031 031 Princess Leia and C-3PO.......................1.60
OCU0032 032 Luke Skywalker / X-Wing interior..............1.60
OCU0033 033 Death Star exhaust port.......................1.60
OCU0034 034 Luke, Leia, and Han...........................1.60
OCU0035 035 Han Solo winking..............................1.60
OCU0036 036 Imperial Probot...............................1.60
OCU0037 037 Luke Skywalker in Wampa lair..................1.60
OCU0038 038 Han Solo with Rebel commander.................1.60
OCU0039 039 Han Solo waving to Snowspeeder.................1.60
OCU0040 040 Han Solo firing at Imperial probe droid 1.60
OCU0041 041 Darth Vader with General Veers................1.60
OCU0042 042 Luke Skywalker.................................1.60

OCU0043 043 Snowspeeder / AT-AT legs......................1.60
OCU0044 044 Millennium Falcon leaving rebel base..........1.60
OCU0045 045 Falcon entering asteroid field................1.60
OCU0046 046 Exploding Tie fighter.........................1.60
OCU0047 047 Yoda..1.60
OCU0048 048 Luke and Yoda.................................1.60
OCU0049 049 Millennium Falcon and Star Destroyer..........1.60
OCU0050 050 Falcon on back of Star Destroyer..............1.60
OCU0051 051 Millennium Falcon cockpit interior............1.60
OCU0052 052 Rebels arriving Besbin........................1.60
OCU0053 053 Darth Vader tortures Han Solo.................1.60
OCU0054 054 Luke's X-Wing approaching Cloud City..........1.60
OCU0055 055 Han Solo / Carbon freezing chamber 1.60
OCU0056 056 Luke and Darth Vader duel.....................1.60
OCU0057 057 Slave I leaving Cloud City....................1.60
OCU0058 058 Darth Vader...................................1.60
OCU0059 059 Luke Skywalker................................1.60
OCU0060 060 Luke Skywalker / Reactor shaft................1.60
OCU0061 061 Luke and Vader dueling / reactor shaft........1.60
OCU0062 062 Darth Vader reaching out to Luke..............1.60
OCU0063 063 Luke Skywalker................................1.60
OCU0064 064 Millennium Falcon and Cloud City..............1.60
OCU0065 065 R2-D2 repairing C-3PO.........................1.60
OCU0066 066 Luke / Millennium Falcon main hold 1.60
OCU0067 067 Leia / Millennium Falcon's cockpit 1.60
OCU0068 068 Luke Skywalker's bionic hand..................1.60
OCU0069 069 R2-D2 with C-3PO..............................1.60
OCU0070 070 Luke, Leia, R2-D2, and C-3PO..................1.60
OCU0071 071 Shuttle leaving Star Destroyer................1.60
OCU0072 072 Darth Vader with Grand Moff Jerjerod..........1.60
OCU0073 073 Jabba's Palace................................1.60
OCU0074 074 Jabba The Hutt................................1.60
OCU0075 075 Boushh the bounty hunter......................1.60
OCU0076 076 Han Solo escaping the carbonite...............1.60
OCU0077 077 Luke with Bib Fortuna.........................1.60
OCU0078 078 Luke Skywalker in Rancor's grip...............1.60
OCU0079 079 Luke, Han, and Chewbacca......................1.60
OCU0080 080 Luke Skywalker................................1.60
OCU0081 081 Boba Fett.....................................1.60
OCU0082 082 Han Solo reaches for Lando 1.60
OCU0083 083 C-3PO and Salacious Crumb 1.60
OCU0084 084 Luke and Leia on Jabba's Sail Barge 1.60
OCU0085 085 The Emperor Palpatine 1.60
OCU0086 086 Yoda Instructing Luke 1.60
OCU0087 087 Mon Mothma and Admiral Ackbar 1.60
OCU0088 088 Shuttle Tydirium / Cockpit 1.60
OCU0089 089 Luke and Leia on Speeder Bike 1.60
OCU0090 090 Luke tackles a Scout Trooper..................1.60
OCU0091 091 Luke, Han, and Chewie surrounded 1.60
OCU0092 092 Luke and Leia at the Ewok village 1.60
OCU0093 093 The Rebel fleet...............................1.60
OCU0094 094 Vader and Luke before the Emperor 1.60
OCU0095 095 Ackbar watching the Rebel fleet..............1.60
OCU0096 096 Battle above the Death Star...................1.60
OCU0097 097 Han plants explosive charges.................1.60
OCU0098 098 The Death Star fires on the Rebels 1.60
OCU0099 099 Lightsaber's clash............................1.60
OCU0100 100 Darth Vader is defeated.......................1.60
OCU0101 101 The Emperor / Throne room 1.60
OCU0102 102 Millennium Falcon / Int. Death Star...........1.60
OCU0103 103 Anakin Skywalker..............................1.60
OCU0104 104 The Death Star explodes.......................1.60
OCU0105 105 Anakin, Ben, and Yoda.........................1.60
OCU0106 106 Luke Skywalker................................1.60
OCU0107 107 Han Solo......................................1.60
OCU0108 108 Leia Organa...................................1.60
OCU0109 109 Obi-Wan Kenobi................................1.60
OCU0110 110 Chewbacca.....................................1.60
OCU0111 111 C-3PO...1.60
OCU0112 112 R2-D2...1.60
OCU0113 113 Darth Vader...................................1.60
OCU0114 114 Yoda..1.60
OCU0115 115 Boba Fett.....................................1.60
OCU0116 116 X-Wing fighter................................1.60
OCU0117 117 Death Star....................................1.60
OCU0118 118 Sandcrawler...................................1.60
OCU0119 119 Millennium Falcon.............................1.60
OCU0120 120 Tie fighter...................................1.60
OCU0121 121 Imperial Shuttle..............................1.60
OCU0122 122 AT-AT...1.60
OCU0123 123 Star Destroyer................................1.60

Cards: UK

OCU0124 124 Vader's Tie fighter 1.60
OCU0125 125 Check List 1.60
OCU0126 P1 same as card #76 .... 3.50
OCU0127 P2 same as card #27 .... 3.50
OCU0128 P3 same as card #69 .... 3.50

Walkers

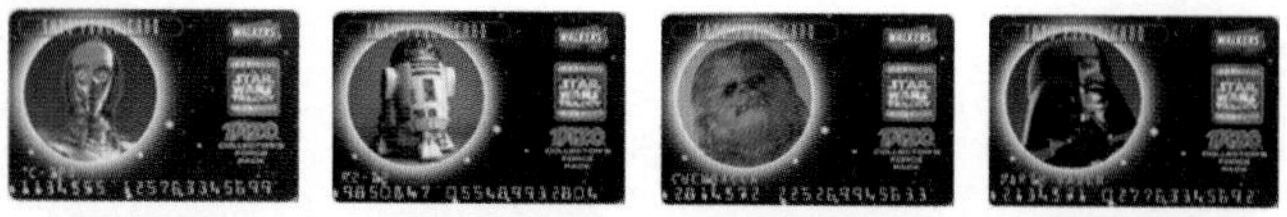

OCU0135 OCU0136 OCU0137 OCU0138

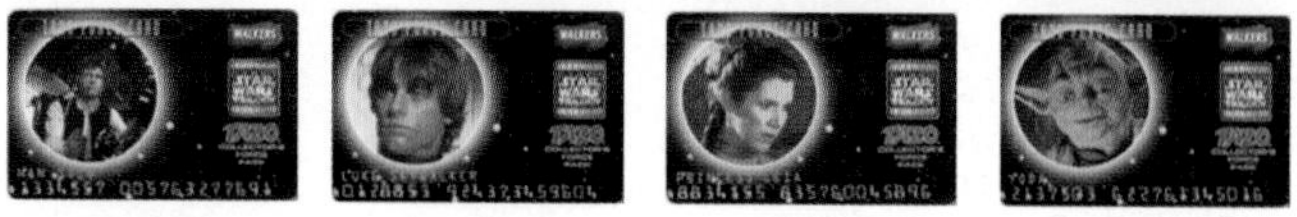

OCU0139 OCU0140 OCU0141 OCU0142

OCU0135 C-3PO 4.00
OCU0137 Chewbacca 4.00
OCU0138 Darth Vader 4.00
OCU0139 Han Solo 4.00
OCU0140 Luke Skywalker 4.00
OCU0141 Princess Leia 4.00
OCU0136 R2-D2 .... 4.00
OCU0142 Yoda 4.00

CARDS: VEHICLE

Topps

OAV0077 #01 (3Di) Luke and Shuttle 3.50
OAV0078 #02 (3Di) Leia and X-Wing 3.50
OAV0001 01 Title Card 1.00
OAV0002 02 Millennium Falcon 1.00
OAV0003 03 A-Wing 1.00
OAV0004 04 B-Wing 1.00
OAV0005 05 Y-Wing 1.00
OAV0006 06 Z-95 Headhunter 1.00
OAV0007 07 X-Wing 1.00
OAV0008 08 V-Wing Air Speeder 1.00
OAV0009 09 E-Wing Fighter 1.00
OAV0010 10 Rebel Snowspeeder 1.00
OAV0011 11 Rebel Blockade Runner 1.00
OAV0012 12 Escape Pod 1.00
OAV0013 13 Rebel Cruiser 1.00
OAV0014 14 Rebel Transport 1.00
OAV0015 15 Mon Cal Cruiser 1.00
OAV0016 16 Nebulon Ranger 1.00
OAV0017 17 T-16 Skyhopper 1.00
OAV0018 18 Luke's Landspeeder 1.00
OAV0019 19 Jawa Sandcrawler 1.00
OAV0020 20 Sail Barge 1.00
OAV0021 21 Lady Luck 1.00
OAV0022 22 Twin-Pod Cloud Car 1.00
OAV0023 23 Slave I 1.00
OAV0024 24 IG-2000 .... 1.00
OAV0025 25 Hound's Tooth 1.00
OAV0026 26 S-Swoop 1.00
OAV0027 27 Outrider 1.00
OAV0028 28 Virago 1.00
OAV0029 29 Stinger 1.00
OAV0030 30 AT-PT 1.00
OAV0031 31 AT-ST 1.00
OAV0032 32 AT-AT 1.00
OAV0033 33 Speeder Bike 1.00
OAV0034 34 Chariot Lav 1.00
OAV0035 35 Tie Fighter 1.00
OAV0036 36 Tie Bomber 1.00
OAV0037 37 Tie Interceptor 1.00

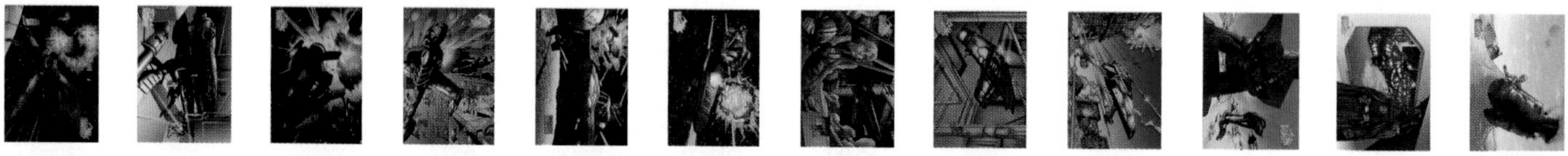

OAV0001 OAV0002 OAV0003 OAV0004 OAV0005 OAV0006 OAV0007 OAV0008 OAV0009 OAV0010 OAV0011 OAV0012

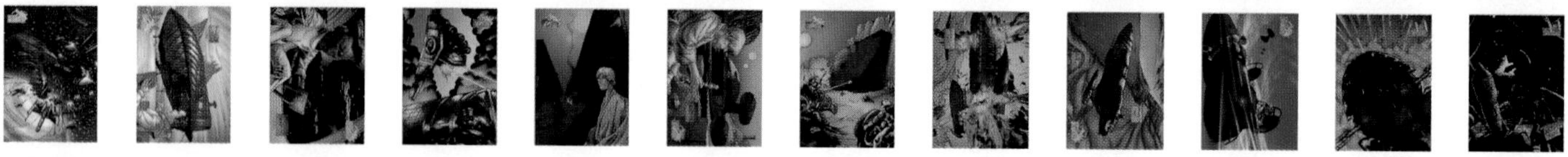

OAV0013 OAV0014 OAV0015 OAV0016 OAV0017 OAV0018 OAV0019 OAV0020 OAV0021 OAV0022 OAV0023 OAV0024

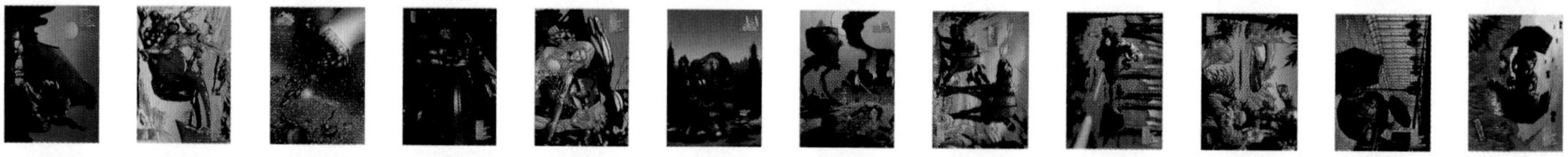

OAV0025 OAV0026 OAV0027 OAV0028 OAV0029 OAV0030 OAV0031 OAV0032 OAV0033 OAV0034 OAV0035 OAV0036

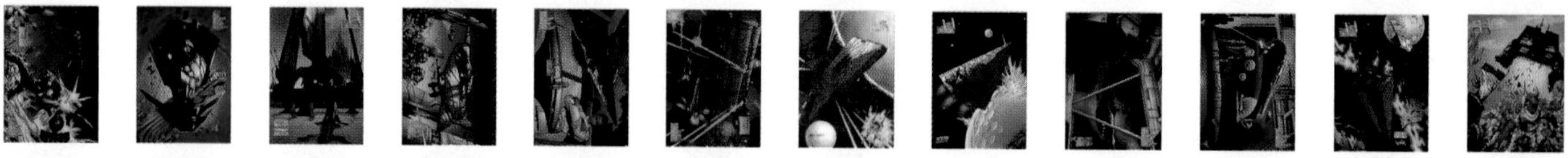

OAV0037 OAV0038 OAV0039 OAV0040 OAV0041 OAV0042 OAV0043 OAV0044 OAV0045 OAV0046 OAV0047 OAV0048

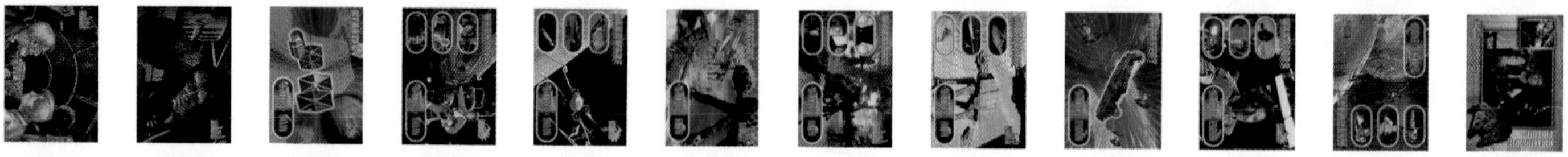

OAV0049 OAV0050 OAV0051 OAV0052 OAV0053 OAV0054 OAV0055 OAV0056 OAV0057 OAV0058 OAV0059 OAV0060

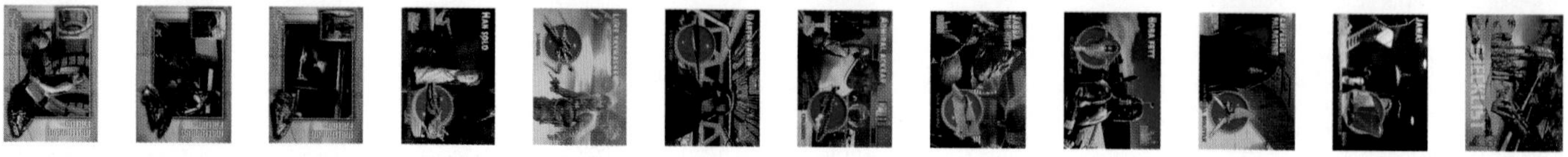

OAV0061 OAV0062 OAV0063 OAV0064 OAV0065 OAV0066 OAV0067 OAV0068 OAV0069 OAV0070 OAV0071 OAV0072

OAV0038 38 Tie Advanced 1.00
OAV0039 39 Lambda-Class Shuttle 1.00
OAV0040 40 I-7 Howlrunner 1.00
OAV0041 41 Interdictor Cruiser 1.00
OAV0042 42 Lancer Frigate 1.00
OAV0043 43 Imperial Star Destroyer 1.00
OAV0044 44 Victory Star Destroyer 1.00
OAV0045 45 Executor 1.00
OAV0046 46 Eclipse Star Destroyer 1.00
OAV0047 47 Sun Crusher 1.00
OAV0048 48 World Devastator 1.00
OAV0049 49 Death Star 1.00
OAV0050 50 Death Star II 1.00
OAV0051 51 Battle of Yavin - Strategy 1.00
OAV0052 52 Battle of Yavin - Warriors 1.00
OAV0053 53 Battle of Yavin - Hardware 1.00
OAV0054 54 Battle of Hoth - Strategy 1.00
OAV0055 55 Battle of Hot - Warriors 1.00
OAV0056 56 Battle of Hoth - Hardware 1.00
OAV0057 57 Battle of Endor - Strategy 1.00
OAV0058 58 Battle of Endor - Warriors 1.00
OAV0059 59 Battle of Endor - Hardware 1.00
OAV0060 60 Gun Port (Falcon subset) 1.00
OAV0061 61 Smuggler's Hold (Falcon subset) 1.00
OAV0062 62 Cockpit (Falcon subset) 1.00
OAV0063 63 Hyperdrive (Falcon subset) 1.00
OAV0064 64 Millennium Falcon (Han Solo) 1.00
OAV0065 65 X-Wing (Luke) 1.00
OAV0066 66 Executor (Darth Vader) 1.00
OAV0067 67 Mon Cal Cruiser (Ackbar) 1.00
OAV0068 68 Sail Barge (Jabba) 1.00
OAV0069 69 Slave 1 (Boba Fett) 1.00
OAV0070 70 Shuttle (Emperor Palpatine) 1.00
OAV0071 71 Jawa Sandcrawler (Jawas) 1.00
OAV0072 72 Checklist 1.00
OAV0073 C1 AT-ST 4.00
OAV0074 C2 Slave I 4.00
OAV0075 C3 X-Wing 4.00
OAV0076 C4 Lambda Shuttle 4.00
OAV0081 P1 Biker Scouts on Speeder Bikes w/Imperial Shuttle (3,200 Produced) 85.00
OAV0082 P1 Refractor Biker Scouts on Speeder Bikes w/Imperial Shuttle (350 Produced) 160.00
OAV0083 P2 Biker Scouts on Speeder Bikes w/Death Star (1,600 Produced) 115.00
OAV0084 P2 Refractor Biker Scouts on Speeder Bikes w/Death Star 175 Produced 175.00
OAV0080 Redeemed Card Oversized 3D Card 9.00
OAV0079 Redemption Card Sketch of Combined 3D Card 6.00
OAV0085 Unopened Retail Box 26.00

CARDS: WIDEVISION, ANH

Topps

OTA0139 #00 Luke by X-Wing (Widevision Binder Only) 5.00
OTA0001 001 Title Card - Art 1.00
OTA0002 002 Star Destroyer Belly 1.00
OTA0003 003 The Tantive IV - Captured 1.00
OTA0004 004 Droids in Hallway 1.00
OTA0005 005 Rebels in Blockade Runner 1.00
OTA0006 006 Battle in Hallway 1.00
OTA0007 007 Leia and R2 .... 1.00
OTA0008 008 Darth and Commander Antilles 1.00
OTA0009 009 Leia 1.00
OTA0010 010 Escape Pod View 1.00
OTA0011 011 Alone in the Desert 1.00
OTA0012 012 Shocked Droid 1.00
OTA0013 013 Sandcrawler 1.00
OTA0014 014 Reunited Droids 1.00
OTA0015 015 "Look Sir, Droids!" 1.00
OTA0016 016 Owen, Luke, and Jawa 1.00
OTA0017 017 Luke Discovers Hologram 1.00
OTA0018 018 Leia's Hologram 1.00
OTA0019 019 Dinner Conversation 1.00
OTA0020 020 Setting Suns 1.00
OTA0021 021 Landspeeder 1.00
OTA0022 022 Tusken Raiders 1.00
OTA0023 023 Tuskens and Bantha 1.00
OTA0024 024 Tusken Challenge 1.00
OTA0025 025 Rescuing Luke 1.00
OTA0026 026 Luke, Obi-Wan, and C-3PO 1.00
OTA0027 027 Luke with New Saber 1.00
OTA0028 028 Discussing the Force 1.00
OTA0029 029 Leia's Hologram 1.00
OTA0030 030 Approaching the Death Star 1.00
OTA0031 031 Imperial Conference 1.00
OTA0032 032 Making a Point 1.00
OTA0033 033 Choking on Vader's Response 1.00
OTA0034 034 Lar's Homestead Destroyed 1.00
OTA0035 035 Vader Interrogates Leia 1.00
OTA0036 036 Ext. Tatooine - Wasteland 1.00
OTA0037 037 Entering Mos Eisley 1.00
OTA0038 038 Cantina Creatures 1.00
OTA0039 039 Bartender Pointing 1.00
OTA0040 040 Wolfman 1.00
OTA0041 041 Mos Eisley Cantina 1.00
OTA0042 042 Obi-Wan's Saber 1.00
OTA0043 043 Han and Chewie 1.00
OTA0044 044 Greedo and Han 1.00
OTA0045 045 Look Greedo 1.00
OTA0046 046 Mos Eisley Street 1.00
OTA0047 047 At the Falcon 1.00
OTA0048 048 The Falcon Takes Off 1.00
OTA0049 049 Star Destroyers in Space 1.00
OTA0050 050 Star Destroyer Chases Falcon 1.00
OTA0051 051 Falcon Cockpit 1.00
OTA0052 052 Tarkin and Leia 1.00
OTA0053 053 Death Star Beam 1.00
OTA0054 054 Taking Aim 1.00
OTA0055 055 Alderaan 1.00
OTA0056 056 Practicing with a Saber 1.00
OTA0057 057 Playing Chess 1.00
OTA0058 058 Remote Vs. Luke 1.00
OTA0059 059 Falcon 1.00
OTA0060 060 In the Cockpit 1.00
OTA0061 061 Approaching the Death Star 1.00
OTA0062 062 Death Star Hangar Bay 1.00
OTA0063 063 Hangar 2037 .... 1.00
OTA0064 064 Darth in Hangar 2037 .... 1.00
OTA0065 065 Out of Hiding - Falcon 1.00
OTA0066 066 Stormtrooper Fires 1.00
OTA0067 067 "She's Rich" 1.00
OTA0068 068 Wookie Prisoner 1.00
OTA0069 069 Detention Area 1.00
OTA0070 070 "Into the Garbage Chute Flyboy" 1.00
OTA0071 071 Garbage Problems 1.00
OTA0072 072 At the Tractor Beam 1.00
OTA0073 073 Firing Across the Chasm 1.00
OTA0074 074 Swinging 1.00
OTA0075 075 Vader and Ben Duel 1.00
OTA0076 076 Luke Fires 1.00
OTA0077 077 Falcon Away 1.00
OTA0078 078 Comforting Luke 1.00
OTA0079 079 Han Mans the Guns 1.00
OTA0080 080 Luke Mans the Guns 1.00
OTA0081 081 Near Yavin 1.00
OTA0082 082 Yavin's Moon 1.00
OTA0083 083 Death Star Near Yavin 1.00
OTA0084 084 Battle Plan 1.00
OTA0085 085 Han and his Reward 1.00
OTA0086 086 Hangar Deck 1.00
OTA0087 087 Sentry 1.00
OTA0088 088 X-Wing Formation 1.00
OTA0089 089 X-Wings Approach Death Star 1.00
OTA0090 090 Tower 1.00
OTA0091 091 Watching the Battle 1.00
OTA0092 092 Ties 1.00
OTA0093 093 Tie Chases X-Wing 1.00
OTA0094 094 War Room 1.00
OTA0095 095 Tie Cockpit View 1.00
OTA0096 096 The Trench 1.00
OTA0097 097 War Room Commanders 1.00
OTA0098 098 Y-Wings 1.00
OTA0099 099 X-Wings 1.00
OTA0100 100 Exploded X-Wing 1.00
OTA0101 101 Vader's Tie 1.00
OTA0102 102 Vader in Cockpit 1.00
OTA0103 103 Vader's View 1.00
OTA0104 104 Death Star War Room 1.00
OTA0105 105 Vader and Wingmen 1.00
OTA0106 106 Falcon 1.00

OTA0001 OTA0002 OTA0003 OTA0004 OTA0005 OTA0006
OTA0007 OTA0008 OTA0009 OTA0010 OTA0011 OTA0012
OTA0013 OTA0014 OTA0015 OTA0016 OTA0017 OTA0018
OTA0019 OTA0020 OTA0021 OTA0022 OTA0023 OTA0024
OTA0025 OTA0026 OTA0027 OTA0028 OTA0029 OTA0030
OTA0031 OTA0032 OTA0033 OTA0034 OTA0035 OTA0036
OTA0037 OTA0038 OTA0039 OTA0040 OTA0041 OTA0042
OTA0043 OTA0044 OTA0045 OTA0046 OTA0047 OTA0048
OTA0049 OTA0050 OTA0051 OTA0052 OTA0053 OTA0054
OTA0055 OTA0056 OTA0057 OTA0058 OTA0059 OTA0060
OTA0061 OTA0062 OTA0063 OTA0064 OTA0065 OTA0066
OTA0067 OTA0068 OTA0069 OTA0070 OTA0071 OTA0072
OTA0073 OTA0074 OTA0075 OTA0076 OTA0077 OTA0078

OTA0107 107 Leia Watches..1.00
OTA0108 108 Luke Uses the Force 1.00
OTA0109 109 Hitting the Target...1.00
OTA0110 110 Exploding Death Star......................................1.00
OTA0111 111 Han and Chewie...1.00
OTA0112 112 Vader Unbalanced...1.00
OTA0113 113 Back to Yavin...1.00
OTA0114 114 Congratulations..1.00
OTA0115 115 Entering Ceremony Hall..................................1.00
OTA0116 116 Han Winks...1.00
OTA0117 117 Heroes...1.00
OTA0118 118 Assembled Heroes...1.00
OTA0119 119 Artwork 1.00
OTA0120 120 Artwork 1.00
OTA0138 5"x7" Han in Gunport (Previews 10/94).................4.00
OTA0121 C01 Droid Prototype Sketch.................................5.00
OTA0122 C02 Luke overlooks canyon...............................5.00
OTA0123 C03 Falcon pulled into Death Star.........................5.00
OTA0127 C07 Death Star Construction................................5.00
OTA0128 C08 Battle in the Trench.......................................5.00
OTA0129 C09 X-Wing in Trench...5.00
OTA0140 K-01 Darth Choking Rebel (From Classic 4-Pack)....3.00
OTA0141 K-02 Luke in Falcon Gun Port (Kenner Classic........3.00
OTA0142 K-03 Interior Falcon Cockpit (Kenner Classic 3.00
OTA0143 K-04 Han Solo in Cantina (Kenner Classic 3.00
OTA0131 SWP0 Luke, Han Chewie enter Award Ceremony 4.00
OTA0132 SWP1 Stormtroopers Stop Landspeeder.................6.00
OTA0133 SWP2 Interior Falcon Cockpit...............................4.00
OTA0134 SWP3 Tie Fighter in Trench.................................4.00
OTA0135 SWP4 Exterior Star Destroyer..............................4.00

OTA0136 SWP5 Darth Choking Rebel................................4.00
OTA0137 SWP6 Leia and C-3PO 4.00

CARDS: WIDEVISION, ESB

Topps
OI0001 #0 Vader in Meditation Chamber (SW Galaxy Magazine #3) 5.00
OI0002 001 Title Card...1.00
OI0003 002 Probe droid..1.00
OI0004 003 Tauntaun and rider..1.00
OI0005 004 Luke on Tauntaun...1.00
OI0006 005 Wampa..1.00
OI0007 006 C-3PO is quieted by Han...................................1.00
OI0008 007 Luke hanging in the cave..................................1.00
OI0009 008 Luke reaches out to ghost Obi............................1.00
OI0010 009 Han waves to rescuers......................................1.00
OI0011 010 Luke in the Bacta tank......................................1.00
OI0012 011 Luke gets a kiss..1.00
OI0013 012 Probe droid..1.00
OI0014 013 The Imperial fleet..1.00
OI0015 014 Vader's helmet 1.00
OI0016 015 The Imperial fleet..1.00
OI0017 016 Vader's meditation chamber..............................1.00
OI0018 017 Leia encourages the troops...............................1.00
OI0019 018 Hoth Cannon 1.00
OI0020 019 Rebel transport away.......................................1.00
OI0021 020 Hoth troops...1.00
OI0022 021 Luke in snowspeeder.......................................1.00
OI0023 022 AT-ATs approach the base................................1.00

OTA0079

OTA0080

OTA0081

OTA0082

OTA0083

OTA0084

OTA0085

OTA0086

OTA0087

OTA0088

OTA0089

OTA0090

OTA0091

OTA0092

OTA0093

OTA0094

OTA0095

OTA0096

OTA0097

OTA0098

OTA0099

OTA0100

OTA0101

OTA0102

OTA0103

OTA0104

OTA0105

OTA0106

OTA0107

OTA0108

OTA0109

OTA0110

OTA0111

OTA0112

OTA0113

OTA0114

OTA0115

OTA0116

OTA0117

OTA0118

OTA0119

OTA0120

OI0002
OI0003
OI0004
OI0005
OI0006
OI0007

OI0008
OI0009
OI0010
OI0011
OI0012
OI0013

OI0014
OI0015
OI0016
OI0017
OI0018
OI0019

OI0020
OI0021
OI0022
OI0023
OI0024
OI0025

OI0026
OI0027
OI0028
OI0029
OI0030
OI0031

OI0032
OI0033
OI0034
OI0035
OI0036
OI0037

OI0038
OI0039
OI0040
OI0041
OI0042
OI0043

OI0044
OI0045
OI0046
OI0047
OI0048
OI0049

OI0050
OI0051
OI0052
OI0053
OI0054
OI0055

OI0056
OI0057
OI0058
OI0059
OI0060
OI0061

OI0062
OI0063
OI0064
OI0065
OI0066
OI0067

OI0068
OI0069
OI0070
OI0071
OI0072
OI0073

OI0024 023 View of AT-AT from snowspeeder....1.00
OI0025 024 AT-ATs on Hoth....1.00
OI0026 025 AT-AT driver....1.00
OI0027 026 Snowspeeders seen from AT-AT....1.00
OI0028 027 AT-AT seen from above....1.00
OI0029 028 Vader in hologram....1.00
OI0030 029 Winding up the legs of an AT-AT....1.00
OI0031 030 An AT-AT falls....1.00
OI0032 031 Snow trench....1.00
OI0033 032 AT-ST....1.00
OI0034 033 Inside a snowspeeder cockpit....1.00
OI0035 034 AT-ATs fire on fleeing rebels....1.00
OI0036 035 AT-AT in the snow....1.00
OI0037 036 An AT-AT explodes....1.00
OI0038 037 Fallen AT-AT....1.00
OI0039 038 AT-ATs attack....1.00
OI0040 039 View from an AT-AT cockpit....1.00
OI0041 040 Falcon leaving the main hangar at Hoth....1.00
OI0042 041 Star Destroyers' near miss....1.00
OI0043 042 The Falcon in an asteroid field....1.00
OI0044 043 Inside the Falcon's cockpit....1.00
OI0045 044 Tie fighters in pursuit....1.00
OI0046 045 Asteroids....1.00
OI0047 046 Tie fighters in asteroid field....1.00
OI0048 047 Into the asteroid field....1.00
OI0049 048 Falcon on an asteroid....1.00
OI0050 049 Falcon on an asteroid....1.00
OI0051 050 Asteroid cave....1.00
OI0052 051 Dagobah swamp....1.00
OI0053 052 Luke cleans up R2....1.00
OI0054 053 Vader's skull....1.00
OI0055 054 Luke confronts Yoda....1.00
OI0056 055 Yoda....1.00
OI0057 056 C-3PO interrupts Han and Leia's kiss.... 1.00
OI0058 057 Vader gives orders....1.00
OI0059 058 Emperor's image....1.00
OI0060 059 Emperor and Vader confer....1.00
OI0061 060 Yoda's house....1.00
OI0062 061 Yoda and Luke in Yoda's house....1.00
OI0063 062 Tie bombers....1.00
OI0064 063 Mynock on the Falcon's window....1.00
OI0065 064 The teeth of a cave....1.00
OI0066 065 Falcon and Space Slug....1.00
OI0067 066 Space Slug....1.00
OI0068 067 Yoda on Luke's back....1.00
OI0069 068 Yoda....1.00
OI0070 069 Duel in the tree cave....1.00
OI0071 070 The face of Luke's future....1.00
OI0072 071 Bossk....1.00
OI0073 072 Vader and Fett....1.00
OI0074 073 Avenger in asteroid field....1.00
OI0075 074 Falcon chased by Star Destroyer....1.00
OI0076 075 Falcon hit!....1.00
OI0077 076 Falcon and Avenger in asteroid field.... 1.00
OI0078 077 Yoda on Luke's foot....1.00
OI0079 078 Yoda....1.00
OI0080 079 X-Wing rises above a bog....1.00
OI0081 080 Falcon on a Star Destroyer....1.00
OI0082 081 Boba Fett....1.00
OI0083 082 Luke does a hand stand....1.00
OI0084 083 The Falcon's cockpit....1.00
OI0085 084 Falcon and cloud cars....1.00
OI0086 085 Falcon....1.00
OI0087 086 The Falcon lands at Cloud City....1.00
OI0088 087 Lando walks out to meet Han....1.00
OI0089 088 Lando greets Han....1.00
OI0090 089 Lando kisses Leia's hand....1.00
OI0091 090 Falcon arrived at Cloud City....1.00
OI0092 091 Luke leaves Yoda in his X-Wing....1.00
OI0093 092 Ghost Obi and Yoda....1.00
OI0094 093 Exterior view Cloud City....1.00
OI0095 094 Darth blocks a blaster shot....1.00
OI0096 095 Darth and Boba....1.00
OI0097 096 Stormtroopers in cloud city....1.00
OI0098 097 Chewbacca reassembles C-3PO....1.00
OI0099 098 Han is tortured....1.00
OI0100 099 Darth confers with Fett....1.00
OI0101 100 Lando....1.00
OI0102 101 X-Wing approaching Cloud City....1.00
OI0103 102 Gathering in the freezing chamber....1.00
OI0104 103 Leia and Han, a last look....1.00
OI0105 104 Leia and Han kiss....1.00
OI0106 105 Solo is prepared for freezing....1.00
OI0107 106 Frozen Han....1.00
OI0108 107 Luke enters the freezing chamber....1.00
OI0109 108 Vader in the freezing chamber....1.00
OI0110 109 Duel in the freezing chamber....1.00
OI0111 110 Chewbacca chokes Lando....1.00
OI0112 111 Captain Solo loaded onto Slave I....1.00
OI0113 112 Slave I leaves Cloud City....1.00
OI0114 113 Leia....1.00
OI0115 114 Vader leaps down....1.00
OI0116 115 Duel in the freezing chamber....1.00
OI0117 116 Luke seeks out Vader....1.00
OI0118 117 Luke flies out a window....1.00
OI0119 118 Luke hangs above the reactor shaft....1.00
OI0120 119 Chewbacca and C-3PO in corridor....1.00
OI0121 120 Falcon on landing platform....1.00
OI0122 121 Falcon leaving Cloud City....1.00
OI0123 122 Cloud City Reactor Shaft....1.00
OI0124 123 Luke and Vader duel....1.00
OI0125 124 Luke and Vader duel....1.00
OI0126 125 Luke loses his hand....1.00
OI0127 126 Vader shakes his fist....1.00
OI0128 127 Luke - "Nooo!"....1.00
OI0129 128 Vader extends a hand....1.00
OI0130 129 Reactor Shaft....1.00
OI0131 130 Luke beneath Cloud City....1.00
OI0132 131 Falcon and Cloud City....1.00
OI0133 132 Falcon beneath Cloud City....1.00
OI0134 133 Millennium Falcon and Tie fighters....1.00
OI0135 134 R2 and C-3PO....1.00
OI0136 135 Chewbacca repairs the Falcon....1.00
OI0137 136 Luke aboard the Falcon....1.00
OI0138 137 Millennium Falcon Cockpit....1.00
OI0139 138 Vader's Star Destroyer Bridge....1.00
OI0140 139 Luke's Mechanical Hand....1.00
OI0141 140 Luke and Leia....1.00
OI0142 141 Space - Millennium Falcon....1.00
OI0143 142 R2 and C-3PO....1.00
OI0144 143 Luke, Leia, and Droids....1.00
OI0145 144 Rebel Star Cruiser - Rebel Ships....1.00
OI0156 5"x7" (Images from P1,P2,P3) (Previews 7/9)....4.25
OI0146 C01 Probot....5.00
OI0147 C02 Luke on Tauntaun....5.00
OI0148 C03 No description available....5.00
OI0149 C04 No description available....5.00
OI0150 C05 Luke and Yoda....5.00
OI0151 C06 No description available....5.00
OI0152 C07 Cloud City....5.00
OI0153 C08 No description available....5.00
OI0154 C09 Luke Under Cloud City....5.00
OI0155 C10 No description available....5.00
OI0157 P1 Vader Tortures Han Solo....4.25
OI0158 P2 AT-AT Walkers....7.00
OI0159 P3 Yoda Surprises Luke....5.75
OI0160 P4 Luke in Cloud City....4.00
OI0161 P5 Slave 1....12.00
OI0162 P6 Closing Scene....4.25

CARDS: WIDEVISION, ROTJ

Topps

OR0155 #0 Ghost Jedi....6.00
OR0156 #0 Ghost Jedi (5x7)....4.25
OR0001 001 Title Card - artwork....1.00
OR0002 002 Star Destroyer, Death Star....1.00
OR0003 003 Shuttle....1.00
OR0004 004 Imperial Shuttle Cockpit....1.00
OR0005 005 The Docking Bay....1.00
OR0006 006 Main Docking Bay View....1.00
OR0007 007 Reviewing the Troops....1.00
OR0008 008 R2 and C-3PO....1.00
OR0009 009 C-3PO Meets a Door....1.00
OR0010 010 Bib Fortuna....1.00
OR0011 011 Jabba....1.00
OR0012 012 Luke's Holo Message....1.00
OR0013 013 Meet EV-9-D9....1.00
OR0014 014 Droid Torture....1.00
OR0015 015 Max Rebo's Band....1.00
OR0016 016 Boushh....1.00

OI0074 OI0075 OI0076 OI0077 OI0078 OI0079
OI0080 OI0081 OI0082 OI0083 OI0084 OI0085
OI0086 OI0087 OI0088 OI0089 OI0090 OI0091
OI0092 OI0093 OI0094 OI0095 OI0096 OI0097
OI0098 OI0099 OI0100 OI0101 OI0102 OI0103
OI0104 OI0105 OI0106 OI0107 OI0108 OI0109
OI0110 OI0111 OI0112 OI0113 OI0114 OI0115
OI0116 OI0117 OI0118 OI0119 OI0120 OI0121
OI0122 OI0123 OI0124 OI0125 OI0126 OI0127
OI0128 OI0129 OI0130 OI0131 OI0132 OI0133
OI0134 OI0135 OI0136 OI0137 OI0138 OI0139
OI0140 OI0141 OI0142 OI0143 OI0144 OI0145

OR0001 OR0002 OR0003 OR0004 OR0005 OR0006
OR0007 OR0008 OR0009 OR0010 OR0011 OR0012
OR0013 OR0014 OR0015 OR0016 OR0017 OR0018
OR0019 OR0020 OR0021 OR0022 OR0023 OR0024
OR0025 OR0026 OR0027 OR0028 OR0029 OR0030
OR0031 OR0032 OR0033 OR0034 OR0035 OR0036
OR0037 OR0038 OR0039 OR0040 OR0041 OR0042
OR0043 OR0044 OR0045 OR0046 OR0047 OR0048
OR0049 OR0050 OR0051 OR0052 OR0053 OR0054
OR0055 OR0056 OR0057 OR0058 OR0059 OR0060
OR0061 OR0062 OR0063 OR0064 OR0065 OR0066
OR0067 OR0068 OR0069 OR0070 OR0071 OR0072

Cards: Widevision, ROTJ

OR0017 017 Boba Fett..1.00
OR0018 018 Jabba's Palace...1.00
OR0019 019 Han Released..1.00
OR0020 020 A Kiss...1.00
OR0021 021 Jabba Looks Over Leia..............................1.00
OR0022 022 Bib and Luke..1.00
OR0023 023 Jabba's Throne...1.00
OR0024 024 Luke in Throne Room................................1.00
OR0025 025 Leia and Lando...1.00
OR0026 026 Rancor..1.00
OR0027 027 Jabba and Fett...1.00
OR0028 028 In the Rancor's Grip..................................1.00
OR0029 029 Dead Rancor..1.00
OR0030 030 Luke and Han..1.00
OR0031 031 Skiff and Sailbarge....................................1.00
OR0032 032 On the Skiff..1.00
OR0033 033 Sarlacc (old version)..................................1.00
OR0034 034 Bib...1.00
OR0035 035 Walking the Plank......................................1.00
OR0036 036 Fighting Fett...1.00
OR0037 037 Firing on the Skiff......................................1.00
OR0038 038 Fett...1.00
OR0039 039 Fett Fires..1.00
OR0040 040 Han and Fett..1.00
OR0041 041 Leia Chokes Jabba....................................1.00
OR0042 042 Dangling to Reach Lando...........................1.00
OR0043 043 Sarlacc has a Meal....................................1.00
OR0044 044 Above the Pitt..1.00
OR0045 045 Damaged C-3PO.......................................1.00
OR0046 046 Salacious Crumb.......................................1.00
OR0047 047 Leia Mans the Guns...................................1.00
OR0048 048 Luke and Leia Swing..................................1.00
OR0049 049 Droids in the Sand.....................................1.00
OR0050 050 A Barge is Blown.......................................1.00
OR0051 051 Shuttle of the Emperor...............................1.00
OR0052 052 The Emperor..1.00
OR0053 053 X-Wing on Dagobah...................................1.00
OR0054 054 Farewell to Yoda.......................................1.00
OR0055 055 Ghost Ben and Luke...................................1.00
OR0056 056 The Rebel Fleet...1.00
OR0057 057 Mon Mothma Speaks..................................1.00
OR0058 058 Ackbar and Endor Map...............................1.00
OR0059 059 Ackbar and Mon Mothma............................1.00
OR0060 060 Revealing the Target..................................1.00
OR0061 061 Death Star Core...1.00
OR0062 062 Lando...1.00
OR0063 063 Inside the Shuttle......................................1.00
OR0064 064 On Endor...1.00
OR0065 065 Bike Chase..1.00
OR0066 066 Luke and Leia Ride Bikes.............................1.00
OR0067 067 Scout Trooper..1.00
OR0068 068 Sparks Fly...1.00
OR0069 069 Leia Vs. Trooper..1.00
OR0070 070 Luke Vs. Trooper.......................................1.00
OR0071 071 Darth in Emperor's Chamber........................1.00
OR0072 072 Meet the Ewoks..1.00
OR0073 073 Ewok Village..1.00
OR0074 074 Baby Ewok..1.00
OR0075 075 Han for Dinner..1.00
OR0076 076 The Regal C-3PO.......................................1.00
OR0077 077 Ewoks with Baby..1.00
OR0078 078 C-3PO Tells a Tale......................................1.00
OR0079 079 Luke and Leia...1.00
OR0080 080 The Shuttle Platform..................................1.00
OR0081 081 Vader and Shuttle......................................1.00
OR0082 082 AT-AT at Platform......................................1.00
OR0083 083 Luke Under Guard......................................1.00
OR0084 084 The Fleet Gathers......................................1.00
OR0085 085 Entering Hyperspace..................................1.00
OR0086 086 The Mon Calamari Bridge.............................1.00
OR0087 087 Ewok Bike Ride...1.00
OR0088 088 Luke, Vader, and Emperor............................1.00
OR0089 089 Falcon Cockpit...1.00
OR0090 090 Ackbar Surveys the Scene...........................1.00
OR0091 091 Approaching the Death Star.........................1.00
OR0092 092 Pulling Up..1.00
OR0093 093 X-Wings and Death Star..............................1.00
OR0094 094 The Battle..1.00
OR0095 095 Falcon Flees...1.00
OR0096 096 Endor Battle...1.00
OR0097 097 Glider...1.00

OR0098 098 Han Fires...1.00
OR0099 099 AT-ST...1.00
OR0100 100 Ties Attack..1.00
OR0101 101 The Battle in Space.....................................1.00
OR0102 102 Death Star Fires..1.00
OR0103 103 Ship Destroyed..1.00
OR0104 104 Another Explosion......................................1.00
OR0105 105 Falcon Moves in Close.................................1.00
OR0106 106 Duel Before the Emperor.............................1.00
OR0107 107 Wookie on an AT-ST....................................1.00
OR0108 108 Crushing an AT-ST......................................1.00
OR0109 109 AT-ST Falls...1.00
OR0110 110 The Duel Continues.....................................1.00
OR0111 111 A Tie is Destroyed.......................................1.00
OR0112 112 Han - No Problem..1.00
OR0113 113 Setting a Timer..1.00
OR0114 114 Raised Saber..1.00
OR0115 115 Vader Loses a Hand.....................................1.00
OR0116 116 Destroyed Bunker.......................................1.00
OR0117 117 Emperor's Lightening...................................1.00
OR0118 118 Luke in Agony..1.00
OR0119 119 Lifted Emperor..1.00
OR0120 120 X-Ray Vader...1.00
OR0121 121 Central Core Shaft.....................................1.00
OR0122 122 Luke and Vader...1.00
OR0123 123 The Falcon...1.00
OR0124 124 Ties..1.00
OR0125 125 Flying in the Shaft......................................1.00
OR0126 126 Falcon..1.00
OR0127 127 Falcon Targets..1.00
OR0128 128 Star Destroyer Bridge Destroyed...................1.00
OR0129 129 Ackbar..1.00
OR0130 130 Vader's Destroyer Nosedives........................1.00
OR0131 131 Vader Revealed...1.00
OR0132 132 X-Wing in the Shaft.....................................1.00
OR0133 133 Explosions...1.00
OR0134 134 The Core Blows..1.00
OR0135 135 Falcon Flees the Destruction........................1.00
OR0136 136 Exploding Free..1.00
OR0137 137 Last Look at Death Star...............................1.00
OR0138 138 Death Star Blows..1.00
OR0139 139 Explosion in the Sky....................................1.00
OR0140 140 Burning Vader's Body...................................1.00
OR0141 141 Ewok Celebration.......................................1.00
OR0142 142 Luke and Leia Celebrate..............................1.00
OR0143 143 3 Ghost Jedi...1.00
OR0144 144 The Final Celebration..................................1.00
OR0145 C01 Darth Vader Leaving Shuttle......................5.00
OR0146 C02 EV-9D9...5.00
OR0147 C03 Jabba's Throne.....................................5.00
OR0148 C04 Luke vs. Rancor......................................5.00
OR0149 C05 Jabba's Sail Barge Destroyed.....................5.00
OR0150 C06 No description available..........................5.00
OR0151 C07 No description available..........................5.00
OR0152 C08 Luke and Darth Vader Duel........................5.00
OR0153 C09 No description available..........................5.00
OR0154 C10 No description available..........................5.00
OR0157 P1 Luke and Han in Jabba's Palace...................6.50
OR0158 P2 Luke on Speeder Bike...............................6.50
OR0159 P3 Han, Leia, and Stormtroopers.....................6.50
OR0160 P4 Emperor Palpatine...................................6.50
OR0161 P5 Jabba and Bib Fortuna..............................6.50
OR0162 P6 Chewbacca, Han, and Luke.........................6.50

CARDS: WIDEVISION, SE HOBBY

Topps

OTB0001 01 Escape Pod Away.....................................1.00
OTB0002 02 Sandtroopers and Dewback.........................1.00
OTB0003 03 Dewback...1.00
OTB0004 04 Sandcrawler...1.00
OTB0005 05 Jawas at Lars Farm...................................1.00
OTB0006 06 Twin Suns..1.00
OTB0007 07 Landspeeder..1.00
OTB0008 08 Mos Eisley Overlook..................................1.00
OTB0009 09 Ranats Near Mos Eisley.............................1.00
OTB0010 10 Entering the City Streets............................1.00
OTB0011 11 A View From Above....................................1.00
OTB0012 12 Rontos in the Distance..............................1.00
OTB0013 13 Droids at Work...1.00

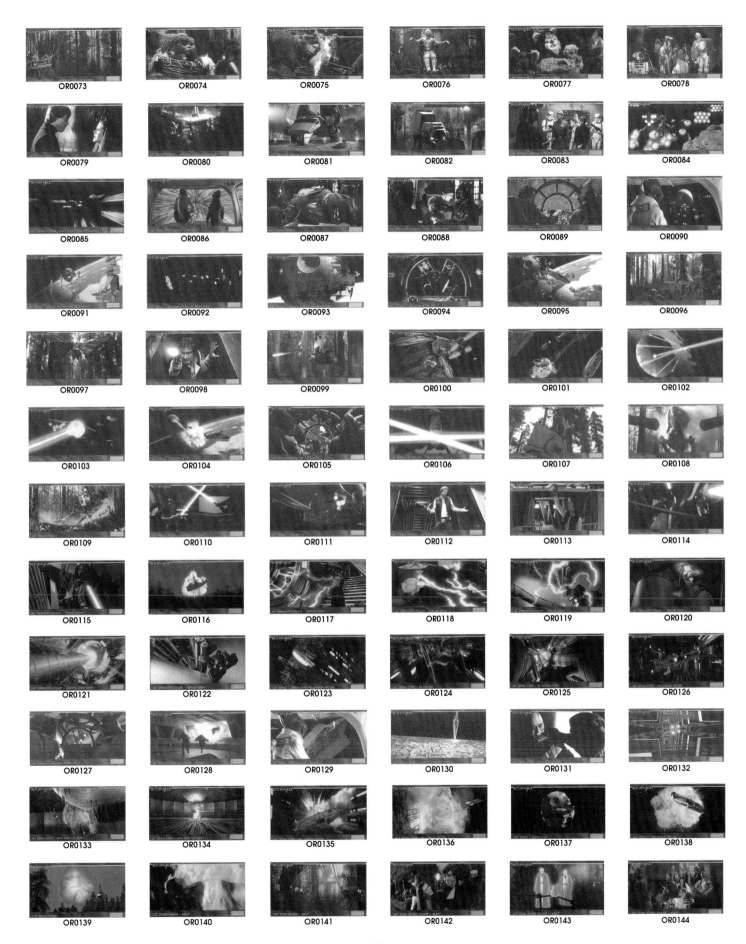

OR0073 OR0074 OR0075 OR0076 OR0077 OR0078
OR0079 OR0080 OR0081 OR0082 OR0083 OR0084
OR0085 OR0086 OR0087 OR0088 OR0089 OR0090
OR0091 OR0092 OR0093 OR0094 OR0095 OR0096
OR0097 OR0098 OR0099 OR0100 OR0101 OR0102
OR0103 OR0104 OR0105 OR0106 OR0107 OR0108
OR0109 OR0110 OR0111 OR0112 OR0113 OR0114
OR0115 OR0116 OR0117 OR0118 OR0119 OR0120
OR0121 OR0122 OR0123 OR0124 OR0125 OR0126
OR0127 OR0128 OR0129 OR0130 OR0131 OR0132
OR0133 OR0134 OR0135 OR0136 OR0137 OR0138
OR0139 OR0140 OR0141 OR0142 OR0143 OR0144

Cards: Widevision, SE Hobby

CARDS: WIDEVISION, SE RETAIL

Topps

OT0082 P4 Sandcrawler 4.00
OT0083 P5 Jawa 4.00
OT0084 P6 Millennium Falcon w/Stormtroopers 4.00
OT0085 P7 Landspeeder at Mos Eisley 1.50
OT0086 P8 Dancers in Jabba's Court 1.50

CARDS: WIDEVISION, SE RETAIL JAPAN

Topps

OTJ0001 01 In the Belly of the Beast 1.30
OTJ0002 02 Leia "Feeds" R2-D2 ....1.30
OTJ0003 03 Demanding an Answer 1.30
OTJ0004 04 A Desolate Desert 1.30
OTJ0005 05 "Look Sir, Droids!" 1.30
OTJ0006 06 A Plea for Help..1.30
OTJ0007 07 Alone in Thought 1.30
OTJ0008 08 Sand People Strike 1.30
OTJ0009 09 Kenobi Gets the Message 1.30
OTJ0010 10 Into Mos Eisley 1.30
OTJ0011 11 Greedo's Unlucky Day 1.30
OTJ0012 12 A Deal is Struck 1.30
OTJ0013 13 Moff Tarkin's Surprise 1.30
OTJ0014 14 Let the Wookie Win! 1.30
OTJ0015 15 Into the Enemy Lair 1.30
OTJ0016 16 A Close - and Smelly - Call....................................1.30
OTJ0017 17 Fight to the End 1.30
OTJ0018 18 Han Hits His Mark 1.30
OTJ0019 19 Preparing For Action 1.30
OTJ0020 20 X-Wings Attack 1.30
OTJ0021 21 The Battle Unfolds 1.30
OTJ0022 22 Into the Trench 1.30
OTJ0023 23 The Dark Lord Attacks...1.30
OTJ0024 24 Hitting Their Target..1.30
OTJ0025 25 Imperial Snoop 1.30
OTJ0026 26 Abominable Wampa..1.30
OTJ0027 27 Rejuvenating Bacta Bath 1.30
OTJ0028 28 Vader's Meditation Ends..1.30
OTJ0029 29 Lumbering Metal Monsters.....................................1.30
OTJ0030 30 Harpooning a Whale 1.30
OTJ0031 31 Fire and Ice 1.30
OTJ0032 32 Han Plays Chicken 1.30
OTJ0033 33 Down in Desolate Dagobah.....................................1.30
OTJ0034 34 Luke Takes Aim 1.30

OTJ0035 35 Vader and His Master 1.30
OTJ0036 36 Shelter From a Storm 1.30
OTJ0037 37 Smoking Them Out 1.30
OTJ0038 38 Size Matters Not 1.30
OTJ0039 39 Vader Hires Boba Fett..1.30
OTJ0040 40 Chasing After Solo...1.30
OTJ0041 41 Luke's Balancing Act 1.30
OTJ0042 42 A Cloud City Welcome 1.30
OTJ0043 43 Friend or Foe? 1.30
OTJ0044 44 A Surprise Dinner Guest 1.30
OTJ0045 45 Loved Ones Part 1.30
OTJ0046 46 Lightsaber Blow 1.30
OTJ0047 47 A Terrible Blow 1.30
OTJ0048 48 A Life Suspended 1.30
OTJ0049 49 Under Construction 1.30
OTJ0050 50 Vader Motivates the Troops.....................................1.30
OTJ0051 51 A Slimy Crime Kingpin 1.30
OTJ0052 52 Han Comes to Life 1.30
OTJ0053 53 A Jedi Tries Reason..1.30
OTJ0054 54 Sarlacc Sightseeing Tour? 1.30
OTJ0055 55 Fighting Fett 1.30
OTJ0056 56 Luke and Leia Swing 1.30
OTJ0057 57 The Emperor Arrives..1.30
OTJ0058 58 Visit to an Old Friend 1.30
OTJ0059 59 Rebel Fleet at the Ready 1.30
OTJ0060 60 Into Enemy Territory 1.30
OTJ0061 61 Chase Through the Forest 1.30
OTJ0062 62 Threepio Tells Tales 1.30
OTJ0063 63 Vader Comes for Luke...1.30
OTJ0064 64 Leading the Attack 1.30
OTJ0065 65 Running for Cover 1.30
OTJ0066 66 Fully Operational! 1.30
OTJ0067 67 Crushing an Enemy 1.30
OTJ0068 68 A Turn to the Darkside? 1.30
OTJ0069 69 The Emperor's Lightning 1.30
OTJ0070 70 The Emperor Goes Soaring 1.30
OTJ0071 71 One Last Look 1.30
OTJ0072 72 Together in the Force 1.30
OTJ0073 Chasecard 1 Leia Hologram 5.00
OTJ0074 Chasecard 2 Falcon into Hyperspace 5.00
OTJ0075 Chasecard 3 Demotion..5.00
OTJ0076 Chasecard 4 The Emperor's Holo.................................5.00
OTJ0077 Chasecard 5 Sarlacc Pitt 5.00
OTJ0078 Chasecard 6 Lightning 5.00

OT0001   OT0002   OT0003   OT0004   OT0005   OT0006

OT0007   OT0008   OT0009   OT0010   OT0011   OT0012

OT0013   OT0014   OT0015   OT0016   OT0017   OT0018

OT0019   OT0020   OT0021   OT0022   OT0023   OT0024

OT0025   OT0026   OT0027   OT0028   OT0029   OT0030

OT0031   OT0032   OT0033   OT0034   OT0035   OT0036

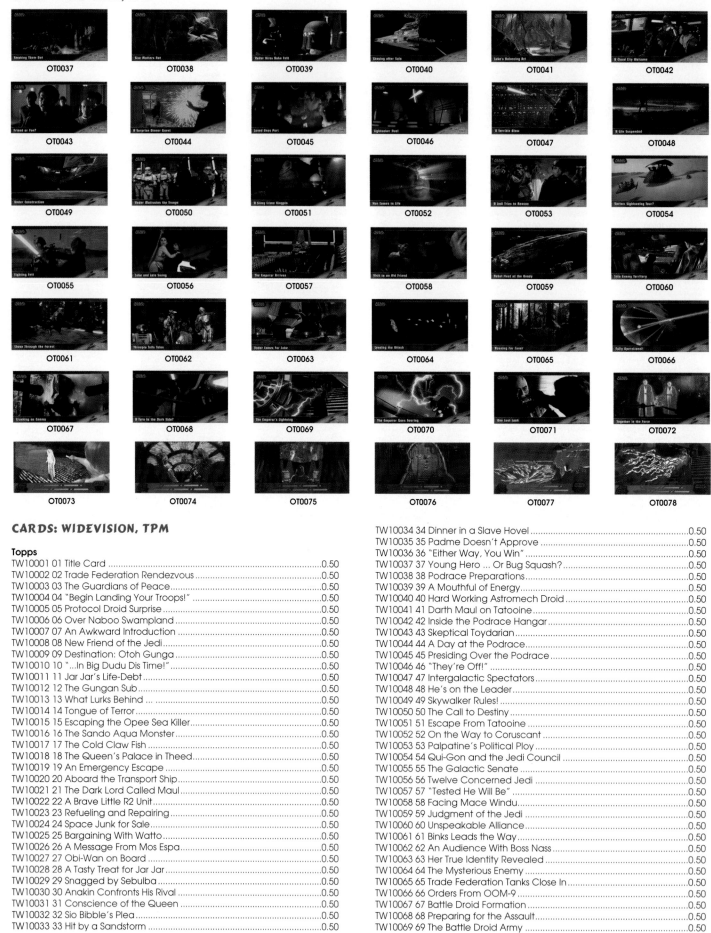

OT0037 OT0038 OT0039 OT0040 OT0041 OT0042
OT0043 OT0044 OT0045 OT0046 OT0047 OT0048
OT0049 OT0050 OT0051 OT0052 OT0053 OT0054
OT0055 OT0056 OT0057 OT0058 OT0059 OT0060
OT0061 OT0062 OT0063 OT0064 OT0065 OT0066
OT0067 OT0068 OT0069 OT0070 OT0071 OT0072
OT0073 OT0074 OT0075 OT0076 OT0077 OT0078

CARDS: WIDEVISION, TPM

Topps

TW10001 TW10002 TW10003 TW10004 TW10005 TW10006
TW10007 TW10008 TW10009 TW10010 TW10011 TW10012
TW10013 TW10014 TW10015 TW10016 TW10017 TW10018
TW10019 TW10020 TW10021 TW10022 TW10023 TW10024
TW10025 TW10026 TW10027 TW10028 TW10029 TW10030
TW10031 TW10032 TW10033 TW10034 TW10035 TW10036
TW10037 TW10038 TW10039 TW10040 TW10041 TW10042
TW10043 TW10044 TW10045 TW10046 TW10047 TW10048
TW10049 TW10050 TW10051 TW10052 TW10053 TW10054
TW10055 TW10056 TW10057 TW10058 TW10059 TW10060

CARDS: WIDEVISION, TPM HOBBY

Topps
Chrome cards.

TW10061

TW10062

TW10063

TW10064

TW10065

TW10066

TW10067

TW10068

TW10069

TW10070

TW10071

TW10072

TW10073

TW10074

TW10075

TW10076

TW10077

TW10078

TW20008 C8 Forces of Justice Closing In 9.00

Bonus Cards.
TW20009 X-01 Pit Droids at Work 4.00
TW20010 X-02 A Jarred Jar Jar 4.00
TW20011 X-03 Droids in Watto's Junk Shop 4.00
TW20012 X-04 Anakin's Podracer 4.00
TW20013 X-05 Watching From on High 4.00
TW20014 X-06 Monitoring the Podrace 4.00
TW20015 X-07 A Final Word From Watto 4.00
TW20016 X-08 Sebulba Gets Ready to Race 4.00
TW20017 X-09 Flying Across the Desert 4.00
TW20018 X-10 Winning the Podrace 4.00
TW20019 X-11 With a Pal Like Jar Jar 4.00
TW20020 X-12 Streets of Mos Espa 4.00
TW20021 X-13 Knights of Light and Dark 4.00
TW20022 X-14 Dark Lord of the Sith 4.00
TW20023 X-15 The Jedi Council 4.00
TW20024 X-16 Can This Boy Be a Jedi? 4.00
TW20025 X-17 Questioning Anakin 4.00
TW20026 X-18 Of Destiny and Great Danger 4.00
TW20027 X-19 The Judgment of Mace Windu 4.00
TW20028 X-20 Holo-View of Darth Sidious 4.00
TW20029 X-21 Jar Jar of Otoh Gunga 4.00
TW20030 X-22 A Toydarian Named Watto 4.00
TW20031 X-23 Four-footed Transportation 4.00
TW20032 X-24 Podrace Fever 4.00
TW20033 X-25 Sebulba Coming up Fast! 4.00
TW20034 X-26 Anakin's Pals and Helpers 4.00
TW20035 X-27 On-Screen Podrace Excitement 4.00
TW20036 X-28 It's All up to Boss Nass 4.00
TW20037 X-29 Citizens of the Sea 4.00
TW20038 X-30 Battle Droid Flanking Viceroy 4.00
TW20039 X-31 Awaiting the Jedi 4.00
TW20040 X-32 Trade Federation Talks Upon the Hill 4.00
TW20041 X-33 Armored Warships Advancing 4.00
TW20042 X-34 OOM-9 Surveys the Battlefield 4.00
TW20043 X-35 The Trade Federation's Finest 4.00
TW20044 X-36 The Reconfigurators 4.00
TW20045 X-37 Wardroids on the March 4.00
TW20046 X-38 Naboo Fighter Surrounded 4.00
TW20047 X-39 No description available 4.00
TW20048 X-40 Day of the Battle Droid 4.00

CARDS: WIDEVISION, TPM RETAIL

Topps
Mirror cards.
TW50001 F01 Anakin Skywalker 9.00
TW50002 F02 Qui-Gon Jinn 9.00
TW50003 F03 Obi-Wan Kenobi 9.00
TW50004 F04 Queen Amidala 9.00
TW50005 F05 Jar Jar Binks 9.00
TW50006 F06 Watto 9.00
TW50007 F07 Darth Maul 9.00
TW50008 F08 Nute Gunray 9.00
TW50009 F09 Battle Droid 9.00
TW50010 F10 C-3PO and R2-D2 ....9.00

Sticker cards.
TW50011 S01 Qui-Gon Jinn 6.00
TW50012 S02 Obi-Wan Kenobi 6.00
TW50013 S03 The Neimoidians 6.00
TW50014 S04 Jar Jar Binks 6.00
TW50015 S05 Darth Sidious 6.00
TW50016 S06 Queen Amidala 6.00
TW50017 S07 C-3PO 6.00
TW50018 S08 Padme Naberrie 6.00
TW50019 S09 Anakin Skywalker 6.00
TW50020 S10 Watto 6.00
TW50021 S11 Darth Maul 6.00
TW50022 S12 Mace Windu 6.00
TW50023 S13 Sebulba 6.00
TW50024 S14 Battle Droids 6.00
TW50025 S15 Boss Nass 6.00
TW50026 S16 The Galactic Senate 6.00

Oversized cards, tin cover art.
TW50027 Anakin Skywalker 4.00
TW50028 Darth Maul 4.00
TW50029 Obi-Wan 4.00
TW50030 Queen Amidala 4.00
TW50031 Qui-Gon Jinn 4.00

CARDS: WIDEVISION, TPM SERIES II

Topps
TW30001 01 Title Card 0.50
TW30002 02 Qui-Gon Jinn 0.50
TW30003 03 Obi-Wan Kenobi 0.50
TW30004 04 Anakin Skywalker 0.50
TW30005 05 Darth Maul 0.50
TW30006 06 Captain Panaka and Queen Amidala 0.50
TW30007 07 Jar Jar Binks 0.50
TW30008 08 The Neimoidians 0.50
TW30009 09 Boss Nass 0.50
TW30010 10 R2-D2 ....0.50
TW30011 11 C-3PO 0.50
TW30012 12 Darth Sidious 0.50
TW30013 13 The Jedi Council 0.50
TW30014 14 Yoda 0.50
TW30015 15 Sebulba 0.50
TW30016 16 Watto 0.50
TW30017 17 Jabba the Hutt 0.50
TW30018 18 Captain Tarpals and the Gungan Warriors 0.50
TW30019 19 Slave Community 0.50
TW30020 20 Atop the Stone Head 0.50
TW30021 21 Podracing Arena 0.50
TW30022 22 Coruscant 0.50
TW30023 23 Landing Ship Interior 0.50
TW30024 24 Theed Power Generator 0.50
TW30025 25 The Walking Droid Fighter 0.50
TW30026 26 Jedi Reprisal 0.50
TW30027 27 Blasted by the Force 0.50
TW30028 28 Qui-Gon Cuts Through 0.50
TW30029 29 Destroyer Droids 0.50
TW30030 30 STAP Warfare 0.50

TW30001 TW30002 TW30003 TW30004 TW30005 TW30006
TW30007 TW30008 TW30009 TW30010 TW30011 TW30012
TW30013 TW30014 TW30015 TW30016 TW30017 TW30018
TW30019 TW30020 TW30021 TW30022 TW30023 TW30024
TW30025 TW30026 TW30027 TW30028 TW30029 TW30030
TW30031 TW30032 TW30033 TW30034 TW30035 TW30036
TW30037 TW30038 TW30039 TW30040 TW30041 TW30042
TW30043 TW30044 TW30045 TW30046 TW30047 TW30048
TW30049 TW30050 TW30051 TW30052 TW30053 TW30054
TW30055 TW30056 TW30057 TW30058 TW30059 TW30060
TW30061 TW30062 TW30063 TW30064 TW30065 TW30066
TW30067 TW30068 TW30069 TW30070 TW30071 TW30072
TW30073 TW30074 TW30075 TW30076 TW30077 TW30078

Cards: Widevision, TPM Series II

TW30031 31 Stampede! 0.50
TW30032 32 The Escape Party 0.50
TW30033 33 Cutting Down Battle Droids 0.50
TW30034 34 Courageous Astromech Droid 0.50
TW30035 35 Encountering Anakin 0.50
TW30036 36 Watto's Gamble 0.50
TW30037 37 Podracing Rivals 0.50
TW30038 38 Teemto Gears Up 0.50
TW30039 39 Podracers in Position 0.50
TW30040 40 Quadinaros Makes Ready 0.50
TW30041 41 Pit Droid Dispute 0.50
TW30042 42 Arriving in the Arena 0.50
TW30043 43 The Crowd Goes Wild 0.50
TW30044 44 Anakin's Challenge 0.50
TW30045 45 Through a Rocky Canyon 0.50
TW30046 46 Sideline Friends 0.50
TW30047 47 Beware of Tusken Raiders! 0.50
TW30048 48 Ratts Tyerell...0.50
TW30049 49 Collision Up Ahead 0.50
TW30050 50 Streaking Across Tatooine 0.50
TW30051 51 Sebulba's Foul Plan 0.50
TW30052 52 High-Speed Climax..0.50
TW30053 53 Fury of the Podrace......................................0.50
TW30054 54 The Winning Podracer...................................0.50
TW30055 55 The Mighty Gungan Army 0.50
TW30056 56 Fantastic Weaponry 0.50
TW30057 57 Blasting Through!..0.50
TW30058 58 Gungan Shields...0.50
TW30059 59 Battlefield: Naboo..0.50
TW30060 60 A Hapless Hero 0.50
TW30061 61 Hostage to Their Will 0.50
TW30062 62 Inside the Theed Central Hangar 0.50
TW30063 63 "Get to Your Ships!" 0.50
TW30064 64 Naboo Starfighters Taking Off 0.50
TW30065 65 The Queen's Volunteer Forces 0.50
TW30066 66 Palace Attack 0.50
TW30067 67 Releasing the Droid Starfighters 0.50
TW30068 68 Blast of the Quadlaser Cannons 0.50
TW30069 69 Celestial Combat 0.50
TW30070 70 Droid Starfighter Assault 0.50
TW30071 71 Droid Control Ship Crisis 0.50
TW30072 72 Immobilizing the Enemy 0.50
TW30073 73 The Menace of Maul......................................0.50
TW30074 74 Fierce Combatants 0.50
TW30075 75 His Moment of Truth 0.50
TW30076 76 Battle to the Death..0.50
TW30077 77 Dueling With Darth Maul 0.50
TW30078 78 Hang On, Obi-Wan 0.50
TW30079 79 A Time to Rejoice 0.50
TW30080 80 Checklist 0.50

CARDS: WIDEVISION, TPM SERIES II HOBBY

Topps
Over-sized box cards.
TW40011 Courageous Astromech Droid 4.00
TW40012 Cutting Down The Battle Droids.........................4.00
TW40013 Darth Maul..4.00

Chrome chase cards.
TW40001 H-C1 Threat of the Destroyer Droids 11.00
TW40002 H-C2 Departing An Underwater World 11.00
TW40003 H-C3 An Appeal To Boss Nass 11.00
TW40004 H-C4 Blasting the Gungans 11.00

Foil embossed chase cards.
TW40005 H-E1 The Neimoidians...14.00
TW40006 H-E2 Battle Droids..14.00
TW40007 H-E3 The Invasion Begins 14.00
TW40008 H-E4 Sebulba On The Move 14.00
TW40009 H-E5 Starpilot Skywalker 14.00
TW40010 H-E6 Darth Maul...14.00

CARDS: WIDEVISION, TPM SERIES II RETAIL

Topps
Chase cards.
TW60001 C1 Sea Creature Peril...5.00
TW60002 C2 Escapees on Tatooine....................................5.00

TW60003 C3 Podrace Excitement 5.00
TW60004 C4 Control Ship Attack 5.00

Embossed foil chase cards.
TW60005 E1 Commander Droid 14.00
TW60006 E2 Jar Jar 14.00
TW60007 E3 Jabba the Hutt..14.00
TW60008 E4 Sebulba...14.00
TW60009 E5 Anakin Skywalker 14.00
TW60010 E6 Boss Nass 14.00

CASSETTES

20th Century Fox
RC20002 Story of Star Wars...11.00

Buena Vista Records

RC20006   RC20008   RC20030   RC20013   RC20014

Read-along stories and adventures.
RC20006 Adventures in ABC 8.00
RC20007 Adventures in Colors and Shapes 8.00
RC20034 Children's Library 3-pack: SW, ESB, ROTJ 16.00
RC20008 Droid World 8.00
RC20009 Empire Strikes Back 8.00
RC20010 Ewoks Join the Fight 8.00
RC20030 Ewoks: The Battle for Endor................................11.00
RC20011 Planet of the Hoojibs 8.00
RC20012 Rebel Mission to Ord Mantell 8.00
RC20013 Return of the Jedi 8.00
RC20014 Star Wars 8.00
RC20015 The Story of Empire Strikes Back 8.00
RC20016 The Story of Return of the Jedi 8.00
RC20017 The Story of Star Wars...8.00

Highbridge Company

RC20025   RC20026   RC20027

RC20023   RC20021

RC20025 Dark Empire Full Cast Audio Drama, 2 cassettes......................18.00
RC20026 Dark Empire II Full Cast Audio Drama, 2 cassettes 18.00
RC20027 Dark Forces: Soldier for the Empire, 2 cassettes........................18.00
RC20022 ESB: Original Radio Drama as heard on National Public Radio, original music/effects; 10 episodes, 5 cassettes 35.00
RC20023 ROTJ: The Original Radio Drama; 3 hours, 3 cassettes 25.00
RC20021 SW: Original Radio Drama as heard on National Public Radio, original music/effects; 13 episodes, 6 cassettes 35.00
RC20024 Trilogy radio drama cassette gift pack, 14 cassettes.................85.00

Polygram Records
RC20001 Star Wars Soundtrack 14.00

Rhino
RC20031 Christmas in the Stars 26.00

RC20031 **RC20028 front and back**

24-page book with read-along cassette. Included vehicles are Galoob/Hasbro Micro-Machines.

RC20028 Star Wars Episode I 8.00
RC20032 Star Wars Episode I with Anakin's Podracer 11.00
RC20033 Star Wars Episode I with Gungan Sub 11.00
RC20029 Star Wars Episode I with Sith Infiltrator 11.00

Skywalkers
RC20035 A Wind to Shake The Stars 21.00

Walt Disney Records
Read-along cassettes.
RC20003 Star Wars 6.00

RC20003 **RC20004** **RC20005**

RC20018 Star Wars with 3 Applause mini-PVC figures 14.00
RC20004 The Empire Strikes Back 6.00
RC20019 The Empire Strikes Back with 3 Applause mini-PVC figures ...14.00
RC20005 Return of the Jedi 6.00
RC20020 Return of the Jedi with 3 Applause mini-pVC figures 14.00

CATALOGS

Borders, Inc.
CL0004 Special edition collector's catalog, 8-page pamphlet of SW titles 5.00

Burger Chef
CL0009 Fun'n Games Booklet (and Kenner catalog) 8.00

Butterick
CL0008 Halloween Catalog 9.00

Estes / Cox
CL0003 Mini-Catalog Activity book 2.00

JC Penney
CL0002 1978 JC Penney toy flyer 7.00

Kenner
CL0006 1980 products, includes ESB toys 12.00
CL0007 1983 products, includes ROTJ toys 12.00

Lego
CL0005 Shop-At-Home catalog, Summer 1999 (Podrace, space battle, and TPM character figures on cover) 4.00

Toys R Us
CL0010 1997 Star Wars Special Edition toys 8.00

CCG: CARDS, 1ST ANTHOLOGY PREVIEWS

EH0001 Boba Fett (D) 8.00

EH0004 Commander Wedge Antilles (L) 5.00
EH0002 Death Star Assault Squadron (D) 5.00
EH0005 Hit And Run (L) 3.00
EH0003 Jabba's Influence (D) 3.00
EH0006 X-wing Assault Squadron (L) 5.00

CCG: CARDS, 2ND ANTHOLOGY PREVIEWS

EM0001 Flagship Operations (D) 4.00
EM0006 Mon Calamari Star Cruiser (L) 6.00
EM0004 Mon Mothma (L) 5.00
EM0005 Rapid Deployment (L) 5.00
EM0002 Sarlacc (D) 5.00
EM0003 Thunderflare (D) 6.00

CCG: CARDS, A NEW HOPE

EA0001 Advance Preparation (L) 0.75
EA0002 Advosze (D) 0.25
EA0003 Alternatives To Fighting (L) 0.75
EA0004 Arcona (L) 0.25
EA0005 Astromech Shortage (D) 0.75
EA0006 Attack Run (D) 4.00
EA0007 Besieged (D) 3.00
EA0008 Bespin Motors Void Spider THX 1138 (D) 0.25
EA0009 Black 4 (D) 0.75
EA0010 Blast The Door, Kid! (L) 0.25
EA0011 Blue Milk (L) 0.25
EA0012 Bowcaster (D) 3.00
EA0013 Brainiac (D) 6.00
EA0014 Captain Khurgee (D) 0.75
EA0015 Cell 2187 (D) 4.00
EA0016 Chewbacca (L) 18.00
EA0017 Clak'dor VII (D) 3.00
EA0018 Come With Me (D) 0.25
EA0019 Commander Evram Lajaie (L) 0.25
EA0020 Commander Vanden Willard (L) 0.75
EA0021 Commence Primary Ignition (D) 5.00
EA0022 Commence Recharging (D) 4.00
EA0023 Conquest (D) 8.00
EA0024 Corellia (D) 4.00
EA0025 Corellian (L) 0.25
EA0026 Corellian Slip (L) 0.25
EA0027 Dannik Jerriko (D) 4.00
EA0028 Danz Borin (D) 0.75
EA0029 Dark Waters (D) 3.00
EA0030 Death Star (D) 12.00
EA0031 Death Star Gunner (D) 0.25
EA0032 Death Star Tractor Beam (D) 3.00
EA0033 Death Star: Conference Room (D) 0.75
EA0034 Death Star: Trench (L) 4.00
EA0035 Defel (D) 0.25
EA0036 Dejarik Hologameboard (L) 4.00
EA0037 Dianoga (Swamp Creature) (L) 4.00
EA0038 Doikk Na'ts (L) 0.75
EA0039 Double Agent (L) 4.00
EA0040 DS-61-4 (L) 4.00
EA0041 Eject! Eject! (L) 0.25
EA0042 Enhanced Tie Laser Cannon (D) 0.25
EA0043 Evader (D) 0.75
EA0044 Fire Extinguisher (L) 0.75
EA0045 Garouf Lafoe (L) 0.75
EA0046 Ghhhk (D) 0.25
EA0047 Gold 2 (L) 0.75
EA0048 Grappling Hook (L) 0.25
EA0049 Greedo (L) 6.00
EA0050 Grimtaash (L) 0.25
EA0051 Hem Dazon (L) 5.00
EA0052 Het Nkik (L) 0.75
EA0053 Houjix (L) 0.25
EA0054 Hunchback (L) 4.00
EA0055 Hyperwave Scan (D) 0.75
EA0056 Hypo (L) 4.00
EA0057 I Have A Very Bad Feeling About This (L) 0.25
EA0058 Ickabel G'ont (L) 0.75
EA0059 I'm Here To Rescue You (L) 0.75
EA0060 I'm On The Leader (L) 4.00
EA0061 Imperial Commander (D) 0.25
EA0062 Imperial Holotable (L) 5.00

CCG: Cards, A New Hope

EA0063 Imperial Justice (D)	0.25
EA0064 Imperial Squad Leader (D)	0.25
EA0065 Incom T-16 Skyhopper (L)	0.25
EA0066 Informant (D)	0.75
EA0067 IT-O (Eyetee-Oh) (L)	4.00
EA0068 Jawa Blaster (D)	0.25
EA0069 Jawa Ion Gun (L)	0.25
EA0070 Kashyyyk (D)	0.25
EA0072 Kiffex (L)	4.00
EA0073 Krayt Dragon Bones (D)	0.75
EA0074 Laser Gate (D)	0.75
EA0075 Leia Seeker (L)	3.00
EA0076 Let The Wookiee Win (L)	4.00
EA0077 Lirin Car'n (D)	0.75
EA0078 Logistical Delay (L)	0.75
EA0079 Lt. Pol Treidum (D)	0.25
EA0080 Lt. Shann Childsen (D)	0.75
EA0081 Luke's Cape (D)	5.00
EA0082 Luke's Hunting Rifle (L)	0.75
EA0083 Magnetic Suction Tube (D)	4.00
EA0085 Maneuver Check (L)	3.00
EA0086 Merc Sunlet (L)	0.25
EA0087 M-HYD 'Binary' Droid (L)	0.75
EA0088 Mobquet A-1 Deluxe Floater (D)	0.25
EA0089 Monnok (D)	0.25
EA0090 Mosep (D)	0.75
EA0091 Motti Seeker (D)	3.00
EA0092 Nalan Cheel (L)	0.75
EA0093 Ng'ok (D)	0.25
EA0094 Officer Evax (D)	0.25
EA0095 Oo-ta Goo-ta, Solo? (D)	0.75
EA0096 Out Of Commission (L)	0.75
EA0097 Program Trap (D)	0.75
EA0098 Quite A Mercenary (L)	0.25
EA0099 R2-D2 (Artoo-Detoo) (D)	14.00
EA0100 R2-Q2 (Artoo-Kyootoo) (D)	0.25
EA0101 R3-T6 (Arthree-Teesix) (D)	5.00
EA0102 R5-A2 (Arfive-Aytoo) (D)	0.25
EA0103 R5-D4 (Arfive-Defour) (L)	0.25
EA0104 RA-7 (Aray-Seven) (L)	0.25
EA0105 Ralltiir (D)	0.25
EA0107 Rebel Commander (L)	0.25
EA0108 Rebel Squad Leader (L)	0.25
EA0109 Rebel Tech (L)	0.25
EA0110 Rectenna (L)	0.25
EA0111 Red 2 (D)	5.00
EA0112 Red 5 (D)	7.00
EA0113 Red 6 (L)	0.75
EA0114 Reegesk (D)	0.75
EA0115 Remote (L)	0.25
EA0116 Reserve Pilot (D)	0.75
EA0117 Retract The Bridge (D)	4.00
EA0118 Rodian (D)	0.25
EA0119 Rogue Bantha (L)	0.75
EA0120 Sabotage (L)	0.75
EA0121 Sandcrawler: Droid Junkheap (D)	4.00
EA0122 Sandcrawler: Loading Bay (D)	4.00
EA0123 Saurin (L)	0.25
EA0124 Scanner Techs (L)	0.75
EA0125 Sensor Panel (L)	0.75
EA0126 Sniper (D)	0.75
EA0127 Solomahal (L)	0.25
EA0128 Sorry About The Mess (L)	0.75
EA0129 Spice Mines Of Kessel (L)	4.00
EA0130 Stunning Leader (D)	0.25
EA0131 Superlaser (L)	5.00
EA0132 SW-4 Ion Cannon (L)	4.00
EA0133 Swilla Corey (D)	0.25
EA0134 Tantive IV (L)	10.00
EA0135 Tatooine: Bluffs (L)	4.00
EA0136 Tech Mo'r (D)	0.75
EA0137 Tentacle (D)	0.25
EA0138 There'll Be Hell To Pay (D)	0.75
EA0139 They're On Dantooine (L)	4.00
EA0140 This Is Some Rescue! (D)	0.75
EA0141 Tie Assault Squadron (D)	0.75
EA0142 Tie Vanguard (D)	0.25
EA0143 Tiree (L)	0.75
EA0144 Tractor Beam (D)	0.75
EA0145 Trooper Davin Felth (L)	4.00
EA0146 Tzizvvt (L)	3.00

EA0147 U-3PO (Yoo-Threepio) (L)	5.00
EA0148 Undercover (D)	0.75
EA0149 Undercover (L)	0.75
EA0150 URoRRuR'R'R (L)	0.75
EA0151 URoRRuR'R'R's Hunting Rifle (D)	0.75
EA0152 Victory-Class Star Destroyer (D)	0.75
EA0153 We Have A Prisoner (D)	0.25
EA0154 WED15-I7 'Septoid' Droid (D)	0.75
EA0155 Wedge Antilles (L)	10.00
EA0156 What're You Tryin' To Push On Us? (L)	0.75
EA0157 Wookiee Roar (L)	4.00
EA0158 Yavin 4: Briefing Room (L)	0.75
EA0159 Yavin 4: Massassi Ruins (L)	0.75
EA0160 You're All Clear Kid! (L)	4.00
EA0161 Y-wing Assault Squadron (L)	0.75
EA0162 Zutton (L)	0.25

CCG: CARDS, CLOUD CITY

EB0001 Ability, Ability, Ability (D)	0.25
EB0002 Abyss (D)	1.00
EB0003 Access Denied (L)	0.25
EB0004 Advantage (L)	3.00
EB0005 Aiiii! Aaa! Aggggggggggg! (D)	3.00
EB0006 All My Urchins (L)	4.00
EB0007 All Too Easy (D)	3.00
EB0008 Ambush (L)	3.00
EB0009 Armed And Dangerous (L)	1.00
EB0010 Artoo, Come Back At Once! (L)	3.00
EB0011 As Good As Gone (L)	0.25
EB0012 Atmospheric Assault (D)	3.00
EB0013 Beldon's Eye (L)	3.00
EB0014 Bespin (D/L)	1.00
EB0017 Bespin: Cloud City (D/L)	1.00
EB0018 Binders (L)	0.25
EB0019 Bionic Hand (L)	4.00
EB0020 Blasted Droid (D)	0.25
EB0021 Blaster Proficiency (L)	0.25
EB0022 Boba Fett (D)	22.00
EB0023 Boba Fett's Blaster Rifle (D)	5.00
EB0024 Bounty (D)	0.25
EB0025 Brief Loss Of Control (D)	3.00
EB0026 Bright Hope (L)	5.00
EB0027 Captain Bewil (D)	4.00
EB0028 Captain Han Solo (L)	23.00
EB0029 Captive Fury (L)	1.00
EB0030 Captive Pursuit (L)	0.25
EB0031 Carbon-Freezing (D)	1.00
EB0032 Carbonite Chamber Console (D)	1.00
EB0033 Chasm (L)	1.00
EB0034 Chief Retwin (D)	4.00
EB0035 Civil Disorder (L)	0.25
EB0036 Clash Of Sabers (L)	1.00
EB0037 Cloud Car (D/L)	0.25
EB0039 Cloud City Blaster (D/L)	0.25
EB0041 Cloud City Engineer (D)	0.25
EB0042 Cloud City Sabacc (D)	1.00
EB0044 Cloud City Technician (L)	0.25
EB0045 Cloud City Trooper (D)	0.25
EB0047 Cloud City: Carbonite Chamber (D/L)	1.00
EB0049 Cloud City: Chasm Walkway (D/L)	0.25
EB0051 Cloud City: Dining Room (D)	3.00
EB0052 Cloud City: East Platform (D)	0.25
EB0053 Cloud City: Guest Quarters (L)	3.00
EB0054 Cloud City: Incinerator (D/L)	0.25
EB0056 Cloud City: Lower Corridor (D/L)	1.00
EB0058 Cloud City: Platform 327 (L)	0.25
EB0059 Cloud City: Security Tower (D)	0.25
EB0060 Cloud City: Upper Plaza Corridor (D/L)	1.00
EB0062 Clouds (D/L)	0.25
EB0064 Commander Desanne (D)	1.00
EB0065 Computer Interface (D)	0.25
EB0066 Courage Of A Skywalker (L)	4.00
EB0067 Crack Shot (L)	1.00
EB0068 Cyborg Construct (L)	1.00
EB0069 Dark Approach (L)	4.00
EB0070 Dark Deal (D)	0.25
EB0071 Dark Strike (D)	0.25
EB0072 Dash (L)	0.25
EB0073 Despair (D)	3.00

EB0074 Desperate Reach (L) 1.00
EB0075 Dismantle On Sight (L) 3.00
EB0076 Dodge (L) 0.25
EB0077 Double Back (D) 1.00
EB0078 Double-Crossing, No-Good Swindler (D) 0.25
EB0079 E Chu Ta (D) 0.25
EB0080 E-3PO (D) 4.00
EB0081 End This Destructive Conflict (D) 4.00
EB0082 Epic Duel (D) 6.00
EB0083 Fall Of The Empire (L) 1.00
EB0084 Fall Of The Legend (L) 1.00
EB0085 Flight Escort (D) 4.00
EB0086 Focused Attack (D) 3.00
EB0087 Force Field (D) 4.00
EB0088 Forced Landing (D) 4.00
EB0089 Frozen Assets (L) 4.00
EB0090 Gambler's Luck (L) 4.00
EB0091 Glancing Blow (L) 4.00
EB0092 Haven (L) 5.00
EB0093 Heart Of The Chasm (D) 1.00
EB0094 Hero Of A Thousand Devices (L) 1.00
EB0095 He's All Yours, Bounty Hunter (D) 4.00
EB0096 Higher Ground (L) 4.00
EB0097 Hindsight (L) 4.00
EB0098 Hopping Mad (L) 3.00
EB0099 Human Shield (D) 0.25
EB0100 I Am Your Father (D) 5.00
EB0101 I Don't Need Their Scum, Either (L) 4.00
EB0102 I Had No Choice (D) 4.00
EB0103 Imperial Decree (D) 1.00
EB0104 Imperial Trooper Guard Dainsom (D) 1.00
EB0105 Impressive, Most Impressive (L) 4.00
EB0106 Innocent Scoundrel (L) 1.00
EB0107 Interrogation Array (D) 4.00
EB0108 Into The Ventilation Shaft, Lefty (L) 3.00
EB0109 It's A Trap! (L) 1.00
EB0110 Kebyc (L) 1.00
EB0111 Keep Your Eyes Open (L) 0.25
EB0112 Lando Calrissian (D) 13.00
EB0113 Lando's Wrist Comlink (L) 1.00
EB0114 Leia Of Alderaan (L) 5.00
EB0115 Levitation Attack (D) 1.00
EB0116 Lieutenant Cecius (D) 1.00
EB0117 Lieutenant Sheckil (D) 4.00
EB0118 Lift Tube Escape (L) 0.25
EB0119 Lobot (L) 6.00
EB0120 Luke's Blaster Pistol (L) 5.00
EB0121 Mandalorian Armor (D) 5.00
EB0122 Mostly Armless (D) 3.00
EB0123 Noooooooo! (L) 3.00
EB0124 Obsidian 7 (D) 6.00
EB0125 Obsidian 8 (D) 6.00
EB0126 Off The Edge (L) 4.00
EB0127 Old Pirates (L) 3.00
EB0128 Out Of Somewhere (L) 1.00
EB0129 Path Of Least Resistance (L) 0.25
EB0130 Point Man (D) 3.00
EB0131 Prepare The Chamber (D) 1.00
EB0132 Princess Leia (L) 21.00
EB0133 Projective Telepathy (D) 1.00
EB0134 Protector (L) 5.00
EB0135 Punch It! (L) 4.00
EB0136 Put That Down (L) 0.25
EB0137 Redemption (L) 9.00
EB0138 Release Your Anger (D) 4.00
EB0139 Rendezvous Point On Tatooine (L) 4.00
EB0140 Rescue In The Clouds (L) 0.25
EB0141 Restricted Access (D) 0.25
EB0142 Rite Of Passage (D) 0.25
EB0143 Shattered Hope (D) 1.00
EB0144 Shocking Information (L) 0.25
EB0145 Shocking Revelation (D) 0.25
EB0146 Slave I (D) 12.00
EB0147 Slip Sliding Away (D) 3.00
EB0148 Smoke Screen (L) 3.00
EB0149 Somersault (L) 0.25
EB0150 Sonic Bombardment (D) 1.00
EB0151 Special Delivery (D) 0.25
EB0152 Surprise (D) 4.00
EB0153 Surreptitious Glance (L) 4.00
EB0154 Swing-And-A-Miss (L) 1.00
EB0155 The Emperor's Prize (D) 4.00
EB0156 This Is Even Better (L) 3.00
EB0157 This Is Still Wrong (D) 3.00
EB0158 Tibanna Gas Miner (D/L) 0.25
EB0159 Tie Sentry Ships (D) 0.25
EB0160 Treva Horme (L) 1.00
EB0161 Trooper Assault (D) 0.25
EB0162 Trooper Jerrol Blendin (D) 1.00
EB0163 Trooper Utris M'toc (L) 1.00
EB0164 Ugloste (D) 4.00
EB0165 Ugnaught (D) 0.25
EB0166 Uncontrollable Fury (L) 4.00
EB0167 Vader's Bounty (D) 5.00
EB0168 Vader's Cape (D) 5.00
EB0169 Weapon Levitation (D) 1.00
EB0170 Weapon Of An Ungrateful Son (D) 1.00
EB0171 Weather Vane (D/L) 1.00
EB0172 We'll Find Han (L) 3.00
EB0173 We're The Bait (D) 3.00
EB0174 Why Didn't You Tell Me? (D) 3.00
EB0175 Wiorkettle (L) 1.00
EB0176 Wookiee Strangle (L) 3.00
EB0177 You Are Beaten (D) 1.00

CCG: CARDS, DAGOBAH

EC0001 3,720 To 1 (D) 0.25
EC0002 4-LOM (D) 7.00
EC0003 4-LOM's Concussion Rifle (D) 5.00
EC0004 A Dangerous Time (D) 0.25
EC0005 A Jedi's Strength (L) 0.75
EC0006 Anger, Fear, Aggression (L) 0.25
EC0007 Anoat (D/L) 0.75
EC0008 Apology Accepted (D) 0.25
EC0009 Asteroid Field (D/L) 0.25
EC0010 Asteroid Sanctuary (L) 0.25
EC0011 Asteroids Do Not Concern Me (L) 3.00
EC0012 Astromech Translator (L) 0.25
EC0013 At Peace (L) 3.00
EC0014 Avenger (D) 10.00
EC0015 Away Put Your Weapon (L) 0.75
EC0016 Awwww, Cannot Get Your Ship Out (D) 0.25
EC0017 Bad Feeling Have I (D) 3.00
EC0018 Big One (D/L) 0.75
EC0019 Big One: Asteroid Cave or Space Slug Belly (D/L) 0.75
EC0020 Blasted Varmints (L) 0.25
EC0021 Bog-wing (D/L) 0.25
EC0022 Bombing Run (D) 3.00
EC0023 Bossk (D) 7.00
EC0024 Bossk's Mortar Gun (D) 4.00
EC0025 Broken Concentration (D) 4.00
EC0026 Captain Needa (D) 5.00
EC0027 Close Call (D) 0.25
EC0028 Closer?! (L) 0.75
EC0029 Comm Chief (D) 0.25
EC0030 Commander Brandei (D) 0.75
EC0031 Commander Gherant (D) 0.75
EC0032 Commander Nemet (D) 0.75
EC0033 Control (D) 0.75
EC0034 Control Lost (L) 0.75
EC0035 Corporal Derdram (D) 0.75
EC0036 Corporal Vandolay (D) 0.75
EC0037 Corrosive Damage (D) 3.00
EC0038 Dagobah (L) 0.75
EC0039 Dagobah: Bog Clearing (L) 4.00
EC0040 Dagobah: Cave (D) 4.00
EC0041 Dagobah: Jungle (L) 0.75
EC0042 Dagobah: Swamp (L) 0.75
EC0043 Dagobah: Training Area (L) 0.25
EC0044 Dagobah: Yoda's Hut (L) 4.00
EC0045 Defensive Fire (D) 0.25
EC0046 Dengar (D) 7.00
EC0047 Dengar's Blaster Carbine (D) 4.00
EC0048 Descent Into The Dark (L) 3.00
EC0049 Do, Or Do Not (L) 0.25
EC0050 Domain Of Evil (L) 0.75
EC0051 Dragonsnake (D) 3.00
EC0052 Droid Sensorscope (L) 0.25
EC0053 Effective Repairs (L) 3.00
EC0054 Egregious Pilot Error (L) 3.00

CCG: Cards, Dagobah

EC0055 Encampment (L)	0.25
EC0056 Executor (D)	18.00
EC0057 Executor: Comm Station (D)	0.75
EC0058 Executor: Control Station (D)	0.75
EC0059 Executor: Holotheatre (D)	4.00
EC0060 Executor: Main Corridor (D)	0.25
EC0061 Executor: Meditation Chamber (D)	4.00
EC0062 Failure At The Cave (D)	4.00
EC0063 Fear (D)	0.25
EC0064 Field Promotion (D)	4.00
EC0065 Flagship (D)	4.00
EC0066 Flash Of Insight (L)	0.75
EC0067 Found Someone You Have (L)	0.75
EC0068 Frustration (D)	3.00
EC0069 Great Warrior (L)	0.25
EC0070 Grounded Starfighter (L)	0.75
EC0071 Han's Toolkit (L)	3.00
EC0072 He Is Not Ready (D)	0.25
EC0073 Hiding In The Garbage (L)	3.00
EC0074 HoloNet Transmission (D)	0.75
EC0075 Hound's Tooth (D)	5.00
EC0076 I Have A Bad Feeling About This (L)	4.00
EC0077 I Want That Ship (D)	3.00
EC0078 IG-2000 (D)	5.00
EC0079 IG-88 (D)	10.00
EC0080 IG-88's Neural Inhibitor (D)	5.00
EC0081 IG-88's Pulse Cannon (D)	4.00
EC0082 Imbalance (D)	0.75
EC0083 Imperial Helmsman (D)	0.25
EC0084 Ineffective Maneuver (L)	0.75
EC0085 It Is The Future You See (L)	3.00
EC0086 Jedi Levitation (L)	3.00
EC0087 Knowledge And Defense (D)	0.25
EC0088 Landing Claw (L)	5.00
EC0089 Lando System? (D)	3.00
EC0090 Levitation (L)	0.75
EC0091 Lieutenant Commander Ardan (D)	0.75
EC0092 Lieutenant Suba (D)	4.00
EC0093 Lieutenant Venka (D)	0.75
EC0094 Light Maneuvers (L)	3.00
EC0095 Location, Location, Location (D)	4.00
EC0096 Lost In Space (D)	4.00
EC0097 Lost Relay (L)	0.25
EC0098 Luke's Backpack (L)	3.00
EC0099 Mist Hunter (D)	5.00
EC0100 Moving To Attack Position (L)	0.25
EC0101 Much Anger In Him (D)	3.00
EC0102 Mynock (D/L)	0.25
EC0103 Never Tell Me The Odds (L)	0.25
EC0104 No Disintegrations! (L)	4.00
EC0105 Nudj (L)	0.25
EC0106 Obi-Wan's Apparition (L)	4.00
EC0107 Order To Engage (L)	3.00
EC0108 Polarized Negative Power Coupling (L)	3.00
EC0109 Portable Fusion Generator (L)	0.25
EC0110 Precision Targeting (D)	0.75
EC0111 Proton Bombs (D)	0.75
EC0112 Punishing One (D)	5.00
EC0113 Quick Draw (L)	0.25
EC0114 Raithal (D/L)	3.00
EC0115 Rebel Flight Suit (L)	0.25
EC0116 Recoil In Fear (L)	0.25
EC0117 Reflection (L)	4.00
EC0118 Report To Lord Vader (L)	3.00
EC0119 Res Luk Ra'auf (D)	3.00
EC0120 Retractable Arm (L)	0.25
EC0121 Rogue Asteroid (D/L)	0.25
EC0122 Rycar's Run (L)	3.00
EC0123 Scramble (L)	0.75
EC0124 Shoo! Shoo! (L)	0.75
EC0125 Shot In The Dark (D)	0.75
EC0126 Shut Him Up Or Shut Him Down (D)	0.75
EC0127 Size Matters Not (L)	3.00
EC0128 Sleen (D)	0.25
EC0129 Smuggler's Blues (L)	4.00
EC0130 Something Hit Us! (D)	0.75
EC0131 Son of Skywalker (D)	23.00
EC0132 Space Slug (D/L)	3.00
EC0133 Star Destroyer: Launch Bay (D)	0.25
EC0134 Starship Levitation (L)	0.75
EC0135 Stone Pile (L)	3.00

EC0136 Sudden Impact (D)	0.75
EC0137 Take Evasive Action (D)	0.25
EC0138 The Dark Path (D)	3.00
EC0139 The Professor (L)	3.00
EC0140 There Is No Try (D)	0.25
EC0141 They'd Be Crazy To Follow Us (L)	0.25
EC0142 This Is More Like It (L)	4.00
EC0143 This Is No Cave (L)	3.00
EC0144 Those Rebels Won't Escape Us (D)	0.25
EC0145 Through The Force Things You Will See (L)	3.50
EC0146 Tie Avenger (L)	0.25
EC0147 Tie Bomber (D)	0.75
EC0148 Tight Squeeze (L)	3.00
EC0149 Transmission Terminated (L)	0.75
EC0150 Tunnel Vision (L)	0.75
EC0151 Uncertain Is The Future (D)	0.25
EC0152 Unexpected Interruption (D)	3.00
EC0153 Vine Snake (D/L)	0.25
EC0154 Visage Of The Emperor (D)	4.00
EC0155 Visored Vision (L)	0.25
EC0156 Voyeur (D)	0.25
EC0157 Warrant Officer M'Kae (D)	0.75
EC0158 Wars Not Make One Great (L)	0.75
EC0159 We Can Still Outmaneuver Them (L)	3.00
EC0160 We Don't Need Their Scum (L)	3.00
EC0161 WHAAAAAAAAAOOOOW! (L)	3.00
EC0162 What Is Thy Bidding, My Master? (L)	3.00
EC0163 Yoda (L)	27.00
EC0164 Yoda Stew (L)	0.75
EC0165 Yoda, You Seek Yoda (L)	4.00
EC0166 Yoda's Gimer Stick (L)	4.00
EC0167 Yoda's Hope (L)	0.75
EC0168 You Do Have Your Moments (L)	0.75
EC0169 Zuckuss (D)	8.00
EC0170 Zuckuss' Snare Rifle (D)	4.00

CCG: CARDS, DEATH STAR II

EO0001 Accuser (D)	5.00
EO0003 Admiral Chiraneau (D)	6.00
EO0005 Anakin Skywalker (D)	7.00
EO0006 Aquaris (L)	0.25
EO0007 A-Wing (L)	0.25
EO0008 A-Wing Cannon (L)	0.25
EO0009 Baron Soontir Fel (D)	4.00
EO0010 Battle Deployment (D)	4.00
EO0011 Black 11 (D)	5.00
EO0012 Blue Squadron 5 (L)	0.50
EO0013 Blue Squadron B-wing (L)	4.00
EO0014 Bring Him Before Me (D)	5.00
EO0015 B-Wing Attack Squadron (L)	4.00
EO0016 B-Wing Bomber (L)	0.25
EO0017 Capital Support (L)	4.00
EO0018 Captain Godherdt (D)	0.50
EO0019 Captain Jonus (D)	1.00
EO0020 Captain Sarkli (D)	4.00
EO0021 Captain Verrack (L)	0.50
EO0022 Captain Yorr (D)	0.50
EO0023 Chimaera (D)	6.00
EO0024 Close Air Support (L)	0.25
EO0025 Colonel Cracken (L)	4.00
EO0026 Colonel Davod Jon (D)	0.50
EO0027 Colonel Jendon (D)	4.00
EO0028 Colonel Salm (L)	0.50
EO0029 Combat Response (D)	0.25
EO0030 Combined Fleet Action (L)	4.00
EO0031 Commander Merrejk (D)	4.00
EO0032 Concentrate All Fire (L)	4.00
EO0033 Concussion Missiles (D/L)	0.25
EO0034 Corporal Marmor (L)	0.50
EO0035 Corporal Midge (L)	0.50
EO0036 Critical Error Revealed (L)	0.25
EO0037 Darth Vader's Lightsaber (D)	7.00
EO0038 Death Star II (D)	8.00
EO0039 Death Star II: Capacitors (D)	0.25
EO0040 Death Star II: Coolant Shaft (D)	0.25
EO0041 Death Star II: Docking Bay (D)	0.25
EO0042 Death Star II: Reactor Core (D)	0.25
EO0043 Death Star II: Throne Room (D)	4.00
EO0044 Defiance (L)	7.00

EO0045 Desperate Counter (D) 0.25
EO0046 Dominator (D) 7.00
EO0047 DS-181-3 (D) 0.50
EO0048 DS-181-4 (D) 0.50
EO0049 Emperor Palpatine (D)R 52.00
EO0050 Emperor's Personal Shuttle (D) 5.00
EO0051 Emperor's Power (D) 0.50
EO0052 Endor Shield (D) 0.50
EO0053 Enhanced Proton Torpedoes (L) 0.25
EO0054 Fighter Cover (D) 4.00
EO0055 Fighters Coming In (D) 4.00
EO0056 First Officer Thaneespi (L) 4.00
EO0057 Flagship Executor (D) 15.00
EO0058 Flagship Operations (D) 4.00
EO0059 Force Lightning (D) 4.00
EO0060 Force Pike (D) 0.25
EO0061 Gall (D) 0.25
EO0062 General Calrissian (L) 10.00
EO0063 General Walex Blissex (L) 0.50
EO0064 Gold Squadron 1 (L) 7.00
EO0065 Gray Squadron 1 (L) 0.50
EO0066 Gray Squadron 2 (L) 0.50
EO0067 Green Leader (L) 4.00
EO0068 Green Squadron 1 (L) 4.00
EO0069 Green Squadron 3 (L) 4.00
EO0070 Green Squadron A-Wing (L) 4.00
EO0071 Green Squadron Pilot (L) 0.25
EO0072 Grey Squadron Y-Wing Pilot (L) 0.25
EO0073 Head Back To The Surface (L) 0.25
EO0074 Heading For The Medical Frigate (L) 0.25
EO0075 Heavy Turbolaser Battery (D/L) 0.25
EO0076 Home One (L) 8.00
EO0077 Home One: Docking Bay (L) 0.25
EO0078 Home One: War Room (L) 4.00
EO0079 Honor Of The Jedi (L) 0.50
EO0179 I Can Save Him (L) 4.00
EO0080 I Feel The Conflict (L) 0.50
EO0081 I'll Take The Leader (L) 4.00
EO0082 I'm With You Too (L) 4.00
EO0083 Imperial Command (D) 4.00
EO0084 Inconsequential Losses (D) 0.25
EO0085 Independence (L) 7.00
EO0086 Insertion Planning (L) 0.25
EO0087 Insignificant Rebellion (D) 0.50
EO0088 Intensify The Forward Batteries (D) 4.00
EO0089 Janus Greejatus (D) 4.00
EO0090 Judicator (D) 7.00
EO0091 Karie Neth (L) 0.50
EO0092 Keir Santage (L) 0.50
EO0093 Kin Kian (L) 0.50
EO0094 Launching The Assault (L) 4.00
EO0095 Leave Them To Me (D) 0.25
EO0096 Let's Keep A Little Optimism Here (L) 0.25
EO0097 Liberty (L) 7.00
EO0098 Lieutenant Blount (L) 4.00
EO0099 Lieutenant Endicott (D) 0.50
EO0100 Lieutenant Hebsly (L) 0.50
EO0101 Lieutenant s'Too Vees (L) 0.50
EO0102 Lieutenant Telsij (L) 0.50
EO0103 Lord Vader (D) 28.00
EO0104 Luke Skywalker, Jedi Knight (L)R 52.00
EO0105 Luke's Lightsaber (L) 9.00
EO0106 Luminous (L) 0.50
EO0107 Major Haash'n (L) 0.50
EO0108 Major Mianda (D) 0.50
EO0109 Major Olander Brit (L) 0.50
EO0110 Major Panno (L) 0.50
EO0111 Major Rhymer (L) 0.50
EO0112 Major Turr Phennir (D) 0.50
EO0113 Masanya (L) 4.00
EO0114 Menace Fades (L) 0.25
EO0115 Mobilization Points (D) 0.25
EO0116 Moff Jerjerrod (D) 5.00
EO0117 Mon Calamari (D/L) 0.25
EO0118 Mon Calamari Star Cruiser (L) 6.00
EO0119 Myn Kyneugh (D) 5.00
EO0120 Nebulon-B Frigate (L) 0.50
EO0121 Nien Nunb (L) 5.00
EO0122 Obsidian 10 (D) 0.50
EO0123 Onyx 1 (D) 4.00
EO0124 Onyx 2 (D) 0.50

EO0125 Operational As Planned (D) 0.25
EO0126 Orbital Mine (L) 0.25
EO0127 Our Only Hope (L) 0.50
EO0128 Overseeing It Personally (D) 4.00
EO0129 Prepared Defenses (D) 0.25
EO0130 Rebel Leadership (L) 4.00
EO0131 Red Squadron 1 (L) 5.00
EO0132 Red Squadron 4 (L) 0.50
EO0133 Red Squadron 7 (L) 0.50
EO0134 Rise, My Friend (L) 4.00
EO0135 Royal Escort (D) 0.25
EO0136 Royal Guard (D) 0.25
EO0137 Saber 1 (D) 5.00
EO0138 Saber 2 (D) 0.50
EO0139 Saber 3 (D) 0.50
EO0140 Saber 4 (D) 0.50
EO0141 Scimitar 1 (D) 0.50
EO0142 Scimitar 2 (D) 0.50
EO0143 Scimitar Squadron Tie (D) 0.25
EO0144 Scythe 1 (D) 0.50
EO0145 Scythe 3 (D) 1.00
EO0146 Scythe Squadron Tie (D) 0.25
EO0147 SFS L-s7.2 Tie Cannon (D) 0.25
EO0148 Sim Aloo (D) 5.00
EO0149 Something Special Planned For Them (D) 0.25
EO0150 Squadron Assignments (L) 0.25
EO0151 Staging Areas (L) 0.25
EO0152 Strike Planning (L) 4.00
EO0153 Strikeforce (L) 0.25
EO0154 Sullust (D/L) 0.25
EO0155 Superficial Damage (L) 0.25
EO0156 Superlaser Mark II (D) 0.50
EO0180 Take Your Father's Place (D) 4.00
EO0157 Taking Them With Us (L) 4.00
EO0158 Tala 1 (L) 4.00
EO0159 Tala 2 (L) 4.00
EO0160 Ten Numb (L) 4.00
EO0161 That Thing's Operational (D) 4.00
EO0162 The Emperor's Shield (D) 5.00
EO0163 The Emperor's Sword (D) 5.00
EO0164 The Time For Our Attack Has Come (L) 0.25
EO0165 The Way Of Things (D) 0.50
EO0166 There Is Good In Him (L) 5.00
EO0167 Thunderflare (D) 5.00
EO0168 Tie Interceptor (D) 0.25
EO0169 Twilight Is Upon Me (L) 4.00
EO0170 Tycho Celchu (L) 4.00
EO0171 Visage (D) 5.00
EO0172 Wedge Antilles, Red Squadron Leader (L) 7.00
EO0173 We're In Attack Position Now (D) 4.00
EO0174 You Cannot Hide Forever (D) 0.50
EO0175 You Must Confront Vader (L) 5.00
EO0176 Young Fool (D) 4.00
EO0177 Your Destiny (D) 0.25
EO0178 Your Insight Serves You Well (L) 0.50

CCG: CARDS, ENDOR

EQ0001 A280 Sharpshooter Rifle (L) 3.50
EQ0002 Accelerate (D) 0.25
EQ0003 Aim High (D) 3.30
EQ0004 Always Thinking With Stomach (D) 3.00
EQ0005 An Entire Legion Of Troops (D) 0.50
EQ0006 Aratech Corporation (D) 3.00
EQ0007 AT-ST Dual Cannon (D) 4.00
EQ0008 AT-ST Pilot (D) 0.25
EQ0009 Battle Order (D) 0.50
EQ0010 Battle Plan (L) 0.50
EQ0011 Biker Scout Gear (D) 0.50
EQ0012 Biker Scout Trooper (D) 0.25
EQ0013 Blastech E-11B Blaster Rifle (L) 0.25
EQ0014 Captain Yutani (L) 0.50
EQ0015 Careful Planning (L) 0.25
EQ0016 Carida (L) 0.50
EQ0017 Chandrila (L) 0.50
EQ0018 Chewbacca Of Kashyyyk (L) 11.00
EQ0019 Chewbacca's Bowcaster (L) 5.00
EQ0020 Chewie's AT-ST (L) 5.00
EQ0021 Chief Chirpa (L) 4.00
EQ0022 Closed Door (D) 3.00

EQ0023 Colonel Dyer (D) 3.00
EQ0024 Combat Readiness (D) 0.25
EQ0025 Commander Igar (D) 4.00
EQ0026 Commando Training (L) 0.25
EQ0027 Compact Firepower (D) 0.25
EQ0028 Corporal Avarik (D) 0.50
EQ0029 Corporal Beezer (L) 0.50
EQ0030 Corporal Delevar (L) 0.50
EQ0031 Corporal Drazin (L) 0.50
EQ0032 Corporal Drelosyn (D) 3.00
EQ0033 Corporal Janse (L) 0.50
EQ0034 Corporal Kensaric (L) 3.00
EQ0035 Corporal Misik (D) 3.00
EQ0036 Corporal Oberk (D) 3.00
EQ0037 Count Me In (L) 3.00
EQ0038 Counterattack (D) 3.00
EQ0039 Covert Landing (L) 0.50
EQ0040 Crossfire (D) 3.00
EQ0041 Daughter Of Skywalker (L) 12.00
EQ0042 Deactivate Shield Generator (L) 5.00
EQ0043 Dead Ewok (D) 0.25
EQ0044 Don't Move! (D) 0.25
EQ0045 Dresselian Commando (L) 0.25
EQ0046 Early Warning Network (D) 4.00
EQ0047 Eee Chu Wawa! (L) 0.25
EQ0048 Elite Squadron Stormtrooper (D) 0.25
EQ0049 Empire's New Order (D) 3.00
EQ0050 Endor (D/L) 0.50
EQ0051 Endor Celebration (L) 3.00
EQ0052 Endor Occupation (D) 3.00
EQ0053 Endor Operations (D) 5.00
EQ0054 Endor Scout Trooper (L) 0.25
EQ0055 Endor: Ancient Forest (D) 0.50
EQ0056 Endor: Back Door (D/L) 0.50
EQ0057 Endor: Bunker (D/L) 0.50
EQ0058 Endor: Chief Chirpa's Hut (L) 3.00
EQ0059 Endor: Dark Forest (D) 3.00
EQ0060 Endor: Dense Forest (D/L) 0.25
EQ0061 Endor: Ewok Village (D/L) 0.50
EQ0062 Endor: Forest Clearing (D) 0.50
EQ0063 Endor: Great Forest (D/L) 0.50
EQ0064 Endor: Hidden Forest Trail (L) 0.50
EQ0065 Endor: Landing Platform (D/L) 0.25
EQ0066 Endor: Rebel Landing Site (L) 4.00
EQ0067 Establish Secret Base (D) 4.00
EQ0068 Ewok And Roll (L) 0.25
EQ0069 Ewok Bow (L) 0.25
EQ0070 Ewok Catapult (L) 0.50
EQ0071 Ewok Glider (L) 0.25
EQ0072 Ewok Log Jam (L) 0.25
EQ0073 Ewok Rescue (L) 0.25
EQ0074 Ewok Sentry (L) 0.25
EQ0075 Ewok Spear (L) 0.25
EQ0076 Ewok Spearman (L) 0.25
EQ0077 Ewok Tribesman (L) 0.25
EQ0078 Explosive Charge (L) 0.50
EQ0079 Firefight (L) 0.25
EQ0080 Fly Casual (L) 3.00
EQ0081 Free Ride (L) 0.50
EQ0082 Freeze! (D) 0.50
EQ0173 Garrison Destroyed (L) 3.00
EQ0083 General Crix Madine (L) 4.00
EQ0084 General Solo (L) 15.00
EQ0085 Get Alongside That One (L) 0.50
EQ0086 Go For Help! (D) 0.25
EQ0087 Graak (L) 4.00
EQ0088 Here We Go Again (L) 4.00
EQ0089 High-speed Tactics (D) 0.50
EQ0090 Hot Pursuit (D) 0.25
EQ0091 I Have A Really Bad Feeling (L) 0.25
EQ0092 I Hope She's All Right (L) 0.50
EQ0093 I Know (L) 4.00
EQ0094 I Wonder Who They Found (L) 0.50
EQ0095 Imperial Academy Training (D) 0.25
EQ0096 Imperial Arrest Order (D) 0.50
EQ0174 Imperial Outpost (D) 4.00
EQ0097 Imperial Tyranny (D) 0.25
EQ0098 Insurrection (L) 0.50
EQ0099 It's An Older Code (D) 3.00
EQ0100 Kazak (L) 3.00
EQ0101 Lambda-Class Shuttle (D) 0.25

EQ0102 Lieutenant Arnet (D) 0.50
EQ0103 Lieutenant Greeve (L) 3.00
EQ0104 Lieutenant Grond (D) 0.50
EQ0105 Lieutenant Page (L) 4.00
EQ0106 Lieutenant Renz (D) 3.00
EQ0107 Lieutenant Watts (D) 0.50
EQ0108 Logray (L) 4.00
EQ0109 Lost In The Wilderness (L) 4.00
EQ0110 Lumat (L) 0.50
EQ0111 Main Course (D) 0.50
EQ0112 Major Hewex (D) 4.00
EQ0113 Major Marquand (D) 4.00
EQ0114 Mon Mothma (L) 5.00
EQ0115 Navy Trooper (D) 0.25
EQ0116 Navy Trooper Fenson (D) 4.00
EQ0117 Navy Trooper Shield Technician (D) 0.25
EQ0118 Navy Trooper Vesden (D) 0.50
EQ0119 Ominous Rumors (D) 4.00
EQ0120 Orrimaarko (L) 5.00
EQ0121 Outflank (D) 0.25
EQ0122 Paploo (L) 0.50
EQ0123 Perimeter Patrol (D) 4.00
EQ0124 Pinned Down (D) 0.50
EQ0125 Pitiful Little Band (D) 0.25
EQ0126 Rabin (L) 0.50
EQ0127 Rapid Deployment (L) 3.00
EQ0128 Rebel Team (L) 5.00
EQ0129 Relentless Tracking (D) 4.00
EQ0130 Romba (L) 3.00
EQ0131 Scout Blaster (D) 0.25
EQ0132 Scout Recon (D) 0.25
EQ0133 Search And Destroy (D) 0.50
EQ0134 Security Precautions (D) 3.00
EQ0135 Sergeant Barich (D) 4.00
EQ0136 Sergeant Brooks Carlson (L) 4.00
EQ0137 Sergeant Bruckman (L) 4.00
EQ0138 Sergeant Elsek (D) 0.50
EQ0139 Sergeant Irol (D) 3.00
EQ0140 Sergeant Junkin (L) 0.50
EQ0141 Sergeant Tarl (D) 0.50
EQ0142 Sergeant Wallen (D) 4.00
EQ0143 Sneak Attack (D) 0.25
EQ0144 Sound The Attack (L) 0.25
EQ0145 Speeder Bike (D/L) 0.25
EQ0146 Speeder Bike Cannon (D) 0.50
EQ0147 Surprise Counter Assault (L) 3.00
EQ0148 Take The Initiative (L) 0.25
EQ0149 Teebo (L) 4.00
EQ0150 Tempest 1 (D) 6.00
EQ0151 Tempest Scout (D) 0.50
EQ0152 Tempest Scout 1 (D) 5.00
EQ0153 Tempest Scout 2 (D) 5.00
EQ0154 Tempest Scout 3 (D) 5.00
EQ0155 Tempest Scout 4 (D) 5.00
EQ0156 Tempest Scout 5 (D) 5.00
EQ0157 Tempest Scout 6 (D) 5.00
EQ0158 That's One (L) 4.00
EQ0159 This Is Absolutely Right (L) 3.00
EQ0160 Threepio (L) 10.00
EQ0161 Throw Me Another Charge (L) 0.50
EQ0162 Tydirium (L) 5.00
EQ0163 Well-earned Command (D) 3.00
EQ0164 Were You Looking For Me? (L) 3.00
EQ0165 Wicket (L) 4.00
EQ0166 Wokling (L) 3.00
EQ0167 Wookiee Guide (L) 0.25
EQ0168 Wounded Warrior (D) 3.00
EQ0169 Wuta (L) 3.00
EQ0170 You Rebel Scum (D) 3.00
EQ0171 YT-1300 Transport (L) 0.25
EQ0172 Yub Yub! (L) 0.25
EQ0173 Biker Scout Trooper (foil) (D) 4.00
EQ0174 Chewbacca Of Kashyyyk (foil) (L) 15.00
EQ0175 Daughter of Skywalker (foil) (L) 22.00
EQ0176 Early Warning Network (foil) (D) 10.00
EQ0177 Elite Squadron Stormtrooper (foil) (D) 5.00
EQ0178 Endor Celebration (foil) (L) 10.00
EQ0179 Endor: Ewok Village (foil) (L) 5.00
EQ0180 Endor: Landing Platform (foil) (D) 5.00
EQ0181 Ewok and Roll (foil) (L) 5.00
EQ0182 Ewok Glider (foil) (L) 5.00

EQ0183 General Solo (foil) (L) 40.00
EQ0184 Hot Pursuit (foil) (D) 10.00
EQ0185 Main Course (foil) (D) 10.00
EQ0186 Paploo (foil) (L) 5.00
EQ0187 Speeder Bike (foil) (D) 5.00
EQ0188 Tempest 1 (foil) (D) 25.00
EQ0189 Tempest Scout 4 (foil) (D) 16.00
EQ0190 Threepio (foil) (L) 28.00

CCG: CARDS, ENHANCED PREMIERE

EI0005 Boba Fett With Blaster Rifle (D) 7.00
EI0006 Darth Vader With Lightsaber (D) 9.00
EI0001 Han With Heavy Blaster Pistol (L) 10.00
EI0002 Leia With Blaster Rifle (L) 10.00
EI0003 Luke With Lightsaber (L) 8.00
EI0004 Obi-Wan With Lightsaber (L) 9.00

CCG: CARDS, ESB

ED0001 AT-AT Driver(3) (D) 0.25
ED0002 Blaster Rifle(2) (D) 0.25
ED0003 Blaster(2) (L) 0.25
ED0004 Chewie(3) (L) 12.00
ED0005 Cold Feet(3) (D) 0.25
ED0006 Commander Evram Lajaie (L) 0.25
ED0007 Corellian (L) 0.25
ED0008 Counter Assault(2) (D) 0.25
ED0009 Echo Base Trooper Officer(2) (L) 0.25
ED0010 Echo Base Trooper(6) (L) 0.25
ED0011 Fall Back!(2) (L) 0.25
ED0012 FX-10 (Effex-Ten) (D) 0.25
ED0013 FX-7 (Effex-Seven) (L) 0.25
ED0014 He Hasn't Come Back Yet(3) (D) 0.25
ED0015 Hoth Survival Gear(2) (L) 0.25
ED0016 Hoth: Defensive Perimeter (3rd Marker)(2) (L) 0.25
ED0017 Hoth: Echo Corridor (L) 0.25
ED0018 Hoth: Echo Docking Bay(2) (L) 0.25
ED0019 Hoth: Echo Med Lab (L) 0.25
ED0020 Hoth: Defensive Perimeter (3rd Marker) (D) 0.25
ED0021 Hoth: Echo Docking Bay (D) 0.25
ED0022 Hoth: Ice Plains (5th Marker) (2) (D) 0.25
ED0023 Hoth: Mountains (6th Marker) (2) (D) 7.00
ED0024 Hoth: North Ridge (4th Marker) (D) 0.25
ED0025 Hoth: Snow Trench (2nd Marker) (L) 0.25
ED0026 Houjix(2) (L) 0.25
ED0027 I'd Just As Soon Kiss A Wookie (D) 0.25
ED0028 Imperial Blaster(2) (D) 0.25
ED0029 Imperial Commander(2) (D) 0.25
ED0030 Imperial Squad Leader(2) (D) 0.25
ED0031 Imperial Trooper Guard(3) (D) 0.25
ED0032 Imperial Walker(3) (D) 7.00
ED0033 Infantry Mine(2) (D/L) 0.25
ED0034 It Can Wait (L) 0.25
ED0035 It Could Be Worse (L) 0.25
ED0036 Ket Maliss (D) 0.25
ED0037 Leia (L) 12.00
ED0038 LIN-V8K (Elleyein-Veeatekay)(2) (L) 0.25
ED0039 LIN-V8M (Elleyein-Veeateemm)(2) (D) 0.25
ED0040 Lone Rogue(3) (L) 7.00
ED0041 Lt. Pol Treidum (D) 0.25
ED0042 Nice Of You Guys To Drop By (L) 0.25
ED0043 Officer Evax (D) 0.25
ED0044 Rebel Commander(2) (L) 0.25
ED0045 Rebel Guard (L) 0.25
ED0046 Rebel Scout(2) (L) 0.25
ED0047 Rebel Snowspeeder(5) (L) 7.00
ED0048 Restraining Bolt (D/L) 0.25
ED0049 Sai'torr Kal Fas (L) 0.25
ED0050 Snowtrooper Officer(2) (D) 0.25
ED0051 Snowtrooper(6) (D) 0.25
ED0052 Stunning Leader(2) (D) 0.25
ED0053 Surprise Assault(2) (L) 0.25
ED0054 Tauntaun Handler(2) (L) 0.25
ED0055 Tauntaun(2) (L) 0.25
ED0056 Timer Mine(2) (D/L) 0.25
ED0057 Veers(3) (D) 9.00
ED0058 Walker Garrison(3) (D) 7.00

CCG: CARDS, HOTH

EE0001 2-1B (Too-Onebee) (L) 4.00
EE0002 A Dark Time For The Rebellion (D) 0.25
EE0003 Admiral Ozzel (D) 5.00
EE0004 Anakin's Lightsaber (L) 10.00
EE0005 Artillery Remote (L) 3.00
EE0006 AT-AT Cannon (D) 0.75
EE0007 AT-AT Driver (D) 0.25
EE0008 Atgar Laser Cannon (L) 0.75
EE0009 Attack Pattern Delta (L) 0.75
EE0010 Bacta Tank (L) 4.00
EE0011 Blizzard 1 (D) 7.00
EE0012 Blizzard 2 (D) 5.00
EE0013 Blizzard Scout 1 (D) 6.00
EE0014 Blizzard Walker (D) 0.75
EE0015 Breached Defenses (D) 0.75
EE0016 Cal Alder (L) 0.75
EE0017 Captain Lennox (D) 0.75
EE0018 Captain Piett (D) 4.00
EE0019 Cold Feet (D) 0.25
EE0020 Collapsing Corridor (D) 4.00
EE0021 Commander Luke Skywalker (L) 19.00
EE0022 ComScan Detection (D) 0.25
EE0023 Concussion Grenade (L) 5.00
EE0024 Crash Landing (L) 0.75
EE0025 Dack Ralter (L) 3.00
EE0026 Dark Dissension (L) 4.00
EE0027 Death Mark (D) 4.00
EE0028 Death Squadron (D) 0.75
EE0029 Debris Zone (D) 3.00
EE0030 Deflector Shield Generators (D) 0.75
EE0031 Derek `Hobbie' Klivian (L) 0.75
EE0032 Direct Hit (D) 0.75
EE0033 Disarming Creature (L) 4.00
EE0034 Dual Laser Cannon (L) 0.75
EE0035 Echo Base Operations (L) 4.00
EE0036 Echo Base Trooper (L) 0.25
EE0037 Echo Base Trooper Officer (L) 0.25
EE0038 Echo Trooper Backpack (L) 0.25
EE0039 EG-4 (Eegee-Four) (L) 0.25
EE0040 Electro-Rangefinder (D) 0.75
EE0041 Evacuation Control (L) 0.75
EE0042 E-web Blaster (D) 0.25
EE0043 Exhaustion (D) 0.75
EE0044 Exposure (D) 0.75
EE0045 Fall Back! (L) 0.25
EE0046 Frostbite (D/L) 0.25
EE0047 Frozen Dinner (D) 4.00
EE0048 Furry Fury (D) 3.00
EE0049 FX-10 (Effex-Ten) (D) 0.25
EE0050 FX-7 (Effex-Seven) (L) 0.25
EE0051 General Carlist Rieekan (L) 4.00
EE0052 General Veers (D) 7.00
EE0053 Golan Laser Battery (L) 0.75
EE0054 He Hasn't Come Back Yet (D) 0.25
EE0055 High Anxiety (D) 4.00
EE0056 Hoth (D/L) 0.75
EE0057 Hoth Survival Gear (L) 0.25
EE0058 Hoth: Defensive Perimeter (D/L) 0.25
EE0059 Hoth: Echo Command Center (D/L) 0.75
EE0152 Hoth: Echo Command War Room (D/L) 0.75
EE0060 Hoth: Echo Corridor (D/L) 0.75
EE0061 Hoth: Echo Docking Bay (D/L) 0.25
EE0062 Hoth: Echo Med Lab (L) 0.25
EE0063 Hoth: Ice Plains (D) 0.75
EE0064 Hoth: Main Power Generators (L) 0.75
EE0065 Hoth: North Ridge (D/L) 0.25
EE0066 Hoth: Snow Trench (L) 0.25
EE0067 Hoth: Wampa Cave (D) 4.00
EE0068 I Thought They Smelled Bad On The Outside (L) 4.00
EE0069 Ice Storm (D/L) 0.75
EE0070 I'd Just As Soon Kiss A Wookiee (D) 0.25
EE0071 Image Of The Dark Lord (D) 4.00
EE0072 Imperial Domination (D) 0.75
EE0073 Imperial Gunner (D) 0.25
EE0074 Imperial Supply (D) 0.25
EE0075 Infantry Mine (D/L) 0.25
EE0076 It Can Wait (L) 0.25
EE0077 Jeroen Webb (L) 0.75
EE0078 K-3PO (Kay-Threepio) (L) 4.00

EE0079 Lieutenant Cabbel (D)	0.75
EE0080 Lightsaber Deficiency (D)	0.75
EE0081 Lucky Shot (L)	0.75
EE0082 Major Bren Derlin (L)	3.00
EE0083 Medium Repeating Blaster Cannon (L)	0.25
EE0084 Medium Transport (L)	0.75
EE0085 Meteor Impact? (D)	4.00
EE0086 Mournful Roar (D)	4.00
EE0087 Nice Of You Guys To Drop By (L)	0.25
EE0088 Oh, Switch Off (L)	0.75
EE0089 One More Pass (L)	0.75
EE0090 Ord Mantell (D/L)	0.25
EE0091 Our First Catch Of The Day (D)	0.25
EE0092 Perimeter Scan (L)	0.25
EE0093 Planet Defender Ion Cannon (L)	4.00
EE0094 Portable Fusion Generator (D)	0.25
EE0095 Power Harpoon (L)	0.75
EE0096 Probe Antennae (D)	0.75
EE0097 Probe Droid (D)	0.25
EE0098 Probe Droid Laser (D)	0.75
EE0099 Probe Telemetry (D)	0.25
EE0100 R2 Sensor Array (L)	0.25
EE0101 R-3PO (Ar-Threepio) (L)	3.00
EE0102 R5-M2 (Arfive-Emmtoo) (L)	0.25
EE0103 Rebel Scout (L)	0.25
EE0104 Responsibility Of Command (D)	4.00
EE0105 Rogue 1 (L)	7.00
EE0106 Rogue 2 (L)	5.00
EE0107 Rogue 3 (L)	6.00
EE0108 Rogue Gunner (L)	0.25
EE0109 Romas Lock ''Navander'' (L)	0.75
EE0110 Rug Hug (L)	4.00
EE0111 Scruffy-Looking Nerf Herder (D)	3.00
EE0112 Self-Destruct Mechanism (D)	0.75
EE0113 Shawn Valdez (L)	0.75
EE0114 Silence Is Golden (D)	0.75
EE0115 Snowspeeder (L)	0.75
EE0116 Snowtrooper (D)	0.25
EE0117 Snowtrooper Officer (D)	0.25
EE0118 Stalker (D)	9.00
EE0119 Stop Motion (D)	0.25
EE0120 Surface Defense Cannon (L)	3.00
EE0121 Tactical Support (D)	3.00
EE0122 Tamizander Rey (L)	0.75
EE0123 Target The Main Generator (D)	4.00
EE0124 Tauntaun (L)	0.25
EE0125 Tauntaun Bones (L)	0.75
EE0126 Tauntaun Handler (L)	0.25
EE0127 That's It, The Rebels Are There! (D)	0.75
EE0128 The First Transport Is Away! (L)	4.00
EE0129 The Shield Doors Must Be Closed (D)	0.75
EE0130 This Is Just Wrong (D)	4.00
EE0131 Tigran Jamiro (L)	0.75
EE0132 Too Cold For Speeders (D)	0.75
EE0133 Toryn Farr (L)	0.75
EE0134 Trample (D)	5.00
EE0135 Turn It Off! Turn It Off! (D)	0.25
EE0136 Tyrant (D)	8.00
EE0137 Under Attack (L)	0.75
EE0138 Vehicle Mine (D/L)	0.25
EE0139 Walker Barrage (D)	0.75
EE0140 Walker Sighting (L)	0.75
EE0141 Wall Of Fire (D)	0.75
EE0142 Wampa (Snow Creature) (D)	4.00
EE0143 Weapon Malfunction (D)	4.00
EE0144 WED-1016 'Techie' Droid (L)	0.25
EE0145 Wes Janson (L)	3.00
EE0146 Who's Scruffy-Looking? (L)	4.00
EE0147 Wyron Serper (L)	0.75
EE0148 Yaggle Gakkle (D)	3.00
EE0149 You Have Failed Me For The Last Time (L)	5.00
EE0150 You Will Go To The Dagobah System (L)	4.00
EE0151 Zev Senesca (L)	3.00

CCG: CARDS, JABBA'S PALACE

EF0001 8D8 (L)	4.00
EF0002 A Gift (L)	0.75
EF0003 Abyssin (D)	0.25
EF0004 Abyssin Ornament (D)	0.75

EF0005 All Wrapped Up (D)	0.75
EF0006 Amanaman (D)	4.00
EF0007 Amanin (D)	0.25
EF0008 Antipersonnel Laser Cannon (D)	0.75
EF0009 Aqualish (D)	0.25
EF0010 Arc Welder (L)	0.75
EF0011 Ardon "Vapor" Crell (L)	4.00
EF0012 Artoo (L)	10.00
EF0013 Artoo, I Have A Bad Feeling About This (L)	0.75
EF0014 Attark (L)	3.00
EF0015 Aved Luun (L)	4.00
EF0016 Bane Malar (D)	6.00
EF0017 Bantha Fodder (D)	0.25
EF0018 Barada (D)	4.00
EF0019 Baragwin (D)	0.25
EF0020 Bargaining Table (L)	0.75
EF0021 Beedo (D)	5.00
EF0022 BG-J38 (L)	3.00
EF0023 Bib Fortuna (D)	6.00
EF0024 Blaster Deflection (D)	4.00
EF0025 Bo Shuda (D)	0.75
EF0026 B'omarr Monk (L)	0.25
EF0027 Bubo (D)	0.75
EF0028 Cane Adiss (D)	0.75
EF0029 Chadra-Fan (L)	0.25
EF0030 Chevin (D)	0.25
EF0031 Choke (L)	0.25
EF0032 Corellian Retort (L)	0.75
EF0033 CZ-4 (D)	0.25
EF0034 Den Of Thieves (D)	0.75
EF0035 Dengar's Modified Riot Gun (D)	4.00
EF0036 Devaronian (D)	0.25
EF0037 Don't Forget The Droids (L)	0.25
EF0038 Double Laser Cannon (D)	4.00
EF0039 Droopy McCool (L)	3.00
EF0040 Dune Sea Sabacc (D/L)	0.75
EF0041 Elom (L)	0.25
EF0042 Ephant Mon (D)	5.00
EF0043 EV-9D9 (D)	4.00
EF0044 Fallen Portal (L)	0.75
EF0045 Florn Lamproid (L)	0.25
EF0046 Fozec (D)	3.00
EF0047 Gailid (D)	4.00
EF0048 Gamorrean Ax (D)	0.25
EF0049 Gamorrean Guard (D)	0.25
EF0050 Garon Nas Tal (L)	3.00
EF0051 Geezum (L)	3.00
EF0052 Ghoel (L)	3.00
EF0053 Giran (D)	4.00
EF0054 Gran (L)	0.25
EF0055 Herat (D)	3.00
EF0056 Hermi Odle (D)	4.00
EF0057 Hidden Compartment (L)	0.75
EF0058 Hidden Weapons (D)	0.75
EF0059 H'nemthe (L)	0.25
EF0060 Holoprojector (L)	0.75
EF0061 Hutt Bounty (L)	4.00
EF0062 Hutt Smooch (D)	0.75
EF0063 I Must Be Allowed To Speak (L)	4.00
EF0064 Information Exchange (D)	0.75
EF0065 Ishi Tib (L)	0.25
EF0066 Ithorian (L)	0.25
EF0067 Jabba The Hutt (D)	16.00
EF0068 Jabba's Palace Sabacc (D/L)	0.75
EF0069 Jabba's Palace: Audience Chamber (D/L)	0.75
EF0070 Jabba's Palace: Droid Workshop (D)	0.75
EF0071 Jabba's Palace: Dungeon (D)	0.75
EF0072 Jabba's Palace: Entrance Cavern (D/L)	0.75
EF0073 Jabba's Palace: Rancor Pit (D)	0.75
EF0074 Jabba's Sail Barge (D)	6.00
EF0075 Jabba's Sail Barge: Passenger Deck (D)	4.00
EF0076 Jedi Mind Trick (L)	4.00
EF0077 Jess (L)	3.00
EF0078 Jet Pack (D)	0.75
EF0079 J'Quille (D)	4.00
EF0080 Kalit (L)	4.00
EF0081 Ke Chu Ke Kukuta? (L)	0.25
EF0082 Kiffex (L)	0.25
EF0083 Kirdo III (L)	3.00
EF0084 Kithaba (D)	3.00
EF0085 Kitonak (L)	0.25

EF0086 Klaatu (D) 3.00
EF0087 Klatooinian Revolutionary (L) 0.25
EF0088 Laudica (L) 3.00
EF0089 Leslomy Tacema (L) 4.00
EF0090 Life Debt (L) 4.00
EF0091 Loje Nella (L) 4.00
EF0092 Malakili (D) 3.00
EF0093 Mandalorian Mishap (L) 0.75
EF0094 Max Rebo (L) 5.00
EF0095 Mos Eisley Blaster (D/L) 0.25
EF0096 Murttoc Yine (D) 3.00
EF0097 Nal Hutta (D) 4.00
EF0098 Nar Shaddaa Wind Chimes (L) 0.75
EF0099 Nikto (D) 0.25
EF0100 Nizuc Bek (D) 3.00
EF0101 None Shall Pass (D) 0.25
EF0102 Nysad (D) 3.00
EF0103 Oola (L) 5.00
EF0104 Ortolan (L) 0.25
EF0105 Ortugg (D) 4.00
EF0106 Palejo Reshad (L) 3.00
EF0107 Pote Snitkin (D) 3.00
EF0108 Princess Leia Organa (L) 17.00
EF0109 Projection Of A Skywalker (L) 0.75
EF0110 Pucumir Thryss (L) 3.00
EF0111 Quarren (D) 0.25
EF0112 Quick Reflexes (D) 0.25
EF0113 Rancor (D) 7.00
EF0114 Rayc Ryjerd (L) 4.00
EF0115 Ree-Yees (D) 4.00
EF0116 Rennek (L) 3.00
EF0117 Resistance (D) 0.75
EF0118 Revealed (L) 0.75
EF0119 R'kik D'nec, Hero Of The Dune Sea (L) 4.00
EF0120 Saelt-Marae (L) 4.00
EF0121 Salacious Crumb (D) 5.00
EF0122 Sandwhirl (D/L) 0.75
EF0123 Scum And Villainy (D) 5.00
EF0124 Sergeant Doallyn (L) 4.00
EF0125 Shasa Tiel (L) 3.00
EF0126 Sic-Six (L) 0.25
EF0127 Skiff (D/L) 0.25
EF0128 Skrilling (D) 0.25
EF0129 Skull (L) 0.75
EF0130 Snivvian (L) 0.25
EF0131 Someone Who Loves You (L) 0.75
EF0132 Strangle (L) 4.00
EF0133 Tamtel Skreej (L) 7.00
EF0134 Tanus Spijek (L) 4.00
EF0135 Tatooine: Desert (D/L) 0.25
EF0136 Tatooine: Great Pit Of Carkoon (D) 0.75
EF0137 Tatooine: Hutt Canyon (L) 0.75
EF0138 Tatooine: Jabba's Palace (D) 0.75
EF0139 Taym Dren-garen (D) 4.00
EF0140 Tessek (L) 3.00
EF0141 The Signal (L) 0.25
EF0142 Thermal Detonator (D) 5.00
EF0143 Thul Fain (D) 4.00
EF0144 Tibrin (L) 3.00
EF0145 Torture (D) 0.25
EF0146 Trandoshan (D) 0.25
EF0147 Trap Door (D) 0.75
EF0148 Twi'lek Advisor (D) 0.25
EF0149 Ultimatum (L) 0.75
EF0150 Unfriendly Fire (L) 4.00
EF0151 Vedain (D) 3.00
EF0152 Velken Tezeri (D) 3.00
EF0153 Vibro-Ax (D/L) 0.25
EF0154 Vizam (D) 3.00
EF0155 Vul Tazaene (L) 3.00
EF0156 Weapon Levitation (L) 0.75
EF0157 Weequay Guard (D) 0.25
EF0158 Weequay Hunter (D) 0.25
EF0159 Weequay Marksman (D) 0.75
EF0160 Weequay Skiff Master (D) 0.25
EF0161 Well Guarded (D) 0.75
EF0162 Whiphid (D) 0.25
EF0163 Wittin (D) 4.00
EF0164 Wooof (D) 3.00
EF0165 Worrt (L) 0.75
EF0166 Wounded Wookiee (D) 0.75
EF0167 Yarkora (L) 0.25
EF0168 Yarna d'al' Gargan (L) 0.75
EF0169 You Will Take Me To Jabba Now (L) 0.25
EF0170 Yoxgit (L) 3.00
EF0171 Yuzzum (D) 0.25

CCG: CARDS, JEDI KNIGHTS

EJK0001 Admiral Motti, Fleet Admiral 0.50
EJK0002 Admiral Motti, Fleet Admiral replacement card P L 0.80
EJK0003 AF-119, Cloud City Garrison 0.25
EJK0004 AF-27, Motivated Trooper 0.25
EJK0005 Artoo, See What You Can Do 0.75
EJK0006 Atgar Laser Cannon 0.75
EJK0007 Bespin System-Cloud City Carbon-Freezing Chamber 1.00
EJK0008 Bespin System-Cloud City Guest Quarters 1.00
EJK0009 Black Two 0.25
EJK0010 Blaster 0.25
EJK0011 Blaster Rifle U S 0.75
EJK0012 Boba Fett, Relentless Hunter R S 5.00
EJK0013 Boba Fett's Blaster Rifle 0.75
EJK0014 C-3PO, The Professor R S 4.00
EJK0015 Come With Me 0.75
EJK0016 Coming Up on Their Sentry Ships 0.25
EJK0017 Commander Kreigg, Tactical Advisor R S 3.00
EJK0018 Concentrate All Fire 0.25
EJK0019 Conquest R S 5.00
EJK0020 Corellian Laser Cannon flip movie card 0.75
EJK0021 Corporal Hakin, Former Skiff Racer 0.25
EJK0022 Corporal Kuep, Seasoned Guard 0.25
EJK0023 Corporal Maer, Tauntaun Handler 0.25
EJK0024 Darth Vader, Agent of the Empire 3.00
EJK0025 Darth Vader, Agent of the Empire tourn. foil card 15.00
EJK0026 Darth Vader, Emperor's Sinister Agent R S 8.00
EJK0027 Darth Vader, Sith Warrior R S 8.00
EJK0028 Darth Vader, Sith Warrior premium card P L 15.00
EJK0029 Destroy Them Ship to Ship R S 3.00
EJK0030 Devastator flip movie card 0.25
EJK0031 Dewback Patrol R S 3.00
EJK0032 Dodonna's Pride R S 3.00
EJK0033 Doikk Na'ts, Beshniquel Soloist R S 3.00
EJK0034 Droid Detector 0.75
EJK0035 DS-61-2, "Mauler Mithel" 0.25
EJK0036 Elis Helrot, Givin Merchant R S 3.00
EJK0037 Ellorrs Madak, Flight Instructor 0.25
EJK0038 Ellorrs Madak's Blaster Pistol 0.25
EJK0039 Emperor Palpatine, Imperial Overlord R S 6.00
EJK0040 Emperor Palpatine, Sith Master league foil card P 15.00
EJK0041 Endor System-Back Door 1.00
EJK0042 Endor System-Dense Forest 1.00
EJK0043 E-Web Repeating Blaster 0.75
EJK0044 Figrin D'an, Bith Band Leader R S 3.00
EJK0045 Force 1 (Force) 0.25
EJK0046 Force 2 (Force) 0.25
EJK0047 Force 3 (Force) 0.75
EJK0048 Force 3 (Force) 0.25
EJK0049 Force 4 (Force) 0.25
EJK0050 Force 5 (Force) 0.25
EJK0051 Force 6 (Force) 0.25
EJK0052 Force 7 (Force) 0.75
EJK0053 Force 7 (Force) 0.25
EJK0054 Force 8 (Force) 0.25
EJK0055 Full Throttle 0.50
EJK0056 Gaffi Stick 0.25
EJK0057 General Tagge, Imperial Commander 0.75
EJK0058 Gold Five 0.25
EJK0059 Gold Two flip movie card 0.75
EJK0060 Good Shooting, Wedge R S 3.00
EJK0061 Grand Moff Tarkin, Destroyer of Alderaan R S 5.00
EJK0062 Grand Moff Tarkin, Destroyer of Alderaan premium card P L 15.00
EJK0063 Grand Moff Tarkin, Imperial Bureaucrat 3.00
EJK0064 Grand Moff Tarkin, Imperial Bureaucrat tourn. foil card 15.00
EJK0065 Greedo, Jabba's Underling R S 3.00
EJK0066 Greedo's Blaster Pistol R S 3.00
EJK0067 Han Solo, Smuggler for Hire 2.00
EJK0068 Han Solo, Smuggler for Hire tourn. foil card 15.00
EJK0069 Han Solo, Unlikely Hero R S 7.00
EJK0070 Han Solo, Unlikely Hero premium card P L 15.00
EJK0071 Han's Blaster Pistol 0.75
EJK0072 He Certainly Is Brave 0.75

EJK0073 Help Me, Obi-Wan Kenobi R S....4.00
EJK0074 Hem Dazon, Salt Fiend....0.75
EJK0075 Hoth System-Frozen Wastes....1.00
EJK0076 Hoth System-North Ridge....1.00
EJK0077 I Have You Now R S....3.00
EJK0078 Iasa, Jawa Merchant....0.75
EJK0079 Iasa's Jawa Blaster....0.75
EJK0080 Imperial Fleet R S....3.00
EJK0081 Imperial Precision....0.75
EJK0082 Jawa Trader....0.75
EJK0083 Just Like Back Home....0.75
EJK0084 Keep the Local Systems In Line R S....4.00
EJK0085 Labria, Slippery Informant R S....3.00
EJK0086 Leia Organa, Your Worshipfulness R S....5.00
EJK0087 Leia's Blaster R S....4.00
EJK0088 Lieutenant Neff, Immigration Officer....0.75
EJK0089 Local Trouble R S....3.00
EJK0090 Luke Skywalker, Hero of Yavin R S....7.00
EJK0091 Luke Skywalker, Hero of Yavin premium card P L....15.00
EJK0092 Luke Skywalker, Jedi Apprentice league card P R....15.00
EJK0093 Luke Skywalker, Moisture Farmer....3.00
EJK0094 Luke Skywalker, Moisture Farmer tourn. foil card....5.00
EJK0095 Luke's Blaster....0.75
EJK0096 Major Millich, Security Chief....0.25
EJK0097 Medal of Alderaan league card P R....20.00
EJK0098 Millennium Falcon, Modified Transport R S....8.00
EJK0099 Millions of Voices R S....4.00
EJK0100 Momaw Nadon, Hammerhead Shepherd....0.75
EJK0101 Nabrun Leids, Morseerian Transport Expert R S....3.00
EJK0102 Nalan Cheel, Bandfill Player R S....3.00
EJK0103 Naval Support flip movie card....0.75
EJK0104 Now I Am the Master....2.00
EJK0105 Now I Am the Master tourn. foil card....15.00
EJK0106 NT-311, Squad Point Man....0.25
EJK0107 Obi-Wan Kenobi, Jedi Knight league card P R....20.00
EJK0108 Obi-Wan Kenobi, Old Ben R S....7.00
EJK0109 Obi-Wan Kenobi, Old Fossil R S....7.00
EJK0110 Obi-Wan's Lightsaber R S....5.00
EJK0111 Outrun Those Imperial Slugs....0.25
EJK0112 Pick Up Some Power Converters....0.25
EJK0113 Ponda Baba, Doesn't Like You R S....3.00
EJK0114 Ponda Baba's Blaster Pistol....0.75
EJK0115 Private Alain, Unit Scrounge....0.25
EJK0116 Proton Torpedoes R S....4.00
EJK0117 PS-29-2, "Mynock" R S....3.00
EJK0118 PS-29-3, "Hammer"....0.75
EJK0119 R2-D2, Feisty Astromech R S....4.00
EJK0120 Rancor's Tooth R S....4.00
EJK0121 Rebel Spies flip movie card....0.75
EJK0122 Red Five, Luke's X-Wing R S....4.00
EJK0123 Red Two....0.25
EJK0124 RGA-972, Assault Specialist....0.50
EJK0125 Senatorial Guard R S....3.00
EJK0126 Sergeant Airten, Alliance Sympathizer....3.00
EJK0127 SFS L-s7.2 Tie Cannon flip movie card....0.75
EJK0128 Shadow Three flip movie card....0.50
EJK0129 Shadow Two R S....3.00
EJK0130 Solomahal, Veteran Scout....0.50
EJK0131 ST-103, Sabacc Player....0.25
EJK0132 ST-4402, Tatooine Garrison....0.25
EJK0133 Stabilize Your Rear Deflectors....0.25
EJK0134 Stalker....0.25
EJK0135 Stand by, Ion Control....0.50
EJK0136 Stay on Target flip movie card....0.25
EJK0137 Taim and Bak IX4 Laser Cannons flip movie card....0.50
EJK0138 Tantive IV flip movie card....0.25
EJK0139 Tatooine System-Lars Moisture Farm....1.00
EJK0140 Tatooine System-Mos Eisley....1.00
EJK0141 Tear This Ship Apart R S....3.00
EJK0142 That's No Moon R S....3.00
EJK0143 The Force Is Strong With This One....2.00
EJK0144 The Force Is Strong With This One tourn. foil card....15.00
EJK0145 The Guns... They've Stopped! R S....3.00
EJK0146 They Came From Behind flip movie card....0.25
EJK0147 Thok, Thug Who Smashes....0.50
EJK0148 Thok's Vibro Ax....0.50
EJK0149 Tiatha, Legendary Scavenger....0.25
EJK0150 Tiatha's Ion Blaster....0.25
EJK0151 TK-420, Inspection Crew....0.25
EJK0152 TK-577, Fire Team Leader....0.25
EJK0153 Trooper Recruit Precht, Green Recruit....0.75
EJK0154 Turbolaser Battery flip movie card....0.50
EJK0155 Ubrikkian 9000....0.25
EJK0156 Ur, Tusken Raider....0.25
EJK0157 Urur, Tusken Warrior....0.25
EJK0158 Vader's Lightsaber, Sith Weapon R S....4.00
EJK0159 Vader's Lightsaber, Sith Weapon premium card P L....15.00
EJK0160 Vader's Tie, Advanced Prototype R S....4.00
EJK0161 Wedge Antilles, X-Wing Ace R S....5.00
EJK0162 X-Wing Laser Cannons....0.50
EJK0163 Yoda, Jedi Master league card P R....15.00
EJK0164 Yoda, Luke's Mentor R S....5.00
EJK0165 You Came in That Thing? R S....3.00
EJK0166 You Like Me Because I'm a Scoundrel....2.00
EJK0167 You Like Me Because I'm a Scoundrel tourn. foil card....15.00
EJK0168 You Overestimate Their Chances....2.00
EJK0169 You Overestimate Their Chances tourn. foil card 15.00
EJK0170 You Should Not Have Come Back....0.25
EJK0171 You're My Only Hope....0.25
EJK0172 Zev Senesca, T-47 Pilot....0.25
EJK0173 Zutton, Holojournalist....0.25

CCG: CARDS, JEDI PACK

EJ0001 Eriadu (D)....0.85
EJ0006 For Luck (L)....0.85
EJ0002 Gravity Shadow (D)....0.75
EJ0007 Han (L)....1.65
EJ0003 Hyperoute Navigation Chart (D)....0.95
EJ0008 Leia (L)....1.35
EJ0009 Luke's T-16 Skyhopper (L)....0.65
EJ0004 Motti (D)....1.25
EJ0005 Tarkin (D)....1.50
EJ0010 Tedn Dahai (L)....0.55

CCG: CARDS, OFFICIAL TOURN. SEALED DECK PREMIUMS

EK0017 Arleil Schous (L)....1.95
EK0001 Black Squadron Tie (D)....7.95
EK0002 Chall Bekan (D)....1.85
EK0003 Corulag (D/L)....1.65
EK0004 Dreadnaught-Class Heavy Cruiser (D)....5.25
EK0005 Faithful Service (L)....2.25
EK0006 Forced Servitude (D)....2.25
EK0007 Gold Squadron Y-Wing (L)....5.25
EK0008 It's A Hit! (L)....2.25
EK0009 Obsidian Squadron Tie (D)....3.25
EK0010 Rebel Trooper Recruit (L)....4.25
EK0011 Red Squadron X-Wing (L)....9.25
EK0012 Stormtrooper Cadet (D)....4.00
EK0013 Tarkin's Orders (D)....2.25
EK0014 Tatooine: Jundland Wastes (L)....4.60
EK0015 Tatooine: Tusken Canyon (D)....4.15
EK0016 Z-95 Headhunter (L)....4.90

CCG: CARDS, PREMIERE DECK (LIMITED)

EG0001 2X-3KPR (Too-Ex) (L)....1.00
EG0002 5D6-RA-7 (Five-De-Six) (D)....4.00
EG0003 A Disturbance In The Force (D)....1.00
EG0004 A Few Maneuvers (L)....0.25
EG0005 A Tremor In The Force (L)....1.00
EG0006 Admiral Motti (D)....4.00
EG0007 Affect Mind (L)....3.00
EG0008 Alderaan (D/L)....2.00
EG0009 Alter (L)....1.00
EG0301 Alter (D)....1.00
EG0010 Assault Rifle (D)....4.00
EG0011 Baniss Keeg (D)....0.25
EG0012 Bantha (D)....0.75
EG0013 Beggar (L)....4.00
EG0014 Beru Lars (L)....0.75
EG0015 Beru Stew (L)....0.75
EG0016 Biggs Darklighter (L)....5.00
EG0017 Black 2 (D)....4.00
EG0018 Black 3 (D)....1.00
EG0019 Blast Door Controls (D)....0.75
EG0020 Blaster (L)....0.25
EG0021 Blaster Rack (D)....1.00

EG0022 Blaster Rifle (L) 0.25	EG0097 Grand Moff Tarkin (D) 22.00
EG0302 Blaster Rifle (D) 0.25	EG0098 Gravel Storm (D) 0.75
EG0023 Blaster Scope (D) 1.00	EG0099 Han Seeker (D) 4.00
EG0024 Boosted Tie Cannon (D) 1.00	EG0100 Han Solo (D) 29.00
EG0025 Boring Conversation Anyway (D) 4.00	EG0101 Han's Back (L) 0.75
EG0026 BoShek (L) 1.00	EG0102 Han's Dice (L) 0.25
EG0027 C-3PO (See-Threepio) (L) 15.00	EG0103 Han's Heavy Blaster Pistol (L) 4.00
EG0028 Caller (L) 0.75	EG0104 Hear Me Baby, Hold Together (L) 0.25
EG0303 Caller (D) 0.75	EG0105 Help Me Obi-Wan Kenobi (L) 4.00
EG0029 Cantina Brawl (L) 4.00	EG0106 How Did We Get Into This Mess? (L) 0.75
EG0030 Charming To The Last (D) 4.00	EG0107 Hydroponics Station (L) 0.75
EG0031 Chief Bast (D) 1.00	EG0108 Hyper Escape (L) 0.25
EG0032 Collateral Damage (D) 0.25	EG0109 I Find Your Lack Of Faith Disturbing (D) 4.00
EG0033 Collision! (L) 0.25	EG0110 I Have You Now (D) 4.00
EG0034 Colonel Wullf Yularen (D) 1.00	EG0111 Imperial Barrier (D) 0.25
EG0035 Combined Attack (L) 0.25	EG0112 Imperial Blaster (D) 0.25
EG0036 Comlink (D) 0.25	EG0113 Imperial Code Cylinder (D) 0.25
EG0037 Commander Praji (D) 0.75	EG0114 Imperial Pilot (D) 0.25
EG0038 Corellian Corvette (L) 0.75	EG0115 Imperial Reinforcements (D) 0.25
EG0039 Counter Assault (L) 0.25	EG0116 Imperial Trooper Guard (D) 0.25
EG0040 Crash Site Memorial (L) 1.00	EG0117 Imperial-Class Star Destroyer (D) 3.00
EG0041 CZ-3 (Seezee-Three) (L) 0.25	EG0118 Into the Garbage Chute, Flyboy (L) 4.00
EG0042 Dantooine (L) 1.00	EG0119 Ion Cannon (D) 1.00
EG0304 Dantooine (D) 1.00	EG0120 It Could Be Worse (L) 0.25
EG0043 Dark Collaboration (D) 4.00	EG0121 It's Worse (D) 0.25
EG0044 Dark Hours (D) 0.75	EG0122 I've Got A Bad Feeling About This (L) 0.25
EG0045 Dark Jedi Lightsaber (D) 1.00	EG0123 I've Got A Problem Here (D) 0.25
EG0046 Dark Jedi Presence (D) 5.00	EG0124 I've Lost Artoo! (D) 1.00
EG0047 Dark Maneuvers (D) 0.25	EG0125 Jawa (L) 0.25
EG0048 Darth Vader (D) 66.00	EG0308 Jawa (D) 0.25
EG0049 Dathcha (L) 1.00	EG0126 Jawa Pack (D) 1.00
EG0050 Dead Jawa (D) 0.25	EG0127 Jawa Siesta (L) 1.00
EG0051 Death Star Plans (L) 5.00	EG0128 Jedi Lightsaber (L) 1.00
EG0052 Death Star Sentry (D) 1.00	EG0129 Jedi Presence (L) 5.00
EG0053 Death Star Trooper (D) 0.25	EG0130 Jek Porkins (L) 1.00
EG0054 Death Star: Central Core (D) 0.75	EG0131 Juri Juice (L) 3.00
EG0055 Death Star: Detention Block Control Room (L) 0.75	EG0132 Kabe (L) 2.00
EG0056 Death Star: Detention Block Corridor (D) 0.25	EG0133 Kal'Falnl C'ndros (L) 5.00
EG0057 Death Star: Docking Bay 327 (L) 0.25	EG0134 Kessel (L) 0.75
EG0305 Death Star: Docking Bay 327 (D) 0.25	EG0309 Kessel (D) 0.75
EG0058 Death Star: Level 4 Military Corridor (D) 1.00	EG0135 Kessel Run (L) 4.00
EG0059 Death Star: Trash Compactor (L) 1.00	EG0136 Ket Maliss (D) 0.25
EG0060 Death Star: War Room (D) 0.75	EG0137 Kintan Strider (D) 0.25
EG0061 Demotion (L) 4.00	EG0138 Kitik Keed'kak (D) 5.00
EG0062 Devastator (D) 15.00	EG0139 K'lor'slug (L) 4.00
EG0063 Dice Ibegon (L) 4.00	EG0140 Krayt Dragon Howl (L) 4.00
EG0064 Disarmed (L) 4.00	EG0141 Labria (L) 3.00
EG0306 Disarmed (D) 4.00	EG0142 Laser Projector (D) 0.75
EG0065 Djas Puhr (D) 3.00	EG0143 Lateral Damage (D) 4.00
EG0066 Don't Get Cocky (L) 5.00	EG0144 Leesub Sirln (L) 4.00
EG0067 Don't Underestimate Our Chances (L) 0.25	EG0145 Leia Organa (L) 25.00
EG0068 Dr. Evazan (D) 4.00	EG0146 Leia's Back (L) 0.75
EG0069 Droid Detector (D) 0.25	EG0147 Leia's Sporting Blaster (L) 1.00
EG0070 Droid Shutdown (L) 0.25	EG0148 Lieutenant Tanbris (D) 0.75
EG0071 DS-61-2 (D) 1.00	EG0149 Lift Tube (L) 0.25
EG0072 DS-61-3 (D) 4.00	EG0310 Lift Tube (D) 0.25
EG0073 Dutch (L) 5.00	EG0150 Light Repeating Blaster Rifle (D) 4.00
EG0074 EG-6 (Eegee-Six) (D) 0.75	EG0151 Lightsaber Proficiency (L) 4.00
EG0075 Electrobinoculars (L) 0.25	EG0152 Limited Resources (D) 0.75
EG0076 Elis Helrot (D) 0.75	EG0153 LIN-V8K (Elleyein-Veeatekay) (L) 0.25
EG0077 Ellorrs Madak (L) 0.25	EG0154 LIN-V8M (Elleyein-Veeateemm) (D) 0.25
EG0078 Emergency Deployment (D) 2.00	EG0155 Local Trouble (D) 5.00
EG0079 Escape Pod (D) 0.75	EG0156 Lone Pilot (D) 3.00
EG0080 Evacuate? (D) 0.75	EG0157 Lone Warrior (D) 3.00
EG0081 Expand The Empire (D) 5.00	EG0158 Look Sir, Droids (D) 5.00
EG0082 Eyes In The Dark (L) 5.00	EG0159 Luke Seeker (D) 4.00
EG0083 Fear Will Keep Them In Line (D) 4.00	EG0160 Luke Skywalker (L) 40.00
EG0084 Feltipern Trevagg (D) 1.00	EG0161 Luke? Luuuuke! (D) 1.00
EG0085 Figrin D'an (L) 0.75	EG0162 Luke's Back (L) 0.75
EG0086 Friendly Fire (L) 0.25	EG0163 Luke's X-34 Landspeeder (L) 1.00
EG0087 Full Scale Alert (D) 0.75	EG0164 Macroscan (D) 0.25
EG0088 Full Throttle (L) 4.00	EG0165 Mantellian Savrip (L) 4.00
EG0089 Fusion Generator Supply Tanks (L) 0.25	EG0166 M'iiyoom Onith (D) 0.75
EG0307 Fusion Generator Supply Tanks (D) 0.25	EG0167 Millennium Falcon (L) 31.00
EG0090 Gaderffii Stick (D) 0.25	EG0168 Molator (D) 4.00
EG0091 Garindan (D) 4.00	EG0169 Momaw Nadon (L) 3.50
EG0092 General Dodonna (L) 1.00	EG0170 Moment of Triumph (D) 4.00
EG0093 General Tagge (D) 5.00	EG0171 Move Along... (D) 4.00
EG0094 Gift Of The Mentor (L) 5.00	EG0172 MSE-6 'Mouse' Droid (D) 1.00
EG0095 Gold 1 (L) 4.00	EG0173 Myo (D) 4.00
EG0096 Gold 5 (L) 4.00	EG0174 Nabrun Leids (L) 0.75

EG0175 Narrow Escape (L) 0.25
EG0176 Nevar Yalnal (D) 4.00
EG0177 Nightfall (L) 1.00
EG0178 Noble Sacrifice (L) 4.00
EG0179 Obi-Wan Kenobi (L) 38.00
EG0180 Obi-Wan's Cape (L) 5.00
EG0181 Obi-Wan's Lightsaber (L) 8.00
EG0182 Observation Holocam (D) 0.75
EG0183 Old Ben (L) 0.25
EG0184 Ommni Box (D) 0.25
EG0185 On The Edge (L) 4.00
EG0186 Organa's Ceremonial Necklace (D) 4.00
EG0187 Our Most Desperate Hour (L) 4.00
EG0188 Out Of Nowhere (L) 0.75
EG0189 Overload (D) 0.25
EG0190 Owen Lars (L) 3.00
EG0191 Panic (L) 1.00
EG0192 Physical Choke (D) 4.00
EG0193 Plastoid Armor (L) 0.75
EG0194 Ponda Baba (D) 1.00
EG0195 Pops (L) 1.00
EG0196 Precise Attack (D) 0.25
EG0197 Presence Of The Force (D) 6.00
EG0198 Prophetess (D) 1.00
EG0199 Proton Torpedoes (L) 0.25
EG0200 Quad Laser Cannon (L) 1.00
EG0201 R1-G4 (Arone-Geefour) (D) 0.25
EG0202 R2-X2 (Artoo-Extoo) (L) 0.25
EG0203 R4-E1 (Arfour-Eeone) (L) 0.25
EG0204 R4-M9 (Arfour-Emmnine) (D) 0.25
EG0205 Radar Scanner (L) 0.25
EG0206 Reactor Terminal (D) 0.75
EG0207 Rebel Barrier (L) 0.25
EG0208 Rebel Guard (L) 0.25
EG0209 Rebel Pilot (L) 0.25
EG0210 Rebel Planners (L) 4.00
EG0211 Rebel Reinforcements (L) 0.25
EG0212 Rebel Trooper (L) 0.25
EG0213 Red 1 (L) 1.00
EG0214 Red 3 (L) 4.00
EG0215 Red Leader (L) 7.00
EG0216 Restraining Bolt (L) 0.25
EG0311 Restraining Bolt (D) 0.25
EG0217 Restricted Deployment (L) 1.00
EG0218 Return Of A Jedi (L) 0.75
EG0219 Revolution (L) 5.00
EG0220 Rycar Ryjerd (L) 1.00
EG0221 Sai'torr Kal Fas (L) 0.25
EG0222 Sandcrawler (L) 5.00
EG0312 Sandcrawler (D) 5.00
EG0223 Scanning Crew (D) 0.25
EG0224 Scomp Link Access (L) 0.25
EG0225 Send A Detachment Down (D) 4.00
EG0226 Sense (L) 1.00
EG0313 Sense (D) 1.00
EG0227 Set For Stun (D) 0.25
EG0228 Shistavanen Wolfman (L) 0.25
EG0229 Skywalkers (L) 5.00
EG0230 Solo Han (L) 4.00
EG0231 SoroSuub V-35 Landspeeder (L) 0.25
EG0232 Spaceport Speeders (L) 0.75
EG0233 Special Modifications (L) 1.00
EG0234 Stormtrooper (D) 0.25
EG0235 Stormtrooper Backpack (D) 0.25
EG0236 Stormtrooper Utility Belt (D) 0.25
EG0237 Sunsdown (D) 1.00
EG0238 Surprise Assault (L) 0.25
EG0239 Tactical Re-Call (D) 4.00
EG0240 Tagge Seeker (L) 4.00
EG0241 Takeel (D) 0.25
EG0242 Tallon Roll (D) 0.25
EG0243 Talz (L) 0.25
EG0244 Targeting Computer (L) 1.00
EG0245 Tarkin Seeker (L) 4.00
EG0246 Tatooine (L) 0.25
EG0314 Tatooine (D) 0.25
EG0247 Tatooine Utility Belt (L) 0.25
EG0248 Tatooine: Cantina (L) 4.00
EG0315 Tatooine: Cantina (D) 4.00
EG0249 Tatooine: Docking Bay 94 (L) 0.25
EG0316 Tatooine: Docking Bay 94 (D) 0.25
EG0250 Tatooine: Dune Sea (L) 0.25
EG0251 Tatooine: Jawa Camp (L) 0.25
EG0317 Tatooine: Jawa Camp (D) 0.25
EG0252 Tatooine: Jundland Wastes (D) 0.25
EG0253 Tatooine: Lars' Moisture Farm (L) 0.75
EG0318 Tatooine: Lars' Moisture Farm (D) 0.75
EG0254 Tatooine: Mos Eisley (L) 0.25
EG0319 Tatooine: Mos Eisley (D) 0.25
EG0255 Tatooine: Obi-Wan's Hut (L) 4.00
EG0256 Thank The Maker (L) 5.00
EG0257 The Bith Shuffle (L) 0.25
EG0258 The Circle Is Now Complete (D) 5.00
EG0259 The Empire's Back (D) 1.00
EG0260 The Force Is Strong With This One (L) 4.00
EG0261 This Is All Your Fault (L) 2.00
EG0262 Tie Advanced x1 (D) 0.75
EG0263 Tie Fighter (D) 0.25
EG0264 Tie Scout (D) 0.25
EG0265 Timer Mine (L) 0.25
EG0320 Timer Mine (D) 0.25
EG0266 Tonnika Sisters (D) 5.00
EG0267 Traffic Control (L) 0.75
EG0268 Trinto Duaba (D) 1.00
EG0269 Trooper Charge (D) 0.75
EG0270 Turbolaser Battery (D) 4.00
EG0271 Tusken Breath Mask (L) 1.00
EG0272 Tusken Raider (D) 0.25
EG0273 Tusken Scavengers (D) 0.25
EG0274 Ubrikkian 9000 Z001 (D) 0.25
EG0275 Utinni ! (L) 4.00
EG0276 Utinni! (D) 4.00
EG0277 Vader's Custom Tie (D) 10.00
EG0278 Vader's Eye (D) 4.00
EG0279 Vader's Lightsaber (D) 14.00
EG0280 Vaporator (L) 0.25
EG0281 Warrior's Courage (L) 4.00
EG0282 WED15-1662 'Treadwell' Droid (D) 5.00
EG0283 WED-9-M1 'Bantha' Droid (L) 4.00
EG0284 We're All Gonna Be A Lot Thinner! (D) 4.00
EG0285 We're Doomed (L) 0.25
EG0286 Wioslea (L) 1.00
EG0287 Wrong Turn (D) 2.00
EG0288 Wuher (D) 0.75
EG0289 X-Wing (L) 0.25
EG0290 Yavin 4 (L) 0.25
EG0321 Yavin 4 (D) 0.25
EG0291 Yavin 4: Docking Bay (L) 0.25
EG0322 Yavin 4: Docking Bay (D) 0.25
EG0292 Yavin 4: Jungle (D/L) 0.75
EG0293 Yavin 4: Massassi Throne Room (L) 5.00
EG0294 Yavin 4: Massassi War Room (L) 0.75
EG0295 Yavin Sentry (L) 0.75
EG0296 Yerka Mig (L) 1.00
EG0297 You Overestimate Their Chances (D) 0.25
EG0298 Your Eyes Can Deceive You (D) 1.00
EG0299 Your Powers Are Weak, Old Man (D) 4.00
EG0300 Y-Wing (L) 0.25

CCG: CARDS, PREMIERE DECK (UNLIMITED)

Decipher

EV0001 2X-3KPR (Tooex) (L) 1.00
EV0002 5D6-RA-7 (Fivedesix) (D) 3.00
EV0003 A Disturbance In The Force (D) 1.00
EV0004 A Few Maneuvers (L) 0.25
EV0005 A Tremor In The Force (L) 1.00
EV0006 Admiral Motti (D) 3.00
EV0007 Affect Mind (L) 3.00
EV0008 Alderaan (D/L) 3.00
EV0009 Alter (L) 1.00
EV0301 Alter (D) 1.00
EV0010 Assault Rifle (D) 3.00
EV0011 Baniss Keeg (D) 0.25
EV0012 Bantha (D) 0.50
EV0013 Beggar (L) 3.00
EV0014 Beru Lars (L) 0.50
EV0015 Beru Stew (L) 0.50
EV0016 Biggs Darklighter (L) 3.00
EV0017 Black 2 (D) 4.00
EV0018 Black 3 (D) 1.00

EV0019 Blast Door Controls (D)	0.50
EV0020 Blaster (L)	0.50
EV0021 Blaster Rack (D)	1.00
EV0022 Blaster Rifle (L)	0.25
EV0302 Blaster Rifle (L)	0.25
EV0023 Blaster Scope (D)	1.00
EV0024 Boosted Tie Cannon (D)	1.00
EV0025 Boring Conversation Anyway (D)	3.00
EV0026 BoShek (L)	1.00
EV0027 C-3PO (See-Threepio) (L)	9.00
EV0028 Caller (L)	0.50
EV0303 Caller (D)	0.50
EV0029 Cantina Brawl (L)	3.00
EV0030 Charming To The Last (D)	3.00
EV0031 Chief Bast (L)	1.00
EV0032 Collateral Damage (D)	0.25
EV0033 Collision! (L)	0.25
EV0034 Colonel Wullf Yularen (D)	1.00
EV0035 Combined Attack (L)	0.25
EV0036 Comlink (D)	0.25
EV0037 Commander Praji (D)	0.50
EV0038 Corellian Corvette (L)	0.50
EV0039 Counter Assault (D)	0.25
EV0040 Crash Site Memorial (L)	1.00
EV0041 CZ-3 (Seezee-Three) (L)	0.25
EV0042 Dantooine (L)	1.00
EV0304 Dantooine (D)	1.00
EV0043 Dark Collaboration (D)	3.00
EV0044 Dark Hours (D)	0.50
EV0045 Dark Jedi Lightsaber (D)	1.00
EV0046 Dark Jedi Presence (D)	4.00
EV0047 Dark Maneuvers (D)	0.25
EV0048 Darth Vader (D)	43.00
EV0049 Dathcha (D)	1.00
EV0050 Dead Jawa (D)	0.25
EV0051 Death Star Plans (L)	4.00
EV0052 Death Star Sentry (D)	1.00
EV0053 Death Star Trooper (D)	0.25
EV0054 Death Star: Central Core (D)	0.50
EV0055 Death Star: Detention Block Control Room (L)	0.50
EV0056 Death Star: Detention Block Corridor (D)	0.25
EV0057 Death Star: Docking Bay 327 (L)	0.25
EV0305 Death Star: Docking Bay 327 (D)	0.25
EV0058 Death Star: Level 4 Military Corridor (D)	1.00
EV0059 Death Star: Trash Compactor (L)	1.00
EV0060 Death Star: War Room (D)	0.50
EV0061 Demotion (D)	3.00
EV0062 Devastator (D)	10.00
EV0063 Dice Ibegon (L)	3.00
EV0064 Disarmed (L)	3.00
EV0306 Disarmed (D)	3.00
EV0065 Djas Puhr (D)	3.00
EV0066 Don't Get Cocky (L)	3.00
EV0067 Don't Underestimate Our Chances (L)	0.25
EV0068 Dr. Evazan (D)	3.00
EV0069 Droid Detector (D)	0.25
EV0070 Droid Shutdown (L)	0.50
EV0071 DS-61-2 (D)	1.00
EV0072 DS-61-3 (D)	4.00
EV0073 Dutch (L)	4.00
EV0074 EG-6 (Eegee-Six) (D)	0.50
EV0075 Electrobinoculars (L)	0.25
EV0076 Elis Helrot (D)	0.50
EV0077 Ellorrs Madak (L)	0.25
EV0078 Emergency Deployment (D)	1.00
EV0079 Escape Pod (L)	0.50
EV0080 Evacuate? (D)	0.50
EV0081 Expand The Empire (D)	3.00
EV0082 Eyes In The Dark (L)	1.00
EV0083 Fear Will Keep Them In Line (D)	3.00
EV0084 Feltipern Trevagg (D)	1.00
EV0085 Figrin D'an (L)	0.50
EV0086 Friendly Fire (L)	0.25
EV0087 Full Scale Alert (D)	0.50
EV0088 Full Throttle (L)	3.00
EV0089 Fusion Generator Supply Tanks (L)	0.25
EV0307 Fusion Generator Supply Tanks (D)	0.25
EV0090 Gaderffii Stick (D)	0.25
EV0091 Garindan (D)	3.00
EV0092 General Dodonna (L)	1.00
EV0093 General Tagge (D)	3.00
EV0094 Gift Of The Mentor (L)	3.00
EV0095 Gold 1 (L)	3.00
EV0096 Gold 5 (L)	3.00
EV0097 Grand Moff Tarkin (D)	10.00
EV0098 Gravel Storm (D)	3.00
EV0099 Han Seeker (D)	3.00
EV0100 Han Solo (L)	16.00
EV0101 Han's Back (L)	0.50
EV0102 Han's Dice (L)	0.25
EV0103 Han's Heavy Blaster Pistol (L)	3.00
EV0104 Hear Me Baby, Hold Together (L)	0.25
EV0105 Help Me Obi-Wan Kenobi (L)	3.00
EV0106 How Did We Get Into This Mess? (L)	0.50
EV0107 Hydroponics Station (L)	0.50
EV0108 Hyper Escape (L)	0.25
EV0109 I Find Your Lack Of Faith Disturbing (D)	3.00
EV0110 I Have You Now (D)	3.00
EV0111 Imperial Barrier (D)	0.25
EV0112 Imperial Blaster (D)	0.25
EV0113 Imperial Code Cylinder (D)	0.25
EV0114 Imperial Pilot (D)	0.25
EV0115 Imperial Reinforcements (D)	0.25
EV0116 Imperial Trooper Guard (D)	0.25
EV0117 Imperial-Class Star Destroyer (D)	1.00
EV0118 Into the Garbage Chute, Flyboy (L)	3.00
EV0119 Ion Cannon (L)	1.00
EV0120 It Could Be Worse (L)	0.25
EV0121 It's Worse (D)	0.25
EV0122 I've Got A Bad Feeling About This (L)	0.25
EV0123 I've Got A Problem Here (D)	0.25
EV0124 I've Lost Artoo! (L)	1.00
EV0125 Jawa (L)	0.25
EV0308 Jawa (D)	0.25
EV0126 Jawa Pack (D)	1.00
EV0127 Jawa Siesta (L)	1.00
EV0128 Jedi Lightsaber (L)	1.00
EV0129 Jedi Presence (L)	3.00
EV0130 Jek Porkins (L)	1.00
EV0131 Juri Juice (D)	3.00
EV0132 Kabe (L)	1.00
EV0133 Kal'Falnl C'ndros (L)	3.00
EV0134 Kessel (L)	0.50
EV0309 Kessel (D)	0.50
EV0135 Kessel Run (L)	3.00
EV0136 Ket Maliss (D)	0.25
EV0137 Kintan Strider (D)	0.25
EV0138 Kitik Keed'kak (D)	3.00
EV0139 K'lor'slug (L)	3.00
EV0140 Krayt Dragon Howl (L)	3.00
EV0141 Labria (D)	3.00
EV0142 Laser Projector (D)	0.75
EV0143 Lateral Damage (D)	3.00
EV0144 Leesub Sirln (L)	3.00
EV0145 Leia Organa (L)	15.00
EV0146 Leia's Back (L)	0.75
EV0147 Leia's Sporting Blaster (L)	1.00
EV0148 Lieutenant Tanbris (D)	0.50
EV0149 Lift Tube (L)	0.25
EV0310 Lift Tube (D)	0.25
EV0150 Light Repeating Blaster Rifle (D)	3.00
EV0151 Lightsaber Proficiency (L)	4.00
EV0152 Limited Resources (D)	0.50
EV0153 LIN-V8K (Elleyein-Veeatekay) (L)	0.25
EV0154 LIN-V8M (Elleyein-Veeateemm) (D)	0.25
EV0155 Local Trouble (D)	3.00
EV0156 Lone Pilot (D)	3.00
EV0157 Lone Warrior (D)	3.00
EV0158 Look Sir, Droids (D)	3.00
EV0159 Luke Seeker (D)	3.00
EV0160 Luke Skywalker (L)	18.00
EV0161 Luke? Luuuuke! (D)	2.00
EV0162 Luke's Back (L)	0.50
EV0163 Luke's X-34 Landspeeder (L)	1.00
EV0164 Macroscan (D)	0.25
EV0165 Mantellian Savrip (L)	3.00
EV0166 M'iiyoom Onith (D)	0.50
EV0167 Millennium Falcon (L)	19.00
EV0168 Molator (D)	3.00
EV0169 Momaw Nadon (L)	0.50
EV0170 Moment of Triumph (D)	3.00
EV0171 Move Along... (L)	3.00

EV0172 MSE-6 'Mouse' Droid (D) 1.00
EV0173 Myo (D) 3.00
EV0174 Nabrun Leids (L) 0.50
EV0175 Narrow Escape (L) 0.25
EV0176 Nevar Yalnal (D) 3.00
EV0177 Nightfall (L) 1.00
EV0178 Noble Sacrifice (L) 3.00
EV0179 Obi-Wan Kenobi (L) 25.00
EV0180 Obi-Wan's Cape (L) 4.00
EV0181 Obi-Wan's Lightsaber (L) 6.00
EV0182 Observation Holocam (D) 0.50
EV0183 Old Ben (L) 0.25
EV0184 Ommni Box (D) 0.25
EV0185 On The Edge (L) 3.00
EV0186 Organa's Ceremonial Necklace (D) 4.00
EV0187 Our Most Desperate Hour (L) 3.00
EV0188 Out Of Nowhere (L) 0.50
EV0189 Overload (D) 0.25
EV0190 Owen Lars (L) 1.00
EV0191 Panic (L) 1.00
EV0192 Physical Choke (D) 3.00
EV0193 Plastoid Armor (L) 0.50
EV0194 Ponda Baba (D) 1.00
EV0195 Pops (L) 1.00
EV0196 Precise Attack (D) 0.25
EV0197 Presence Of The Force (D) 3.00
EV0198 Prophetess (D) 1.00
EV0199 Proton Torpedoes (L) 0.25
EV0200 Quad Laser Cannon (L) 1.00
EV0201 R1-G4 (Arone-Geefour) (D) 0.25
EV0202 R2-X2 (Artoo-Extoo) (L) 0.25
EV0203 R4-E1 (Arfour-Eeone) (L) 0.25
EV0204 R4-M9 (Arfour-Emmnine) (D) 0.25
EV0205 Radar Scanner (L) 0.25
EV0206 Reactor Terminal (D) 0.50
EV0207 Rebel Barrier (L) 0.25
EV0208 Rebel Guard (L) 0.25
EV0209 Rebel Pilot (L) 0.25
EV0210 Rebel Planners (L) 3.00
EV0211 Rebel Reinforcements (L) 0.25
EV0212 Rebel Trooper (L) 0.25
EV0213 Red 1 (L) 1.00
EV0214 Red 3 (L) 3.00
EV0215 Red Leader (L) 4.00
EV0216 Restraining Bolt (L) 0.25
EV0311 Restraining Bolt (L) 0.25
EV0217 Restricted Deployment (L) 1.00
EV0218 Return Of A Jedi (L) 0.50
EV0219 Revolution (L) 4.00
EV0220 Rycar Ryjerd (L) 1.00
EV0221 Sai'torr Kal Fas (L) 0.25
EV0222 Sandcrawler (L) 3.00
EV0312 Sandcrawler (D) 3.00
EV0223 Scanning Crew (D) 0.25
EV0224 Scomp Link Access (L) 0.25
EV0225 Send A Detachment Down (D) 3.00
EV0226 Sense (L) 1.00
EV0313 Sense (D) 1.00
EV0227 Set For Stun (D) 0.25
EV0228 Shistavanen Wolfman (L) 0.25
EV0229 Skywalkers (L) 5.00
EV0230 Solo Han (L) 3.00
EV0231 SoroSuub V-35 Landspeeder (L) 0.25
EV0232 Spaceport Speeders (L) 0.50
EV0233 Special Modifications (L) 1.00
EV0234 Stormtrooper (D) 0.25
EV0235 Stormtrooper Backpack (D) 0.25
EV0236 Stormtrooper Utility Belt (D) 0.25
EV0237 Sunsdown (D) 1.00
EV0238 Surprise Assault (L) 0.25
EV0239 Tactical Re-Call (D) 3.00
EV0240 Tagge Seeker (L) 3.00
EV0241 Takeel (D) 0.25
EV0242 Tallon Roll (D) 0.25
EV0243 Talz (L) 0.25
EV0244 Targeting Computer (L) 1.00
EV0245 Tarkin Seeker (L) 3.00
EV0246 Tatooine (L) 0.25
EV0314 Tatooine (D) 0.25
EV0247 Tatooine Utility Belt (L) 0.25
EV0248 Tatooine: Cantina (L) 3.00

EV0315 Tatooine: Cantina (D) 3.00
EV0249 Tatooine: Docking Bay 94 (L) 0.25
EV0316 Tatooine: Docking Bay 94 (D) 0.25
EV0250 Tatooine: Dune Sea (L) 0.25
EV0251 Tatooine: Jawa Camp (L) 0.25
EV0317 Tatooine: Jawa Camp (D) 0.25
EV0252 Tatooine: Jundland Wastes (D) 0.25
EV0253 Tatooine: Lars' Moisture Farm (L) 0.50
EV0318 Tatooine: Lars' Moisture Farm (D) 0.50
EV0254 Tatooine: Mos Eisley (L) 0.25
EV0319 Tatooine: Mos Eisley (D) 0.25
EV0255 Tatooine: Obi-Wan's Hut (L) 4.00
EV0256 Thank The Maker (L) 3.00
EV0257 The Bith Shuffle (L) 0.25
EV0258 The Circle Is Now Complete (D) 3.00
EV0259 The Empire's Back (D) 1.00
EV0260 The Force Is Strong With This One (L) 3.00
EV0261 This Is All Your Fault (L) 1.00
EV0262 TieAdvanced x1 (D) 0.50
EV0263 Tie Fighter (D) 0.25
EV0264 Tie Scout (D) 0.25
EV0265 Timer Mine (L) 0.25
EV0320 Timer Mine (D) 0.25
EV0266 Tonnika Sisters (D) 4.00
EV0267 Traffic Control (L) 0.50
EV0268 Trinto Duaba (D) 1.00
EV0269 Trooper Charge (D) 0.50
EV0270 Turbolaser Battery (D) 3.00
EV0271 Tusken Breath Mask (L) 1.00
EV0272 Tusken Raider (D) 0.25
EV0273 Tusken Scavengers (D) 0.25
EV0274 Ubrikkian 9000 Z001 (D) 0.25
EV0275 Utinni ! (L) 3.00
EV0276 Utinni! (D) 3.00
EV0277 Vader's Custom Tie (D) 8.00
EV0278 Vader's Eye (D) 4.00
EV0279 Vader's Lightsaber (D) 7.00
EV0280 Vaporator (L) 0.25
EV0281 Warrior's Courage (L) 3.00
EV0282 WED15-1662 'Treadwell' Droid (D) 3.00
EV0283 WED-9-M1 'Bantha' Droid (D) 3.00
EV0284 We're All Gonna Be A Lot Thinner! (D) 3.00
EV0285 We're Doomed (L) 0.25
EV0286 Wioslea (L) 1.00
EV0287 Wrong Turn (D) 1.00
EV0288 Wuher (D) 0.50
EV0289 X-Wing (L) 0.25
EV0290 Yavin 4 (L) 0.25
EV0321 Yavin 4 (D) 0.25
EV0291 Yavin 4: Docking Bay (L) 0.25
EV0322 Yavin 4: Docking Bay (D) 0.25
EV0292 Yavin 4: Jungle (D/L) 0.50
EV0293 Yavin 4: Massassi Throne Room (L) 1.00
EV0294 Yavin 4: Massassi War Room (L) 0.50
EV0295 Yavin Sentry (L) 0.50
EV0296 Yerka Mig (L) 1.00
EV0297 You Overestimate Their Chances (D) 1.00
EV0298 Your Eyes Can Deceive You (D) 1.00
EV0299 Your Powers Are Weak, Old Man (D) 3.00
EV0300 Y-Wing (L) 0.25

CCG: CARDS, PREMIERE 2-PLAYER INTRO SET PREMIUMS

EL0001 Death Star: Docking Control Room 327 (D) 2.00
EL0004 Death Star: Level 6 Core Shaft Corridor (L) 2.00
EL0005 Luke (L) 2.00
EL0006 Run Luke, Run! (L) 2.00
EL0002 Vader (D) 2.00
EL0003 Vader's Obsession (D) 2.00

CCG: CARDS, REBEL LEADERS

EN0001 Gold Leader in Gold 1 (L) 2.00
EN0002 Red Leader in Red 1 (L) 2.00

CCG: CARDS, REFLECTIONS

ER10015 2-1B (Hoth) (L) 5.00

ER10071 4-LOM (Dagobah) (D) 5.00
ER10072 Admiral Ozzel (Hoth) (D) 5.00
ER10016 All Wings Report In (Special Edition) (L) 5.00
ER10017 Anakin's Lightsaber (Hoth) (L) 5.00
ER10018 Artoo (Jabba's Palace) (L) 6.00
ER10019 Attack Run (A New Hope) (L) 5.00
ER10073 Avenger (Dagobah) (D) 5.00
ER10074 Bane Malar (Jabba's Palace) (D) 5.00
ER10002 Ben Kenobi (Special Edition) (L) 25.00
ER10075 Bib Fortuna (Jabba's Palace) (D) 5.00
ER10020 Biggs Darklighter (Premiere) (L) 5.00
ER10076 Black 2 (Premiere) (D) 5.00
ER10077 Blizzard 1 (Hoth) (D) 5.00
ER10078 Blizzard 2 (Hoth) (D) 5.00
ER10079 Blizzard Scout 1 (Hoth) (D) 5.00
ER10059 Boba Fett (Cloud City) (D) 24.00
ER10080 Boba Fett's Blaster Rifle (Cloud City) (D) 5.00
ER10081 Bossk (Dagobah) (D) 5.00
ER10082 Bossk in Hounds Tooth (Special Edition) (D) 5.00
ER10021 Braniac (A New Hope) (L) 5.00
ER10003 C-3PO (Premiere) (L) 18.00
ER10004 Captain Han Solo (Cloud City) (L) 22.00
ER10005 Chewbacca (A New Hope) (L) 23.00
ER10022 Cloud City: Downtown Plaza (Special Edition) (L) 5.00
ER10023 Cloud City: Guest Quarters (Cloud City) (L) 5.00
ER10024 Commander Luke Skywalker (Hoth) (L) 9.00
ER10083 Commence Primary Ignition (A New Hope) (D) 5.00
ER10084 Conquest (A New Hope) (D) 5.00
ER10025 Coruscant Celebration (Special Edition) (L) 5.00
ER10026 Dagobah: Yoda's Hut (Dagobah) (L) 5.00
ER10058 Darth Vader (Premiere) (D)RF 77.00
ER10060 Darth Vader, Dark Lord Of The Sith (Special Edition) (D) 25.00
ER10085 Death Squadron Star Destroyer (Special Edition) (D) 5.00
ER10061 Death Star (A New Hope) (D) 10.00
ER10027 Death Star (Special Edition) (L) 6.00
ER10028 Death Star Plans (Premiere) (L) 5.00
ER10029 Death Star: Trench (A New Hope) (L) 5.00
ER10086 Dengar (Dagobah) (D) 5.00
ER10062 Devastator (Premiere) (D) 9.00
ER10087 DS-61-3 (Premiere) (D) 5.00
ER10030 Dutch (Premiere) (L) 5.00
ER10088 Epic Duel (Cloud City) (D) 5.00
ER10063 Executor (Dagobah) (D) 15.00
ER10089 Expand The Empire (Premiere) (D) 5.00
ER10064 General Veers (Hoth) (D) 14.00
ER10065 Grand Moff Tarkin (Premiere) (D) 14.00
ER10090 Greedo (A New Hope) (D) 5.00
ER10006 Han Solo (Premiere) (L) 17.00
ER10031 Haven (Cloud City) (L) 5.00
ER10091 IG-2000 (Dagobah) (D) 5.00
ER10092 IG-88 (Dagobah) (D) 5.00
ER10032 It Is The Future You See (Dagobah) (L) 5.00
ER10093 IT-O (A New Hope) (D) 5.00
ER10094 Jabba (Special Edition) (D) 8.00
ER10066 Jabba The Hutt (Jabba's Palace) (D) 15.00
ER10095 Jabba's Sail Barge (Jabba's Palace) (D) 5.00
ER10033 Landing Claw (Dagobah) (L) 5.00
ER10007 Lando Calrissian (Cloud City) (L) 10.00
ER10067 Lando Calrissian (Cloud City) (D) 10.00
ER10008 Leia Organa (Premiere) (L) 18.00
ER10034 Lightsaber Proficiency (Premiere) (L) 5.00
ER10035 Lobot (Cloud City) (L) 5.00
ER10096 Lobot (Special Edition) (D) 5.00
ER10001 Luke Skywalker (Premiere) (L)RF 65.00
ER10036 Mechanical Failure (Special Edition) (L) 5.00
ER10009 Millennium Falcon (Premiere) (L) 24.00
ER10097 Mist Hunter (Dagobah) (D) 5.00
ER10010 Obi-Wan Kenobi (Premiere) (L) 17.00
ER10037 Obi-Wan's Lightsaber (Premiere) (L) 6.00
ER10098 Obsidian 7 (Cloud City) (D) 5.00
ER10099 Obsidian 8 (Cloud City) (D) 5.00
ER10038 Oola (Jabba's Palace) (L) 5.00
ER10100 Presence of the Force (Premiere) (D) 5.00
ER10039 Princess Leia (Cloud City) (L) 5.00
ER10011 Princess Leia Organa (Jabba's Palace) (L) 16.00
ER10040 Princess Organa (Special Edition) (L) 5.00
ER10101 Punishing One (Dagobah) (D) 5.00
ER10012 R2-D2 (A New Hope) (L) 14.00
ER10102 Rancor (Jabba's Palace) (D) 5.00
ER10041 Red 2 (A New Hope) (L) 5.00
ER10042 Red 5 (A New Hope) (L) 5.00
ER10043 Red Leader (Premiere) (L) 5.00
ER10044 Redemption (Cloud City) (L) 5.00
ER10045 Reflection (Dagobah) (L) 5.00
ER10046 Rendezvous Point (Special Edition) (L) 5.00
ER10047 Revolution (Premiere) (L) 5.00
ER10048 Rogue 1 (Hoth) (L) 5.00
ER10049 Rogue 3 (Hoth) (L) 5.00
ER10103 Salacious Crumb (Jabba's Palace) (D) 5.00
ER10050 Skywalkers (Premiere) (L) 5.00
ER10068 Slave I (Cloud City) (D) 14.00
ER10104 Slip Sliding Away (Cloud City) (D) 5.00
ER10013 Son Of Skywalker (Dagobah) (L) 18.00
ER10051 Spiral (Special Edition) (L) 5.00
ER10105 Stalker (Hoth) (D) 5.00
ER10106 Superlaser (A New Hope) (D) 5.00
ER10052 Tamtel Skreej (Jabba's Palace) (L) 5.00
ER10053 Tantive IV (A New Hope) (L) 5.00
ER10107 The Circle Is Now Complete (Premiere) (D) 5.00
ER10054 TK-422 (Special Edition) (L) 6.00
ER10108 Tonnika Sisters (Premiere) (D) 5.00
ER10109 Tyrant (Hoth) (D) 6.00
ER10110 U-3PO (A New Hope) (D) 5.00
ER10055 Uncontrollable Fury (Cloud City) (L) 5.00
ER10069 Vader's Custom Tie (Premiere) (D) 11.00
ER10070 Vader's Lightsaber (Premiere) (D) 14.00
ER10111 Vengeance (Special Edition) (D) 6.00
ER10112 Visage Of The Emperor (Dagobah) (D) 5.00
ER10113 Wampa (Hoth) (D) 5.00
ER10056 Wedge Antilles (A New Hope) (L) 7.00
ER10057 What Is Thy Bidding, My Master? (Dagobah) (L) 5.00
ER10014 Yoda (Dagobah) (L) 24.00
ER10114 Zuckuss (Dagobah) (D) 5.00

CCG: CARDS, SPECIAL EDITION

EP0001 2X-7KPR (Tooex) (D) 0.25
EP0002 A Bright Center To The Universe (D) 0.75
EP0003 A Day Long Remembered (D) 0.75
EP0004 A Real Hero (D) 4.00
EP0005 Air-2 Racing Swoop (L) 0.25
EP0006 Ak-rev (D) 0.75
EP0007 Alderaan Operative (L) 0.25
EP0008 Alert My Star Destroyer! (D) 0.25
EP0009 All Power To Weapons (D) 0.25
EP0010 All Wings Report In (L) 4.00
EP0011 Anoat Operative (D/L) 0.25
EP0012 Antilles Maneuver (L) 0.25
EP0013 ASP-707 (L) 5.00
EP0014 Balanced Attack (L) 0.75
EP0015 Bantha Herd (D) 3.00
EP0016 Barquin D'an (D) 0.75
EP0017 Ben Kenobi (L) 21.00
EP0018 Blast Points (D) 0.25
EP0019 Blown Clear (D) 0.75
EP0020 Boba Fett (D) 15.00
EP0021 Boelo (D) 5.00
EP0022 Bossk In Hound's Tooth (D) 8.00
EP0023 Bothan Spy (L) 0.25
EP0024 Bothawui (L) 5.00
EP0025 Bothawui Operative (L) 0.25
EP0026 Brangus Glee (D) 4.00
EP0027 Bren Quersey (L) 0.75
EP0028 Bron Burs (L) 4.00
EP0029 B-Wing Attack Fighter (L) 3.00
EP0030 Camie (L) 4.00
EP0031 Carbon Chamber Testing (D) 5.00
EP0032 Chyler (D) 0.75
EP0033 Clak'dor VII Operative (L) 0.75
EP0034 Cloud City Celebration (L) 4.00
EP0035 Cloud City Occupation (D) 4.00
EP0036 Cloud City: Casino (D/L) 0.75
EP0037 Cloud City: Core Tunnel (L) 0.75
EP0038 Cloud City: Downtown Plaza (D/L) 4.00
EP0039 Cloud City: Interrogation Room (D) 0.25
EP0040 Cloud City: North Corridor (L) 0.25
EP0041 Cloud City: Port Town District (D) 0.75
EP0042 Cloud City: Upper Walkway (D) 0.25
EP0043 Cloud City: West Gallery (D/L) 0.25
EP0044 Colonel Feyn Gospic (L) 4.00
EP0045 Combat Cloud Car (D) 5.00

EP0046 Come Here You Big Coward! (D) 0.25
EP0047 Commander Wedge Antilles (L) 6.00
EP0048 Coordinated Attack (D) 0.25
EP0049 Corellia Operative (L) 0.75
EP0050 Corellian Engineering Corporation (L) 4.00
EP0051 Corporal Grenwick (D) 3.00
EP0052 Corporal Prescott (D) 0.75
EP0053 Corulag Operative (D) 0.25
EP0054 Coruscant (D/L) 4.00
EP0055 Coruscant Celebration (L) 4.00
EP0056 Coruscant: Docking Bay (D) 0.25
EP0057 Coruscant: Imperial City (D) 0.75
EP0058 Coruscant: Imperial Square (D) 3.00
EP0059 Counter Surprise Assault (D) 4.00
EP0060 Dagobah (D) 0.75
EP0061 Dantooine Base Operations (L) 5.00
EP0062 Dantooine Operative (D) 0.25
EP0063 Dark Lord Of The Sith, Darth Vader (D) 30.00
EP0064 Darklighter Spin (L) 0.25
EP0065 Death Squadron Star Destroyer (D) 6.00
EP0066 Death Star (D) 8.00
EP0067 Death Star Assault Squadron (D) 6.00
EP0068 Death Star: Detention Block Control Room (D) 0.25
EP0069 Death Star: Detention Block Corridor (L) 0.25
EP0070 Debnoli (L) 4.00
EP0071 Desert (D/L) 5.00
EP0072 Desilijic Tattoo (D) 0.75
EP0073 Desperate Tactics (L) 0.25
EP0074 Destroyed Homestead (D) 3.00
EP0075 Dewback (D) 0.25
EP0076 Direct Assault (L) 0.25
EP0077 Disruptor Pistol (D/L) 5.00
EP0078 Docking And Repair Facilities (L) 4.00
EP0079 Dodo Bodonawieedo (D) 0.75
EP0080 Don't Tread On Me (L) 3.00
EP0081 Down With The Emperor! (L) 0.75
EP0082 Dr. Evazan's Sawed-off Blaster (D) 0.75
EP0083 Draw Their Fire (L) 0.75
EP0084 Dreaded Imperial Starfleet (D) 4.00
EP0085 Droid Merchant (L) 0.25
EP0086 Dune Walker (D) 5.00
EP0087 Echo Base Trooper Rifle (L) 0.25
EP0088 Elyhek Rue (L) 0.75
EP0307 Empire's Sinister Agents (D) 0.25
EP0089 Entrenchment (L) 3.00
EP0090 Eriadu Operative (D) 0.25
EP0091 Executor: Docking Bay (D) 0.75
EP0092 Farm (L) 5.00
EP0093 Feltipern Trevagg's Stun Rifle (D) 0.75
EP0094 Firepower (D) 0.25
EP0095 Firin Morett (L) 0.75
EP0096 First Aid (L) 5.00
EP0097 First Strike (D) 0.75
EP0098 Flare-S Racing Swoop (D) 0.25
EP0099 Flawless Marksmanship (D) 0.25
EP0100 Floating Refinery (D) 0.25
EP0101 Fondor (D) 0.75
EP0102 Forest (D/L) 5.00
EP0103 Gela Yeens (D) 0.75
EP0104 General McQuarrie (L) 4.00
EP0105 Gold 3 (L) 0.75
EP0106 Gold 4 (L) 0.75
EP0107 Gold 6 (L) 0.75
EP0108 Goo Nee Tay (L) 4.00
EP0109 Greeata (D) 0.75
EP0110 Grondorn Muse (L) 3.00
EP0111 Harc Seff (L) 0.75
EP0112 Harvest (L) 4.00
EP0113 Heavy Fire Zone (D) 0.25
EP0114 Heroes Of Yavin (L) 4.00
EP0115 Heroic Sacrifice (L) 0.75
EP0116 Hidden Base (L) 5.00
EP0117 Hit And Run (L) 4.00
EP0118 Hol Okand (L) 0.75
EP0119 Homing Beacon (D) 3.00
EP0120 Hoth Sentry (L) 0.75
EP0121 Hunt Down And Destroy The Jedi (D) 5.00
EP0122 Hunting Party (D) 3.00
EP0123 I Can't Shake Him! (D) 0.25
EP0124 Iasa, The Traitor of Jawa Canyon (D) 4.00
EP0125 IM4-099 (D) 5.00

EP0126 Imperial Atrocity (L) 3.00
EP0179 Imperial Control (D) 5.00
EP0127 Imperial Occupation (D) 5.00
EP0128 Imperial Propaganda (D) 6.00
EP0129 In Range (D) 0.25
EP0206 In The Hands of the Empire (D) 5.00
EP0130 Incom Corporation (L) 3.00
EP0131 Incom Engineer (L) 0.25
EP0132 Intruder Missile (D/L) 5.00
EP0133 ISB Operations (D) 5.00
EP0134 It's Not My Fault! (L) 5.00
EP0135 Jabba (D) 9.00
EP0136 Jabba's Influence (D) 4.00
EP0137 Jabba's Space Cruiser (D) 5.00
EP0138 Jabba's Through With You (D) 0.75
EP0139 Jabba's Twerps (D) 0.75
EP0140 Joh Yowza (L) 4.00
EP0141 Jungle (D/L) 5.00
EP0142 Kalit's Sandcrawler (L) 4.00
EP0143 Kashyyyk Operative (D/L) 0.75
EP0144 Kessel Operative (D) 0.75
EP0145 Ketwol (L) 3.00
EP0146 Kiffex Operative (D/L) 0.75
EP0147 Kirdo III Operative (L) 0.25
EP0148 Koensayr Manufacturing (L) 3.00
EP0149 Krayt Dragon (D) 5.00
EP0150 Kuat (D) 0.75
EP0151 Kuat Drive Yards (D) 3.00
EP0152 Lando's Blaster Rifle (L) 4.00
EP0153 Legendary Starfighter (L) 0.25
EP0154 Leia's Blaster Rifle (L) 4.00
EP0308 Liberation (L) 0.25
EP0155 Lieutenant Lepira (L) 0.75
EP0156 Lieutenant Naytaan (L) 0.75
EP0157 Lieutenant Tarn Mison (L) 3.00
EP0158 Lobel (D) 0.25
EP0159 Lobot (D) 4.00
EP0160 Local Defense (L) 0.75
EP0161 Local Uprising (L) 5.00
EP0162 Lyn Me (D) 0.75
EP0163 Major Palo Torshan (L) 4.00
EP0164 Makurth (D) 5.00
EP0165 Maneuvering Flaps (L) 0.25
EP0166 Masterful Move (D) 0.25
EP0167 Mechanical Failure (L) 4.00
EP0168 Meditation (L) 4.00
EP0169 Medium Bulk Freighter (L) 0.75
EP0170 Melas (L) 4.00
EP0171 Mind What You Have Learned (L) 5.00
EP0172 Moisture Farmer (L) 0.25
EP0309 More Dangerous Then You Realize (L) 0.25
EP0310 My Favorite Decoration (D) 0.25
EP0173 Nal Hutta Operative (D) 0.25
EP0174 Neb Dulo (L) 0.75
EP0175 Nebit (D) 3.00
EP0176 Niado Duegad (D) 0.75
EP0177 Nick Of Time (L) 0.75
EP0178 No Bargain (D) 0.75
EP0180 Old Times (L) 3.00
EP0181 On Target (L) 0.25
EP0182 One-Arm (D) 3.00
EP0183 Operations, Ralltiir (D) 5.00
EP0184 Oppressive Enforcement (D) 0.75
EP0185 Ord Mantell Operative (D) 0.25
EP0186 Organized Attack (L) 0.25
EP0187 OS-72-1 In Obsidian 1 (D) 5.00
EP0188 OS-72-10 (D) 5.00
EP0189 OS-72-2 In Obsidian 2 (D) 5.00
EP0190 Outer Rim Scout (D) 6.00
EP0191 Overwhelmed (D) 0.25
EP0192 Patrol Craft (D/L) 0.25
EP0193 Planetary Subjugation (D) 0.75
EP0194 Ponda Baba's Hold-out Blaster (D) 0.75
EP0195 Portable Scanner (D) 0.25
EP0196 Power Pivot (L) 0.25
EP0197 Precise Hit (L) 0.25
EP0198 Pride Of The Empire (D) 0.25
EP0199 Princess Organa (L) 13.00
EP0200 Put All Sections On Alert (D) 0.75
EP0201 R2-A5 (D) 0.75
EP0202 R3-A2 (L) 0.75

EP0203 R3-T2 (L)	3.00
EP0204 Raithal Operative (D)	0.25
EP0205 Ralltiir Freighter Captain (L)	5.00
EP0207 Ralltiir Operative (L)	0.25
EP0208 Rapid Fire (L)	0.25
EP0209 Rappertunie (D)	0.75
EP0210 Rebel Ambush (L)	0.25
EP0211 Rebel Base Occupation (D)	5.00
EP0212 Rebel Fleet (L)	4.00
EP0213 Red 10 (L)	0.75
EP0214 Red 7 (L)	0.75
EP0215 Red 8 (L)	0.75
EP0216 Red 9 (L)	0.75
EP0217 Relentless Pursuit (D)	0.25
EP0218 Rendezvous Point (L)	5.00
EP0219 Rendili (D)	5.00
EP0220 Rendili StarDrive (D)	4.00
EP0221 Rescue The Princess (L)	5.00
EP0222 Return To Base (D)	4.00
EP0223 Roche (L)	0.75
EP0224 Rock Wart (D)	5.00
EP0225 Rogue 4 (L)	4.00
EP0226 Ronto (D/L)	0.25
EP0227 RR'uruurrr (D)	4.00
EP0228 Ryle Torsyn (L)	0.75
EP0229 Rysttl (D)	4.00
EP0230 Sacrifice (D)	5.00
EP0231 Sandspeeder (L)	5.00
EP0232 Sandtrooper (D)	5.00
EP0233 Sarlacc (D)	4.00
EP0311 Save You It Can (L)	0.25
EP0234 Scrambled Transmission (L)	0.75
EP0235 Scurrier (L)	5.00
EP0236 Secret Plans (D)	0.75
EP0237 Sentinel-Class Landing Craft (D)	5.00
EP0238 Sergeant Edian (L)	0.75
EP0239 Sergeant Hollis (L)	3.00
EP0240 Sergeant Major Bursk (D)	0.75
EP0241 Sergeant Major Enfield (D)	4.00
EP0242 Sergeant Merril (D)	0.75
EP0243 Sergeant Narthax (D)	4.00
EP0244 Sergeant Torent (D)	4.00
EP0245 S-foils (L)	0.25
EP0246 SFS L-s9.3 Laser Cannons (D)	0.25
EP0247 Short-range Fighters (D)	4.00
EP0248 Sienar Fleet Systems (D)	5.00
EP0249 Slayn and Korpil Facilities (L)	3.00
EP0250 Slight Weapons Malfunction (L)	0.25
EP0312 Sometimes I Amaze Even Myself (L)	0.25
EP0251 Soth Petikkin (L)	3.00
EP0252 Spaceport City (D/L)	5.00
EP0253 Spaceport Docking Bay (D/L)	5.00
EP0254 Spaceport Prefect's Office (D)	5.00
EP0255 Spaceport Street (D/L)	5.00
EP0313 Spaceport Street (D)	0.25
EP0256 Spiral (L)	6.00
EP0257 Star Destroyer! (L)	4.00
EP0258 Stay Sharp! (L)	0.75
EP0259 Steady Aim (L)	0.25
EP0260 Strategic Reserves (D)	4.00
EP0261 Suppressive Fire (L)	0.25
EP0262 Surface Defense (D)	3.00
EP0263 Swamp (D/L)	5.00
EP0264 Swoop Mercenary (D)	5.00
EP0265 Sy Snootles (D)	4.00
EP0314 Systems Will Slip Through Your Fingers (D)	0.25
EP0266 T-47 Battle Formation (L)	4.00
EP0267 Tarkin's Bounty (D)	0.75
EP0268 Tatooine Celebration (L)	4.00
EP0269 Tatooine Occupation (D)	4.00
EP0270 Tatooine: Anchorhead (L)	5.00
EP0271 Tatooine: Beggar's Canyon (L)	4.00
EP0272 Tatooine: Jabba's Palace (L)	0.25
EP0273 Tatooine: Jawa Canyon (D/L)	0.75
EP0274 Tatooine: Krayt Dragon Pass (D)	5.00
EP0275 Tatooine: Tosche Station (L)	0.25
EP0276 Tauntaun Skull (D)	0.25
EP0277 Tawss Khaa (L)	4.00
EP0315 Their Fire Has Gone Out Of The Universe (D)	0.25
EP0278 The Planet That It's Farthest From (L)	0.75
EP0279 Thedit (L)	3.00
EP0280 Theron Nett (L)	0.75
EP0281 They're Coming In Too Fast! (D)	0.25
EP0282 They're Tracking Us (D)	0.25
EP0283 They've Shut Down The Main Reactor (D)	0.25
EP0284 Tibrin Operative (L)	0.25
EP0285 Tie Defender Mark I (D)	3.00
EP0286 TK-422 (L)	9.00
EP0287 Trooper Sabacc (D/L)	5.00
EP0288 Uh-oh! (L)	0.75
EP0289 Umpass-stay (D)	3.00
EP0290 URoRRuR'R'R's Bantha (D)	3.00
EP0291 Ur'Ru'r (D)	4.00
EP0292 Uutkik (D)	3.00
EP0293 Vader's Personal Shuttle (D)	6.00
EP0294 Vengeance (D)	7.00
EP0295 Wakeelmui (D)	0.75
EP0296 Watch Your Back! (D)	0.25
EP0297 Weapons Display (D)	0.25
EP0298 Wise Advice (D)	0.75
EP0299 Wittin's Sandcrawler (D)	4.00
EP0300 Womp Rat (D)	0.25
EP0301 Wookiee (L)	3.00
EP0302 Wrist Comlink (L)	0.25
EP0303 X-Wing Assault Squadron (L)	5.00
EP0304 X-Wing Laser Cannon (L)	0.25
EP0305 Yavin 4 Trooper (L)	5.00
EP0306 Yavin 4: Massassi Headquarters (L)	4.00

CCG: CARDS, YOUNG JEDI: BATTLE OF NABOO

E1C0001 A Thousand Terrible Things (D)	0.25
E1C0002 After Her! (D)	0.25
E1C0003 Alderaan Diplomat, Senator (L)	0.25
E1C0005 Amidala's Starship, Royal Transport (Foil) (L)	9.00
E1C0004 Amidala's Starship, Royal Transport (L)	4.00
E1C0006 Anakin Skywalker, Padawan (L)	5.00
E1C0007 Aqualish, Galactic Senator (D)	0.25
E1C0008 Armored Assault (D)	0.25
E1C0009 Aurra Sing, Mercenary (D)	4.00
E1C0010 Aurra Sing, Mercenary (Foil) (D)R	24.00
E1C0011 Battle Droid Blaster Rifle (D)	0.25
E1C0012 Battle Droid Squad, Guard Unit (D)	4.00
E1C0013 Battle Droid Squad, Guard Unit (Foil) (D)	10.00
E1C0014 Battle Droid: Infantry, Defense Division (D)	0.25
E1C0015 Battle Droid: Infantry, Patrol Division (D)	0.25
E1C0016 Battle Droid: Officer, Defense Division (D)	0.25
E1C0017 Battle Droid: Officer, Patrol Division (D)	0.25
E1C0018 Battle Droid: Pilot, Defense Division (D)	0.25
E1C0019 Battle Droid: Pilot, Patrol Division (D)	0.25
E1C0020 Battle Droid: Security, Defense Division (D)	0.25
E1C0021 Battle Droid: Security, Patrol Division (D)	0.25
E1C0022 Battleship, Trade Federation Transport (D)	0.25
E1C0023 Bith, Musician (D)	0.50
E1C0024 Blaster (D/L)	0.25
E1C0025 Blaster Rifle (D)	0.25
E1C0026 Bombad General (L)	0.50
E1C0027 Boss Nass, Gungan Chief (L)	0.50
E1C0028 Bravo 3, Naboo Starfighter (L)	0.50
E1C0029 Bravo Pilot, Ace Flyer (L)	0.25
E1C0030 Captain Panaka, Veteran Leader (L)	4.00
E1C0031 Captain Tarpals' Electropole (L)	0.50
E1C0032 Captain Tarpals, Gungan Officer (L)	0.50
E1C0033 Capture The Viceroy (L)	0.25
E1C0034 Celebration (L)	0.25
E1C0035 Coruscant - Capital City (D)	4.00
E1C0036 Coruscant - Galactic Senate (L)	4.00
E1C0037 Coruscant Guard, Chancellor's Escort (L)	0.25
E1C0038 Council Member, Naboo Governor (L)	0.25
E1C0039 Da Dug Chaaa! (D)	0.50
E1C0040 Darth Maul, Dark Lord of the Sith (D)	8.00
E1C0041 Darth Maul, Dark Lord of the Sith (Foil) (D)R	28.00
E1C0042 Darth Maul, Evil Sith Lord (D)	4.00
E1C0043 Darth Maul's Electrobinoculars (D)	0.50
E1C0045 Darth Maul's Lightsaber (Foil) (D)	8.00
E1C0044 Darth Maul's Lightsaber (D)	4.00
E1C0046 Darth Sidious, Sith Manipulator (D)	6.00
E1C0047 Daultay Dofine, Neimoidian Attendant (D)	0.50
E1C0048 Death From Above (D)	0.25
E1C0049 Destroyer Droid Squad, Guard Division (D)	4.00
E1C0050 Destroyer Droid Squad, Guard Division (Foil) (D)	8.00

CCG: Cards, Young Jedi: Battle of Naboo

E1C0051 Destroyer Droid, MTT Infantry (D) 0.25
E1C0052 Destroyer Droid, Vanguard Droid (D) 0.25
E1C0053 Diva Funquita, Dancer (D) 0.50
E1C0054 Diva Shaliqua, Singer (D) 0.50
E1C0055 Don't Spect A Warm Welcome (D) 0.25
E1C0056 Droid Control Ship, Trade Federation Transport (D) 0.50
E1C0057 Droid Starfighter (D) 0.25
E1C0058 Eeth Koth's Lightsaber (L) 0.50
E1C0059 Electropole (L) 0.25
E1C0060 Fambaa (L) 0.25
E1C0061 Flash Speeder (L) 0.25
E1C0062 Guardians Of The Queen (L) 0.50
E1C0063 Gunga City (L) 0.25
E1C0064 Gungan Battle Cry (L) 0.50
E1C0065 Gungan General, Army Leader (L) 0.25
E1C0066 Gungan Guard, Lookout (L) 0.25
E1C0067 Gungan Soldier, Infantry (L) 0.25
E1C0068 Gungan Warrior, Veteran (L) 0.25
E1C0069 Heavy Blaster (L) 0.25
E1C0070 How Wude! (L) 0.50
E1C0071 I Will Make It Legal (D) 0.25
E1C0072 I Will Take Back What Is Ours (L) 0.25
E1C0073 Jabba The Hutt, Crime Lord (D) 4.00
E1C0074 Jar Jar Binks, Bombad Gungan General (L) 4.00
E1C0075 Jedi Force Push (L) 0.50
E1C0076 Kaadu (L) 0.25
E1C0077 Kiss Your Trade Franchise Goodbye (L) 0.50
E1C0078 Mace Windu, Jedi Speaker (L) 4.00
E1C0080 Mace Windu's Lightsaber (Foil) (L) 6.00
E1C0079 Mace Windu's Lightsaber (L) 3.00
E1C0081 Meeeesa Lika Dis! (L) 0.25
E1C0082 Multi Troop Transport (D) 0.50
E1C0083 Naboo - Battle Plains (L) 4.00
E1C0084 Naboo - Theed Palace (D) 4.00
E1C0085 Naboo Bureaucrat, Official (L) 0.25
E1C0086 Naboo Officer, Commander (L) 0.25
E1C0087 Naboo Officer, Squad Leader (L) 0.50
E1C0088 Naboo Security, Defender (L) 0.25
E1C0089 Naboo Security, Trooper (L) 0.25
E1C0090 Naboo Starfighter (L) 0.25
E1C0091 Neimoidian Advisor, Bureaucrat (D) 4.00
E1C0092 Nikto, Slave (D) 0.25
E1C0093 NOOOOOOOOOOOO! (L) 3.00
E1C0094 Not For A Sith (D) 3.00
E1C0095 Not For A Sith (Foil) (D) 7.00
E1C0096 Now There Are Two Of Them (D) 0.50
E1C0097 Nute Gunray, Neimoidian Despot (D) 4.00
E1C0098 Nute Gunray, Neimoidian Despot (Foil) (D) 6.00
E1C0099 Obi-Wan Kenobi (L) 5.00
E1C0100 Obi-Wan Kenobi, Jedi Knight (Foil) (L)R 18.00
E1C0101 Obi-Wan Kenobi, Jedi Negotiator (L) 4.00
E1C0102 OOM-9, Battle Droid Commander (D) 0.50
E1C0103 P-59, Destroyer Droid Commander (D) 0.50
E1C0104 Pacithhip, Prospector (D) 0.25
E1C0105 Padme Naberrie, Amidala's Handmaiden (L) 4.00
E1C0106 Planetary Shuttle (L) 0.25
E1C0107 Quarren, Smuggler (D) 0.50
E1C0108 Queen Amidala, Keeper of the Peace (L) 4.00
E1C0109 Queen Amidala, Keeper of the Peace (Foil) (L) 14.00
E1C0110 Queen Amidala, Resolute Negotiator (L) 3.00
E1C0111 Queen Amidala, Resolute Negotiator (Foil) (L) 14.00
E1C0112 Qui-Gon Jinn, Jedi Ambassador (L) 5.00
E1C0113 Qui-Gon Jinn, Jedi Ambassador (Foil) (L)R 33.00
E1C0114 R2-D2, The Queen's Hero (L) 3.00
E1C0115 R2-D2, The Queen's Hero (Foil) (L) 10.00
E1C0116 Rep Officer, Gungan Diplomat (L) 4.00
E1C0117 Republic Cruiser, Transport (L) 0.25
E1C0118 Ric Olie, Bravo Leader (L) 0.50
E1C0119 Rune Haako, Neimoidian Deputy (D) 4.00
E1C0120 Sabe, Handmaiden Decoy Queen (L) 0.50
E1C0121 Sache, Handmaiden (L) 0.50
E1C0122 Sando Aqua Monster (D) 0.25
E1C0123 Sebulba, Dangerous Podracer Pilot (D) 4.00
E1C0124 Sio Bibble, Governor of Naboo (L) 0.50
E1C0125 Sith Force Push (D) 0.50
E1C0126 Sith Infiltrator, Starfighter (D) 0.50
E1C0127 Sith Lightsaber (D) 4.00
E1C0128 Sith Probe Droid, Remote Tracker (D) 0.25
E1C0129 STAP (D) 0.50
E1C0130 Tatooine - Desert Landing Site (L) 4.00
E1C0131 Tatooine - Mos Espa (D) 4.00

E1C0132 Thanks, Artoo! (L) 0.50
E1C0133 The Chancellor's Ambassador (L) 0.50
E1C0134 The Phantom Menace (D) 0.50
E1C0135 The Will Of The Force (L) 3.00
E1C0136 The Will Of The Force (Foil) (L) 8.00
E1C0137 There's Always A Bigger Fish (L) 0.25
E1C0138 They Will Not Stay Hidden For Long (D) 0.25
E1C0139 They Win This Round (D) 0.25
E1C0140 This Is Too Close! (D) 0.50
E1C0141 Toonbuck Toora, Senator (D) 0.50
E1C0142 Trade Federation Tank Laser Cannon (D) 0.50
E1C0143 Trade Federation Tank, Guard Division (D) 4.00
E1C0144 Trade Federation Tank, Guard Division (Foil) (D) 10.00
E1C0145 Trade Federation Tank, Patrol Division (D) 4.00
E1C0146 Trade Federation Tank, Patrol Division (Foil) (D) 8.00
E1C0147 Twi'lek Diplomat, Senator (D) 0.25
E1C0148 Uh-Oh! (L) 0.25
E1C0149 Watto, Toydarian Gambler (D) 3.00
E1C0150 We Are Sending All Troops (D) 0.25
E1C0151 We Wish To Form An Alliance (L) 0.25
E1C0152 Weequay, Enforcer (D) 0.25
E1C0153 Yane, Handmaiden (L) 0.50
E1C0154 Yoda, Jedi Elder (L) 5.00
E1C0155 Yoda, Jedi Elder (Foil) (L) 14.00
E1C0156 Young Skywalker (L) 0.50
E1C0157 Your Occupation Here Has Ended (L) 0.25

CCG: CARDS, YOUNG JEDI: JEDI COUNCIL

E1B0001 Adi Gallia, Corellian Jedi Master (L) 0.50
E1B0002 Adi Gallia's Lightsaber (L) 0.50
E1B0003 Aks Moe, Senator (D) 0.25
E1B0005 Amidala's Blaster (Foil) (L) 5.00
E1B0004 Amidala's Blaster (L) 3.00
E1B0006 Anakin Skywalker, Child of Prophecy (L) 6.00
E1B0007 Ascension Gun (L) 0.25
E1B0008 Balance To The Force (L) 0.50
E1B0009 Battle Droid Blaster Rifle (D) 0.25
E1B0010 Battle Droid Squad, Escort Unit (D) 4.00
E1B0011 Battle Droid: Infantry, Assault Division (D) 0.25
E1B0012 Battle Droid: Infantry, Guard Division (D) 0.25
E1B0013 Battle Droid: Officer, Assault Division (D) 0.25
E1B0014 Battle Droid: Officer, Guard Division (D) 0.25
E1B0015 Battle Droid: Pilot, Assault Division (D) 0.25
E1B0016 Battle Droid: Pilot, Guard Division (D) 0.25
E1B0017 Battle Droid: Security, Assault Division (D) 0.25
E1B0018 Battle Droid: Security, Guard Division (D) 0.25
E1B0019 Battleship, Trade Federation Transport (D) 0.25
E1B0020 Blaster (D/L) 0.25
E1B0021 Blaster Rifle (D/L) 0.25
E1B0022 Boss Nass, Gungan Leader (L) 0.50
E1B0023 Brave Little Droid (L) 0.50
E1B0024 Bravo 2, Naboo Starfighter (L) 0.50
E1B0025 Bravo Pilot, Naboo Volunteer (L) 0.25
E1B0026 Captain Panaka, Amidala's Bodyguard (L) 4.00
E1B0027 Captain Panaka, Amidala's Bodyguard (Foil) (L) 8.00
E1B0028 Captain Tarpals, Gungan Battle Leader (L) 0.50
E1B0029 Clegg Holdfast, Podracer Pilot (D) 0.50
E1B0030 Clegg Holdfast's Podracer (D) 0.50
E1B0031 Coruscant – Galactic Senate (D) 4.00
E1B0032 Coruscant – Jedi Council Chamber (L) 4.00
E1B0033 Coruscant Guard Blaster Rifle (D) 0.50
E1B0034 Coruscant Guard, Chancellor's Guard (L) 0.25
E1B0035 Coruscant Guard, Coruscant Detachment (L) 0.25
E1B0036 Coruscant Guard, Officer (L) 0.25
E1B0037 Coruscant Guard, Peacekeeper (L) 0.25
E1B0038 Darth Maul, Master of Evil (D) 8.00
E1B0039 Darth Maul, Master of Evil (Foil) (D)R 38.00
E1B0040 Darth Maul, Sith Warrior (D) 4.00
E1B0042 Darth Maul's Lightsaber (Foil) (D) 6.00
E1B0041 Darth Maul's Lightsaber (D) 4.00
E1B0044 Darth Maul's Sith Speeder (Foil) (D) 5.00
E1B0043 Darth Maul's Sith Speeder (D) 4.00
E1B0045 Darth Sidious, Lord of the Sith (D) 5.00
E1B0046 Darth Sidious, Lord of the Sith (Foil) (D)R 26.00
E1B0047 Depa Billaba, Jedi Master (L) 0.50
E1B0048 Destroyer Droid Squad, Defense Division (D) 4.00
E1B0049 Destroyer Droid, Assault Droid (D) 0.25
E1B0050 Destroyer Droid, Battleship Security (D) 0.25
E1B0051 Dos Mackineeks No Comen Here! (L) 0.25

E1B0052 Droid Starfighter (D) 0.25
E1B0053 Dud Bolt, Podracer Pilot (D)........................0.50
E1B0054 Dud Bolt's Podracer (D)..............................0.50
E1B0055 Edcel Bar Gane, Roona Senator (D)...............0.25
E1B0056 Eeth Koth, Zabrak Jedi Master (L)................0.50
E1B0057 Eirtae', Handmaiden (L)..............................0.50
E1B0058 Electropole (L)..0.25
E1B0059 Even Piell, Lannik Jedi Master (L).................0.50
E1B0060 Flash Speeder (L).......................................0.25
E1B0061 Fode and Beed, Podrace Announcer (D)...........3.00
E1B0062 Galactic Chancellor (L)................................0.25
E1B0063 Galactic Delegate, Representative (D).............0.25
E1B0064 Galactic Senator, Delegate (L).....................4.00
E1B0065 Gian Speeder (L).......................................0.25
E1B0066 Hate Leads To Suffering (L)........................0.50
E1B0067 Horox Ryyder, Senator (D)..........................0.25
E1B0068 I Object! (D)..0.25
E1B0069 I Will Deal With Them Myself (D)..................0.25
E1B0070 I Will Not Cooperate (L).............................0.50
E1B0071 Invasion! (L)...0.25
E1B0072 Jabba the Hutt, Gangster (D)......................4.00
E1B0073 Jabba the Hutt, Gangster (Foil) (D)..............8.00
E1B0074 Jar Jar Binks, Gungan Outcast (L)...............4.00
E1B0075 Kaadu (L)..0.25
E1B0076 Ki-Adi-Mundi, Cerean Jedi Knight (L)............4.00
E1B0077 Let Them Make The First Move (D)...............4.00
E1B0078 Lott Dod, Neimoidian Senator (D)................3.00
E1B0079 Lott Dod, Neimoidian Senator (Foil) (D).........5.00
E1B0080 Mace Windu, Senior Jedi Council Member (L)....5.00
E1B0081 Mace Windu, Senior Jedi Council Member (Foil) (L)...9.00
E1B0082 Mars Guo, Podracer Pilot (D)........................0.50
E1B0083 Mars Guo's Podracer (D).............................0.50
E1B0084 May The Force Be With You (L)......................0.25
E1B0085 Move Against The Jedi First (D).....................0.25
E1B0086 Multi Troop Transport (D)............................0.50
E1B0087 Naboo * Battle Plains (D)............................4.00
E1B0088 Naboo * Gungan Swamp (L).........................4.00
E1B0089 Naboo Blaster (L)......................................0.25
E1B0090 Naboo Officer, Liberator (L).........................0.25
E1B0091 Naboo Security, Amidala's Guard (L)...............0.25
E1B0092 Naboo Starfighter (L).................................0.25
E1B0093 Neimoidian Aide Federation Delegate (D)..........4.00
E1B0094 Nute Gunray, Neimoidian Viceroy (D)..............4.00
E1B0095 Nute Gunray, Neimoidian Viceroy (Foil) (D).......7.00
E1B0096 Obi-Wan Kenobi, Jedi Apprentice (L)...............8.00
E1B0097 Obi-Wan Kenobi, Jedi Apprentice (Foil) (L)R......35.00
E1B0098 Obi-Wan Kenobi, Jedi Warrior (L)...................4.00
E1B0099 Ody Mandrell, Podracer Pilot (D)...................0.50
E1B0100 Ody Mandrell's Podracer (D).........................0.50
E1B0101 Open Fire! (D)..0.50
E1B0102 Oppo Rancisis, Jedi Master (L)......................0.50
E1B0104 Padme Naberrie, Queen's Handmaiden (L).........4.00
E1B0103 Padme Naberrie, Queen's Handmaiden (Foil) (L)....9.00
E1B0105 Plo Koon, Jedi Master (L)............................0.50
E1B0106 Queen Amidala, Representative of Naboo (L).......5.00
E1B0107 Queen Amidala, Representative of Naboo (Foil) (L)...9.00
E1B0108 Queen Amidala, Voice of Her People (L)............5.00
E1B0109 Qui-Gon Jinn, Jedi Protector (L)....................6.00
E1B0110 Qui-Gon Jinn, Jedi Protector (Foil) (L)R...........24.00
E1B0112 Qui-Gon Jinn's Lightsaber (Foil) (L)................6.00
E1B0111 Qui-Gon Jinn's Lightsaber (L)........................5.00
E1B0113 R2-D2, Loyal Droid (L)................................5.00
E1B0114 R2-D2, Loyal Droid (Foil) (L)........................7.00
E1B0115 Radiant VII, Republic Cruiser Transport (L)........0.25
E1B0116 Ratts Tyerell, Podracer Pilot (D)....................0.50
E1B0117 Ratts Tyerell's Podracer (D)..........................0.50
E1B0118 Republic Captain, Officer (L)........................0.25
E1B0119 Republic Pilot, Veteran (L)..........................0.25
E1B0120 Ric Olie, Chief Pilot (L).............................0.50
E1B0121 Rodian, Mercenary (D)................................0.25
E1B0122 Rune Haako, Neimoidian Advisor (D)................4.00
E1B0123 Rune Haako, Neimoidian Advisor (Foil) (D).........6.00
E1B0124 Saesee Tiin, Iktotchi Jedi Master (L)...............0.50
E1B0125 Sci Taria, Chancellor's Aide (L).....................0.25
E1B0126 Seal Off The Bridge (D)..............................0.50
E1B0127 Sebulba, Podracer Pilot (D)..........................4.00
E1B0128 Senator Palpatine (L).................................0.25
E1B0129 Sith Infiltrator, Starfighter (D)....................0.50
E1B0130 Sith Probe Droid, Hunter Droid (D)................0.25
E1B0131 STAP (D)..0.50
E1B0132 Start Your Engines! (D)..............................0.50

E1B0133 Switch To Bio (D) 0.25
E1B0134 Take Them To Camp Four (D)........................0.25
E1B0135 Tatooine – Mos Espa (L)..............................4.00
E1B0136 Tatooine – Podrace Arena (D)........................4.00
E1B0137 The Might Of The Republic (L).......................0.25
E1B0138 Thermal Detonator (D)................................0.50
E1B0139 Trade Federation Tank Laser Cannon (D)...........0.50
E1B0140 Trade Federation Tank, Assault Division (D).......4.00
E1B0141 Valorum, Supreme Chancellor (D)...................0.25
E1B0142 Very Unusual (D)......................................0.25
E1B0143 Vote Of No Confidence (D)...........................0.25
E1B0144 Watto, Junk Merchant (D)............................4.00
E1B0145 Watto, Junk Merchant (Foil) (D).....................8.00
E1B0146 We Are Meeting No Resistance (D)..................0.25
E1B0147 We Don't Have Time For This (L).....................0.25
E1B0148 We Have Them On The Run (D).......................0.50
E1B0149 We Wish To Board At Once (L)........................0.25
E1B0150 Wisdom Of The Council (L)...........................3.00
E1B0151 Wookiee Senator, Representative (L)................0.25
E1B0152 Yaddle, Jedi Master (L)...............................0.50
E1B0153 Yarael Poof, Quermian Jedi Master (L)..............0.50
E1B0154 Yoda, Jedi Council Member (L).......................5.00
E1B0155 Yoka To Bantha Poodoo (D)...........................0.25
E1B0156 Your Little Insurrection Is At An End (D)...........0.50

CCG: CARDS, YOUNG JEDI: MENACE OF MAUL

E1A0001 Anakin Skywalker, Meet Obi-Wan Kenobi (L) 0.50
E1A0002 Anakin Skywalker, Podracer Pilot (L)...............6.00
E1A0004 Anakin Skywalker's Podracer (Foil) (L)..............4.00
E1A0003 Anakin Skywalker's Podracer (L).....................5.00
E1A0005 Ann and Tann Gella, Sebulba's Attendants (D)......0.50
E1A0006 Are You An Angel? (L)................................0.50
E1A0007 At Last We Will Have Revenge (D)...................0.50
E1A0008 Aurra Sing, Bounty Hunter (D).......................5.00
E1A0009 Aurra Sing's Blaster Rifle (D).......................4.00
E1A0010 Battle Droid Blaster Rifle (D)........................0.25
E1A0011 Battle Droid Squad (Foil) (D)........................10.00
E1A0012 Battle Droid Squad, Assault Unit (D)................4.00
E1A0013 Battle Droid: Infantry, AAT Division (D).............0.25
E1A0014 Battle Droid: Infantry, MTT Division (D).............0.25
E1A0015 Battle Droid: Officer, AAT Division (D)..............0.25
E1A0016 Battle Droid: Officer, MTT Division (D)..............0.25
E1A0017 Battle Droid: Pilot, AAT Division (D)................0.25
E1A0018 Battle Droid: Pilot, MTT Division (D)................0.25
E1A0019 Battle Droid: Security, AAT Division (D).............0.25
E1A0020 Battle Droid: Security, MTT Division (D).............0.25
E1A0021 Battleship, Trade Federation Transport (D)..........0.25
E1A0022 Begin Landing Your Troops (D).......................0.25
E1A0023 Ben Quadinaros' Podracer (Foil) (D).................4.00
E1A0024 Ben Quadinaros' Podracer (D)........................0.50
E1A0025 Ben Quadinaros, Podracer Pilot (D)..................0.50
E1A0026 Bib Fortuna, Twi'lek Advisor (D).....................0.50
E1A0027 Blaster (D/L)...0.25
E1A0028 Blaster Rifle (D/L).....................................0.25
E1A0029 Boonta Eve Podrace (D)...............................0.50
E1A0030 Boss Nass, Leader of the Gungans (L)...............0.50
E1A0031 Bravo 1, Naboo Starfighter (Foil) (L)................4.00
E1A0032 Bravo 1, Naboo Starfighter (L).......................0.50
E1A0033 Bravo Pilot, Veteran Flyer (L).......................0.25
E1A0034 C-3PO (Foil) (L)..11.00
E1A0035 C-3PO, Anakin's Creation (L).........................4.00
E1A0036 Captain Panaka, Protector of the Queen (L).........3.00
E1A0037 Captain Panaka's Blaster (L).........................0.25
E1A0038 Captain Tarpals, Gungan Guard (L)..................0.50
E1A0039 Cha Skrunee Da Pat, Sleemo (L).....................0.25
E1A0040 Coruscant – Capital City (L)..........................4.00
E1A0041 Coruscant – Jedi Council Chamber (D) 4.00
E1A0042 Counterparts (L).......................................0.50
E1A0043 Da Beings Hereabouts Cawazy (L)...................0.25
E1A0044 Darth Maul (Foil) (D).................................40.00
E1A0045 Darth Maul Starfighter, Sith Infiltrator (D).........4.00
E1A0046 Darth Maul, Sith Apprentice (D).....................10.50
E1A0047 Darth Maul, Sith Lord (D)............................5.00
E1A0048 Darth Sidious (Foil) (D)..............................30.00
E1A0049 Darth Sidious, Sith Master (D).......................8.00
E1A0050 Destroyer Droid Squad (Foil) (D)....................10.00
E1A0051 Destroyer Droid Squad, Security Division (D).......4.00
E1A0052 Destroyer Droid, Defense Droid (D)..................0.25
E1A0053 Destroyer Droid, Wheel Droid (D)....................0.25

E1A0054 Droid Starfighter (D) 0.25
E1A0055 Electropole (L) 0.25
E1A0056 Enough Of This Pretense (L) 0.50
E1A0057 Eopie (L) 0.25
E1A0058 Fear Attracts The Fearful (L) 0.50
E1A0059 Flash Speeder (L) 0.25
E1A0060 Gardulla the Hutt, Crime Lord (D) 0.50
E1A0061 Gasgano, Podracer Pilot (D) 0.50
E1A0062 Gasgano's Podracer (Foil) (D) 4.00
E1A0063 Gasgano's Podracer (D) 0.50
E1A0064 Gragra, Chuba Peddler (D) 0.25
E1A0065 Grueling Contest (D) 0.50
E1A0066 Gungan Curiosity (L) 0.25
E1A0067 Gungan Guard (L) 0.25
E1A0068 Gungan Official, Bureaucrat (L) 0.25
E1A0069 Gungan Soldier, Scout (L) 0.25
E1A0070 Gungan Soldier, Veteran (L) 0.25
E1A0071 Gungan Warrior, Infantry (L) 0.25
E1A0072 He Was Meant To Help You (L) 0.50
E1A0073 I Have A Bad Feeling About This (L) 0.50
E1A0074 In Complete Control (D) 0.25
E1A0075 Ishi Tib, Warrior (L) 0.25
E1A0076 Ithorian, Merchant (L) 0.25
E1A0077 I've Been Trained In Defense (L) 0.50
E1A0078 Jabba the Hutt, Vile Crime Lord (D) 5.00
E1A0079 Jar Jar Binks' Electropole (L) 0.50
E1A0080 Jar Jar Binks, Gungan Chuba Thief (L) 5.00
E1A0081 Jar-Jar Binks (Foil) (L) 25.00
E1A0082 Jawa Ion Blaster (L) 0.25
E1A0083 Jawa, Bargainer (L) 4.00
E1A0084 Jawa, Thief (L) 0.25
E1A0085 Jedi Lightsaber, Ki-Adi-Mundi's (L) 0.50
E1A0086 Kaa Bazza Kundee Hodrudda! (D) 0.50
E1A0087 Kaadu (L) 0.25
E1A0088 Mace Windu (Foil) (L) 14.00
E1A0089 Mace Windu, Jedi Master (L) 7.00
E1A0090 Mas Amedda, Vice Chancellor (L) 0.50
E1A0091 Mawhonic, Podracer Pilot (D) 0.50
E1A0092 Mawhonic's Podracer (Foil) (D) 4.00
E1A0093 Mawhonic's Podracer (D) 0.50
E1A0094 Multi Troop Transport (D) 0.50
E1A0095 Naboo – Gungan Swamp (D) 4.00
E1A0096 Naboo – Theed Palace (L) 4.00
E1A0097 Naboo Blaster (L) 0.25
E1A0098 Naboo Officer, Battle Planner (L) 0.50
E1A0099 Naboo Security, Guard (L) 0.25
E1A0100 Naboo Starfighter (L) 0.25
E1A0101 Neimoidian, Trade Federation Pilot (D) ...4.00
E1A0102 Obi-Wan Kenobi (Foil) (L) 35.00
E1A0103 Obi-Wan Kenobi, Jedi Padawan (L) 4.00
E1A0104 Obi-Wan Kenobi, Young Jedi (L) 8.00
E1A0105 Obi-Wan Kenobi's Lightsaber (Foil) (L) ...3.00
E1A0106 Obi-Wan Kenobi's Lightsaber (L) 4.00
E1A0107 Opee Sea Killer (D) 0.25
E1A0108 Padme Naberrie, Handmaiden (L) 4.00
E1A0109 Passel Argente, Senator (D) 0.25
E1A0110 Pit Droid, Engineer (D) 0.25
E1A0111 Pit Droid, Heavy Lifter (D) 0.25
E1A0112 Pit Droid, Mechanic (D) 0.25
E1A0113 Podrace Preparation (D) 0.50
E1A0114 Queen Amidala (Foil) (L) 10.00
E1A0115 Queen Amidala, Royal Leader (L) 5.00
E1A0116 Queen Amidala, Ruler of Naboo (L) 4.00
E1A0117 Qui-Gon Jinn, Jedi Master (L) 5.00
E1A0118 R2-D2, Astromech Droid (L) 4.00
E1A0119 Rabe, Handmaiden (L) 0.50
E1A0120 Rep Been, Gungan (L) 0.50
E1A0121 Republic Cruiser, Transport (Foil) (L) 4.00
E1A0122 Republic Cruiser, Transport (L) 0.25
E1A0123 Ric Olie, Ace Pilot (L) 0.50
E1A0124 Royal Guard, Leader (L) 0.25
E1A0125 Royal Guard, Veteran (L) 0.25
E1A0126 Sandstorm (D) 0.25
E1A0127 Sebulba, Bad-Tempered Dug (D) 4.00
E1A0128 Sebulba's Podracer (Foil) (D) 9.00
E1A0129 Sebulba's Podracer (D) 3.00
E1A0130 Security Volunteers (L) 0.25
E1A0131 Shmi's Pride (L) 0.50
E1A0132 Sith Lightsaber (D) 4.00
E1A0133 Sith Probe Droid, Spy Drone (D) 0.25
E1A0134 Sniper (D) 0.25

E1A0135 STAP (D) 0.50
E1A0136 Tatooine – Desert Landing Site (D) 4.00
E1A0137 Tatooine – Podrace Arena (L) 4.00
E1A0138 Tatooine Thunder Rifle (D) 0.25
E1A0139 Teemto Pagalies, Podracer (Foil) (D) ...4.00
E1A0140 Teemto Pagalies, Podracer (D) 0.50
E1A0141 Teemto Pagalies, Podracer Pilot (D) 0.50
E1A0142 The Federation Has Gone Too Far (L) ...0.25
E1A0143 The Invasion Is On Schedule (D) 0.25
E1A0144 The Negotiations Were Short (L) 0.25
E1A0145 The Queen's Plan (L) 0.25
E1A0146 Trade Federation Tank Laser Cannon (D) ...0.50
E1A0147 Trade Federation Tank, Armored Division (D) ...4.00
E1A0148 Tusken Raider, Marksman (D) 0.25
E1A0149 Tusken Raider, Nomad (D) 0.25
E1A0150 Vile Gangsters (D) 0.50
E1A0151 Watto, Slave Owner (D) 4.00
E1A0152 Watto's Wager (D) 0.50
E1A0153 We're Not In Trouble Yet (L) 0.50
E1A0154 Yoda, Jedi Master (L) 6.00
E1A0155 You Have Been Well Trained (D) 4.00
E1A0156 Yousa Guys Bombad! (L) 4.00

CD WALLETS

American Covers

CW0001 front and back   CW0002 front and back

CW0001 "Darth Vader/Boba Fett" 17.00
CW0002 Episode I Collage 18.00

World Wide Licenses Ltd.

CW0003   CW0004   CW0006

CW0006 Darth Maul 16.00
CW0003 Space Battle 16.00
CW0004 Star Wars logo on metal plate.....................14.00
CW0005 Star Wars logo on metal plate, double wallet.....19.00

CD-PLAYERS

CD0001 in package and close-up

Tiger Electronics
CD0001 Darth Maul CD Player..98.00

CDS

Alec Empire
RC40026 Generation Star Wars, music..................................15.00

Arista Records
RC40003 SW Trilogy: The Original Soundtrack Anthology 4 CD set..........26.00

BMG Entertainment
RC40004 Max Rebo Band: Jedi Rocks, selected from the Original Motion Picture Soundtrack ROTJ:SE 8.00

Force Records
RC40002 Soundtrack from Caravan of Courage and Ewok Adventure ...8.00

Highbridge Company
RC40006 ESB: Original Radio Drama as heard on National Public Radio, original music/effects; 10 episodes, 5 CDs 55.00
RC40007 ROTJ: The Original Radio Drama; 3 hours, 3 CDs 35.00
RC40005 SW: Original Radio Drama as heard on National Public Radio, original music/effects; 13 episodes, 7 CDs 60.00
RC40024 Trilogy radio drama CD set; 29 episodes on 15 CDs 110.00
RC40008 Trilogy radio drama deluxe CD set; 15 CDs in a foil-stamped slipcase 160.00

Kid Rhino
RC40028 Junior Jedi Training Manual read-along.....................................23.00

KRB Music Company
RC40001 Music from the Star Wars Trilogy performed by the New World Orchestra 10.00

Mercury Records
RC40009 The Best of Meco 9.00

Oglio Entertainment Group
RC40010 Cocktails in the Cantina music 12.00

RCA Victor
RC40012 ANH Special Edition Original Soundtrack Recording 24.00
RC40011 ANH Special Edition Original Soundtrack Recording, deluxe edition packaging 28.00
RC40018 Cantina Band picture disc CD single....................................18.00
RC40017 Darth Vader helmet-shaped CD single 22.00
RC40014 ESB Special Edition Original Soundtrack Recording 24.00
RC40013 ESB Special Edition Original Soundtrack Recording, deluxe edition packaging 28.00
RC40019 Rebo Band picture disc CD single....................................18.00
RC40016 ROTJ Special Edition Original Soundtrack Recording 24.00
RC40015 ROTJ Special Edition Original Soundtrack Recording, deluxe edition packaging..28.00

Rhino
RC40020 Star Wars Episode I 24-page book and CD read-along............12.00
RC40022 Star Wars Episode I 24-page book and CD read-along with Anakin's Podracer MicroMachine 14.00
RC40021 Star Wars Episode I 24-page book and CD read-along with Gungan Sub MicroMachine..15.00
RC40025 Star Wars Episode I 24-page book and CD read-along with Sith Infiltrator MicroMachine...14.00

Style Wars

RC40026

RC40004

RC40002

RC40024

RC40006

RC40008

RC40013

RC40027

RC40023

RC40027 Style Wars, Free The Funk, music 14.00
RC40023 Christmas in the Stars 16.00

CELPHONE FACEPLATES

CFP0001   CFP0002   CFP0003   CFP0004

CFP0003 Darth Maul / movie poster art, fits Nokia 3210 ....25.00
CFP0004 Queen Amidala, fits Nokia 3210 ....25.00
CFP0001 Queen Amidala, fits Nokia 5100 ....25.00
CFP0002 Yoda, fits Nokia 5100 ....25.00

CELPHONE STRAPS

CPS0001

CPS0002

Mafuyu
CPS0001 Chewbacca..18.00
CPS0002 Princess Leia 18.00

CENTERPIECES

PFE0001   PFE0002   PFE0003   PFE0004

Drawing Board
PFE0001 Cloud City...15.00
PFE0002 Darth Vader and Luke Duel 15.00
PFE0003 Ewoks in Forest...12.00

Party Express
PFE0004 EPI:TPM party table centerpiece 6.00

CERAMIC BOXES

HOC0001   HOC0002

Sigma
HOC0001 Stormtrooper...55.00
HOC0002 Yoda in Backpack 65.00

CERTIFICATES

TCT0001

TCT0002

Toys R Us
TCT0001 Episode I Toy Premiere, May 3, 1999 ....9.00

Walmart
TCT0002 Jedi Lightsaber Building Contest (Lego) 7.00

CHAIRS

American Toy and Furniture Co.
FUC0001 Wicket the Ewok rocker 80.00

Pipsqueaks

FUC0002 front & back

FUC0003 front & back

FUC0004 front & back

FUC0005 front & back

Hand painted hardwood. FAO Schwartz exclusive.
FUC0002 EPI: Anakin 175.00
FUC0003 EPI: Jar Jar 175.00
FUC0004 EPI: Sebulba 175.00
FUC0005 EPI: Watto 175.00

CHALKBOARDS

American Toy and Furniture Co.
SUC0003 Ewoks chalkboard and easel.......................................116.00

Manton
SUC0001 R2-D2 and Wicket the Ewok...57.00

CHARM BRACELETS

JCB0002

Factors, Etc.
JCB0001 C-3PO, Chewbacca, R2-D2 ....35.00
JCB0002 C-3PO, Darth Vader, R2-D2 ....35.00
JCB0003 Chewbacca, Stormtrooper, X-Wing.................................35.00

CHECKBOOK COVERS

CBC0001

CBC0002

CBC0001 Darth Vader tooled into vinyl......................................12.00
CBC0002 Star Wars logo set against starfield on blue vinyl......................10.00

CHESS GAMES

ND0001 board and stored pieces

ND0003

ND0005

ND0004

ND0002

A La Carte
Classic trilogy characters. Sculpted plastic pieces.
ND0003 Chess 85.00
ND0005 Chess, revised pkg. 65.00

Danbury Mint
ND0001 Star Wars Chess Set, pewter pieces with storage/playing
     board...980.00

Really Useful
ND0004 Chess, Episode I characters...65.00

Tiger Electronics
ND0002 Galactic Chess, electronic 79.00

CIGAR BANDS

Morrita
Available in sets with background colors: blue, gray, purple, red, or white.
CGB0002 01 Han Solo 2.00
CGB0007 02 Obi-Wan Kenobi 2.00
CGB0012 03 Darth Vader 2.00
CGB0017 04 Han Solo 2.00
CGB0022 05 Luke Skywalker 2.00
CGB0027 06 C-3PO 2.00
CGB0032 07 Yoda 2.00
CGB0037 08 Obi-Wan Kenobi 2.00
CGB0042 09 R2-D2 C-3PO 2.00
CGB0047 10 Boba Fett..2.00
CGB0052 11 R2-D2 C-3PO 2.00
CGB0057 12 Luke Skywalker 2.00
CGB0062 13 R2-D2 ....2.00
CGB0067 14 Ewok 2.00
CGB0072 15 Jawa 2.00
CGB0077 16 Emperor 2.00
CGB0082 17 Luke Skywalker 2.00

CGB0002

CGB0007

CGB0012

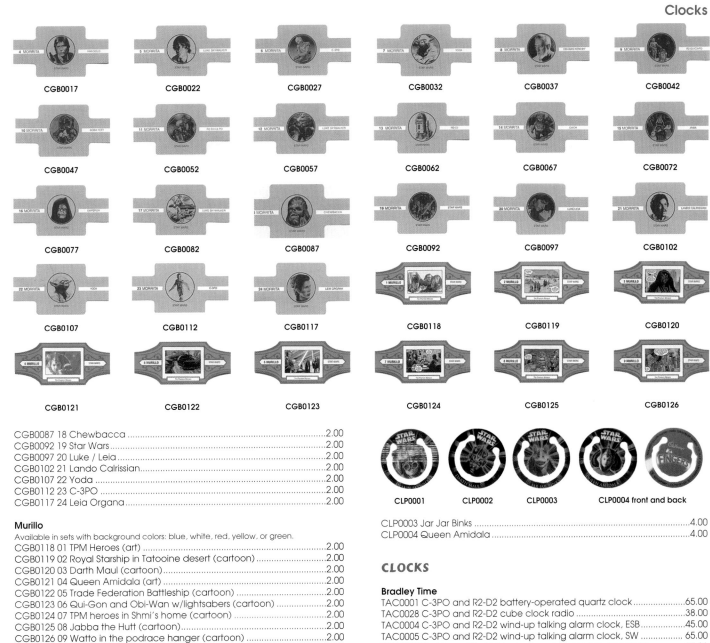

CGB0017	CGB0022	CGB0027	CGB0032	CGB0037	CGB0042
CGB0047	CGB0052	CGB0057	CGB0062	CGB0067	CGB0072
CGB0077	CGB0082	CGB0087	CGB0092	CGB0097	CGB0102
CGB0107	CGB0112	CGB0117	CGB0118	CGB0119	CGB0120
CGB0121	CGB0122	CGB0123	CGB0124	CGB0125	CGB0126

CGB0087 18 Chewbacca 2.00
CGB0092 19 Star Wars............2.00
CGB0097 20 Luke / Leia............2.00
CGB0102 21 Lando Calrissian............2.00
CGB0107 22 Yoda 2.00
CGB0112 23 C-3PO 2.00
CGB0117 24 Leia Organa 2.00

Murillo
Available in sets with background colors: blue, white, red, yellow, or green.
CGB0118 01 TPM Heroes (art) 2.00
CGB0119 02 Royal Starship in Tatooine desert (cartoon) 2.00
CGB0120 03 Darth Maul (cartoon)............2.00
CGB0121 04 Queen Amidala (art) 2.00
CGB0122 05 Trade Federation Battleship (cartoon) 2.00
CGB0123 06 Qui-Gon and Obi-Wan w/lightsabers (cartoon) 2.00
CGB0124 07 TPM heroes in Shmi's home (cartoon) 2.00
CGB0125 08 Jabba the Hutt (cartoon)............2.00
CGB0126 09 Watto in the podrace hanger (cartoon) 2.00
CGB0127 10 Darth Maul releases probe droids (cartoon) 2.00

CLIP-A-LONGS

VCL0001 · VCL0002 · VCL0003

Craft Master
VCL0002 Compass with crayon, R2-D2............12.00
VCL0001 Crayon holder and sharpener, Darth Vader 12.00
VCL0003 Wicket magnifying glass............16.00

CLIPPOS

Cadbury
CLP0001 Anakin Skywalker 4.00
CLP0002 Darth Maul............4.00

CLP0001 CLP0002 CLP0003 CLP0004 front and back

CLP0003 Jar Jar Binks 4.00
CLP0004 Queen Amidala 4.00

CLOCKS

Bradley Time
TAC0001 C-3PO and R2-D2 battery-operated quartz clock............65.00
TAC0028 C-3PO and R2-D2 cube clock radio 38.00
TAC0004 C-3PO and R2-D2 wind-up talking alarm clock, ESB............45.00
TAC0005 C-3PO and R2-D2 wind-up talking alarm clock, SW 65.00
TAC0007 Droids and Tie Fighter battery-operated quartz clock 75.00
TAC0011 Space Battle Scene and 2nd Death Star, black frame under glass............45.00
TAC0010 Super Live Adventure Clock, digital tabletop clock............75.00

Clock-Wise
TAC0017 Death Star battle (ROTJ) artwork, beveled glass quartz clock.19.00

Micro Games of America
TAC0008 Darth Vader AM/FM clock radio 32.00

Nelsonic
Desktop mini-clocks.
TAC0018 Darth Maul on Sith Speeder 16.00

TAC0001 box and opened · TAC0028

Clocks

TAC0007 TAC0008 TAC0023 boxed and opened TAC0022 TAC0018 TAC0019 TAC0020 TAC0021

TAC0024 TAC0025 TAC0026 TAC0027

TAC0019 Jar Jar Binks 25.00
TAC0020 Naboo Fighter 25.00
TAC0021 Queen Amidala 34.00
TAC0024 Qui-Gon Jinn 34.00

Pepsi Cola
TAC0023 R2-D2 Alarm Clock, promotional 38.00

Thinkway
TAC0022 Jar Jar Binks Wake Up System, includes pit-droid clock 39.00

Welby Elgin
Empire Strikes Back battery-operated wall clocks.
TAC0002 C-3PO and R2-D2 ....40.00
TAC0006 Darth Vader and Stormtroopers 45.00

TAC0009 C-3PO and R2-D2 "Anywhere" clock; pendant, clip-on, or
   stick-on 35.00
TAC0003 C-3PO and R2-D2 portable clock radio, ROTJ 35.00
TAC0025 Darth Maul alarm clock, round, light-up face 23.00
TAC0026 Darth Maul with lightsaber pendulum, plays theme.................27.00
TAC0015 Empire Strikes Back Special Edition, 9"x11" 36.00
TAC0027 EP1 Battleship alarm clock, sculpted Naboo Fighter flies over, digi-
   tal display 18.00
TAC0016 Return of the Jedi Special Edition, 9"x11".......................36.00
TAC0014 Star Wars Special Edition, 9"x11" 36.00

CLOTHES HOOKS

HOK0001 Boba Fett 25.00
HOK0002 C-3PO 25.00
HOK0003 Darth Vader 25.00
HOK0004 Emperor's Royal Guard 25.00

CLOTHES RACKS
Adam Joseph Industries
FUR0001 C-3PO and R2-D2 ....45.00
FUR0003 Max Rebo Band 45.00

FUR0002 front and back

American Toy and Furniture Co.
FUR0002 Luke and Darth Vader Dueling 65.00

COASTERS

CST0010 CST0002 front and back CST0003 CST0004

CST0006 CST0007 CST0008 CST0009

Disney / MGM
CST0010 Cantina: Mos Eisley Tatooine, set of 12 ....18.00

Pizza Hut
"Jedi Tricks", 4" diameter.
CST0001 Levitating Straw 3.00
CST0002 Mind Reading 3.00
CST0003 Presidential Flip 3.00
CST0004 Salt Shaker Teleportation....................................3.00
CST0005 Straw Telekinesis...3.00

Zak Designs
Round, 4" diameter.
CST0006 Anakin Skywalker...4.00
CST0007 Darth Maul...4.00
CST0008 Jar Jar Binks...4.00
CST0009 Queen Amidala...4.00

COIN PURSES
Applause

PET0002 PET0003 PET0004 PET0001

Treasure Keepers.
PET0001 Jar Jar Binks...6.00
PET0002 Queen Amidala 8.00
PET0003 R2-D2 ....6.00
PET0004 Yoda 6.00

Touchline

PET0005 PET0006 PET0007 PET0008

3" round, any color.
PET0005 Admiral Ackbar 10.00

PET0009	PET0010	PET0011

PET0012 C-3PO 10.00
PET0006 Chewbacca 10.00
PET0007 Darth Vader 10.00
PET0008 Ewok 10.00
PET0009 Jabba the Hutt 10.00
PET0010 R2-D2 ....10.00
PET0011 Stormtrooper 10.00

COINS: ACTION FIGURE

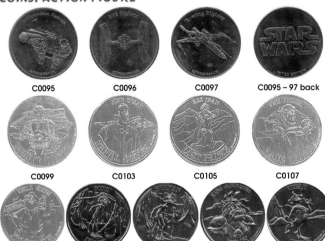

C0095	C0096	C0097	C0095 – 97 back
C0099	C0103	C0105	C0107
C0110	C0111	C0114	C0112	C0115

Just Toys (Bend Ems)
C0095 Millennium Falcon 12.00
C0096 Tie Fighter 12.00
C0097 X-Wing Fighter 12.00

Kenner (Droids)
C0098 A-Wing Pilot 35.00
C0099 Boba Fett 65.00
C0100 C-3PO Droids 12.00
C0101 C-3PO Protocol Droid 20.00
C0102 Jann Tosh 10.00
C0103 Jord Dusat 10.00
C0104 Kea Moll 10.00
C0105 Kez-Iban 10.00
C0106 RD-D2 Droids 12.00
C0107 Sise Fromm 10.00
C0108 Thall Joben 10.00
C0109 Tig Fromm 10.00
C0110 Uncle Gundy 10.00

Kenner (Ewoks)
C0111 Dulok Scout 10.00
C0114 Dulok Shaman 10.00
C0112 King Gorneesh 10.00
C0113 Logray 17.00
C0115 Urgah Lady Gorneesh 10.00
C0116 Wicket W. Warrick 17.00

Kenner (POTF)
C0027 2-1B 100.00
C0028 Amanaman 17.00
C0029 Anakin Skywalker 70.00

C0030 AT-AT 50.00
C0031 AT-ST Driver 15.00
C0032 A-Wing Pilot 10.00
C0033 Barada 10.00
C0024 Bib Fortuna 143.00
C0034 Biker Scout 15.00
C0035 Boba Fett 305.00
C0085 B-Wing Pilot 12.00
C0038 C-3PO 15.00
C0040 Cantina Creatures, "at local cantinas" 76.00
C0025 Chewbacca 18.00
C0042 Chief Chirpa 35.00
C0043 Darth Vader 18.00
C0044 Droids (R2-D2 and Power Droid) 58.00
C0045 Emperor 12.00
C0046 Emperor's Royal Guard 55.00
C0047 EV-9D9 ....10.00
C0048 FX-7 ....75.00
C0049 Gamorrean Guard 24.00
C0050 Greedo 102.00
C0051 Han Solo, Carbon Freeze 10.00
C0052 Han Solo, Rebel 20.00
C0053 Han Solo, Rebel Fighter 75.00
C0054 Han Solo, Rebel Hero 65.00
C0055 Hans Solo, Rebel (misspelling) 250.00
C0056 Hoth Stormtrooper 225.00
C0057 Imperial Commander 46.00
C0058 Imperial Dignitary 15.00
C0059 Imperial Gunner 15.00
C0060 Jawas 22.00
C0061 Lando Calrissian, Rebel General (Cloud City) 67.00
C0062 Lando Calrissian, Rebel General (Falcon) 10.00
C0063 Logray 32.00
C0064 Luke Skywalker in Stormtrooper armor 26.00
C0065 Luke Skywalker in Stormtrooper armor w/o eyes 12.00
C0066 Luke Skywalker on Scout Bike 10.00
C0067 Luke Skywalker on Tauntaun 140.00
C0068 Luke Skywalker w/Landspeeder 35.00
C0069 Luke Skywalker, Jedi Knight 20.00
C0070 Luke Skywalker, Jedi Knight on Dagobah 75.00
C0071 Luke Skywalker, Jedi w/X-Wing 25.00
C0072 Lumat 12.00
C0073 Millennium Falcon 65.00
C0074 Millennium Falcon (misspelling) 175.00
C0075 Obi-Wan Kenobi 15.00
C0076 Paploo 11.00
C0077 Princess Leia, Boushh 149.00
C0078 Princess Leia in Endor Fatigues 12.00
C0079 Princess Leia w/R2-D2 ....73.00
C0080 R2-D2 ....16.00
C0081 Romba 10.00
C0082 Sail Barge 225.00
C0083 Sail Skiff 255.00
C0084 Sail Skiff w/o Star Wars logo 175.00
C0086 Stormtrooper 50.00
C0087 Teebo 12.00
C0088 Tie Fighter Pilot 39.00
C0089 Tusken Raider 85.00
C0090 Warok 10.00
C0091 Wicket 15.00
C0092 Yak Face 90.00
C0093 Yoda 24.00
C0094 Zuckuss 195.00

Toy Fair
C0117 Darth Vader, Toy Fair exclusive 25.00

COINS: MINTED

Disney / MGM
CPM0035 Star Wars Weekends, R2-D2 projecting hologram Mickey, limited
to 1,200 ....65.00

C0028	C0029	C0031	C0032	C0033	C0085	C0038	C0025	C0043

Coins: Minted

C0045	C0047	C0052	C0058	C0059	C0061	C0062	C0066	C0069
C0070	C0071	C0076	C0078	C0079	C0080	C0081	C0086	C0090

CPM0035 front and back close-up, mounted

CPM0007 front and back close-up, mounted

Rarities Mint

CPM0029 10th Anniversary (Leia and Luke), gold .10 oz 160.00
CPM0014 10th Anniversary (Leia and Luke), gold .25 oz. 325.00
CPM0015 10th Anniversary (Leia and Luke), gold 1 oz. 1,500.00
CPM0007 10th Anniversary (Leia and Luke), silver 1 oz. 50.00
CPM0001 10th Anniversary (Leia and Luke), silver 5 oz. 175.00
CPM0008 15th Anniversary (Leia and Luke), silver 1 oz. 75.00
CPM0030 Ben Kenobi and Darth Vader, gold .10 oz. 160.00
CPM0016 Ben Kenobi and Darth Vader, gold .25 oz. 325.00
CPM0017 Ben Kenobi and Darth Vader, gold 1 oz. 1,250.00
CPM0009 Ben Kenobi and Darth Vader, silver 1 oz. 50.00
CPM0002 Ben Kenobi and Darth Vader, silver 5 oz. 175.00
CPM0031 C-3PO and R2-D2, gold .10 oz. 160.00
CPM0018 C-3PO and R2-D2, gold .25 oz. 325.00
CPM0019 C-3PO and R2-D2, gold 1 oz. 1,250.00
CPM0010 C-3PO and R2-D2, silver 1 oz. 50.00
CPM0003 C-3PO and R2-D2, silver 5 oz. 175.00
CPM0032 Chewbacca and Han Solo, gold .10 oz. 160.00
CPM0020 Chewbacca and Han Solo, gold .25 oz. 325.00
CPM0021 Chewbacca and Han Solo, gold 1 oz. 1,250.00
CPM0011 Chewbacca and Han Solo, silver 1 oz. 50.00
CPM0004 Chewbacca and Han Solo, silver 5 oz. 175.00
CPM0033 Mos Eisley Cantina Band, gold .10 oz. 160.00
CPM0022 Mos Eisley Cantina Band, gold .25 oz. 325.00
CPM0023 Mos Eisley Cantina Band, gold 1 oz. 1,250.00
CPM0012 Mos Eisley Cantina Band, silver 1 oz. 50.00
CPM0005 Mos Eisley Cantina Band, silver 5 oz. 175.00
CPM0034 Stormtroopers, gold .10 oz. 160.00
CPM0024 Stormtroopers, gold .25 oz. 325.00
CPM0025 Stormtroopers, gold 1 oz. 1,250.00
CPM0013 Stormtroopers, silver 1 oz. 50.00
CPM0006 Stormtroopers, silver 5 oz. 175.00

Rawcliffe

4" pewter medallion.
CPM0026 Darth Vader 35.00
CPM0027 Obi-Wan Kenobi 35.00
CPM0028 Yoda 35.00

COLLECTOR FLEET TOYS

YC0001	YC0002	YC0003

Kenner

YC0001 Imperial Star Destroyer 30.00
YC0002 Rebel Blockade Runner 25.00
YC0003 Super Star Destroyer 93.00

COLORING SETS

COL0002	COL0003	COL0004

Craft House

Mega-Fuzz coloring set.
COL0003 AT-AT 7.00
COL0004 Darth Vader 7.00
COL0002 Death Star Battle 5.00

Craft Master

COL0001

COL0001 Color N' Clean Machine, 50" roll of reusable scenes to color, four
crayons and wipe cloth 35.00

Rose Art Industries

COL0005	COL0006	COL0007	COL0008

COL0005 A New Hope: 3-D Crayon by Number 7.00
COL0009 Deluxe Light-Up Drawing Desk 18.00
COL0007 Designer Desk 16.00
COL0008 Droid Factory 12.00
COL0006 Light Up Drawing Desk 12.00

COMBS

Adam Joseph Industries

TOC0001 C-3PO and R2-D2 pop-up comb 10.00
TOC0002 Darth Vader pop-up comb 10.00

| TOC0001 | TOC0002 | TOC0003 | TOC0004 | TOC0007 |

TOC0003 Landspeeder Comb-n-Keeper 10.00
TOC0004 Max Rebo Band Comb-n-Keeper 12.00
TOC0005 Princess Kneesaa and Wicket Comb-n-Keeper 8.00
TOC0006 Princess Kneesaa Comb-n-Keeper 8.00
TOC0007 Princess Leia as Jabba's Prisoner pop-up comb 16.00

COMFORTERS

CMF0001 EPI Pod Racing, any size 46.00

COMIC BOOKS

| CB0001 | CB0004 | CB0005 | CB0006 | CB0007 |

Blackthorne Publishing
3D comic books.
CB0001 01 Star Wars 12.00
CB0002 02 Havoc on Hoth 12.00
CB0003 03 The Dark Side of Dantooine 12.00

Entity Comics
CB0004 Fart Wars, parody 4.00
CB0005 Return of One-Eye, parody 4.00

Manga
CB0012 A New Hope, issue 1 ....14.00
CB0013 A New Hope, issue 2 ....14.00
CB0014 A New Hope, issue 3 ....14.00
CB0015 A New Hope, issue 4 ....14.00
CB0016 Empire Strikes Back, issue 1 ....14.00
CB0017 Empire Strikes Back, issue 2 ....14.00
CB0018 Empire Strikes Back, issue 3 ....14.00
CB0019 Empire Strikes Back, issue 4 ....14.00
CB0008 Return of the Jedi, issue 1 ....14.00
CB0009 Return of the Jedi, issue 2 ....14.00
CB0010 Return of the Jedi, issue 3 ....14.00
CB0011 Return of the Jedi, issue 4 ....14.00
CB0006 Star Wars Episode I: The Phantom Menace 28.00

YPS
CB0007 Der Stormtrooper des Imperiums 43.00

COMIC BOOKS: DARK HORSE COMICS

Dark Horse Comics
CBD0021 A New Hope - Trade Paperback (reprints Marvel Comics issues 1-3) 12.00

CBD0366 A New Hope - Trade Paperback (reprints Marvel Comics issues 4-6) 12.00
CBD0369 A New Hope: Special Edition - trade paperback 10.00
CBD0017 A New Hope: Special Edition, Issue 1 ....6.00
CBD0018 A New Hope: Special Edition, Issue 2 ....6.00
CBD0019 A New Hope: Special Edition, Issue 3 ....6.00
CBD0020 A New Hope: Special Edition, Issue 4 ....6.00
CBD0006 Boba Fett: #1/2 gold foil edition 18.00
CBD0005 Boba Fett: #1/2 Wizard mail-away 12.00
CBD0397 Boba Fett: Agent of Doom 3.00
CBD0007 Boba Fett: Bounty on Bar-Kooda 6.00
CBD0011 Boba Fett: Death, Lies, and Trechery (trade paperback) 14.00
CBD0342 Boba Fett: Enemy of the Empire - trade paperback 12.00
CBD0287 Boba Fett: Enemy of the Empire, Issue 1 ....3.00
CBD0288 Boba Fett: Enemy of the Empire, Issue 2 ....3.00
CBD0289 Boba Fett: Enemy of the Empire, Issue 3 ....3.00
CBD0290 Boba Fett: Enemy of the Empire, Issue 4 ....3.00
CBD0008 Boba Fett: Murder Most Foul (double-sized) 6.00
CBD0009 Boba Fett: Twin Engines of Destruction 8.00
CBD0010 Boba Fett: When The Fat Lady Swings 6.00
CBD0377 Bounty Hunters, Issue 1: Scoundrel's Wages 5.00
CBD0373 Bounty Hunters, Issue 2: Kenix Kil 5.00
CBD0318 Chewbacca, Issue 1 ....5.00
CBD0319 Chewbacca, Issue 2 ....5.00
CBD0320 Chewbacca, Issue 3 ....5.00
CBD0321 Chewbacca, Issue 4 ....5.00
CBD0236 Classic Star Wars Issue 01 ....6.00
CBD0237 Classic Star Wars Issue 02 ....6.00
CBD0238 Classic Star Wars Issue 03 ....6.00
CBD0239 Classic Star Wars Issue 04 ....6.00
CBD0240 Classic Star Wars Issue 05 ....6.00
CBD0241 Classic Star Wars Issue 06 ....6.00
CBD0242 Classic Star Wars Issue 07 ....6.00
CBD0243 Classic Star Wars Issue 08 ....6.00
CBD0244 Classic Star Wars Issue 09 ....6.00
CBD0245 Classic Star Wars Issue 10 ....6.00
CBD0246 Classic Star Wars Issue 11 ....6.00
CBD0247 Classic Star Wars Issue 12 ....6.00
CBD0248 Classic Star Wars Issue 13 ....6.00
CBD0249 Classic Star Wars Issue 14 ....6.00
CBD0250 Classic Star Wars Issue 15 ....6.00
CBD0251 Classic Star Wars Issue 16 ....6.00
CBD0252 Classic Star Wars Issue 17 ....6.00
CBD0253 Classic Star Wars Issue 18 ....6.00
CBD0254 Classic Star Wars Issue 19 ....6.00
CBD0255 Classic Star Wars Issue 20 ....6.00
CBD0257 Classic SW, The Early Adventures, Issue 1 ....5.00
CBD0258 Classic SW, The Early Adventures, Issue 2 ....5.00
CBD0259 Classic SW, The Early Adventures, Issue 3 ....5.00
CBD0260 Classic SW, The Early Adventures, Issue 4 ....5.00
CBD0261 Classic SW, The Early Adventures, Issue 5 ....5.00
CBD0262 Classic SW, The Early Adventures, Issue 6 ....5.00
CBD0263 Classic SW, The Early Adventures, Issue 7 ....5.00
CBD0264 Classic SW, The Early Adventures, Issue 8 ....5.00
CBD0265 Classic SW, The Early Adventures, Issue 9 ....5.00
CBD0343 Classic Star Wars, The Early Adventures, trade paperback 17.00
CBD0336 Classic Star Wars, The Rebel Storm, trade paperback 16.00
CBD0256 Classic Star Wars, The Vandelhelm Mission 5.00
CBD0337 Classic Star Wars, trade paperback 16.00
CBD0028 Crimson Empire - trade paperback 18.00
CBD0281 Crimson Empire Handbook 3.00
CBD0029 Crimson Empire II, Issue 1 ....6.00
CBD0030 Crimson Empire II, Issue 2 ....6.00
CBD0282 Crimson Empire II, Issue 3 ....6.00
CBD0283 Crimson Empire II, Issue 4 ....6.00
CBD0284 Crimson Empire II, Issue 5 ....6.00
CBD0285 Crimson Empire II, Issue 6 ....6.00
CBD0022 Crimson Empire, Issue 1 ....7.00
CBD0023 Crimson Empire, Issue 2 ....6.00

| CBD0021 | CBD0366 | CBD0017 | CBD0018 | CBD0019 | CBD0020 | CBD0005 | CBD0397 | CBD0007 | CBD0011 |

CBD0287 CBD0288 CBD0289 CBD0290 CBD0008 CBD0009 CBD0010 CBD0377 CBD0373 CBD0318

CBD0319 CBD0320 CBD0321 CBD0236 CBD0237 CBD0238 CBD0239 CBD0240 CBD0241 CBD0242

CBD0243 CBD0244 CBD0245 CBD0246 CBD0247 CBD0248 CBD0249 CBD0250 CBD0251 CBD0252

CBD0253 CBD0254 CBD0255 CBD0257 CBD0258 CBD0259 CBD0260 CBD0261 CBD0262 CBD0263

CBD0264 CBD0265 CBD0343 CBD0336 CBD0256 CBD0337 CBD0281 CBD0029 CBD0030 CBD0282

CBD0283	CBD0284	CBD0285	CBD0022	CBD0023	CBD0024	CBD0025	CBD0026	CBD0027	CBD0053
CBD0067	CBD0055	CBD0057	CBD0059	CBD0061	CBD0063	CBD0065	CBD0031	CBD0036	CBD0037
CBD0040	CBD0044	CBD0074	CBD0068	CBD0069	CBD0070	CBD0071	CBD0072	CBD0073	CBD0269
CBD0270	CBD0271	CBD0272	CBD0273	CBD0274	CBD0291	CBD0358	CBD0359	CBD0381	CBD0382

CBD0269 Dark Horse Classics: Dark Empire, Issue 1 ....4.00
CBD0270 Dark Horse Classics: Dark Empire, Issue 2 ....4.00
CBD0271 Dark Horse Classics: Dark Empire, Issue 3 ....4.00
CBD0272 Dark Horse Classics: Dark Empire, Issue 4 ....4.00
CBD0273 Dark Horse Classics: Dark Empire, Issue 5 ....4.00
CBD0274 Dark Horse Classics: Dark Empire, Issue 6 ....4.00
CBD0291 Dark Horse Comics #7: "Beginning an All New Star Wars Adventure" 5.00
CBD0358 Darth Maul 1 of 4 ....5.00
CBD0359 Darth Maul 2 of 4 ....3.00
CBD0381 Darth Maul 3 of 4 ....3.00
CBD0382 Darth Maul 4 of 4 ....3.00
CBD0175 Devil Worlds, Issue 1 ....6.00
CBD0371 Devil Worlds, Issue 2 ....6.00
CBD0081 Droids - trade paperback............18.00
CBD0075 Droids, Issue 1 ....5.00
CBD0076 Droids, Issue 2 ....5.00
CBD0077 Droids, Issue 3 ....5.00
CBD0078 Droids, Issue 4 ....5.00
CBD0079 Droids, Issue 5 ....5.00
CBD0080 Droids, Issue 6 ....5.00
CBD0372 Droids, Special Edition 8.00
CBD0090 Droids: 2nd Series - trade paperback 8.00
CBD0082 Droids: 2nd Series, Issue 1 ....5.00
CBD0083 Droids: 2nd Series, Issue 2 ....4.00
CBD0084 Droids: 2nd Series, Issue 3 ....4.00
CBD0085 Droids: 2nd Series, Issue 4 ....4.00
CBD0086 Droids: 2nd Series, Issue 5 ....4.00
CBD0087 Droids: 2nd Series, Issue 6 ....4.00
CBD0088 Droids: 2nd Series, Issue 7 ....4.00
CBD0089 Droids: 2nd Series, Issue 8 ....4.00
CBD0338 Droids: Rebellion, trade paperback 16.00
CBD0334 Empire Strikes Back - trade paperback (reprints Marvel Comics issues 39-41) 12.00
CBD0367 Empire Strikes Back - trade paperback (reprints Marvel Comics issues 42-44) 12.00

CBD0227 Empire Strikes Back: Manga Issue 1 ....12.00
CBD0228 Empire Strikes Back: Manga Issue 2 ....12.00
CBD0229 Empire Strikes Back: Manga Issue 3 ....12.00
CBD0230 Empire Strikes Back: Manga Issue 4 ....12.00
CBD0176 Empire Strikes Back: Special Edition - trade paperback 10.00
CBD0093 Empire's End - trade paperback 6.00
CBD0091 Empire's End, Issue 1 ....4.00
CBD0092 Empire's End, Issue 2 ....4.00
CBD0351 Episode I: Adventures, trade paperback 13.00
CBD0309 Episode I: The Phantom Menace, Issue 1/2 ....12.00
CBD0310 Episode I: The Phantom Menace, Issue 1 ....3.00
CBD0311 Episode I: The Phantom Menace, Issue 2 ....3.00
CBD0312 Episode I: The Phantom Menace, Issue 3 ....3.00
CBD0313 Episode I: The Phantom Menace, Issue 4 ....3.00
CBD0314 Episode I: The Phantom Menace: Anakin Skywalker 3.00
CBD0379 Episode I: The Phantom Menace: Obi-Wan Kenobi 3.00
CBD0316 Episode I: The Phantom Menace: Obi-Wan Kenobi, photo cover 3.00
CBD0378 Episode I: The Phantom Menace: Queen Amidala 3.00
CBD0315 Episode I: The Phantom Menace: Queen Amidala, photo cover 3.00
CBD0380 Episode I: The Phantom Menace: Qui-Gon Jinn 3.00
CBD0317 Episode I: The Phantom Menace: Qui-Gon Jinn, photo cover 3.00
CBD0266 Han Solo at Star's End, Issue 1 ....3.00
CBD0267 Han Solo at Star's End, Issue 2 ....3.00
CBD0268 Han Solo at Star's End, Issue 3 ....3.00
CBD0339 Han Solo at Star's End, trade paperback 16.00
CBD0100 Heir to the Empire - trade paperback 20.00
CBD0094 Heir to the Empire, Issue 1 ....4.00
CBD0095 Heir to the Empire, Issue 2 ....4.00
CBD0096 Heir to the Empire, Issue 3 ....4.00
CBD0097 Heir to the Empire, Issue 4 ....4.00
CBD0098 Heir to the Empire, Issue 5 ....4.00
CBD0099 Heir to the Empire, Issue 6 ....4.00
CBD0409 Infinities: A New Hope, issue 1 ....5.00
CBD0410 Infinities: A New Hope, issue 2 ....5.00

CBD0175	CBD0371	CBD0081	CBD0075	CBD0076	CBD0077	CBD0078	CBD0079	CBD0080	CBD0372
CBD0082	CBD0083	CBD0084	CBD0085	CBD0086	CBD0087	CBD0088	CBD0089	CBD0338	CBD0334
CBD0367	CBD0227	CBD0228	CBD0229	CBD0230	CBD0091	CBD0092	CBD0310	CBD0309	CBD0311
CBD0312	CBD0313	CBD0314	CBD0379	CBD0316	CBD0378	CBD0315	CBD0380	CBD0317	CBD0266
CBD0267	CBD0268	CBD0339	CBD0100	CBD0094	CBD0095	CBD0096	CBD0097	CBD0098	CBD0099
CBD0409	CBD0410	CBD0286	CBD0012	CBD0016	CBD0013	CBD0015	CBD0014	CBD0101	CBD0102
CBD0103	CBD0104	CBD0350	CBD0360	CBD0361	CBD0362	CBD0363	CBD0402	CBD0403	CBD0404
CBD0105	CBD0106	CBD0107	CBD0108	CBD0109	CBD0110	CBD0346	CBD0111	CBD0112	CBD0113

CBD0114   CBD0307   CBD0308   CBD0389   CBD0390   CBD0391   CBD0172   CBD0368   CBD0232   CBD0233

CBD0234   CBD0235   CBD0370   CBD0115   CBD0116   CBD0117   CBD0118   CBD0374   CBD0173   CBD0119

CBD0411 Infinities: A New Hope, issue 3 ....5.00
CBD0412 Infinities: A New Hope, issue 4 ....5.00
CBD0286 Jabba the Hutt: The Jabba Tape 4.00
CBD0012 Jabba the Hutt: Betrayal 4.00
CBD0016 Jabba the Hutt: The Art of the Deal, trade paperback 10.00
CBD0013 Jabba the Hutt: The Dynasty Trap 4.00
CBD0014 Jabba the Hutt: The Gaar Suppoon Hit 4.00
CBD0015 Jabba the Hutt: The Hunger of Princess Nampi 4.00
CBD0101 Jedi Acadamy: Leviathan, Issue 1 ....4.00
CBD0102 Jedi Acadamy: Leviathan, Issue 2 ....4.00
CBD0103 Jedi Acadamy: Leviathan, Issue 3 ....4.00
CBD0104 Jedi Acadamy: Leviathan, Issue 4 ....4.00
CBD0350 Jedi Acadamy: Leviathan, trade paperback 12.00
CBD0360 Jedi Council: Acts of War, Issue 1 ....3.00
CBD0361 Jedi Council: Acts of War, Issue 2 ....3.00
CBD0362 Jedi Council: Acts of War, Issue 3 ....3.00
CBD0363 Jedi Council: Acts of War, Issue 4 ....3.00
CBD0402 Jedi vs. Sith, Issue 1 ....3.00
CBD0403 Jedi vs. Sith, Issue 2 ....3.00
CBD0404 Jedi vs. Sith, Issue 3 ....3.00
CBD0405 Jedi vs. Sith, Issue 4 ....3.00
CBD0406 Jedi vs. Sith, Issue 5 ....3.00
CBD0407 Jedi vs. Sith, Issue 6 ....3.00
CBD0105 Last Command, Issue 1 ....4.00
CBD0106 Last Command, Issue 2 ....4.00
CBD0107 Last Command, Issue 3 ....4.00
CBD0108 Last Command, Issue 4 ....4.00
CBD0109 Last Command, Issue 5 ....4.00
CBD0110 Last Command, Issue 6 ....4.00
CBD0346 Last Command, trade paperback 15.00
CBD0111 Mara Jade: By The Emperor's Hand, Issue 1 ....6.00
CBD0112 Mara Jade: By The Emperor's Hand, Issue 2 ....5.00
CBD0113 Mara Jade: By The Emperor's Hand, Issue 3 ....5.00
CBD0114 Mara Jade: By The Emperor's Hand, Issue 4 ....5.00
CBD0307 Mara Jade: By The Emperor's Hand, Issue 5 ....5.00
CBD0308 Mara Jade: By The Emperor's Hand, Issue 6 ....5.00
CBD0347 Mara Jade: By The Emperor's Hand, trade paperback 13.00
CBD0389 Qui-Gon and Obi-Wan, Issue 01: Last Stand on Ord Mantell, Issue 1 ....3.00
CBD0390 Qui-Gon and Obi-Wan, Issue 02: Last Stand on Ord Mantell, Issue 2 ....3.00
CBD0391 Qui-Gon and Obi-Wan, Issue 03: Last Stand on Ord Mantell, Issue 3 ....3.00
CBD0172 Return of the Jedi, trade paperback (reprints Marvel Comics issues 1-2) 10.00
CBD0368 Return of the Jedi, trade paperback (reprints Marvel Comics issues 3-4) 10.00
CBD0232 Return of the Jedi: Manga Issue 1 ....10.00
CBD0233 Return of the Jedi: Manga Issue 2 ....10.00
CBD0234 Return of the Jedi: Manga Issue 3 ....10.00
CBD0235 Return of the Jedi: Manga Issue 4 ....10.00
CBD0370 Return of the Jedi: Special Edition, trade paperback 10.00
CBD0115 River of Chaos, Issue 1 ....6.00
CBD0116 River of Chaos, Issue 2 ....6.00
CBD0117 River of Chaos, Issue 3 ....6.00
CBD0118 River of Chaos, Issue 4 ....6.00
CBD0374 Sergio Aragonis Stomps Star Wars 14.00
CBD0173 Shadow Stalker 4.00

CBD0125 Shadows of the Empire, trade paperback 18.00
CBD0119 Shadows of the Empire, Issue 1 ....8.00
CBD0120 Shadows of the Empire, Issue 2 ....6.00
CBD0121 Shadows of the Empire, Issue 3 ....6.00
CBD0122 Shadows of the Empire, Issue 4 ....5.00
CBD0123 Shadows of the Empire, Issue 5 ....5.00
CBD0124 Shadows of the Empire, Issue 6 ....5.00
CBD0126 Shadows of the Empire: Evolution, Issue 1 ....3.00
CBD0127 Shadows of the Empire: Evolution, Issue 2 ....3.00
CBD0128 Shadows of the Empire: Evolution, Issue 3 ....3.00
CBD0129 Shadows of the Empire: Evolution, Issue 4 ....3.00
CBD0130 Shadows of the Empire: Evolution, Issue 5 ....3.00
CBD0135 Splinter of the Mind's Eye, trade paperback 15.00
CBD0131 Splinter of the Mind's Eye, Issue 1 ....4.00
CBD0132 Splinter of the Mind's Eye, Issue 2 ....4.00
CBD0133 Splinter of the Mind's Eye, Issue 3 ....4.00
CBD0134 Splinter of the Mind's Eye, Issue 4 ....5.00
CBD0353 Star Wars Handbook, Vol. 3 Dark Empire 5.00
CBD0340 Star Wars Issue 0, Princess Leia cover 11.00
CBD0388 Star Wars Issue 0, Luke and Leia cover 14.00
CBD0279 Star Wars Tales, Issue 1 ....7.00
CBD0280 Star Wars Tales, Issue 2 ....7.00
CBD0364 Star Wars Tales, Issue 3 ....7.00
CBD0365 Star Wars Tales, Issue 4 ....9.00
CBD0383 Star Wars Tales, Issue 5 ....6.00
CBD0401 Star Wars Tales, Issue 5 photo cover 6.00
CBD0392 Star Wars Tales, Issue 6 ....6.00
CBD0398 Star Wars Tales, Issue 7 ....6.00
CBD0400 Star Wars Tales, Issue 7 photo cover 6.00
CBD0413 Star Wars Tales, Issue 8 ....6.00
CBD0414 Star Wars Tales, Issue 8 photo cover 6.00
CBD0221 Star Wars, Issue 01: Prelude to Rebellion, Issue 1 ....8.00
CBD0222 Star Wars, Issue 02: Prelude to Rebellion, Issue 2 ....3.00
CBD0223 Star Wars, Issue 03: Prelude to Rebellion, Issue 3 ....3.00
CBD0224 Star Wars, Issue 04: Prelude to Rebellion, Issue 4 ....3.00
CBD0225 Star Wars, Issue 05: Prelude to Rebellion, Issue 5 ....3.00
CBD0226 Star Wars, Issue 06: Prelude to Rebellion, Issue 6 ....3.00
CBD0322 Star Wars, Issue 07: Outlander, Issue 1 ....3.00
CBD0323 Star Wars, Issue 08: Outlander, Issue 2 ....3.00
CBD0324 Star Wars, Issue 09: Outlander, Issue 3 ....3.00
CBD0325 Star Wars, Issue 10: Outlander, Issue 4 ....3.00
CBD0326 Star Wars, Issue 11: Outlander, Issue 5 ....3.00
CBD0327 Star Wars, Issue 12: Outlander, Issue 6 ....3.00
CBD0328 Star Wars, Issue 13: Emissaries to Malastare, Issue 1 ....3.00
CBD0329 Star Wars, Issue 14: Emissaries to Malastare, Issue 2 ....3.00
CBD0330 Star Wars, Issue 15: Emissaries to Malastare, Issue 3 ....3.00
CBD0331 Star Wars, Issue 16: Emissaries to Malastare, Issue 4 ....3.00
CBD0332 Star Wars, Issue 17: Emissaries to Malastare, Issue 5 ....3.00
CBD0333 Star Wars, Issue 18: Emissaries to Malastare, Issue 6 ....3.00
CBD0354 Star Wars, Issue 19: Twilight, Issue 1 ....3.00
CBD0355 Star Wars, Issue 20: Twilight, Issue 2 ....3.00
CBD0356 Star Wars, Issue 21: Twilight, Issue 3 ....3.00
CBD0357 Star Wars, Issue 22: Twilight, Issue 4 ....3.00
CBD0384 Star Wars, Issue 23: Infinity's End, Issue 1 ....3.00
CBD0385 Star Wars, Issue 24: Infinity's End, Issue 2 ....3.00
CBD0386 Star Wars, Issue 25: Infinity's End, Issue 3 ....3.00
CBD0387 Star Wars, Issue 26: Infinity's End, Issue 4 ....3.00
CBD0399 Star Wars, Issue 27: Starcrash 3.00

Comic Books: Dark Horse Comics

CBD0120	CBD0121	CBD0122	CBD0123	CBD0124	CBD0126	CBD0127	CBD0128	CBD0129	CBD0130
CBD0135	CBD0131	CBD0132	CBD0133	CBD0134	CBD0353	CBD0340	CBD0388	CBD0279	CBD0280
CBD0364	CBD0365	CBD0383	CBD0401	CBD0392	CBD0398	CBD0400	CBD0413	CBD0221	CBD0222
CBD0223	CBD0224	CBD0225	CBD0226	CBD0322	CBD0324	CBD0325	CBD0326	CBD0327	CBD0328
CBD0329	CBD0330	CBD0331	CBD0332	CBD0333	CBD0354	CBD0355	CBD0356	CBD0357	CBD0384

CBD0294   CBD0295   CBD0296   CBD0297   CBD0335   CBD0231   CBD0177   CBD0393   CBD0394   CBD0395

CBD0396   CBD0408   CBD0303   CBD0304   CBD0306   CBD0275   CBD0276   CBD0277   CBD0278   CBD0375

CBD0376   CBD0180   CBD0178   CBD0218   CBD0219   CBD0181   CBD0182   CBD0183   CBD0184   CBD0185

CBD0186   CBD0187   CBD0188   CBD0189   CBD0190   CBD0191   CBD0192   CBD0193   CBD0194   CBD0195

CBD0196   CBD0197   CBD0198   CBD0199   CBD0200   CBD0201   CBD0202   CBD0203   CBD0204   CBD0205

CBD0206   CBD0207   CBD0208   CBD0209   CBD0210   CBD0211   CBD0212   CBD0213   CBD0214   CBD0215

CBD0216   CBD0341   CBD0217   CBD0345   CBD0348

CBD0205 X-Wing Rogue Squadron, Issue 24: In the Empire's Service, Issue 4 ..4.00
CBD0206 X-Wing Rogue Squadron, Issue 25: The Making of Baron Fel (double-sized) 6.00
CBD0207 X-Wing Rogue Squadron, Issue 26: Family Ties, Issue 1 ....4.00
CBD0208 X-Wing Rogue Squadron, Issue 27: Family Ties, Issue 2 ....4.00
CBD0209 X-Wing Rogue Squadron, Issue 28: Masquerade, Issue 1............4.00
CBD0210 X-Wing Rogue Squadron, Issue 29: Masquerade, Issue 2............4.00

CBD0211 X-Wing Rogue Squadron, Issue 30: Masquerade, Issue 3............4.00
CBD0212 X-Wing Rogue Squadron, Issue 31: Masquerade, Issue 4............4.00
CBD0213 X-Wing Rogue Squadron, Issue 32: Mandatory Retirement, Issue 1...4.00
CBD0214 X-Wing Rogue Squadron, Issue 33: Mandatory Retirement, Issue 2...4.00
CBD0215 X-Wing Rogue Squadron, Issue 34: Mandatory Retirement, Issue 3...4.00
CBD0216 X-Wing Rogue Squadron, Issue 35: Mandatory Retirement, Issue 4...4.00
CBD0217 X-Wing Rogue Squadron: Handbook...4.00

COMIC BOOKS: MARVEL

Marvel Comics
CBM0190 3-Pack, Star Wars Issues 7-9, reprints 19.00
CBM0193 4-Pack, Return of the Jedi Issues 1-4 ....26.00
CBM0118 Droids Issue 1, April 8.00
CBM0119 Droids Issue 2, June 7.00

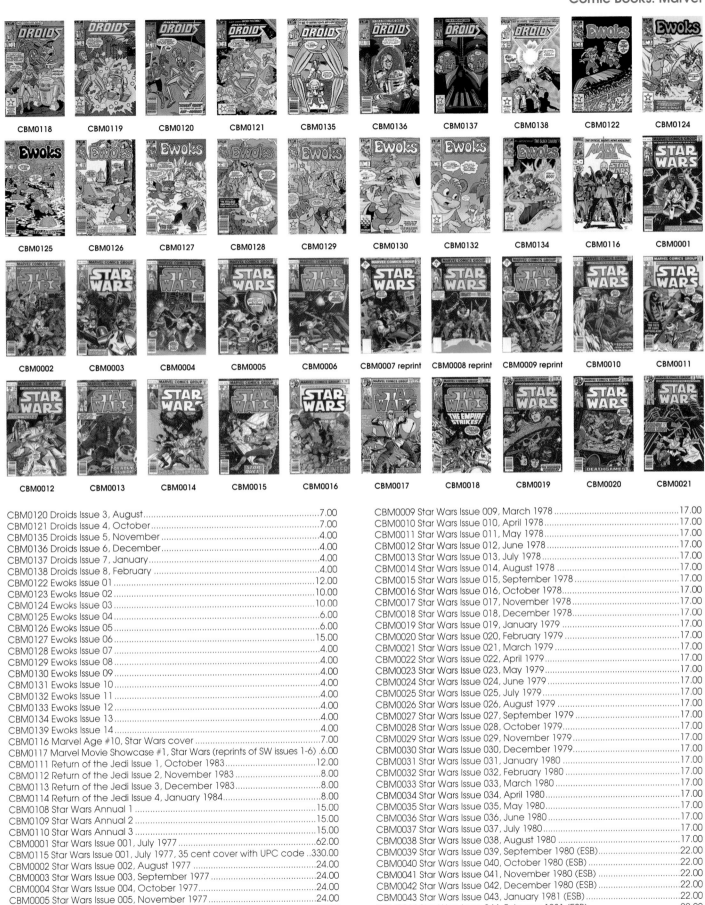

CBM0118   CBM0119   CBM0120   CBM0121   CBM0135   CBM0136   CBM0137   CBM0138   CBM0122   CBM0124

CBM0125   CBM0126   CBM0127   CBM0128   CBM0129   CBM0130   CBM0132   CBM0134   CBM0116   CBM0001

CBM0002   CBM0003   CBM0004   CBM0005   CBM0006   CBM0007 reprint   CBM0008 reprint   CBM0009 reprint   CBM0010   CBM0011

CBM0012   CBM0013   CBM0014   CBM0015   CBM0016   CBM0017   CBM0018   CBM0019   CBM0020   CBM0021

CBM0120 Droids Issue 3, August...7.00
CBM0121 Droids Issue 4, October...7.00
CBM0135 Droids Issue 5, November 4.00
CBM0136 Droids Issue 6, December...4.00
CBM0137 Droids Issue 7, January...4.00
CBM0138 Droids Issue 8, February 4.00
CBM0122 Ewoks Issue 01..12.00
CBM0123 Ewoks Issue 02..10.00
CBM0124 Ewoks Issue 03..10.00
CBM0125 Ewoks Issue 04..6.00
CBM0126 Ewoks Issue 05..6.00
CBM0127 Ewoks Issue 06..15.00
CBM0128 Ewoks Issue 07..4.00
CBM0129 Ewoks Issue 08..4.00
CBM0130 Ewoks Issue 09..4.00
CBM0131 Ewoks Issue 10..4.00
CBM0132 Ewoks Issue 11..4.00
CBM0133 Ewoks Issue 12..4.00
CBM0134 Ewoks Issue 13..4.00
CBM0139 Ewoks Issue 14..4.00
CBM0116 Marvel Age #10, Star Wars cover 7.00
CBM0117 Marvel Movie Showcase #1, Star Wars (reprints of SW issues 1-6) .6.00
CBM0111 Return of the Jedi Issue 1, October 1983....................12.00
CBM0112 Return of the Jedi Issue 2, November 1983 ....8.00
CBM0113 Return of the Jedi Issue 3, December 1983....................8.00
CBM0114 Return of the Jedi Issue 4, January 1984......................8.00
CBM0108 Star Wars Annual 1 ....15.00
CBM0109 Star Wars Annual 2 ....15.00
CBM0110 Star Wars Annual 3 ....15.00
CBM0001 Star Wars Issue 001, July 1977.................................62.00
CBM0115 Star Wars Issue 001, July 1977, 35 cent cover with UPC code ..330.00
CBM0002 Star Wars Issue 002, August 1977.............................24.00
CBM0003 Star Wars Issue 003, September 1977 ....24.00
CBM0004 Star Wars Issue 004, October 1977............................24.00
CBM0005 Star Wars Issue 005, November 1977..........................24.00
CBM0006 Star Wars Issue 006, December 1977..........................24.00
CBM0007 Star Wars Issue 007, January 1978 ....17.00
CBM0008 Star Wars Issue 008, February 1978 ....17.00

CBM0009 Star Wars Issue 009, March 1978 ....17.00
CBM0010 Star Wars Issue 010, April 1978................................17.00
CBM0011 Star Wars Issue 011, May 1978................................17.00
CBM0012 Star Wars Issue 012, June 1978................................17.00
CBM0013 Star Wars Issue 013, July 1978 ....17.00
CBM0014 Star Wars Issue 014, August 1978 ....17.00
CBM0015 Star Wars Issue 015, September 1978 ....17.00
CBM0016 Star Wars Issue 016, October 1978............................17.00
CBM0017 Star Wars Issue 017, November 1978..........................17.00
CBM0018 Star Wars Issue 018, December 1978..........................17.00
CBM0019 Star Wars Issue 019, January 1979 ....17.00
CBM0020 Star Wars Issue 020, February 1979 ....17.00
CBM0021 Star Wars Issue 021, March 1979 ....17.00
CBM0022 Star Wars Issue 022, April 1979................................17.00
CBM0023 Star Wars Issue 023, May 1979................................17.00
CBM0024 Star Wars Issue 024, June 1979................................17.00
CBM0025 Star Wars Issue 025, July 1979 ....17.00
CBM0026 Star Wars Issue 026, August 1979 ....17.00
CBM0027 Star Wars Issue 027, September 1979 ....17.00
CBM0028 Star Wars Issue 028, October 1979............................17.00
CBM0029 Star Wars Issue 029, November 1979..........................17.00
CBM0030 Star Wars Issue 030, December 1979..........................17.00
CBM0031 Star Wars Issue 031, January 1980 ....17.00
CBM0032 Star Wars Issue 032, February 1980 ....17.00
CBM0033 Star Wars Issue 033, March 1980 ....17.00
CBM0034 Star Wars Issue 034, April 1980................................17.00
CBM0035 Star Wars Issue 035, May 1980................................17.00
CBM0036 Star Wars Issue 036, June 1980................................17.00
CBM0037 Star Wars Issue 037, July 1980 ....17.00
CBM0038 Star Wars Issue 038, August 1980 ....17.00
CBM0039 Star Wars Issue 039, September 1980 (ESB)...................22.00
CBM0040 Star Wars Issue 040, October 1980 (ESB) 22.00
CBM0041 Star Wars Issue 041, November 1980 (ESB) 22.00
CBM0042 Star Wars Issue 042, December 1980 (ESB)....................22.00
CBM0043 Star Wars Issue 043, January 1981 (ESB)......................22.00
CBM0044 Star Wars Issue 044, February 1981 (ESB).....................22.00
CBM0045 Star Wars Issue 045, March 1981 ....16.00
CBM0046 Star Wars Issue 046, April 1981................................16.00

CBM0022   CBM0023 reprint   CBM0024   CBM0025   CBM0026   CBM0027   CBM0028   CBM0029   CBM0030   CBM0031

CBM0032   CBM0033   CBM0034   CBM0035   CBM0036   CBM0037   CBM0038   CBM0039   CBM0040   CBM0041

CBM0042   CBM0043   CBM0044   CBM0045   CBM0046   CBM0047   CBM0048   CBM0049   CBM0050   CBM0051

CBM0052   CBM0053   CBM0054   CBM0055   CBM0056   CBM0057   CBM0058   CBM0059   CBM0060   CBM0061

CBM0047 Star Wars Issue 047, May 1981.................................16.00
CBM0048 Star Wars Issue 048, June 1981.................................16.00
CBM0049 Star Wars Issue 049, July 1981.................................16.00
CBM0050 Star Wars Issue 050, August 1981..............................16.00
CBM0051 Star Wars Issue 051, September 1981 ....16.00
CBM0052 Star Wars Issue 052, October 1981.............................16.00
CBM0053 Star Wars Issue 053, November 1981............................16.00
CBM0054 Star Wars Issue 054, December 1981............................16.00
CBM0055 Star Wars Issue 055, January 1982.............................16.00
CBM0056 Star Wars Issue 056, February 1982............................16.00
CBM0057 Star Wars Issue 057, March 1982...............................15.00
CBM0058 Star Wars Issue 058, April 1982...............................16.00
CBM0059 Star Wars Issue 059, May 1982.................................16.00
CBM0060 Star Wars Issue 060, June 1982.................................16.00
CBM0061 Star Wars Issue 061, July 1982.................................16.00
CBM0062 Star Wars Issue 062, August 1982..............................16.00
CBM0063 Star Wars Issue 063, September 1982 ....16.00
CBM0064 Star Wars Issue 064, October 1982.............................16.00
CBM0065 Star Wars Issue 065, November 1982............................16.00
CBM0066 Star Wars Issue 066, December 1982............................16.00
CBM0067 Star Wars Issue 067, January 1983.............................16.00
CBM0068 Star Wars Issue 068, February 1983 (Origin: Boba Fett) 34.00
CBM0069 Star Wars Issue 069, March 1983...............................15.00
CBM0070 Star Wars Issue 070, April 1983...............................15.00
CBM0071 Star Wars Issue 071, May 1983.................................15.00
CBM0072 Star Wars Issue 072, June 1983.................................15.00
CBM0073 Star Wars Issue 073, July 1983.................................15.00
CBM0074 Star Wars Issue 074, August 1983..............................15.00
CBM0075 Star Wars Issue 075, September 1983 ....15.00
CBM0076 Star Wars Issue 076, October 1983.............................15.00
CBM0077 Star Wars Issue 077, November 1983............................15.00
CBM0078 Star Wars Issue 078, December 1983............................15.00
CBM0079 Star Wars Issue 079, January 1984.............................15.00
CBM0080 Star Wars Issue 080, February 1984............................15.00
CBM0081 Star Wars Issue 081, March 1984...............................20.00
CBM0082 Star Wars Issue 082, April 1984...............................20.00
CBM0083 Star Books Issue 083, May 1984................................20.00
CBM0084 Star Wars Issue 084, June 1984.................................20.00

CBM0085 Star Wars Issue 085, July 1984.................................20.00
CBM0086 Star Wars Issue 086, August 1984..............................20.00
CBM0087 Star Wars Issue 087, September 1984 ....20.00
CBM0088 Star Wars Issue 088, October 1984.............................20.00
CBM0089 Star Wars Issue 089, November 1984............................20.00
CBM0090 Star Wars Issue 090, December 1984............................20.00
CBM0091 Star Wars Issue 091, January 1985.............................20.00
CBM0092 Star Wars Issue 092, February 1985............................20.00
CBM0093 Star Wars Issue 093, March 1985...............................20.00
CBM0094 Star Wars Issue 094, April 1985...............................20.00
CBM0095 Star Wars Issue 095, May 1985.................................20.00
CBM0096 Star Wars Issue 096, June 1985.................................20.00
CBM0097 Star Wars Issue 097, July 1985.................................20.00
CBM0098 Star Wars Issue 098, August 1985..............................20.00
CBM0099 Star Wars Issue 099, September 1985 ....20.00
CBM0100 Star Wars Issue 100, October 1985.............................35.00
CBM0101 Star Wars Issue 101, November 1985............................20.00
CBM0102 Star Wars Issue 102, December 1985............................20.00
CBM0103 Star Wars Issue 103, January 1986.............................20.00
CBM0104 Star Wars Issue 104, March 1986...............................20.00
CBM0105 Star Wars Issue 105, May 1987.................................20.00
CBM0106 Star Wars Issue 106, July 1986.................................20.00
CBM0107 Star Wars Issue 107, September 1986...........................58.00
CBM0191 Star Wars Special Edition, 1 of 2 oversized 9.00
CBM0192 Star Wars Special Edition, 2 of 2 oversized 9.00
CBM0198 Star Wars triple comic, any issue 3.50
CBM0199 Star Wars Weekly Issue 001....................................55.00
CBM0200 Star Wars Weekly Issue 002....................................20.00
CBM0201 Star Wars Weekly Issue 003....................................20.00
CBM0202 Star Wars Weekly Issue 004....................................20.00
CBM0203 Star Wars Weekly Issue 005....................................20.00
CBM0204 Star Wars Weekly Issue 006....................................20.00
CBM0205 Star Wars Weekly Issue 007....................................20.00
CBM0206 Star Wars Weekly Issue 008....................................20.00
CBM0207 Star Wars Weekly Issue 009....................................20.00
CBM0208 Star Wars Weekly Issue 010....................................20.00
CBM0209 Star Wars Weekly Issue 011....................................20.00
CBM0210 Star Wars Weekly Issue 012....................................20.00

CBM0062 CBM0063 CBM0064 CBM0065 CBM0066 CBM0067 CBM0068 CBM0069 CBM0070 CBM0071

CBM0072 CBM0111 CBM0112 CBM0113 CBM0114 CBM0073 CBM0074 CBM0075 CBM0076 CBM0077

CBM0078 CBM0079 CBM0080 CBM0081 CBM0082 CBM0083 CBM0084 CBM0085 CBM0086 CBM0087

CBM0088 CBM0089 CBM0090 CBM0091 CBM0092 CBM0093 CBM0094 CBM0095 CBM0096 CBM0097

CBM0098   CBM0099   CBM0100   CBM0101   CBM0102   CBM0103   CBM0104   CBM0105   CBM0106   CBM0107

CBM0199   CBM0200   CBM0201   CBM0202   CBM0204   CBM0205   CBM0206   CBM0207   CBM0211   CBM0213

CBM0224   CBM0227   CBM0228   CBM0230   CBM0231   CBM0233   CBM0237   CBM0242   CBM0244   CBM0245

CBM0248   CBM0249   CBM0250   CBM0251   CBM0253   CBM0255   CBM0256   CBM0271   CBM0276   CBM0279

CBM0285	CBM0291	CBM0292	CBM0293	CBM0294	CBM0295	CBM0296	CBM0298	CBM0299	CBM0300
CBM0303	CBM0304	CBM0305	CBM0307	CBM0308	CBM0309	CBM0312	CBM0313	CBM0314	CBM0315
CBM0316	CBM0317	CBM0326	CBM0332	CBM0333	CBM0334	CBM0336	CBM0337	CBM0339	CBM0348
CBM0356	CBM0358	CBM0362	CBM0364	CBM0193	CBM0198	CBM0108	CBM0109	CBM0110	CBM0365

COMPLETE GALAXY
Kenner

CG0001	CG0002	CG0003	CG0004

CONSTRUCTION PAPER

PPH0001

Stuart Hall
PPH0001 Biker Scout Contruction Paper pad...17.00

CONTAINERS, FIGURAL

AFC0001   AFC0002

Applause
AFC0001 Darth Maul, PVC...18.00
AFC0002 R2-D2, PVC...18.00

COOKIE JARS

CJ0001 front and back   CJ0004

Roman Ceramics
CJ0001 C-3PO...195.00
CJ0004 R2-D2..145.00

Sigma

CJ0002 front and back

CJ0002 Darth Vader and Droids, ceramic 2-sided hexagonal...............125.00

Star Jars

CJ0007   CJ0006   CJ0003   CJ0008

CJ0005 Ben Kenobi 200.00
CJ0007 C-3PO 200.00
CJ0006 Chewbacca..200.00
CJ0009 Jabba the Hutt...275.00
CJ0003 Princess Leia 200.00
CJ0008 Wicket the Ewok...275.00

COOLERS

Bluebird

COO0002   COO0004

COO0004 Cool Bag, Darth Vader art 21.00
COO0002 Cool Bag, Stormtrooper art 18.00

Pepsi Cola

COO0003 side and opened   COO0005   COO0001

COO0003 MMT, holds 10 350ml cans, comes with Battle Droid can
  holders 315.00
COO0005 R2-D2 cooler 425.00
COO0001 R2-D2, approx 2½' tall 75.00

CORK BOARDS

Manton Cork
CK0001 AT-AT, glow-in-dark dome 18.00
CK0002 Boba Fett, Darth Vader, Stormtroopers 26.00

CK0001   CK0015   CK0004   CK0006   CK0009

CK0003   CK0010   CK0020   CK0005

CK0013   CK0016   CK0011

CK0003 C-3PO and R2-D2, 2-piece set 28.00
CK0004 C-3PO and R2-D2, glow-in-dark dome 18.00
CK0005 C-3PO, Chewbacca, Han, Leia, Luke, R2-D2.........24.00
CK0006 Chewbacca, glow-in-dark dome 18.00
CK0007 Darth Vader 24.00
CK0008 Darth Vader and Luke Skywalker Duel 18.00
CK0009 Darth Vader, glow-in-dark dome 18.00
CK0010 Darth Vader, helmet and shoulders.....................24.00
CK0011 Ewok Hut 18.00
CK0012 Jabba the Hutt 18.00
CK0013 Jabba's Palace 18.00
CK0014 Luke on Tauntaun 24.00
CK0015 Luke on Tauntaun, glow-in-dark dome.................18.00
CK0016 Max Rebo Band 18.00
CK0017 Millennium Falcon "May The Force Be With You"...23.00
CK0018 Paploo, Wicket, C-3PO and R2-D2 ....18.00
CK0019 Star Wars logo, Millennium Falcon, Tie Fighters, X-Wing.............22.00
CK0020 Yoda 24.00
CK0021 Yoda, glow-in-dark 25.00
CK0022 Yoda, glow-in-dark dome 18.00

COSTUMES

Acamas
CT0037 C-3PO 28.00
CT0038 Chewbacca 28.00
CT0039 Darth Vader...28.00
CT0040 Gamorrean Guard...28.00
CT0041 Klattu...28.00
CT0042 Luke Skywalker...28.00
CT0043 Princess Leia..28.00
CT0044 Stormtrooper...28.00
CT0045 Wicket..28.00
CT0046 Yoda...28.00

Ben Cooper
CT0002 Admiral Ackbar, Revenge 85.00
CT0001 Admiral Ackbar, ROTJ.....................................26.00
CT0003 Boba Fett, ESB...35.00
CT0004 Boba Fett, ROTJ..35.00
CT0007 C-3PO (Golden Robot)......................................30.00
CT0006 C-3PO (Golden Robot), ESB...............................16.00
CT0005 C-3PO (Golden Robot), SW................................25.00
CT0009 Chewbacca, ESB..20.00
CT0010 Chewbacca, ROTJ..30.00
CT0008 Chewbacca, SW...25.00
CT0066 Chewbacca, SW 3-piece disguise kit...................22.00
CT0012 Gamorrean Guard, Revenge...............................85.00
CT0011 Gamorrean Guard, ROTJ 28.00
CT0014 Klattu, Revenge 85.00
CT0013 Klattu, ROTJ 25.00
CT0016 Lord Darth Vader, ESB......................................20.00
CT0017 Lord Darth Vader, ROTJ....................................30.00
CT0015 Lord Darth Vader, SW.......................................25.00
CT0022 Luke Skywalker (X-Wing Pilot), ESB....................18.00
CT0023 Luke Skywalker (X-Wing Pilot), ROTJ...................30.00
CT0021 Luke Skywalker (X-Wing Pilot), SW.....................20.00
CT0019 Luke Skywalker, ESB..16.00
CT0020 Luke Skywalker, ROTJ......................................30.00
CT0018 Luke Skywalker, SW...25.00
CT0025 Princess Leia, ESB...35.00
CT0026 Princess Leia, ROTJ...30.00
CT0024 Princess Leia, SW..35.00
CT0028 R2-D2, ESB..20.00
CT0029 R2-D2, ROTJ..35.00
CT0027 R2-D2, SW...30.00
CT0031 Stormtrooper, ESB...25.00
CT0032 Stormtrooper, ROTJ...28.00
CT0030 Stormtrooper, SW..23.00

CT0034 Wicket, Revenge..95.00
CT0033 Wicket, ROTJ..30.00
CT0035 Yoda, ESB..35.00
CT0036 Yoda, ROTJ..35.00

Croner Toys
CT0065 Stormtrooper, children's size 35.00

Len Hunter Trading
CT0067 Darth Vader helmet, mask, vest, cape, lightsaber 7.00

Rubies
CT0061 C-3PO children's size 12.00
CT0047 C-3PO, adult...55.00
CT0053 C-3PO, children's deluxe....................................35.00
CT0048 Chewbacca, adult...70.00
CT0054 Chewbacca, children's deluxe..............................35.00
CT0062 Chewbacca, children's size.................................12.00
CT0049 Darth Vader, adult..60.00
CT0055 Darth Vader, children's deluxe.............................35.00
CT0063 Darth Vader, children's size................................12.00
CT0059 Jabba the Hutt, children's deluxe.........................35.00
CT0050 Princess Leia, adult..45.00
CT0056 Princess Leia, children's deluxe...........................25.00
CT0051 Stormtrooper, adult..55.00
CT0057 Stormtrooper, children's deluxe...........................40.00
CT0064 Stormtrooper, children's size...............................12.00
CT0060 Tusken Raider, children's deluxe..........................40.00
CT0052 Yoda, adult...60.00
CT0058 Yoda, children's deluxe.....................................25.00

COSTUMES: ACCESSORIES

CTA0003   CTA0002

Rubies
CTA0003 Anakin Skywalker Neckpiece 4.00
CTA0001 Jedi Braid, Anakin Skywalker's, clip-on................3.00
CTA0002 Jedi Braid, Obi-Wan Kenobi's, clip-on.................3.00
CTA0004 Queen Amidala super deluxe headpiece w/attached wig and
    braids 48.00

COSTUMES: TPM

Rubies
CT10001 Anakin Skywalker actionwear: PVC mask and jumpsuit 25.00
CT10002 Anakin Skywalker deluxe actionwear: PVC helmet, tunic, pants
    with attached boot tops, belt 38.00

CT0003   CT0008   CT0009   CT0022

CT0018   CT0024   CT0027   CT0033   CT0035   CT0065   CT0050   CT0064

CT10003 Anakin Skywalker Jedi Apprentice children's deluxe: tunic, shirt, pants with attached boot tops, printed vinyl belt 40.00

CT10004 Anakin Skywalker Jedi Apprentice children's super deluxe: tunic, shirt, pants with attached boot tops, sash, rubber 3D belt 60.00

CT10005 Anakin Skywalker Jedi Apprentice children's: tunic, pants with attached boot tops 20.00

CT10006 Anakin Skywalker Podrace children's deluxe: PVC headpiece, tunic, pants with attached boot tops, printed vinyl belt 40.00

CT10007 Anakin Skywalker Podrace children's super deluxe: vinyl headpiece, tunic, pants with attached boot tops, belt 60.00

CT10008 Anakin Skywalker Podrace children's: PVC headpiece, tunic, pants with attached boot tops 20.00

CT10009 Darth Maul actionwear deluxe: PVC mask, hooded tunic, pants with attached boot tops, molded 3D rubber belt 38.00

CT10010 Darth Maul actionwear: PVC mask and jumpsuit 25.00

CT10011 Darth Maul adult deluxe: mask, hooded tunic, pants with attached boot tops, rubber 3D belt 50.00

CT10012 Darth Maul adult super deluxe: latex mask, hooded tunic, pants with attached boot tops, sashes, rubber 3D belt 80.00

CT10013 Darth Maul adult: PVC mask, hooded tunic, pants with attached boot tops, belt 25.00

CT10014 Darth Maul children's blister card costume kit: PVC mask, lightsaber, hooded cloak, belt 14.00

CT10015 Darth Maul children's boxed costume kit: PVC mask, lightsaber, hooded cloak, belt 16.00

CT10016 Darth Maul children's deluxe: mask, hooded tunic, pants with attached boot tops, belt 45.00

CT10017 Darth Maul children's super deluxe: vinyl 3/4 mask, hooded tunic, pants with attached boot tops, sashes, rubber 3D belt 75.00

CT10018 Darth Maul children's: PVC mask, hooded tunic, pants with attached boot tops 20.00

CT10019 Jar Jar Binks actionwear: PVC mask and jumpsuit 25.00

CT10020 Jar Jar Binks adult: PVC mask, tunic, pants 30.00

CT10021 Jar Jar Binks children's deluxe: PVC mask, jumpsuit with attached shoe covers 40.00

CT10022 Jar Jar Binks children's: PVC mask, tunic, pants 20.00

CT10023 Jar Jar Binks deluxe actionwear: PVC mask, tunic, pants 38.00

CT10024 Jedi Robe adult 20.00

CT10025 Jedi Robe adult deluxe 30.00

CT10026 Jedi Robe children's 15.00

CT10027 Jedi Robe children's deluxe 25.00

CT10028 Obi-Wan Kenobi actionwear: PVC mask and jumpsuit 25.00

CT10029 Obi-Wan Kenobi adult deluxe: tunic, shirt, pants with attached boot tops, sash, rubber 3D belt 60.00

CT10030 Obi-Wan Kenobi adult: tunic, pants with attached boot tops, belt 35.00

CT10031 Obi-Wan Kenobi children's blister card costume kit: PVC mask, lightsaber, hooded cloak, belt 14.00

CT10032 Obi-Wan Kenobi children's boxed costume kit: PVC mask, lightsaber, hooded cloak, belt 16.00

CT10033 Obi-Wan Kenobi children's deluxe: tunic, shirt, pants with attached boot tops, printed vinyl belt 40.00

CT10034 Obi-Wan Kenobi children's super deluxe: tunic, shirt, pants with attached boot tops, sash, rubber 3D belt 60.00

CT10035 Obi-Wan Kenobi children's: tunic, pants with attached boot tops.20.00

CT10036 Obi-Wan Kenobi deluxe actionwear: tunic, pants with attached boot tops, molded 3D rubber belt 38.00

CT10037 Queen Amidala actionwear: PVC mask and dress 25.00

CT10038 Queen Amidala adult deluxe: PVC headpiece, dress 40.00

CT10039 Queen Amidala adult supreme: headpiece, velvet dress, lights .80.00

CT10040 Queen Amidala adult: PVC headpiece, dress 20.00

CT10041 Queen Amidala children's deluxe: PVC headpiece, dress 35.00

CT10042 Queen Amidala children's super deluxe: headpiece, dress, lights 55.00

CT10043 Queen Amidala children's supreme: headpiece, velvet dress, lights70.00

CT10044 Queen Amidala children's: PVC headpiece, dress 20.00

CT10045 Queen Amidala deluxe actionwear: PVC headpiece, dress, make-up kit 38.00

CT10046 Qui-Gon Jinn actionwear: PVC mask and jumpsuit 25.00

CT10047 Qui-Gon Jinn adult deluxe: tunic, shirt, pants with attached boot tops, sash, rubber 3D belt 60.00

CT10048 Qui-Gon Jinn adult: tunic, pants with attached boot tops, belt..35.00

CT10049 Qui-Gon Jinn children's blister card costume kit: PVC mask, lightsaber, hooded cloak, belt 14.00

CT10050 Qui-Gon Jinn children's boxed costume kit: PVC mask, lightsaber, hooded cloak, belt 16.00

CT10051 Qui-Gon Jinn children's deluxe: tunic, shirt, pants with attached boot tops, printed vinyl belt 40.00

CT10052 Qui-Gon Jinn children's super deluxe: tunic, shirt, pants with attached boot tops, sash, rubber 3D belt 60.00

CT10053 Qui-Gon Jinn children's: tunic, pants with attached boot tops20.00

CT10054 Qui-Gon Jinn deluxe actionwear: tunic, pants with attached boot tops, molded 3D rubber belt 38.00

CRACKERS

CKS0001

CKS0001 TPM, package of 6 ....22.00

CREATURES: ACTION FIGURE, POTF2

Hasbro

P2B0012 Dewback and Sandtrooper, scaled for 12" figures, Toys R Us exclusive..95.00

Kenner

P2B0001 Bantha and Tusken Raider .00 ....47.00

P2B0002 Dewback and Sandtrooper .00..................23.00

P2B0003 Dewback and Sandtrooper .01 ....18.00

P2B0004 Jabba the Hutt and Han Solo .00 ....34.00

P2B0005 Jabba the Hutt and Han Solo .01 ....27.00

P2B0006 Jabba the Hutt and Han Solo .02 ....16.00

P2B0007 Rancor and Luke Skywalker .00 ....50.00

P2B0008 Ronto and Jawa .00 ....19.00

P2B0009 Tauntaun and Han Solo .00..................38.00

P2B0010 Tauntaun and Luke Skywalker .00 ....16.00

P2B0011 Wampa and Luke Skywalker .00 ....27.00

CREATURES: ACTION FIGURE, TPM

Hasbro

P3B0005 Ammo Wagon with Falumpaset 34.00

P3B0008 Captain Tarpals and Kaadu, scaled for 12" figures, Target exclusive..................60.00

P3B0007 Eopie and Qui-Gon Jinn 95.00

P3B0006 Fambaa with Shield Generator and Gungan Warrior, FAO Schwarz exclusive..................85.00

P3B0001 Jabba Glob 14.00

P3B0004 Jabba the Hutt with 2-Headed Announcer (Hex and Rex) 36.00

P3B0002 Kaadu and Jar Jar Binks 17.00

P3B0003 Opee and Qui-Gon Jinn 18.00

CREATURES: ACTION FIGURE, VINTAGE

Kenner

AVB0001 Patrol Dewback, SW pkg..................80.00

AVB0002 Patrol Dewback, ESB pkg...................225.00

AVB0003 Patrol Dewback, loose 12.00

AVB0001

AVB0002

AVB0009

AVB0007

AVB0014

AVB0005

P2B0008

P2B0003

P2B0006

P2B0010

P2B0009

P2B0011

P2B0001

P2B0007

P3B0001

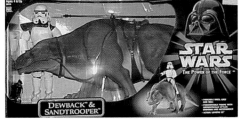

P2B0012

P3B0006

P3B0002

P3B0003

P3B0004

P3B0005

P3B0007

AVB0005 Rancor Monster, ROTJ pkg. 75.00
AVB0006 Rancor Monster, loose 15.00
AVB0007 Tauntaun (Open Belly), ESB pkg. 73.00
AVB0008 Tauntaun (Open Belly), loose 18.00
AVB0009 Tauntaun (Solid Belly), ESB pkg. 77.00
AVB0010 Tauntaun (Solid Belly), loose 22.00
AVB0012 Wampa, ESB pkg. (Box shows Luke in Hoth Gear) 60.00
AVB0014 Wampa, ESB pkg. (Box shows Rebel Commander)...................95.00
AVB0013 Wampa, ROTJ pkg. (Box shows Luke in Hoth Gear)...............42.00
AVB0011 Wampa, loose 15.00

Kenner (UK)
AVB0004 Patrol Dewback, tri-logo pkg. 99.00

Lili Ledy
AVB0016 Rancor Monster, ROTJ pkg. 115.00

Palitoy
AVB0015 Tauntaun (Open Belly), ESB pkg. 135.00

CRYSTALS: CEREAL PREMIUMS

KP0001

KP0002

KP0003

KP0004

KP0005

KP0006

Crystals: Cereal Premiums

Kellogg's
KP0001 Blue - Naboo space battle 5.00
KP0002 Green - Gungan army 5.00
KP0003 Orange - Podrace 5.00
KP0004 Purple - Jedi vs. Sith 5.00
KP0005 Red - Jedi 5.00
KP0006 Yellow - Battle droids 5.00

CUFFLINKS

CLK0001   CLK0004   CLK0002

CLK0003 C-3PO and R2-D2, lenticular 16.00
CLK0001 Darth Maul 31.00
CLK0004 Jar Jar Binks 14.00
CLK0002 R2-D2 ....24.00

CUP TOPPERS

CUT0003   CUT0001   CUT0002   CUT0004

CUT0009   CUT0011   CUT0013   CUT0014   CUT0015

CUT0016   CUT0017   CUT0018   CUT0019   CUT0020

Kentucky Fried Chicken
Episode I figural cup topper with matching cup.
CUT0009 Boss Nass 4.00
CUT0010 Capt. Tarpals 4.00
CUT0011 Queen Amidala 4.00
CUT0012 R2-D2 ....4.00
CUT0003 R2-D2, SW:SE promotion 12.00
CUT0004 Stormtrooper, SW:SE promotion 10.00

Pizza Hut
Episode I figural cup topper with matching cup.
CUT0013 Jar Jar Binks 4.00
CUT0014 Mace Windu 4.00
CUT0015 Nute Gunray 4.00
CUT0016 Yoda 4.00

Taco Bell
Episode I figural cup topper with matching cup.
CUT0020 Anakin Skywalker 4.00

CUT0019 Darth Maul 4.00
CUT0017 Sebulba 4.00
CUT0018 Watto 4.00
CUT0001 C-3PO, SW:SE promotion 11.00
CUT0002 Darth Vader, SW:SE promotion 11.00

CUPS

CU0096   CU0097   CU0091

CU0105   CU0090   CU0098

CU0099   CU0092   CU0089

Applause
CU0096 Anakin Skywalker, figural 6.00
CU0097 C-3PO (TPM), figural 6.00
CU0091 C-3PO, figural 7.00
CU0105 Darth Maul tumbler with no-spill travel lid and handle 12.00
CU0090 Darth Vader, figural 7.00
CU0098 Jar Jar Binks, figural 7.00
CU0099 Queen Amidala, figural 7.00
CU0092 Stormtrooper, figural 7.00
CU0089 Wicket the Ewok, figural 7.00

Coca-Cola

CU0045   CU0046   CU0048   CU0051

CU0045 Ben Kenobi 10.00
CU0046 Boba Fett 10.00
CU0047 C-3PO and R2-D2 ....10.00
CU0048 Chewbacca 10.00
CU0049 Darth Vader and Tarkin 10.00
CU0050 Han Solo 10.00
CU0051 Luke Skywalker and Princess Leia 10.00
CU0052 Tie Fighter vs. X-Wing Fighter 10.00

Coca-Cola / 7-11

CU0055 front and back   CU0056 front and back

CU0057 front and back   CU0059 front and back

CU0060 front and back   CU0063 front and back

CU0053 Admiral Ackbar / Lando Calrissian and Nien Nunb 7.00
CU0054 Admiral Ackbar, Lando, Luke and Droids / Han Solo in Carbonite 8.00
CU0055 Bib Fortuna, Gamorrean Guard, Jabba / Max Rebo 7.00
CU0056 Biker Scouts / Biker Scout and Han Solo 7.00
CU0057 Chewbacca, Han and Leia / C-3PO and R2-D2 ....7.00
CU0058 Chewbacca, Han, Lando, Luke (skiff) / Ben Kenobi and Luke 7.00
CU0059 Darth Vader and Luke Duel / Darth Vader, Emperor 7.00
CU0060 Emperor's Throne Room / Emperor's Royal Guards 7.00
CU0061 Imperial Moff / Imperial Dignitaries 8.00
CU0062 Ishi Tibb, Jawas and Klaatu / Lando Calrissian 7.00
CU0063 Jabba Sail Barge / C-3PO, Ree-Yees and Yak Face 7.00
CU0064 Wicket / Ewok, Wicket, and AT-ST 7.00

Coca-Cola / Frozen Coke / 7-11

CU0040   CU0044   CU0042   CU0041

CU0039   CU0038   CU0043   CU0037

CU0040 1 Han Solo / Chewbacca 8.00
CU0044 2 The Final Chase 8.00
CU0042 3 Tusken Raiders / Jawas 8.00
CU0041 4 Darth Vader 8.00
CU0039 5 R2-D2 / C-3PO 8.00
CU0038 6 Ben (Obi-Wan) Kenobi 8.00
CU0043 7 Luke Skywalker / Princess Leia Organa 8.00
CU0037 8 The Light Sabers 8.00

Coca-Cola / Koolee
CU0017 Battle Above The Death Star 12.00
CU0018 Ben and Darth Vader Duel 12.00
CU0019 Ben Kenobi 12.00
CU0020 C-3PO and R2-D2 ....12.00
CU0021 Chewbacca and Han Solo 12.00
CU0022 Chewbacca, Han and Luke in Disguise 12.00
CU0023 Darth Vader Questions Rebel Soldier 12.00
CU0024 Darth Vader, Leia and Tarkin 12.00
CU0025 Han Solo, Luke, and Princess Leia 12.00
CU0026 Jawas and R2-D2 ....12.00

CU0027 Leia and Luke Swing to Safety 12.00
CU0028 Luke in Falcon Gunwell 12.00
CU0029 Luke Skywalker 12.00
CU0030 Luke Training with Remote 12.00
CU0031 Mos Eisley 12.00
CU0032 Princess Leia 12.00
CU0033 Stormtrooper 12.00
CU0034 Trash Compactor 12.00
CU0035 Tusken Raider Attacks Luke 12.00
CU0036 Tusken Raiders and Bantha 12.00

Deka
CU0088 Return of the Jedi 6 oz., 11 oz., or 17 oz. 9.00
CU0086 Star Wars 6 oz., 11 oz., or 17 oz. 15.00
CU0087 The Empire Strikes Back 6 oz., 11 oz., or 17 oz. 12.00

Hallmark
CU0108 Star Wars: Qui-Gon and Darth Maul, 17 oz. 3.00

Jay Franco and Sons
CU0103 Mos Espa Arena Podracing tumbler, features pit droids 8.00

Kentucky Fried Chicken
CU0106 Character cup, EPI:TPM promotion, any 6.00

Pepperidge Farms

CU0065   CU0066   CU0067   CU0068   CU0069

CU0066 The Creatures 12.00
CU0065 The Endor Forest 8.00
CU0068 The Rebels 12.00
CU0069 The Vehicles 12.00
CU0067 The Villains 12.00

Pepsi Cola

CU0072   CU0073   CU0074   CU0075

CU0072 C-3PO 10.00
CU0077 C-3PO, Taco Bell medium 3.00
CU0073 Darth Vader 10.00
CU0070 Darth Vader, AT-AT, Deathstar SW:SE promotion 6.00
CU0076 Darth Vader, Taco Bell large 3.00
CU0074 R2-D2 ....10.00
CU0078 R2-D2, Taco Bell, small 3.00
CU0114 Star Wars Cantina: FAO Schwarz, Las Vegas 10.00
CU0075 Stormtrooper 10.00
CU0125 TPM: Battle Droid 44 oz. fluted, ridged 4.00
CU0119 TPM: C-3PO 44 oz. fluted, ridged 4.00
CU0126 TPM: C-3PO 44 oz. tapered, smooth 4.00
CU0120 TPM: Darth Sidious 44 oz. tapered, smooth 4.00
CU0121 TPM: Jar Jar Binks 44 oz. tapered, smooth 4.00
CU0122 TPM: Obi-Wan Kenobi 44 oz. fluted, ridged 4.00
CU0127 TPM: Obi-Wan Kenobi 44 oz. tapered, smooth 4.00
CU0128 TPM: Padme 44 oz. fluted, ridged 4.00
CU0123 TPM: Queen Amidala 44 oz. fluted, ridged 4.00
CU0129 TPM: Queen Amidala 44 oz. tapered, smooth 4.00
CU0124 TPM: Sebulba 44 oz. fluted, ridged 4.00
CU0130 TPM: Sebulba 44 oz. tapered, smooth 4.00

Cups

Pizza Hut

| CU0071 | CU0115 | CU0116 | CU0117 |

CU0071 Luke and Darth Vader on Bespin Gantry Take-Out Cup w/lid 4.00
CU0115 C-3PO, SW trilogy 5.00
CU0116 Chewbacca, SW trilogy 5.00
CU0117 Darth Vader, SW trilogy 5.00
CU0118 R2-D2, SW trilogy 5.00

Spearmark Int.
CU0113 Star Wars classic sport tumbler with flip-top lid 12.00

Super Live Adventure
CU0104 R2-D2 cup with coin slot in top; use as bank when emptied......15.00

Taco Bell

| CU0131 | CU0133 | CU0134 | CU0107 |

Special Edition logo with lenticular scenes.
CU0131 Star Wars 7.00
CU0132 A New Hope 7.00
CU0133 Empire Strikes Back 7.00
CU0134 Return of the Jedi 7.00
CU0107 Defeat the Dark Side character cup, any 6.00

Theater Promo 1982

| CU0080 front and back | CU0082 | CU0083 |

Plastics with both Star Wars and Empire Strikes Back artwork.
CU0079 20-oz. Cup 7.00
CU0080 32-oz. Cup 9.00
CU0081 50-oz. Pitcher 14.00

Theater Promo 1983
Plastics with Darth Vader and Luke Dueling, and Jabba's Throne Room.
CU0082 20-oz. Cup 7.00
CU0083 50-oz. Pitcher 17.00

Zak Designs

| CU0102 | CU0095 | CU0093 | CU0100 | CU0101 | CU0094 |

| CU0104 | CU0070 | CU0106 | CU0114 |

| CU0113 | CU0108 | CU0088 | CU0103 |

| CU0111 | CU0112 | CU0109 | CU0110 |

CU0111 Anakin Skywalker / Sebulba sport tumbler with lid.........................7.00
CU0102 Anakin Skywalker Juice cup, blue, 8 oz.....................................7.00
CU0112 Darth Maul sport tumbler with lid 8.00
CU0093 Darth Maul tumbler with no-spill travel lid 11.00
CU0100 Jar Jar Binks tumbler with no-spill travel lid 8.00
CU0095 Pod Race Juice cup, transparent blue, 8 oz. 5.00
CU0109 Podracer half-sculpted sports bottle 8.00
CU0110 Podracer sport tumbler with lid 7.00
CU0101 Qui-Gon Jinn tumbler with no-spill travel lid..................................8.00
CU0094 Space Battle tumbler with no-spill travel lid 10.00

CUPS: PAPER

| PFL0023 front and back | PFL0003 | PFL0004 | PFL0010 |

Coca-Cola
PFL0023 Advertises Kenner Toys with game piece attached, theater promo-
tion 26.00

Coca-Cola / 7-11
PFL0007 Darth Vader 2.00
PFL0008 Stormtrooper 2.00
PFL0009 Yoda 2.00

Deeko
PFL0006 Illustrated Star Wars scenes, pkg. of 8...14.00

Drawing Board
PFL0001 Classic Characters, 8-pack..10.00
PFL0002 Cloud City, 8-pack..10.00
PFL0003 Darth Vader and Luke Duel, 8-pack 10.00
PFL0005 Ewoks Hang-Gliding, 8-pack 8.00

Kentucky Fried Chicken
PFL0011 Boss Nass 16 oz. 2.00
PFL0012 Boss Nass 20 oz. 2.00
PFL0013 Boss Nass 32 oz. 2.00
PFL0014 Jar Jar Binks 16 oz. 2.00
PFL0015 Jar Jar Binks 20 oz. 2.00
PFL0016 Jar Jar Binks 32 oz. 2.00

PFL0017 Jedi 16 oz. 2.00
PFL0018 Jedi 20 oz. 2.00
PFL0019 Jedi 32 oz. 2.00
PFL0020 Queen Amidala 16 oz. 2.00
PFL0021 Queen Amidala 20 oz. 2.00
PFL0022 Queen Amidala 32 oz. 2.00

Party Express
PFL0004 Dogfight over Death Star, 8-pack...........6.00
PFL0010 Qui-Gon Jinn, Obi-Wan Kenobi , Jedi vs. Sith, 8-pack...........4.00

CURTAINS

Bibb Co.
CCR0001 ESB: Boba Fett 22.00
CCR0002 ESB: Boba Fett (J.C. Penney)...........24.00
CCR0003 ESB: Darth's Den...........20.00
CCR0004 ESB: Ice Planet...........16.00
CCR0005 ESB: Lord Vader...........20.00
CCR0006 ESB: Lord Vader's Chamber 20.00
CCR0007 ESB: Spectre...........18.00
CCR0008 ESB: Yoda...........20.00
CCR0009 ROTJ: Jabba the Hutt, Ewoks, etc. 20.00
CCR0010 ROTJ: logos from all 3 films...........18.00
CCR0011 ROTJ: Luke and Darth Vader Duel, AT-ST, etc...........20.00
CCR0012 ROTJ: Star Wars Saga 16.00
CCR0013 SW: Aztec Gold...........16.00
CCR0014 SW: Galaxy 18.00
CCR0015 SW: Jedi Knights 20.00
CCR0016 SW: Lord Vader 20.00
CCR0017 SW: Space Fantasy...........16.00

Westpoint Stevens
CCR0019 Character study drapery with tiebacks...........45.00
CCR0018 EPI: Podracers, valance...........17.00

DANGLERS

Applause

DA0001 DA0002 DA0003 DA0004 DA0005 DA0006

DA0007 DA0008 DA0009 DA0010 DA0011 DA0012 DA0013

DA0007 Anakin's Podracer...........6.00
DA0001 Death Star 7.00
DA0002 Millennium Falcon 7.00
DA0008 Naboo Starfighter...........6.00
DA0009 Sebulba's Podracer 6.00
DA0010 Sith Infiltrator...........6.00
DA0003 Star Destroyer...........7.00
DA0004 Tie Fighter 7.00
DA0011 Trade Federation Droid Fighter...........6.00
DA0012 Trade Federation Tank 6.00
DA0013 Unopened box of 12, EPI 73.00
DA0005 X-Wing Fighter...........7.00
DA0006 Y-Wing Fighter...........7.00

DATEBOOKS

Antioch
PED0003 1996 Star Wars "Book of Days" 14.00

Cedco
PED0001 1996 Wide Image...........12.00
PED0002 1997 Art of Star Wars...........10.00

PED0004 1998 Trilogy Special Edition...........10.00

PED0003   PED0002   PED0004   PED0006

Day Runner
PED0006 2-Year Monthly Planner, Obi-Wan and Qui-Gonn Jinn on cover..6.00

Trielle Corporation
PED0007 1997 Diary, includes early sketches of the characters and ideas...9.00

DECALS

DE0007   DE0002   DE0004

Fan Club
DE0001 Bounty Hunters, 4"x5" 12.00
DE0007 Star Wars cling 8.00
DE0006 Yoda, 4"x5" 10.00

Image Marketing
DE0002 C-3PO and R2-D2...........8.00
DE0003 Darth Vader...........8.00
DE0004 Millennium Falcon under Attack...........8.00
DE0005 Yoda...........8.00

Liquid Blue

DE0008 DE0009 DE0010 DE0011 DE0012 DE0013

DE0014 DE0015 DE0016 DE0017 DE0018 DE0019

Series 1.
DE0008 #1 Queen Amidala 3.00
DE0009 #2 Anakin Skywalker 3.00
DE0010 #3 Jar Jar Binks 3.00
DE0011 #4 Darth Maul 3.00
DE0012 #5 Qui-Gon Jinn 3.00
DE0013 #6 Obi-Wan Kenobi 3.00

Series 2.
DE0014 #1 Jedi vs. Sith 3.00
DE0015 #2 Jedi 3.00
DE0016 #3 Anakin's Podracer 3.00
DE0017 #4 Battle Droid...........3.00
DE0018 #5 Naboo Space Battle...........3.00
DE0019 #6 Federation Droid Fighter 3.00

DESKS

American Toy and Furniture Co.
FUD0001 Ewoks 2-sided desk with benches...........85.00
FUD0002 Return of the Jedi student desk and chair 85.00
FUD0003 Wicket activity desk and bench...........65.00

Desks

FUD0002 FUD0003 FUD0004

Born to Play
FUD0004 Episode I desk and stool 94.00

DESKTOP ORGANIZERS

DTO0001

Impact, Inc.
DTO0001 Trade Federation Tank organizer 18.00

DIARIES

DR0001 DR0002 DR0003 DR0004

Antioch
DR0001 Queen Amidala, inset photo 8.00
DR0005 Queen Amidala, photo framed 8.00

Charles Letts and Co.
DR0002 Star Wars Limited Edition Diary 14.00

Ink Group
DR0003 Episode I 2000 Diary...16.00

Q-Stat
DR0004 Queen Amidala..8.00

DINNERWARE SETS

DID0001 DID0004 DID0005

Deka
DID0001 3-piece children's set, Wicket.................................35.00
DID0002 ROTJ: Baby's First Feeding Set..................................45.00
DID0003 ROTJ: Dinnerware set 35.00

Sigma
DID0004 "The World of Star Wars Fantasy Childset" ceramic, boxed 85.00

Zak Designs
DID0005 EPI: Podracer plate, bowl, tumbler, boxed 12.00

DISCS, GALACTICOS

OQ0001 01 C-3PO 1.00
OQ0002 02 R2-D2..1.00
OQ0003 03 Tusken Raider 1.00

OQ0004 04 Cockpit of the Falcon...1.00
OQ0005 05 Luke with Saber 1.00
OQ0006 06 Darth Vader 1.00
OQ0007 07 Grand Moff Tarkin..1.00
OQ0008 08 Luke in Stormtrooper Gear 1.00
OQ0009 09 Stormtroopers..1.00
OQ0010 10 Obi-Wan 1.00
OQ0011 11 Han Solo 1.00
OQ0012 12 Ties in Death Star Trench.......................................1.00
OQ0013 13 SE Logo in Spanish 1.00
OQ0014 14 Luke...1.00
OQ0015 15 C-3PO 1.00
OQ0016 16 R2-D2...1.00
OQ0017 17 Darth Vader 1.00
OQ0018 18 Painting of Luke and Vader Dueling.......................1.00
OQ0019 19 C-3PO with Luke and Ben 1.00
OQ0020 20 Dewback on Patrol 1.00
OQ0021 21 Han and Leia 1.00
OQ0022 22 Darth Vader Set Against Stars.................................1.00
OQ0023 23 Chasing Vader's Tie 1.00
OQ0024 24 Leia..1.00
OQ0025 25 Luke and R2 on Dagobah......................................1.00
OQ0026 26 AT-ATs..1.00
OQ0027 27 Leia and Lando 1.00
OQ0028 28 Lando and Frozen Han 1.00
OQ0029 29 Luke and Yoda 1.00
OQ0030 30 Darth Vader 1.00
OQ0031 31 Luke Enters the Cave 1.00
OQ0032 32 Chewbacca 1.00
OQ0033 33 Yoda...1.00
OQ0034 34 Luke Exits Snowspeeder 1.00
OQ0035 35 Jabba 1.00
OQ0036 36 Droids Approach the Palace....................................1.00
OQ0037 37 Jabba 1.00
OQ0038 38 Leia..1.00
OQ0039 39 Han and Chewbacca 1.00
OQ0040 40 Han Captured by Ewoks 1.00
OQ0041 41 Wicket..1.00
OQ0042 42 Vader and Luke 1.00
OQ0043 43 Scout Bike Trooper...1.00
OQ0044 44 Luke and Leia Prepare to Swing...............................1.00
OQ0045 45 The Emperor 1.00
OQ0046 46 The Falcon..1.00
OQ0047 47 Vader..1.00
OQ0048 48 Chewbacca 1.00
OQ0049 49 No Description Available..1.00
OQ0050 50 B-Wings 1.00

DISPENSERS: CANDY

DSP0001 DSP0002

Cap Candy
DSP0002 Naboo Fighter, includes display stand and Skittles.....................8.00
DSP0001 R2-D2, includes M and M's candies 8.00

DISPENSERS: SOAP / LOTION

DSQ0001 DSQ0002

Jay Franco and Sons
DSQ0001 Darth Maul 16.00
DSQ0002 Jar Jar Binks 14.00

DISPLAY STANDS: ACTION FIGURE, VINTAGE

AVA2005

AVA2004

Kenner
AVA2001 Display Arena, Mailer packaging 230.00
AVA2004 Display Stand, SW pkg. 225.00
AVA2002 Display Stand, ESB pkg. 135.00
AVA2005 Display Stand, Mail-in Premium, Mailer packaging 85.00
AVA2003 Display Stand, loose 34.00

DOG TAGS

DT0001 front and back

Applause
DT0001 Darth Maul 7.00
DT0002 Droid Starfighter 7.00
DT0003 Naboo Starfighter 7.00
DT0004 Obi-Wan Kenobi 7.00

DOODLE KITS

DOD0001   DOD0002   DOD0003   DOD0004   DOD0005

Trends International Corp.
DOD0001 3-D Doodle Kit..6.00
DOD0002 Doodle Bag, 6 Posters, and 6 Colored Pens, Bonus 10-Pen Pack
   Shown 8.00
DOD0003 Doodle Clings with 6 Markers 8.00
DOD0004 Jar Jar Binks Velvet Doodle 11"x15" plus 6 color pens.......7.00
DOD0005 Podrace doodle poster, six markers, bonus magnet, bonus full-
   color movie poster 14.00

DOORKNOB HANGERS

DH0005

Antioch
DH0001 C-3PO / Do Not Disturb..4.00
DH0002 Darth Vader / Do Not Disturb.......................................4.00

Scholastic
DH0003 Endor Rebel Heroes / This Room is Protected By The Force 1.00
DH0005 Endor Rebel Heroes and Jabba the Hut sheet of 4 doorknob hang-
   ers 4.00
DH0004 Jabba the Hutt / Please Knock Before Entering My Galaxy 1.00

DRAPES

Black Falcon
D0001 Empire Strikes Back, pleated top 10.00
D0002 Return of the Jedi, pleated top 15.00
D0004 EPI Naboo space battle scenes......................................18.00
D0003 Star Wars, pleated top 18.00

DRAWING INSTRUMENTS

Helix
SUA0001 C-3PO and R2-D2 illustration on tin containing drawing instruments 46.00

DUFFEL BAGS
Adam Joseph Industries
LD0001 C-3PO and R2-D2 ....18.00
LD0002 Darth Vader 18.00
LD0003 Millennium Falcon 18.00
LD0004 Wicket the Ewok 18.00
LD0005 Yoda 18.00

LD0006

Pyrazmid
LD0007 Boba Fett..12.00
LD0006 Jedi vs. Sith 12.00

DUST COVERS
World Wide Licenses Ltd.
DC0001 Darth Maul, for monitor and keyboard..................16.00

DC0001

DVDS

20th Century Fox

DVD0001 front and back   DVD0002 front and back

DVD0003 front and back   DVD0004

DVD0001 Episode 4: The New Hope...59.00
DVD0002 Episode 5: The Empire Strikes Back 59.00
DVD0003 Episode 6: Return of the Jedi....................................59.00
DVD0004 The Phantom Menace..45.00

EARMUFFS

Rayman/Ridless Products Group
AA0001 ROTJ Earmuffs 36.00

Earrings

EARRINGS

JER0004   JER0006   JER0008   JER0009

Factors, Etc.
JER0001 C-3PO 12.00
JER0002 C-3PO, clip-on 16.00
JER0003 Chewbacca 12.00
JER0004 Darth Vader 12.00
JER0005 Darth Vader, clip-on 16.00
JER0006 R2-D2 ....12.00
JER0007 R2-D2, clip-on 16.00
JER0008 Stormtrooper 12.00
JER0010 Stormtrooper, clip-on 12.00
JER0009 X-Wing 16.00
JER0011 X-Wing, clip-on 16.00

ELECTRONIC GAMES

NE0004

NE0002 boxed and opened   NE0009

Kenner
NE0002 Electronic Battle Command 55.00
NE0004 Laser Battle 45.00
NE0009 X-Wing Aces Target Game 690.00

Micro Games of America

NE0001   NE0003   NE0005

NE0028   NE0027   NE0025   NE0018   NE0007

NE0027 Empire Strikes Back Electronic LCD Game 26.00
NE0003 Empire Strikes Back hand-held game 25.00
NE0025 Return of the Jedi Electronic LCD Game......................26.00
NE0005 Return of the Jedi hand-held game 25.00
NE0018 Shakin' Pinball 35.00
NE0028 Star Wars Electronic LCD Game 26.00
NE0006 Star Wars Game Wizard 2-in-1 ....15.00
NE0007 Star Wars Game Wizard 3-in-1 ....17.00
NE0001 Star Wars hand-held game 25.00

Palitoy
NE0010 Destroy Death Star 135.00

NE0010

Tiger Electronics

NE0026   NE0013   NE0011   NE0016   NE0017

NE0021   NE0022   NE0023   NE0015   NE0014   NE0020

NE0011 Death Star Escape 12.00
NE0026 Galactic Laser Pinball 63.00
NE0012 Imperial Assault w/Darth Vader joystick 12.00
NE0022 Jedi Adventure R-Zone headgear Game 18.00
NE0014 Millennium Falcon Challenge LCD game....................16.00
NE0021 Millennium Falcon Challenge R-Zone headgear Game 18.00
NE0017 Millennium Falcon "Sounds of the Force" 18.00
NE0013 Quiz Whiz 11.00
NE0016 R2-D2 Ditto Droid 14.00
NE0015 Rebel Forces Laser Game 26.00

R-Zone cartridges.
NE0024 Imperial Assault 8.00
NE0019 Jedi Adventure..8.00
NE0020 Millennium Falcon Challenge............................8.00
NE0023 Rebel Forces 8.00

ELECTRONIC GAMES, TPM

NE10018   NE10017   NE10010   NE10012   NE10004

NE10005   NE10006   NE10007   NE10011   NE10003

NE10001   NE10009   NE10015   NE10013   NE10014

NE10002   NE10020   NE10008   NE10016

Hasbro
NE10018 Ask The Force, over 50 Star Wars phrases 12.00
NE10021 Sith Droid Attack Game 22.00

Thinkway
NE10017 Dancing Jar Jar Binks..18.00

Tiger Electronics
NE10010 Battle of Naboo game with Capt. Tarples and Battle Droid joysticks..12.00

NE10012 Battle Tank Attack game 14.00
NE10004 Destroyer Droid game 30.00
NE10005 Droid Fighter Attack keychain game 9.00
NE10006 Gian Speeder Chase keychain game 7.00
NE10007 Gungan Sub Escape keychain game 7.00
NE10011 Jedi Hunt game with Darth Maul and Qui-Gon Jinn joysticks...12.00
NE10003 Lightsaber Duel game 24.00
NE10001 Lightsaber Duel pen game 9.00
NE10016 Naboo Defence game 21.00
NE10009 Naboo Escape game 12.00
NE10015 Naboo Fighter game with exclusive Anakin Pilot figure (figure on right of card) 29.00
NE10019 Naboo Fighter game with exclusive Anakin Pilot figure (figure on center of card) 36.00
NE10013 Podrace Challenge game 15.00
NE10014 Podrace game 24.00
NE10002 Sith Infiltrator pen game 9.00
NE10020 Sith Speeder game with Darth Maul action figure 30.00
NE10008 Underwater Race to Theed game 16.00

ERASERS

| SUE0001 | SUE0002 | SUE0003 | SUE0005 | SUE0006 | SUE0007 | SUE0008 |

| SUE0009 | SUE0010 | SUE0011 | SUE0012 | SUE0013 | SUE0004 | SUE0014 |

Butterfly Originals
SUE0001 Admiral Ackbar 7.00
SUE0002 Baby Ewok 7.00
SUE0003 Bib Fortuna 7.00
SUE0014 C-3PO, Darth Vader, Millennium Falcon, 3-pack ...15.00
SUE0004 C-3PO, Darth Vader, Millennium Falcon, 3-pack glow-in-dark....9.00
SUE0005 Darth Vader 7.00
SUE0006 Emperor's Royal Guard 7.00
SUE0013 Emperor's Royal Guard, flat rectangular with decal.......10.00
SUE0007 Gamorrean Guard 7.00
SUE0043 Gamorrean Guard, Jabba, Speederbike Trooper 18.00
SUE0008 Jabba the Hutt 7.00
SUE0009 Max Rebo 7.00
SUE0010 R2-D2 ....7.00
SUE0011 Wicket the Ewok 7.00
SUE0012 Yoda 7.00

HC Ford

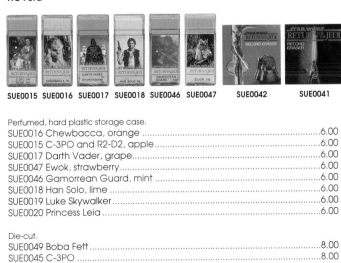

| SUE0015 | SUE0016 | SUE0017 | SUE0018 | SUE0046 | SUE0047 | SUE0042 | SUE0041 |

Perfumed, hard plastic storage case.
SUE0016 Chewbacca, orange 6.00
SUE0015 C-3PO and R2-D2, apple 6.00
SUE0017 Darth Vader, grape 6.00
SUE0047 Ewok, strawberry 6.00
SUE0046 Gamorrean Guard, mint 6.00
SUE0018 Han Solo, lime 6.00
SUE0019 Luke Skywalker 6.00
SUE0020 Princess Leia 6.00

Die-cut.
SUE0049 Boba Fett 8.00
SUE0045 C-3PO 8.00

SUE0048 Gamorrean Guard 8.00
SUE0044 R2-D2 ....8.00
SUE0050 Wicket the Ewok 8.00

Record erasers.
SUE0042 Luke and Vader on Bespin gantry............................8.00
SUE0041 ROTJ movie poster art 8.00

Impact, Inc.

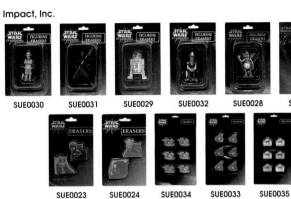

| SUE0030 | SUE0031 | SUE0029 | SUE0032 | SUE0028 | SUE0027 |

| SUE0023 | SUE0024 | SUE0034 | SUE0033 | SUE0035 |

| SUE0026 | SUE0025 | SUE0022 | SUE0021 |

SUE0023 2-Pack flat: Anakin Skywalker and Jar Jar Binks 4.00
SUE0024 2-Pack flat: Darth Maul and Qui-Gon Jinn 4.00
SUE0026 3-Pack figurine: Anakin, R2-D2, Jar Jar Binks 8.00
SUE0025 3-Pack figurine: Watto, Darth Maul, Sebulba 8.00
SUE0035 6-Pack flat mini Anakin in Podracer 4.00
SUE0034 6-Pack flat mini Jedi vs. Sith 4.00
SUE0033 6-Pack flat mini Space Battle 4.00
SUE0030 Anakin figurine 5.00
SUE0031 Darth Maul figurine 6.00
SUE0027 Lightsaber 5.00
SUE0022 Naboo Fighter 2.50
SUE0029 R2-D2 figurine 5.00
SUE0032 Sebulba figurine 6.00
SUE0021 Trade Federation Droid Fighter 2.50
SUE0028 Watto figurine 5.00

Q-Stat

| SUE0036 | SUE0037 | SUE0038 | SUE0039 | SUE0040 |

SUE0036 Obi-Wan eraser with Darth Maul pencil sharpener on card........7.00
SUE0037 Artoo-Detoo, sculpted bust 4.00
SUE0051 C-3PO on Death Star card 6.00
SUE0038 C-3PO, sculpted bust 4.00
SUE0052 Darth Vader on Death Star card 6.00
SUE0039 Darth Vader, sculpted bust 4.00
SUE0053 R2-D2 on Death Star card 6.00
SUE0040 Stormtrooper, sculpted bust 4.00

EWOK PRESCHOOL TOYS

| TYO0002 | TYO0003 | TYO0004 |

Ewok Preschool Toys

TYO0005 front/back   TYO0006   TYO0007

Kenner
Ewok preschool toys.
TYO0002 Family Hut	85.00
TYO0003 Fire Cart	63.00
TYO0004 Music Box Radio	22.00
TYO0005 Talking Telephone	45.00
TYO0006 Teaching Clock	75.00
TYO0001 The Ewok Family	34.00
TYO0007 Woodland Wagon	66.00

FIGURE MAKERS

FGM0002   FGM0003   FGM0001   FGM0004   FGM0005

Kenner
FGM0001 Droids	6.00
FGM0004 Jedi	6.00
FGM0002 Millennium Falcon	10.00
FGM0003 Slave I	10.00
FGM0005 Space Creatures	6.00

Supercast

FGM0006   FGM0007   FGM0008

FGM0008 Badge and Magnet figure molding set	27.00
FGM0006 Heroes 3D plaster molding set	24.00
FGM0007 Villains 3D plaster molding set	24.00

FIGURES: 12"

TF0001

Hot Toys
TF0001 George Lucas likeness, limited to 500	79.00

FIGURES: 12" POTF2

P210077   P210079   P210080   P210072   P210078

P210074   P210075

Hasbro
P210077 1999 Portrait Edition, 1 of 3, Princess Leia, Ceremonial Gown	35.00
P210079 Chewbacca (molded)	20.00
P210080 Han Solo (Endor) with magnetic detonators	39.00
P210072 Luke Skywalker (Stormtrooper disguise)	24.00
P210074 Obi-Wan Kenobi with glow-in-the-dark lightsaber	30.00
P210075 Ponda Baba with Removable Arm	36.00
P210078 Princess Leia as Jabba's Prisoner	22.00

Kenner
P210066 2-Pack C-3PO and R2-D2 electronic	54.00
P210068 2-Pack Death Star Gunner and Grand Moff Tarkin, FAO Schwarz exclusive, ltd. to 15,000	95.00
P210063 2-Pack Emperor Palpatine and Emperor's Royal Guard, Target exclusive	45.00
P210024 2-Pack Han Solo and Luke Skywalker in Stormtrooper Disguises, KB Toys exclusive, limited to 20,000	140.00
P210029 2-Pack Luke and Bib Fortuna w/gloves, FAO Schwarz exclusive	115.00
P210069 2-Pack Luke and Bib Fortuna w/o gloves, FAO Schwarz exclusive	160.00
P210030 2-Pack Luke and Wampa, Target exclusive	59.00
P210061 2-Pack Princess Leia as Jabba's Prisoner and Bartender R2-D2, FAO Schwarz exclusive	95.00
P210067 2-Pack Wedge Antilles and Biggs Darklighter, FAO Schwarz exclusive	82.00
P210060 3-Pack Luke Skywalker, Princess Leia as Boushh, Han Solo in Bespin Outfit, KB Toys exclusive	120.00
P210004 4-Pack Luke Skywalker (Hoth), Han Solo (Hoth), Snowtrooper, AT-AT Driver	95.00
P210001 Admiral Ackbar	24.00
P210003 AT-AT Driver	28.00
P210002 AT-AT Driver, Service Merchandise exclusive	65.00
P210062 Barquin D'an	28.00
P210005 Boba Fett	74.00
P210064 Boba Fett 14", Electronic, KB Toys exclusive	65.00
P210006 C-3PO	25.00
P210007 Cantina Band Alien	24.00
P210008 Chewbacca	84.00
P210009 Chewbacca (Boushh's Bounty)	55.00
P210013 Darth Vader, 14" Electronic	40.00
P210010 Darth Vader, dark blue card, black lightsaber handle	46.00
P210012 Darth Vader, light blue card, black and silver lightsaber handle	26.00
P210011 Darth Vader, light blue card, black lightsaber handle	33.00
P210014 Doikk N'ats, Wal-Mart exclusive	30.00
P210015 Emperor Palpatine	24.00
P210016 Figrin D'an, Wal-Mart exclusive	30.00
P210018 Grand Moff Tarkin with Interrogation Droid	32.00
P210020 Greedo	22.00

P210066   P210068   P210063

P210024   P210029   P210004

P210069   P210030   P210061   P210067   P210060   P210001   P210003

P210002   P210062   P210005   P210064   P210006   P210008   P210009   P210013   P210010   P210014

P210015   P210016   P210018   P210020   P210019   P210023   P210025   P210065   P210071

P210021   P210026   P210028   P210035   P210036   P210037   P210038   P210039   P210073   P210031

P210040   P210041   P210045   P210059   P210049   P210048   P210050   P210051   P210052   P210053

P210054   P210056   P210027   P210046   P210047   P210057   P210058

Figures: 12" POTF2

P210045 Princess Leia 57.00
P210059 Princess Leia in Hoth Gear, Service Merchandise exclusive 34.00
P210046 R2-D2, 6" 24.00
P210047 R5-D4, 6" 27.00
P210049 Sandtrooper with Imperial Droid 24.00
P210048 Sandtrooper, Diamond exclusive 55.00
P210050 Snowtrooper...34.00
P210051 Stormtrooper 45.00
P210052 Tech, Wal-Mart exclusive 30.00
P210053 Tech, Wal-Mart exclusive 30.00
P210054 Tie Fighter Pilot 28.00
P210055 Tusken Raider with Blaster and Macrobinoculars.....................34.00
P210056 Tusken Raider with Gaderffii Stick...........................38.00
P210057 Wicket, 6", Wal-Mart exclusive 20.00
P210058 Yoda, 6" 28.00

FIGURES: 12" POTJ

P430001

P430005

P430006

P430002

P430003

P430010

P430011

P430012

P430004

Hasbro
P430001 2-Pack Sith Lords, Darth Vader and Darth Maul 65.00
P430002 4-LOM...34.00
P430003 Bossk with blaster rifle 34.00
P430005 Captain Tarpals and Kaadu, Target exclusive 75.00
P430010 Death Star Droid 34.00
P430011 Death Star Trooper 34.00
P430012 Han Solo in Stormtrooper Disguise 34.00
P430004 IG-88...34.00

P430006 Luke Skywalker, 100th Figure 67.00

FIGURES: 12" TPM

Hasbro
P320002 1999 Portrait Edition, 2 of 3, Queen Amidala, Black Travel Gown .65.00
P320003 1999 Portrait Edition, 3 of 3, Queen Amidala, Red Senate Gown .65.00
P320018 2000 Portrait Edition, 1 of 4, Queen Amidala, Return to Naboo ..100.00
P320028 2000 Portrait Edition, 2 of 4, 2-pack Qui-Gon Jinn and Queen Amidala, Defense of Naboo 135.00
P320026 2-Pack Chancellor Valorum and Senate Guard, Fan Club exclusive 95.00
P320005 Anakin Skywalker..15.00
P320030 Anakin Skywalker, podracer pilot 38.00
P320006 Battle Droid 20.00
P320023 Battle Droid Commander 22.00
P320029 Beautiful Braids Padme 26.00
P320031 Boss Nass..36.00
P320025 C-3PO, electronic 28.00
P320007 Darth Maul...42.00
P320027 Darth Maul with Sith Speeder 45.00
P320008 Darth Maul, Electronic 35.00
P320009 Jar Jar Binks...30.00
P320010 Jar Jar Binks, Electronic 28.00
P320021 Mace Windu..38.00
P320011 Obi-Wan Kenobi..30.00
P320012 Pit Droids 18.00
P320001 Queen Amidala Hidden Majesty fashion doll...............12.00
P320017 Queen Amidala Royal Elegance fashion Doll 15.00
P320004 Queen Amidala Ultimate Hair fashion Doll................15.00
P320013 Qui-Gon Jinn..34.00
P320014 Qui-Gon Jinn, Electronic 28.00
P320022 Qui-Gon Jinn, Tatooine Poncho 30.00
P320015 R2-A6 ....24.00
P320032 Sebulba 30.00
P320020 TC-14, electronic, KayBee exclusive 28.00
P320016 Watto 18.00

Robert Tonner
P320019 Queen Amidala Trunk Set, FAO Schwarz exclusive, limited to 200..1,475.00

FIGURES: 12" VINTAGE

Kenner
AV10004 Ben Kenobi..375.00
AV10005 Ben Kenobi, loose 180.00
AV10002 Boba Fett, ESB pkg. 625.00

P320002

P320003

P320018

P320028

P320026

P320027

P320030

P320006

P320023

P320029

P320031

P320025

P320007

P320008

P320009

P320010

P320021

P320011

P320001

P320017

P320004

P320013   P320014

P320022   P320032   P320020

P320016

P320005

P320012

P320015

AV10003 Boba Fett, loose...195.00
AV10001 Boba Fett, SW pkg...570.00
AV10006 C-3PO...190.00
AV10007 C-3PO, loose..63.00
AV10008 Chewbacca...215.00
AV10009 Chewbacca, loose..59.00
AV10010 Darth Vader..270.00
AV10011 Darth Vader, loose..95.00
AV10012 Han Solo..555.00
AV10013 Han Solo, loose..275.00
AV10014 IG-88...740.00
AV10015 IG-88, loose..205.00
AV10016 Jawa...265.00
AV10017 Jawa, loose...96.00
AV10018 Leia Organa...390.00
AV10019 Leia Organa, loose...155.00
AV10020 Luke Skywalker..400.00
AV10021 Luke Skywalker, loose...175.00
AV10022 R2-D2..165.00
AV10023 R2-D2, loose..60.00
AV10024 Stormtrooper..345.00
AV10025 Stormtrooper, loose...115.00

Lili Ledy

AV10004   AV10001   AV10010   AV10012

AV10014   AV10018   AV10020   AV10024

AV10027 Darth Vader 1,050.00
AV10026 Han Solo 980.00
AV10032 Jawa 950.00
AV10028 Luke Skywalker 1,050.00
AV10030 Princess Leia 1,050.00
AV10031 R2-D2 ....1,000.00
AV10029 Tusken Raider 1,140.00

FIGURES: CERAMIC

CLF001   CLF002   CLF003   CLF004   CLF005   CLF007   CLF008

CLF009   CLF010   CLF011   CLF012   CLF013   CLF014

Sigma
CLF0001 Bib Fortuna 28.00
CLF0002 Boba Fett...55.00
CLF0003 C-3PO and R2-D2 ....45.00
CLF0004 Darth Vader 45.00
CLF0005 Emperor Palpatine 38.00
CLF0007 Gamorrean Guard...35.00

CLF0008 Han Solo 40.00
CLF0009 Jabba the Hutt 27.00
CLF0010 Klaatu 28.00
CLF0011 Lando Calrissian 35.00
CLF0012 Luke Skywalker...40.00
CLF0013 Princess Leia Boushh Disguise 35.00
CLF0014 Wicket the Ewok 40.00

FIGURES: EPIC FORCE

ZPF0010   ZPF0007   ZPF0002   ZPF0006

ZPF0008   ZPF0003   ZPF0009   ZPF0001   ZPF0004   ZPF0005

Kenner
ZPF0010 3-Pack: Ben Kenobi, Chewbacca, Han Solo, FAO Schwarz exclu-
    sive..90.00
ZPF0007 Ben Kenobi, FAO Schwarz exclusive....................25.00
ZPF0002 Boba Fett..24.00
ZPF0006 C-3PO..17.00
ZPF0008 Chewbacca, FAO Schwarz exclusive 25.00
ZPF0003 Darth Vader..17.00
ZPF0009 Han Solo, FAO Schwarz exclusive 25.00
ZPF0001 Luke Skywalker, Bespin fatigues 17.00
ZPF0004 Princess Leia 18.00
ZPF0005 Stormtrooper..17.00

FIGURES: EPIC FORCE, TPM

P3F0002   P3F0003   P3F0004

Hasbro
P3F0002 Darth Maul...25.00
P3F0003 Obi-Wan Kenobi 25.00
P3F0004 Qui-Gon Jinn 30.00

FIGURES: MEGA ACTION, POTJ

PJF0001   PJF0002   PJF0003

Hasbro
PJF0001 Darth Maul 11.00
PJF0003 Destroyer Droid..16.00
PJF0002 Obi-Wan Kenobi 11.00

Figures: Mega Action, POTJ

TYF003 TYF004 TYF005 TYF006 TYF007 TYF008 TYF009 TYF010 TYF011 TYF0024 TYF012 TYF013 TYF014

TYF015 TYF016 TYF017 TYF018 TYF019 TYF020 TYF021 TYF022 TYF023 TYF0032 TYF0033 TYF0034

FIGURES: MINI

Applause
TYF0046 5-Pack..16.00
TYF0001 5-Pack with bonus 6th figure, Blockbuster exclusive...................23.00
TYF0002 6-Pack with display base..................................26.00
TYF0048 7-Pack, includes exclusive Boba Fett 24.00
TYF0003 Admiral Ackbar 4.00
TYF0004 Boba Fett 4.00
TYF0005 Bosk 4.00
TYF0006 C-3PO 4.00
TYF0047 C-3PO and R2-D2 on platform.................................6.00
TYF0007 Chewbacca 4.00
TYF0008 Darth Vader 4.00
TYF0009 Emperor Palpatine 4.00
TYF0010 Greedo 4.00
TYF0011 Han Solo 4.00
TYF0024 Han Solo and Jabba the Hutt.................................7.00
TYF0012 Lando Calrissian 4.00
TYF0013 Luke Skywalker..4.00
TYF0014 Obi-Wan Kenobi..4.00
TYF0015 Obi-Wan Kenobi, spirit 4.00
TYF0016 Princess Leia 4.00
TYF0017 R2-D2 ....4.00
TYF0032 Read-Along Playpack ANH: C-3PO, R2-D2, Stormtrooper 14.00
TYF0033 Read-Along Playpack ESB: Boba Fett, Chewbacca, Han Solo .14.00
TYF0034 Read-Along Playpack ROTJ: Emperor, Luke Skywalker, Princess Leia 14.00
TYF0018 Snowtrooper 4.00
TYF0019 Stormtrooper 4.00
TYF0020 Tie Fighter Pilot 4.00
TYF0021 Tusken Raider 4.00
TYF0022 Wedge Antillies 4.00
TYF0023 Yoda 4.00

Comics Spain
TYF0026 C-3PO 12.00
TYF0029 Ewok carrying spear 10.00
TYF0027 Ewok wearing hat with green feather 10.00
TYF0028 Ewok wearing hat with pink feather 10.00
TYF0030 Ewok with horn 10.00
TYF0031 Kez-Iban 10.00
TYF0025 R2-D2 ....12.00

Disney / MGM

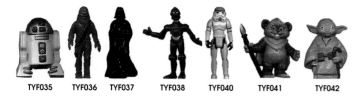

TYF035 TYF036 TYF037 TYF038 TYF040 TYF041 TYF042

TYF0035 Artoo Detoo 8.00
TYF0036 Chewbacca 8.00
TYF0037 Darth Vader 8.00
TYF0038 See Threepio 8.00
TYF0039 Stormtrooper 8.00
TYF0040 Stormtrooper, gray dome 10.00
TYF0041 Wicket the Ewok 8.00
TYF0042 Yoda 8.00

Makura

TYF0043   TYF0044   TYF0045   TYF0049

TYF0043 Darth Vader's Tie Fighter, rubber 9.00
TYF0049 Millennium Falcon, rubber 9.00
TYF0044 X-Wing Fighter, rubber 9.00
TYF0045 Y-Wing Fighter, rubber 9.00

FIGURES: MINI, TPM

Applause

TYG0010   TYG0001   TYG0002   TYG0003   TYG0004

TYG0005   TYG0007   TYG0008   TYG0006

TYG0009 4-Pack: Anakin Skywalker, Destroyer Droid, Jar Jar Binks, Queen Amidala..12.00
TYG0010 4-Pack: Darth Maul, Obi-Wan Kenobi, Qui-Gon Jinn, battle droid ground commander.....................................12.00
TYG0005 Anakin Skywalker (Tatooine) 3.00
TYG0008 Darth Maul...5.00
TYG0001 Destroyer Droid 4.00
TYG0003 Jar Jar Binks..4.00
TYG0006 Obi-Wan..5.00
TYG0002 Pit Droid..4.00
TYG0004 Queen Amidala (Naboo) 3.00
TYG0007 Qui-Gon 5.00

Tomy

TYG021   TYG022   TYG023   TYG024   TYG025

TYG026   TYG027   TYG028   TYG029   TYG030

TYG0027 Anakin and Sebulba 4.00
TYG0028 Anakin and Watto 4.00
TYG0021 Battle Droid on Stap 4.00
TYG0022 Darth Maul on Sith Speeder 4.00
TYG0023 Destroyer Droid 5.00
TYG0029 Nute Gunray and Senator Palpatine 4.00
TYG0026 Obi-Wan and Darth Maul 4.00
TYG0024 Obi-Wan and TC-14..4.00
TYG0025 Qui-Gon and Jar Jar Binks 4.00
TYG0030 Qui-Gon with lightsaber and Jar Jar Binks 4.00

TYG0011   TYG0012   TYG0013   TYG0014   TYG0015

TYG0016   TYG0017   TYG0018   TYG0019   TYG0020

TYG0011 Anakin Skywalker, 2" 3.00
TYG0012 Battle Droid, 2"..3.00
TYG0013 Boss Nass, 2" 3.00
TYG0014 Darth Maul, 2"...3.00
TYG0015 Darth Sidious, 2" 3.00
TYG0016 Darth Vader, 2" 3.00
TYG0017 Jabba the Hutt, 2"...3.00
TYG0018 Jar Jar Binks, 2" 3.00
TYG0019 Qui-Gon Jinn, 2" 3.00
TYG0020 Yoda, 2"...3.00

FIGURES: PAINTABLE CRAFTS

CRF0001   CRF0003   CRF0004

CRF0005   CRF0006   CRF0008

Craft Master
CRF0001 Admiral Ackbar...20.00
CRF0002 Boba Fett 20.00
CRF0003 C-3PO and R2-D2 ....20.00
CRF0004 Han Solo 20.00
CRF0005 Luke on Tauntaun 20.00
CRF0006 Princess Leia 20.00
CRF0007 Wicket 20.00
CRF0008 Yoda...20.00

FIGURES: PAINTABLE CRAFTS, TPM

Hasbro
3D figure painters.
CRZ0002 Darth Maul..9.00

CRZ0001   CRZ0002   CRZ0003

CRZ0003 Obi-Wan Kenobi 9.00
CRZ0001 Qui-Gon Jinn 9.00

FIGURES: PLASTIC/PVC/VINYL

FG027   FG003   FG005   FG007   FG008   FG009   FG011

FG012   FG039   FG015   FG016   FG017   FG018

FG021   FG023   FG024   FG025   FG026

Applause
FG0027 Boba Fett 24.00
FG0034 C-3PO..15.00
FG0003 Chewbacca with C-3PO in cargo net..........................18.00
FG0005 Darth Vader...23.00
FG0006 Darth Vader, cloth cape 18.00
FG0007 Dash Rendar..18.00
FG0008 Emperor Palpatine 18.00
FG0009 Greedo 18.00
FG0011 Han Solo in Stormtrooper disguise 18.00
FG0012 Lando Calrissian in Skiff disguise.................................18.00
FG0039 Leia as Jabba's Prisoner 24.00
FG0035 Luke Skywalker in X-Wing Pilot Gear............................17.00
FG0033 Luke Skywalker, Jedi Training with glow-in-dark lightsaber and
     removable blastshield helmet 17.00
FG0015 Luke with Yoda in backpack 18.00
FG0055 Luke with Yoda in backpack, pewter-colored plastic.................24.00
FG0016 Obi-Wan Kenobi 18.00
FG0017 Obi-Wan Kenobi, glow-in-dark...................................20.00
FG0018 Prince Xizor 26.00
FG0020 Princess Leia and R2-D2 ....22.00
FG0021 Princess Leia, Endor outfit 18.00
FG0023 R2-D2 ....18.00
FG0024 Tie Fighter Pilot..18.00
FG0025 Tusken Raider 18.00
FG0026 Wedge Antillies 20.00

Figures, approximately 7" in height.
FG0040 Anakin Skywalker 8.00
FG0041 Darth Maul with binoculars..8.00
FG0042 Jar Jar Binks 8.00
FG0043 Watto 8.00

Figures: Plastic/PVC/Vinyl

Collectibles Characters. Approximately 10" in height.
FG0044 Darth Maul...11.00
FG0045 Obi-Wan Kenobi..11.00
FG0046 Queen Amidala..11.00
FG0047 Qui-Gon Jinn..11.00

Mega Collectibles with lighted sabers. Approximately 14" in height. Limited edition numbered packaging.
FG0048 Darth Maul...50.00
FG0049 Obi-Wan Kenobi..50.00
FG0050 Qui-Gon Jinn..50.00

FG0040   FG0041   FG0042   FG0043

FG0044   FG0045   FG0046   FG0047

FG0048   FG0049   FG0050

Out of Character

FG0001 FG0002 FG0004 FG0010 FG0013 FG0019 FG0022 FG0014

FG0001 C-3PO..19.00
FG0002 Chewbacca..17.00
FG0004 Darth Vader...18.00
FG0010 Han Solo..17.00
FG0013 Luke Skywalker, Jedi.................................17.00
FG0028 Obi-Wan Kenobi..18.00
FG0019 Princess Leia...17.00
FG0022 R2-D2..19.00
FG0014 Stormtrooper...18.00

Takara
FG0029 C-3PO..245.00
FG0030 Chewbacca..245.00
FG0031 Darth Vader...245.00
FG0032 Stormtrooper...245.00

4" Deformed plastic figures.

FG0051   FG0052   FG0053   FG0054

FG0051 Anakin Skywalker 7.00
FG0052 Darth Maul..9.00
FG0053 Sebulba, swivels at neck...............................7.00
FG0054 Watto, swivels at waist 7.00

FIGURINES: PORCELAIN

PF0001   PF0002   PF0003 PF0004   PF0005

PF0006   PF0007   PF0009   PF0010

PF0008   PF0011   PF0012   PF0013

PF0001 AT-AT 7.00
PF0002 A-Wing fighter 7.00
PF0003 C-3PO 10.00
PF0004 Darth Vader...10.00
PF0005 Darth Vader's Tie Fighter 7.00
PF0006 Imperial Star Destroyer 7.00
PF0007 Millennium Falcon 8.00
PF0008 R2-D2 ....10.00
PF0009 Sandcrawler 7.00
PF0010 Slave I 7.00
PF0011 Snowspeeder 7.00
PF0012 Star Wars classic logo 8.00
PF0013 X-Wing Fighter 7.00

FILM, CAMERA

FPF0001   FPF0002

Agfa
FPF0001 3-pack with free frisbee...............................21.00
FPF0002 3-pack with free yo-yo 18.00

FILM FRAMES

FC0005 samples

224

Willetts Design
FC0005 Star Wars 70mm frame mounted in Lucite block with color photo insert, any frame...26.00

FC0001 ANH 70mm, any frame...20.00
FC0002 ESB 70mm, any frame..15.00
FC0004 Revenge of the Jedi, 70mm title frame 45.00
FC0003 ROTJ 70mm, any frame...15.00

FILMS

JEF Films
FL0011 Empire Strikes Back theatrical trailer 675.00
FL0012 Return of the Jedi theatrical trailer 575.00
FL0010 Star Wars theatrical trailer 1,300.00

Ken Films

FL0001   FL0004   FL0008

FL0009   FL0016

FL0001 SW: Black and White / Silent, 8mm 17.00
FL0002 SW: Color / Silent, 8mm 25.00
FL0003 SW: Color / 4 minutes, 8mm 38.00
FL0004 SW: Color / 8 minutes, 8mm 45.00
FL0005 SW: Color / 17 minutes, 8mm 80.00
FL0006 ESB: Color / 4 minutes, 8mm 17.00
FL0007 ESB: Color / 8 minutes, 8mm 35.00
FL0008 ESB: Color / 17 minutes, 8mm 65.00
FL0009 ESB: Color / 17 minutes Part 2, 8mm........................65.00
FL0014 Empire Strikes Back SE theatrical trailer 350.00
FL0016 Filmstrip with audio cassette and workbook..............135.00
FL0015 Return of the Jedi SE theatrical trailer......................350.00
FL0013 Star Wars SE theatrical trailer 625.00

FLAGS

FB0002   FB0004

Great Scott
FB0001 Darth Vader 28"x40"...18.00
FB0002 Darth Vader, Star Wars Trilogy art 20"x36" 18.00
FB0003 Stormtrooper, Empire Strikes Back Trilogy Art, 20"x36".....18.00
FB0004 X-wing fighter 28"x40" 18.00
FB0005 Yoda, Return of the Jedi Trilogy art 20"x36" 18.00

FLASHLIGHTS

LG0002 front and back

Tiger Electronics
LG0002 Lightsaber FX Torchlight 12.00

FLIGHT CONTROLLERS

MMM0001   MMM0005   MMM0002

MMM0003   MMM0006   MMM0004

Galoob
MMM0001 Darth Vader's Tie Fighter, Imperial 14.00
MMM0005 Darth Vader's Tie Fighter with bonus X-Wing fighter targets, Imperial...61.00
MMM0002 Tie Interceptor, Imperial 14.00
MMM0003 X-Wing Fighter, Rebel 14.00
MMM0006 X-Wing Fighter with bonus Tie fighter targets 64.00
MMM0004 Y-Wing Fighter, Rebel 14.00

FLIGHT SIMULATORS

YJ0001

Kenner
YJ0001 X-Wing..16.00

FOLDERS

SUF0040   SUF0046   SUF0042   SUF0047

SUF0048   SUF0043   SUF0044   SUF0045   SUF0049

Impact, Inc.
SUF0040 Anakin Skywalker 2.00
SUF0046 Darth Maul / Darth Sidious 2.00
SUF0042 Jar Jar 2.00
SUF0047 Jedi vs. Sith 3.00
SUF0048 Pod Race..3.00
SUF0043 Queen Amidala 2.00
SUF0044 Qui-Gon Jinn 2.00
SUF0045 R2-D2 / C-3PO..2.00
SUF0049 Space Battle..3.00

Mead
SUF0034 "Freeze You Rebel Scum".......................................3.00
SUF0018 "May The Force Be With You" 4.00
SUF0029 "May The Force Be With You" 3.00
SUF0030 "Never Underestimate The Power Of The Dark Side" 3.00
SUF0001 Ben Kenobi and Stormtroopers................................11.00

Folders

SUF0010 front and back   SUF0034   SUF0029

SUF0030   SUF0039   SUF0033   SUF0028   SUF0031

SUF0036   SUF0032   SUF0035   SUF0037   SUF0038

SUF0055 Bounty Hunters neon: IG-88, Greedo, Boba Fett 6.00
SUF0050 B-Wing Attack 4.00
SUF0015 C-3PO 4.00
SUF0002 C-3PO and R2-D2 ....11.00
SUF0052 C-3PO R2-D2 neon 6.00
SUF0039 C-3POs Phrases / C-3PO 3.00
SUF0005 Chewbacca, Han, and Luke 11.00
SUF0016 Darth Vader 4.00
SUF0006 Darth Vader and Stormtroopers 11.00
SUF0033 Darth Vader, Dark Lord of the Sith 3.00
SUF0028 Han / Millennium Falcon 3.00
SUF0017 Han Solo 4.00
SUF0054 He's No Good To Me Dead neon, Boba Fett, Darth Vader 6.00
SUF0051 Jabba's Palace neon: Jabba the Hutt, Bib Fortuna, Gamorrean guard 6.00
SUF0010 Leia and Luke 11.00
SUF0031 Luke Skywalker 3.00
SUF0036 Opening Crawl / Stormtrooper / Tanavive IV 3.00
SUF0019 Princess Leia 4.00
SUF0032 Princess Leia 3.00
SUF0035 Princess Leia's Plea / R2-D2 ....3.00
SUF0020 R2-D2 ....4.00
SUF0021 Space Ships 4.00
SUF0037 Starfighters 3.00
SUF0053 Tatooine neon: Bantha, Tusken Raider, Jawa 6.00
SUF0022 Title Crawl 4.00
SUF0013 X-Wing and Tie Fighter 11.00
SUF0023 Yoda 4.00
SUF0038 Yoda's speech / Yoda 3.00

Stuart Hall

SUF0004   SUF0012

SUF0024 Bounty Hunters 11.00
SUF0003 C-3PO and R2-D2 ....11.00
SUF0004 C-3PO, R2-D2, and Wicket the Ewok 8.00
SUF0025 Character collage 11.00
SUF0026 Chewbacca 11.00
SUF0027 Darth Vader 11.00
SUF0007 Darth Vader and Stormtroopers 11.00
SUF0008 Darth Vader, Emperor Palpatine, Luke Skywalker 8.00
SUF0009 Jabba the Hutt and Salicious Crumb 8.00
SUF0011 Max Rebo Band 8.00
SUF0012 Speeder Bikes, B-Wing, and Tie Fighter 8.00
SUF0014 Yoda and Luke on Dagobah 11.00

FOLDING PICTURE CUBES

FPC0001

Disney / MGM
FPC0001 Folding Picture Cube, classic trilogy scenes 9.00

FORTUNE TELLING TOYS

FT0001 front and back

Kenner
FT0001 Yoda the Jedi Master magic answer fortune telling 54.00

FRISBEES

Burger King

FRI0010   FRI0012   FRI0011   FRI0009

FRI0010 Darth Vader, ESB 25.00

Kentucky Fried Chicken
Flying bucket toppers.
FRI0011 Battle Droid 4.00
FRI0012 Jar Jar Binks 4.00

Pine-Sol

FRI0001   FRI0003   FRI0005   FRI0006

Character or scene line-drawing with logo on silver plastic. Mail-in premium.
FRI0001 C-3PO 16.00
FRI0002 Chewbacca 16.00
FRI0003 Darth Vader 16.00
FRI0004 R2-D2 ....16.00
FRI0005 Stormtrooper 16.00
FRI0006 X-Wing Fighter 16.00

Spectra Star
FRI0007 Star Wars logo above raised images of Star Destroyer and Millennium Falcon 8.00

Worlds Apart
FRI0009 Darth Maul E. Pix flying disc, glows in the dark 11.00
FRI0008 Whizza Performance Disc, Star Wars logo and X-wings on colored sticker 18.00

FURNITURE, INFLATABLE

Intex Recreation Corp.
IPF0001 C-3PO Junior Chair 30"x22½"x22" 10.00

IPF0001　　　　　　　IPF0002

IPF0003　　　　　　　IPF0004　　　　　　　IPF0005

IPF0002 Darth Maul Chair 48"x42"x36"...20.00
IPF0003 Jar Jar Chair 37"x32"x31½" 15.00
IPF0004 Queen Amidala Chair 38"x32"x31½" 15.00
IPF0005 R2-D2 Junior Chair 30½"x23"x22½" 10.00

GAME PIECES: PROMOTIONAL

Kellogg's
GM0047 Ewok Adventure Collect-a-Prize game piece...........................14.00
GM0045 Picture Name Decoder Disc: C-3PO and Logray 18.00
GM0046 Picture Name Decoder Disc: Squidhead.....................................16.00

Toys R Us

GM0048

GM0048 Destroy The Death Star scratch-off game piece 4.00

Tricon Global Restaurants, Inc.
GM0001 #01 Ric Olie, $10,000 winner...0.50
GM0002 #02 Daultay Dofine, $10,000 winner, 50 produced.....................75.00
GM0003 #03 R2-D2, $10,000 winner...0.50
GM0004 #04 Yoda, $1,000 winner, 1,500 produced.............................60.00
GM0005 #05 Mace Windu, $1,000 winner...0.50
GM0006 #06 Sebulba, $1,000,000 winner...0.50
GM0007 #07 Anakin Skywalker, $1,000,000 winner...............................0.50
GM0008 #08 Watto, $1,000,000 winner 0.50
GM0009 #09 C-3PO, $1,000,000 winner...0.50
GM0010 #10 Shmi Skywalker, $1,000,000 winner, only 1 produced - not
　　　　redeemed..7,500.00
GM0011 #11 Darth Maul, $1,000,000 winner..0.50
GM0012 #12 Qui-Gon Jinn, $1,000,000 winner 0.50
GM0013 #13 Battle Droid, $1,000,000 winner, only 1 produced - not
　　　　redeemed..7,500.00

GM0014 #14 Jar Jar Binks, $1,000,000 winner 0.50
GM0015 #15 Boss Nass, $1,000,000 winner......................................0.50
GM0016 #16 Queen Amidala, $1,000,000 winner...............................0.50
GM0017 #17 Senator Palpatine, $1,000,000 winner...........................0.50
GM0018 #18 Obi-Wan Kenobi, $1,000,000 winner 0.50
GM0019 #19 Darth Sidious, $1,000,000 winner...................................0.50
GM0020 #20 Chancellor Velorum, $1,000,000 winner, only 1 produced - not
　　　　redeemed.. 7,500.00
GM0021 Instant Winner: $10,000 VISA shopping spree, 10 produced 50.00
GM0022 Instant Winner: 2 pc. chicken meal/KFC; or combo meal/Taco Bell,
　　　　1.6m produced..4.00
GM0023 Instant Winner: 3 pc. chicken snack/KFC; or nachos supreme/Taco
　　　　Bell, 1.3m produced..4.00
GM0024 Instant Winner: Apple Imac computer, 125 produced 10.00
GM0025 Instant Winner: Bread sticks/Pizza Hut; or regular nachos/Taco Bell,
　　　　2.7m produced..4.00
GM0026 Instant Winner: Crispy strip/KFC; or original taco/Taco Bell, 5.3m
　　　　produced..4.00
GM0027 Instant Winner: Crispy Strip/KFC; or soft taco/Taco Bell, 4.1m pro-
　　　　duced..4.00
GM0028 Instant Winner: Darth Maul CD-player, 2000 produced..............7.00
GM0029 Instant Winner: Indiv. side item/KFC; or regular nachos/Taco Bell,
　　　　5.3m produced 4.00
GM0030 Instant Winner: Indiv. side item/KFC; Pepsi 2 liter or 2 dine-in bever-
　　　　ages/Pizza Hut, 1m produced..4.00
GM0031 Instant Winner: Individual dessert/KFC; or cinnamon twists/Taco
　　　　Bell, 2.2m produced..4.00
GM0032 Instant Winner: Lincoln Navagator, 4 produced.......................55.00
GM0033 Instant Winner: Lucas Learning SW:EPI PC/Mac game, 200 pro-
　　　　duced..7.00
GM0034 Instant Winner: LucasArt Entertainment SW:EPI CD-Rom game, 200
　　　　produced..8.00
GM0035 Instant Winner: Meade refracting telescope, 150 produced......9.00
GM0036 Instant Winner: Medium 3 topping pizza/Pizza Hut; or 8 pc. chicken
　　　　meal/KFC, 1.6m produced 4.00
GM0037 Instant Winner: Nintendo 64 w/EPI Racer cartridge, 1000 pro-
　　　　duced..4.00
GM0038 Instant Winner: Official SW Fan Club membership, 50k produced.. 5.00
GM0039 Instant Winner: Pepsi 2 liter or 2 dine-in beverages/Pizza Hut; or
　　　　original taco/Taco Bell, 7.7m produced 4.00
GM0040 Instant Winner: Pepsi 2 liter or 2 dine-in beverages/Pizza Hut; or reg-
　　　　ular nachos/Taco Bell, 7.7m produced.....................................4.00
GM0041 Instant Winner: Seneca Sports wheeled sports pkg., 300 pro-
　　　　duced 10.00
GM0042 Instant Winner: Star Wars Speeder, 1 produced 1,100.00
GM0043 Instant Winner: THX home entertainment system, 75 produced12.00
GM0044 Instant Winner: Trip for 2 around the world, 3 produced............75.00

GIFT BAGS

GFB0001　　　　　　　GFB0002　　　　　　　GFB0003

GM0001　　　GM0003　　　GM0005　　　GM0006　　　GM0008　　　GM0009　　　GM0011　　　GM0012

GM0014　　　GM0015　　　GM0016　　　GM0017　　　GM0018　　　GM0019　　　GM0031 front and back

Gift Bags

GFB0004   GFB0005   GFB0006

GFB0003 B-Wing fighter attack 7.00
GFB0001 Chewbacca 8.00
GFB0002 Darth Vader with stormtroopers 8.00
GFB0006 Droids, R2-D2 and C-3PO 22.00
GFB0004 Space battle above second Death Star.............7.00
GFB0005 X-Wings 7.00

GIFT CARDS

Borders, Inc.
GTC0001 Anakin in podracer helmet, $25 gift card.............7.00
GTC0002 Darth Maul, $50 gift card 12.00

K-Mart
$50 cash cards.
GTC0003 Anakin in podracer helmet.............................8.00
GTC0007 Darth Maul, September 1999...........................8.00
GTC0004 Jar Jar Binks, June 1999 ....8.00
GTC0006 Queen Amidala, August 1999 ....8.00
GTC0005 Qui-Gon Jinn, July 1999 ....8.00

GIFT CERTIFICATES

GC0001

Clarks
GC0001 Clarks, featuring Star Wars images to promote SW line of Clarks
shoes..14.00

GIFT TAGS

PFF0012   PFF0003   PFF0011

Cleo
PFF0012 30 Foil-Leaf Gift Tags, EPI.............................5.00

Drawing Board
PFF0001 C-3PO and R2-D2, card art...........................5.00
PFF0002 C-3PO and R2-D2, card photo........................5.00
PFF0003 C-3PO and R2-D2, tag, self-adhesive, 5-pack........12.00
PFF0004 Cloud City, card 6.00
PFF0005 Darth Vader and Luke Duel, card 5.00
PFF0006 Ewoks Hang-Gliding, tag...............................5.00
PFF0007 Leia, Luke, and Han, card 5.00
PFF0008 R2-D2, stick-on decoration 9.00
PFF0009 X-Wing Fighter, card 4.00
PFF0010 Yoda, stick-on decoration 8.00

Hallmark
PFF0011 TPM C-3PO and R2-D2, 2"x3".......................2.00

GIFT WRAP

PFG0022   PFG0005   PFG0006   PFG0009

Ambassador
Each roll contains 15 square feet of paper.
PFG0019 Star Wars Classic Trilogy, blue starfield background, roll 6.00
PFG0020 Star Wars Classic Trilogy, neon action art, roll 5.00
PFG0022 Star Wars Classic Trilogy, starship battles on blue technical background, folded 8.00
PFG0021 TPM character art, roll....................................4.00

Cleo
PFG0017 Pod Racer, red sparkled 8 sq. ft. roll...............7.00
PFG0018 Space Battle, black sparkled 8 sq. ft. roll..........7.00

Drawing Board
PFG0015 "Happy Birthday" w/photos, folded 8.00
PFG0016 "Happy Birthday" w/photos, roll......................10.00
PFG0001 C-3PO, R2-D2, Darth Vader, and battle scene, 12 ft. roll 15.00
PFG0002 C-3PO, R2-D2, Darth Vader, and battle scene, 16 ft. roll 25.00
PFG0003 C-3PO, R2-D2, Darth Vader, and battle scene, 5 ft. roll 10.00
PFG0004 C-3PO, R2-D2, Darth Vader, and battle scene, folded 8.00
PFG0006 Characters ESB, folded 10.00
PFG0005 Characters SW, folded 8.00
PFG0007 Cloud City, folded 8.00
PFG0008 Cloud City, roll..10.00
PFG0009 Darth Vader and Luke Duel, folded 6.00
PFG0010 Darth Vader and Luke Duel, roll 8.00
PFG0011 Dogfight, folded 8.00
PFG0012 Dogfight, roll..10.00
PFG0013 Ewoks Hang-Gliding, folded 6.00
PFG0014 Ewoks Hang-Gliding, roll 8.00

GIGAPETS

GP0001   GP0002   GP0003

Tiger Electronics
GP0001 R2-D2...11.00
GP0002 Rancor...11.00
GP0003 Yoda 11.00

GLASSES

GA0031 front and back

Amora
GA0031 Chewbacca and Ewok 19.00

Burger King
GA0019 Empire Strikes Back C-3PO and R2-D2....................10.00
GA0020 Empire Strikes Back Darth Vader..........................10.00
GA0021 Empire Strikes Back Lando Calrissian 10.00
GA0022 Empire Strikes Back Luke Skywalker 10.00
GA0024 Return of the Jedi Emperor's Throne Room 8.00

GA0015   GA0016   GA0017   GA0018   GA0019   GA0020   GA0021

GA0022   GA0023   GA0024   GA0028   GA0025   GA0029   GA0026

GA0023 Return of the Jedi Ewok Village 8.00
GA0026 Return of the Jedi Jabba's Palace..................................... 8.00
GA0025 Return of the Jedi Jabba's Sail Barge 8.00
GA0028 Return of the Jedi, Emperor's Throne Room, plastic 10.00
GA0027 Return of the Jedi, Ewok Village, plastic 10.00
GA0030 Return of the Jedi, Jabba's Palace, plastic 10.00
GA0029 Return of the Jedi, Jabba's Sail Barge, plastic 10.00
GA0015 Star Wars C-3PO and R2-D2.. 12.00
GA0017 Star Wars Chewbacca.. 12.00
GA0016 Star Wars Darth Vader.. 12.00
GA0018 Star Wars Luke Skywalker 12.00

Pepsi Cola

GA0014   GA0041   GA0036 filled   GA0037 filled   GA0042   GA0043

GA0044   GA0045   GA0039 front and back   GA0040 front and back

GA0046 front and back   GA0047 front and back

GA0041 C-3PO, Hong Kong exclusive 16.00
GA0032 C-3PO icon on blue background 18.00
GA0001 C-3PO Star Wars Trilogy (Holland) 13.00
GA0033 Darth Vader icon on yellow background 20.00
GA0014 Darth Vader, Hong Kong exclusive 16.00
GA0042 EPI: Anakin Skywalker 8.00
GA0044 EPI: Queen Amidala 8.00
GA0045 EPI: Qui-Gon Jinn 8.00
GA0043 EPI: R2-D2 .... 8.00
GA0034 R2-D2 icon on red background 20.00
GA0035 Stormtrooper icon on red background 22.00
GA0036 TPM heroes, clear etched glass 16.00
GA0037 TPM villains, clear etched glass 16.00

GA0002 Artoo-Detoo, glazed 12.00
GA0009 C-3PO, glazed 12.00
GA0005 Chewbacca, glazed 12.00
GA0008 Darth Vader, glazed 12.00
GA0038 Darth vader vs. Luke Skywalker 12.00
GA0010 Emperor's Royal Guard, glazed 12.00
GA0040 EPI: Anakin Skywalker 6.00
GA0039 EPI: Battle Droid 6.00
GA0047 EPI: Jar Jar 6.00
GA0046 EPI: Jedi Knight (Obi-Wan) 6.00
GA0012 Han Solo, glazed 12.00
GA0004 Luke Skywalker, glazed 12.00
GA0006 Obi-Wan Kenobi, glazed 12.00
GA0007 Princess Leia, glazed 12.00
GA0003 Stormtrooper, glazed 12.00
GA0011 Yoda, glazed 12.00

GLOVES

AG0007   AG0006

Handcraft Mfg. Corp.
AG0007 Darth Maul, fleece... 12.00
AG0006 Star Wars logo, fleece 12.00

Sales Corp. of America
AG0001 C-3PO 12.00
AG0002 Chewbacca... 12.00
AG0003 Darth Vader... 12.00
AG0004 R2-D2 .... 14.00

GLOW-IN-THE-DARK DECORATIONS

Glow Zone

HD0001 front and back   HD0023   HD0022 front and back

HD0001 8 Glow-in-the-dark decorations: Luke, Millennium Falcon, Vader,
     Tie, X-Wing, R2-D2, C-3PO, Boba Fett 7.00
HD0023 Wall Plaque, Anakin Skywalker 11.00
HD0022 Wall Plaque, Darth Maul... 9.00

Illuminations

HD0002 back   HD0003 back   HD0004 back   HD0005 back

Action Wall Scenes in plastic envelope packaging with 36 pieces.
HD0002 Droids 6.00
HD0003 Jedi vs. Sith 6.00
HD0004 Land Battle 6.00
HD0005 Space Battle 6.00

Large box of 79 pieces.
HD0025 Battle Zone 18.00
HD0024 Characters 16.00

Small boxes of 38-41 pieces.
HD0017 Characters 7.00

Glow-in-the-Dark Decorations

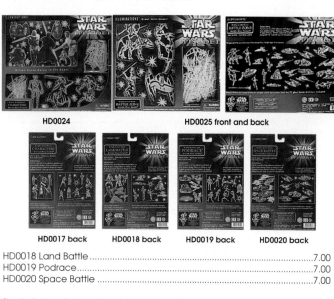

HD0024   HD0025 front and back

HD0017 back   HD0018 back   HD0019 back   HD0020 back

HD0018 Land Battle 7.00
HD0019 Podrace..7.00
HD0020 Space Battle 7.00

Sheet of character head decals in plastic envelope.

HD0013   HD0014   HD0015   HD0016

HD0015 C-3PO 7.00
HD0014 Darth Maul 7.00
HD0013 Jar Jar Binks 7.00
HD0016 Obi-Wan Kenobi...7.00

Action Wall Scene decals, flat 10"x9½".

HD0006   HD0007   HD0008

HD0009   HD0010   HD0021

HD0009 Droids..12.00
HD0010 Gugan Adventure 12.00
HD0021 "Jedi vs. Sith" 12.00
HD0007 Podrace 12.00
HD0006 Space Battle 12.00
HD0008 Trade Federation Invasion................................12.00

Action Wall Scene decals, flat 13"x10½".

HD0011   HD0012

HD0012 Battle Droids 12.00
HD0011 Jedi..12.00

GLUE

SUG0002   SUG0001   SUG0003   SUG0004

Beecham Italia S.p.A.
SUG0002 UHU glue stick with Kenner Ewok figure.....................................295.00

Butterfly Originals
SUG0001 ROTJ Color Glue 8.00

Impact, Inc.
SUG0003 R2-D2 Gluestick...2.00

Rose Art Industries
SUG0004 Lightsaber gluestick 7.00

GOODIE BAGS

GB0003   GB0001   GB0002

Look-o-Look
GB0003 Chupa Chup sucker, sticker, and Chewbacca head sucker
    holder...6.00

Tapper Candies
GB0002 Anakin mask, Darth Maul sticker, Smarties candy, Chupa-Chup lol-
    lipop, Jedi vs. Sith Coin Battle game 5.00
GB0001 Darth Maul mask and sticker, Smarties candy, Chupa-Chup lol-
    lipop, Jedi vs. Sith Coin Battle game 5.00

GREETING CARDS

GR0058   GR0007   GR0059   GR0066

GR0060   GR0067   GR0061   GR0062   GR0016   GR0038

GR0063   GR0041   GR0042   GR0046   GR0065   GR0050

Drawing Board

GR0058 C-3PO and Luke Skywalker in Ben's Hut, "They don't make 'em like you anymore!" 7.00
GR0007 C-3PO holding birthday cake, and R2-D2, "Have a Happy Birthday." / ".it's the human thing to do" 8.00
GR0059 C-3PO Lost on Tatooine, "Lost without you!" 7.00
GR0066 C-3PO, "Feeling Kinda Rusty" / "How about a warm lubricant bath?" 7.00
GR0060 C-3PO, "Sorry haven't written" / ".but I'm only human!" 7.00
GR0067 Chewbacca, "Not feeling well?" / "May you soon have the strength of a Wookie!" 7.00
GR0061 Chewbacca, "You're Weird" / ".but wonderful!" 7.00
GR0062 Darth Vader, "Don't Play Games With Me!!!" / "Write!!!" 7.00
GR0016 Darth Vader, "Happy Birthday, Earthling!" 7.00
GR0038 Luke Skywalker, "Hold it right there..." / ".and have a happy birthday" 7.00
GR0063 Millennium Falcon, "Greetings from Tatooine" 7.00
GR0041 Obi-Wan, "May the force be with you" 10.00
GR0042 R2-D2 and C-3PO, "29 Again!?!?" / "It boggles the memory bank!" 9.00
GR0046 R2-D2, "From Your Faithful Droid" / "Within the innards of me is a message." 7.00
GR0065 Space Dogfight, "Would have written sooner..." / "But I just haven't had a minute!" 7.00
GR0050 Trash Compactor, "There's no escaping." / ".another birthday" 8.00

Fan Club

GR0103 C-3PO, R2-D2, Santa, 1999 Christmas reproduction of Star Wars Christmas album cover 2.00
GR0081 Jawas Christmas, 1999 reproduction of original card Lucas sent to employees 2.00

Hallmark / Expressions

GR0111 "Damn! Where's the Force when you need it?" / "On your birthday may you not suffer the humiliation of saber-droop." 8.00
GR0110 "Have a speed-chasing, podracing." / ".wizard cool BLAST of a Birthday!" 5.00
GR0108 "May The Force Be With You / Mighty Blasters / At Last We Will Have Revenge" / "Wishing you an Adventure-filled Birthday." 4.00
GR0112 C-3PO, "Oh, dear- I can't bear to watch you suffer." / "Hope you're FULLY operational soon." 6.00
GR0107 Darth Vader, "It is useless to resist. There is no escape. It is your destiny. It is." / "Your Birthday! Hope it's happy!" 5.00
GR0113 Darth Vader, "Valentine, there's a disturbance in the Force" / "Must be all these Valentine wishes coming your way" 5.00
GR0109 Leia, "Me? Forget Your Birthday?" / "I'd Just As Soon Kiss A Wookie!" 4.00

Hallmark / Shoebox Greetings

| GR0107 | GR0109 | GR0110 | GR0111 | GR0112 | GR0113 |

GR0097 "Darn! 'There it goes again" 3.00
GR0084 "Got It!" 3.00
GR0088 "Hi!" 3.00
GR0101 "I am ready." 3.00
GR0091 "I'm the luckiest girl in the galaxy" 3.00
GR0085 "Intergalactic PMS hits Princess Leia" 3.00
GR0099 "It's your birthday. Party like Chewbacca" 3.00
GR0092 "Like it?" 3.00
GR0086 "Luke learns that true friends put up with a lot" 3.00
GR0090 "Party" 3.00
GR0094 "Think about a flowing cape. Seriously." 3.00
GR0102 "True friends never let each other get cut in half by a lightsaber". 3.00
GR0098 "Vader, get away from my office, now!" 3.00
GR0083 "You want to know where your destiny lies, Luke?" 3.00
GR0089 "You will regret this rash assault, Luke!" 3.00
GR0087 "You! See a stylist!" 3.00
GR0096 (Artoo-Detoo with a heart) 3.00
GR0100 (Chewbacca) 3.00
GR0093 (Luke Smiling) 3.00
GR0095 (Yoda Standing) 3.00

Skywalkers

| GR0114 front and inside | GR0015 front and inside |

GR0114 "Happy Birthday" / "From All Of Us In The Rebel Alliance" 12.00
GR0115 "Seasons Greetings" / "From All Of Us In The Rebel Alliance" 12.00
GR0001 Boba Fett, die-cut 12.00
GR0002 C-3PO and Ewoks 7.00
GR0003 C-3PO and R2-D2 floating away with balloons 7.00
GR0004 C-3PO and R2-D2, "Enjoy the Holidays" 10.00
GR0005 C-3PO and R2-D2, "For A Fine Boy", embossed 7.00
GR0053 C-3PO and R2-D2, "For An Earthling Girl" 7.00
GR0006 C-3PO and R2-D2, "Have a Happy Birthday" 7.00
GR0054 C-3PO and R2-D2, "Peace and Goodwill " 7.00
GR0078 C-3PO and R2-D2, "To Son On Valentine's Day" 7.00
GR0008 C-3PO sitting and thinking, embossed 9.00
GR0068 C-3PO with Mask 8.00
GR0009 C-3PO, 12th birthday 8.00
GR0010 C-3PO, die-cut 10.00
GR0055 C-3PO, "For An Out Of This World Grandson" 7.00
GR0011 C-3PO, R2-D2, Aliens, Gamorrean Guard, embossed 6.00
GR0079 C-3PO, "Valentine Greetings" 7.00
GR0013 Chewbacca 10.00
GR0012 Chewbacca, 7th birthday 8.00
GR0069 Chewbacca, "Do Not Fear" 8.00
GR0014 Chewbacca, Han, and Leia, fold-out game card, birthday 8.00
GR0070 Chewbacca, Han, and Luke, "From The Alliance" 8.00
GR0015 Chewbacca, Han, Leia, R2-D2, C-3PO, Jabba the Hutt, Wicket.4.00
GR0017 Darth Vader and Emperor's Royal Guards 6.00
GR0018 Darth Vader lightsaber drawn, die-cut 10.00
GR0071 Darth Vader with bats 9.00
GR0019 Darth Vader with Drawn Lightsaber 7.00
GR0020 Darth Vader, 11th birthday 8.00
GR0021 Darth Vader, fold-out game card, birthday 8.00
GR0080 Darth Vader, "Space Bulletin for Grandson" 7.00
GR0022 Ewok and Princess Leia 7.00
GR0023 Ewok with Ewok Children 7.00
GR0024 Ewoks: Archery Range 7.00
GR0025 Ewoks: Baby Ewoks 8.00
GR0026 Ewoks: Ewok in Glider 7.00
GR0027 Ewoks: Fishing 7.00
GR0028 Ewoks: Kenner Preschool Birthday Club Card 12.00
GR0029 Ewoks: Nature Study 7.00
GR0030 Ewoks: Playing Music 7.00
GR0031 Ewoks: Princess Kneesaa and Baga 7.00

Hallmark / Shoebox Greetings

GR0097	GR0101	GR0091	GR0085	GR0099	GR0092

GR0094	GR0102	GR0098	GR0096	GR0093	GR0095

GR0084	GR0088	GR0086	GR0090

GR0083	GR0089	GR0087	GR0108

Greeting Cards

GR0032 Ewoks: Swimming 7.00
GR0033 Female Ewok, "For A Very Special Girl" 6.00
GR0106 Han, Leia, and Luke 6.00
GR0034 Han, Leia, and Luke, die-cut 10.00
GR0035 Hoojibs and R2-D2, embossed 7.00
GR0036 Leia and Luke on Speederbike 7.00
GR0037 Luke on Tauntaun, die-cut 10.00
GR0072 Luke Skywalker, "For An Out Of This World Son" 8.00
GR0039 Max Rebo Band 7.00
GR0073 Millennium Falcon, "For An Earthling Girl" 8.00
GR0040 Obi-Wan Kenobi, 10th birthday 8.00
GR0074 Obi-Wan Kenobi, "Happy Halloween" 8.00
GR0064 Obi-Wan Kenobi, "Happy Holidays" 7.00
GR0104 Princess Leia and R2-D2, "For An Out Of This World Granddaughter" 8.00
GR0075 Princess Leia, "For An Out Of This World Daughter" 8.00
GR0043 R2-D2 and Wicket 7.00
GR0056 R2-D2 with wreath 7.00
GR0044 R2-D2, 9th birthday 8.00
GR0082 R2-D2, "A Valentine Message for You" 7.00
GR0045 R2-D2, die-cut 11.00
GR0047 R2-D2, "Happy Birthday to You", embossed 7.00
GR0076 Space Dogfight, "For An Earthling Boy" 8.00
GR0048 Stormtrooper, 8th birthday 8.00
GR0049 Stormtrooper, die-cut 11.00
GR0057 X-Wing Fighters, "Intergalactic Greetings" 7.00
GR0105 X-Wing Fighters, "To An Out-Of-This-World Boy" 8.00
GR0077 Yoda delivering presents using the Force, 10 cards with envelopes 19.00
GR0051 Yoda, die-cut 9.00
GR0052 Yoda, fold-out game card, birthday 8.00

GROWTH CHARTS

PEG0001 boxed and opened

Random House
PEG0001 Star Wars "Grow" chart 12.00

GYM SETS

GY0004 opened

Gym Dandy
GY0002 Scout Walker Command Tower Swingset with Speederbike ride..725.00
GY0003 Scout Walker Command Tower with 7 ft. slide 475.00
GY0001 Scout Walker Command Tower with Speederbike ride 525.00
GY0004 Speederbike swing add-on..............................185.00

HANGERS

Adam Joseph Industries
HOH0001 Admiral Ackbar..24.00
HOH0002 C-3PO..24.00
HOH0003 Stormtrooper 24.00

HATS

Fresh Caps
PH0001 Anakin Skywalker, Podrace 8.00

PH0001   PH0002

PH0002 Jar Jar...8.00

HATS: PARTY

PFH0006   PFH0005

Drawing Board
PFH0001 Cloud City, 8-pack cones 10.00
PFH0002 Darth Vader and Luke Duel, 8-pack cones 10.00
PFH0003 Ewoks Hang-Gliding, 8-pack cones 8.00
PFH0004 Star Wars punch-out, 8-pack 17.00

Party Express
PFH0005 Battle above Death Star, 8-pack cones................4.00
PFH0007 Droids with Star Wars logo, neon 8-pack cones 5.00
PFH0006 Jar Jar Binks, 8-pack cones 3.00

HEADPHONES

HP0001   HP0002   HP0003

Philips
Earphones.
HP0001 C-3PO...26.00
HP0003 Darth Vader...26.00
HP0002 Luke Skywalker..26.00

HELMETS: MINIATURE

HN0001   HN0002   HN0003   HN0004   HN0005

Riddell
HN0001 Boba Fett...75.00
HN0002 C-3PO...60.00
HN0003 Darth Vader 70.00
HN0004 Stormtrooper 70.00
HN0005 X-Wing Pilot 60.00

HELMETS: SPORTS

HGH0001   HGH0002   HGH0004

Dynacraft
HGH0001 Darth Maul multisport, children's 17.00
HGH0002 Queen Amidala multisport, children's 17.00

MV Sports
HGH0003 Darth Maul 35.00
HGH0004 Jar Jar Binks 31.00

HOLOGRAMS

3D Arts
2"x2" in 3¾"x2¾" acrylic stand.
HG0004 C-3PO and R2-D2 ....12.00
HG0005 Darth Vader 12.00
HG0006 Millennium Falcon 12.00
HG0007 X-Wing Fighter 12.00

4"x6" in matted frame.
HG0008 Darth Vader 30.00
HG0009 Millennium Falcon 30.00

A.H. Prismatic
HG0001 Millennium Falcon, 5"x7" matted 23.00

Fantasma
8"x10" matted.
HG0002 Darth Vader 35.00
HG0003 Space Battle 35.00

ICE SKATES

Brookfield Athletic
SKI0001 Darth Vader and Emperor's Royal Guards 50.00
SKI0002 Wicket the Ewok 35.00

INFLATABLES

Pepsi Cola
INT0002 Inflatable display can 11.00

Pizza Hut
INT0003 Royal Starship, 12' cold-air inflatable 1,150.00

Takara
INT0001 Inflatable X-Wing 260.00

INVITATIONS

PF1001   PF1003   PF1004   PF1007   PF1008   PF1009   PF1010

Drawing Board
PFI0001 C-3PO and R2-D2, 8-pack 10.00
PFI0002 C-3PO and R2-D2, 8-pack postcards 8.00
PFI0003 Cloud City, 8-pack 10.00
PFI0004 Darth Vader and Luke Duel, 8-pack 10.00
PFI0005 Ewoks Hang-Gliding, 8-pack 8.00
PFI0006 Heroes and Villains, 8-pack 10.00
PFI0007 R2-D2, 8-pack 10.00

Party Express
PFI0011 Droids with Star Wars logo, neon 8-pack 5.00
PFI0009 Obi-Wan, Qui-Gon, "Nothing can stop us." 4.00
PFI0008 R2-D2, 8-pack 8.00

Unique
PFI0010 Qui-Gon vs. Maul art, 8 invitations w/envelopes 4.00
PFI0012 C-3PO, R2-D2, Naboo Fighter: Invitaciones te Invito a mi Fiesta...9.00

IRON-ON TRANSFERS

Factors, Etc.
IO0007 "Darth Vader Lives" 4.00
IO0009 "May The Force Be With You" 4.00
IO0014 Boba Fett 3.00
IO0001 C-3PO and Luke 4.00
IO0002 C-3PO and R2-D2, blue background 4.00
IO0003 C-3PO and R2-D2, ship's corridor 4.00
IO0004 Chewbacca 4.00
IO0027 Chewbacca 4.00
IO0005 Chewbacca and Han Solo 4.00
IO0008 Darth Vader 4.00
IO0006 Darth Vader helmet and ships 4.00
IO0015 Empire Strikes Back logo 3.00
IO0016 Empire Strikes Back poster art 3.00
IO0017 Han Solo 3.00
IO0010 Jawas 4.00
IO0018 Lando Calrissian 3.00
IO0019 Luke and Yoda 3.00
IO0020 Luke on Tauntaun 3.00
IO0021 Luke with X-Wing 3.00
IO0022 Millennium Falcon 3.00
IO0011 Princess Leia 4.00
IO0028 R2-D2 ....4.00
IO0023 Star Destroyer 3.00
IO0013 Star Wars poster art 4.00
IO0012 Star Was logo, glitter 4.00
IO0024 Tie Fighter 3.00
IO0025 X-Wing Fighter 3.00
IO0026 Yoda 3.00

JACKETS

Adam Joseph Industries
AJ0001 Rain jacket, Darth Vader and Royal Guards 25.00
AJ0002 Rain jacket, R2-D2 and C-3PO 25.00
AJ0003 Rain poncho, Darth Vader and Royal Guards. 17.00
AJ0004 Rain poncho, R2-D2 and C-3PO 17.00

B/W Character Merchandising
AJ0005 Rain cape, plastic ESB 31.00

Baltro Italiana
AJ0006 Wool jacket SW 65.00

Bright Red Group
AJ0007 Unlined jacket, black with white trim and "Darth Vadar Lives"
  patch 25.00
AJ0008 Unlined jacket, blue with white trim and logo patch 25.00
AJ0009 Windbreaker, quilted. Any solid color w/white trim 15.00
AJ0010 Windbreaker, quilted. Blue w/white trim, SW logo patch 30.00
AJ0011 Windbreaker, quilted. Red w/white trim, "Darth Vadar Lives"
  patch 25.00
AJ0012 Windbreaker, quilted. White w/black trim, "MTFBWY" patch......25.00

Galoob

AJ0018 front and back

AJ0018 1999 Toy Design Team 575.00

Jackets

SW Fan Club
AJ0013 Han Solo Vest..125.00
AJ0014 Luke Skywalker Fatigue Jacket..................... 150.00

The Fan Club, Inc.
AJ0015 Boba Fett embroidered on back of denim jacket 165.00
AJ0016 Darth Vader's Helmet embroidered on back of denim jacket.135.00

JOURNALS, BLANK

PPJ0001 PPJ0010 PPJ0013 PPJ0014 PPJ0011

PPJ0007 PPJ0004 PPJ0005 PPJ0015 PPJ0006

Antioch
PPJ0001 20th Anniversary w/Rystall bookmark and 2 wallet cards 18.00
PPJ0002 Book of Days 12.00
PPJ0010 Episode I limited edition journal, free bookmark and bookplate, 50,000 produced...11.00
PPJ0013 Queen Amidala journal, free bookmark and bookplate, 50,000 produced...10.00
PPJ0014 Qui-Gon Jinn journal, free bookmark and bookplate, 50,000 produced...10.00
PPJ0011 Sith journal, free bookmark and bookplate, 50,000 produced .11.00
PPJ0008 Space Battle w/bookmark 10.00
PPJ0007 Star Wars poster art w/bookmark 10.00
PPJ0004 The Courtship of Princess Leia w/bookmark...................10.00
PPJ0005 The Crystal Star w/bookmark 10.00
PPJ0015 Trade Federation journal, free bookmark and bookplate, 50,000 produced...10.00
PPJ0006 Truce at Bakura w/bookmark 10.00

Ballantine

PPJ0003 PPJ0009

PPJ0003 My Jedi Journal...18.00

Chronicle Books
PPJ0009 Star Wars Logbook..14.00

Tokyo Queen
PPJ0012 Darth Vader cover, C-3PO on back 24.00

KEYCHAINS

3D Arts
Square lasergrams.
KE0073 C-3PO and R2-D2 ....28.00
KE0007 Darth Vader 28.00
KE0026 X-Wing Fighter 28.00
KE0030 Yoda 28.00

A.H. Prismatic
Holograms encased in 2" square plastic.

KE0031 C-3PO and R2-D2 ....6.00
KE0032 Darth Vader 6.00
KE0033 Millennium Falcon...6.00
KE0034 X-Wing Fighter..6.00

Adam Joseph Industries

KE0004 KE0012 KE0017 KE0018 KE0024

KE0004 Darth Vader 9.00
KE0012 Millennium Falcon...9.00
KE0017 Princess Kneesaa..8.00
KE0018 R2-D2 ....9.00
KE0024 Wicket 8.00
KE0027 Yoda 9.00

Applause

KE0087 KE0085 KE0086 KE0108 KE0167 KE0166

KE0121 KE0110 KE0120 KE0165

PVC figures.
KE0110 Anakin Skywalker..8.00
KE0166 Destroyer Droid 8.00
KE0119 Jar Jar Binks 8.00
KE0120 Obi-Wan Kenobi 8.00
KE0167 Pit Droid..8.00
KE0121 Queen Amidala 8.00
KE0122 Qui-Gon Jinn 8.00

Flat die-cut vinyl characters.
KE0084 Boba Fett 4.00
KE0108 Darth Maul 4.00
KE0085 Darth Vader 4.00
KE0086 Greedo 4.00
KE0109 Jar Jar Binks 4.00
KE0087 Stormtrooper 4.00

Metal 3D jointed characters.
KE0111 Jar Jar Binks 12.00
KE0112 Pit Droid..14.00
KE0113 Watto 12.00
KE0165 Jedi vs. Sith on blue oval 4.00

Creative Conventions
1½"x2" white background.
KE0006 Darth Vader in flames 8.00
KE0011 Luke Skywalker, "A New Hope" triangular logo...............8.00
KE0028 Yoda, round 8.00

Crystal Craft
KE0168 Bravo Squadron..6.00
KE0171 JEDI 7.00
KE0169 Podracing..6.00
KE0170 Star Wars Episode I logo...................................7.00

Disney / MGM
KE0172 Star Wars Weekends, May 2001, R2-D2 projecting hologram
   Mickey 24.00

Downpace Ltd.
KE0175 Battle Droid...6.00
KE0176 Darth Maul...6.00
KE0177 Jar Jar Binks 6.00
KE0178 Obi-Wan Kenobi 6.00
KE0179 Qui-Gon Jinn 6.00

Factors, Etc.
KE0002 C-3PO...12.00
KE0003 Chewbacca 12.00
KE0005 Darth Vader helmet, 1¼" painted black 12.00
KE0020 R2-D2 1" unpainted metal 12.00
KE0023 Stormtrooper helmet, 1" painted white 12.00
KE0025 X-Wing Fighter, 2" unpainted.......................12.00

Fan Club
KE0052 10th Anniversary 1½" square plastic 11.00
KE0173 Official Star Wars Fan Club, 1977.................18.00

Hollywood Pins
KE0001 "20-Years 1977-1997"..................................9.00
KE0016 "Power of the Dark Side".............................6.00
KE0008 Darth Vader, mask 7.00
KE0009 Darth Vader, mask (small)...........................5.00
KE0010 Darth Vader, portrait..................................5.00
KE0013 Millennium Falcon.......................................6.00
KE0014 New Republic..6.00
KE0015 New Republic, antique finish 6.00
KE0019 R2-D2 ....7.00
KE0021 Rebel Forces..6.00
KE0022 Rebel Forces, antique finish........................6.00
KE0029 Yoda 5.00

Lego
KE0115 Darth Maul lego..7.00
KE0116 Darth Vader lego 8.00
KE0114 Luke, X-Wing pilot lego 8.00

Pepsi Cola
KE0174 Star Wars Trilogy, presented to Taco Bell managers 23.00

Playco Toys
KE0061 4-Pack Artoo-Detoo, Darth Vader, Luke Skywalker, See-
   Threepio 18.00
KE0062 4-Pack Boba Fett, Han Solo, Obi-Wan Kenobi, Yoda 18.00
KE0063 Admiral Ackbar 6.00
KE0064 Artoo-Detoo 5.00
KE0065 Artoo-Detoo painted gold, boxed 6.00
KE0066 Boba Fett 5.00
KE0067 Chewbacca 6.00
KE0068 Darth Vader 5.00
KE0069 Darth Vader painted gold, boxed 6.00
KE0070 Emperor Palpatine......................................6.00
KE0071 Greedo..6.00
KE0072 Han Solo..5.00
KE0104 Han Solo in Carbonite (FAO Schwarz numbered exclusive)........12.00
KE0074 Luke Skywalker 5.00
KE0075 Luke Skywalker in X-Wing Gear.....................6.00
KE0076 Luke Skywalker painted gold, boxed.............6.00

KE0077 Obi-Wan Kenobi 5.00
KE0078 Princess Leia 6.00
KE0079 See-Threepio 5.00
KE0080 See-Threepio painted gold, boxed................6.00
KE0081 Stormtrooper..6.00
KE0082 Tie Fighter Pilot 6.00
KE0083 Yoda 5.00

Rawcliffe

KE0088   KE0095   KE0093   KE0099   KE0094

KE0050   KE0041   KE0046

KE0035   KE0036   KE0047   KE0049   KE0051

KE0124   KE0037   KE0091   KE0048

KE0152 20-Year Anniversary..8.00
KE0154 Anakin Skywalker emblem 8.00
KE0035 AT-AT, pewter..12.00
KE0036 AT-ST, pewter..12.00
KE0144 Battle Droid blaster..12.00
KE0037 Blaster Pistol pewter, sculpted 12.00
KE0038 Blaster Rifle pewter, sculpted..........................12.00
KE0088 Boba Fett helmet, red Galactic Empire blister card 7.00
KE0089 Boba Fett with gun, red Galactic Empire blister card 7.00
KE0090 Boba Fett, red Galactic Empire blister card 7.00
KE0155 Darth Maul's face..10.00
KE0091 Darth Vader (fist)...7.00
KE0092 Darth Vader / Lightsaber 7.00
KE0093 Darth Vader helmet, red Galactic Empire blister card........7.00
KE0039 Darth Vader pewter, "Never Underestimate the Dark Side." 12.00
KE0040 Death Star pewter, sculpted..........................12.00
KE0094 Death Star, red Galactic Empire blister card......7.00
KE0041 Empire Strikes Back logo pewter......................12.00
KE0146 Episode I logo..12.00

KE0172   KE0061   KE0062   KE0065   KE0069   KE0076   KE0080   KE0104   Pkg. Sample

KE0063   KE0064   KE0066   KE0067   KE0068   KE0070   KE0071   KE0072   KE0074   KE0075   KE0077   KE0078   KE0079   KE0081   KE0082   KE0083

Keychains

KE0151 Episode I: Phantom Menace 7.00
KE0157 Gungan Sub 8.00
KE0042 Imperial emblem, pewter 12.00
KE0150 Jar Jar Binks 10.00
KE0159 Magic of Myth 15.00
KE0095 Millennium Falcon, blue Rebel Alliance blister card 7.00
KE0096 Millennium Falcon, CompUSA promotion, boxed 10.00
KE0097 Obi-Wan Kenobi / Lightsaber, blue Rebel Alliance blister card 7.00
KE0043 Obi-Wan Kenobi, pewter 12.00
KE0148 Obi-Wan's lightsaber 10.00
KE0153 Pit Droid..10.00
KE0149 Podracing...7.00
KE0098 Princess Leia, blue Rebel Alliance blister card 7.00
KE0145 Queen Amidala's Gun..12.00
KE0044 R2-D2 pewter, sculpted 12.00
KE0099 R2-D2, blue Rebel Alliance blister card.................7.00
KE0045 Rebel Alliance emblem, pewter 12.00
KE0046 Return of the Jedi logo, pewter 12.00
KE0158 Royal Starship 10.00
KE0047 Sand Skiff, pewter 12.00
KE0048 Shadows of the Empire logo, pewter...................12.00
KE0049 Shuttle Tyderium, pewter 12.00
KE0050 Star Wars logo, pewter..12.00
KE0124 Star Wars Special Edition, painted pewter 9.00
KE0100 Stormtrooper, red Galactic Empire blister card......7.00
KE0156 The Dark Side 7.00
KE0051 Tie Fighter, pewter..12.00
KE0101 Tie Squadron, red Galactic Empire blister card.....7.00
KE0147 Trade Federation Starfighter badge 8.00
KE0103 Yoda, pewter...12.00

Tiger Electronics

| KE0053 | KE0054 | KE0055 | KE0056 | KE0057 |

| KE0058 | KE0060 | KE0107 | KE0117 | KE0118 |

KE0107 Boba Fett, speaks one phrase 7.00
KE0053 C-3PO, flashlight 7.00
KE0117 Chewbacca, plays sound 6.00
KE0054 Darth Vader, speaks one phrase...........................6.00
KE0055 Death Star, records voice and plays back 7.00
KE0102 Jabba the Hutt sculpted, makes laughing sound ...6.00
KE0056 Lightsaber, lights and makes sound, extends and retracts............7.00
KE0118 Luke Skywalker, speaks one phrase......................6.00
KE0057 Millennium Falcon, plays sound............................6.00
KE0058 R2-D2, digital clock...7.00
KE0059 Star Destroyer, lights and plays sound 6.00
KE0060 Stormtrooper, speaks one phrase 6.00

Unlicensed

KE0125 – KE0143

KE0143 6-Pack, any 6 hanging off header copied from Hasbro header 36.00
KE0130 Anakin Skywalker, PVC 6.00
KE0136 Battle Droid, PVC 6.00
KE0125 Boss Nass, PVC 6.00
KE0141 C-3PO, PVC 6.00
KE0127 Chancellor Velorum, PVC 6.00
KE0133 Darth Maul, PVC 6.00
KE0140 Darth Sidious, PVC 6.00
KE0129 Gasgano, PVC 6.00
KE0132 Jar Jar Binks, PVC 6.00
KE0126 Ki-Adi-Mundi, PVC 6.00
KE0128 Mace Windu, PVC 6.00
KE0131 Obi-Wan Kenobi, PVC 6.00
KE0142 Padme, PVC 6.00
KE0134 Queen Amidala, PVC 6.00
KE0135 Qui-Gon Jinn, PVC 6.00
KE0139 Ric Olie, PVC 6.00
KE0138 Senator Palpatine, PVC 6.00
KE0137 Watto, PVC 6.00

Williams

| KE0160 | KE0161 | KE0164 |

| KE0163 | KE0162 |

KE0160 C-3PO, Star Wars Episode I Pinball...........................14.00
KE0161 Darth Maul, Star Wars Episode I Pin, 2000 ....14.00
KE0164 R2-D2 ....7.00
KE0163 Trade Federation Droid Starfighter 16.00
KE0162 Wrench, Official pinball pit droid 12.00
KE0123 Lightsaber, Qui-Gon's, part of Jedi Power Battle for Playstation promotion 5.00
KE0105 Mandelorian Emblem, pewter................................8.00
KE0106 Princess Leia w/Blaster on Square background, pewter 8.00

KITES

KI0019

General Mills
KI0019 Star Wars delta-wing flyer, mail-in premium 19.00

Palitoy
KI0011 Wing-shaped kite with X-Wing and Tie Fighter.........42.00

Spectra Star
KI0001 8-Panel with characters, box 17.00
KI0012 Boba Fett 32", diamond 6.00
KI0013 Darth Vader, delta-wing 11.00
KI0015 Darth Vader, diamond 16.00
KI0002 Darth Vader, character 14.00
KI0017 Darth Vader, parasail 12.00
KI0003 Death Star Trench, delta wing 8.00
KI0004 Droids, streamer 12.00
KI0005 Ewoks on Gliders 80"...10.00
KI0006 Luke Skywalker, character 14.00
KI0007 Luke Skywalker vs. Darth Vader 8.00
KI0016 Millennium Falcon, diamond 16.00
KI0008 Speeder Bike 50 ft., dragon 22.00
KI0009 Star Wars characters, delta-wing 8.00
KI0014 Wacky Winder, Darth Vader pkg. 5.00

KI0010 Wicket the Ewok, character 12.00

Worlds Apart
KI0018 Naboo Fighter stunt kite.......................... 8.00

KOOSH BALLS

KB0001   KB0002   KB0003   KB0004

Hasbro
KB0002 Captain Tarpals w/Kaadu 9.00
KB0001 Jar Jar Binks...9.00
KB0003 Sebulba 9.00
KB0004 Watto 9.00

LAMP SHADES

Hay Jax
LMS0001 Return of the Jedi characters on brown background..............38.00

LAMPS

Windmill Ceramics
LM0001 Chewbacca 9½" tall 57.00
LM0002 Darth Vader 12" tall 72.00
LM0003 R2-D2 8½" tall 55.00

LAPEL PINS

Factors, Etc.
Set 1.
JLP0001 C-3PO 6.00
JLP0003 Darth Vader 6.00
JLP0004 R2-D2 ....6.00

Set 2.
JLP0002 Chewbacca 6.00
JLP0005 Stormtrooper 6.00
JLP0006 X-Wing 6.00

LASER DISCS

VL0015   VL0016

VL0001   VL0009   VL0010

International Video Co. Ltd.
VL0014 A New Hope 75.00
VL0015 Empire Strikes Back......................................75.00

VL0016 Return of the Jedi...75.00
VL0013 Episode I: The Phantom Menace 115.00
VL0011 Ewoks-The Battle for Endor 45.00
VL0009 Making of Star Wars / ESB Special Effects........85.00
VL0007 Return of the Jedi, extended play 70.00
VL0012 Star Wars Special Edition, widescreen 115.00
VL0001 Star Wars, extended play 40.00
VL0002 Star Wars, extended play letterbox................65.00
VL0003 Star Wars, standard play 50.00
VL0004 The Empire Strikes Back, extended play 40.00
VL0005 The Empire Strikes Back, extended play letterbox 65.00
VL0006 The Empire Strikes Back, standard play 50.00
VL0010 The Ewok Adventure 45.00
VL0008 Trilogy Boxed Set: Special Collectors Edition, book, certificate, gift box 250.00

LASER LIGHT SPINNER

LLS0001 front and back and spinner

Fantasma
LLS0001 Star Wars logo and ships on defractive foil, covering 3¾" metal disc 10.00

LATCHHOOK CRAFT KITS

CRL0007 boxed and completed   CRL0009 completed

Leewards Creative Crafts
CRL0001 C-3PO and R2-D2 rug 24"x36" 35.00
CRL0002 C-3PO rug 35.00
CRL0003 Chewbacca rug, 20"x27" 35.00
CRL0004 Dart Vader pillow, 15"x15" (head only) 35.00
CRL0005 Darth Vader rug, 20"x27" (full figure)...........35.00
CRL0006 R2-D2 pillow, 15"x15" 35.00
CRL0007 R2-D2 rug, 20"x27" 35.00
CRL0008 Stormtrooper rug 24"x36" 35.00
CRL0009 Yoda rug 20"x27" 35.00

LAUNDRY BAGS

Adam Joseph Industries
LL0001 C-3PO and R2-D2 ....18.00
LL0002 Darth Vader and Emperor's Royal Guards 18.00
LL0003 Princess Kneesaa and Wicket........................10.00
LL0004 Wicket the Ewok 10.00

LEG WARMERS

Sales Corp. of America
AL0005 "Jedi"...10.00
AL0001 C-3PO 10.00
AL0007 Chewbacca 12.00
AL0008 Darth Vader 12.00
AL0002 Ewok 10.00
AL0004 R2-D2 ....12.00
AL0009 Return of the Jedi logo, applique 14.00
AL0003 Return of the Jedi logo, knit 12.00
AL0006 SW high socks...8.00

LEGO TOYS

Lego

LO0039 #1 Mini-figure 3-pack: Emperor, Darth Vader, Darth Maul (3340) 12.00
LO0040 #2 Mini-figure 3-pack: Han, Luke, Boba Fett (3341) 12.00
LO0041 #3 Mini-figure 3-pack: Chewbacca, two biker scout troops (3342) 12.00
LO0042 #4 Mini-figure 3-pack: OOM-9, two battle droids (3343) 12.00
LO0013 Anakin's Podracer (7131) 55.00
LO0014 A-Wing Fighter (7134) 25.00
LO0034 Battle Droid Carrier (7126) 45.00
LO0027 Battle Droid, Technics (8001) 30.00
LO0020 B-Wing at Rebel Control Center (7180)...............................45.00
LO0053 C-3PO, Technics (8007) 25.00
LO0043 Darkside Developer by Mindstorm 115.00
LO0009 Desert Skiff (7104) 12.00
LO0028 Destroyer Droid, Technics (8002)..50.00
LO0008 Droid Developer by Mindstorm 120.00
LO0033 Droid Escape (7106) 18.00
LO0010 Droid Fighter (7111) 10.00
LO0012 Flash Speeder (7124) 16.00
LO0011 Gungan Patrol (7115) 12.00
LO0018 Gungan Sub (7161) 65.00
LO0052 Imperial AT-ST (7127) 18.00
LO0048 Imperial Shuttle (7166) 35.00
LO0001 Landspeeder (7110) 9.00
LO0030 Lego building block embossed w/SW logo and TPM Lego characters; distributed at the SW Celebration in Denver, CO 18.00
LO0006 Lightsaber Duel (7101)...9.00
LO0024 Millennium Falcon (7190) 115.00
LO0019 Mos Espa Podrace (7171) 120.00
LO0015 Naboo Fighter (7141) 28.00
LO0007 Naboo Swamp (7121) 35.00
LO0026 Pit Droid, Technics (8000) 20.00
LO0049 Podrace Brick (7159) 24.00
LO0054 Promotion brick, with classic and current characters..................5.00
LO0017 Sith Infiltrator (7151) 38.00
LO0016 Slave I (7144) 26.00
LO0003 Snow Speeder (7130) 20.00

LO0002 Speeder Bikes (7128) 14.00
LO0051 Stormtrooper, Technics (8008)...25.00
LO0035 Tie Fighter (7146) 35.00
LO0005 Tie Fighter and Y-Wing (7150) 65.00
LO0022 Tie Interceptor, Technics (7181) 135.00
LO0029 Toy Fair promotion: 4"x5"x2" box with Luke and Vader figures and sound chip, labeled "Building a New Galaxy in 1999" 77.00
LO0021 Trade Federation AAT (7155) 30.00
LO0023 Trade Federation MTT (7184) 55.00
LO0050 Watto's Junk Yard (7186) 35.00
LO0004 X-Wing Fighter (7140) 36.00
LO0025 X-Wing, Technics (7191) 175.00

Similar in design to Kubricks by Mediacom.
LO0047 Han in Carbonite Block, single figure promotion 16.00
LO0044 ANH: R2-D2, C-3PO, Princess Leia, Ben Kenobi 45.00
LO0045 ESB: Stormtrooper, Han, Chewbacca, Boba Fett 52.00

LO0044

LO0045

LO0046

LO0057

LO0039   LO0040   LO0041   LO0042   LO0013   LO0014   LO0034   LO0027   LO0020

LO0043   LO0009   LO0028   LO0008   LO0033   LO0010

LO0012   LO0011   LO0018   LO0001   LO0006   LO0024

LO0019   LO0015   LO0007   LO0017   LO0016   LO0003   LO0002

LO0035   LO0005   LO0022   LO0021   LO0023   LO0004   LO0025

LO0046 ROTJ: Darth Vader, Luke, Yoda, Emperor.........................45.00
LO0057 Death Star Escape: Luke and Han in Stormtrooper disguise, Chewbacca 45.00

LICENSE PLATES

Disney / MGM
LCP0001 Jedi Training Academy 12.00

LIGHTERS

CGL0001

Kingsway
CGL0001 Splinter of the Mind's Eye art 10.00

LIP BALM

LPB0006 LPB0001 LPB0007 LPB0008 LPB0009 LPB0005 LPB0010 LPB0002 LPB0003 LPB0004

Minnetonka
Picture of character on barrel.
LPB0001 Darth Vader...5.00
LPB0006 Anakin Skywalker 5.00
LPB0007 Darth Maul..5.00
LPB0008 Jar Jar Binks 5.00
LPB0009 Queen Amidala 5.00

Sculpt of figure for cap.
LPB0002 Darth Vader...7.00
LPB0005 Anakin Skywalker 7.00
LPB0010 Darth Maul..7.00
LPB0003 Jar Jar Binks 7.00
LPB0004 Queen Amidala 7.00

LITE-BRITE REFILL SHEETS

Hasbro
LBR0001 12 Sheets from SW Trilogy, and 8 free-form sheets.........6.00

LBR0001 front and back

LITHOGRAPHY

LTG0001   **LTG0006**

20th Century Fox
LTG0001 Special Edition Video Covers, free w/purchase of SW:SE 12.00

Disney / MGM
LTG0007 Star Wars Weekends, May 2001....................................49.00

Gifted Images Publishing
LTG0002 Darth Vader from box artwork of Topps SW Galaxy cards, 23½"x30" signed by the artist, 500 produced numbered 560.00
LTG0003 Luke and Yoda signed by the artist, 500 produced numbered ...410.00

Score Board
LTG0004 Yoda sitting at his desk by Michael Whelan, 18"x17" signed, 850 produced...130.00

Star Struck
LTG0005 ROTJ lithograph: 3 X-Wings flying toward Death Star II with planets all around, signed and numbered, 3,000 produced..........................325.00
LTG0006 Episode I: Premium for pre-ordering EPI video.............................11.00

LOTION

LOT0001 front and back

Minnetonka
LOT0001 Queen Amidala bottle with sculpted character cap 6.00

LOTTERY TICKETS

WIN0001   WIN0002   WIN0003   WIN0004

WIN0005   WIN0006   WIN0007   WIN0008   WIN0009

La Francaise des Jeux
Scratch-off lottery tickets.
WIN0001 C-3PO...3.00
WIN0002 Dark Maul..3.00
WIN0003 Jar Jar Binks 3.00
WIN0004 Mace Windu...3.00
WIN0005 Obi-Wan Kenobi 3.00
WIN0006 Qui-Gon Jinn 3.00
WIN0007 R2-D2 ....3.00
WIN0008 Reine Amidala 3.00
WIN0009 Yoda...3.00

LUNCH BOXES

Calego International
LX0022 Starfighters, vinyl 8.00

Canadian Thermos Products

LX0003   LX0038   LX0039   LX0034

LX0003 ANH: movie art, plastic 34.00
LX0034 Dogfight over Deathstar...34.00
LX0038 ESB: movie art, plastic 34.00
LX0039 ROTJ: movie art, plastic..34.00

Lunch Boxes

King Seeley-Thermos

LX0011

LX0005

LX0004

LX0006

LX0007

LX0012

LX0010

LX0001

LX0002

LX0011 DROIDS: Plastic. Cartoon C-3PO and R2-D2 on lid. Thermos with cartoon droids 45.00
LX0005 ESB: Metal. Dagobah Swamp and Hoth Battle. Thermos with Yoda 85.00
LX0004 ESB: Metal. Millennium Falcon and Luke, R2-D2 and Yoda. Thermos with Yoda 55.00
LX0006 ESB: Plastic. Chewbacca, Han, Leia, and Luke on lid. Thermos with Yoda. 35.00
LX0007 ESB: Plastic. Logo with photo inserts. Thermos with Yoda. 43.00
LX0012 EWOKS: plastic. Ewoks on lid. Thermos with Ewok 32.00
LX0008 ROTJ: Metal. Jabba's Palace and Space Battle. Thermos with Ewok 35.00
LX0010 ROTJ: Plastic. Luke and Jabba's Palace Creatures. Plain thermos. 41.00
LX0009 ROTJ: Plastic. R2-D2 and Wicket on lid. Thermos with Ewok 32.00
LX0041 SW: Metal. Space Battle and Mos Eisley, no art on top, bottom, or sides 85.00
LX0001 SW: Metal. Space Battle and Mos Eisley. Thermos w/C-3PO and R2-D2 ....63.00
LX0042 SW: Plastic. Darth Vader and stormtroopers on paper decal......45.00
LX0002 SW: Plastic. Darth Vader, C-3PO, and R2-D2 on Paper Decal. Thermos w/C-3PO and R2-D2 ....57.00

Pyramid

LX0026

LX0023

LX0029

LX0040 Anakin Skywalker podracer, includes bottle................................12.00
LX0036 Darth Maul bust, includes bottle...12.00
LX0037 Darth Maul full-body, includes bottle...12.00
LX0013 Darth Maul, Style A 6.00
LX0014 Darth Maul, Style B 7.00
LX0015 Darth Maul, Style C 7.00
LX0026 Jar Jar, style A 6.00
LX0027 Jar Jar, style B 7.00
LX0028 Jar Jar, style C 7.00
LX0019 Jedi vs. Sith, Style A 6.00
LX0020 Jedi vs. Sith, Style B 7.00
LX0021 Jedi vs. Sith, Style C 7.00
LX0023 Jedi, style A..6.00
LX0024 Jedi, style B 7.00
LX0025 Jedi, style C 7.00
LX0016 Podracing featuring Anakin and Sebulba, Style A.........................6.00
LX0017 Podracing featuring Anakin and Sebulba, Style B 7.00
LX0018 Podracing featuring Anakin and Sebulba, Style C 7.00
LX0029 Podracing, style A...6.00
LX0030 Podracing, style B 7.00
LX0031 Podracing, style C 7.00

Spearmark Int.

LX0032

LX0035

LX0033

LX0032 Classic art decal featuring Luke and Leia, Vader and Stormtrooper, on plastic lunchbox 15.00
LX0035 Anakin Skywalker-shaped, includes bottle and wrench-shaped cooler block 18.00
LX0033 Darth Maul-shaped, includes bottle and sandwich case 18.00

MAGNETIC PLAYSET

MAG0001 front and back

MAG0001 Mix 'N' Match Adventure Playset, Deathstar Interior.................9.00

MAGNETS

A.H. Prismatic

HOX0089

HOX0090

HOX0089 Darth Vader, hologram...7.00
HOX0090 X-Wing Fighter in combat, hologram 7.00

Adam Joseph Industries

HOX0001

HOX0002

HOX0001 Chewbacca, Darth Vader, R2-D2, and Yoda 12.00
HOX0002 Wicket and Kneesaa..8.00

Applause

HOX0114

HOX0043

HOX0045

HOX0044

HOX0114 3D Magnets: Naboo Fighter, Battle Droid on Stap, Jar Jar Binks, Watto, boxed 21.00
HOX0038 AT-AT, die-cut 4.00
HOX0043 Battle Droid, 3D 6.00
HOX0044 Jar Jar Binks, 3D 6.00
HOX0039 Millennium Falcon, die-cut 4.00

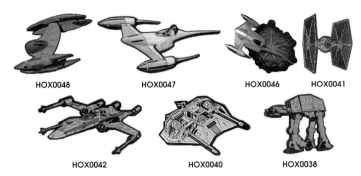

HOX0048   HOX0047   HOX0046   HOX0041

HOX0042   HOX0040   HOX0038

HOX0046 Naboo Fighter, 3D 5.00
HOX0047 Naboo starfighter, die-cut 4.00
HOX0040 Snowspeeder, die-cut 4.00
HOX0041 Tie Fighter, die-cut 4.00
HOX0048 Trade Federation Droid fighter, die-cut 4.00
HOX0045 Watto, 3D...6.00
HOX0042 X-Wing Fighter, die-cut......................................4.00

Ata-Boy

HOX0027   HOX0064   HOX0066

HOX0006 ANH Falcon cockpit 4.00
HOX0007 Ben holding lightsaber 4.00
HOX0008 Ben Kenobi 4.00
HOX0009 Ben Kenobi portrait..4.00
HOX0010 Boba Fett in Cloud City corridor 4.00
HOX0011 Bounty hunter line-up 4.00
HOX0012 B-wings in battle..4.00
HOX0013 C-3PO portrait...4.00
HOX0014 Chewbacca, snow covered 4.00
HOX0015 Darth Vader flanked by two stormtroopers.......4.00
HOX0016 Darth Vader portrait 4.00
HOX0017 Darth Vader portrait (shuttle ramp in background) 4.00
HOX0018 Darth Vader reaches out on Cloud City gantry ...4.00
HOX0019 Darth Vader silhouetted in ESB freeze chamber.........4.00
HOX0020 Darth Vader with beige background 4.00
HOX0021 Droids in Blockade Runner corridor 4.00
HOX0022 Droids in Hoth base corridor 4.00
HOX0023 Emperor Palpatine portrait 4.00
HOX0024 ESB 'A' poster with credits.................................4.00
HOX0025 ESB Luke in the tree..4.00
HOX0026 Falcon in flight 4.00
HOX0027 Han and Chewbacca blasting (publicity shot) 4.00
HOX0028 Han and Leia kiss (ESB) 4.00
HOX0029 Han blasting...4.00
HOX0030 Han in gunner chair 4.00
HOX0031 Han on Tauntaun 4.00
HOX0032 Han portrait...4.00
HOX0033 Han Solo 4.00
HOX0049 Holochess aboard the Falcon 4.00
HOX0050 Interior of Ben's house 4.00
HOX0051 Leia consoles Luke 4.00
HOX0052 Leia hand on hip, gun up 4.00
HOX0053 Leia on Falcon...4.00
HOX0054 Leia programming R2-D2 ....4.00
HOX0055 Luke and Leia ROTJ swing 4.00
HOX0056 Luke and X-Wing in swamp 4.00
HOX0057 Luke looking at the sunsets...............................4.00
HOX0058 Luke playing with T-16 ....4.00
HOX0059 Luke portrait..4.00
HOX0060 Luke sees charred relatives 4.00
HOX0061 Luke, Leia, and Han in Death Star 4.00
HOX0062 R2-D2 ....4.00
HOX0063 ROTJ 'A' poster with credits..............................4.00
HOX0064 Sandtrooper on dewback 4.00
HOX0065 Stormtrooper in freeze chamber 4.00
HOX0066 Stormtroopers blasting 4.00
HOX0067 SW 'C' poster with credits..................................4.00

HOX0068 Tie Interceptor 4.00
HOX0069 Tie shooting Falcon amid asteroids 4.00
HOX0070 X-Wing in flight 4.00
HOX0071 X-Wing shooting Vader's Tie Fighter 4.00
HOX0072 Yoda 4.00
HOX0073 Yoda in his house 4.00
HOX0074 Yoda on Luke's back 4.00

Disney / MGM
Star Tours.
HOX0035 C-3PO 4.00
HOX0036 R2-D2 ....4.00
HOX0034 Star Tours logo 4.00

Galoob
HOX0037 Magnetic base with 200 mini-Millennium Falcons, Toy Fair give-away 1997...24.00

Giftware International

HOX0099   HOX0100   HOX0101

HOX0102   HOX0103   HOX0104

Resin fridge magnets.
HOX0099 Anakin Skywalker 8.00
HOX0100 C-3PO 12.00
HOX0101 Chewbacca..12.00
HOX0102 Darth Maul 10.00
HOX0103 Darth Vader...12.00
HOX0104 Queen Amidala 10.00

Glow Zone

HOX0075   HOX0076

HOX0075 Darkside / Jedi refrigerator magnets, sheet of 10 .....8.00
HOX0076 Naboo Battle refrigerator magnets, sheet of 7 ....8.00

Howard Eldon
HOX0003 A New Hope, triangular logo 8.00
HOX0005 Return of the Jedi, Yoda in circle 8.00
HOX0004 The Empire Strikes Back, Darth Vader in flames 8.00

Kentucky Fried Chicken
HOX0095 Anakin Skywalker 5.00
HOX0097 Darth Maul..5.00

HOX0095   HOX0097   HOX0096   HOX0098

Magnets

HOX0096 Jar Jar Binks 5.00
HOX0098 Queen Amidala 5.00

Pepsi Cola

HOX0077   HOX0078   HOX0079   HOX0106   HOX0080

HOX0081   HOX0082   HOX0083   HOX0084   HOX0085

HOX0086   HOX0087   HOX0088   HOX0107   HOX0105

HOX0077 Anakin Skywalker 5.00
HOX0078 Battle Droid 5.00
HOX0079 Boss Nass 5.00
HOX0106 C-3PO 5.00
HOX0080 Captain Tarpals...5.00
HOX0081 Darth Maul..5.00
HOX0082 Darth Vader...5.00
HOX0083 Episode I Logo 5.00
HOX0084 Jar Jar Binks 5.00
HOX0085 Mace Windu..5.00
HOX0086 Nute Gunray 5.00
HOX0087 R2-D2 ....5.00
HOX0088 Sebulba 5.00
HOX0107 Watto 5.00
HOX0105 Yoda..5.00

Pizza Hut

HOX0091   HOX0092   HOX0093   HOX0094

HOX0091 Anakin Skywalker 3.00
HOX0093 Darth Maul..3.00
HOX0092 Jar Jar Binks 3.00
HOX0094 Queen Amidala 3.00

MAKE-UP KITS

MUK0002   MUK0003   MUK0004

Rubies

MUK0002 Darth Maul, deluxe 12.00
MUK0001 Darth Maul..7.00
MUK0003 Queen Amidala Jewelry and Make-Up......................12.00

MUK0004 Queen Amidala 7.00

MARBLES

MRB0001   MRB0002   MRB0003   MRB0004

MRB0005   MRB0006   MRB0007   MRB0008

MRB0009   MRB0010 front and back

Starbles

Classic trilogy scene viewable from front, marble collection set information viewable from back. 1¾"

MRB0008 C-3PO and R2-D2 on Hoth 15.00
MRB0005 Chewbacca..15.00
MRB0002 Darth Vader on Bespin gantry..................................15.00
MRB0001 Dogfight over Deathstar 15.00
MRB0006 Han Solo..15.00
MRB0003 Jabba the Hutt...15.00
MRB0004 Princess Leia (Jabba's prisoner)...............................15.00
MRB0010 Princess Leia and R2-D2 ....15.00
MRB0009 Wicket the Ewok..15.00
MRB0007 Yoda...15.00

MARKERS

SUH0002   SUH0003

Butterfly Originals

SUH0001 C-3PO card with Marker 6.00
SUH0002 Darth Vader (black or blue) 8.00
SUH0003 Darth Vader helmet on clip (any color)......................6.00

Mead

SUH0004 front and back

SUH0004 8-pack, each color has own character illustration on barrel......7.00

242

Rose Art Industries

SUH0005

SUH0005 Super Stamper, washable..................................7.00

MASCOT STRAPS

MS0001 C-3PO 14.00
MS0002 Darth Vader 14.00

MASKS

Ben Cooper
MA0001 Admiral Ackbar...9.00
MA0012 Chewbacca 8.00
MA0025 Gamorrean Guard 9.00
MA0029 Klaatu 9.00
MA0047 Wicket 9.00
MA0051 Yoda...10.00

Cesar

MA0054　　　　MA0056

MA0053 C-3PO...35.00
MA0054 Chewbacca 35.00
MA0055 Darth Vader 35.00
MA0056 Stormtrooper 35.00
MA0057 Tusken Raider 35.00

Don Post
MA0002 Admiral Ackbar...35.00
MA0003 Admiral Ackbar, hands....................................25.00
MA0004 Boba Fett...60.00
MA0005 Boba Fett, deluxe 975.00
MA0006 Boba Fett, retail 1998.....................................35.00
MA0007 C-3PO, black latex; gold paint, 1978 ....60.00
MA0008 C-3PO, copyright by Lucas Films Ltd., 1993 .....50.00
MA0009 C-3PO, gold latex, 1977 ....195.00
MA0010 Cantina Band Member....................................45.00
MA0011 Cantina Band Member, hands.........................25.00
MA0013 Chewbacca, closed mouth, 1978 ....100.00
MA0014 Chewbacca, snarling, 1977 ....425.00
MA0072 Chewbacca, vinyl with hair 35.00
MA0015 Darth Vader Deluxe helmet, fiberglass 1995 ....800.00
MA0016 Darth Vader helmet w/plastic nose and respirator tips, 1994....50.00
MA0017 Darth Vader helmet, copyright by 20th Century Fox, 1978......125.00

MA0002　　　MA0008　　　MA0010　　　MA0019

MA0022　　MA0024　　MA0026　　MA0028　　MA0030　　MA0042　　MA0048　　MA0052

MA0018 Darth Vader helmet, copyright by Lucas Films Ltd., 1993...........50.00
MA0019 Darth Vader helmet, original w/sticker, 1977 ....250.00
MA0020 Darth Vader helmet, retail distribution, 1998......................35.00
MA0021 Darth Vader helmet, w/o respirator tips, 1983 ....50.00
MA0022 Emperor 125.00
MA0023 Emperor, copyright by Lucas Films Ltd., 1994....................60.00
MA0024 Emperor's Royal Guard 95.00
MA0026 Gamorrean Guard 35.00
MA0027 Gamorrean Guard, copyright by Lucas Films Ltd. 60.00
MA0028 Greedo 50.00
MA0073 Jawa 40.00
MA0030 Klaatu 45.00
MA0031 Klaatu, copyright by Lucas Films Ltd., 1994 ....60.00
MA0032 Nien Nunb 30.00
MA0033 Prince Xizor 50.00
MA0034 Prince Xizor, hands...25.00
MA0070 Scout Trooper helmet, retail distribution, 1998 ....55.00
MA0035 Stormtrooper helmet, copyright by Lucas Films Ltd., 1993 ....50.00
MA0036 Stormtrooper helmet, lighter eye lenses 1978 ....85.00
MA0037 Stormtrooper helmet, molded band 45.00
MA0038 Stormtrooper helmet, original 1977 ....100.00
MA0039 Stormtrooper helmet, painted eyes, 1988 ....55.00
MA0040 Stormtrooper helmet, retail distribution, 1998.......35.00
MA0041 Tie Pilot Helmet...110.00
MA0071 Tie Pilot Helmet and Chest Plate....................1,200.00
MA0042 Tie Pilot Helmet, retail 1998............................40.00
MA0074 Tusken Raider 40.00
MA0075 Tusken Raider 40.00
MA0043 Tusken Raider, 1977 ....125.00
MA0044 Tusken Raider, copyright by Lucas Films Ltd., 1993...........50.00
MA0045 Ugnaught 75.00
MA0046 Weequay 95.00
MA0048 Wicket, molded fur 85.00
MA0049 Wicket, real fur 70.00
MA0050 X-Wing Pilot..110.00
MA0052 Yoda...40.00

Micro Games of America

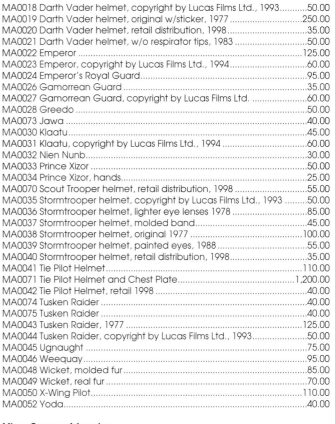

MA0069 front and back

MA0069 Power Talker, Darth Vader mask with microphone and belt-clipped speaker..36.00

Rubies
MA0061 Boba Fett, covers head, flexible rubber 23.00
MA0058 C-3PO, children's PVC 4.00
MA0062 C-3PO, covers head, flexible rubber..................23.00
MA0059 Chewbacca, children's PVC 4.00
MA0063 Chewbacca, covers head, flexible rubber...........23.00
MA0060 Darth Vader, children's PVC 4.00
MA0065 Darth Vader, covers head, 2-piece molded plastic 18.00
MA0064 Darth Vader, covers head, flexible rubber...........23.00
MA0066 Stormtrooper, covers head, flexible rubber.........23.00
MA0067 Tusken Raider, covers head, flexible rubber 23.00
MA0068 Yoda, covers head, flexible rubber....................23.00

MASKS, TPM

Don Post
MAS0001 Anakin's Pod Helmet 60.00
MAS0006 Darth Maul...44.00

Masks, TPM

MAS0010 Even Piell 60.00
MAS0005 Jar Jar Binks 55.00
MAS0011 Jar Jar Binks (Deluxe).............................. 125.00
MAS0009 Ki-Adi-Mundi 60.00
MAS0002 Naboo Starfighter Helmet 55.00
MAS0013 Nute Gunray...95.00
MAS0003 Queen Amidala-Senate Headpiece............ 55.00
MAS0004 Queen Amidala-Theed...............................55.00
MAS0014 Rune Haako..95.00
MAS0007 Sebulba..44.00
MAS0012 Sebulba (Deluxe) 75.00
MAS0008 Watto..44.00

Rubies

MAS0018   MAS0016   MAS0021   MAS0020   MAS0023

MAS0031 Anakin Skywalker, children's 5.00
MAS0025 Boss Nass deluxe overhead latex, adult 43.00
MAS0018 Boss Nass vinyl 3/4, adult......................22.00
MAS0024 Darth Maul deluxe overhead latex, adult 43.00
MAS0032 Darth Maul PVC, adult.............................5.00
MAS0033 Darth Maul PVC, children's......................5.00
MAS0016 Darth Maul vinyl 3/4, adult.....................22.00
MAS0017 Darth Maul vinyl 3/4, children's 8.00
MAS0028 Jar Jar Binks deluxe overhead latex, adult....................40.00
MAS0021 Jar Jar Binks vinyl 3/4, adult.................. 18.00
MAS0022 Jar Jar Binks vinyl 3/4, children's 8.00
MAS0034 Jar Jar Binks, adult.................................5.00
MAS0035 Jar Jar Binks, children's 5.00
MAS0027 Nute Gunray deluxe overhead latex, adult 45.00
MAS0020 Nute Gunray vinyl 3/4, adult..................26.00
MAS0036 Queen Amidala, children's 5.00
MAS0029 Sebulba deluxe overhead latex, adult.......43.00
MAS0023 Sebulba vinyl 3/4, adult........................20.00
MAS0026 Watto deluxe overhead latex, adult.........36.00
MAS0019 Watto vinyl 3/4, adult............................18.00
MAS0030 Yoda deluxe overhead latex, adult 43.00

Tapper Candies

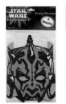

MAS0015 front and back

MAS0015 Party Mask 4-pack: Anakin's Pod Race Helmet, Jar Jar, Queen Amidala Headdress, Darth Maul..3.00

MATCHBOXES

MBC0002   MBC0003   MBC0004   MBC0005   MBC0006

MBC0007   MBC0008   MBC0009   MBC0010   MBC0011

MBC0012   MBC0013   MBC0014   MBC0015   MBC0016

MBC0017   MBC0018   MBC0019   MBC0020   MBC0021

Hollywood Match Company.
MBC0022 10-pack: characters 35.00
MBC0001 10-pack: movie posters 35.00
MBC0003 ANH international art 3.00
MBC0004 ANH SE poster art 3.00
MBC0020 C-3PO 3.00
MBC0018 Chewbacca 3.00
MBC0016 Darth Vader 3.00
MBC0009 ESB classic international art 3.00
MBC0010 ESB international art 3.00
MBC0005 ESB SE poster art 3.00
MBC0017 Han Solo 3.00
MBC0013 Luke Skywalker...3.00
MBC0014 Obi-Wan Kenobi 3.00
MBC0015 Princess Leia 3.00
MBC0019 R2-D2 ....3.00
MBC0008 ROTJ classic international art 3.00
MBC0011 ROTJ international art 3.00
MBC0006 ROTJ SE poster art 3.00
MBC0021 Stormtrooper 3.00
MBC0007 SW classic international art 3.00
MBC0012 SW: movie poster art 3.00
MBC0002 SW:SE Trilogy Logo 3.00

MATS

MT0001 package and mat

Recticel Sutcliffe Ltd.
MT0001 Play mat, artwork from all 3 movies, 24½"x39"...........................135.00

MEDALLIONS

MDC0001   MDC0002   MDC0003

Craft House
MDC0001 C-3PO and R2-D2 / Darth Vader 12.00
MDC0002 Han Solo / Princess Leia 12.00
MDC0003 Luke Skywalker / Yoda 12.00

MEMO BOARDS

Day Runner
Wipe-off board with pen and paper calendar.

SUI0008   SUI0013

SUI010 Darth Maul, large...14.00
SUI006 Darth Maul, small..8.00
SUI011 Jar Jar Binks, large 14.00
SUI007 Jar Jar Binks, small..8.00
SUI012 R2-D2, large..14.00
SUI008 R2-D2, small..8.00
SUI013 Yoda, large...14.00
SUI009 Yoda, small...8.00

Icarus
Wipe-clean with marker.
SUI002 Chewbacca, Han Solo, and Lando Calrissian................................22.00
SUI003 Darth Vader and Stormtroopers 24.00
SUI004 Han Solo, Luke Skywalker, and Princess Leia................................22.00

Junior Achievment
SUI001 Message Center, limited to 500 .... 135.00

Union
SUI005 10th anniversary, plastic with pocket for paper and pen, magnetic
back 20.00

MEMO PADS

SUM0010   SUM0013   SUM0011   SUM0012

SUM0008   SUM0009   SUM0007

Impact, Inc.
50 sheets, die-cut.
SUM0007 Darth Maul 3.00
SUM0008 Jar Jar 3.00
SUM0009 Queen Amidala 3.00

3"x5", 60 sheets.
SUM0010 Anakin 2.00
SUM0013 Darth Maul 2.00
SUM0011 Jar Jar 2.00
SUM0012 Obi-Wan 2.00

Stuart Hall
SUM0001 Aliens memo pad...6.00
SUM0002 Boba Fett memo pad...8.00
SUM0003 C-3PO and R2-D2 memo pad 8.00
SUM0004 Darth Vader and Stormtroopers memo pad...........................8.00
SUM0005 Luke Skywalker in Bepin Fatigues memo pad 8.00
SUM0006 Yoda memo pad 8.00

MICE: COMPUTER

CM0010   CM0001   CM0002   CM0003

CM0010 Anakin Skywalker, sculpted...35.00

American Covers
CM0001 C-3PO, sculpted 35.00
CM0002 Darth Vader, sculpted 35.00
CM0003 Stormtrooper, sculpted 35.00

World Wide Licenses Ltd.

CM0007   CM0011   CM0009   CM0004   CM0012

CM0005   CM0006   CM0008

CM0005 "Computer Gift Set", C-3PO sculpted mouse with C-3PO and R2-D2 mousepad...29.00
CM0007 "Computer Gift Set", Darth Maul mouse with Darth Maul mousepad 21.00
CM0006 "Computer Gift Set", Darth Vader sculpted mouse with Darth Vader mousepad...29.00
CM0011 "Computer Gift Set", Jar Jar Binks mouse with Naboo mousepad...21.00
CM0008 "Computer Gift Set", Stormtrooper sculpted mouse with Stormtrooper mousepad...29.00
CM0009 Anakin Skywalker 11.00
CM0004 Darth Maul 16.00
CM0012 Jar Jar Binks 12.00

MICRO COLLECTION TOYS

TYM0001   TYM0003   TYM0004   TYM0006

TYM0009   TYM0010   TYM0011

TYM0012   TYM0017   TYM0018   TYM0019   TYM0020

Kenner
TYM0001 Bespin Control Room..26.00
TYM0002 Bespin Freeze Chamber 63.00
TYM0003 Bespin Gantry..22.00
TYM0004 Bespin World...135.00
TYM0005 Build Your Armys (Set of 6)...35.00
TYM0006 Death Star Escape..30.00
TYM0007 Death Star Trash Compactor 75.00
TYM0008 Death Star World...110.00
TYM0009 Hoth Generator Attack..34.00

Micro Collection Toys

TYM0010 Hoth Ice Cannon..35.00
TYM0011 Hoth Turret Defense.....................................27.00
TYM0012 Hoth Wampa Cave.......................................25.00
TYM0013 Hoth World...115.00
TYM0014 Individual Figures, ea.....................................3.00
TYM0015 Individual Figures, unpainted ea. 2.00
TYM0016 Millennium Falcon (Sears exclusive)..............225.00
TYM0017 Snowspeeder (J.C. Penney exclusive)............165.00
TYM0018 Tie Fighter...65.00
TYM0019 Tie Fighter with alternate Background............85.00
TYM0020 X-Wing Fighter 44.00
TYM0021 X-Wing Fighter with Background 85.00

MICROMACHINES

MCM0003   MCM0005   MCM0002

MCM0001   MCM0010   MCM0008

Galoob

MCM0001 A-Wing Starfighter 7.00
MCM0009 Death Star 7.00
MCM0010 Death Star II 12.00
MCM0002 Imperial AT-AT...7.00
MCM0003 Imperial Star Destroyer 7.00
MCM0004 Millennium Falcon.......................................12.00
MCM0005 Snowspeeder..12.00
MCM0006 Tie Starfighter...10.00
MCM0008 Tie Starfighter, bronze 20th Century Fox promo 26.00
MCM0007 X-Wing Starfighter 10.00

MICROMACHINES, TPM

MCN0004   MCN0005   MCN0006   MCN0007   MCN0008

Galoob

MCN0001 Anakin's Podracer 12.00
MCN0002 Gasgano's Podracer....................................12.00
MCN0003 Gungan Sub (Bongo)..................................12.00
MCN0004 Mars Guo's Podracer...................................12.00
MCN0005 Naboo Fighter 12.00
MCN0006 Sebulba's Podracer.....................................12.00
MCN0007 Sith Infiltrator...12.00
MCN0008 Trade Federation MTT..................................12.00

MICROMACHINES: ACTION FLEET

MMA0011   MMA0012   MMA0018   MMA0021

MMA0019   MMA0002   MMA0006   MMA0003

MMA0001   MMA0034   MMA0013   MMA0005

MMA0009   MMA0014   MMA0030   MMA0020

MMA0008   MMA0023   MMA0022   MMA0017

Galoob

MMA0011 2-Pack: Luke's Landspeeder / AT-ST (KB Toys exclusive)..........25.00
MMA0012 AT-AT, remote control (KB Toys exclusive) 24.00
MMA0004 A-Wing Starfighter with C-3PO and Rebel Pilot 18.00
MMA0018 A-Wing with Mon Mothma and Pilot........................11.00
MMA0021 Bespin Cloud Car with Cloud Car Pilot and Lobot...................10.00
MMA0019 B-Wing Starfighter with Rebel Pilot and Admiral Ackbar.........10.00
MMA0002 Darth Vader's Tie Fighter with Darth Vader and Imperial Pilot..17.00
MMA0033 Darth Vader's Tie Fighter, white box (Avon exclusive) 14.00
MMA0031 E-Wing Starfighter with Rebel Pilot and R7 Astromech Droid..85.00
MMA0006 Imperial AT-AT with Imperial Driver and Snowtrooper..............17.00
MMA0026 Imperial Landing Craft.....................................38.00
MMA0003 Imperial Shuttle Tyderium with Han Solo and Chewbacca 18.00
MMA0029 Jabba's Sail Barge with Saelt-Marae (Yak Face) and R2-D2..10.00
MMA0010 Jawa Sandcrawler with Jawa and Scavenger Droid.............10.00
MMA0032 Luke's X-Wing from Dagobah Swamp (Toyfare exclusive) 14.00
MMA0001 Luke's X-Wing Starfighter with Luke Skywalker and R2-D2.......10.00
MMA0034 Luke's X-Wing Starfighter, white box (Avon exclusive) 14.00
MMA0025 Millennium Falcon with Han Solo and Chewbacca 10.00
MMA0013 Rancor with Gamorrean Guard and Luke Skywalker..............10.00
MMA0027 Rebel Blockade Runner with Princess Leia and Rebel Fleet
    Trooper...30.00
MMA0005 Rebel Snowspeeder with Luke Skywalker and Rebel Gunner..16.00
MMA0009 Slave I with Boba Fett and Han Solo 10.00
MMA0028 T-16 Skyhopper wiith Biggs Darklighter and Luke Skywalker....10.00
MMA0014 Tie Bomber with Imperial Pilot and Imperial Naval Trooper 10.00
MMA0030 Tie Defender with Imperial Tie Pilot and Moff Jerjerrod 95.00
MMA0020 Tie Fighter with Imperial Pilot and Grand Moff Tarkin..........10.00
MMA0008 Tie Interceptor with 2 Imperial Pilots.........................12.00
MMA0015 Virago with Prince Xizor and Guri 48.00
MMA0023 X-Wing with Porkins and R2-Unit............................12.00
MMA0016 X-Wing with Wedge and R2 Unit............................12.00
MMA0007 Y-Wing Starfighter with Rebel Pilot and R2 unit......................10.00
MMA0022 Y-Wing with Blue Leader and R2 Unit.......................11.00
MMA0017 Y-Wing with Gold Leader and R2 Unit 11.00

MICROMACHINES: ACTION FLEET BATTLE PACK

MMB0001   MMB0002   MMB0003   MMB0004   MMB0005

MMB0006   MMB0007   MMB0008   MMB0009   MMB0010

MMB0011 MMB0013 MMB0016 MMB0017 MMB0018

MMP0006 MMP0009 MMP0001

MMP0010 MMP0003 MMP0002

MMP0012 MMP0008 MMP0013

MMP0005 MMP0004 MMP0007

Galoob

MMB0001 #01: Speeder Bikes, Lando, Luke, Leia, Rebel Trooper, Echo base Trooper 8.00
MMB0002 #02: AT-ST, AT-ST Pilot, Scout Trooper, Darth Vader, Sandtrooper 8.00
MMB0003 #03: Bantha, Tusken Raider, Gamorrean Guard, Bib Fortuna, Brea Tonnika 8.00
MMB0004 #04: Dewback, Sandtrooper, Boba Fett, Greedo, Bossk............8.00
MMB0005 #05: Swoops, Dash Rendar, Prince Xizor, Guri, LE-BO2D9, Jix.....8.00
MMB0006 #06: Desert Skiff, Boba Fett, Nikto, Chewbacca, Han, Luke 8.00
MMB0007 #07: Escape Pod, R2-D2, Obi-Wan Kenobi, C-3PO, Sandtrooper, Darth Vader 8.00
MMB0008 #08: Jabba the Hutt, Ishi Tibb, Princess Leia (Boushh), Lando, Sy Snootles 8.00
MMB0009 #09: Hang Glider, Speeder Bike, Luke, Scout Trooper, Wicket, Rebel Trooper, Ewok...............8.00
MMB0010 #10: Ronto, Luke, Ben, Jawa, Dr. Evazan, Garindan 8.00
MMB0011 #11: Landspeeder, C-3PO, Ben, Figrin D'an, Muftak, Han 8.00
MMB0012 #12: LakSivrak, Duros, Labria, Momaw Nadon, Arcona, Wuher, Nabrun Leids, Advozsec...............8.00
MMB0013 #13: Tauntaun, General Veers, Wampa, Han Solo with Tauntaun, Luke, Snowtrooper...............8.00
MMB0014 #14: General Tagge, Admiral Motti, Princess Leia, Han, Ben, Darth Vader, R2-D2............... 8.00
MMB0015 #15: Yoda (Glow-In-The-Dark), Obi-Wan (GITD), Anakin (GITD), Luke, Leia, Han, Chewbacca...............8.00
MMB0016 #16: Lars Family Landspeeder, Uncle Owen, Aunt Beru, Luke, EG-6, Jawa...............8.00
MMB0017 #17: Speeder Bike, Scout Troopers, Stormtrooper, Snowtrooper, Sandtrooper...............8.00
MMB0018 #18: Echo Base Troopers, Rebel Troopers, Endor Trooper, X-Wing Pilot, Y-Wing Pilot, Y-Wing Gunner............... 8.00

MMP0006 Cloud City, 2nd release 14.00
MMP0009 Death Star 12.00
MMP0001 Death Star, 2nd release 14.00
MMP0010 Endor Planetary Power Station......................12.00
MMP0003 Endor Planetary Power Station, 2nd release 14.00
MMP0011 Hoth Base......................12.00
MMP0002 Hoth Base, 2nd release 14.00
MMP0012 Millennium Falcon carry playset 18.00
MMP0008 Millennium Falcon carry playset, 2nd release 14.00
MMP0013 Planet Dagobah 12.00
MMP0005 Planet Dagobah, 2nd release 14.00
MMP0014 Planet Tatooine 12.00
MMP0004 Planet Tatooine, 2nd release 14.00
MMP0015 Rebel Transport 12.00
MMP0007 Rebel Transport, 2nd release 14.00

MICROMACHINES: ACTION FLEET MINI SCENES, TPM

MMO0004 MMO0001 MMO0002 MMO0003

MMO0009 MMO0010 MMO0011 MMO0012

Galoob

MMO0005 #01: STAP Invasion.........................8.00
MMO0004 #01: STAP Invasion (First Edition) 10.00
MMO0006 #02: Destroyer Droid Ambush 8.00
MMO0001 #02: Destroyer Droid Ambush (First Edition)............................10.00
MMO0007 #03: Gungan Assault 8.00
MMO0002 #03: Gungan Assault (First Edition) 10.00
MMO0008 #04: Sith Pursuit 8.00
MMO0003 #04: Sith Pursuit (First Edition) 10.00
MMO0009 #05: Trade Federation Raid 8.00
MMO0010 #06: Throne Room Reception 8.00
MMO0011 #07: Watto's Deal........................8.00
MMO0012 #08: Generator Core Duel 8.00

MICROMACHINES: ACTION FLEET PLAYSETS

Galoob

MMP0016 Cloud City...........................12.00

MICROMACHINES: ACTION FLEET PLAYSETS, DOUBLE-TAKES

MMDT0001 front and back

Galoob

MMDT001 Double-Takes Death Star 45.00

MICROMACHINES: ACTION FLEET PLAYSETS, TPM

Galoob

MMI0001 Gian Speeder and Theed Palace (Sneak Preview)...................24.00
MMI0002 Mos Espa Market......................15.00

MMI0001 MMI0002

MMI0006   MMI0005   MMI0007

MMI0003 Mos Espa Market (First Edition) 17.00
MMI0006 Otoh Gunga 24.00
MMI0004 Pod Racer Hangar Bay...15.00
MMI0005 Pod Racer Hangar Bay (First Edition) 17.00
MMI0007 Theed Palace 22.00

MICROMACHINES: ACTION FLEET, TPM

MMQ0001   MMQ0011   MMQ0004   MMQ0005

MMQ0006   MMQ0007   MMQ0008   MMQ0009

MMQ0002   MMQ0010   MMQ0003   MMQ0014

Galoob
MMQ0001 Anakin's Pod Racer 12.00
MMQ0011 Fambaa with remote control 17.00
MMQ0004 Flash Speeder 12.00
MMQ0005 Gungan Submarine 12.00
MMQ0006 Mars Guo's Pod Racer 12.00
MMQ0007 Naboo Fighter 12.00
MMQ0008 Republic Cruiser 12.00
MMQ0009 Sebulba's Pod Racer 12.00
MMQ0002 Trade Federation Droid Fighter 12.00
MMQ0010 Trade Federation Landing Ship 12.00
MMQ0003 Trade Federation MTT 12.00
MMQ0014 Trade Federation Tank with remote control 17.00

Hasbro

MMQ0012   MMQ0016   MMQ0013   MMQ0015

MMQ0012 Royal Starship 15.00
MMQ0016 Sith Infiltrator 18.00
MMQ0013 Trade Federation Droid Control Ship 15.00
MMQ0015 Trade Federation Tank 15.00

MICROMACHINES: ACTION MASTERS

Galoob
MMD0001 4-Pack: C-3PO, Princess Leia, R2-D2, Obi-Wan........................30.00

MMD0001   MMD0002

MMD0003   MMD0006   MMD0004

MMD0005   MMD0008   MMD0009   MMD0010   MMD0011

MMD0002 4-Pack: C-3PO, Princess Leia, R2-D2, Obi-Wan; POTF style pkg. . 33.00
MMD0003 6-Pack: Boba Fett, Han, Chewbacca, Darth Vader, Luke,
    Stormtrooper...36.00
MMD0004 6-Pack: Boba Fett, Han, Chewbacca, Darth Vader, Luke,
    Stormtrooper; POTF style pkg. 45.00
MMD0005 C-3PO 9.00
MMD0006 C-3PO, Gold (mail-in exclusive)..22.00
MMD0008 Darth Vader 12.00
MMD0013 Darth Vader, tri-logo 7.00
MMD0009 Luke Skywalker..8.00
MMD0010 R2-D2...10.00
MMD0012 R2-D2, tri-logo 7.00
MMD0011 Stormtrooper 10.00

MICROMACHINES: ADVENTURE GEAR

MME0003   MME0001   MME0002

Galoob
MME0003 Luke's Binoculars/Yavin Rebel Base..12.00
MME0001 Luke's Binoculars/Yavin Rebel Base, 2nd release 14.00
MME0004 Vader's Lightsaber/Death Star Trench 12.00
MME0002 Vader's Lightsaber/Death Star Trench, 2nd release.................14.00

MICROMACHINES: BOXED SETS

MMF0001   MMF0002   MMF0003   MMF0010

MMF0004   MMF0018   MMF0007

MMF0016   MMF0005   MMF0019   MMF0009

Galoob
MMF0001 Collector's Edition A New Hope...7.00
MMF0002 Collector's Edition Empire Strikes Back 7.00
MMF0003 Collector's Edition Return of the Jedi 7.00
MMF0004 Collector's Gift Set, bronze finish (Toys R Us exclusive) 24.00

MMF0005 Darth Vader / Star Destroyer 2-pack (Fan Club exclusive) 19.00
MMF0019 Droids...18.00
MMF0006 Eleven-Piece Collector's Gift Set (KB Toys exclusive)................17.00
MMF0007 Galaxy Battle Collector's Set (K-Mart exclusive) 18.00
MMF0008 Galaxy Battle Collector's Set 2nd edition (K-Mart exclusive) ..18.00
MMF0009 Han Solo / Millennium Falcon (Fan Club exclusive) 36.00
MMF0011 Imperial Forces Gift Set 2nd edition with exclusive Darth Vader fig-
ure (Target exclusive) 13.00
MMF0010 Imperial Forces Gift Set with exclusive Emperor figure (Target
exclusive) 13.00
MMF0012 Master Collector's Edition (Toys R Us exclusive)........................27.00
MMF0013 Micro 3-pack (Film and Toy Fair exclusive) 37.00
MMF0015 Rebel Forces Gift Set 2nd edition (Target exclusive) 14.00
MMF0014 Rebel Forces Gift Set with exclusive Admiral Ackbar figure (Target
exclusive) 14.00
MMF0016 Rebel vs. Imperial Gift Set...15.00
MMF0018 Trilogy Gift Set 24.00

MICROMACHINES: CLASSIC DUELS

MMG0001

MMG0002

Galoob
MMG0001 Millennium Falcon vs. Tie Interceptor (Toys R Us exclusive).....36.00
MMG0002 X-Wing Fighter vs. Tie Fighter (Toys R Us exclusive)..................36.00

MICROMACHINES: DIECAST VEHICLES

MMZ0019   MMZ0020   MMZ0021

Galoob
MMZ0019 24k 2-pack (plated): Imperial Logo and Shuttle Tyderium.......35.00
MMZ0021 24k 2-pack (plated): Millennium Falcon and Darth Vader's Tie
Fighter...35.00
MMZ0020 24k 2-pack (plated): X-Wing and Slave I.................................35.00
MMZ0001 A-Wing Fighter 7.00
MMZ0002 Death Star 24.00
MMZ0003 Executor with Star Destroyer 15.00
MMZ0014 Imperial Star Destroyer 7.00
MMZ0004 Imperial Star Destroyer, 2nd release 7.00
MMZ0005 Jawa's Sandcrawler 7.00
MMZ0006 Landspeeder 7.00
MMZ0015 Millennium Falcon 7.00
MMZ0007 Millennium Falcon, 2nd release 7.00
MMZ0008 Slave I 15.00
MMZ0009 Snowspeeder 7.00
MMZ0010 Tie Bomber 18.00
MMZ0016 Tie Fighter 7.00
MMZ0011 Tie Fighter, 2nd release 7.00
MMZ0017 X-Wing Fighter...7.00

MMZ0005

MMZ0015

MMZ0016

MMZ0017

MMZ0018

MMZ0001

MMZ0002

MMZ0003

MMZ0004

MMZ0006

MMZ0007

MMZ0008

MMZ0009

MMZ0011

MMZ0012

MMZ0013

MMZ0012 X-Wing Fighter, 2nd release 7.00
MMZ0018 Y-Wing Fighter..7.00
MMZ0013 Y-Wing Fighter, 2nd release 7.00

MICROMACHINES: DIECAST VEHICLES, TPM

MAI0005

MAI0001

MAI0006

MAI0002

MAI0007

MAI0008

MAI0003

MAI0004

Galoob
MA10005 Federation Tank 14.00
MA10001 Gian Speeder 7.00
MA10009 Gian Speeder (First Edition) 9.00
MA10006 Republic Cruiser 14.00
MA10002 Royal Starship 7.00
MA10010 Royal Starship (First Edition) 9.00
MA10007 Sebulba's Pod Racer 14.00
MA10008 Sith Infiltrator 14.00
MA10003 Trade Federation Battleship 7.00
MA10011 Trade Federation Battleship (First Edition)...........................9.00
MA10004 Trade Federation Droid Starfighter 7.00
MA10012 Trade Federation Droid Starfighter (First Edition)................ 9.00

MICROMACHINES: EPIC COLLECTIONS

MMJ0001

MMJ0002

MMJ0003

MMJ0004

MMJ0005

MMJ0006

Galoob
MMJ0001 I: Heir to the Empire..5.00
MMJ0002 II: Jedi Search 5.00
MMJ0003 III: Truce at Bakura...5.00
MMJ0004 IV: Dark Apprentice 45.00
MMJ0005 V: Dark Force Rising 45.00
MMJ0006 VI: The Courtship of Princess Leia 45.00

MICROMACHINES: FIGURES

Galoob
MMK0014 Bounty Hunters 18.00
MMK0025 Classic Characters..6.00
MMK0011 Classic Characters, 2nd release 7.00
MMK0021 Echo Base Troops 6.00
MMK0007 Echo Base Troops, 2nd release 7.00
MMK0012 Endor Rebel Strike Team 6.00
MMK0016 Ewoks 18.00

Micromachines: Figures

MMK0015	MMK0016	MMK0020	MMK0021
MMK0014	MMK0011	MMK0007	MMK0012
MMK0008	MMK0006	MMK0004	MMK0001
MMK0005	MMK0009	MMK0003	MMK0010

MMN0001	MMN0002	MMN0003	MMN0004

MMN00011	MMN00012	MMN00013	MMN00014

MMN0005	MMN0006	MMN0007	MMN0008

MMN0009	MMN0010	MMN0015

MMK0002 Ewoks, 2nd release 135.00
MMK0022 Imperial Naval Troopers 6.00
MMK0008 Imperial Naval Troopers, 2nd release 7.00
MMK0020 Imperial Officers...6.00
MMK0006 Imperial Officers, 2nd release......................7.00
MMK0018 Imperial Pilots 6.00
MMK0004 Imperial Pilots, 2nd release 7.00
MMK0013 Imperial Scout Troopers..............................6.00
MMK0015 Imperial Stormtroopers................................6.00
MMK0001 Imperial Stormtroopers, 2nd release.............7.00
MMK0019 Jawas 6.00
MMK0005 Jawas, 2nd release....................................7.00
MMK0023 Rebel Fleet Troopers 6.00
MMK0009 Rebel Fleet Troopers, 2nd release...............7.00
MMK0017 Rebel Pilots...6.00
MMK0003 Rebel Pilots, 2nd release............................7.00
MMK0024 Tusken Raiders 6.00
MMK0010 Tusken Raiders, 2nd release........................7.00

MICROMACHINES: INSIDE ACTION SETS, TPM

MA60001	MA60002

Galoob
MA60002 Darth Maul / Theed Generator 28.00
MA60001 Gungan Sub / Otoh Gunga 28.00

MICROMACHINES: MEGA-DELUXE PLAYSETS, TPM

MA70001

Galoob
MA70001 Trade Federation MTT / Naboo Battlefield 38.00

MICROMACHINES: MINI-ACTION SETS

Galoob
MMN0001 I: Boba Fett, Admiral Ackbar, Gamorrean Guard...................12.00

MMN0011 I: Boba Fett, Admiral Ackbar, Gamorrean Guard, 2nd release .16.00
MMN0002 II: Nien Nunb, Greedo, Tusken Raider 9.00
MMN0012 II: Nien Nunb, Greedo, Tusken Raider, 2nd release...............16.00
MMN0003 III: Jawa, Yoda, Princess Leia as Boushh 9.00
MMN0013 III: Jawa, Yoda, Princess Leia as Boushh, 2nd release..............16.00
MMN0004 IV: Bib Fortuna, Figrin D'an, Scout Trooper 9.00
MMN0014 IV: Bib Fortuna, Figrin D'an, Scout Trooper, 2nd release.........16.00
MMN0005 V: Bossk, Duros, Sandtrooper.......................55.00
MMN0006 VI: 2-1B, Weequay, Emperor's Royal Guard 55.00
MMN0007 VII: 4-LOM, Rebel Pilot, Snowtrooper............55.00
MMN0008 VIII: Wampa, Wicket, Tie Fighter Pilot 55.00
MMN0009 IX: Salacious Crumb, Jabba the Hutt, AT-AT Driver 55.00
MMN0015 Mini-Action Boxed C-3PO Set (7 Figure Heads)....................124.00
MMN0010 Mini-Action Boxed Yoda Set (7 Figure Heads).........................12.00

MICROMACHINES: PLATFORM ACTION SETS, TPM

MA40001	MA40002	MA40003

MA40004	MA40005	MA40006

Galoob
MA40004 Galactic Dogfight: Trade Federation Droid Fighter, Naboo Fighter, Daultay Dofine 12.00
MA40002 Galactic Senate: Coruscant Taxi, Senator Palpatine, Chancellor Valorum..12.00
MA40003 Naboo Temple Ruins: Gungan guard, Boss Nass, Gian Speeder 12.00
MA40001 Pod Race Arena: Flagman, Aldar Beedo's Pod Racer, Jabba the Hutt 12.00
MA40005 Tatooine Desert: Royal Starship, Qui-Gon Jinn, Qui-Gon Jimm on Eopie 12.00
MA40006 Theed Rapids: Gungan Sub (Bongo), Qui-Gon Jinn, Obi-Wan Kenobi 12.00

MICROMACHINES: PLAYSETS, TPM

Galoob
MNP0001 Naboo Hangar, Final Combat.......................18.00

MNP0001 MNP0002 MNP0003

MNP0002 Royal Starship Repair..18.00
MNP0003 Theed Palace Assault 25.00

MICROMACHINES: POD RACERS, TPM

MA20008 MA20009 MA20011

MA20001 MA20002 MA20003 MA20004

MA20005 MA20006 MA20007

Galoob
MA20008 Build Your Own Pod Racer (blue) 9.00
MA20010 Build Your Own Pod Racer (red)...................................7.00
MA20009 Build Your Own Pod Racer (teal)...................................7.00
MA20011 Build Your Own Pod Racer (yellow)................................7.00
MA20006 Gasgano Turbo Pod Racer 12.00
MA20005 Launcher 2-pack w/Gasgano/Teemto Pagalies.....................14.00
MA20007 Ody Mandrell Turbo Pod Racer 12.00
MA20001 Pod Racer Pack I : Anakin Skywalker / Ratts Tyerell 7.00
MA20002 Pod Racer Pack II : Sebulba / Clegg Holdfast 7.00
MA20003 Pod Racer Pack III : Dud Bolt / Mars Guo 7.00
MA20004 Pod Racer Pack IV : Boles Roor / Neva Kee...........................7.00

Hasbro

MA20012 MA20013 MA20014 MA20015

MA20013 Build Your Own Pod Racer (black)..................................7.00
MA20012 Build Your Own Pod Racer (crystal blue)...........................8.00
MA20014 Build Your Own Pod Racer (orange)................................7.00
MA20015 Build Your Own Pod Racer (yellow)................................7.00

MICROMACHINES: SERIES ALPHA

MMR0001 MMR0002 MMR0003 MMR0004 MMR0006

Galoob
MMR0001 B-Wing Fighter 18.00
MMR0002 Imperial AT-AT 17.00
MMR0003 Imperial Shuttle 17.00
MMR0004 Snowspeeder 17.00
MMR0005 Twin-Pod Cloud Car 18.00

MMR0006 X-Wing Starfighter 17.00
MMR0007 Y-Wing Fighter 18.00

MICROMACHINES: SERIES ALPHA, TPM

MMV0001 MMV0002

MMV0003 MMV0004

Hasbro
MMV0001 Naboo Fighter..20.00
MMV0002 Royal Starship..20.00
MMV0003 Sith Infiltrator..18.00
MMV0004 Trade Federation Droid Fighter....................................17.00

MICROMACHINES: TRANSFORMING ACTION SETS

MMS0001 MMS0005 MMS0004

MMS0006 MMS0015 MMS0013

MMS0007 MMS0017 MMS0008

MMS0011 MMS0012 MMS0009

MMS0010 MA50001 MA50002

Galoob
MMS0006 Boba Fett / Cloud City..16.00
MMS0001 C-3PO / Cantina 19.00
MMS0014 C-3PO / Cantina, 2nd release 16.00
MMS0005 Chewbacca / Endor 16.00
MMS0002 Darth Vader / Bespin 19.00
MMS0015 Darth Vader / Bespin, 2nd release 16.00
MMS0013 Jabba / Mos Eisley Space Port 14.00
MMS0007 Luke Skywalker / Hoth...16.00
MMS0003 R2-D2 / Jabba's Desert Palace 19.00
MMS0009 R2-D2 / Jabba's Desert Palace, 2nd release..........................16.00
MMS0008 Royal Guard / Death Star II 16.00
MMS0011 Slave I / Tatooine..16.00
MMS0012 Star Destroyer / Space Fortress 16.00

Micromachines: Transforming Action Sets

MMS0004 Stormtrooper / Death Star..16.00
MMS0016 Stormtrooper / Death Star, 2nd release 16.00
MMS0009 Tie Fighter Pilot / Academy.....................................16.00
MMS0010 Yoda / Dagobah 16.00

MICROMACHINES: TRANSFORMING ACTION SETS, TPM

Galoob
MA50001 Battle Droid / Trade Federation Control Ship 17.00
MA50002 Jar Jar / Naboo..17.00

MICROMACHINES: VEHICLE / FIGURE COLLECTIONS, SOTE

MMY0001 **MMY0002** **MMY0003**

Galoob
MMY0001 I: IG-2000, Guri, Darth Vader, ASP, Stinger 9.00
MMY0002 II: Outrider, Dash Rendar, Luke Skywalker, LE-BO2D9, Hound-
stooth 9.00
MMY0003 III: Virago, Xizor, Emperor, Swoop with Rider................9.00

MICROMACHINES: VEHICLE / FIGURE COLLECTIONS, TPM

MA30001 **MA30011** **MA30002** **MA30012**

MA30013 **MA30014** **MA30005** **MA30006**

MA30007 **MA30008** **MA30009** **MA30010**

Galoob
MA30011 Collection 01: Anakin's Pod Racer, Anakin, Flash Speeder, Sio
Bibble 7.00
MA30001 Collection 01: Anakin's Pod Racer, Anakin, Flash Speeder, Sio Bib-
ble (First Edition) 14.00
MA30012 Collection 02: Gungan Sub, Boss Nass, Federation Tank AAT, Nute
Gunray 7.00
MA30002 Collection 02: Gungan Sub, Boss Nass, Federation Tank AAT, Nute
Gunray (First Edition) 14.00
MA30013 Collection 03: Gasgano's Pod Racer, Gasgano, Fambaa, Jar Jar
Binks 7.00
MA30003 Collection 03: Gasgano's Pod Racer, Gasgano, Fambaa, Jar Jar
Binks (First Edition) 14.00
MA30014 Collection 04: Coruscant Taxi, Ki-Adi-Mundi, Sith Infiltrator, Darth
Sidious 7.00
MA30004 Collection 04: Coruscant Taxi, Ki-Adi-Mundi, Sith Infiltrator, Darth
Sidious (First Edition) 14.00
MA30015 Collection 05: Gungans 7.00
MA30005 Collection 05: Gungans (First Edition)........................14.00
MA30016 Collection 06: Battle Droids 7.00
MA30006 Collection 06: Battle Droids (First Edition)...................14.00
MA30007 Collection 07: Sebulba, Sebulba's Pod Racer, Kitster, Eopie 8.00
MA30008 Collection 08: Darth Maul, Sith Speeder with Darth Maul, Naboo
Fighter, Naboo Pilot 8.00
MA30009 Collection 09: Jar Jar Binks, Falumpaset with Cart, Mars Guro,
Mars Guro's Podracer..8.00
MA30010 Collection 10: Battle Droid, Trade Federation MTT, Rune Haako,
Gian Speeder 8.00

MICROMACHINES: VEHICLES

Galoob
MMT0001 #1: X-Wing, Millennium Falcon, Star Destroyer 7.00
MMT0002 #2: Tie Fighter, AT-AT, Snowspeeder 7.00
MMT0003 #3: AT-ST, Jabba's Sail Barge, B-Wing........................7.00
MMT0004 #4: Blockade Runner, Sandcrawler, Y-Wing..................7.00
MMT0005 #5: Slave I, Twin-Pod Cloud Car, Tie Bomber................7.00
MMT0006 #6: Speeder Bike with Rebel, Shuttle Tyderium, A-Wing..............7.00
MMT0007 I: Tie Interceptor, Star Destroyer, Blockade Runner 6.00
MMT0022 I: Tie Interceptor, Star Destroyer, Blockade Runner, 2nd release 6.00
MMT0008 II: Landspeeder, Millennium Falcon, Jawa Sandcrawler............6.00

MMX0001 **MMX0002** **MMX0003** **MMX0004**

MMT0022 **MMT0023** **MMT0024** **MMT0025** **MMT0026** **MMT0027** **MMT0028**

MMT0030 **MMT0031** **MMT0018** **MMT0019** **MMT0020** **MMT0014** **MMT0016** **MMT0017**

MMT0032 **MMT0001** **MMT0002** **MMT0003** **MMT0007** **MMT0008** **MMT0009** **MMT0011** **MMT0013**

MMT0023 II: Landspeeder, Millennium Falcon, Jawa Sandcrawler, 2nd release 6.00
MMT0009 III: Darth Vader's Tie Fighter, Y-Wing, X-Wing 6.00
MMT0024 III: Darth Vader's Tie Fighter, Y-Wing, X-Wing, 2nd release 6.00
MMT0010 IV: Probot, AT-AT, Snowspeeder 6.00
MMT0025 IV: Probot, AT-AT, Snowspeeder, 2nd release 6.00
MMT0011 V: Rebel Transport, Tie Bomber, AT-ST 6.00
MMT0026 V: Rebel Transport, Tie Bomber, AT-ST, 2nd release 6.00
MMT0012 VI: Escort Frigate, Slave I, Twin-Pod Cloud Car 6.00
MMT0027 VI: Escort Frigate, Slave I, Twin-Pod Cloud Car, 2nd release 6.00
MMT0013 VII: Mon Calamari Star Cruiser, Jabba's Sail Barge, Speeder Bike with Rebel 6.00
MMT0028 VII: Mon Calamari Star Cruiser, Jabba's Sail Barge, Speeder Bike with Rebel, 2nd release 6.00
MMT0014 VIII: Speeder Bike with Imperial, Shuttle Tyderium, Tie Fighter 6.00
MMT0029 VIII: Speeder Bike with Imperial, Shuttle Tyderium, Tie Fighter, 2nd release 6.00
MMT0015 IX: Executor, B-Wing, A-Wing 6.00
MMT0030 IX: Executor, B-Wing, A-Wing, 2nd release 6.00
MMT0016 X: T-16 Skyhopper, Lars Family Landspeeder, Death Star II 6.00
MMT0031 X: T-16 Skyhopper, Lars Family Landspeeder, Death Star II, 2nd release 6.00
MMT0017 XI: Cloud City, Mon Calamari Rebel Cruiser, Escape Pod 6.00
MMT0018 XII: A-Wing, Tie Fighter, Y-Wing...............................6.00
MMT0019 XIII: Battle Damaged X-Wings (Red, Blue, Green) 8.00
MMT0020 XIV: Landing Craft, Death Star, Speeder Swoop 6.00
MMT0021 XV: Outrider, Tibanna Refinery, V-35 Landspeeder 6.00
MMT0032 3-pack: AT-AT, Snowspeeder, X-Wing, bronze-colored 19.00
MMT0033 Classic Series I: X-Wing Fingter and Slave I (J.C. Penney exclusive) 16.00
MMT0034 Classic Series II: Imperial Shuttle and Imperial Emblem (FAO Schwarz exclusive) 16.00
MMT0035 Classic Series III: Darth Vader's Tie Fighter and Millennium Falcon (SW Catalog exclusive) 16.00
MMT0036 The Balance of Power: X-Wing Fighter and Tie Fighter 19.00

MICROMACHINES: X-RAY FLEET

Galoob
Photos on previous page.
MMX0001 I: Darth Vader's Tie Fighter and A-Wing 7.00
MMX0002 II: X-Wing and AT-AT..8.00
MMX0003 III: Millennium Falcon and Sandcrawler 7.00
MMX0004 IV: Slave I and Y-Wing 7.00
MMX0005 V: Tie-Bomber and B-Wing..62.00
MMX0006 VI: AT-ST and Snowspeeder 62.00
MMX0007 VII: Tie Fighter and Land Speeder.............................62.00
MMX0008 VIII: Death Star and Imperial Shuttle.........................75.00
MMX0009 Trilogy Gift Set (J.C. Penney exclusive) 58.00

MILK CAPS

MC0001

Stanpac
MC0001 Darth Vader, "The Force is With You" 26.00

MINI-MOVIES

MM0001   MM0002   MM0003   MM0004   MM0005   MM0006

Interlace4D
24-frame lenticular flip-movies. Limited to 10,000 each.
MM0001 Attack on Battleship 20.00
MM0002 Darth Maul 20.00
MM0003 Explosion: Pod Racer Cockpit 20.00
MM0004 Jedi vs. Battledroids 20.00
MM0005 Pod Racer Crash..20.00
MM0006 Pod Racer Through Arches 20.00
MM0007 Qui-Gon vs. Battledroids 20.00
MM0008 Space Battle 24.00

MIRRORS

HOM0003   HOM0005

Lightline Industries
Silver frame 20"x30".
HOM0002 C-3PO and R2-D2 ....57.00
HOM0003 Chewbacca and Han Solo 57.00
HOM0004 Darth Vader 57.00
HOM0005 Dogfight...62.00

Sigma

HOM0001

HOM0001 Darth Vader mirror..35.00

MITTENS

Sales Corp. of America
AM0001 C-3PO..10.00
AM0002 Chewbacca 10.00
AM0003 Darth Vader 10.00
AM0004 Paploo 8.00
AM0005 R2-D2 ....11.00
AM0006 Wicket 8.00

MOBILES

MBL0001 front and back

Glow Zone
MBL0001 Episode I glow-in-the-dark mobile, Naboo Fighter, Droid Fighter, Naboo, Trade Federation Battleship 8.00

Kentucky Fried Chicken
MBL0004 Anakin Skywalker circle danglers, Naboo fighter on back 4.00
MBL0005 Boss Nass circle danglers, Naboo fighter on back 4.00
MBL0006 Jar Jar Binks circle danglers, Naboo fighter on back 4.00
MBL0007 Obi-Wan Kenobi circle danglers, Naboo fighter on back 4.00
MBL0008 Queen Amidala circle danglers, Naboo fighter on back 4.00
MBL0009 Qui-Gon Jinn circle danglers, Naboo fighter on back 4.00
MBL0003 TPM cup topper mobile, 2 pieces with slots for toppers 3.00

Pepsi Cola
MBL0002 Mobile: X-Wings vs. Ties, Star Wars SE Trilogy 11.00

MODEL ROCKETS

Estes
MR0014 A-Wing starter set 45.00

Model Rockets

MR0001   MR0002   MR0018   MR0019

MR0025   MR0027   MR0028   MR0029   MR0034

MR0031   MR0035   MR0036

MR0037 Darth Vader's Tie Fighter complete launch set, flies over 500 feet ..45.00
MR0001 Darth Vader's Tie Fighter, boxed 35.00
MR0015 Death Star starter set 35.00
MR0002 Death Star, boxed...25.00
MR0020 Millennium Falcon 18.00
MR0032 Naboo Fighter with R2-D2 launcher, flies up to 330 feet.............40.00
MR0028 Naboo Fighter, flies up to 330 feet...9.00
MR0027 Naboo Royal Starship mini, flies up to 300 feet 8.00
MR0036 Naboo Royal Starship, flies up to 300 feet 45.00
MR0003 Proton Torpedo, boxed..35.00
MR0034 R2-D2 EPI Flying Model Rocket Starter Set, flies up to 100 feet ...16.00
MR0035 R2-D2 EPI, flies up to 100 feet..9.00
MR0004 R2-D2 Flying, bagged..35.00
MR0005 R2-D2 Flying, bagged 15th Anniversary 25.00
MR0006 R2-D2 Flying, boxed 40.00
MR0024 R2-D2 with recovery parachute 30.00
MR0025 Red Squadron X-Wing Starfighter, prebuilt 11.00
MR0021 Shuttle Tyderium 23.00
MR0031 Sith Infilterator, flies up to 200 feet...45.00
MR0007 Star Destroyer 24.00
MR0022 Tie Fighter with recovery parachute...25.00
MR0008 Tie Fighter, bagged...29.00
MR0009 Tie Fighter, bagged 15th Anniversary 25.00
MR0030 Trade Federation Battleship..40.00
MR0033 Trade Federation Droid Fighter 40.00
MR0029 Trade Federation Droid Fighter, flies up to 215 feet......................9.00
MR0016 X-Wing and Darth Vader's Tie Fighter starter set........................65.00
MR0026 X-Wing Fighter North Coast Rocketry, 20"x18" with recovery para-
    chute, deluxe 130.00
MR0010 X-Wing Fighter, bagged 26.00
MR0011 X-Wing Fighter, bagged 15th Anniversary 28.00
MR0012 X-Wing Fighter, boxed 40.00
MR0017 X-Wing starter set 35.00
MR0023 X-Wing with recovery parachute 20.00
MR0013 X-Wing, boxed Maxi-Brute..65.00
MR0019 X-Wing, mini in blister pkg..9.00
MR0018 Y-Wing starter set...45.00

MODELS: METAL

MOM0008

AMT/Ertl
MOM0008 Naboo Fighter, 1:48 scale, pre-painted w/stand.....................24.00

MOM0001   MOM0002

Remco
MOM0001 Millennium Falcon, Steel Tec 50.00
MOM0002 X-Wing Fighter, Steel tec...35.00

Tsukuda

MOM0004   MOM0005

MOM0003 AT-AT and Snowspeeder..115.00
MOM0004 AT-ST and Snowspeeder 115.00
MOM0005 Millennium Falcon and Slave I..115.00
MOM0006 Star Destroyer with Millennium Falcon and Rebel Transport.115.00
MOM0007 Tie Fighter and X-Wing Fighter...120.00

MODELS: PLASTIC

MOP0001   MOP0098   MOP0099

MOP0013   MOP0015   MOP0095

MOP0028   MOP0030   MOP0031

MOP0033   MOP0043   MOP0051

MOP0055   MOP0061   MOP0074

MOP0097   MOP0079   MOP0081

Airfix
MOP0100 Luke Skywalker's Snowspeeder, ESB 28.00

AMT/Ertl
MOP0001 3-Piece Set: B-Wing, X-Wing, Tie Interceptor, ROTJ Snap-
    together 25.00
MOP0004 AT-AT, ROTJ 20.00
MOP0098 AT-AT, Snap-Fast..8.00
MOP0099 AT-ST, Snap-Fast...8.00
MOP0013 Battle on Ice Planet Hoth, ESB 15.00
MOP0015 B-Wing Fighter, ROTJ limited edition gold 36.00
MOP0095 Cantina Action Scene...24.00
MOP0021 Darth Vader, SW..12.00
MOP0025 Darth Vader's Tie Fighter, SW..12.00

MOP0006

MOP0007

MOP0009

MOP0010

MOP0017

MOP0018

MOP0011

MOP0016

MOP0019

MOP0023

MOP0032

MOP0036

MOP0038

MOP0041

MOP0046

MOP0049

MOP0054

MOP0052

MOP0058

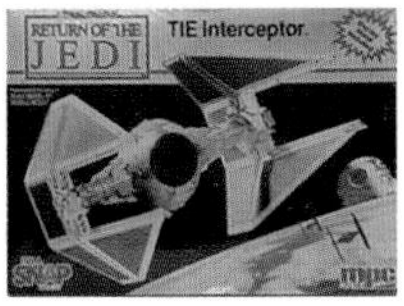
MOP0069

MOP0060

MOP0062

MOP0073

MOP0028 Darth Vader's Tie Fighter, SW flight display 22.00
MOP0030 Darth Vader's Tie Fighter, SW w/paint 17.00
MOP0094 Death Star 22.00
MOP0031 Encounter with Yoda on Dagobah, ESB 16.00
MOP0093 Imperial Tie Fighters 14.00
MOP0033 Jabba's Throne Room, ROTJ 15.00
MOP0035 Luke Skywalker's Snowspeeder, ESB 16.00
MOP0040 Millennium Falcon, ROTJ 18.00
MOP0043 Millennium Falcon, ROTJ cut-away 35.00
MOP0096 Rancor, Collector's Edition 39.00
MOP0048 Rebel base, ESB 18.00
MOP0051 Shuttle Tyderium, ROTJ 15.00
MOP0055 Slave I, ESB 16.00
MOP0057 Speeder Bike, ROTJ 20.00
MOP0061 Star Destroyer, ESB 12.00
MOP0064 Star Destroyer, ESB w/fiber optic lights 75.00
MOP0066 Tie Interceptor, ROTJ limited edition gold 45.00
MOP0068 Tie Interceptor, ROTJ Snap-together 16.00
MOP0074 Xizor's Virago, SOTE 20.00
MOP0097 X-Wing Fighter, Electronic 24.00
MOP0075 X-Wing Fighter, ROTJ 12.00
MOP0078 X-Wing Fighter, ROTJ flight display 20.00
MOP0079 X-Wing Fighter, ROTJ limited edition gold 35.00
MOP0084 X-Wing Fighter, ROTJ w/paint 15.00
MOP0081 X-Wing Fighter, Snap-together 12.00

MPC

MOP0003 AT-AT, ESB 35.00
MOP0006 AT-AT, ROTJ Structor wind-up 27.00
MOP0007 AT-ST, ROTJ 15.00
MOP0009 AT-ST, ROTJ Mirr-a-Kit 16.00
MOP0010 AT-ST, ROTJ Structor wind-up 27.00
MOP0011 A-Wing Fighter, ROTJ Snap-together 22.00
MOP0014 Battle on Ice Planet Hoth, ESB 36.00
MOP0016 B-Wing Fighter, ROTJ Snap-together 35.00
MOP0017 C-3PO, ROTJ 15.00
MOP0018 C-3PO, ROTJ Structor wind-up 27.00
MOP0019 C-3PO, SW 48.00
MOP0020 C-3PO, SW reduced box 35.00
MOP0023 Darth Vader, SW with Glo-Light saber 55.00
MOP0024 Darth Vader, SW action model 75.00
MOP0026 Darth Vader's Tie Fighter, SW 45.00
MOP0029 Darth Vader's Tie Fighter, SW reduced box 35.00
MOP0032 Encounter with Yoda on Dagobah, ESB 50.00
MOP0034 Jabba's Throne Room, ROTJ 43.00
MOP0036 Luke Skywalker's Snowspeeder, ESB 40.00
MOP0038 Luke Skywalker's X-Wing, SW 45.00
MOP0039 Luke Skywalker's X-Wing, SW reduced box 35.00
MOP0041 Millennium Falcon, ROTJ 45.00
MOP0044 Millennium Falcon, SW w/lights 125.00
MOP0045 R2-D2, ROTJ 22.00
MOP0046 R2-D2, SW 45.00
MOP0047 R2-D2, SW reduced box 35.00
MOP0049 Rebel base, ESB 24.00
MOP0052 Shuttle Tyderium, ROTJ 38.00

MOP0082

MOP0085

MOP0054 Shuttle Tyderium, ROTJ Mirr-a-Kit 16.00
MOP0056 Slave I, ESB 75.00
MOP0058 Speeder Bike, ROTJ 28.00
MOP0060 Speeder Bike, ROTJ Mirr-a-Kit 16.00
MOP0062 Star Destroyer, ESB 35.00
MOP0065 Tie Fighter, ROTJ 18.00
MOP0067 Tie Interceptor, ROTJ Mirr-a-Kit 16.00
MOP0069 Tie Interceptor, ROTJ Snap-together 20.00
MOP0071 Van, Darth Vader, SW Snap-together 50.00
MOP0072 Van, Luke Skywalker, SW Snap-together 50.00
MOP0073 Van, R2-D2, SW Snap-together 50.00
MOP0076 X-Wing Fighter, ROTJ 20.00
MOP0080 X-Wing Fighter, ROTJ Mirr-a-Kit 16.00
MOP0082 X-Wing Fighter, ROTJ Snap-together 20.00
MOP0085 Y-Wing Fighter, ROTJ 50.00
MOP0087 Y-Wing Fighter, ROTJ Mirr-a-Kit 16.00

MPC/Ertl

MOP0002 3-Piece Set: B-Wing, X-Wing, Tie Interceptor, ROTJ Snap-together .36.00
MOP0005 AT-AT, ROTJ 20.00
MOP0008 AT-ST, ROTJ 10.00
MOP0012 A-Wing Fighter, ROTJ Snap-together 17.00
MOP0022 Darth Vader, SW 15.00
MOP0027 Darth Vader's Tie Fighter, SW 15.00
MOP0037 Luke Skywalker's Snowspeeder, ESB 20.00
MOP0042 Millennium Falcon, ROTJ 20.00
MOP0050 Rebel base, ESB 15.00
MOP0053 Shuttle Tyderium, ROTJ 17.00
MOP0059 Speeder Bike, ROTJ 18.00
MOP0063 Star Destroyer, ESB 15.00
MOP0070 Tie Interceptor, ROTJ Snap-together 14.00
MOP0077 X-Wing Fighter, ROTJ 12.00
MOP0083 X-Wing Fighter, ROTJ Snap-together 12.00
MOP0086 Y-Wing Fighter, ROTJ 35.00

Polydata

MOP0088

MOP0089

MOP0090

MOP0091

MOP0092

1/6 scale, pre-painted, limited to 9,000.

MOP0088 Ben Kenobi 25.00
MOP0089 Lando Calrissian 27.00

Models: Plastic

MOP0090 Luke Skywalker 25.00
MOP0091 Princess Leia...25.00
MOP0092 Tusken Raider...33.00

MODELS: PLASTIC, TPM

MOZ0001   MOZ0002   MOZ0003

MOZ0004   MOZ0005   MOZ0006   MOZ0007

MOZ0008   MOZ0009   MOZ0010

AMT/Ertl
MOZ0001 Anakin's Pod Racer...12.00
MOZ0003 Droid Fighters (3 in kit)..14.00
MOZ0010 Gungan Sub...39.00
MOZ0005 Landing Ship, Snapfast Mini, 5 parts.......................................6.00
MOZ0004 Large Transport, Snapfast Mini, 8 parts 5.00
MOZ0002 Naboo Fighter..12.00
MOZ0006 Republic Cruiser, Snapfast Mini, 7 parts...................................6.00
MOZ0007 Sith Infiltrator, Snapfast Mini, 5 parts...................................7.00
MOZ0009 STAP...16.00
MOZ0008 Trade Federation Battle Tank...18.00

MODELS: RESIN

Kaiyodo
MDR0002 Han Solo 1/15 scale..66.00
MDR0003 Stormtrooper 1/15 scale 74.00

MODELS: VINYL

MOV0006   MOV0009   MOV0010   MOV0013   MOV0015

AMT/Ertl
MOV0006 Darth Vader 23.00
MOV0009 Emperor Palpatine, SOTE 34.00
MOV0010 Han Solo...23.00
MOV0013 Luke Skywalker...23.00
MOV0015 Prince Xizor, SOTE 20.00

Kaiyodo
MOV0027 R2-D2 1/6 ....50.00
MOV0026 Stormtrooper 1/6...45.00

Marmit

MOV0022   MOV0023   MOV0024   MOV0025

Action figure kits.
MOV0024 Boba Fett 175.00
MOV0022 Sandtrooper 175.00
MOV0023 Stormtrooper 155.00
MOV0025 Tie Fighter Pilot 135.00

Screamin' Products Inc

MOV0001   MOV0003   MOV0005   MOV0016   MOV0019

MOV0001 Boba Fett 1/4..75.00
MOV0002 Boba Fett 1/6..65.00
MOV0003 C-3PO 1/4..55.00
MOV0004 C-3PO 1/6..50.00
MOV0005 Chewbacca 1/4..75.00
MOV0007 Darth Vader 1/4..55.00
MOV0008 Darth Vader 1/6..50.00
MOV0011 Han Solo 1/4...65.00
MOV0012 Han Solo 1/6...50.00
MOV0014 Luke Skywalker 1/4...70.00
MOV0020 Luke Skywalker 1/6...70.00
MOV0021 Princess Leia 1/6..75.00
MOV0016 Stormtrooper 1/4...60.00
MOV0017 Stormtrooper 1/6...45.00
MOV0018 Tusken Raider 1/4..75.00
MOV0019 Yoda 1/4...75.00

MODELS: WOOD / BALSA

MOB0001   MOB0002   MOB0003   MOB0004   MOB0009   MOB0010

Estes
MOB0001 A-Wing Fighter...6.00
MOB0009 Naboo fighter..11.00
MOB0010 Naboo Royal Starship 11.00
MOB0002 Star Destroyer 3.00
MOB0003 X-Wing Fighter...3.00
MOB0004 Y-Wing Fighter...3.00

Takara

MOB0005 front and back   MOB0007 front and back

MOB0005 Landspeeder 85.00
MOB0006 R2-D2 ....85.00
MOB0007 Tie Fighter 85.00
MOB0008 X-Wing Fighter 85.00

MONEY, NOVELTY

Die-cut image on real US $1.00 bill.
PM0010 Anakin Skywalker 3.00
PM0009 Boba Fett...3.00
PM0002 C-3PO and R2-D2 ....3.00
PM0003 Chewbacca 3.00
PM0004 Darth Vader 3.00
PM0013 Grand Moff Tarkin 3.00
PM0005 Han Solo 3.00
PM0006 Luke Skywalker..3.00
PM0011 Obi-Wan Kenobi 3.00
PM0007 Princess Leia...3.00

PM0010   PM0009   PM0002

PM0003   PM0004   PM0013

PM0005   PM0006   PM0011

PM0007   PM0012   PM0014

PM0012 Queen Amidala 3.00
PM0014 Yoda (EPI)..3.00

MOUSEPADS

CMP0011   CMP0009   CMP0010   CMP0013   CMP0012

CMP0015   CMP0020   CMP0018   CMP0021   CMP0022

American Covers
CMP0011 "Darth Vader / Boba Fett" 12.00
CMP0009 "Death Star"..12.00
CMP0010 "Droids" 12.00
CMP0013 "Jump to Lightspeed" 3D Motion Mat 12.00
CMP0012 "Yoda"..12.00
CMP0015 3-D Lightsaber Battle..7.00
CMP0016 Anakin Podracer...7.00
CMP0017 Darth Maul 7.00
CMP0018 Episide I Logo...7.00
CMP0019 Jar Jar 7.00
CMP0020 Jedi vs. Sith 7.00
CMP0021 Naboo Space Battle..7.00
CMP0014 Photo Mat..12.00
CMP0022 Queen Amidala 7.00

Long Island Distributing Co. Ltd.
Mousepads include built-in solar calculators.
CMP0025 Bounty Hunters...16.00

CMP0023   CMP0024   CMP0025   CMP0029

CMP0030   CMP0031   CMP0032

CMP0030 B-Wing Fighter Attack 16.00
CMP0024 Death Star Trench 16.00
CMP0031 Dogfight above 2nd Death Star...................................16.00
CMP0032 Luke vs. the Emperor...16.00
CMP0029 Tie Attack...16.00
CMP0023 X-Wing fighters...16.00

Mousetrak

CMP0004   CMP0005   CMP0007   CMP0008

CMP0001 Bounty Hunters...14.00
CMP0002 C-3PO and R2-D2 ....14.00
CMP0003 Dark Forces 14.00
CMP0004 Darth Vader 14.00
CMP0005 Leia and Luke on Jabba's sail barge 14.00
CMP0006 Millennium Falcon 14.00
CMP0007 Rebel Assault 14.00
CMP0008 Yoda 14.00

World Wide Licenses Ltd.

CMP0026   CMP0028

CMP0028 Battle Droid with Trade Federation tank 9.00
CMP0026 Darth Maul 9.00

MUGS

Applause

MUM0002   MUM0005   MUM0008   MUM0011   MUM0023   MUM0025

MUM0016   MUM0017   MUM0033   MUM0036   MUM0038

MUM0044   MUM0045   MUM0066   MUM0067   MUM0068

MUM0002 Bib Fortuna 18.00
MUM0005 Boba Fett...20.00
MUM0008 C-3PO..18.00
MUM0011 Chewbacca 18.00
MUM0066 Darth Maul 17.00
MUM0014 Darth Vader 18.00
MUM0016 Darth Vader, metalized 22.00
MUM0017 Emperor Palpatine..18.00
MUM0023 Gamorrean Guard 18.00
MUM0025 Han Solo..18.00
MUM0067 Jar Jar Binks 17.00
MUM0033 Luke Skywalker 18.00
MUM0036 Obi-Wan Kenobi 18.00

Mugs

MUM0038 Princess Leia 18.00
MUM0068 R2-D2 (TPM) 17.00
MUM0044 Stormtrooper 18.00
MUM0045 Tusken Raider 20.00

California Originals

MUM0050   MUM0051   MUM0052

MUM0052 Ben Kenobi, 6¾" tall, holds 36 ounces; blue inside by Jim
   Rumph 115.00
MUM0050 Chewbacca, 6¾" tall, holds 36 ounces; black rim/inside by Jim
   Rumph 155.00
MUM0069 Darth Vader, 5½" tall, black inside 45.00
MUM0070 Darth Vader, 5½" tall, white inside 47.00
MUM0051 Darth Vader, 7¼" tall, holds 52 ounces by Jim Rumph 115.00
MUM0071 R2-D2 stein with flip-top lid, prototype only 1,725.00

Deka

MUM0006 front and back   MUM0009   MUM0047

MUM0015 front and back   MUM0041 front and back

MUM0004 Boba Fett and Darth Vader 10 oz. 10.00
MUM0006 C-3PO, Chewbacca and R2-D2 10 oz. 10.00
MUM0009 C-3PO, R2-D2 and Wicket / Princess Leia and Ewoks 12.00
MUM0015 Darth Vader, Emperor's Royal Guard, Luke Skywalker and
   Yoda 12.00
MUM0026 Han Solo, Princess Leia and Luke Skywalker 10 oz. 10.00
MUM0041 Star Wars 10 oz. 10.00
MUM0047 Yoda 10 oz. 10.00

Disney / MGM

MUM0057

MUM0058 C-3PO and Star Tours logo 10.00
MUM0059 R2-D2 and Star Tours logo 10.00
MUM0057 Star Tours logo, silver metallic finish 8.00

Downpace Ltd.

MUM0063   MUM0064   MUM0065

MUM0063 C-3PO 8.00
MUM0064 Darth Vader 12.00
MUM0065 Luke Skywalker 10.00

Kinnerton Confectionery
Mugs include chocolate Death Star.

MUM0084   MUM0062

MUM0084 Battle above Death Star...18.00
MUM0062 Lightsaber Duel 17.00

Long Island Distributing Co. Ltd.

MUM0095   MUM0085   MUM0086

MUM0095 Anakin Skywalker, podracer 7.00
MUM0085 Imperial Insignia 7.00
MUM0086 Rebel Insignia 7.00

Rawcliffe
Emblems are pewter attached to 15 ounce black mugs.

MUM0061   MUM0072   MUM0074

MUM0075   MUM0076   MUM0078   MUM0080

MUM0082   MUM0083   MUM0089

MUM0078 20th Anniversary 12.00
MUM0073 Boba Fett with gun 12.00
MUM0072 Boba Fett's Helmet 12.00
MUM0075 Darth Vader with clenched fist 12.00
MUM0081 Darth Vader 12.00
MUM0077 Darth Vader's lightsaber 12.00
MUM0080 Imperial emblem 12.00
MUM0076 Mandalorean emblem 12.00
MUM0083 Obi-Wan Kenobi 12.00
MUM0074 Princess Leia 12.00
MUM0079 Rebel logo 12.00
MUM0061 Star Wars logo 12.00
MUM0089 The Magic of Myth 22.00
MUM0082 Yoda..12.00

Sigma
MUM0001 10th Anniversary 15.00
MUM0003 Biker Scout, figural 35.00
MUM0053 Boba Fett and Chewbacca 17.00
MUM0054 C-3PO and R2-D2 ....17.00

MUM0013   MUM0029   MUM0034   MUM0007   MUM0010

MUM0022   MUM0027   MUM0030   MUM0031   MUM0046

MUM0053 front and back   MUM0054 front and back

MUM0055 front and back   MUM0056 front and back

MUM0007 C-3PO, figural 35.00
MUM0010 Chewbacca, figural 35.00
MUM0013 Darth Vader, figural..35.00
MUM0055 Darth Vader, Princess Leia, Stormtrooper.........17.00
MUM0022 Gamorrean Guard, figural 35.00
MUM0027 Han, figural 35.00
MUM0029 Klaatu, figural 35.00
MUM0030 Lando, figural 35.00
MUM0031 Leia, figural...35.00
MUM0056 Luke Skywalker and Yoda 17.00
MUM0034 Luke, figural 35.00
MUM0042 Star Wars w/thermal ink 15.00
MUM0043 Stormtrooper, figural 35.00
MUM0046 Wicket, figural...35.00
MUM0048 Yoda, figural..35.00

The Hamilton Collection

MUM0012   MUM0024   MUM0028   MUM0032

MUM0035   MUM0037   MUM0039   MUM0040

MUM0087 front and side   MUM0060   MUM0088 front and side

MUM0049 front and back

MUM0012 Darth Vader and Luke Skywalker 12.00
MUM0024 Han Solo...12.00
MUM0028 Imperial Walkers..12.00
MUM0032 Luke Skywalker and Yoda 12.00
MUM0035 Millennium Falcon Cockpit 12.00
MUM0037 Princess Leia 12.00

MUM0039 R2-D2 and Wicket..12.00
MUM0040 Space Battle Scene 12.00
MUM0091 Anakin Skywalker, thermal 7.00
MUM0087 C-3PO ceramic 9.00
MUM0096 Darth Maul with Obi-Wan and Qui-Gon...............8.00
MUM0093 Darth Maul, thermal 7.00
MUM0088 Darth Vader ceramic...9.00
MUM0060 Darth Vader ceramic, stars in eyes 8.00
MUM0092 Jar Jar Binks, thermal.......................................7.00
MUM0094 Queen Amidala, thermal 7.00
MUM0090 R2-D2 ceramic hand-painted..............................3.00
MUM0049 Special Edition art..14.00

MUSIC BOXES

CLM0001   CLM0002   CLM0003

Sigma
CLM0001 Ion Turret with C-3PO 85.00
CLM0002 Max Rebo Band 100.00
CLM0003 Wicket and Princess Kneesaa 75.00

NAME BADGES

PFJ0001   PFJ0002

Drawing Board
PFJ0001 Darth Vader, 16-pack...16.00
PFJ0002 Star Wars logo, 16-pack 16.00

Kentucky Fried Chicken
Employee name badges, "Welcome to Naboo."

PFJ0003   PFJ0005   PFJ0006

PFJ0003 Anakin Skywalker 7.00
PFJ0004 Darth Maul...7.00
PFJ0005 Jar Jar Binks..7.00
PFJ0006 Obi-Wan Kenobi 7.00
PFJ0007 Queen Amidala 7.00

NAPKINS

Drawing Board
PFK0001B C-3PO and R2-D2, beverage................................8.00
PFK0001D C-3PO and R2-D2, dinner..................................10.00
PFK0002B Cloud City, beverage 6.00
PFK0002D Cloud City, dinner 8.00
PFK0003B Darth Vader and Luke Duel, beverage 6.00
PFK0003D Darth Vader and Luke Duel, dinner.......................8.00
PFK0005B Ewoks Hang-Gliding, beverage.............................8.00
PFK0005D Ewoks Hang-Gliding, dinner................................10.00

PFK0001   PFK0002   PFK0003   PFK0005

Napkins

| PFK0004 | 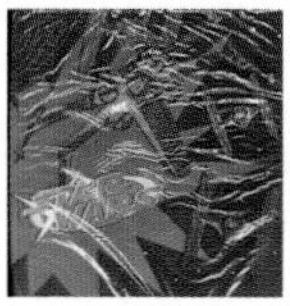 PFK0006 |  PFK0007 |  PFK0008 |

Party Express
PFK0006B Classic Trilogy Ships in neon colors, beverage............................4.00
PFK0006D Classic Trilogy Ships in neon colors, dinner...............................5.00
PFK0004B Dogfight over Death Star, beverage 6.00
PFK0004D Dogfight over Death Star, dinner.......................................8.00
PFK0008B Obi-Wan Kenobi, Jedi vs. Sith scene, beverage 2.00
PFK0008D Obi-Wan Kenobi, Jedi vs. Sith scene, dinner 3.00
PFK0007B Qui-Gon Jinn, Jedi vs. Sith scene, beverage 3.00
PFK0007D Qui-Gon Jinn, Jedi vs. Sith scene, dinner 4.00

NECKLACES

| JNK0014 |  JNK0029 |  JNK0020 |

| JNK0012 |  JNK0019 |  JNK0021 |  JNK0028 |

Adam Joseph Industries
JNK0014 "May The Force Be With You", gold 8.00
JNK0001 C-3PO bust 1" gold...10.00
JNK0012 Darth Vader, painted 12.00
JNK0031 Emperor's Royal Guard 1¼" gold 10.00
JNK0032 Ewok 1" gold..10.00
JNK0015 R2-D2 1" gold...10.00
JNK0019 R2-D2, painted 12.00
JNK0029 Rebel Alliance Logo 8.00
JNK0020 Return of the Jedi logo 8.00
JNK0021 Salacious Crumb 1¼" gold 10.00
JNK0026 X-Wing Pilot 8.00
JNK0033 Yoda, 1" gold 10.00
JNK0028 Yoda, 1" painted 12.00

Creative Conventions
JNK0013 "A New Hope", McQuarrie art, 10th anniversary..........................8.00
JNK0008 Darth Vader in Flames, 10th anniversary..................................8.00
JNK0027 Yoda, 10th anniversary..8.00

Factors, Etc.

| JNK0025 | JNK0022 | JNK0004 | JNK0003 JNK0010 JNK0024 |

JNK0004 C-3PO pendant, 1½" gold plated, articulated...........................12.00
JNK0003 C-3PO pendant, 2" gold plated, articulated..............................18.00
JNK0007 Chewbacca pendant, 1½" painted, articulated 12.00
JNK0006 Chewbacca pendant, 2" painted, articulated 18.00
JNK0010 Darth Vader pendant, 1¼" 18.00
JNK0011 Darth Vader pendant ¾" 12.00
JNK0018 R2-D2 pendant, 1", articulated..12.00

JNK0017 R2-D2 pendant, 1½", articulated..18.00
JNK0022 Stormtrooper pendant, 1¼" 18.00
JNK0023 Stormtrooper pendant ¾" 12.00
JNK0025 X-Wing Fighter pendant, 1" 14.00
JNK0024 X-Wing Fighter pendant, 2" 20.00

Unlicensed
JNK0034 C-3PO 1.25" enamel..11.00
JNK0036 Millennium Falcon (small)..12.00
JNK0035 R2-D2 .75" enamel...11.00
JNK0030 Star Wars logo and stars..9.00
JNK0038 Star Wars logo, trapezoid design...8.00
JNK0037 Tie Fighter (small)...17.00

Wallace Berrie and Co.
Enameled pendants.
JNK0002 C-3PO and R2-D2 ....17.00
JNK0005 Chewbacca 17.00
JNK0009 Darth Vader 17.00
JNK0016 R2-D2 ....17.00

NECKTIES

Ralph Marlin and Co.
AQ0002 All Character Icons (character vignettes repeating pattern in green, orange, red, black, and blue), silk..16.00
AQ0056 Anakin Skywalker icons repeating, silk 19.00
AQ0037 Anakin Skywalker in podracer gear, polyester/blend.................15.00
AQ0011 ANH 1995 international video artwork, polyester/blend.............12.00
AQ0012 ANH style "A" poster art (Vader's lightsaber extends along length of tie), polyester/blend...12.00
AQ0013 AT-AT McQuarrie art, polyester/blend 15.00
AQ0046 Battle Above Naboo, polyester/blend 15.00
AQ0039 Battle Droid art over Federation tank, polyester/blend..............15.00
AQ0060 Battle Droid icons repeating, silk...19.00
AQ0014 Bounty hunters artwork, polyester/blend 15.00
AQ0003 Cantina (on orange tie), silk..16.00
AQ0015 Darth Maul (name and drawings), polyester/blend 12.00
AQ0016 Darth Maul face repeating, silk...12.00
AQ0041 Darth Maul line-art bust over repeating name, polyester/blend .15.00
AQ0042 Darth Maul photo over Tatooine duel scene, polyester/blend .15.00
AQ0017 Darth Vader from SW novel cover artwork repeating pattern, silk, limited edition in tin...14.00
AQ0018 Darth Vader line art, polyester/blend 15.00
AQ0019 Darth Vader video art (same as 1995 ANH video release), polyester/blend 14.00
AQ0004 Death Star Assault (McQuarrie art of Tie chasing X-Wing), polyester/blend 12.00
AQ0005 Death Star Rising (X-Wings attack Death Star), polyester/blend ..16.00
AQ0020 Droids line art and square photo on sage green, polyester/blend 10.00
AQ0021 ESB 1995 international video artwork, polyester/blend..............12.00
AQ0022 Gold and black Darth Vader helmet repeating pattern, ...12.00
AQ0055 Han and Chewbacca line art and square photo on navy, polyester/blend 15.00
AQ0023 Imperial vehicles "blueprints", silk..11.00
AQ0038 Invasion Army, battle droids on STAPs and tanks, polyester/blend 15.00
AQ0061 Jar Jar Binks icons repeating - black, silk....................................19.00
AQ0062 Jar Jar Binks icons repeating - navy, silk.....................................19.00
AQ0043 Jar Jar Binks over bubble pattern on blue background, polyester/blend 15.00
AQ0045 Jar Jar Binks pictured above Anakin's podracer, polyester/blend 15.00
AQ0044 Jar Jar posed over repeating name, polyester/blend 15.00
AQ0063 Jedi icons repeating - black, silk..19.00
AQ0064 Jedi icons repeating - navy, silk...19.00
AQ0024 Jedi Obi-Wan Kenobi, polyester/blend 18.00
AQ0048 Jedi Qui-Gon Jinn, polyester/blend 15.00
AQ0066 Jedi vs. Sith pattern repeating, silk...19.00
AQ0006 Jung Poster Art, silk 16.00
AQ0047 Qui-Gon Jinn Jedi Master, polyester/blend 15.00
AQ0049 Qui-Gon Jinn, polyester/blend 15.00
AQ0050 Race to Freedom, polyester/blend 15.00
AQ0007 Rebel Alliance blueprint, silk..14.00
AQ0025 ROTJ 1995 international video artwork, polyester/blend 18.00
AQ0026 Silver and black Darth Vader helmet repeating pattern, silk.....18.00
AQ0027 Sith Darth Maul (photos of character), polyester/blend 18.00
AQ0052 Sith Lord, polyester/blend 15.00
AQ0065 Sith, The Dark Side pattern repeating, silk.................................19.00

AQ0051 Sith, The Dark Side, polyester/blend 15.00
AQ0028 Space Battle (Naboo fighters), polyester/blend 18.00
AQ0057 Starfighter blueprints - black, silk 19.00
AQ0058 Starfighter blueprints - navy, silk 19.00
AQ0059 Starfighter blueprints - olive, silk 19.00
AQ0053 Starfighters (TPM), polyester/blend.......................................15.00
AQ0029 Stormtrooper video art (same as 1995 ESB video release), polyester/blend 15.00
AQ0030 SW characters (character photos and SW logo at bottom), polyester/blend 16.00
AQ0008 SW Characters II (from top to bottom: Han, Ben, Leia, Luke, Vader), polyester/blend 14.00
AQ0031 SW Original Illustration (McQuarrie SW novel cover artwork of Vader looming over Luke and Leia), polyester/blend 14.00
AQ0009 SW Vehicles - black, silk 14.00
AQ0010 SW Vehicles (multicolor line drawings on black tie), silk 12.00
AQ0032 T.I.E. tie (3 Ties in trench), polyester/blend............................15.00
AQ0040 TPM characters, polyester/blend...15.00
AQ0033 TPM Ships repeating, silk..14.00
AQ0034 Yoda artwork, silk..32.00
AQ0035 Yoda line art and square Luke/Yoda photo on emerald, polyester/blend 16.00
AQ0036 Yoda video art (same as 1995 ROJ video release), polyester/blend 15.00
AQ0054 Young Skywalker, polyester/blend 15.00
AQ0072 Battle Droids repeating 19.00
AQ0068 Darth Maul icons repeating 17.00
AQ0070 Darth Maul in front of repeating pattern of probe droids 17.00
AQ0073 Jar Jar Binks making faces, square icons....................................19.00
AQ0067 Jedi icon between crossed sabers..17.00
AQ0069 Naboo fighter icons repeating 19.00
AQ0071 R2-D2 icons repeating..19.00
AQ0001 Scenes from Trilogy, plastic..8.00

NESTED DOLLS

ND10001

Fan Made
ND10001 Nested dolls, set of 5-7 any style, hand crafted 75.00

NEWSPAPER STRIPS

NS0001

NS0002 B/W, any day, trimmed 1.00
NS0001 Color, any day, trimmed..1.50

NIGHTGOWNS

Wilker Bros.
APN0001 Darth Vader...10.00
APN0002 Darth Vader and Death Star 10.00
APN0003 Darth Vader and Luke Skywalker..10.00
APN0004 Luke Skywalker and Princess Leia...10.00
APN0005 Luke Skywalker and Yoda 12.00
APN0006 Princess Kneesaa 15.00
APN0007 R2-D2 and C-3PO..10.00
APN0008 R2-D2, C-3PO, and Starfield 10.00
APN0009 Yoda 15.00

AQ0072 AQ0068 AQ0070 AQ0073 AQ0067 AQ0069 AQ0071 AQ0001

AQ0002 AQ0006 AQ0007 AQ0008 AQ0009 AQ0010 AQ0011 AQ0012 AQ0013 AQ0014 AQ0015 AQ0016 AQ0017 AQ0018 AQ0019 AQ0020 AQ0021 AQ0023 AQ0024

AQ0025 AQ0027 AQ0028 AQ0029 AQ0030 AQ0032 AQ0033 AQ0035 AQ0037 AQ0038 AQ0039 AQ0040 AQ0041 AQ0042 AQ0043 AQ0045 AQ0044 AQ0046 AQ0047

AQ0048 AQ0049 AQ0050 AQ0051 AQ0052 AQ0053 AQ0054 AQ0055 AQ0056 AQ0057 AQ0058 AQ0059 AQ0060 AQ0061 AQ0062 AQ0063 AQ0064 AQ0065 AQ0066

NIGHTLIGHTS

HON0001 HON0002 HON0003 HON0005

HON0007 HON0008 HON0004 HON0006

Adam Joseph Industries
HON0001 C-3PO disc-cut 10.00
HON0002 C-3PO sculpted 12.00
HON0003 Darth Vader sculpted 12.00
HON0004 Princess Kneesaa sculpted...8.00
HON0005 R2-D2 die-cut 10.00
HON0006 Wicket sculpted..8.00
HON0007 Yoda die-cut..10.00
HON0008 Yoda sculpted 12.00

NIGHTSTANDS

American Toy and Furniture Co.
FUN0001 Return of the Jedi nightstand...145.00

NOTE CUBES

N0001

Impact, Inc.
N0001 Darth Maul...4.00

NOTEBOOKS

SUN0001

Antioch
SUN0001 Mini-Notebook with "Lost City of the Jedi" art.............................5.00

HC Ford
Mini-memo pads.
SUN0030 C-3PO and R2-D2..8.00
SUN0032 Darth Vader...8.00
SUN0029 Han Solo 8.00

SUN0030 SUN0032 SUN0029 SUN0002

SUN0028 SUN0031 SUN0021

SUN0002 Luke Skywalker 8.00
SUN0028 Princess Leia 8.00
SUN0031 Yoda..8.00

Pocket memo pads.
SUN0021 3-pack: Droids, Han / Chewbacca, Luke / Yoda.....................15.00
SUN0003 C-3PO and R2-D2..6.00
SUN0004 Han and Chewbacca..6.00
SUN0005 Luke and Yoda...6.00

Letraset

SUN0006 SUN0007 SUN0008 SUN0026

SUN0026 C-3PO's Exercise Book...14.00
SUN0006 Chewbacca's Space Notes...10.00
SUN0007 Princess Leia's Rebel Jotter..10.00
SUN0009 R2-D2's Memory Book 10.00
SUN0008 Stormtrooper Manual...10.00

Mead
180 ruled sheets, 5½"x3½".

SUN0022 SUN0023 SUN0024 SUN0025

SUN0022 "Freeze You Rebel Scum!" 4.00
SUN0025 "May The Force Be With You" 4.00
SUN0024 "Never Underestimate The Power of the Dark Side" 4.00
SUN0023 Star Wars Star Fighters 4.00

Palitoy

SUN0027

SUN0027 Bounty Hunter Capture Log 27.00

Stuart Hall
3"x5" pocket memo notebooks.
SUN0016 Biker Scouts...4.00
SUN0010 Boba Fett 6.00
SUN0011 C-3PO and R2-D2..6.00
SUN0017 C-3PO, R2-D2, and Wicket..4.00
SUN0012 Character montage 6.00
SUN0018 Darth Vader and Luke Skywalker 4.00
SUN0013 Darth Vader and Stormtroopers 6.00
SUN0019 Jabba the Hutt..4.00
SUN0014 Luke Skywalker..6.00
SUN0020 Max Rebo Band 4.00
SUN0015 Space battle scene..4.00

NOTEBOOKS, SPIRAL

Impact, Inc.
50 sheets, 8"x10½" wide ruled.

SN0034   SN0046   SN0044   SN0036

SN0037   SN0039   SN0045

SN0034 Anakin Skywalker 3.00
SN0046 Anakin Skywalker, Podracer 3.00
SN0035 Jar Jar 3.00
SN0044 Jedi vs. Sith 3.00
SN0036 Queen Amidala 3.00
SN0037 Qui-Gon Jinn...3.00
SN0038 R2-D2 / C-3PO 3.00
SN0039 Sith Lord 3.00
SN0045 Space Battle over Naboo 3.00

90 sheets 6"x9" wide ruled; black rubber cover with riveted character.

SN0040   SN0041   SN0042   SN0043

SN0040 Anakin Skywalker 4.00
SN0041 Darth Maul 4.00
SN0042 Jar Jar Binks..4.00
SN0043 Queen Amidala 4.00

Mead

SN0017   SN0025   SN0002

SN0013   SN0014   SN0018   SN0028

SN0017 "Freeze You Rebel Scum" 3.00
SN0032 "May The Force Be With You".............................3.00
SN0025 "Never Underestimate The Power of the Dark Side" 3.00
SN0002 Ben, Han, Leia, and Luke 8.00
SN0005 C-3PO and R2-D2...8.00
SN0009 Chewbacca and Han...8.00
SN0013 Darth Vader 8.00
SN0014 Darth Vader, Dark Lord of Sith 3.00
SN0018 Han and Millennium Falcon 3.00
SN0028 Starships...3.00
SN0029 Stormtroopers (vintage) 8.00
SN0033 Stormtroopers 3.00

Stuart Hall
SN0001 2-1B, Aliens, Bounty Hunters, Probot, Ugnaught 8.00
SN0003 Boba Fett...11.00
SN0004 B-Wing and Tie Fighter 7.00
SN0006 C-3PO and R2-D2 ....8.00
SN0007 C-3PO 6.00
SN0008 C-3PO, R2-D2, and Wicket 5.00
SN0010 Chewbacca 9.00

SN0003   SN0004   SN0006   SN0019   SN0002

SN0011 Darth Vader and Stormtroopers.................................8.00
SN0012 Darth Vader on Bespin 9.00
SN0016 Darth Vader, Emperor Palpatine, Luke Skywalker........7.00
SN0015 Darth Vader, Han, Lando, Leia, and Luke 9.00
SN0019 Han, Leia, and Luke on Hoth 9.00
SN0020 Jabba and Salicious Crumb 8.00
SN0048 Leia and Luke on Bespin, Hoth snowtroopers..............9.00
SN0021 Luke and Stormtroopers on Bespin 8.00
SN0022 Luke on Dagobah 8.00
SN0023 Max Rebo Band 6.00
SN0024 Millennium Falcon and Star Destroyer 10.00
SN0047 Princess Leia, Luke, Ben, Han 9.00
SN0026 R2-D2 and Wicket the Ewok 8.00
SN0027 Speeder Bikers 6.00
SN0030 Vader Silhouette 9.00
SN0031 Yoda 9.00

NOTECARDS

PPN0001   front and back   PPN0002   PPN0005

Drawing Board
PPN0001 C-3PO and R2-D2, box of 10 w/envelopes..................17.00
PPN0002 C-3PO, Chewbacca, and Darth Vader, assorted box of 12.....18.00
PPN0003 Ewoks, 4 assorted designs......................................4.00
PPN0004 Hildebrandt Art, box of 10 w/envelopes.....................18.00
PPN0005 R2-D2 fold covers, box of 12..................................23.00

NOTEPADS

PPK0007 10th Anniversary notepads 8.00

Drawing Board

PPK0002   PPK0003

PPK0002 Darth Vader Official Duty Roster 7.00
PPK0003 Ewok with horn, "Notes" 7.00
PPK0004 Ewoks notepad, "Droppin' a Line" 7.00
PPK0006 Wookie Doodle Pad 7.00

Stuart Hall
PPK0001 C-3PO and R2-D2..10.00
PPK0005 Millennium Falcon and Star Destroyer 10.00

NUTCRACKERS

NTC0001

Steinbach
NTC0001 Darth Vader nutcracker, limited to 2,000 ....260.00

OIL LAMPS

OLM0001 front and close-ups of base art

Lamplight Farms Inc.
OLM0001 Star Wars oil lamp, base shows drawings of Darth Vader, R2-D2, C-3PO; originally shipped with fuel, wick, and wax seal 122.00

ORNAMENTS

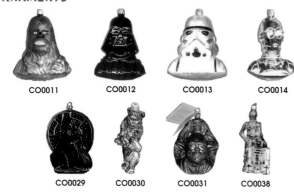

CO0011   CO0012   CO0013   CO0014

CO0029   CO0030   CO0031   CO0038

Christopher Radko
Individually mouth-blown glass ornament.
CO0038 C-3PO and R2-D2 ....32.00
CO0014 C-3PO 34.00
CO0011 Chewbacca 34.00
CO0029 Darth Vader on second Death Star 28.00
CO0012 Darth Vader 34.00
CO0030 Ewoks 28.00
CO0013 Stormtrooper 34.00
CO0031 Yoda 36.00

Hallmark
CO0032 Anakin Skywalker (2001) 15.00
CO0033 Battle of Naboo, set of 3 (2001) 15.00
CO0008 Boba Fett (1998) 44.00

CO0004 C-3PO and R2-D2 (1997)................................27.00
CO0016 Chewbacca (1999)...16.00
CO0023 Darth Maul (2000)...14.00
CO0006 Darth Vader (1997)..34.00
CO0018 Darth Vader's Tie Fighter (1999)....................25.00
CO0037 Empire Strikes Back Lunchbox (2001) 15.00
CO0005 Ewoks, set of 3 (1998) 35.00
CO0024 Gungan Sub (2000)...10.00
CO0017 Han Solo (1999)...18.00
CO0034 Jar Jar Binks (2001)...15.00
CO0026 Jedi Council (2000)...14.00
CO0003 Luke Skywalker, Lightsaber drawn (1997).....36.00
CO0019 Max Rebo Band, set of 3 (1999).....................14.00
CO0001 Millennium Falcon (1996)...............................47.00
CO0021 Naboo Fighter (1999)......................................20.00
CO0035 Naboo Royal Starship (2001)..........................20.00
CO0027 Obi-Wan Kenobi (2000)..................................14.00
CO0010 Princess Leia (1998)..24.00
CO0020 Queen Amidala (1999)....................................15.00
CO0028 Qui-Gon Jinn (2000) 10.00
CO0036 R2-D2 (2001) 15.00
CO0009 Star Wars Lunchbox (1998)............................24.00
CO0025 Stormtrooper (2000)..15.00
CO0002 Vehicles: AT-AT, Tie Fighter, X-Wing (1996) ...44.00
CO0015 X-Wing Fighter (1998).....................................26.00
CO0007 Yoda (1997)..27.00

Rawcliffe
Ornaments made of pewter.

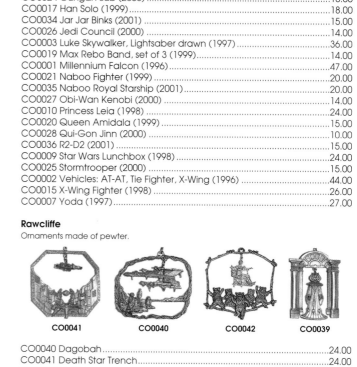

CO0041   CO0040   CO0042   CO0039

CO0040 Dagobah...24.00
CO0041 Death Star Trench...24.00
CO0042 Endor...24.00
CO0039 Queen Amidala...24.00
CO0022 Royal Starship...24.00

OUTFITS: 2-PIECE

Kids Headquarters
Shirt with either pants or shorts.

CO0001   CO0002   CO0003   CO0004   CO0005   CO0006   CO0007   CO0008

CO0009   CO0010   CO0015   CO0016   CO0017   CO0018   CO0019

CO0020   CO0021   CO0023   CO0024   CO0025   CO0027   CO0028

CMC0001 Anakin Skywalker, dark blue / gray, shorts 14.00
CMC0002 Bravo Squadron polyester black / black, pants 16.00
CMC0003 Bravo Squadron polyester blue / blue, pants 16.00
CMC0004 Darth Maul black polyester / white nylon, pants 16.00
CMC0005 Darth Maul, gray / black, shorts 14.00
CMC0006 Darth Maul, white / black, shorts 14.00
CMC0007 Droids sweats, gray and blue / blue, pants 16.00
CMC0008 Droids, yellow / dark blue, shorts 14.00
CMC0009 Jar Jar (4 faces), blue / gray, shorts 14.00
CMC0010 Jar Jar nylon jogger, green / blue, pants 16.00
CMC0012 Jar Jar sweats, gray and blue / blue, pants...........16.00
CMC0013 Jar Jar, light blue / dark blue, shorts 14.00
CMC0014 Jedi duel, black / gray, shorts 14.00
CMC0015 Jedi vs. Sith, gray and blue / dark blue, shorts...........14.00
CMC0016 Jedi vs. Sith, red / gray, shorts..........14.00
CMC0017 Naboo starfighter embroidered on knit polo shirt, shorts 14.00
CMC0019 Naboo starfighter, dark blue / gray, shorts 14.00
CMC0018 Naboo starfighter, white polyester over black nylon, pants...16.00
CMC0020 Pit Droid, yellow / dark blue, shorts 14.00
CMC0021 Pit Droids, blue / red, shorts 14.00
CMC0022 Podracing, gray / red, shorts 14.00
CMC0023 R2-D2, Pit Droid, C-3PO knit shirt, sweat pants 17.00

OVERALLS

Bibb Co.
ALS0001 Toddler suit 12.00

Kids Headquarters
ALS0004 Jar Jar overalls and long sleeve shirt set.....................18.00

Liberty Trouser Co.
ALS0002 Short pants sun suit 12.00
ALS0003 Star Wars overalls.................12.00

PACHINKO GAMES

PG0001 front, back, and opened   PG0002

PG0001 Star Wars Jedi Knights, handheld blue 35.00
PG0002 Star Wars Jedi Knights, handheld red 35.00

PACKAGING: ACTION FIGURES, VINTAGE

AVA3001 certificate box and mailer figures

Kenner
AVA3002 Earlybird mailer w/certificate..................400.00
AVA3001 Earlybird mailer w/figures, mailer packaging..........650.00

PACKAGING: BAGS

Kentucky Fried Chicken
PAO0003 Take-out bag, Queen Amidala 2.00

Taco Bell
PAO0001 Large bag, C-3PO..........2.00
PAO0002 Small bag, R2-D2..........2.00

PACKAGING: BEVERAGE

Fan Club
PAB0035 EPI Anakin's Destiny in acrylic case, Fan Club exclusive 50.00

PAB0034 EPI Soda Pop storage case, two-door front, Naboo fighter handles, Fan Club exclusive 100.00

Hi-C
PAB0001 Hi-C Can label w/droids pictured. T-shirt and cap offer..........7.00
PAB0002 Hi-C Cans w/droids pictured. T-shirt & cap offer..........25.00

Nestle
PAB0003 Nestle's Quik can w/pendant offer on label..........20.00

Pepsi Cola

PAB0010 PAB0011 PAB0012 PAB0013 PAB0014 PAB0015 PAB0016 PAB0017
PAB0018 PAB0019 PAB0020 PAB0021 PAB0022 PAB0023 PAB0024 PAB0025
PAB0026 PAB0027 PAB0028 PAB0029 PAB0030 PAB0031 PAB0032 PAB0033
PAB0190 PAB0191 PAB0192 PAB0193 PAB0036 PAB0037 PAB0038 PAB0189

PAB0036 EPI #00 Luke Skywalker, production sample 240.00
PAB0010 EPI #01 Pepsi Anakin Skywalker 1.00
PAB0011 EPI #02 Pepsi Sebulba 1.00
PAB0012 EPI #03 Pepsi Qui-Gon Jinn 1.00
PAB0013 EPI #04 Pepsi Watto 1.00
PAB0014 EPI #05 Pepsi Jabba the Hutt..........1.00
PAB0015 EPI #06 Pepsi Senator Palpatine 1.00
PAB0016 EPI #07 Pepsi R2-D2 ....1.00
PAB0017 EPI #08 Pepsi Darth Sidious..........1.00
PAB0018 EPI #09 Mountain Dew Darth Maul 1.00
PAB0019 EPI #10 Mountain Dew Jar Jar 1.00
PAB0020 EPI #11 Mountain Dew Mace Windu 1.00
PAB0021 EPI #12 Mountain Dew Obi-Wan Kenobi 1.00
PAB0022 EPI #13 Mountain Dew Captain Panaka 1.00
PAB0023 EPI #14 Mountain Dew Rune Haako 1.00
PAB0024 EPI #15 Mountain Dew Ric Olie 1.00
PAB0025 EPI #16 Mountain Dew Destroyer Droid 1.00
PAB0026 EPI #17 Diet Pepsi Queen Amidala 1.00
PAB0027 EPI #18 Diet Pepsi Padme 1.00
PAB0028 EPI #19 Diet Pepsi Shmi Skywalker 1.00
PAB0029 EPI #20 Diet Pepsi Battle Droid 1.00
PAB0030 EPI #21 Pepsi One Chancellor Valorum 1.00
PAB0031 EPI #22 Pepsi One C-3PO 1.00
PAB0032 EPI #23 Pepsi One Nute Gunray 1.00
PAB0033 EPI #24 Pepsi One Boss Nass 1.00
PAB0189 EPI Destiny Can, limited to 1:900 cases 125.00
PAB0037 EPI Jar Jar Binks, Storm 3.00
PAB0038 EPI Qui-Gon Jinn, Storm..........3.00
PAB0005 Pepsi products 12-pack carton w/character, any..........4.00
PAB0006 Pepsi products 2 liter bottles w/character, any..........1.00
PAB0007 Pepsi products 20-oz. bottles w/character, any 1.00
PAB0008 Pepsi products 24-pack carton w/character, any 2.00
PAB0190 SW:SE Darth Vader, Pepsi 2.00
PAB0192 SW:SE R2-D2, Diet Pepsi..........2.00
PAB0193 SW:SE Stormtrooper, Diet Pepsi 2.00
PAB0191 SW:SE logo, Pepsi..........2.00

Packaging: Beverage

Pepsi Cola (Argentina)

PAB0039 PAB0040 PAB0041 PAB0042 PAB0043 PAB0044

All cans are 325ml.

PAB0039 Anakin Skywalker 5.00
PAB0040 Darth Maul 5.00
PAB0041 Jar Jar Binks 5.00
PAB0042 Obi-Wan Kenobi 5.00
PAB0043 Queen Amidala 5.00
PAB0044 Qui-Gon Jinn 5.00

Pepsi Cola (Australia)

PAB0045 PAB0046 PAB0047 PAB0048 PAB0049 PAB0050 PAB0051 PAB0052

PAB0045 Anakin Skywalker, Pepsi 4.00
PAB0046 C-3PO, 7-Up 4.00
PAB0047 Darth Maul, Pepsi 4.00
PAB0048 Jar Jar Binks, Pepsi Max 4.00
PAB0049 Obi-Wan Kenobi, Pepsi 4.00
PAB0050 Queen Amidala, Diet Pepsi 4.00
PAB0051 Qui-Gon Jinn, Pepsi 4.00
PAB0052 Watto, Mountain Dew 4.00

Pepsi Cola (Austria)

PAB0053 PAB0054 PAB0055 PAB0056 PAB0057

PAB0053 Anakin Skywalker, Pepsi 5.00
PAB0054 Yoda, 7-Up 5.00
PAB0055 Jar Jar Binks, Pepsi Max 5.00
PAB0056 Queen Amidala, Diet Pepsi 5.00
PAB0057 Qui-Gon Jinn, Pepsi 5.00

Pepsi Cola (Brazil)

PAB0058 PAB0059 PAB0060 PAB0061 PAB0062 PAB0063 PAB0064 PAB0065

PAB0058 Anakin Skywalker, Pepsi 5.00
PAB0059 Darth Maul, Pepsi 5.00
PAB0060 Jar Jar Binks, Pepsi 5.00
PAB0061 Obi-Wan Kenobi, Pepsi 5.00
PAB0062 Qui-Gon Jinn, Pepsi 5.00
PAB0063 Rainha Amidala, Diet Pepsi 5.00
PAB0064 Rainha Amidala, Pepsi 5.00
PAB0065 Yoda, 7-Up 5.00

Pepsi Cola (Canada)

PAB0066 #01 Anakin Skywalker, Pepsi 1.00
PAB0067 #02 Sebulba, Pepsi 1.00
PAB0068 #03 Qui-Gon Jinn, Pepsi 1.00
PAB0069 #04 Watto, Pepsi 1.00
PAB0070 #05 Jabba, Pepsi 1.00
PAB0071 #06 Senator Palpatine, Pepsi 1.00
PAB0072 #07 R2-D2, Pepsi 1.00

PAB0066 PAB0067 PAB0068 PAB0069 PAB0070 PAB0071 PAB0072

PAB0073 PAB0074 PAB0075 PAB0076 PAB0077 PAB0078

PAB0079 PAB0080 PAB0081 PAB0082 PAB0083 PAB0084 PAB0085

PAB0073 #08 Darth Sidious, Pepsi 1.00
PAB0074 #09 Darth Maul, Mountain Dew 1.00
PAB0075 #10 Jar Jar Binks, Mountain Dew 1.00
PAB0076 #11 Mace Windu, Mountain Dew 1.00
PAB0077 #12 Obi-Wan Kenobi, Mountain Dew 1.00
PAB0078 #13 Queen Amidala, Diet Pepsi 1.00
PAB0079 #14 Padme, Diet Pepsi 1.00
PAB0080 #15 Shmi Skywalker, Diet Pepsi 1.00
PAB0081 #16 Battle Droid, Diet Pepsi 1.00
PAB0082 #17 Chancellor Valorum, 7-Up 1.00
PAB0083 #18 C-3PO, 7-Up 1.00
PAB0084 #19 Nute Gunray, 7-Up 1.00
PAB0085 #20 Boss Nass, 7-Up 1.00

Pepsi Cola (France)

All cans are 330ml.

PAB0086 PAB0087 PAB0088

PAB0086 Anakin Skywalker 5.00
PAB0087 Darth Maul 5.00
PAB0088 Queen Amidala 5.00

Pepsi Cola (Germany)

PAB0095 PAB0096 PAB0097 PAB0098 PAB0099 PAB0100 PAB0101

PAB0095 Darth Maul, Pepsi 500ml 5.00
PAB0096 Jar Jar Binks, Pepsi Boom 330ml 4.00
PAB0097 Qui-Gon Jinn, Pepsi 330ml 4.00
PAB0098 R2-D2, Pepsi Max 500ml 5.00
PAB0099 Rainha Amidala, Pepsi Light 330ml 4.00
PAB0100 Watto, Mirando 330ml 4.00
PAB0101 Yoda, 7-Up 330ml 4.00

Pepsi Cola (Holland)

PAB0089 PAB0090 PAB0091 PAB0092 PAB0093 PAB0094

PAB0089 Anakin Skywalker, Pepsi 3.00

PAB0090 Jar Jar Binks, Pepsi Max................................3.00
PAB0091 Qui-Gon Jinn, Pepsi 3.00
PAB0092 R2-D2, Pepsi Max 3.00
PAB0093 Watto, Sisi................................3.00
PAB0094 Yoda, 7-Up................................3.00

Pepsi Cola (Italy)
All cans are 330ml.

PAB0102   PAB0103   PAB0104   PAB0105   PAB0106

PAB0102 Anakin Skywalker, Pepsi 4.00
PAB0103 C-3PO, 7-Up................................4.00
PAB0104 Darth Maul, Pepsi 4.00
PAB0105 Qui-Gon Jinn, Pepsi 4.00
PAB0106 R2-D2, Pepsi Max 4.00

Pepsi Cola (Japan)

PAB0107 PAB0108 PAB0109 PAB0110 PAB0111 PAB0112 PAB0113 PAB0114

PAB0117 PAB0120 PAB0123 PAB0124 PAB0127 PAB0128 PAB0129

PAB0116 PAB0119 PAB0122 PAB0125 PAB0131 PAB0133
PAB0115 PAB0118 PAB0121 PAB0126 PAB0130 PAB0132

PAB0107 Anakin Skywalker, 350ml................................6.00
PAB0108 Anakin Skywalker, 500ml................................6.00
PAB0109 C-3PO, 350ml gold rim 6.00
PAB0110 C-3PO, 350ml gold rim, celebration 2000 ....7.00
PAB0111 C-3PO, 500ml gold rim 6.00
PAB0112 C-3PO, 500ml gold rim, celebration 2000 ....7.00
PAB0113 Darth Maul, 350ml................................6.00
PAB0114 Darth Maul, 500ml................................6.00
PAB0115 Darth Maul, full-body bottom................................4.00
PAB0116 Darth Maul, full-body top 7.00
PAB0117 Jar Jar Binks, 350ml 6.00
PAB0118 Nute Gunray, full-body bottom 4.00
PAB0119 Nute Gunray, full-body top 7.00
PAB0120 Obi-Wan Kenobi, 350ml 6.00
PAB0121 Obi-Wan Kenobi, full-body bottom 4.00
PAB0122 Obi-Wan Kenodi, full-body top 7.00
PAB0123 Queen Amidala, 350ml 6.00
PAB0124 Queen Amidala, 500ml 6.00
PAB0125 Queen Amidala, full-body bottom................................4.00
PAB0126 Queen Amidala, full-body top................................7.00
PAB0127 R2-D2, 350ml................................6.00
PAB0128 R2-D2, 350ml gold rim................................6.00
PAB0129 R2-D2, 500ml gold rim................................6.00
PAB0130 R2-D2, full-body bottom................................4.00

PAB0131 R2-D2, full-body top................................7.00
PAB0132 Watto, full-body bottom 4.00
PAB0133 Watto, full-body top 7.00

Pepsi Cola (Korea)
All cans are 250ml.

PAB0134   PAB0135   PAB0136   PAB0137

PAB0134 Darth Maul................................4.00
PAB0135 Jar Jar Binks 4.00
PAB0136 Queen Amidala 4.00
PAB0137 Qui-Gon Jinn 4.00

Pepsi Cola (Malaysia)
All cans are 325ml.

PAB0141   PAB0138   PAB0139   PAB0140

PAB0141 Anakin Skywalker 4.00
PAB0138 Darth Maul................................4.00
PAB0139 Jar Jar Binks 4.00
PAB0140 Queen Amidala................................4.00

Pepsi Cola (Mexico)
All cans are 355ml.

PAB0142   PAB0143   PAB0144   PAB0145

PAB0142 Anakin Skywalker 3.00
PAB0143 Darth Maul................................3.00
PAB0144 Jar Jar Binks 3.00
PAB0145 Queen Amidala................................3.00

Pepsi Cola (New Zealand)

PAB0146   PAB0147   PAB0148   PAB0149   PAB0150   PAB0151

PAB0146 Anakin Skywalker, Pepsi 4.00
PAB0147 Jar Jar Binks, Pepsi Max................................4.00
PAB0148 Queen Amidala, Diet Pepsi................................4.00
PAB0149 Sebulba, Miranda................................4.00
PAB0150 Watto, Mountain Dew................................4.00
PAB0151 Yoda, 7-Up................................4.00

Pepsi Cola (Portugal)

PAB0152   PAB0153   PAB0154   PAB0155

PAB0152 Anakin Skywalker, Pepsi 4.00
PAB0153 C3-PO, 7-Up................................4.00

Packaging: Beverage

PAB0154 Qui-Gon Jinn, Pepsi 4.00
PAB0155 Yoda, 7-Up 4.00

Pepsi Cola (Singapore)

PAB0156 PAB0157 PAB0158 PAB0159

PAB0156 Anakin Skywalker Podrace 64.00
PAB0157 Darth Maul 5.00
PAB0158 Jar Jar Binks 5.00
PAB0159 Qui-Gon Jinn 5.00

Pepsi Cola (Spain)

PAB0160 PAB0161 PAB0162 PAB0163 PAB0164 PAB0165 PAB0166 PAB0167

PAB0160 #01 Anakin Skywalker, Pepsi 6.00
PAB0161 #02 Qui-Gon Jinn, Pepsi 6.00
PAB0162 #03 Reina Amidala, Diet Pepsi 6.00
PAB0163 #04 R2-D2, Pepsi Max 6.00
PAB0164 #05 Darth Maul, Kas Limon 6.00
PAB0165 #06 Obi-Wan Kenobi, Kas Narania 6.00
PAB0166 #07 Yoda, 7-Up 6.00
PAB0167 #08 Jar Jar Binks, Pepsi Boom 6.00

Pepsi Cola (Turkey)

All cans are 350ml.

PAB0168 PAB0169 PAB0170 PAB0171 PAB0172

PAB0168 Anakin Skywalker 4.00
PAB0169 C-3PO 4.00
PAB0170 Darth Maul 4.00
PAB0171 Jar Jar Binks 4.00
PAB0172 Kralice Amidala 4.00

Pepsi Cola (UK)

PAB0173 PAB0174 PAB0175 PAB0176 PAB0177 PAB0178 PAB0179 PAB0180

PAB0181 PAB0182 PAB0183 PAB0184 PAB0185 PAB0186 PAB0187 PAB0188

PAB0173 Anakin Skywalker, Pepsi 4.00
PAB0174 Anakin Skywalker, Pepsi 150ml 3.00
PAB0175 C3-PO, 7-Up 4.00
PAB0176 C3-PO, 7-Up Lite 4.00
PAB0177 Jar Jar Binks, Pepsi Max 4.00
PAB0178 Jar Jar Binks, Pepsi Max 150ml 3.00
PAB0179 Obi-Wan Kenobi, Diet Pepsi 4.00
PAB0180 Obi-Wan Kenobi, Diet Pepsi 150ml 3.00
PAB0181 Queen Amidala, Diet Pepsi 4.00
PAB0182 Queen Amidala, Diet Pepsi 150ml 3.00
PAB0183 Qui-Gon Jinn, Pepsi 4.00
PAB0184 Qui-Gon Jinn, Pepsi 150ml 3.00
PAB0185 R2-D2, Pepsi Max 4.00
PAB0186 R2-D2, Pepsi Max 150ml 3.00
PAB0187 Yoda, 7-Up 4.00
PAB0188 Yoda, 7-Up Lite 4.00

PACKAGING: BREAD

Wonder Bread

PAR0001 Wonder Bread wrapper w/Star Wars trading card premium....35.00

PACKAGING: CANDY

PAC0070 front and side

Bazooka Bubblegum

PAC0070 Darth Vader Counter Display Dispenser 26.00

Cap Candy

Battle Pop with pushbutton battle action.

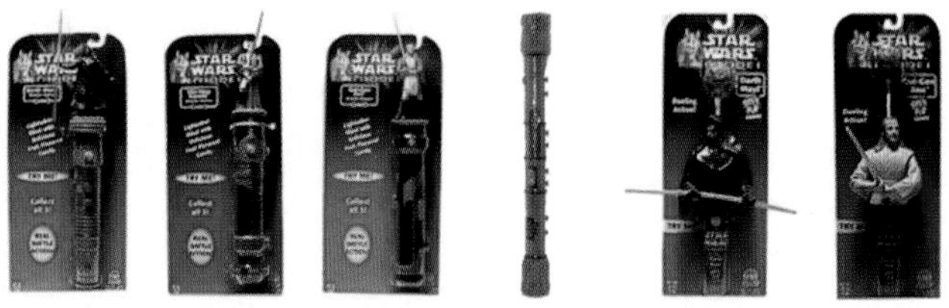

PAC0003 PAC0004 PAC0005 PAC0008 PAC0001 PAC0002

PAC0003 Darth Maul 10.00
PAC0004 Obi-Wan Kenobi 10.00
PAC0005 Qui-Gon Jinn 10.00
PAC0008 Darth Maul Saber Stick 3.00

Spin Pop with motorized dueling action.

PAC0001 Darth Maul 6.00
PAC0002 Qui-Gon Jinn 6.00

Film action containers.

PAC0038 PAC0039 PAC0040 PAC0041

PAC0006

PAC0007

PAC0037 Anakin Skywalker 2.00
PAC0039 Darth Sidious 2.00
PAC0040 Jar Jar Binks 2.00
PAC0038 Queen Amidala 2.00
PAC0041 R2-D2 ....2.00
PAC0006 Jar Jar Binks Monster Mouth candy 4.00
PAC0007 Obi-Wan Kenobi Lightsaber Pop candy 3.00

Chupa Chups

Lollipop wrappers.

PAC0072 Anakin Skywalker 2.00

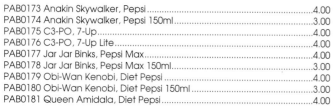

PAC0047   PAC0052   PAC0073   PAC0074

PAC0073 Battle Droid 2.00
PAC0047 C-3PO 2.00
PAC0074 Darth Maul 2.00
PAC0048 Emperor 2.00
PAC0049 Han 2.00
PAC0075 Jar Jar Binks 2.00
PAC0050 Leia 2.00
PAC0051 Luke 2.00
PAC0076 Queen Amidala 2.00
PAC0052 R2 ....2.00
PAC0053 Stormtrooper 2.00
PAC0077 Watto 2.00
PAC0054 Yoda 2.00

Crazy Planet
Wrapper: 4 Mega Stickers, 2 Gum, 1 Sticker.

PAC0140

PAC0146 Anakin Skywalker 6.00
PAC0148 Battle Droid 6.00
PAC0145 Darth Maul 6.00
PAC0143 Jar Jar Binks 6.00
PAC0140 Obi-Wan Kenobi 6.00
PAC0142 Queen Amidala 6.00
PAC0144 Qui-Gon Jinn 6.00
PAC0147 Watto 6.00

Frito-Lay

PAC0081

PAC0081 Cracker Jack tin, oversized replica of Pepsi can #1, Anakin Skywalker, TRU exclusive 8.00

Hersheys
ESB Photo on candybar 6-pack.

PAC0055   PAC0056   PAC0059   PAC0060

PAC0057 Kit Kat (Luke on Tauntaun) 16.00
PAC0055 Milk Chocolate (C-3PO and R2-D2) 16.00
PAC0056 Milk Chocolate with Almonds (Chewbacca) 16.00
PAC0060 Reese's Crunchy Peanut Butter Cups (Darth Vader) 16.00
PAC0059 Reese's Peanut Butter Cups (Boba Fett) 16.00
PAC0058 Whatchamacallit (Darth Vader) 16.00

Kinnerton Confectionery
Jelly shapes in tin with decorative character bust.
PAC0139 R2-D2 ....5.00
PAC0078 Anakin 5.00

PAC0139   PAC0078   PAC0079   PAC0080

PAC0013   PAC0063   PAC0141

PAC0079 Darth Maul 5.00
PAC0080 Jar Jar Binks 5.00
PAC0013 Hollow chocolate eggs with Star Wars jelly shapes, cut-out book-
mark on box 17.00
PAC0063 Jelly Shapes 100g in R2-D2 shaped tin 9.00
PAC0141 Jelly Shapes in R2-D2 container, cardboard 5.00

Meiji

PAC0136 front and back   PAC0138 front and back

PAC0136 Star Wars movie candy 32.00
PAC0138 The Phantom Menace, with bonus trading card 11.00

Nestle
PAC0010 Nestle's chocolate candybar wrapper w/pendant offer 12.00

Pez Candy, Inc.
PAC0012 Pez Display Box 14.00
PAC0036 Trilogy: 4-Pack of sculpted candy dispensers with Topps trading
cards 12.00
PAC0031 Trilogy: C-3PO's head sculpted candy dispenser with Topps trad-
ing card 2.50
PAC0032 Trilogy: Chewbacca's head sculpted candy dispenser with Topps
trading card 2.50
PAC0033 Trilogy: Darth Vader's head sculpted candy dispenser with Topps
trading card 2.50
PAC0035 Trilogy: Unopened box of 24 sculpted head candy dispensers with
Topps trading cards 50.00
PAC0034 Trilogy: Yoda's head sculpted candy dispenser with Topps trading
card 2.50

Sellos

PAC0135

PAC0135 Candy-filled rubber stamper 2.00

Sonrics
PAC0071 Bombiux Death Star shaped candy holders, from Star Wars Sepe-
cial Edition 3.00

Topps
PAC0086 Box, empty ESB I sculpted candy dispensers 3.00
PAC0087 Box, empty ESB II: sculpted candy dispensers 3.00
PAC0102 Box, empty ESB wax packs, series 1 ....4.00
PAC0103 Box, empty ESB wax packs, series 2 ....4.00
PAC0104 Box, empty ESB wax packs, series 3 ....4.00
PAC0107 Box, empty ROTJ wax packs, series 1 ....4.00
PAC0108 Box, empty ROTJ wax packs, series 2 ....4.00
PAC0088 Box, empty ROTJ: sculpted candy dispensers 2.00
PAC0094 Box, empty SW wax packs, series 1 ....18.00

Packaging: Candy

PAC0018

PAC0109

PAC0111

PAC0113

PAC0127

PAC0128

PAC0129

PAC0130

PAC0131

PAC0132

PAC0133

PAC0134

PAC0095 Box, empty SW wax packs, series 2 ....18.00
PAC0096 Box, empty SW wax packs, series 3 ....18.00
PAC0097 Box, empty SW wax packs, series 4 ....18.00
PAC0098 Box, empty SW wax packs, series 5 ....18.00
PAC0018 Box, unopened ESB I sculpted candy dispensers 34.00
PAC0023 Box, unopened ESB II: sculpted candy dispensers 36.00
PAC0099 Box, unopened ESB wax packs, series 1 ....108.00
PAC0100 Box, unopened ESB wax packs, series 2 ....108.00
PAC0101 Box, unopened ESB wax packs, series 3 ....108.00
PAC0105 Box, unopened ROTJ wax packs, series 1 ....108.00
PAC0106 Box, unopened ROTJ wax packs, series 2 ....108.00
PAC0029 Box, unopened ROTJ: sculpted candy dispensers 34.00
PAC0089 Box, unopened SW wax packs, series 1 ....325.00
PAC0090 Box, unopened SW wax packs, series 2 ....245.00
PAC0091 Box, unopened SW wax packs, series 3 ....245.00
PAC0092 Box, unopened SW wax packs, series 4 ....245.00
PAC0093 Box, unopened SW wax packs, series 5 ....175.00
PAC0014 Dispenser, sculpted ESB I: Boba Fett 2.00
PAC0015 Dispenser, sculpted ESB I: C-3PO 2.00
PAC0016 Dispenser, sculpted ESB I: Chewbacca 2.00
PAC0017 Dispenser, sculpted ESB I: Darth Vader 2.00
PAC0030 Dispenser, sculpted ESB I: Stormtrooper 2.00
PAC0019 Dispenser, sculpted ESB II: 2-1B 2.00
PAC0020 Dispenser, sculpted ESB II: Bossk 2.00
PAC0021 Dispenser, sculpted ESB II: Tauntaun 2.00
PAC0022 Dispenser, sculpted ESB II: Yoda..............2.00
PAC0024 Dispenser, sculpted ROTJ: Admiral Ackbar 2.00
PAC0025 Dispenser, sculpted ROTJ: Darth Vader 2.00
PAC0026 Dispenser, sculpted ROTJ: Ewok 2.00
PAC0027 Dispenser, sculpted ROTJ: Jabba the Hutt 2.00
PAC0028 Dispenser, sculpted ROTJ: Sy Snootles..............2.00
PAC0082 Sculpted C-3PO head with trading card..............3.00
PAC0083 Sculpted Chewbacca head with trading card..............3.00
PAC0084 Sculpted Darth Vader head with trading card..............3.00
PAC0085 Sculpted Yoda head with trading card..............3.00
PAC0119 Wax pack, ESB series 1 ....3.00
PAC0120 Wax pack, ESB series 2 ....3.00
PAC0121 Wax pack, ESB series 3 ....3.00
PAC0125 Wax pack, ROTJ series 1 ....3.00
PAC0126 Wax pack, ROTJ series 2 ....3.00
PAC0109 Wax pack, SW series 1 ....9.00
PAC0110 Wax pack, SW series 2 ....7.00
PAC0111 Wax pack, SW series 3 ....7.00
PAC0112 Wax pack, SW series 4 ....7.00
PAC0113 Wax pack, SW series 5 ....5.00
PAC0122 Wax wrapper, ESB series 1 ....2.00
PAC0123 Wax wrapper, ESB series 2 ....2.00
PAC0124 Wax wrapper, ESB series 3 ....2.00
PAC0127 Wax wrapper, ROTJ series 1: Darth Vader 2.00
PAC0128 Wax wrapper, ROTJ series 1: Jabba the Hutt 2.00
PAC0129 Wax wrapper, ROTJ series 1: Luke Skywalker..............2.00
PAC0130 Wax wrapper, ROTJ series 1: Wicket the Ewok 2.00
PAC0132 Wax wrapper, ROTJ series 2: Baby Ewok 2.00
PAC0131 Wax wrapper, ROTJ series 2: C-3PO 2.00
PAC0133 Wax wrapper, ROTJ series 2: Lando as Skiff Guard 2.00
PAC0134 Wax wrapper, ROTJ series 2: Princess Leia 2.00
PAC0114 Wax wrapper, SW series 1 ....5.00

PAC0115 Wax wrapper, SW series 2 ....5.00
PAC0116 Wax wrapper, SW series 3 ....4.00
PAC0117 Wax wrapper, SW series 4 ....4.00
PAC0118 Wax wrapper, SW series 5 ....4.00
PAC0137 Anakin Skywalker in podracer gear, hexagon container..............14.00
PAC0061 Box of 9 Chocolate Shapes 14.00
PAC0062 Darth Vader and Death Star on blue background 11.00

PACKAGING: CEREAL

General Mills

PAD0008 front and back

PAD0010

PAD0001 Cheerios box w/16-oz. tumbler mail-in offer 25.00
PAD0002 Cheerios box with promotion / toy rebate 45.00
PAD0005 Lucky Charms box with mobile premium 45.00
PAD0008 Any box with Collector Cards premium 40.00
PAD0009 Any box with Mini-Poster premium 32.00
PAD0010 Any box with Stick-Ons premium 46.00

Kellogg's

PAD0020 front and back

PAD0015

PAD0014

PAD0021 Any box with ROTJ Decoder Game Piece inside..............11.00
PAD0020 Any box with SOTE cut-out cards on back 18.00
PAD0015 Any box with video tape mail-in 12.00
PAD0011 Apple Jacks box with comic book mail-in offer..............10.00
PAD0012 C-3PO's with plastic rebel-rocket premium 25.00
PAD0013 C-3PO's with Stick'R trading card premium 30.00
PAD0014 C-3PO's with character cut-out mask on back 35.00
PAD0018 Corn Flakes box with Empire Strikes Back SE Trilogy hologram ...7.00
PAD0019 Corn Pops box with Return of the Jedi SE Trilogy hologram 7.00
PAD0017 Frosted Flakes box with Star Wars SE Trilogy hologram 7.00
PAD0016 Fruit Loops box w/Han Solo figure mail-in offer 16.00

PACKAGING: CHEESE

Dairylea
PAH0001 Cheese spread, illustrated with droids and Ewok figures 16.00

Paper covering cheese wedge.
PAH0002 Baga 6.00
PAH0003 C-3PO 6.00
PAH0004 Chief Chirpa..............6.00
PAH0005 Latara 6.00
PAH0006 Logray..............6.00
PAH0007 Malani 6.00
PAH0008 Princess Kneesaa 6.00
PAH0009 R2-D2 ....6.00
PAH0010 Shodu..............6.00
PAH0011 Teebo..............6.00
PAH0012 Wicket 6.00
PAH0013 Winda 6.00

PACKAGING: CLEANERS

Pine-Sol
PAE0001 Pine-Sol Bottle w/Star Wars Label..............25.00

PACKAGING: COOKIES

Burtons
PAG0004 Star Wars Biscuits 14.00

Gamesa

PAG0011   **PAG0012**

PAG0011 Arcoiris, marshmallow with free premium..........................5.00
PAG0012 Emperador, chocolate with free premium 5.00

Nabisco

PAG0005   **PAG0008**   **PAG0009**   **PAG0010**

PAG0007 Anakin in Podrace Helmet 4.00
PAG0009 C-3PO and R2-D2 ....4.00
PAG0010 Darth Maul on Sith Speeder 4.00
PAG0005 Jedi vs. Jedi 4.00
PAG0008 Obi-Wan with Maul Background 4.00
PAG0006 Trade Federation Battleship 4.00

Pepperidge Farms

PAG0001   **PAG0002**   **PAG0003**

PAG0001 Rebel Alliance I, vanilla..22.00
PAG0002 Rebel Alliance II, peanut butter..............................22.00
PAG0003 The Imperial Forces, chocolate 22.00

PACKAGING: FOOD WRAPPERS

Heinz

PAF0034
front and back

PAF0034 Star Wars pasta shapes in tomato sauce 5.00

Kentucky Fried Chicken
PAF0003 Boss Nass large paper barrel...................................4.00
PAF0004 Boss Nass medium paper bucket.............................3.00
PAF0005 Jar Jar Binks large paper barrel...............................4.00
PAF0006 Jar Jar Binks medium paper bucket 3.00
PAF0007 Jedi large paper barrel..4.00
PAF0008 Jedi medium paper bucket 3.00
PAF0009 Queen Amidala large paper barrel 4.00
PAF0010 Queen Amidala medium paper bucket.....................3.00
PAF0002 Star Wars SE chicken bucket, cardboard 5.00

Meiji
PAF0033 Seasoning packets, with bonus trading card.............11.00

PAF0033
front and back

Nagatanien

PAF0011 front and back   **PAF0012**   **PAF0013**   **PAF0014**   **PAF0015**

PAF0016 front and back   **PAF0017 front and back**   **PAF0018 front and back**

PAF0019   **PAF0020 front and back**   **PAF0021 front and back**   **PAF0022**

PAF0027 Curry Box, contains individual packets 23.00
PAF0011 Anakin Skywalker - salmon......................................3.00
PAF0012 Battle Droid - salmon 4.00
PAF0013 C-3PO - salmon 3.00
PAF0014 Darth Maul - okaka 4.00
PAF0035 Darth Maul - salmon 3.00
PAF0015 Darth Sidious - salmon 3.00
PAF0016 Obi-Wan Kenobi - okaka 3.00
PAF0017 Obi-Wan Kenobi - salmon 3.00
PAF0018 Queen Amidala - okaka 3.00
PAF0019 Queen Amidala (Senate) - salmon 3.00
PAF0020 Qui-Gon Jinn - okaka 3.00
PAF0032 Sebulba - salmon 3.00
PAF0021 Shmi Skywalker - salmon.......................................3.00
PAF0022 Yoda - okaka...4.00

Pizza Hut
Pizza boxes.

PAF0028   **PAF0029**   **PAF0030**   **PAF0031**

PAF0031 Anakin Skywalker 7.00
PAF0023 C-3PO and Millennium Falcon, medium 3.00
PAF0028 Darth Maul 9.00
PAF0024 Darth Vader and Star Destroyer................................5.00
PAF0029 Jar Jar Binks...9.00
PAF0030 Queen Amidala 9.00
PAF0025 R2-D2 and X-Wing Fighter, medium...........................4.00
PAF0026 Stormtrooper, large...4.00

Taco Bell
PAF0001 Taco Bell C-3PO 2.00

PACKAGING: FRUIT SNACKS

Farley's

DDS0001   **DDS0002**   **DDS0003**

DDS0004 Fruit Snacks, bag 2.25 oz..1.00
DDS0001 Fruit Snacks, box, 10 pouches 9 oz. 4.00

DDS0003 Glitter Roll, Galactic Watermelon flavor, box, 8 pouches 5 oz...4.00
DDS0002 Mega-duals, box, 8 pouches 8.8 oz. 4.00

PACKAGING: ICE CREAM

Campina Ijsfabbrieken

PAJ0002

PAJ0002 ROTJ promotion on wrapper, premium stickers were ESB...........6.00

Pauls
PAJ0004 SW Popsicles 10-pack..42.00

Peters
PAJ0003 ROTJ with Jedi Jelly 25.00

Wells
PAJ0001 Battle Droid Ice (Ice-Cream on a stick) Wrapper..................3.00

PAJ0004   **PAJ0003**

PAJ0001 wrapper and contents

PACKAGING: KIDS MEALS

Burger Chef

PAK0001   **PAK0002**   **PAK0005**

Funmeal trays.
PAK0001 C-3PO puppet 30.00
PAK0002 Darth Vader card game 30.00
PAK0003 Flight game with spinner..30.00
PAK0004 Punch-out Landspeeder...30.00
PAK0005 R2-D2 puppet...30.00
PAK0006 Table tent...30.00
PAK0007 Tie Fighter...30.00
PAK0008 X-Wing fighter...30.00

Kentucky Fried Chicken
Kid's meal boxes, full color.
PAK0012 SW:SE 4.00
PAK0013 SW:TPM 3.00

Taco Bell
Fun Meal boxes.
PAK0009 Empire Strikes Back 4.00
PAK0010 Return of the Jedi 4.00
PAK0011 Star Wars 4.00

PACKAGING: PAPER CUPS

Dixie/Northern Inc.
Unopened boxes.
PAP0001 ESB, AT-AT and Snowspeeder...20.00
PAP0002 ESB, Darth Vader...20.00
PAP0003 ESB, Luke on Tauntaun 20.00

PAP0002   **PAP0003**   **PAP0007**   **PAP0009**   **PAP0013**

PAP0015   **PAP0016**   **PAP0017**   **PAP0023**   **PAP0024**

PAP0004 ESB, Millennium Falcon...20.00
PAP0005 ESB, Star Destroyer 20.00
PAP0006 ESB, Twin-pod Cloud Car 20.00
PAP0007 ESB, X-Wing in Swamp 20.00
PAP0008 ESB, Yoda...20.00
PAP0009 ROTJ, B-Wing, Luke Skywalker and Yoda.....................................15.00
PAP0010 ROTJ, Darth Vader, Emperor, Royal Guard 15.00
PAP0011 ROTJ, Ewoks...15.00
PAP0012 ROTJ, Jabba the Hutt and Princess Leia 15.00
PAP0017 SW, Chewbacca and Han Solo 25.00
PAP0018 SW, Darth Vader..25.00
PAP0019 SW, Death Star, Tie Fighter, X-Wing..25.00
PAP0020 SW, Droids..25.00
PAP0021 SW, Luke Skywalker...25.00
PAP0022 SW, Obi-Wan Kenobi..25.00
PAP0023 SW, Princess Leia...35.00
PAP0024 SW, Stormtrooper...25.00
PAP0013 SW Saga, C-3PO, and R2-D2...15.00
PAP0014 SW Saga, Darth Vader 15.00
PAP0015 SW Saga, Han Solo, Leia, Stormtroopers.....................................15.00
PAP0016 SW Saga, Luke Skywalker, and Yoda 15.00

PACKAGING: SHOES

Stride Rite
SHA0002 Stride Rite Shoe Bag 12.00
SHA0001 Stride Rite Shoebox..18.00

PACKAGING: SNACK CHIPS

Frito-Lay
PAS0001 Cheetos 13.5 oz. with 3D motion card inside 3.00
PAS0002 Cheetos 15.5 oz. with 3D motion card inside 3.00
PAS0003 Doritos Cooler Ranch 14.5 oz. with 3D motion card inside 3.00
PAS0008 Doritos Nacho Cheesier 14.5 oz. with 3D motion card inside 3.00
PAS0004 Doritos Nacho Cheesier 2.125 oz. with 3D motion disc inside 3.00
PAS0009 Doritos Nacho Cheesier 25 oz. R2-D2 art with game card inside ..3.00
PAS0005 Doritos Nacho Cheesier 3.5 oz. R2-D2 art with game card inside .3.00
PAS0006 Doritos Nacho Cheesier 3.5 oz. with 3D motion disc inside 3.00
PAS0012 Doritos Nacho Cheesier 3Ds 10 oz. with game card inside 3.00
PAS0010 Doritos Nacho Cheesier 3Ds 2.5 oz. with game card inside 3.00
PAS0011 Doritos Nacho Cheesier 3Ds 6 oz. with game card inside 3.00
PAS0015 Doritos Pizza Cravers 14.5 oz. with 3D motion card inside...........3.00
PAS0013 Doritos Pizza Cravers 2.125 oz. with 3D motion disc inside 3.00
PAS0014 Doritos Pizza Cravers 3.5 oz. with 3D motion motion disc inside ..3.00
PAS0017 Doritos Smokey Red BBQ 14.5 oz. Qui-Gon Jinn art with game card inside..3.00
PAS0016 Doritos Smokey Red BBQ 3.5 oz. Qui-Gon Jinn art 2.00
PAS0020 Doritos Taco Supreme 14.5 oz. with 3D motion card inside 3.00
PAS0018 Doritos Taco Supreme 2.125 oz. with 3D motion disc inside 3.00
PAS0019 Doritos Taco Supreme 3.5 oz. with 3D motion disc inside 3.00
PAS0025 Lay's Classic Potato Chips 12.25 oz. Anakin Skywalker photo.....2.00
PAS0007 Doritos Nacho Cheesier 14.5 oz. R2-D2 art with game card inside ..3.00
PAS0026 Lay's Classic Potato Chips 13.25 oz. Anakin Skywalker photo with game card inside..3.00
PAS0027 Lay's Classic Potato Chips 21.5 oz. Qui-Gon Jinn photo with poster offer 5.00

PAS0021 Lay's Classic Potato Chips 3 oz. Anakin Skywalker photo............2.00
PAS0022 Lay's Classic Potato Chips 5.5 oz. Anakin Skywalker photo.........2.00
PAS0023 Lay's Classic Potato Chips 5.5 oz. Anakin Skywalker photo with game card inside 3.00
PAS0024 Lay's Classic Potato Chips 7.5 oz. Anakin Skywalker photo.........2.00
PAS0028 Lay's Pizza Flavored Potato Chips 1.75 oz. with Obi-Wan Kenobi action figure offer 4.00
PAS0032 Lay's Pizza Flavored Potato Chips 14 oz. with Obi-Wan Kenobi action figure offer 4.00
PAS0029 Lay's Pizza Flavored Potato Chips 3.25 oz. with Obi-Wan Kenobi action figure offer 4.00
PAS0030 Lay's Pizza Flavored Potato Chips 6 oz. with Obi-Wan Kenobi action figure offer 4.00
PAS0031 Lay's Pizza Flavored Potato Chips 9 oz. with Obi-Wan Kenobi action figure offer 4.00
PAS0033 Lay's Potato Chips 1.75 oz. with Obi-Wan Kenobi action figure offer 4.00
PAS0037 Lay's Potato Chips 14 oz. with Obi-Wan Kenobi action figure offer ...4.00
PAS0034 Lay's Potato Chips 3.25 oz. with Obi-Wan Kenobi action figure offer 4.00
PAS0035 Lay's Potato Chips 6 oz. with Obi-Wan Kenobi action figure offer 4.00
PAS0036 Lay's Potato Chips 9 oz. with Obi-Wan Kenobi action figure offer 4.00
PAS0040 Lay's Salt and Vinegar Potato Chips 13.5 oz. Jar Jar Binks photo with game card inside...3.00
PAS0038 Lay's Salt and Vinegar Potato Chips 5.5 oz. Jar Jar Binks photo with game card inside...3.00
PAS0039 Lay's Salt and Vinegar Potato Chips 7.5 oz. Jar Jar Binks photo.2.00
PAS0044 Lay's Sour Cream and Onion Potato Chips 13.5 oz. Queen Amidala photo with game card inside..3.00
PAS0041 Lay's Sour Cream and Onion Potato Chips 3 oz. Queen Amidala photo 2.00
PAS0042 Lay's Sour Cream and Onion Potato Chips 5.5 oz. Queen Amidala photo with game card inside..2.00
PAS0043 Lay's Sour Cream and Onion Potato Chips 7.5 oz. Queen Amidala photo 2.00
PAS0047 Lay's Toasted Onion and Cheese Potato Chips 13.5 oz. Obi-Wan Kenobi photo with game card inside..3.00
PAS0045 Lay's Toasted Onion and Cheese Potato Chips 3 oz. Obi-Wan Kenobi photo...2.00
PAS0046 Lay's Toasted Onion and Cheese Potato Chips 5.5 oz. Obi-Wan Kenobi photo with game card inside..3.00
PAS0048 Multi-pack boxes with ANH adventure game printed inside box with cut-out game pieces on insert card 8.00
PAS0049 Multi-pack boxes with ESB adventure game printed inside box with cut-out game pieces on insert card..8.00
PAS0050 Multi-pack boxes with ROTJ adventure game printed inside box with cut-out game pieces on insert card 8.00

Matutano Snack Ventures
PAS0051 Boca Bits, 15g with Jar Jar toy offer on back 4.00
PAS0052 Boca Bits, 27g with Queen Amidala photo 3.00
PAS0053 Boca Bits, 50g with Queen Amidala photo 3.00
PAS0054 Bugles 3-D's, 36g with Jar Jar photo...3.00
PAS0055 Bugles 3-D's, 65g with Jar Jar photo...3.00
PAS0056 Bugles 3-D's, 85g with Jar Jar photo...3.00
PAS0057 Cheetos Pandilla, 14g with Jar Jar toy offer on back 4.00
PAS0058 Cheetos Pandilla, 31g with Anakin Skywalker photo 3.00
PAS0059 Cheetos Pandilla, 75g with Anakin Skywalker photo 3.00
PAS0060 Cheetos Pelotazos, 22g with Jar Jar toy offer on back...............4.00
PAS0061 Cheetos Rizos, 14g with Jar Jar toy offer on back 4.00
PAS0062 Cheetos Rizos, 27g with Anakin Skywalker photo 3.00
PAS0063 Cheetos Rizos, 57g with Anakin Skywalker photo 3.00
PAS0064 Cheetos Sticks, 18g with Jar Jar toy offer on back......................4.00
PAS0065 Cheetos Sticks, 36g with Anakin Skywalker photo 3.00
PAS0066 Cheetos Sticks, 70g with Anakin Skywalker photo 3.00
PAS0068 Churreria Santa Ana, 120g with Qui-Gon photo.........................3.00
PAS0069 Churreria Santa Ana, 170g with Qui-Gon photo.........................3.00
PAS0067 Churreria Santa Ana, 41g with Qui-Gon photo...........................3.00
PAS0071 Doritos Rock and Cream, 110g with Darth Maul photo 3.00
PAS0070 Doritos Rock and Cream, 80g with Darth Maul photo 3.00
PAS0075 Doritos Tex-Mex, 110g with Darth Maul photo............................3.00
PAS0072 Doritos Tex-Mex, 30g with Darth Maul photo..............................3.00
PAS0073 Doritos Tex-Mex, 44g with Darth Maul photo..............................3.00
PAS0074 Doritos Tex-Mex, 80g with Darth Maul photo..............................3.00
PAS0078 Fritos Matutano Barbacoa, 130g with Jar Jar photo 3.00
PAS0076 Fritos Matutano Barbacoa, 50g with Jar Jar photo 3.00
PAS0077 Fritos Matutano Barbacoa, 95g with Jar Jar photo 3.00
PAS0079 Fritos Matutano Ketchup, 25g with Jar Jar toy offer on back 4.00
PAS0080 Lay's a la Vinagreta, 110g with Qui-Gon photo 3.00
PAS0081 Lay's a la Vinagreta, 160g with Qui-Gon photo 3.00
PAS0083 Lay's Doradas con Cebolleta, 110g with Qui-Gon photo 3.00
PAS0084 Lay's Doradas con Cebolleta, 160g with Qui-Gon photo 3.00
PAS0082 Lay's Doradas con Cebolleta, 44g with Qui-Gon photo 3.00

PAS0087 Lay's Ligeras 33% Menos Grasa, 140g with Qui-Gon photo 3.00
PAS0085 Lay's Ligeras 33% Menos Grasa, 30g with Qui-Gon photo 3.00
PAS0086 Lay's Ligeras 33% Menos Grasa, 44g with Qui-Gon photo 3.00
PAS0088 Lay's Receta Campesina, 110g w/Qui-Gon photo.....................3.00
PAS0089 Lay's Receta Campesina, 160g w/Qui-Gon photo.....................3.00
PAS0092 Lay's, 125g with Qui-Gon photo 3.00
PAS0093 Lay's, 170g with Qui-Gon photo 3.00
PAS0090 Lay's, 30g with Qui-Gon photo 3.00
PAS0091 Lay's, 44g with Qui-Gon photo 3.00
PAS0095 Ruffles Alioli ole, 110g with Obi-Wan photo 3.00
PAS0096 Ruffles Alioli ole, 160g with Obi-Wan photo 3.00
PAS0094 Ruffles Alioli ole, 44g with Obi-Wan photo 3.00
PAS0099 Ruffles Jamon Jamon, 110g with Obi-Wan photo 3.00
PAS0097 Ruffles Jamon Jamon, 30g with Obi-Wan photo 3.00
PAS0098 Ruffles Jamon Jamon, 44g with Obi-Wan photo 3.00
PAS0101 Ruffles Onduladas, 125g with Obi-Wan photo 3.00
PAS0102 Ruffles Onduladas, 170g with Obi-Wan photo 3.00
PAS0100 Ruffles Onduladas, 44g with Obi-Wan photo 3.00
PAS0104 Ruffles Pimenton Molon, 110g w/Obi-Wan photo 3.00
PAS0105 Ruffles Pimenton Molon, 160g w/Obi-Wan photo 3.00
PAS0103 Ruffles Pimenton Molon, 44g w/Obi-Wan photo 3.00
PAS0107 Ruffles Queso y eso, 110g with Obi-Wan photo 3.00
PAS0108 Ruffles Queso y eso, 160g with Obi-Wan photo 3.00
PAS0106 Ruffles Queso y eso, 44g with Obi-Wan photo 3.00

Smith's Snackfood
PAS0110 Doritos Corn Chips Cheese Supreme 230g with Yoda photo 3.00
PAS0109 Doritos Corn Chips Cheese Supreme 50g with Yoda photo 3.00
PAS0112 Doritos Corn Chips Cool Tang 230g w/C-3PO photo 3.00
PAS0111 Doritos Corn Chips Cool Tang 50g w/C-3PO photo 3.00
PAS0113 Doritos Corn Chips Nacho Cheese 230g with Qui-Gon photo ...3.00
PAS0114 Doritos Corn Chips Original 230g with Amidala photo................3.00
PAS0115 Lay's 12 packs Flavour Mix with C-3PO photo.............................3.00
PAS0116 Lay's 12 packs Original with Anakin photo..................................3.00
PAS0117 Lay's 12 packs Texas BBQ with Jar Jar photo 3.00
PAS0118 Lay's 18 packs Flavour Mix with Yoda photo...............................3.00
PAS0120 Lay's Cheddar Cheese and Onion 100g with Amidala photo ...3.00
PAS0121 Lay's Cheddar Cheese and Onion 200g with Amidala photo ...3.00
PAS0119 Lay's Cheddar Cheese and Onion 50g with Amidala photo 3.00
PAS0123 Lay's Original 100g with Anakin photo 3.00
PAS0122 Lay's Original 50g with Anakin photo 3.00
PAS0125 Lay's Roast Chicken 100g with Obi-Wan photo.........................3.00
PAS0126 Lay's Roast Chicken 250g with Obi-Wan photo.........................3.00
PAS0124 Lay's Roast Chicken 50g with Obi-Wan photo...........................3.00
PAS0128 Lay's Salt and Vinegar 250g with R2-D2 photo 3.00
PAS0127 Lay's Salt and Vinegar 50g with R2-D2 photo 3.00
PAS0130 Lay's Texas BBQ 100g with Jar Jar photo 3.00
PAS0131 Lay's Texas BBQ 200g with Jar Jar photo 3.00
PAS0129 Lay's Texas BBQ 50g with Jar Jar photo 3.00

UFO
PAS0132 ESB promotion with sticker premiums 8.00

Walkers

PAS0138   PAS0139   PAS0140   PAS0137   PAS0136

PAS0141   PAS0142   PAS0133   PAS0145

PAS0144   PAS0146   PAS0134   PAS0135   PAS0143

PAS0138 Crisps, beef and onion, SW:SE C-3PO..............................3.00
PAS0139 Crisps, cheese and onion, SW:SE C-3PO 3.00

Packaging: Snack Chips

PAS0140 Crisps, cream cheese and chive, SW:SE C-3PO 3.00
PAS0137 Crisps, Worchester sauce, SW:SE C-3PO 3.00
PAS0136 Doritos, original, SW:SE Darth Vader 3.00
PAS0141 Doritos, sizzlin' barbeque, SW:SE Darth Vader 3.00
PAS0142 Doritos, tangy cheese, SW:SE Darth Vader 3.00
PAS0133 French Fries, SW:SE Chewbacca..........................3.00
PAS0145 Lites, cheese and onion, SW:SE C-3PO 3.00
PAS0144 Lites, salt and vinegar, SW:SE C-3PO 3.00
PAS0146 Lites, salted, SW:SE C-3PO 3.00
PAS0134 Quavers, cheese, SW:SE R2-D2..........................3.00
PAS0135 Quavers, salt and vinegar, SW:SE R2-D2 ....3.00
PAS0143 Quavers, tangy tomato, SW:SE R2-D2 ....3.00

PACKAGING: SUGAR-FREE GUM

SFG0058

Topps

SFG0001 01) Jawas..........................5.00
SFG0002 02) Han Solo aiming blaster 5.00
SFG0003 03) C-3PO full body..........................5.00
SFG0004 04) Ben Kenobi 5.00
SFG0005 05) C-3PO above the knees 5.00
SFG0006 06) Jawa sitting..........................5.00
SFG0007 07) Han and Chewbacca..........................5.00
SFG0008 08) Luke 5.00
SFG0009 09) R2-D2 and C-3PO 5.00
SFG0010 10) Luke in gunner chair 5.00
SFG0011 11) Han on Falcon ramp 5.00
SFG0012 12) Stormtroopers..........................5.00
SFG0013 13) Han on Falcon's ramp 5.00
SFG0014 14) X-Wings and Y-Wing 5.00
SFG0015 15) Luke in X-Wing helmet 5.00
SFG0016 16) Ben with lightsaber 5.00
SFG0017 17) Luke holding gun 5.00
SFG0018 18) R2-D2 ....5.00
SFG0019 19) Han 5.00
SFG0020 20) Tusken Raider, gaffi stick over head..........................5.00
SFG0021 21) Stormtrooper 5.00
SFG0022 22) R2-D2 ....5.00
SFG0023 23) Princess Leia 5.00
SFG0024 24) Tusken pointing gaffi stick 5.00
SFG0025 25) Ben Kenobi 5.00
SFG0026 26) C-3PO, dirty, shoulders up 5.00
SFG0027 27) Chewbacca headshot 5.00
SFG0028 28) Alien (not seen in movie)..........................6.00
SFG0029 29) Grand Moff Tarkin 5.00
SFG0030 30) Han with collar open..........................5.00
SFG0031 31) Darth Vader airbrush portrait 5.00
SFG0032 32) Luke in X-Wing, no helmet 5.00
SFG0033 33) Tusken Raider headshot 5.00
SFG0034 34) Sandtrooper 5.00
SFG0035 35) Stormtrooper 5.00
SFG0036 36) Leia in Yavin war room..........................5.00
SFG0037 37) Cantina band member 5.00
SFG0038 38) Luke as stormtrooper, no helmet 5.00
SFG0039 39) C-3PO..........................5.00
SFG0040 40) Luke 5.00
SFG0041 41) Millennium Falcon..........................5.00
SFG0042 42) Han shooting 5.00
SFG0043 43) Tarkin, face only..........................5.00
SFG0044 44) Luke in X-Wing gear 5.00
SFG0045 45) Luke 5.00
SFG0046 46) R2-D2 and C-3PO 5.00
SFG0047 47) C-3PO..........................5.00
SFG0048 48) Escape pod rear view..........................5.00
SFG0049 49) Leia and Luke after Death Star escape 5.00
SFG0050 50) Luke and Leia 5.00
SFG0051 51) Chewbacca and Han 5.00

SFG0052 52) Ben and Luke 5.00
SFG0053 53) Stormtroopers 5.00
SFG0054 54) Luke (X-Wing gear) and Leia 5.00
SFG0055 55) Uncle Owen and Luke 5.00
SFG0056 56) Luke and C-3PO 5.00
SFG0057 Unopened box 230.00
SFG0058 Unopened pkg., any of 4 wrappers: Han Solo, Darth Vader, Luke
  Skywalker, Princess Leia 5.00

PACKAGING: YOGURT

Dairylea
PAY0001 Admiral Ackbar pineapple 8.00
PAY0002 Chewbacca fudge 8.00
PAY0003 Darth Vader black cherry 8.00
PAY0004 Ewoks banana 8.00
PAY0005 Jabba the Hutt peach melba 8.00
PAY0006 Luke Skywalker raspberry 8.00
PAY0007 Princess Leia strawberry 8.00
PAY0008 Yoda gooseberry 8.00

PADS: SPORTS

SFT0001　　　　**SFT0002**　　　　**SFT0003**

Dynacraft
SFT0001 Darth Maul glove, knee and elbow pad set..........................16.00
SFT0002 Queen Amidala glove, knee and elbow pad set..........................16.00

MV Sports
SFT0005 Darth Maul knee and elbow pads 14.00

Seneca Sports Inc.
SFT0003 Imperial Assault protective gear backpack with knee pads, elbow
  pads, wrist guards, water bottle 14.00
SFT0004 R2-D2 protective gear backpack with knee pads, elbow pads, wrist
  guards, water bottle 16.00

PAINT-BY-NUMBER CRAFT KITS

Craft House

CRP0016　　　　**CRP0017**　　　　**CRP0018**

Acrylic paint-by-number.
CRP0018 AT-ST and Speeder Bike 5.00
CRP0016 Darth Vader and Boba Fett 6.00
CRP0017 Luke and Han 3.00

Craft Master
CRP0001 Battle on Hoth..........................16.00
CRP0002 Boba Fett 16.00
CRP0003 C-3PO and R2-D2 ....16.00
CRP0004 Chase Through Astroids 16.00
CRP0005 Darth Vader 16.00
CRP0006 Ewok Gliders..........................16.00
CRP0007 Ewok Village 16.00
CRP0015 Han Solo and Princess Leia 16.00
CRP0008 Jabba the Hutt 16.00
CRP0009 Lando Calrissian and Boushh 16.00
CRP0010 Luke Skywalker..........................16.00

CRP0001   CRP0004   CRP0015

CRP0010 front and back   CRP0008   CRP0014

CRP0014 Max Rebo band 16.00
CRP0012 Wicket and Baga 16.00
CRP0013 Yoda 16.00

Rose Art Industries

CRP0019

CRP0019 A New Hope 8.00

PAJAMAS

Long Eddies
APJ0062 Anakin Skywalker, long sleeves and legs 16.00
APJ0057 Darth Vader and Luke Skywalker................................18.00
APJ0063 Jedi vs. Sith, long sleeves and legs 16.00

PCA Apparel
APJ0058 Darth Vader, 100% polyester with velcro-attached cape........29.00
APJ0060 Jedi vs. Sith, white T-shirt tops with blue shorts............18.00
APJ0061 Lightsaber duel, T-shirt tops with black shorts 18.00
APJ0059 STAPs and battle droids, button front red and white tops 18.00

Wilker Bros.
APJ0021 "Darth Vader Lives" 20.00
APJ0001 Admiral Ackbar 20.00
APJ0002 Baby Ewoks 23.00
APJ0003 Boba Fett...30.00
APJ0004 Boba Fett and Darth Vader..30.00
APJ0005 Boba Fett, C-3PO, Chewbacca, and R2-D2 ....22.00
APJ0006 Boker Scouts 25.00
APJ0007 C-3PO and Darth Vader 21.00
APJ0008 C-3PO and Ewoks 20.00
APJ0009 C-3PO and Luke Skywalker 20.00
APJ0010 C-3PO and R2-D2 ....22.00
APJ0011 C-3PO, R2-D2 and X-Wing 23.00
APJ0012 C-3PO, R2-D2, and Chewbacca 20.00
APJ0013 C-3PO, R2-D2, and Emperor's Guards..........................23.00
APJ0014 Cantina Band 24.00
APJ0015 Chewbacca 20.00
APJ0016 Chewbacca and Millennium Falcon 22.00
APJ0017 Darth Vader 21.00
APJ0018 Darth Vader and Death Star 22.00
APJ0019 Darth Vader and Emperor's Guards...............................25.00
APJ0020 Darth Vader and Luke Skywalker 23.00
APJ0022 Droopy McCool 23.00
APJ0023 Ewoks in Village 20.00
APJ0024 Gamorrean Guards 20.00
APJ0025 Han Solo and Chewbacca 22.00
APJ0026 Han Solo and Darth Vader 21.00

APJ0027 Jabba the Hutt 20.00
APJ0028 Jabba the Hutt and Bib Fortuna 20.00
APJ0029 Jabba the Hutt and Boba Fett 24.00
APJ0030 Latara 21.00
APJ0031 Luke Skywalker and Princess Leia 20.00
APJ0032 Luke Skywalker on Tauntaun 20.00
APJ0033 Max Rebo..25.00
APJ0034 Paploo on Speeder Bike...20.00
APJ0035 Princess Kneesaa 20.00
APJ0036 Princess Kneesaa on swing 20.00
APJ0037 Princess Kneesaa skipping rope 20.00
APJ0039 Stormtrooper...20.00
APJ0038 Stormtrooper and R2-D2 ....20.00
APJ0040 Wicket and Princess Kneesaa in bush 20.00
APJ0041 Wicket and Princess Kneesaa on skateboard................20.00
APJ0042 Wicket and Princess Kneesaa on teeter-totter...............20.00
APJ0043 Wicket and Princess Kneesaa on vine............................20.00
APJ0044 Wicket and Princess Kneesaa playing musical instruments.......20.00
APJ0045 Wicket and Princess Kneesaa tug-of-war 20.00
APJ0046 Wicket and Princess Kneesaa w/flowers..........................20.00
APJ0047 Wicket and R2-D2 ....20.00
APJ0048 Wicket in basket 20.00
APJ0049 Wicket on vine 20.00
APJ0050 Wicket the Ewok..20.00
APJ0051 Wicket w/balloons 20.00
APJ0052 Wicket w/butterfly net 20.00
APJ0053 Wicket w/walking stick 20.00
APJ0054 Wiley the Ewok 20.00
APJ0055 Yoda 20.00
APJ0056 Yoda and Luke Skywalker..20.00

PANTS

Bibb Co.
AP0001 Chambray jeans, SW 10.00
AP0002 Corduroy jeans, SW 10.00

Gans Enterprises
AP0003 Denim jeans, Darth Vader 8.00
AP0004 Denim jeans, Droids 8.00
AP0005 Denim jeans, Jedi logo 10.00
AP0006 Denim jeans, Paploo 8.00

Liberty Trouser Co.
AP0007 Jeans, SW w/overall pattern 16.00
AP0008 Shorts, fleece gym w/Jedi logo 12.00
AP0009 Shorts, gym w/Jedi logo 10.00
AP0010 Shorts, SW w/overall pattern...10.00

Mr. Seb Sportswear
AP0011 Shorts, athletic w/Jedi logo 10.00

PAPER REINFORCEMENTS

SUJ0001 front and back

Butterfly Originals
SUJ0001 Foil Loose-Leaf Paper Reinforcers, 48-pack...................7.00

PAPERWEIGHTS

PEP0003   PEP0004

3D Arts
PEP0001 Darth Vader hologram 15.00
PEP0002 Yoda hologram 15.00

Paperweights

PEP0005 10th Anniversary paperclip, spring hinge with magnetic back.24.00
PEP0003 Chewbacca, sculpted under glass 24.00
PEP0004 Yoda, sculpted under glass 24.00

PARTY DECORATIONS

PD0001 front and back   PD0002

Party Express

PD0002 Jedi and Sith silhouette crepe paper streamer 3.00
PD0003 Jedi vs. Sith set of 3 wallhangings 7.00
PD0001 Millennium Falcon, Tie Fighter, X-Wing Fighter wallhangings 9.00

PARTY GAMES

NF0001

Party Express

NF0001 Space Battle 7.00

PASSPORTS

PPP0001 front with stickers

Ballantine

PPP0001 The Star Wars Intergalactic Passport...24.00

Pepsi Cola

PPP0003   PPP0004   PPP0005   PPP0002

PPP0003 Anakin...3.00
PPP0004 Qui-Gon Jinn..3.00
PPP0005 Watto...3.00
PPP0002 Passport to universe, Star Wars SE 18.00

PATCHES

PT0036

Boy Scouts of America

PT0036 Sith Park Empire Council, 2001 National Jamboree 19.00
PT0025 Yoda, green border..35.00
PT0026 Yoda, yellow border...56.00

Crew

PT0024 Revenge logo...45.00

Factors, Etc.

PT0004 "Darth Vader Lives" 23.00
PT0010 "May the Force be with You"...12.00
PT0002 Brotherhood of Jedi Knights, 3" wide....................................21.00
PT0003 Brotherhood of Jedi Knights, 3½" wide...................................12.00
PT0012 Rebel Forces..24.00
PT0018 SW Outline logo, 3½" wide...18.00
PT0019 SW Outline logo, 4" wide..14.00
PT0020 SW Pyramid Logo w/o TM..23.00
PT0021 SW Pyramid Logo w/TM..20.00

Fan Club

PT0001 A New Hope, triangular 15.00
PT0005 Darth Vader in Flames...15.00
PT0006 Empire Strikes Back: 10th anniversary...................................16.00
PT0007 ESB logo with Star Wars outlined, any variation 15.00
PT0008 Lucasfilm Fan Club, any variation..8.00
PT0009 Lucasfilm Fan Club, blue on maroon......................................10.00
PT0011 Official Star Wars Fan Club, any variation...............................15.00
PT0014 Revenge logo, rounded corners...35.00
PT0015 ROTJ logo...14.00
PT0017 Star Wars: The First Ten Years..17.00
PT0022 Yoda, Revenge...65.00
PT0023 Yoda, ROTJ...14.00

ILM / Crew

PT0027   PT0028   PT0029

PT0030   PT0031   PT0032

PT0033   PT0034   PT0035

PT0034 Anakin's Podracer 18.00
PT0029 Boss Nass 24.00
PT0030 Darth Maul..24.00
PT0035 Jar Jar Binks...24.00
PT0032 Naboo Fighter...18.00
PT0027 Queen Amidala...24.00
PT0028 SWI...28.00
PT0031 Trade Federation Tank...18.00
PT0033 Watto...22.00

Kenner

PT0013 Return of the Jedi...75.00
PT0016 Star Wars: The Empire Strikes Back 65.00

PATTERNS

Buttericks

APA0006 Darth Vader (5186) 14.00

APA0006

APA0001   APA0002   APA0003   APA0005

McCall's

APA0001 Ewok Costume...18.00
APA0002 Five Patterns (ESB) 35.00
APA0003 Night Wear (ROTJ)....................................12.00
APA0005 Robes and Cloaks.......................................4.00
APA0004 Shirt (ROTJ) 12.00

PENCIL CASES / BOXES

3D Arts
SUK0023 Holographic sticker affixed to lid of metal box 7.00

A.H. Prismatic
SUK0016 Holographic sticker affixed to lid of black metal box..................8.00

Butterfly Originals

SUK0003

SUK0003 Vader and Luke duel, zippered pouch...12.00

Creata Promotions
SUK0025 C-3PO and R2-D2 ....9.00

Grand Toys
SUK0032 Darth Maul character shaped, zippered 8.00

HC Ford
SUK0015 Darth Vader, spaceships, and ROTJ logo, zippered plastic.......12.00

Helix
Zippered plastic.
SUK0007 Ben Kenobi...16.00
SUK0008 C-3PO 16.00
SUK0009 Darth Vader 16.00
SUK0010 Han Solo 16.00
SUK0011 Luke Skywalker 16.00
SUK0012 Princess Leia 16.00
SUK0013 R2-D2 ....16.00
SUK0014 Stormtrooper...16.00

Impact, Inc.

SUK0022   SUK0024

SUK0026

SUK0022 "Jedi vs. Sith" Qui-Gonn Jinn, Obi-Wan, Darth Sidious, Darth Maul, tin box...4.00
SUK0024 "Tatooine" Anakin, Jar Jar, Sebulba, and Watto, tin box 4.00
SUK0026 Jar Jar Transformable Pencil Case: sharpener, glue, eraser, ruler, tape, paper clips....................................12.00
SUK0028 Podracer pencil pouch 6.00

Mead
Zipper pouch with reinforced holes for use in binder.
SUK0020 Darth Vader on black.....................................5.00

SUK0017   SUK0019

SUK0020   SUK0021

SUK0019 Darth Vader on blue...................................5.00
SUK0017 Darth Vader patch centered 5.00
SUK0021 Star Wars patch on blueprint 5.00

Metal Box Ltd.
Tin boxes.

SUK0001   SUK0002   SUK0004

SUK0001 C-3PO 12.00
SUK0002 Chewbacca 12.00
SUK0004 Darth Vader 12.00
SUK0005 R2-D2 ....12.00
SUK0006 Yoda 12.00

SUK0027   SUK0029

SUK0030

Q-Stat
Tin pencil boxes.
SUK0029 Anakin Skywalker...5.00
SUK0030 Darth Maul 5.00
SUK0027 Queen Amidala..5.00

Rose Art Industries

SUK0031   SUK0037   SUK0033

SUK0018

SUK0018 Lightsaber pencil case 6.00
SUK0034 Anakin Skywalker Podracing, zippered 4.00
SUK0031 Darth Maul pencil tin, shaped 7.00

Pencil Cases/Boxes

SUK0034

SUK0035

SUK0036

SUK0037 Darth Maul tin 5.00
SUK0035 Darth Maul, zippered...4.00
SUK0033 Jedi vs. Sith, zippered..4.00
SUK0038 Queen Amidala tin 5.00
SUK0036 Queen Amidala, zippered 6.00

PENCIL CUPS
HC Ford
SUL0002 Artwork of characters, 4" high metal...16.00

SUL0001

Sigma
SUL0001 Yoda pencil cup 65.00

PENCIL SHARPENERS

SUP0002

SUP0003

SUP0005

SUP0006

Butterfly Originals
SUP0001 Baby Ewoks, plastic 4.00
SUP0002 Darth Vader, sculpted 8.00
SUP0003 R2-D2, sculpted 8.00
SUP0004 Tie Fighter, round plastic..5.00
SUP0006 Wicket the Ewok sharpener with deal and die-cut eraser in blister
    pack 12.00
SUP0005 Yoda, sculpted 8.00

HC Ford
Character drawing on dome-shaped sharpener.
SUP0008 C-3PO and R2-D2 ....17.00
SUP0009 Darth Vader and Stormtrooper 17.00
SUP0010 Han Solo and Chewbacca 17.00
SUP0011 Luke and Leia 17.00

Picture on oval-shaped sharpener.
SUP0012 Darth Vader 10.00
SUP0013 X-Wing Fighter...10.00
SUP0007 Death Star-shaped..26.00

Impact, Inc.
SUP0016 Destroyer Droid sharpener/eraser combo 6.00

SUP0015

SUP0016

SUP0015 Federation Tank sculpted...4.00

Rose Art Industries
SUP0014 Millennium Falcon sculpted 6.00

SUP0014

PENCIL TOPS

Butterfly Originals
PNT0012 C-3PO, without pencil..4.00
PNT0013 Darth Vader, without pencil 4.00
PNT0014 Emperor's Royal Guard, without pencil...4.00
PNT0015 Wicket, without pencil 4.00

HC Ford

PNT0001

PNT0002

PNT0004

PNT0005

PNT0007

PNT0010

PNT0001 Admiral Ackbar 5.00
PNT0002 Bib Fortuna 5.00
PNT0003 Chewbacca 5.00
PNT0004 Darth Vader (2 different)..5.00
PNT0005 Gamorrean Guard 5.00
PNT0006 Han Solo 5.00
PNT0007 Imperial Guard 5.00
PNT0008 Luke Skywalker..5.00
PNT0009 R2-D2 ....5.00
PNT0010 Wicket 5.00
PNT0011 Yoda 5.00

PENCIL TRAYS

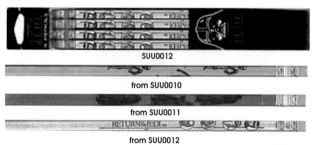
SUQ0001

Sigma
SUQ0001 C-3PO pencil tray...20.00

PENCILS

Butterfly Originals
SUU0010 C-3PO 4-pack, blister packed on Darth Vader header card with
    ROTJ logo 6.00

SUU0012

from SUU0010

from SUU0011

from SUU0012

SUU0003

SUU0004

SUU0005

SUU0006

SUU0007

SUU0003 C-3PO ROTJ character-topped pencils 6.00
SUU0011 Darth Vader 4-pack, blister packed on Darth Vader header card
    with ROTJ logo 6.00
SUU0004 Darth Vader ROTJ character-topped pencils 6.00
SUU0005 Emperor's Royal Guard ROTJ character-topped pencils 6.00
SUU0007 Pop-a-Point Pencils, 2-pack, red sparkle plastic embossed with
    "May The Force Be With You"..8.00
SUU0008 Pop-a-Point Pencils, 6-pack, red sparkle plastic embossed with
    "May The Force Be With You"..11.00
SUU0002 Pop-a-Point, red sparkle plastic embossed with "May The Force Be
    With You" 14.00
SUU0012 ROTJ logo 4-pack, blister packed on Darth Vader header card
    with ROTJ logo 5.00
SUU0006 Wicket the Ewok ROTJ character-topped pencils........................6.00

Fan Club
SUU0001 Empire Strikes Back logo and Character Strip 5.00
SUU0009 Star Wars logo and Character strip 5.00

Fantasma
Line art on foil background.
SUU0013 Star Wars logo...3.00
SUU0014 Star Wars logo, fringe topped 4.00

HC Ford
Character tag-topped pencils.
SUU0015 C-3PO and R2-D2..6.00
SUU0016 Chewbacca and Han Solo 6.00
SUU0017 Darth Vader and Stormtroopers 6.00
SUU0018 Luke Skywalker and Princess Leia 6.00

Helix
SUU0024 "May The Force Be With You" in gold on blue 2.00
SUU0023 Stormtrooper packaging, 10 colored pencils 8.00

Character-topped pencils.
SUU0019 C-3PO character-topped pencil 3.00
SUU0020 Darth Vader character-topped pencil 3.00
SUU0021 R2-D2 character-topped pencil..............................3.00
SUU0022 Stormtrooper character-topped pencil.......................3.00

Mead

SUU0026

SUU0026 Star Wars 4-pack of character pencils 3.00

Pentech
2-pack of pencils with character pencil toppers.
SUU0030 Anakin and Amidala, EPI 4.00
SUU0029 Darth Maul and Jar Jar 4.00

SUU0027   SUU0028   SUU0029   SUU0030

SUU0028 2-pack of character pencils with lightsaber pencil sharpener ...5.00
SUU0027 Episode I 8-pack of character pencils 6.00

Q-Stat
Pencil sets. Include: 2 pencils, pencil pouch, sharpener, and eraser.
SUU0031 Jedi vs. Sith..6.00
SUU0032 Pod Race 6.00

Rose Art Industries

SUU0025

SUU0025 Star Wars 6-pack foil pencils 5.00

PENNANTS

PEN0001 10th Anniversary pennant...................................20.00

PENS

Butterfly Originals

SUV0001

SUV0002 ROTJ "May The Force Be With You", felt-tip, Darth Vader clip 6.00
SUV0001 ROTJ w/logo and Characters, blue ink, 2-pack...............11.00

Chupa Chups

SUV0013 loose and in package   SUV0014 loose and in package

Pen with motorized spinning lollipop.
SUV0013 Darth Vader..8.00
SUV0014 Stormtrooper..8.00

Disney / MGM
SUV0008 Star Tours logo and stars.................................3.00

Fan Club
SUV0015 Floaty Pen, Star Wars Insider renewal premium 25.00

Fantasma
SUV0003 Star Wars logo and line art on foil background, ballpoint...........4.00

Fisher
SUV0004 Rebel Fighter pen, black rubberized grip, "Star Wars" on clip, and
    Rebel emblem on end 16.00

SUV0028 pen

front and back

279

Pens

SUV0005 Titanium space pen, "Star Wars" and "May The Force Be With You" imprinted on barrel 45.00
SUV0028 Titanium space pen, "Star Wars" and "May The Force Be With You" imprinted on barrel, Dave Prowse autographed, limited edition of 200 ....70.00

Helix

SUV0006 Colored felt tips, boxed set of five...............................25.00
SUV0007 Colored felt tips, boxed set of ten 36.00

Mead

SUV0016 | SUV0017 | SUV0018 | SUV0019

SUV0016 C-3PO "They've Shut Down The Main Reactor..." 3.00
SUV0018 Darth Vader "I Find Your Lack of Faith Disturbing" 3.00
SUV0017 Princess Leia and R2-D2 "Help Me Obi-Wan Kenobi." 3.00
SUV0019 Stormtroopers "Freeze You Rebel Scum" 3.00

Penline

Packaged on Tie-fighter backer card.

SUV0022 | SUV0023 | SUV0024 | SUV0025

SUV0023 Darth Vader cap 5.00
SUV0024 Han Solo cap..5.00
SUV0025 Luke Skywalker cap 5.00
SUV0022 R2-D2 cap..5.00

Pentech

SUV0020 | SUV0021 | SUV0026

SUV0026 Darth Maul ballpoint, includes collector's tin.....................15.00
SUV0021 3-pack of ballpoint pens, sculpted as lightsabers, Episode I......5.00
SUV0020 6-pack of character ballpoint pens, Episode I.....................4.00

Super Live Adventure

SUV0027

SUV0027 3-pen set: Indiana Jones, Star Wars, and SLA 16.00

Tiger Electronics

Character speaks phrase, plus record-and-playback function.

SUV0009 | SUV0010 | SUV0012 | SUV0011

SUV0009 C-3PO 8.00
SUV0010 Darth Vader..8.00

SUV0012 X-Wing Pilot...8.00
SUV0011 Lightsaber, 4 Sound FX, 12 second record/playback, voice changer 12.00

PEWTER

Danbury Mint

Chess pieces.

PEW0067 PEW0068 PEW0069 PEW0066 PEW0070 PEW0065 PEW0073

PEW0072 PEW0071 PEW0060 PEW0064 PEW0058

PEW0062 PEW0059 PEW0057 PEW0063 PEW0061 PEW0094

PEW0067 AT-ST, rook 38.00
PEW0068 Boba Fett with blaster, bishop 38.00
PEW0062 C-3PO, rook 38.00
PEW0060 Chewbacca in seat with control stick, knight 38.00
PEW0069 Darth Vader with red lightsaber, bishop 38.00
PEW0066 Death Star, queen 38.00
PEW0070 Emperor, king 38.00
PEW0064 Ewok with spear, pawn 38.00
PEW0058 Han with blaster, bishop 38.00
PEW0065 Imperial Probot, rook 38.00
PEW0059 Leia on speeder bike, knight 38.00
PEW0057 Luke with blue lightsaber, bishop 38.00
PEW0063 Millennium Falcon, queen 38.00
PEW0061 Obi-Wan and Yoda, king 38.00
PEW0094 R2-D2, rook 38.00
PEW0073 Stormtrooper kneeling, pawn 38.00
PEW0072 Trooper on speederbike, knight 38.00
PEW0071 Tusken Raider on Bantha, knight.........................38.00

Franklin Mint

PEW0001 PEW0002

PEW0074 "Duel of the Jedi" with glass dome 85.00
PEW0001 AT-AT...260.00
PEW0002 Millennium Falcon 260.00

Heritage / Star Trek Galore

PEW0003 Bantha with two Sand People riders.......................38.00
PEW0093 Bantha, no riders or saddle.................................32.00
PEW0004 C-3PO 15.00

PEW0003 PEW0004 PEW0005 PEW0006 PEW0008 PEW0012

PEW0009   PEW0010   PEW0011   PEW0013   PEW0014   PEW0015

PEW0005 Chewbacca 15.00
PEW0006 Darth Vader 20.00
PEW0007 Han Solo (STG only) 45.00
PEW0008 Jawa 20.00
PEW0009 Luke Skywalker 15.00
PEW0010 Obi-Wan Kenobi 20.00
PEW0011 Princess Leia 15.00
PEW0012 R2-D2 ....15.00
PEW0013 Sand Person, standing 15.00
PEW0014 Snitch (Grindan) 20.00
PEW0015 Stormtrooper 20.00

Rawcliffe
PEW0031 Admiral Ackbar 20.00
PEW0087 Anakin Skywalker 24.00
PEW0055 Anakin Skywalker (Boxed with Hasbro's Deluxe Monopoly CD
     Game) 12.00
PEW0016 A-Wing Fighter 40.00
PEW0097 Battle Droid 24.00
PEW0032 Bib Fortuna 20.00
PEW0033 Boba Fett 24.00
PEW0017 B-Wing Fighter 45.00
PEW0034 C-3PO 20.00
PEW0035 Chewbacca 22.00
PEW0076 Darth Maul 36.00
PEW0036 Darth Vader 34.00
PEW0018 Darth Vader's Tie Fighter, deluxe limited to 15,000 ....125.00
PEW0089 Death Star, limited to 4,500 ....86.00
PEW0054 Droopy McCool 19.00
PEW0037 Emperor 20.00
PEW0078 Federation Droid Starfighter 48.00
PEW0077 Federation Large Transport 62.00
PEW0086 Federation Tank 62.00

PEW0039 Gamorrean Guard 20.00
PEW0040 Han Solo 20.00
PEW0019 Imperial Star Destroyer 75.00
PEW0050 Jabba and Leia, limited to 2,005 ....200.00
PEW0088 Jabba the Hutt 48.00
PEW0079 Jar Jar Binks 29.00
PEW0041 Lando Calrissian 20.00
PEW0042 Luke Skywalker 22.00
PEW0052 Max Rebo 29.00
PEW0020 Millennium Falcon 50.00
PEW0021 Millennium Falcon, deluxe limited to 15,000 ...110.00
PEW0080 Naboo Starfighter 48.00
PEW0098 Naboo Starfighter, deluxe limited to 1,000 .....200.00
PEW0081 Nute Gunray 29.00
PEW0043 Obi-Wan Kenobi 23.00
PEW0082 Obi-Wan Kenobi (TPM) 29.00
PEW0022 Outrider 35.00
PEW0044 Princess Leia 20.00
PEW0051 Princess Leia as Jabba's prisoner 20.00
PEW0049 Princess Leia as Jabba's prisoner promotion (round base) 15.00
PEW0084 Qui-Gon Jinn 29.00
PEW0096 Queen Amidala 24.00
PEW0045 R2-D2 ....22.00
PEW0085 Royal Starship 48.00
PEW0023 Sail Barge 45.00
PEW0024 Shuttle Tyderium 50.00
PEW0025 Slave I 40.00
PEW0051 Slave Leia 18.00
PEW0026 Snowspeeder 35.00
PEW0091 Speeder Bike 48.00
PEW0046 Stormtrooper 23.00
PEW0048 Stormtrooper Dark Forces promotion 14.00
PEW0053 Sy Snootles 19.00
PEW0092 Tie Bomber 40.00
PEW0027 Tie Fighter 42.00
PEW0090 Tie Interceptor, deluxe limited to 7,500 ....125.00
PEW0083 Watto 29.00
PEW0038 Wicket 20.00
PEW0028 X-Wing Fighter 45.00
PEW0029 X-Wing Fighter, deluxe limited to 15,000 ....95.00
PEW0047 Yoda 20.00
PEW0030 Y-Wing Fighter 50.00
PEW0056 Princess Leia and Luke, classic logo pose 450.00

PEW0031   PEW0055   PEW0032   PEW0033   PEW0034   PEW0035   PEW0036   PEW0054   PEW0037   PEW0039   PEW0050   PEW0088   PEW0040

PEW0041   PEW0042   PEW0052   PEW0043   PEW0044   PEW0051   PEW0049   PEW0045   PEW0046   PEW0048   PEW0053   PEW0038   PEW0047   PEW0016

PEW0017   PEW0019   PEW0020   PEW0022   PEW0023   PEW0024   PEW0025   PEW0026   PEW0091   PEW0092

PEW0027   PEW0028   PEW0030   PEW0018   PEW0089   PEW0021   PEW0090   PEW0029   PEW0087   PEW0097   PEW0076   PEW0079   PEW0081

PEW0082   PEW0096   PEW0084   PEW0083   PEW0078   PEW0077   PEW0086   PEW0080   PEW0085   PEW0098

Pewter

PEW0075 Qui-Gon figurine and lightsaber keychain, Jedi Power Battle for Playstation promotion 16.00

PEZ DISPENSERS

PEZ0031

Cap Candy
PEZ0031 Jar Jar Binks PEZ Handler, battery operated 15.00

Pez Candy, Inc.
PEZ0025 Boba Fett, bagged...4.00
PEZ0032 Boba Fett, carded (C-3PO, Chewbacca, and Yoda)................6.00
PEZ0021 Boba Fett, carded (Darth Vader and Stormtrooper)...................5.00
PEZ0001 C-3PO, bagged..3.00
PEZ0006 C-3PO, carded (C-3PO, Chewbacca, and Yoda) 3.00
PEZ0016 C-3PO, carded (Darth Vader and Stormtrooper) 3.00
PEZ0002 Chewbacca, bagged...3.00
PEZ0007 Chewbacca, carded (C-3PO, Chewbacca, and Yoda) 3.00
PEZ0017 Chewbacca, carded (Darth Vader and Stormtrooper) 3.00
PEZ0003 Darth Vader, bagged...3.00
PEZ0029 Darth Vader, carded (Darth Vader and Stormtrooper, blue)......4.00
PEZ0008 Darth Vader, carded (Darth Vader and Stormtrooper, purple)..3.00
PEZ0023 Luke in X-Wing Gear, bagged 4.00
PEZ0019 Luke in X-Wing Gear, carded (Darth Vader and Stormtrooper)..5.00
PEZ0027 Pez Dispenser C-3PO, plated gold color, limited to 500 ....115.00
PEZ0028 Pez Dispenser Darth Vader, plated chrome color, limited to 500 ..115.00
PEZ0024 Princess Leia, bagged...4.00
PEZ0020 Princess Leia, carded (Darth Vader and Stormtrooper) 5.00
PEZ0004 Stormtrooper, bagged...3.00
PEZ0030 Stormtrooper, carded (Darth Vader and Stormtrooper, blue) 4.00
PEZ0009 Stormtrooper, carded (Darth Vader and Stormtrooper, purple).3.00
PEZ0026 Wickett, bagged 4.00
PEZ0022 Wickett, carded (Darth Vader and Stormtrooper).......................5.00
PEZ0005 Yoda, bagged 3.00
PEZ0010 Yoda, carded (C-3PO, Chewbacca, and Yoda) 3.00
PEZ0018 Yoda, carded (Darth Vader and Stormtrooper) 3.00

Pez Candy, Inc. (UK)
Packaged on blue backer card featuring Darth Vader.
PEZ0012 Chewbacca..4.00
PEZ0011 C-3PO..4.00
PEZ0013 Darth Vader..4.00
PEZ0014 Stormtrooper 4.00

PEZ0015 Yoda...4.00

PEZ REFILLS

Pez Candy, Inc.
8-pack with free Star Wars character sticker.

PZ10001   **PZ10002**   **PZ10003**   **PZ10004**

PZ10001 Darth Vader...7.00
PZ10002 Han Solo..7.00
PZ10003 Luke Skywalker 7.00
PZ10004 Princess Leia 7.00

PICTURE FRAMES

HOP0001   **HOP0002**   **HOP0003**

Sigma
HOP0001 C-3PO..35.00
HOP0002 Darth Vader...25.00
HOP0003 R2-D2...30.00

PILLOWCASES

CPC0002

PEZ0021 PEZ0006 PEZ0016 PEZ0007 PEZ0017 PEZ0029 PEZ0008 PEZ0019 PEZ0020 PEZ0030 PEZ0009 PEZ0022

PEZ0010 PEZ0018 PEZ0025 PEZ0001 PEZ0023 PEZ0024 PEZ0026 PEZ0005 PEZ0011 PEZ0012 PEZ0013 PEZ0014 PEZ0015

Bibb Co.

Reversible, one character on each side.
CPC0001 Boba Fett / Darth Vader.........................35.00
CPC0002 C-3PO / R2-D2 ....30.00
CPC0003 Chewbacca / Yoda 26.00

Westpoint Stevens

CPC0006

CPC0006 Space Battle pillow sham 14.00

2-packs. Pillowcases are gold, black and red overlaid on Rebel Alliance emblem.
CPC0007 C-3PO and R2-D2 ....18.00
CPC0008 Han and Chewbacca 18.00
CPC0004 Luke and Leia.....................................18.00
CPC0005 Yoda and Obi-Wan Kenobi.........................18.00

PILLOWS

Adam Joseph Industries

Die-cut.
PIL0002 Darth Vader.......................................26.00
PIL0003 R2-D2 ....26.00

Bibb Co.

PIL0001

PIL0001 C-3PO and R2-D2 / Darth Vader 15" square, quilted 24.00

Liebhardt, Inc.

16" square.

PIL0004   **PIL0007**   **PIL0008**

PIL0009   **PIL0010**   **PIL0011**

PIL0005   **PIL0006**

PIL0004 Anakin 8.00
PIL0007 Darth Maul.......................................8.00
PIL0010 Jar Jar 8.00

PIL0011 Queen Amidala 8.00
PIL0008 Qui-Gon 8.00
PIL0009 Space Battle 8.00
PIL0005 Chewbacca, square 5.00
PIL0006 Han Solo, square 7.00

PINBALL GAMES

NG0001

Data East

NG0001 Star Wars pinball, coin-operated.....................1,650.00

NG0004 cabinet, backglass, playboard

Sega

NG0004 SW:SE Trilogy, coin-operated.........................3,800.00

Williams

NG0003 Star Wars Episode I, coin-operated 5,400.00
NG0002 Star Wars Special Edition pinball, coin-operated 3,600.00

PINS

3D Arts

Square lasergram.
PI0086 C-3PO and R2-D2 ....6.00
PI0087 Darth Vader 6.00
PI0088 Millennium Falcon..................................6.00
PI0089 X-Wing Fighter.....................................6.00

Adam Joseph Industries

PI0011   **PI0055**   **PI0070**   **PI0040**

PI0036 "May The Force Be With You", brass 8.00
PI0011 C-3PO, brass......................................8.00
PI0023 Emperor's Royal Guard, brass........................8.00
PI0040 Princess Kneesaa, painted plastic 3.00
PI0044 R2-D2, brass......................................8.00
PI0054 Return of the Jedi logo, brass.........................8.00
PI0055 Salacious Crumb, brass..............................8.00
PI0059 Star Wars logo, brass...............................8.00
PI0065 The Force, brass 8.00
PI0069 Wicket the Ewok, brass 8.00
PI0070 Wicket the Ewok, painted plastic 3.00
PI0072 X-Wing Fighter, brass 8.00
PI0078 Yoda, brass.......................................8.00

Applause

PI0090 Anakin Skywalker 3.00

Pins

PI0091 Battle Droid...4.00
PI0092 C-3PO..3.00
PI0093 Darth Maul..3.00
PI0094 Episode I: TPM Logo....................................5.00
PI0095 Jar Jar Binks...3.00
PI0096 Naboo Starfighter..3.00
PI0097 Obi-Wan Kenobi..3.00
PI0098 Queen Amidala..3.00
PI0099 Qui-Gon Jinn..3.00
PI0100 R2-D2..4.00
PI0101 Trade Federation Droid Fighter.......................3.00
PI0126 Dark Side Collection: Darth Maul, Darth Sidious, Battle Droid, Droid Starship, EPI Logo framed....................35.00

Atari
Promotional pins.
PI0080 C-3PO black and silver.................................23.00
PI0081 Darth Vader black and silver..........................23.00
PI0082 R2-D2 black and silver.................................23.00

Castoline

PI0141 Darth Vader..6.00
PI0142 Logo, SW...6.00
PI0143 Logo, SW:SE...6.00
PI0144 Millennium Falcon..6.00
PI0145 Princess Leia and R2-D2................................6.00
PI0146 R2-D2..6.00
PI0147 Stormtrooper...6.00

Disney / MGM
PI0084 C-3PO / Disneyland 35-year anniversary............18.00
PI0105 Disney Weekends May 2000, Anakin dangler, limited to 3000......18.00
PI0119 Disney Weekends May 2000, Boba Fett dangler, limited to 3000 ..26.00
PI0103 Disney Weekends May 2000, Chewbacca dangler, autographed by designer, limited to 3000............18.00
PI0102 Disney Weekends May 2000, Chewbacca dangler, limited to 3000..18.00
PI0106 Disney Weekends May 2000, Darth Vader dangler, limited to 3000 ...18.00
PI0104 Disney Weekends May 2000, Mickey head with laser light, limited to 7500......11.00
PI0123 Disney Weekends May 2000, Princess Leia dangler, limited to 3000 .18.00
PI0107 Disney Weekends May 2000, R2-D2 dangler, limited to 3000........18.00
PI0134 Disney Weekends May 2001, Darth Vader's Tie Fighter, limited to 2001......24.00
PI0138 Disney Weekends May 2001, Han Solo, limited to 2001.................24.00
PI0139 Disney Weekends May 2001, Luke Skywalker, limited to 2001.........24.00
PI0133 Disney Weekends May 2001, Millennium Falcon, limited to 2001 .24.00
PI0131 Disney Weekends May 2001, Naboo Fighter, limited to 2001 ....24.00

PI0136 Disney Weekends May 2001, Obi-Wan Kenobi, limited to 2001....18.00
PI0135 Disney Weekends May 2001, R2-D2 projecting hologram Mickey, limited to 2001......30.00
PI0137 Disney Weekends May 2001, X-Wing Fighter, limited to 2001 ....24.00
PI0132 Disney Weekends May 2001, Yoda, ltd. to 2001.........18.00
PI0083 Star Tours logo..14.00
PI0129 Star Tours Tatooine Express.............................9.00
PI0128 Star Tours The Leader In Galactic Sightseeing........9.00

Fan Club

PI0130

PI0130 Star Wars Celebration, Denver, Colorado, brass...........18.00

Hollywood Pins

PI0003   PI0006   PI0076

PI0026 "Freeze You Rebel Scum!"...............................6.00
PI0035 "May The Force Be With You".............................5.00
PI0063 "Taking the Galaxy by Storm" (SW Summit excl.)..........65.00
PI0001 Admiral Ackbar..7.00
PI0002 AT-AT...8.00
PI0003 Ben Kenobi...8.00
PI0004 Black Sun logo...4.00
PI0005 Boba Fett..10.00
PI0007 Boba Fett Insignia (Round)...............................7.00
PI0006 Boba Fett, "He's No Good To Me Dead"...................6.00
PI0009 C-3PO...8.00
PI0012 C-3PO, "We're Doomed."..................................7.00
PI0013 Chewbacca..12.00
PI0015 Darth Vader...12.00
PI0017 Darth Vader helmet..4.00
PI0018 Darth Vader helmet, sculpted............................6.00
PI0020 Darth Vader, "Power of the Dark Side.".................7.00
PI0021 Emperor..10.00
PI0022 Emperor's Royal Guard....................................6.00
PI0025 Far Star...3.00
PI0027 Gamorrean Guard..6.00
PI0028 Imperial Emblem...6.00
PI0029 Jabba the Hutt...6.00
PI0030 Jabba the Hutt...6.00
PI0031 Lando Calrissian...8.00
PI0032 Lightsabers crossed of Star Wars logo..................8.00
PI0033 Luke on Tauntaun...12.00
PI0034 Max Rebo Band..12.00
PI0037 Millennium Falcon...8.00
PI0039 Millennium Falcon, round..................................9.00
PI0041 Princess Leia..8.00
PI0042 R2-D2...8.00

PI0045 Rebel Alliance logo, large..5.00
PI0046 Rebel Alliance logo, large gold...................................7.00
PI0047 Rebel Alliance logo, mini...6.00
PI0048 Rebel Alliance logo, small..6.00
PI0049 Rebel Alliance logo, small gold....................................5.00
PI0050 Rebel Alliance logo, small red......................................5.00
PI0051 Rebel Forces...5.00
PI0052 Return of the Jedi...15.00
PI0056 Slave I...9.00
PI0057 Star Wars 20th Anniversary...8.00
PI0060 Star Wars Trilogy Special Edition, antique finish............6.00
PI0061 Star Wars: A New Hope..15.00
PI0062 Stormtrooper...10.00
PI0064 The Empire Strikes Back...15.00
PI0066 Tie Fighter..9.00
PI0067 Tie Fighter, round...8.00
PI0068 Wicket the Ewok..8.00
PI0071 X-Wing Fighter..6.00
PI0074 X-Wing Fighter, round...8.00
PI0075 X-Wing Fighter, sculpted..6.00
PI0076 Yoda..8.00
PI0079 Yoda, "Try Not..."..7.00

Howard Eldon
PI0010 C-3PO, 10th anniversary, enameled............................7.00
PI0019 Darth Vader, 10th anniversary, enameled.....................7.00
PI0024 Empire Strikes Back logo, 10th anniversary, enameled...................8.00
PI0043 R2-D2, 10th anniversary, enameled.............................7.00
PI0053 Return of the Jedi logo, 10th anniversary, enameled......................8.00
PI0058 Star Wars logo, 10th anniversary, enameled................8.00

McDonald's

PI0127

PI0127 May The Fries Be With You 26.00

Wallace Berrie and Co.
PI0008 Boba Fett, dangle 11.00
PI0014 Chewbacca, dangle..11.00
PI0016 Darth Vader / ESB logo, dangle.................................11.00
PI0038 Millennium Falcon..11.00
PI0073 X-Wing Fighter 11.00
PI0077 Yoda / "May The Force Be With You", dangle 11.00
PI0112 Boba Fett pin badge...6.00
PI0116 Boba Fett with gun pin badge......................................6.00
PI0085 C-3PO and R2-D2 on square blue background with white logo....5.00
PI0115 C-3PO pin badge...6.00
PI0113 Darth Vader helmet pin badge.....................................7.00
PI0114 Darth Vader profile pin badge......................................7.00

PI0008   PI0016   PI0073

PI0112   PI0116   PI0115   PI0113   PI0114

PI0117   PI0108   PI0109   PI0110   PI0111

PI0117 Darth Vader reaching pin badge 7.00
PI0108 Princess Leia pin badge..6.00
PI0109 R2-D2 pin badge..6.00
PI0140 Star Wars Episode I logo..6.00
PI0110 Stormtrooper pin badge..6.00
PI0111 Yoda pin badge..6.00

PITCHERS

DIP0001

Deka
90 ounce pitcher with lid.
DIP0001 Star Wars 22.00
DIP0002 The Empire Strikes Back 90 oz. with top 22.00
DIP0003 Return of the Jedi...22.00

PLACE CARDS

PFM0001

Drawing Board
PFM0001 C-3PO and R2-D2, 8-pack...9.00

PLACEMATS

Burger King

PFN0009   PFN0010

PFN0009 ESB glasses, promotional...7.00
PFN0010 Everybody Wins game, ESB promotional 8.00

Dixie
PFN0007 AT-AT, Luke and Darth Vader, Space Battle, and Yoda............32.00

PFN0002

Drawing Board
PFN0002 Maze, 8-pack 26.00

Icarus
PFN0003 C-3PO and R2-D2; Chewbacca, Han, and Lando; Bounty Hunters ..25.00
PFN0004 Darth Vader and Stormtroopers; Luke on Tauntaun; Yoda 25.00
PFN0005 Darth Vader, Luke, Imperial Guards, and Speeder Bikes...........25.00
PFN0006 Jabba the Hutt, Princess Leia, Lando Calrissian, and Wicket....25.00

Pizza Hut

PFN0008   PFN0011

Placemats

PFN0008 Placemat promoting Kids Pack with Mini-Transforming Playsets.4.00
PFN0011 Placemat: Jedi Trivia / Jedi Wisdom..2.00

Sigma

PFN0001

PFN0001 ESB, 4-pack: Luke and Yoda, C-3PO and R2-D2, Darth Vader and
Leia, Chewbacca and Boba Fett..65.00

PLANNERS

PLN0003　　**PLN0005**　　**PLN0016**　　**PLN0017**　　**PLN0018**

Day Runner

2-year planner, 1/00-12/01.
PLN0023 Darth Maul..6.00
PLN0024 Obi-Wan Kenobi...6.00
PLN0025 Queen Amidala...6.00

Academic planning calendars with assignment pages, 7/99-7/00.
PLN0012 Anakin Skywalker, 5½"x8½"..4.00
PLN0019 Anakin Skywalker, 8½"x11""...7.00
PLN0013 Darth Maul, 5½"x8½"..4.00
PLN0020 Darth Maul, 8½"x11"..7.00
PLN0021 Obi-Wan Kenobi, 8½"x11"..7.00
PLN0014 Queen Amidala, 5½"x8½"...4.00
PLN0022 Queen Amidala, 8½"x11"...7.00

Dated assignment books.
PLN0008 Anakin Skywalker 8.00
PLN0009 Darth Maul 8.00
PLN0010 Jedi 8.00

Monthly planners, 5½"x8½".
PLN0015 Anakin Skywalker 5.00
PLN0016 Darth Maul 5.00
PLN0017 Obi-Wan Kenobi...5.00
PLN0018 Queen Amidala 5.00

Student planners.
PLN0002 Darth Maul 13.00
PLN0003 Jar Jar Binks 13.00
PLN0007 Obi-Wan Kenobi...13.00
PLN0006 Queen Amidala (travel gown)..13.00
PLN0004 Queen Amidala student planner 13.00
PLN0005 Qui-Gon Jinn student planner 13.00
PLN0011 Queen Amidala weekly planner w/assignments Aug 1999 to July
2000, spiral bound 6.00

Mead

PLN0001　　**PLN0026**　　**PLN0027**　　**PLN0028**　　**PLN0029**

Student day planner.
PLN0026 Darth Vader 8.00
PLN0027 Darth Vader inset art 8.00
PLN0001 Technology design with snap latch 8.00
PLN0028 Technology design with velcro latch...............................8.00
PLN0029 Yoda inset art 8.00

Q-Stat

PLN0030 Queen Amidala address book, datebook, notepad....6.00

PLN0030

PLATES

DIL0001　　　**DIL0003**

Deka

Compartment plates.
DIL0001 Star Wars...14.00
DIL0002 The Empire Strikes Back..14.00
DIL0003 Return of the Jedi 14.00

Zak Designs

DIL0004　　　**DIL0005**

DIL0005 Pod Race, features Anakin and Sebulba, round 3.00
DIL0004 Pod Race, features Anakin and Sebulba, shaped 4.00

PLATES: COLLECTOR

PL0001　　　**PL0002**　　　**PL0003**　　　**PL0004**

PL0005　　　**PL0006**　　　**PL0007**　　　**PL0008**

PL0009　　　**PL0010**　　　**PL0011**　　　**PL0012**

PL0013　　　**PL0014**　　　**PL0015**　　　**PL0016**

PL0017　　　**PL0018**　　　**PL0019**　　　**PL0020**

PL0021　　　**PL0022**　　　**PL0023**　　　**PL0024**

PL0025	PL0026	PL0027	PL0028
PL0029	PL0030	PL0031	PL0032
PL0033	PL0034	PL0035	PL0036

The Hamilton Collection

PL0001 CS1 Han Solo 65.00
PL0002 CS2 Darth Vader and Luke Skywalker...............................65.00
PL0003 CS3 Princess Leia..65.00
PL0004 CS4 Imperial Walkers 65.00
PL0005 CS5 Luke and Yoda 65.00
PL0006 CS6 Space Battle 65.00
PL0007 CS7 R2-D2 and Wicket 65.00
PL0008 CS8 Millennium Falcon Cockpit 65.00
PL0009 HV01 Luke Skywalker 55.00
PL0010 HV02 Han Solo 75.00
PL0011 HV03 Darth Vader...75.00
PL0012 HV04 Princess Leia 75.00
PL0013 HV05 Obi-Wan Kenobi 75.00
PL0014 HV06 Emperor Palpatine 75.00
PL0015 HV07 Yoda 150.00
PL0016 HV08 Boba Fett 115.00
PL0033 HV09 Chewbacca...225.00
PL0034 HV10 Jabba The Hutt 180.00
PL0035 HV11 Lando Calrissian 225.00
PL0036 HV12 R2-D2 ....180.00
PL0017 SV01 Millennium Falcon 55.00
PL0018 SV02 Tie Fighter 55.00
PL0019 SV03 Red Five 55.00
PL0020 SV04 Imperial Shuttle 55.00
PL0021 SV05 Star Destroyer..85.00
PL0022 SV06 Snowspeeders..55.00
PL0023 SV07 B-Wing Fighter 75.00
PL0024 SV08 Slave I...90.00
PL0025 SV09 Medical Frigate 95.00
PL0026 SV10 Jabba's Sail Barge 110.00
PL0027 SV11 Y-Wing Fighter 115.00
PL0028 SV12 Death Star 125.00
PL0029 TA1 10th Anniversary 160.00
PL0030 TR1 Star Wars 175.00
PL0031 TR2 Empire Strikes Back 150.00
PL0032 TR3 Return of the Jedi...150.00

PLATES: PAPER

| PFP0004 | PFP0006 | PFP0008 | PFP0010 |

Drawing Board

PFP0003 ESB: Cloud City, 7" pack 12.00
PFP0004 ESB: Cloud City, 9" pack 15.00
PFP0005 Ewoks, 7" pack 8.00
PFP0006 Ewoks, 9" pack 10.00
PFP0007 ROTJ: Darth Vader and Luke Duel, 7" pack 12.00
PFP0008 ROTJ: Darth Vader and Luke Duel, 9" pack 15.00

PFP0009 SW: C-3PO, R2-D2 and X-Wing Fighters, 9" pack 15.00
PFP0010 SW: Darth Vader, Death Star, and Tie Fighters, 7" pack..............12.00

Party Express

| PFP0002 | PFP0011 | PFP0012 |

PFP0001 Dogfight over Death Star, 7" pack 6.00
PFP0002 Dogfight over Death Star, 9" pack 8.00
PFP0012 Obi-Wan Kenobi, Jedi vs. Sith scene, 7" pack.....................5.00
PFP0011 Qui-Gon Jonn, Jedi vs. Sith scene, 9" pack 5.00

PLAY HOUSES

| PYH0001 | PHY0003 | PHY0002 |

ERO Industries

PYH0001 EPI:TPM 40"x30"x44"..25.00

Worlds Apart

PYH0002 Pop'n'Fun Pop-Out Play Tunnel with Episode I Space Battle
Scenes..37.00
PYH0003 Pop'n'Fun Pop-Up Naboo Fighter 54.00

PLAY-DOH SETS

| YD0001 | YD0006 |

Kenner

YD0001 Attack the Death Star 45.00
YD0002 Empire Strikes Back action set: Dagobah...........................50.00
YD0003 Empire Strikes Back action set: Ice Planet Hoth 45.00
YD0004 Return of the Jedi: Jabba the Hutt................................35.00
YD0005 Star Wars action set..45.00
YD0006 Wicket the Ewok 27.00

PLAYING CARDS

CP0002

Glow Zone

CP0002 Glow-in-the-Dark 18.00

International Playing Card Company

CP0001 2 Decks (Heroes / Villains) in Collector tin, English/French, limited to
200,000..17.00

| CP0001 | CP0003 | CP0004 |

Playing Cards

PLAYSETS: ACTION FIGURE, POTF2

P2P0007

Hasbro

Kenner

P2P0001   P2P0002   P2P0003

P2P0004   P2P0005   P2P0006

PLAYSETS: ACTION FIGURE, POTJ

P3P0001 front and back

Hasbro

PLAYSETS: ACTION FIGURE, TPM

Hasbro

P3PO001   P3PO002

PLAYSETS: ACTION FIGURE, VINTAGE

Kenner

AVP0037   AVP0003   AVP0005

AVP0024   AVP0022   AVP0014

AVP0011   AVP0001   AVP0036

AVP0033   AVP0007   AVP0031

AVP0029

AVP0009 front and back   AVP0027

Lili Ledy
AVP0038 Jabba the Hutt playset, ROTJ pkg. 155.00

Palitoy

AVP0034   AVP0035

AVP0034 Creature Cantina, SW pkg. 335.00
AVP0035 Death Star, SW pkg. 535.00

PLUSH TOYS

Applause
TYN0036 Jar Jar Binks, 12" 12.00
TYN0023 Jar Jar Binks, 18" 29.00
TYN0033 Jar Jar Binks, 48" tall, FAO Schwarz exclusive 95.00
TYN0037 Watto, 12" 12.00
TYN0024 Watto, 18" 29.00
TYN0022 Wicket the Ewok 13" tall, limited to 6,000 ....75.00

Disney / MGM
Star Tours souvenirs.
TYN0015 Ewok, dark brown with pink cowl.....................................12.00
TYN0014 Ewok, light brown with green cowl 15.00

Douglass Toys
TYN0026 Ewok, life-sized plush with yellow cowl 375.00

Frito-Lay

TYN0038

TYN0038 Ewok, 28" SW:SE promotion 43.00

Hasbro

TYN0025   TYN0034   TYN0035

TYN0025 Jar Jar Binks Hungry Hero 24.00
TYN0034 Jar Jar Binks, FAO Schwarz exclusive 22.00
TYN0035 Watto, FAO Schwarz exclusive 22.00

Idea Factory
Farce Wars parody characters.

TYN0027   TYN0028   TYN0029   TYN0030

TYN0031   TYN0032

TYN0027 Anteater Dirtwalker 7.00
TYN0028 Dark Gator 7.00
TYN0029 Dark Mole 7.00
TYN0030 Goata 7.00
TYN0031 Queen Armadillo 7.00
TYN0032 Slabba the Mutt...7.00

Kenner
TYN0008 Gwig, wokling 12.00
TYN0004 Latara 29.00
TYN0009 Leeni, wokling 12.00
TYN0010 Malani, wokling 12.00
TYN0011 Mookiee, wokling 12.00
TYN0012 Nippet, wokling; white or brown 12.00
TYN0005 Paploo 29.00
TYN0006 Princess Kneesaa 25.00
TYN0003 R2-D2 ....65.00
TYN0007 Wicket 25.00
TYN0013 Wiley, wokling 12.00

Kenneth Feld
TYN0016 Yoda, plastic head, tan robe, brown belt, 12" tall 135.00

Regal

TYN0001   TYN0002

TYN0001 Chewbacca 78.00
TYN0002 Jawa 195.00

Takara

TYN0017   TYN0018   TYN0019   TYN0020   TYN0021

7" tall (except R2-D2), comic style, gold hang string.
TYN0017 C-3PO 65.00
TYN0018 Chewbacca 65.00
TYN0019 Darth Vader 65.00
TYN0020 Luke Skywalker 65.00
TYN0021 R2-D2, 5" tall 65.00

POG SLAMMERS

Canada Games
Available in red, yellow, blue, green, purple, bronze, silver, and gold.

TZB0001   TZB0002   TZB0003   TZB0004

TZB0005   TZB0006   TZB0007   TZB0008

TZB0001 1 Star Wars..3.00
TZB0002 2 Empire Strikes Back..3.00
TZB0003 3 Return of the Jedi...3.00
TZB0004 4 Luke..3.00

Pog Slammers

TZB0005 5 Leia 3.00
TZB0006 6 Han...3.00
TZB0007 7 Darth Vader 3.00
TZB0008 8 Jabba the Hutt 3.00

Topps

Available in black, silver, and gold.

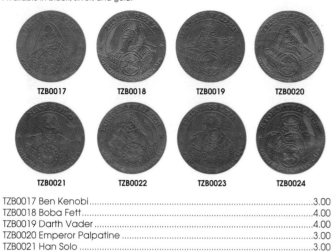

| TZB0017 | TZB0018 | TZB0019 | TZB0020 |
| TZB0021 | TZB0022 | TZB0023 | TZB0024 |

TZB0017 Ben Kenobi...3.00
TZB0018 Boba Fett...4.00
TZB0019 Darth Vader 4.00
TZB0020 Emperor Palpatine 3.00
TZB0021 Han Solo 3.00
TZB0022 Luke Skywalker...3.00
TZB0023 Princess Leia...4.00

TZB0024 Stormtrooper..3.00

POGS

Canada Games

TZA0001 09 Luke on Tauntaun..1.00
TZA0002 10 Han / Falcon Montage 1.00
TZA0003 11 Jawa and Tusken Raider 1.00
TZA0004 12 Obi Wan Kenobi 1.00
TZA0005 13 Darth Vader 1.00
TZA0006 14 Darth Vader 1.00
TZA0007 15 Luke and X-Wing...1.00
TZA0008 16 Storm Trooper 1.00
TZA0009 17 C-3PO and R2 ....1.00
TZA0010 18 Princess Leia 1.00
TZA0011 19 Millennium Falcon..1.00
TZA0012 20 Han Solo...1.00
TZA0013 21 Tusken Raider 1.00
TZA0014 22 Darth Vader 1.00
TZA0015 23 Luke in Landspeeder 1.00
TZA0016 24 C-3PO and R2 ....1.00
TZA0017 25 Lightsaber 1.00
TZA0018 26 Ben and Luke 1.00
TZA0019 27 Princess Leia 1.00
TZA0020 28 Chewbacca 1.00
TZA0021 29 Star Wars Logo 1.00
TZA0022 30 Empire Strikes Back 1.00
TZA0023 31 Han and Probe Droid 1.00
TZA0024 32 Luke - Leia - Yoda 1.00
TZA0025 33 Star Wars 1.00

TZA0001	TZA0002	TZA0003	TZA0004	TZA0005	TZA0006	TZA0007	TZA0008	TZA0009
TZA0010	TZA0011	TZA0012	TZA0013	TZA0014	TZA0015	TZA0016	TZA0017	TZA0018
TZA0019	TZA0020	TZA0021	TZA0022	TZA0023	TZA0024	TZA0025	TZA0026	TZA0027
TZA0028	TZA0029	TZA0030	TZA0031	TZA0032	TZA0033	TZA0034	TZA0035	TZA0036
TZA0037	TZA0038	TZA0039	TZA0040	TZA0041	TZA0042	TZA0043	TZA0044	TZA0045
TZA0046	TZA0047	TZA0048	TZA0049	TZA0050	TZA0051	TZA0052	TZA0053	TZA0054

TZA0055 TZA0056 TZA0057 TZA0058 TZA0059 TZA0060 TZA0061 TZA0062 TZA0063

TZA0064 TZA0065 TZA0066 TZA0067 TZA0068 TZA0069 TZA0070 TZA0228 TZA0226

TZA0145 TZA0146 TZA0148 TZA0149 TZA0150 TZA0151 TZA0152 TZA0153 TZA0154

TZA0155 TZA0156 TZA0157 TZA0158 TZA0159 TZA0160 TZA0161 TZA0162 TZA0163

TZA0164 TZA0165 TZA0166 TZA0167 TZA0168 TZA0169 TZA0170 TZA0171 TZA0172

TZA0173 TZA0174 TZA0175 TZA0176 TZA0177 TZA0178 TZA0179 TZA0180 TZA0181

TZA0182 TZA0183 TZA0184 TZA0185 TZA0186 TZA0187 TZA0188 TZA0189 TZA0190

TZA0191 TZA0192 TZA0193 TZA0194 TZA0195 TZA0196 TZA0197 TZA0198 TZA0199

TZA0200 TZA0201 TZA0202 TZA0203 TZA0205 TZA0206 TZA0207 TZA0208 TZA0209

TZA0210 TZA0211 TZA0212 TZA0213 TZA0214 TZA0215 TZA0216 TZA0217 TZA0218

Pogs

TZA0219	TZA0220	TZA0221	TZA0222	TZA0223	TZA0224	TZA0225

TZA0026 34 Luke and Yoda 1.00
TZA0027 35 Darth with Empire Logo 1.00
TZA0028 36 Luke, Yoda, R2 ....1.00
TZA0029 37 Boba Fett 1.00
TZA0030 38 21-B Medical Droid 1.00
TZA0031 39 Luke in Dagobah fatigues 1.00
TZA0032 40 Darth Vader and Snow Trooper 1.00
TZA0033 41 Yoda 1.00
TZA0034 42 Millennium Falcon 1.00
TZA0035 43 R2 ....1.00
TZA0036 44 Empire Strikes Back 1.00
TZA0037 45 X-Wing approaching planet 1.00
TZA0038 46 Darth, Boba Fett, and Lando 1.00
TZA0039 47 Star Destroyer and Falcon 1.00
TZA0040 48 Leia 1.00
TZA0041 49 X-Wings 1.00
TZA0042 50 Falcon, Tie, asteroid..............................1.00
TZA0043 51 ROTJ Logo 1.00
TZA0044 52 Slave Leia Montage 1.00
TZA0045 53 Luke / B-Wing Montage 1.00
TZA0046 54 Emperor 1.00
TZA0047 55 Luke / Gamorrean Guard.........................1.00
TZA0048 56 Jabba 1.00
TZA0049 57 Rancor 1.00
TZA0050 58 Max Rebo 1.00
TZA0051 59 Sy Snootles, Jabba's palace 1.00
TZA0052 60 Boba Fett 1.00
TZA0053 61 Ewok 1.00
TZA0054 62 Luke and Leia 1.00
TZA0055 63 Trooper on speeder bike 1.00
TZA0056 64 Royal Guard 1.00
TZA0057 65 Chewbacca 1.00
TZA0058 66 Admiral Ackbar 1.00
TZA0059 67 Luke 1.00
TZA0060 68 Salacious Crumb...................................1.00
TZA0061 69 Emperor 1.00
TZA0062 70 AT-ST 1.00
TZA0063 71 Luke with Stormtroopers 1.00
TZA0064 72 Salacious Crumb...................................1.00
TZA0065 73 X-Wing 1.00
TZA0066 74 Yoda 1.00
TZA0067 75 Leia and Han 1.00
TZA0068 76 C-3PO 1.00
TZA0069 77 Darth Vader 1.00
TZA0070 78 Star Wars 1.00
TZA0071 Checklist Boba Fett 1.00
TZA0072 Checklist Darth Vader.................................1.00
TZA0073 Checklist Han 1.00
TZA0074 Checklist Luke 1.00

Schmidt

TZA0075 01 Darth Vader 1.80
TZA0076 02 Darth and Luke Duel 1.80
TZA0077 03 The Falcon's Cockpit...............................1.80
TZA0078 04 Lando Calrissian 1.80
TZA0079 05 Star Destroyer 1.80
TZA0080 06 Han and Chewbacca 1.80
TZA0081 07 Bib Fortuna 1.80
TZA0082 08 Jabba 1.80
TZA0083 09 Stormtrooper 1.80
TZA0084 10 Stormtroopers Cloud City 1.80
TZA0085 11 Chewbacca 1.80
TZA0086 12 Han 1.80
TZA0087 13 Yoda..1.80
TZA0088 14 Luke 1.80
TZA0089 15 Chewbacca 1.80
TZA0090 16 Falcon 1.80
TZA0091 17 Salacious Crumb....................................1.80
TZA0092 18 R2-D2 ....1.80
TZA0093 19 Jabba Band Member 1.80
TZA0094 20 AT-ATs 1.80
TZA0095 21 Luke and Yoda 1.80
TZA0096 22 Luke eats Root Stew 1.80
TZA0097 23 Darth Vader - Snowtrooper (glittered)...................1.80

TZA0098 24 Vader-Lando-Boba (glittered) 1.80
TZA0099 25 Vader (saber is glittered) 1.80
TZA0100 26 Luke and Leia 1.80
TZA0101 27 2-1B (glittered)....................................1.80
TZA0102 28 AT-AT (glittered) 1.80
TZA0103 29 Max Rebo 1.80
TZA0104 30 Slave Leia and Jabba 1.80
TZA0105 31 Rancor 1.80
TZA0106 32 Han in Carbonite 1.80
TZA0107 33 Luke (silvery background) 1.80
TZA0108 34 Gamorrean Guard (w/glitter) 1.80
TZA0109 35 Luke (glittered saber) 1.80
TZA0110 36 Sail Barge 1.80
TZA0111 37 Boba Fett (glittered) 1.80
TZA0112 38 Leia (glitter background)..........................1.80
TZA0113 39 Surveying the Troops 1.80
TZA0114 40 Royal Guard 1.80
TZA0115 41 Stormtroopers 1.80
TZA0116 42 Luke on Tauntaun 1.80
TZA0117 43 Probot (glitter on ground) 1.80
TZA0118 44 Luke (glittered)....................................1.80
TZA0119 45 Luke (glittered saber) 1.80
TZA0120 46 Leia 1.80
TZA0121 47 Darth (glitter arm) 1.80
TZA0122 48 Darth (glitter chest) 1.80
TZA0123 49 Trench Battle Artwork 1.80
TZA0124 50 C-3PO and R2 ....1.80
TZA0125 51 Han 1.80
TZA0126 52 Obi-Wan 1.80
TZA0127 53 R2 (glittered dome) 1.80
TZA0128 54 AT-ATs (glitter) 1.80
TZA0129 55 R2 (glittered parts) 1.80
TZA0130 56 Han 1.80
TZA0131 57 Mon Calamari (glittered hat)......................1.80
TZA0132 58 Tusken (glittered gaffi stick) 1.80
TZA0133 59 Bantha 1.80
TZA0134 60 Wicket 1.80
TZA0135 61 Ackbar and aide 1.80
TZA0136 62 Scout Trooper 1.80
TZA0137 63 Stormtroopers (glitter wall)........................1.80
TZA0138 64 Darth (glitter chest) 1.80
TZA0139 65 Obi-Wan (glittered saber) 1.80
TZA0140 66 Luke 1.80
TZA0141 67 Darth (glitter in places) 1.80
TZA0142 68 Luke and Trooper (glittered) 1.80
TZA0143 69 Jawa 1.80
TZA0144 70 AT-ST 1.80

Topps

TZA0228 00-A C-3PO and R2-D2.................................6.00
TZA0226 00-B Darth Vader (promo)..............................6.00
TZA0145 01 Luke Skywalker 0.45
TZA0146 02 Darth Vader 0.45
TZA0147 03 Yoda..0.45
TZA0148 04 Emperor Palpatine 0.45
TZA0149 05 Obi-Wan Kenobi 0.45
TZA0150 06 Grand Moff Tarkin 0.45
TZA0151 07 Princess Leia Organa 0.45
TZA0152 08 Moff Jerjerrod 0.45
TZA0153 09 Mon Mothma 0.45
TZA0154 10 General Tagge 0.45
TZA0155 11 Han Solo 0.45
TZA0156 12 Boba Fett 0.45
TZA0157 13 Chewbacca 0.45
TZA0158 14 General Veers 0.45
TZA0159 15 General Dodonna 0.45
TZA0160 16 Admiral Motti.......................................0.45
TZA0161 17 Admiral Ackbar 0.45
TZA0162 18 Imperial Guard 0.45
TZA0163 19 Lando Calrissian 0.45
TZA0164 20 Garindan (long snoot) 0.45
TZA0165 21 Nien Nunb 0.45
TZA0166 22 Imperial Advisor 0.45
TZA0167 23 Wedge Antilles......................................0.45

TZA0168 24 Tie Fighter Pilot..0.45
TZA0169 25 Biggs Darklighter 0.45
TZA0170 26 Scout Trooper 0.45
TZA0171 27 C-3PO 0.45
TZA0172 28 Stormtrooper 0.45
TZA0173 29 R2-D2 ....0.45
TZA0174 30 Snowtrooper 0.45
TZA0175 31 Ugnaught 0.45
TZA0176 32 Han Solo 0.45
TZA0177 33 Boba Fett 0.45
TZA0178 34 Taggor Bren 0.45
TZA0179 35 Leia on Speeder Bike 0.45
TZA0180 36 Lando 0.45
TZA0181 37 C-3PO Blasted 0.45
TZA0182 38 Han Solo Tortured 0.45
TZA0183 39 Obi-Wan 0.45
TZA0184 40 Too-Onebee 0.45
TZA0185 41 Tusken Raider 0.45
TZA0186 42 Grand Moff Tarkin 0.45
TZA0187 43 Luke in Battle 0.45
TZA0188 44 Boba Fett and Dengar 0.45
TZA0189 45 Jabba 0.45
TZA0190 46 Salacious Crumb..0.45
TZA0191 47 Vader and Luke 0.45
TZA0192 48 Rancor 0.45
TZA0193 49 Max Rebo Band 0.45
TZA0194 50 Swamp Creature 0.45
TZA0195 51 Oola 0.45
TZA0196 52 Vader Before Emperor 0.45
TZA0197 53 Wookie 0.45
TZA0198 54 Empire Poster...0.45
TZA0199 55 Rancor 0.45
TZA0200 56 Gamorrean Guard 0.45
TZA0201 57 Luke and Vader 0.45
TZA0202 58 Angry Chewbacca 0.45
TZA0203 59 Luke and Vader 0.45
TZA0204 60 Yoda 0.45
TZA0205 61 Luke and Leia Swinging 0.45
TZA0206 62 Luke 0.45
TZA0207 63 Ewok 0.45
TZA0208 64 Luke on Dagobah 0.45
TZA0209 65 Vader Unmasked 0.45
TZA0210 66 Jawas 0.45
TZA0211 67 Snowtrooper 0.45
TZA0212 68 Luke on Adventure 0.45
TZA0213 69 Salacious Crumb...0.45
TZA0214 70 George Lucas 0.45
TZA0215 Galaxy foil 01 Luke ready for flight 05
TZA0216 Galaxy foil 02 Luke Skywalker...........................05
TZA0217 Galaxy foil 03 C-3PO 05
TZA0218 Galaxy foil 04 Han Solo in Carbonite 05
TZA0219 Galaxy foil 05 Greedo 05
TZA0220 Galaxy foil 06 Luke on Speeder Bike 05
TZA0221 Galaxy foil 07 Luke and Darth Vader Duel...........05
TZA0222 Galaxy foil 08 Princess Leia in Disguise 05
TZA0223 Galaxy foil 09 Darth Vader 05
TZA0224 Galaxy foil 10 Boba Fett 05
TZA0225 Packaging (Milk Caps)....................................3.00

TZA0227

TZA0227 Sheet of 6 using SW Galaxy art 3.00

POGS: TPM

Nagatanien
TZL0001 01 Obi-Wan Kenobi 1.20
TZL0002 02 Qui-Gon Jinn 1.20
TZL0003 03 Queen Amidala 1.20
TZL0004 04 Darth Maul...1.20
TZL0005 05 R2-D2...1.20
TZL0006 06 C-3PO...1.20
TZL0007 07 Padme 1.20
TZL0008 08 Rune Haako...1.20

TZL0001 **TZL0002** **TZL0003** **TZL0004** **TZL0005**

TZL0006 **TZL0007** **TZL0008** **TZL0009** **TZL0010**

TZL0011 **TZL0012** **TZL0013** **TZL0014** **TZL0015**

TZL0016 **TZL0017** **TZL0018** **TZL0019** **TZL0020**

TZL0009 09 Battle Droid...1.20
TZL0010 10 Mace Windu...1.20
TZL0011 11 Nute Gunray..1.20
TZL0012 12 Jar Jar Binks...1.20
TZL0013 13 Senator Palpatine......................................1.20
TZL0014 14 Sebulba 1.20
TZL0015 15 Shmi Skywalker...1.20
TZL0016 16 Jabba the Hutt..1.20
TZL0017 17 Yoda...1.20
TZL0018 18 Darth Sidious...1.20
TZL0019 19 Anakin Skywalker.......................................1.20
TZL0020 20 Boss Nass..1.20

PONCHOS

CPT0001 **CPT0002** **CPT0002 alt. packaging**

Ben Cooper
CPT0001 C-3PO 18.00
CPT0002 Darth Vader...18.00

Pyramid
CPT0003 Darth Maul rain poncho....................................6.00
CPT0004 Jedi vs. Sith rain poncho 6.00

POOL TOYS

Intex Recreation Corp.
IPT0001 Anakin's Pod Racer Lounge 82"x37½" 20.00
IPT0002 Darth Maul Sno-Tube 39" 9.00
IPT0003 Gungan Sub Ride-In 53½"x35½" 9.00

IPT0004 **IPT0005** **IPT0006**

Pool Toys

IPT0007   IPT0008

IPT0004 Jar Jar 2 Person Ride-In 58½"x27" 14.00
IPT0005 Landspeeder Boat Lounge 70"x55" 20.00
IPT0006 Millennium Falcon Island/River Raft 66"x52" 20.00
IPT0010 Naboo Starfighter Ride-In 40"x28½" 12.00
IPT0007 Naboo Starfighter Ride-On 71"x41" 14.00
IPT0009 Trade Federation Droid Starfighter Ride-In 37"x29"...12.00
IPT0008 Trade Federation Droid Starfighter Ride-On 56"x37"...14.00

POOLS

SWP0002   SWP0003

Intex Recreation Corp.
SWP0001 Jar Jar's World Aquarium Pool 18"x60" 25.00
SWP0002 Pod Racing Snapset Pool 15"x84" 25.00
SWP0003 Trade Federation Droid Control Ship Spray Pool 13"x73" 25.00

POPCORN BUCKET

POP0001

POP0001 Plastic popcorn pail, theater promotion during SWSE 7.00

POSTCARDS

PSC0097   PSC0098   PSC0096   PSC0095   PSC0090

20th Century Fox
PSC0097 A New Hope...4.00
PSC0098 Empire Strikes back.....................................4.00
PSC0096 Return of the Jedi 4.00
PSC0095 SW:SE logo 4.00
PSC0090 The Phantom Menace promotional........................4.00

3D Arts
PSC0023 C-3PO and R2-D2, lasergram 3.00
PSC0024 Darth Vader, lasergram 3.00
PSC0025 Millennium Falcon, lasergram 3.00
PSC0026 X-Wing Fighter, lasergram 3.00

A.H. Prismatic
PSC0001 Darth Vader holographic foil image......................6.00
PSC0003 Millennium Falcon and Tie Fighters holographic foil image ...6.00
PSC0002 Millennium Falcon in Astroid Field holographic foil image ...6.00

Classico
PSC0027 ASP Droid, SW:SE 2.00
PSC0028 A-Wing fighter 2.00
PSC0084 Battle in the Asteroids (Magic Eye).......................4.00
PSC0029 Ben and Luke 2.00
PSC0030 Ben Kenobi 2.00
PSC0115 Ben with lightsaber 2.00

PSC0104 Ben, Luke, and C-3PO view Mos Eisley..................2.00
PSC0031 Boba Fett portrait...2.00
PSC0085 B-Wing Attack (Magic Eye) 4.00
PSC0105 C-3PO aboard Millennium Falcon 2.00
PSC0032 C-3PO above oil bath.......................................2.00
PSC0075 C-3PO and R2-D2 face EV-99..............................2.00
PSC0033 C-3PO, Chewie, and Leia in forest 2.00
PSC0034 Chewbacca...2.00
PSC0035 Chewbacca and C-3PO in parts 2.00
PSC0102 Darth Vader and Princess Leia............................2.00
PSC0036 Darth Vader and troops in Cloud City 2.00
PSC0127 Darth Vader on Cloud City 2.00
PSC0037 Darth Vader on the Blockade Runner 2.00
PSC0114 Darth Vader pointing 2.00
PSC0038 Darth Vader silhouette in carbon chamber...............2.00
PSC0039 Dewback, SW:SE 2.00
PSC0040 Droids on the Blockade Runner 2.00
PSC0041 Emperor extreme close-up 2.00
PSC0042 Emperor on ramp, pointing 2.00
PSC0043 ESB Japanese movie poster artwork (Lando and Falcon prominent) ...2.00
PSC0044 ESB:SE poster..2.00
PSC0045 Falcon blasting out of Mos Eisley, SW:SE 2.00
PSC0046 Han and Jabba, SW:SE 2.00
PSC0047 Han and Leia kiss (ESB)....................................2.00
PSC0113 Han and Leia kiss (ROTJ) 2.00
PSC0117 Han in Rebel base 2.00
PSC0048 Han portrait 2.00
PSC0106 Han Solo on Endor 2.00
PSC0086 Heroes collage (Magic Eye)................................4.00
PSC0083 Hoth Asteroid Field (Magic Eye) 4.00
PSC0049 Jabba the Hutt 2.00
PSC0121 Jabba the Hutt close-up from SW:SE 2.00
PSC0050 Jabba the Hutt from SW:SE 2.00
PSC0051 Jawas blasting 2.00
PSC0052 Lando extreme close-up 2.00
PSC0053 Leia as Jabba prisoner 2.00
PSC0100 Luke and Han in the trash compactor 2.00
PSC0054 Luke and Leia on barge 2.00
PSC0118 Luke and Vader duel 2.00
PSC0101 Luke boards X-Wing on Yavin 4............................2.00
PSC0055 Luke carrying Yoda 2.00
PSC0112 Luke in Falcon's gunwell 2.00
PSC0108 Luke in front of moisture vaparator 2.00
PSC0110 Luke in stormtrooper disguise 2.00
PSC0056 Luke in the tree on Dagobah 2.00
PSC0081 Luke on Dagobah (Magic Eye) 4.00
PSC0116 Luke on Tauntaun 2.00
PSC0057 Luke shooting 2.00
PSC0058 Luke slicing Fett's gun.....................................2.00
PSC0103 Luke standing (promo).....................................2.00
PSC0125 Luke under Cloud City 2.00
PSC0059 Luke, Leia, and Han in Death Star 2.00
PSC0060 Princess Leia in ceremonial gown 2.00
PSC0061 R2-D2 in canyon...2.00
PSC0124 Ronto in Mos Eisley 2.00
PSC0062 ROTJ `B' movie poster 2.00
PSC0063 ROTJ:SE poster 2.00
PSC0064 Sandcrawler, SW:SE 2.00
PSC0065 Sandtrooper, SW:SE 2.00
PSC0119 Sandtroopers and dewback 2.00
PSC0087 Starships, Stormtroopers, Droids (Magic Eye) 4.00
PSC0066 Stormtroopers 2.00
PSC0082 Stormtroopers (Magic Eye).................................4.00
PSC0067 Stormtroopers blasting 2.00
PSC0068 SW `A' movie poster 2.00
PSC0069 SW:SE poster 2.00
PSC0120 Swoop scares Ronto in Mos Eisley.........................2.00
PSC0111 Tie Fighters in Death Star trench..........................2.00
PSC0070 Tusken Raider 2.00
PSC0107 Vader in Hoth rebel base 2.00
PSC0071 Wicket 2.00
PSC0122 X-Wing fleet...2.00

PSC0092   PSC0093   PSC0094   PSC0091   PSC0074

PSC0027 PSC0028 PSC0084 PSC0029 PSC0030 PSC0115 PSC0104 PSC0031 PSC0085 PSC0105 PSC0032 PSC0075 PSC0033

PSC0034 PSC0035 PSC0102 PSC0036 PSC0127 PSC0114 PSC0038 PSC0040 PSC0041 PSC0042 PSC0045 PSC0046 PSC0047

PSC0113 PSC0117 PSC0048 PSC0106 PSC0086 PSC0083 PSC0049 PSC0121 PSC0050 PSC0051 PSC0052 PSC0053 PSC0100

PSC0054 PSC0118 PSC0101 PSC0055 PSC0112 PSC0108 PSC0110 PSC0056 PSC0081 PSC0116 PSC0057 PSC0058 PSC0103

PSC0125 PSC0059 PSC0060 PSC0061 PSC0124 PSC0064 PSC0065 PSC0119 PSC0087 PSC0066 PSC0082 PSC0067 PSC0120

PSC0111 PSC0070 PSC0107 PSC0071 PSC0122 PSC0123 PSC0072 PSC0126 PSC0076 PSC0109 PSC0073 PSC0077

PSC0123 X-Wing fleet, SW:SE 2.00
PSC0072 X-Wing launch, SW:SE 2.00
PSC0126 X-Wings approach Death Star 2.00
PSC0076 X-Wings in Death Star trench....................................2.00
PSC0109 Yoda...2.00
PSC0073 Yoda in his house 2.00

Disney / MGM
PSC0092 Bespin 4.00
PSC0011 C-3PO and R2-D2 Star Tours, 8"x10" 3.00
PSC0093 Endor 4.00
PSC0012 Han Solo Star Tours, 8"x10".....................................3.00
PSC0013 Luke Skywalker Star Tours, 8"x10" 3.00
PSC0017 Star Tours, 4"x6" 2.00
PSC0014 Stormtroopers Star Tours, 8"x10" 3.00
PSC0094 Tatooine 4.00
PSC0091 The Ultimate Adventure, Star Tours 4.00

Icons Authentic Replicas
PSC0074 Advertisement for Ben's lightsaber and Han's blaster 4.00

Lego
PSC0080 Just Imagine. Speeder Bikes 2.00

PSC0080 PSC0079 PSC0078

PSC0079 Just Imagine. X-Wing Fighter 2.00
PSC0078 Use The Force, shows Darth Vader 3.00

Lucasarts

PSC0089 front and back   PSC0099

PSC0089 Dark Forces promotional 4.00
PSC0099 X-Wing vs. Tie Fighter 4.00

Oral-B
PSC0006 C-3PO and R2-D2 dental check-up reminders 4.00
PSC0007 Ewoks dental check-up reminders 4.00
PSC0008 Luke and Darth Vader dental check-up reminders 4.00
PSC0009 Star Wars heroes dental check-up reminders 4.00

Pop-Shots

PSC0020   PSC0019

Postcards

PSC0018   **PSC0021**   **PSC0022 front and back**

PSC0020 Birthday Greetings from Mos Eisley 8.00
PSC0019 C-3PO and R2-D2, We've Been Through A Lot Together............7.00
PSC0018 C-3PO and R2-D2, You Artoo Older Then Me, Happy Birthday ..7.00
PSC0021 The Duel, You Have Learned Much, Young One, Happy Birthday ..7.00
PSC0022 Yoda, When 900 Years Old You Reach., Happy Birthday 8.00

POSTER ART KITS

Craft Master

CRA0003

CRA0001 Dagobah and Yoda / Battle on Hoth 22.00
CRA0002 Darth Vader 3D 35.00
CRA0003 Darth Vader Lives / May The Force Be With You 25.00
CRA0004 Galactic Dogfight / Forces of Good and Evil 25.00
CRA0005 Heroes and Villains / Cantina and Aliens...............28.00

Kenner
CRA0006 Playnts, 5-poster set 35.00

Merlin Publishing Internat'l Ltd.

CRA0008

CRA0008 Star Wars, 4 posters with crayons 11"x17" 12.00

Rose Art Industries

CRA0007

CRA0007 A New Hope, 4 Exciting Scenes to Color 8.00

POSTERS
20th Century Fox

X0023

X0023 Star Wars, originally sold in lobby 1977........................415.00

At-A Glance
X0008 Anakin...6.00
X0009 Darth Maul 6.00
X0010 Jar Jar 6.00
X0011 Jedi Battle 6.00
X0012 Pod Race 6.00

X0013 Queen Amidala...6.00
X0014 Space Battle 6.00

Burger King
Empire Strikes Back, 18"x24".

X0029   **X0030**   **X0031**

X0029 Bespin...14.00
X0030 Dagobah...14.00
X0031 Hoth...14.00

Coca-Cola
1977 Star Wars; distributed through fast food franchises.

X0004   **X0005**   **X0006**   **X0007**

X0006 Chewbacca 16.00
X0004 Darth Vader 16.00
X0007 Luke Skywalker..16.00
X0005 R2-D2 and C-3PO 16.00

Esso
Co-produced with Pepsi and Walkers.

X0024   **X0025**   **X0026**   **X0027**

X0026 Anakin Skywalker..5.00
X0027 Darth Maul 5.00
X0025 Jar Jar Binks...5.00
X0024 Obi-Wan Kenobi 5.00

Pepsi Cola
Distributed through Pizza Hut.
X0002 1997 Empire Strikes Back SE 8.00
X0003 1997 Return of the Jedi SE 8.00
X0001 1997 Star Wars SE 8.00

SciPubTech
Cut-away posters, 36"x24".
X0015 AT-AT and snowspeeder, deluxe..............................40.00
X0016 AT-AT and snowspeeder, regular 20.00
X0017 Millennium Falcon, deluxe.....................................40.00
X0018 Millennium Falcon, regular....................................20.00
X0019 X-Wing Fighter, deluxe 40.00
X0020 X-Wing Fighter, regular 20.00

Skywalkers

X0033   **X0034**

X0033 The Empire Strikes Back.......................................32.00
X0034 Your pictorial guide to the major characters 25.00

Smithsonian Institute

X0032

X0032 SW: The Magic of Myth, Oct. 1997 - Oct. 1998 ....24.00

Star Wars Insider
X0021 136 Vintage Action Figures with common variations.....................22.00

Williams

X0028   X0022

X0028 Don't Panic - You've Got Flippers......................................24.00
X0022 "All I needed to know about life I learned from Star Wars" 12.00

POSTERS: PLANETARY MAPS

Kenner
PPM0001 Death Star planetary map..11.00
PPM0002 Endor planetary map 8.00
PPM0003 Tatooine planetary map 8.00

PRESS KITS

20th Century Fox

PK0003   PK0004

PK0003 ESB:SE CD-ROM multi-media presskit 55.00
PK0001 ROTJ: Special Edition, includes booklet and 14 slides...................35.00
PK0004 Star Wars Pressbook 85.00
PK0002 SW:SE CD-ROM multi-media presskit 53.00

PROGRAMS

George Fenmore Associates

PRG0001   PRG0003   PRG0006

PRG0001 Star Wars, first edition smooth cover................................45.00
PRG0002 Star Wars, second edition textured cover..............................24.00
PRG0003 The Empire Strikes Back 45.00
PRG0006 Return of the Jedi, Official Collectors Edition 22.00

PRG0004   PRG0005   PRG0007

San Diego Museum of Art
PRG0005 Star Wars The Magic of Myth: 9/25/99 - 2/2/00 ....4.00

Washington Museums
PRG0007 Star Wars The Magic of Myth 10.00

Yerba Buena Gardens
PRG0004 The Art of Star Wars: 12/27/94 - 3/12/95 ....4.00

PROJECTORS / VIEWERS

TYV0015

Chad Valley
TYV0015 Slide Projector Set..120.00

Harbert

TYV0012 cover and contents

TYV0012 Star Wars movie strip viewer......................................180.00

Kenner

TYV0001 boxed and opened   TYV0006

TYV0002 Assault on Death Star...25.00
TYV0003 Battle in Hyperspace 25.00
TYV0004 Danger at the Cantina 25.00
TYV0005 Destroy Death Star 25.00
TYV0007 ESB Give-a-Show Projector...95.00
TYV0008 ESB Give-a-Show Projector w/Scooby Doo Offer.......................97.00
TYV0009 Ewoks Give-a-Show Projector 80.00
TYV0001 Star Wars Movie Viewer w/"May The Force Be With You" Cassette...60.00
TYV0006 SW Give-a-Show Projector 115.00

Meccano

TYV0013   TYV0014

TYV0014 Star Wars Cinevue 342.00
TYV0013 Star Wars movie-frame cassette..87.00

Projectors/Viewers

Smith's Snackfood

TYV0011 binder not shown

TYV0011 50 film cels, 3-ring storage binder, flashlight projector..............166.00

Tiger Electronics

TYV0010 Lightsaber Image Projector, flashlight or slide projector, makes 4 authentic sounds...................................16.00

TYV0016 front, back, and contents

Toltoys

TYV0016 Give-A-Show projector 115.00

PUBLICATIONS

20th Anniversary Commemorative Magazine
PB0002 Collector's version: Gold foil Star Wars logo 15.00
PB0003 Collector's version: Gold foil Star Wars logo, bagged with trading card 19.00
PB0001 Newsstand version: flat ink Star Wars logo 8.00
PB0004 Special Collectors version: Blue foil Star Wars logo 45.00

20th Anniversary Poster Magazine
PB0005 Star Wars Heroes...6.00
PB0006 Star Wars Villains 6.00

20th Century Fox
PB0333 Empire Strikes Back pressbook 74.00

321 Contact
PB0352 1980 March/April, "Amazing Movies! Could They Really Happen?"..8.00

Adastra
PB0365 Issue 11, ESB cover...6.00

Amazing Heroes
PB0007 #13"Star Wars in Comics" cover 6.00

American Cinematographer
PB0008 1977 July Star Wars cover 85.00
PB0009 1980 June Empire Strikes Back cover 45.00
PB0010 Return of the Jedi, R2-D2 and C-3PO on cover............35.00

American Film
PB0011 1977 April "George Lucas Goes Far Out".....................12.00
PB0012 1983 June Return of the Jedi special effects articles......................7.00

Bantha Tracks
PB0014 Issue 34, includes soundtrack record 14.00
PB0013 Issues 1-35 ea. 6.00

Best of Starlog
PB0015 Vol. 1: Luke from ESB on cover, assorted articles..............7.00
PB0016 Vol. 2: Yoda on cover, assorted articles.......................7.00
PB0017 Vol. 4: Jabba on cover, assorted articles.....................7.00
PB0018 Vol. 5: Luke and Darth Vader duel on cover, assorted articles.....7.00
PB0357 Vol. 6: Empire Strikes back articles 7.00

Chicago Tribune
PB0020 1980 May 4 Headline "Empire Strikes Back" 12.00

Cinefantastique
PB0338 20th Anniversary, SW:SE 9.00
PB0022 Vol. 10, No. 2 Review of Empire Strikes Back 8.00
PB0023 Vol. 12, No. 5 / Vol 12, No. 6 (Double Issue) "The Revenge of the Jedi".....................................23.00
PB0024 Vol. 13, No. 4 Jedi Plot Revealed 10.00
PB0021 Vol. 6, No. 4 / Vol. 7, No. 1 (Double Issue) "Making Star Wars"....35.00

Cinefex
PB0025 No. 02, August 1980, special effects articles.....................65.00
PB0026 No. 03, Empire Strikes Back cover.............................57.00
PB0027 No. 13, Return of the Jedi film production...........................35.00
PB0028 No. 65, ILM 20th anniversary, Millennium Falcon cover 20.00

Cinemacabre
PB0359 No. 6, Summer 1984, Luke Skywalker on Sailbarge Deck 5.00

Cinescape
PB0341 1996 February, "Star Wars Forever" 4.00

Collecting Toys
PB0350 1995 August, "Star Wars breaks loose!" 3.00
PB0351 1997 February, "Star Wars Forever" 3.00

Collector's Universe
PB0363 The Definitive Star Wars Secondary Market Price Guide................5.00

Comic Collector's Magazine
PB0029 No. 139, October 1977, Star Wars interviews, behind the scenes and comic era 8.00

Comics Journal
PB0030 No. 2, Empire Strikes Back issue 8.00
PB0031 No. 37, Star Wars comics and movie issue 8.00

Comics Scene
PB0032 Darth Vader on cover and article on ROTJ comic 11.00

Commodore User's Magazine
PB0033 No. 3, Star Wars cover, SW games issue 4.00

Cracked Magazine
PB0345 "Phantom Menace Exposed" 5.00
PB0034 No. 146, November 1977, C-3PO and R2-D2 on cover, Star Wars parody...17.00
PB0343 No. 149, March 1978, "Bionic Man in Star Wars" 12.00
PB0344 No. 152, August 1978, "Star Wars has a Close Encounter"...........12.00
PB0035 No. 173, November 1980, "The Empire Strikes It Out".....................15.00
PB0036 No. 174, December 1980, "The Empire Strikes It Rich" 15.00
PB0037 No. 199, November 1983, "Returns of the Jedi Eye" 13.00

Crash
PB0038 No. 54, July 1988, Empire Strikes Back game on cover, with related article..9.00

Crazy
PB0039 Vol. 1, No. 32, December 1977, Star Wars cover, parody issue ...16.00

Creative Computing
PB0040 Vol. 8, No. 8, August 1982, Darth Vader on cover........................9.00

Current Science
PB0331 1980 April 30, Han, Leia, and C-3PO on cover................................4.00

Daily Record
PB0367 SW: EPI, The Ultimate Guide, part 1.......................5.00
PB0368 SW: EPI, The Ultimate Guide, part 2.......................5.00

Delap's Fiction and SF Review
PB0041 Vol. 3, No. 7, July 1977, Star Wars cover story with movie articles...22.00

Discover
PB0042 Vol. 5, No. 8, August 1984, George Lucas and Droids on Cover, "Computerizing the Movies" 18.00

Dreamwatch
PB0043 April 1997, Star Wars partial cover and article................................4.00

Dynamite
PB0047 No. 114, 1983, Luke and Princess Leia on cover 12.00
PB0044 No. 41, 1977, Star Wars article 14.00
PB0045 No. 63, Empire Strikes Back cover and article................................10.00
PB0046 No. 76, 1980, Luke Skywalker cover, Empire Strikes Back article..10.00

Electric Company
PB0296 1980 July, Darth Vader Cover, "Will The Bad Guys Win?" 8.00
PB0048 April / May 1983, Yoda cover, Star Wars articles............................7.00

Electronic Gaming Monthly
PB0327 Featuring: "Super Star Wars" 3.00

Empire Strikes Back
PB0049 Empire Strikes Back Official Collector's Edition..............................8.00
PB0050 Empire Strikes Back Poster Album..16.00

Empire Strikes Back Poster Book
PB0051 No. 1, "Back In Action" 6.00
PB0052 No. 2, "The Dark Lord, The Forces of the Empire" 6.00
PB0053 No. 3, "The Mysteries of Yoda, The Indignities of Artoo Detoo"....6.00
PB0054 No. 4, "AT-AT Attack, The Magic Factory" 6.00
PB0055 No. 5, "Han Solo - Hero and Scoundrel"..7.00

Enterprise Spotlight
PB0056 No. 4, Star Wars special 3.00

Entertainment Weekly
PB0057 1997 January 10, Luke Skywalker cover, SE articles.........................7.00
PB0290 1999 June 11, Inside the New Star Wars.......................................6.00
PB0329 1999 May 21, Inside Star Wars 6.00

Epic Illustrated
PB0299 1980 October, "Special Preview: Revenge of the Jedi" 12.00

Family Circle
PB0294 1980 August 5, "The Empire Strikes Back" 4.00

Famous Monsters
PB0073 Movie Aliens: Darth Vader cover, reprinted articles from "Famous Monsters" 12.00
PB0060 No, 140, Star Wars articles 10.00
PB0058 No. 137, Star Wars special issue 24.00
PB0059 No. 138, Star Wars cover, articles 20.00
PB0061 No. 142, Darth Vader cover...7.00
PB0062 No. 145, Empire Strikes Back article 13.00
PB0326 No. 146, Star Wars Article 7.00
PB0063 No. 147, Star Wars cover, articles 7.00
PB0064 No. 148, Darth Vader cover..12.00
PB0065 No. 153, David Prowse interview 7.00
PB0066 No. 156, Empire Strikes Back cover, articles 12.00
PB0067 No. 165, Empire Strikes Back special issue 20.00
PB0068 No. 166, Empire Strikes Back cover..12.00
PB0069 No. 167, Empire Strikes Back cover..12.00
PB0070 No. 174, Star Wars cover..12.00
PB0071 No. 177, Yoda cover 12.00
PB0072 No. 190, Empire Strikes Back cover..12.00

Fantascene
PB0074 No. 3, 1977, "The Star Wars" 16.00

Fantastic Films
PB0075 Vol. 1, No. 1, April 1978, articles and interviews............................12.00
PB0291 Vol. 1, No. 4, August 1978, The Weapons of Star Wars.................12.00
PB0076 Vol. 1, No. 8, April 1979, "Star Wars Strikes Back" 10.00
PB0077 Vol. 2, No. 2, June 1979, "One Last Time Down The Death Trench"..8.00
PB0078 Vol. 3, No. 2, July 1980, interviews Larry Kasdan and Dennis Muren (effects photographer) 8.00
PB0079 Vol. 3, No. 3, September 1980, Chewbacca cover, Gary Kurtz interview 10.00
PB0080 Vol. 3, No. 4, October 1980, Yoda cover, articles 8.00
PB0081 Vol. 3, No. 5, December 1980, Clone wars explained 16.00
PB0082 Vol. 3, No. 7, February 1981, articles..8.00
PB0083 Vol. 3, No. 8, April 1981, articles 8.00
PB0084 Vol. 3, No. 9, June 1981, cover of characters on radio, "Star Wars Comes To Radio" 14.00
PB0085 Vol. 4, No. 1, August 1981, articles..8.00
PB0086 Vol. 4, No. 4, April 1982, "From Star Wars to Empire to Revenge of the Jedi" 10.00
PB0087 Vol. 5, No. 2, "Revenge of the Jedi" 9.00
PB0088 Vol. 5, No. 3, Return of the Jedi cover and articles.........................8.00
PB0089 Vol. 5, No. 4, Return of the Jedi cover and articles.........................8.00
PB0090 Vol. 5, No. 5, Return of the Jedi cover and articles.........................8.00

Fantasy Film Preview
PB0091 1977, Star Wars special effects 5.00

Fantasy Modeling
PB0092 No. 6, Star Wars miniature models...4.00

Film Review
PB0095 1980 August, "Carrie Fisher and Mark Hamill Talk About Their Roles in Empire" 8.00
PB0094 1980 July, "More Photos from the Empire Strikes Back" 5.00
PB0093 1980 June, "Star Wars Rage Again Against the Empire" 5.00
PB0096 1983 July, "Star Wars - The Final Force Filled Phase" 6.00

Films and Filming
PB0302 Vol. , No. , February 1978, Mark Hamill Interview 11.00
PB0097 Vol. 23, No. 11, August 1977, Star Wars preview 11.00

Finescale Modeler
PB0098 No. 43, Summer 1983, Jedi diorama cover 5.00

Fortune
PB0099 1980 October 6, "The Empire Pays Off" 9.00

Future
PB0100 No. 1, April 1978, Star Wars advertising posters...........................16.00
PB0101 No. 19, Empire Strikes Back preview..8.00
PB0102 No. 20, Empire Strikes Back cover and article................................8.00

Gateways
PB0103 No. 6, Star Wars role-playing game 6.00

PB0002 PB0003 PB0005 PB0333 PRESSBOOK PB0008 PB0009 PB0010 PB0012

PB00338 PB0022 PB0021 PB0026 PB0341 PB0343 PB0344 PB0345

Publications

High Drive Publications, Inc.
PB0313 SW Generation fanzine 1992 #1, black-and-white photocopied issue 5.00
PB0314 SW Generation fanzine 1992, #2, black-and-white photocopied issue 5.00
PB0315 SW Generation fanzine 1997 #1 Vol. 2 "quarterly" with a color glossy cover 4.00

Hollywood Studio Magazine
PB0104 Vol. 12, No. 5, June 1978, articles 6.00

Hot Dog
PB0105 No. 17, 1983, Star Wars action figures article 7.00

House of Hammer
PB0106 No. 13, article 4.00
PB0107 No. 16, articles and poster 8.00

Jack and Jill
PB0348 Carrie Fisher, Princess Leia in The Empire Strikes Back 6.00
PB0349 Yoda, the Jedi Master in The Empire Strikes Back 6.00

Kitbuilders
PB0358 Issue 2, Spring 1997, "Customizing Kaiyodo's Boba Fett" 22.00

Kuifje
PB0108 Vol. 38, No. 5, Return of the Jedi articles 6.00

LA Life
PB0330 1996 June 10, "May The Force Continue" 4.00

LA Times
PB0109 1977 June 14, George Lucas on Opening Night 24.00

Ladies Home Journal
PB0110 1983 September, "Jedimania: Why We Love Those Star Warriors" ..9.00

L'ecran Fantastique
PB0111 No. 13, Empire Strikes Back articles 12.00
PB0112 No. 31, Jedi cover and articles 12.00
PB0113 No. 33, Empire Strikes Back cover and special effects articles....12.00
PB0114 No. 37, Return of the Jedi cover and articles 12.00
PB0115 No. 38, Return of the Jedi cover and articles 12.00
PB0116 No. 86, 10th Anniversary article 7.00

Lego Mania
PB0316 1999 March-April: cover and 10 full pages of SW coverage 3.00
PB0317 1999 May-June: cover and 8 full pages of Star Wars..............3.00
PB0318 2000 March-April: cover (Slave I) and 9 full pages of Star Wars coverage 3.00

Life
PB0301 1977: The Year In Pictures 21.00
PB0117 Vol. 4, No. 1, January 1981, Yoda cover 26.00
PB0118 Vol. 6, No. 6, June 1983, "Father of the Jedi" 12.00

Lucasfilm Fan Club
PB0120 Any issue with non-Star Wars cover 5.00

PB0119 Any issue with Star Wars cover................................8.00

Mad Magazine
PB0121 1978 January No. 196, "Star Bores" 16.00
PB0123 1979 December No. 203, "The Mad Star Wars Musical".............18.00
PB0122 1979 March No. 197, "A 'Mad' Look at Star Wars" 15.00
PB0124 1981 January No. 220, "The Empire Strikes Out" 13.00
PB0125 1982 April No. 230, "The Star Wars Log-Mad's version of George Lucas' presonal log"...10.00
PB0126 1983 October No. 242, "Star Bores - Rehash of the Jedi" 10.00
PB0127 1983 Summer, Mad Superspecial.................................11.00
PB0293 1996 Star Wars Spectacular....................................6.00
PB0336 Star Wars Macarena 6.00

Mad Movies
PB0128 1980 No. 20, Empire Strikes Back cover..........................10.00

Mediascene Preview
PB0129 Vol. 1, No. 22, November 1976, Star Wars cover and feature news . 35.00
PB0131 Vol. 2, No. 11, "Darth Vader returns with a new ally, Boba Fett"...8.00
PB0130 Vol. 2, No. 4, August 1980, interview with Mark Hamill 12.00
PB0132 Vol. 3, No. 2, interview with Brian Johnson (special effects) 5.00

Midnight Marquee
PB0133 No. 29, Yoda cover, Empire Strikes Back review..............7.00

Military Modeler
PB0134 Vol. 7, No. 11, Millennium Falcon cover.......................6.00

Modesto Bee
PB0135 1977 June 5, Star Wars 7.00

Movie Aliens Illustrated
PB0332 1979 Darth Vader on cover.....................................3.00

Movie Monsters
PB0136 Vol. 1, No. 3, Fall 1981, Darth Vader and Bounty Hunters cover....8.00

Movie News
PB0366 1977 Sept / Oct., "Star Wars" The Smash Hit of the Year! 16.00

Muppet Magazine
PB0137 Vol. 1, No. 3, Summer 1983, Muppets dressed as Star Wars characters on cover..14.00

National Enquirer
PB0138 1983 June 21, cover shows Shuttle Tyderium, story 5.00

New Voyager
PB0140 No. 4, Summer 1983, Return of the Jedi articles 5.00

New Yorker
PB0141 1997 January 6, George Lucas interview and Star Wars articles...6.00

Newsweek
PB0287 1977 Special Issue: Pictures of '77...................................18.00
PB0139 Vol. 89, No. 22, May 30, 1977, "Fun In Space" 32.00

PB0331

PB0045

PB0046

PB0047

PB0296

PB0327

PB0290

PB0329

PB0299

PB0294

PB0060

PB0062

PB0063

PB0064

PB0326

PB0291

Nickelodeon
PB0289 1997 March, Star Wars Strikes Back 6.50

NY Times
PB0142 1980 December 20, Saga beyond Star Wars....................................4.00

Orbit
PB0143 No. 13, Winter 1981, Empire Strikes Back cover and articles 8.00

Orbit and SF Terra Presenteren
PB0144 Return of the Jedi special issue 8.00

Parade
PB0364 Issue 324, November 1977, "Elvis - and other Pop tragedies"........4.00

Paris Match
PB0346 Queen Amidala on cover...2.00

People
PB0146 1977 Vol. 8, No. 26, R2-D2 cover, article 14.00
PB0145 1977 July 18, article 10.00
PB0147 1978 August 14, Carrie Fisher and Darth Vader on cover, article ...14.00
PB0148 1980 June 9, Yoda cover, article...14.00
PB0149 1980, July 7, 1980, Empire Strikes Back on cover and article 14.00
PB0152 1981 August 31, Vol. 16, No. 9, Mark Hamill and Yoda cover, Hamill
    interview 12.00
PB0151 1983 June 20, Vol. 19, No. 24, Darth Vader cover, article 8.00
PB0150 1983 June 6, Carrie Fisher cover, article 14.00
PB0153 1997 February 3, 20th Anniversary article, focusing on actors.......7.00

Photoplay
PB0155 1978 February, Star Wars cover 6.00
PB0154 1978 January, Star Wars cover..6.00
PB0156 1980 June, Empire Strikes Back cover 8.00

Pizzazz
PB0157 No. 1, C-3PO and R2-D2 on cover 9.00

Popular Mechanics
PB0320 The machines of Star Wars Episode I..5.00

Posters Monthly
PB0158 ANH No. 01 C-3PO and R2-D2 ....8.00
PB0159 ANH No. 02 Darth Vader 8.00
PB0160 ANH No. 03 C-3PO and R2-D2 in Death Star.................................8.00
PB0161 ANH No. 04 Chewbacca 8.00
PB0162 ANH No. 05 Darth Vader 8.00
PB0163 ANH No. 06 C-3PO..8.00
PB0164 ANH No. 07 R2-D2...8.00
PB0165 ANH No. 08 Stormtrooper 8.00
PB0166 ANH No. 09 Darth Vader 8.00
PB0167 ANH No. 10 Star Wars photo collage 8.00
PB0168 ANH No. 11 R2-D2...8.00
PB0169 ANH No. 12 Dogfight above the Death Star 8.00
PB0170 ANH No. 13 C-3PO and Luke 8.00
PB0171 ANH No. 14 Death Star trench 8.00
PB0172 ANH No. 15 C-3PO..8.00
PB0173 ANH No. 16 C-3PO and R2-D2 ....12.00
PB0380 ESB No. 1, "Back In Action!" 5.00
PB0381 ESB No. 2, "The Dark Lord"...5.00
PB0382 ESB No. 3, "The Mysteries of Yoda"..5.00
PB0383 ESB No. 4, "AT-AT Attack"...5.00
PB0384 ESB No. 5, "Han Solo - Hero and Scoundrel".....................................5.00
PB0385 ROTJ No. 1, "At Last The Waiting Is Over!"...6.00
PB0386 ROTJ No. 2, "Inside Jabba the Hutt's Court".......................................6.00

PB0380   PB0381   PB0382   PB0383   PB0384

PB0078   PB0079   PB0080   PB0081   PB0083   PB0088   PB0302   PB0100   PB0315

PB0348   PB0349   PB0330   PB0301   PB0118   PB0119   PB0121   PB0123   PB0124

PB0293   PB0336   PB0129   PB0332   PB0366   PB0287   PB0289   PB0364

PB0346   PB0145   PB0147   PB0150   PB0152   PB0157   PB0320   PB0158   PB0160

Publications

PB0387 ROTJ No. 3, "Two Fantastic Posters" Rancor and Han Solo............6.00
PB0388 ROTJ No. 4, "Two Fantastic Posters" Darth Vader and Space Battle...6.00

Premiere
PB0174 1997 February, 20th Anniversary article 3.00

Preview
PB0298 1983 Vol. 2, No. 2, Luke and Leia on Desert Skiff Cover..................4.00

Questar
PB0175 No. 1, 1978, "The Triumph of Star Wars" 12.00
PB0176 No. 8, August 1980, "The Making of an Empire: Star Wars Returns"..12.00

Radio Times
PB0324 1999 July 3-9, Darth Maul cover 2.00
PB0322 1999 July 3-9, Obi-Wan Kenobi cover 2.00
PB0323 1999 July 3-9, Queen Amidala cover..2.00
PB0321 1999 July 3-9, Qui-Gon Jinn cover 2.00

Reel Fantasy
PB0177 No. 1, Star Wars articles 8.00

Republic Scene
PB0334 1981 George Lucas standing behind Star Destroyer model 14.00

Return of the Jedi Poster Book
PB0178 No. 1 Death Star battle..7.00
PB0179 No. 2 Wicket...7.00
PB0180 No. 3 Rancor / Han Solo 7.00
PB0181 No. 4 Darth vader / Space Battle...8.00

Review
PB0182 Vol. 2, No. 12, Luke and Leia cover, interview with Richard Marquand...9.00
PB0183 Vol. 2, No. 14, Interview w/Billy Dee Williams................................10.00

Rolling Stone
PB0184 1977 August 25, The Force Behind George Lucas.........................15.00
PB0185 1980 August 12, The Empire Strikes Back...................................15.00
PB0186 1980 July 24, Han, Lando, Leia, and Luke in plain clothes cover, "Slaves to the Empire"...17.00
PB0360 1999 June 24, Free 18"x22" Star Wars poster..........................12.00
PB0187 No. 400/401, Darth Vader, Princess Leia on Beach, interviews with George Lucas and Carrie Fisher 25.00

Scholastic Action
PB0342 1977 October 8, Luke in Landspeeder on cover 11.00

Science and Fantasy
PB0188 1977 Winter, Interviews with actors and article on music 3.00

Science Fiction Age
PB0297 1997 March, "Star Wars Special Issue" 5.00

Science Fiction, Horror and Fantasy
PB0189 Vol. 1, No. 1, Fall 1997, Star Wars collector edition 6.00

Sci-Fi Entertainment
PB0190 1997 February, Star Wars cover 6.00

PB0292 1998 February, George Lucas Speaks 7.00

Sci-Fi Universe
PB0191 1994 July, The Next Star Wars Trilogy cover story 9.00
PB0192 1995 November, Star Wars Lives cover...................................6.00

Scintillation
PB0193 No. 13, June 1977, "George Lucas brings the excitement back".9.00

Screen Superstars
PB0194 No. 8, 1977, Star Wars articles 10.00

Seventeen
PB0195 1983 March 19, interview with actors on location...........................6.00

SFTV
PB0196 No. 7, Star Wars costumes article 8.00

SFX
PB0288 1997 June 1, 4 Stunning FX Shots from Star Wars Trilogy Special Edition 7.00

Sky
PB0361 2000 March, "All four hits together on British television" 8.00

Space Wars
PB0197 1977 October, Star Wars articles..10.00
PB0198 1978 June, Star Wars vs. Close Encounters comparison article ...10.00

Star Blaster
PB0199 Vol. 1, No. 2, Darth Vader cover, article on Star Wars droids 8.00

Star Encounters
PB0223 Vol. 1, No. 1, April 1978, Making of Star Wars article 7.00

Star Force
PB0227 1981 October, Revenge of the Jedi article 10.00
PB0225 Vol. 1, No. 1, "Star Wars II: The Empire Fights Back Again!" 6.00
PB0226 Vol. 2, No. 3, Darth Vader, Lando, and ESB scenes on cover, Return of the Jedi article..8.00

Star Quest Comix
PB0339 Star Wars revisited 4.00

Star Warp
PB0263 1978 April, includes posters 7.00

Star Wars Galaxy Magazine
PB0264 No. 01...15.00
PB0265 No. 02...12.00
PB0266 No. 03...12.00
PB0267 No. 04...12.00
PB0268 No. 05...10.00
PB0269 No. 06...10.00
PB0270 No. 07...10.00
PB0271 No. 08...10.00
PB0272 No. 09..7.00
PB0273 No. 10..7.00
PB0274 No. 11..7.00

PB0298   PB0321   PB0322   PB0323   PB0324   PB0334   PB0184   PB0342

PB0188   PB0297   PB0189   PB0190   PB0292   PB0193   PB0288   PB0197

Star Wars Insider
PB0200 Starts at Issue #23 (1-22 are Lucasfilm Fan Club), each.................5.00

Star Wars Kids
PB0308 Issue #01...3.00
PB0309 Issue #02...3.00
PB0310 Issue #03...3.00
PB0311 Issue #04...3.00
PB0312 Issue #05...3.00

Star Wars Kids, Insider Insert
PB0319 #00 Preview Issue..2.00

Star Wars Newspaper
PB0275 1977 Single issue 14.00

Star Wars Spectacular
PB0276 Tribute magazine to Star Wars 12.00

Star Wars: The Making of the World's Greatest Movie
PB0277 1977 Behind the scenes articles..17.00

Starblazer
PB0201 1986 December, Darth Vader cover 6.00

Starburst
PB0220 1987 Winter Special, Star Tours and 10th Anniversary articles......12.00
PB0221 1993 Classic Sci-Fi Special, Star Wars cover 10.00
PB0222 1996 Outer Space Special, Star Wars Special Edition article 8.00
PB0202 No. 1, Star Wars cover...18.00
PB0203 No. 2, "3PO Unmasked" article...15.00
PB0217 No. 208, Snowtrooper cover...8.00
PB0206 No. 22, Empire Strikes Back article...10.00
PB0218 No. 223, Darth Vader cover, George Lucas interview...................10.00
PB0219 No. 225, Present and future of Star Wars article 8.00
PB0207 No. 23, Empire Strikes Back articles and poster 10.00
PB0208 No. 24, Star Wars interviews..8.00
PB0209 No. 25, Empire interviews...8.00
PB0210 No. 26, Empire Strikes Back special effects article 10.00
PB0204 No. 3, Star Wars article..12.00
PB0211 No. 43, Star Wars article..8.00
PB0212 No. 58, Return of the Jedi articles..10.00
PB0213 No. 59, Return of the Jedi articles..10.00
PB0214 No. 60, C-3PO article...8.00
PB0215 No. 61, Carrie Fisher interview...10.00
PB0205 No. 8, Empire Strikes Back article..12.00
PB0216 No. 93, Return of the Jedi Video article...5.00

Starfix
PB0224 1980, Return of the Jedi issue 8.00

Starlog
PB0228 No. 007, X-Wing and Tie fighter on cover 34.00
PB0295 No. 008, Star Wars (Sept. 1977)..26.00
PB0229 No. 016, "Invisible Visions of Star Wars" article 8.00
PB0230 No. 017, Effects and Ralph McQuarrie articles...............................9.00
PB0340 No. 018, "Star Wars" sequel...7.00
PB0231 No. 019, Cantina creatures on cover, Star Wars Holiday Special article 15.00

Starlog (continued)
PB0355 No. 024, Science Fiction Spectacular...8.00
PB0232 No. 031, Empire Strikes Back cover, review 12.00
PB0233 No. 035, Darth Vader cover...9.00
PB0234 No. 036, Boba Fett and Darth Vader cover 10.00
PB0235 No. 037, Millennium Falcon cover..8.00
PB0236 No. 040, Luke and Yoda cover...8.00
PB0237 No. 041, Luke and Yoda cover, Mark Hamill interview 9.00
PB0238 No. 048, Luke and Yoda cover...8.00
PB0239 No. 050, Boba Fett cover..10.00
PB0240 No. 051, Luke Skywalker cover...8.00
PB0241 No. 056, Darth Vader cover...8.00
PB0242 No. 065, Luke Skywalker cover...8.00
PB0243 No. 069, Return of the Jedi cast cover..9.00
PB0244 No. 071, Han, Leia, and Luke cover, ROTJ articles and interviews.12.00
PB0245 No. 072, Mark Hamill interview..8.00
PB0246 No. 074, Return of the Jedi creatures article....................................9.00
PB0247 No. 076, Return of the Jedi preview article..9.00
PB0248 No. 080, Return of the Jedi special effects cover and article 8.00
PB0249 No. 082, Return of the Jedi special effects article and interview with Emperor 10.00
PB0250 No. 084, Frank Oz discusses Yoda article..9.00
PB0251 No. 086, Return of the Jedi special effects article............................8.00
PB0252 No. 090, Ewok Adventure article...9.00
PB0253 No. 093, Return of the Jedi speeder bike special effects article ..7.00
PB0254 No. 094, Return of the Jedi special effects article............................7.00
PB0255 No. 096, Peter Cushing interview...16.00
PB0256 No. 099, C-3PO cover..8.00
PB0257 No. 100, George Lucas interview...10.00
PB0353 No. 101, Ewoks live action TV movie 11.00
PB0258 No. 104, Chewbacca cover, Peter Mayhew interview 9.00
PB0259 No. 115, Star Tours articles...7.00
PB0260 No. 118, George Lucas / Star Tours cover..7.00
PB0261 No. 120, 10th Anniversary cover...12.00
PB0262 No. 127, George Lucas interview...7.00
PB0354 No. 237, George Lucas explains why he did SW:SE 7.00
PB0356 No. 274, Defining Yodaisms..7.00
PB0335 Starlog Scrap Book Vol. 1 ....18.00

Stripschrift
PB0278 No. 142, December 1980, Empire Strikes Back cover, Ralph McQuarrie article 12.00

Sunday Mirror
PB0369 Episode I: The Phantom Menace part 1 ....5.00
PB0370 Episode I: The Phantom Menace part 2 ....5.00

Sunday Times
PB0371 The New Star Wars..5.00

Time Magazine
PB0279 1977 May 30, "Years Best Movie: Star Wars"..................................26.00
PB0280 1980 May 19, "The Empire Strikes Back" 14.00
PB0281 1983 May 23, "Star Wars III: Return of the Jedi"..............................14.00
PB0282 1997 February 10, The Return of Star Wars cover 8.00
PB0325 1999 April 26, "The Complete Guide to The Phantom Menace" ..4.00

Today's Collector
PB0362 1999, Vol. 7 No. 6, "Collecting Star Wars"..5.00

PB0223   PB0339   PB0264   PB0265   PB0267   PB0310   PB0312   PB0319

PB0275   PB0276   PB0228   PB0340   PB0239   PB0243   PB0249   PB0260

Publications

PB0261

PB0295

PB0335

PB0280

PB0281

PB0282

PB0325

PB0284

PB0285

PB0300

PB0328

PB0347

PB0303

PB0337

Total Film
PB0389 Star Wars, `70s Haircuts, `90s action! 3.00

True-UFOs and Outer Space Quarterly
PB0283 No. 19, Fall 1980, AT-Ats on cover, "The Empire Strikes Back But Not Out!" 4.00

TV Guide
PB0376 June 12-18 1 of 4...3.00
PB0377 June 12-18 2 of 4...3.00
PB0378 June 12-18 3 of 4...3.00
PB0379 June 12-18 4 of 4...3.00
PB0372 May 15-21 1 of 4..3.00
PB0373 May 15-21 2 of 4..3.00
PB0374 May 15-21 3 of 4..3.00
PB0375 May 15-21 4 of 4..3.00

TV This Week
PB0306 1978 November 12, Washington Star TV Listing with article on 1978 SW Holiday Special 9.00

US
PB0284 Vol. 4, No. 7, July 22, 1980, "The Good Guys of Star Wars" 10.00
PB0285 Vol. 8, No. 13, June 20, 1983, Return of the Jedi cover and articles.. 8.00

Vanity Fair
PB0300 1999 February, "The Force Is Back At Last!" with Bonus Foldout....7.00

Variety
PB0286 1997 February 3, "Star Wars in Outer Space"................................7.00

Video Gaming Illustrated
PB0328 1983 February "Star Wars Spectacular" 5.00

Vogue
PB0307 Natalie Portman - Star Wars Queen.......................................5.00

Who Weekly
PB0347 2000 Sept. 30, "The new Darth Vader unmasked and on-set secrets revealed" 12.00

World Publishers
PB0303 1998 UK Souvenir Annual 17.00

WOW
PB0337 1978 Issue 21, Luke and droids in desert on cover 4.00

PUPPETS

YE0003

YE0004

Applause
YE0003 Jar Jar Binks 20.00
YE0004 Yoda 20.00

Kenner

YE0001 boxed, front, and back

YE0001 Yoda hand puppet 55.00

Regal
YE0002 Chewbacca hand puppet...73.00

PURSES / CARRY BAGS

PC0001

PC0002

PC0003

Giftware International
PC0001 Chewbacca 17.00
PC0002 Darth Vader 17.00
PC0003 Jar Jar Binks 14.00

Kathrine Baumann Design

PC0004

PC0004 Queen Amidala miniaudiere, limited to 75.................................475.00

PUSH PINS

Rose Art Industries
PP0001 Star Wars push pins, 12 per set...7.00

PP0001 front and back

PUZZLES

TYP0013   TYP0015   TYP0017   TYP0018

TYP0021   TYP0022   TYP0023   TYP0024

TYP0011   TYP0012   TYP0014

TYP0016   TYP0006   TYP0019

Craft Master
TYP0011 Battle on Endor, 170 pieces 10.00
TYP0012 B-Wing Fighters, 170 pieces 10.00
TYP0013 Darth Vader, tray...6.00
TYP0014 Death Star, 70 pieces...8.00
TYP0015 Ewok Gliders, tray...6.00
TYP0016 Ewok Leaders, 170 pieces 10.00
TYP0017 Ewok Village, tray 6.00
TYP0004 Ewoks: Fishing, 35 pieces...7.00
TYP0005 Ewoks: Lessons 7.00
TYP0006 Ewoks: Swimming Hole, 35 pieces..................................7.00
TYP0018 Gamorrean Guard, tray...6.00
TYP0019 Jabba's Henchmen, 70 pieces...8.00
TYP0020 Jabba's Throne Room, 70 pieces 8.00
TYP0032 Luke Inspects Droids 8.00
TYP0021 Princess Kneesaa and Baga, tray.....................................6.00
TYP0022 Princess Leia and Wicket, tray..6.00
TYP0023 R2-D2 and Wicket, tray 6.00
TYP0024 Wicket the Ewok, tray..6.00

Hasbro
TYP0085 Anakin Skywalker slivers 8.00
TYP0104 Bravo Squadron Assault, 750 pieces, puzzle printed on front and back...7.00
TYP0084 Darth Maul Rubik's Cube Puzzle 7.00

TYP0084   TYP0085   TYP0086   TYP0099

TYP0091   TYP0092   TYP0093   TYP0094

TYP0088   TYP0089   TYP0090

TYP0095   TYP0096   TYP0097   TYP0098   TYP0100

TYP0102   TYP0103   TYP0104   TYP0101

TYP0086 Darth Maul slivers 8.00
TYP0096 Darth Maul, 100 piece shaped puzzle, includes theme shaped pieces 5.00
TYP0100 Gungan Sub 66 pieces, 3D mini-puzzle.............................9.00
TYP0103 Gungan Sub Escape, 750 pieces, puzzle printed on front and back 7.00
TYP0087 Jar Jar Binks slivers..8.00
TYP0095 Jar Jar Binks, 100 piece shaped puzzle, includes theme shaped pieces 5.00
TYP0088 Jedi vs. Sith, 200 pieces, hidden image glows in the dark............7.00
TYP0091 Jedi vs. Sith, 50 piece mini-puzzle, 5"x7" 2.00
TYP0089 Mos Espa Podrace, 200 pieces, hidden image glows in the dark..7.00
TYP0090 Opee Sea Creature, 200 pieces, hidden image glows in the dark ..7.00
TYP0093 Pit Droids, 50 piece mini-puzzle, 5"x7" 2.00
TYP0102 Podrace Challenge, 750 pieces, puzzle printed on front and back..7.00
TYP0092 Queen Amidala , 50 piece mini-puzzle, 5"x7".....................2.00
TYP0097 R2-D2, 100 piece shaped puzzle, includes theme shaped pieces..5.00
TYP0094 Sebulba, 50 piece mini-puzzle, 5"x7"................................2.00
TYP0101 Sith Infiltrator 73 pieces, 3D mini-puzzle...........................9.00
TYP0099 TPM: Movie Teaser Poster, 300 extra-large pieces 8.00
TYP0098 Yoda, 100 piece shaped puzzle, includes theme shaped pieces...5.00

Kenner

TYP0007   TYP0038   TYP0026 with alternate box

TYP0027   TYP0030   TYP0009   TYP0040

TYP0031   TYP0077   TYP0010   TYP0041

Puzzles

| TYP0029 | TYP0033 | TYP0035 | TYP0037 |

TYP0007 Aboard Millennium Falcon, 1,000 pieces 24.00
TYP0025 Any SW Series 1 in Black Box 12.00
TYP0038 Bantha, 140 pieces 10.00
TYP0026 C-3PO and R2-D2, 140 pieces 15.00
TYP0039 Cantina Band, 500 pieces 12.00
TYP0027 Chewbacca and Han Solo, 140 pieces 15.00
TYP0008 Corridor of Light, 1500 pieces 26.00
TYP0030 Darth Vader and Obi-Wan Duel, 500 pieces 10.00
TYP0009 Hildebrandt Movie Poster Art, 1000 pieces........................17.00
TYP0040 Jawas and R2-D2 ....10.00
TYP0031 Luke and Leia, 500 pieces 10.00
TYP0077 Luke Meets R2-D2, 140 pieces 15.00
TYP0028 Luke, 500 pieces 15.00
TYP0010 Millennium Falcon, 1500 pieces...24.00
TYP0041 Purchase of the Droids, 500 pieces 12.00
TYP0034 Sandtroopers in Mos Eisley, 140 pieces...............................8.00
TYP0029 Space Battle, 500 pieces 15.00
TYP0033 Trash Compactor, 140 pieces 8.00
TYP0035 Tusken Raider, 140 pieces 8.00
TYP0036 Victory Celebration, 500 pieces 10.00
TYP0037 X-Wing Hangar, 500 pieces 10.00

Milton Bradley

| TYP0045 | TYP0046 | TYP0047 |

| TYP0078 | TYP0079 | TYP0080 | TYP0081 | TYP0109 |

| TYP0002 | TYP0003 | TYP0082 | TYP0083 |

| TYP0042 | TYP0043 | TYP0044 | TYP0001 |

TYP0045 C-3PO and R2-D2 in desert, 100 pieces 8.00
TYP0047 C-3PO, Chewbacca, Han, and Leia in Shuttle Tyderium, 100
  pieces 8.00
TYP0001 Darth Vader 3D...35.00
TYP0046 Darth Vader, 100 pieces 8.00
TYP0109 Death Star trench scene, 100 pieces 12.00
TYP0002 Imperial Star Destroyer 3D 35.00
TYP0083 Jar Jar Binks, 3D..25.00
TYP0003 Millennium Falcon 3D 35.00
TYP0078 Mural Puzzle, Scene 1: A New Hope, 221 pieces 6.00
TYP0079 Mural Puzzle, Scene 2: Empire Strikes Back, 221 pieces 6.00
TYP0080 Mural Puzzle, Scene 3: Return of the Jedi, 221 pieces 6.00
TYP0081 Mural Puzzle, Scene 4: Trilogy, 221 pieces 6.00
TYP0082 R2-D2, 3D w/electronic sounds 35.00
TYP0044 Return of the Jedi, 550 pieces with foil highlights 12.00
TYP0042 Star Wars: A New Hope, 550 pieces with foil highlights.........12.00

TYP0043 The Empire Strikes Back, 550 pieces with foil highlights 12.00

Pizza Hut

Episode I puzzle games.

| TYP0110 |

TYP0110 Get Into It!, red border 5.00
TYP0112 Get Into It!, blue border 5.00

Really Useful

| TYP0105 | TYP0106 | TYP0107 | TYP0108 |

TYP0108 Anakin Skywalker 3D sculpture mini 14.00
TYP0105 Jar Jar Binks 3D scukpture...32.00
TYP0106 Obi-Wan Kenobi 3D sculpture mini...................................14.00
TYP0107 Qui-Gon Jinn 3D sculpture mini...14.00

Rose Art Industries

| TYP0048 | TYP0049 |

TYP0051 Empire Strikes back, 550 pieces 8.00
TYP0048 Luke and Leia, 100 pieces 8.00
TYP0052 Return of the Jedi, 550 pieces...8.00
TYP0049 Star Wars poster art, 100 pieces 8.00
TYP0050 Star Wars, 550 pieces 8.00

Schmid

TYP0053 Return of the Jedi 2-in-1, Jabba the Hutt and Luke in Jabba's
  Court 36.00

Springbok

TYP0055 Empire Strikes Back, 1,000 pieces.....................................24.00
TYP0054 Star Wars, 1,500 pieces...24.00

T. Theophanides and Son

TYP0062 Mini-Puzzles, 63 pieces, 14x18cm, eight different pictures, each...24.00

Takara

TYP0056 60 pieces, six different pictures, each...................................18.00
TYP0057 100 pieces, six different pictures, each.................................23.00
TYP0058 500 pieces, six different pictures, each.................................25.00
TYP0059 700 pieces, six different pictures, each.................................35.00
TYP0060 Frame tray puzzle..25.00
TYP0061 Plastic frame tray puzzle 30.00

Waddington

| TYP0067 | TYP0069 |

TYP0067 Action figures and Land Speeder, 350 pieces 65.00
TYP0068 Action figures, Land Speeder, X-Wing and Tie Fighter, 350 pieces ..65.00
TYP0063 C-3PO and R2-D2, 150 pieces...25.00
TYP0064 Chewbacca and Han, 150 pieces..25.00

| TYP0064 | TYP0065 | TYP0066 | TYP0111 |

TYP0069 Darth Vader, 150 pieces 16.00
TYP0065 Entering Mos Eisley, 150 pieces 25.00
TYP0073 Ewoks at home, 150 pieces 14.00
TYP0076 Ewoks in woods 14.00
TYP0074 Ewoks sledding, 150 pieces 14.00
TYP0075 Ewoks swimming 14.00
TYP0066 Inside the Millennium Falcon, 150 pieces 25.00
TYP0071 Jabba's Throne Room, 150 pieces 16.00
TYP0072 Luke with blaster, 150 pieces 16.00
TYP0111 Star Wars: Special Edition logo, 300 extra-large pieces, 2'x3' 12.00

PUZZLES: BLOCK

Craft Master

| PZB0001 | PZB0002 |

PZB0001 Ewoks, 9 block..12.00
PZB0002 Return of the Jedi characters, 9 block......................12.00

Pepsi Cola
Episode I premiums.

| PZB0003 | PZB0004 | PZB0005 | PZB0006 | PZB0007 |

PZB0003 Anakin Skywalker 7.00
PZB0004 C-3PO 7.00
PZB0005 Darth Maul...7.00
PZB0006 Jar Jar Binks 7.00
PZB0007 Obi-Wan Kenobi 7.00

R2-D2 TOYS MISC.

| RBO0004 | RBO0002 | RBO0001 | RBO0003 |

Micro Games of America
RBO0004 Talking R2-D2, says four different phrases....................14.00

Palitoy
RBO0002 Talking R2-D2, says four different phrases...................225.00

Takara
RBO0001 Bump-and-Go battery powered R2-D2........................264.00
RBO0003 Missile Firing R2-D2 ....285.00

RACING SETS

Fundimensions
YF0001 Duel at Death Star...125.00
YF0002 Duel at Death Star, white box with line-art..................165.00

| YF0001 | YF0002 | YF0003 |
| YF0004 | YF0005 |

Galoob
YF0005 Arch Canyon Adventure, includes Dud Bolt's and Clegg Holdfast's
podracers...16.00
YF0004 Beggars Canyon Challenge, includes Mars Guo's and Ratts Tyrell's
podracers...16.00
YF0003 Boonta Eve Challenge, includes Anakin Skywalker's and Sebulba's
podracers...24.00

RACING VEHICLE TOYS

Action / Revell
YL0016 "Pedal car bank" with trailer, 6.2" long; 2,500 produced 55.00
YL0006 1/18 scale racing car, 1,500 produced 100.00
YL0007 1/18 scale racing car, 4,000 produced 250.00
YL0011 1/18 scale "standard limited edition" racing car 45.00
YL0014 1/24 scale "clear window bank" racing car, 8.3" long; 10,000 pro-
duced...75.00
YL0013 1/24 scale "Elite" racing car....................................26.00
YL0008 1/24 scale racing car, 12,500 produced 36.00
YL0005 1/24 scale racing car, 8.3" long, 3,500 produced...........42.00
YL0012 1/24 scale "standard limited edition" racing car 24.00
YL0009 1/43 scale racing car, 5,500 produced 44.00
YL0015 1/64 scale diecast racing car, 3.1" long; 15,000 produced..........14.00
YL0010 1/64 scale racing car, 20,000 produced 8.00

Kenner

| YL0002 | YL0003 |

| YL0004 | YL0001 |

YL0002 Darth Vader SSP Van..85.00
YL0003 Luke Skywalker SSP Van...85.00
YL0001 Power Racing Speeder Bike.....................................20.00
YL0004 SSP Van Set, both van, cones, obstacles.....................275.00

Winner's Circle

| YL0017 |

YL0017 Star Wars Episode I, Pit Row 17.00

RADIO CONTROLLED TOYS

Foodland
YG0006 Mr. Grocer, licensed variation on the Cobot 185.00

Radio Controlled Toys

YG0006

Hitari

YG0008

YG0008 Darth Vader 75.00

Kenner

YG0002   YG0003

YG0007

YG0007 Imperial Speeder Bike 87.00
YG0002 Jawa Sandcrawler 365.00
YG0003 R2-D2 ....165.00
YG0004 R2-D2 w/obstacle course 410.00

Takara

YG0005 front and open   YG0001 box and opened

YG0005 R2-D2, fires toy discs and top of body turns 425.00
YG0001 Cobot (R2-D2 robot with Coca-Cola can body) 325.00

RADIOS AND CASSETTE PLAYERS

Kenner

HM0001   HM0003

HM0001 Luke Skywalker AM headset radio 475.00
HM0003 R2-D2 radio 95.00

Micro Games of America
HM0007 C-3PO AM/FM Radio 30.00

HM0006

HM0006 Darth Vader AM/FM Radio..18.00
HM0005 Millennium Falcon cassette player 34.00

Tiger Electronics

HM0004   HM0002

HM0004 R2-D2 cassette player, flat with belt clip.........................24.00
HM0002 R2-D2 Data Droid cassette player 35.00

RECORDS

20th Century Fox

RC10019   RC10003

RC10019 1977 Star Wars radio spots, 30 seconds each, on 7" 33rpm l.p. ..117.00
RC10001 Star Wars Soundtrack, 2 albums 18.00
RC10002 Story of Star Wars..14.00
RC10003 Story of Star Wars, picture disc album 21.00

Buena Vista Records

RC10006   RC10007   RC10008   RC10009

RC10011   RC10012   RC10014   RC10015

RC10004 Adventures in ABC read-along...9.00
RC10005 Adventures in Colors and Shapes read-along...................9.00
RC10006 Droid World read-along..9.00
RC10007 Empire Strikes Back read-along...9.00
RC10008 Ewoks Join the Fight read-along..9.00
RC10009 Planet of the Hoojibs read-along......................................9.00
RC10010 Rebel Mission to Ord Mantell 9.00
RC10011 Return of the Jedi read-along..7.00
RC10012 Star Wars read-along..7.00
RC10013 The Story of Empire Strikes Back...7.00
RC10014 The Story of Return of the Jedi 7.00
RC10015 The Story of ROTJ, Special Edition Picture Disc (Ewok picture on
    record)..16.00
RC10016 The Story of Star Wars..7.00

Kid Stuff
RC10026 Star Wars..5.00

Polydor
RC10021 Empire Strikes Back soundtrack 64.00

RCA
RC10024 Music from John Williams' Close Encounters / SW.......................5.00
RC10017 "What can you get a Wookie for Christmas?" 16.00
RC10020 Christmas in the Stars 65.00
RC10018 Meco plays music from The Empire Strikes Back 4.00
RC10025 Music from Star Wars performed by The Electric Moog Orchestra 5.00
RC10023 Star Wars and other Galactic Funk by Meco 18.00

| RC10026 | RC10021 | Not Listed | RC10018 |

| RC10017 | RC10020 | RC10022 | RC10023 |

RC10027 Star Wars Episode I Soundtrack 9.00
RC10022 Star Wars Theme / Cantina Band by Meco, 45rpm 15.00

REEL-TO-REEL TAPES

RC50002

20th Century Fox
RC50001 Star Wars Soundtrack 11.00
RC50003 SW Soundtrack / Story of SW, boxed set.....................34.00
RC50002 Story of Star Wars...18.00

REMOTE CONTROLLED TOYS

| YH0003 | YH0004 | YH0001 |

Bandpresto
YH0004 Millennium Falcon 23.00
YH0003 R2-D2 ....18.00

Kenner
YH0001 R2-D2 ....28.00

REMOTE CONTROLS

RMC0001

Kash 'N' Gold
RMC0001 Lightsaber, universal w/sound effects 35.00

Telemania
RMC0002 Darth Maul's Sith Infiltrator, universal 40.00

RMC0002

REPLICAS

Don Post
REP0007 Boba Fett Life Size, cast from original props..........................6,000.00
REP0008 Stormtrooper Life Size, cast from original props, limited to 500
    pieces...4,500.00

Icons Authentic Replicas
Lightsabers. Plexiglass display case included. Limited to 10,000 each.
REP0002 Darth Vader's lightsaber 350.00
REP0004 Luke Skywalker's lightsaber 350.00
REP0003 Obi-Wan Kenobi's lightsaber 350.00

Starfighters. Miniature replicas. Plexiglass display case included. Limited to 1,977 each.
REP0005 Tie Fighter 1,500.00
REP0006 X-Wing Fighter..1,500.00

Illusive Originals
REP0001 Han Solo in Carbonite prop replica, limited to 2,500.............1,250.00

Rubies
REP0009 Darth Vader Life Size display figure.........................4,500.00

RINGS

Adam Joseph Industries
JNR0011 X-Wing Pilot...14.00

Factors, Etc.
Set 1.

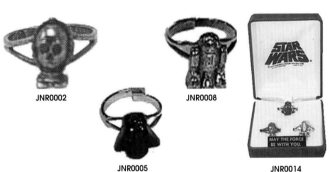

| JNR0002 | JNR0008 |
| JNR0005 | JNR0014 |

JNR0002 C-3PO 8.00
JNR0003 Chewbacca 8.00
JNR0008 R2-D2 ....8.00
JNR0014 Set 1 with display box 30.00

Set 2.
JNR0005 Darth Vader..8.00
JNR0009 Stormtrooper...8.00
JNR0012 X-Wing 8.00
JNR0015 Set 2 with display box 30.00

Wallace Berrie and Co.

| JNR0007 | JNR0010 | JNR0013 |

JNR0006 "May The Force Be With You" 10.00
JNR0001 C-3PO and R2-D2...10.00
JNR0004 Darth Vader..10.00
JNR0007 R2-D2 ....10.00
JNR0010 X-Wing Fighter 10.00
JNR0013 Yoda...10.00

Plastic children's rings from gumball-type vending machines. Red or blue.
JNR0016 Stormtrooper..3.00
JNR0017 Tie Fighter 3.00

ROLE PLAYING GAME

West End Games

RPG0017 #01 A New Hope galaxy guide 14.00
RPG0018 #02 Yavin and Bespin galaxy guide.................................14.00
RPG0019 #03 The Empire Strikes Back galaxy guide 14.00
RPG0020 #04 Alien Races galaxy guide 14.00
RPG0021 #05 Return of the Jedi galaxy guide 14.00
RPG0022 #06 Tramp Freighters galaxy guide 14.00
RPG0023 #07 Mos Eisley galaxy guide 14.00
RPG0024 #08 Scouts galaxy guide 14.00
RPG0025 #09 Fragments from the Rim galaxy guide 14.00
RPG0026 #10 Bounty Hunters galaxy guide 14.00
RPG0027 #11 Criminal Organizations galaxy guide 14.00
RPG0028 #12 Aliens galaxy guide...14.00
RPG0089 Adventure Journal 01 (B-Wing cover) 17.00
RPG0090 Adventure Journal 02 (Rancor cover)........................14.00
RPG0091 Adventure Journal 03 (Stormtrooper cover)............15.00
RPG0092 Adventure Journal 04 (Royal Guard cover) 12.00
RPG0093 Adventure Journal 05 (2-1B cover) 12.00
RPG0094 Adventure Journal 06 (Millennium Falcon cover) ..12.00
RPG0095 Adventure Journal 07 (X-Wing / Tie Fighter cover) 12.00
RPG0096 Adventure Journal 08 (Santa Yoda cover).............12.00
RPG0097 Adventure Journal 09 (Bounty hunters cover)........12.00
RPG0098 Adventure Journal 10 (Hoth battle cover).............12.00
RPG0099 Adventure Journal 11 (Speederbike cover).............12.00
RPG0100 Adventure Journal 12 (Mos Eisley cover) 12.00
RPG0101 Adventure Journal 13 (Star Destroyer cover) 12.00
RPG0102 Adventure Journal 14 (Y-Wing cover) 15.00
RPG0103 Adventure Journal 15 (Pilot Luke cover) 15.00
RPG0043 Battle for the Golden Sun adventure supplement........12.00
RPG0044 Black Ice adventure supplement..................................12.00
RPG0088 Black Sands of Socorro 14.00
RPG0003 Campaign Pack...14.00
RPG0045 Classic Adventures adventure supplement 16.00

RPG0046 Classic Adventures II adventure supplement............15.00
RPG0047 Classic Adventures III adventure supplement..........16.00
RPG0076 Classic Adventures IV adventure supplement..........15.00
RPG0029 Cracken's Rebel Field Guide background book........18.00
RPG0030 Cracken's Rebel Operatives background book........18.00
RPG0031 Creatures of the Galaxy background book................18.00
RPG0048 Crisis on Cloud City adventure supplement..............12.00
RPG0007 Dark Empire Sourcebook 17.00
RPG0008 Dark Force Rising Sourcebook..17.00
RPG0049 Darkstryder Campaign adventure supplement..........14.00
RPG0050 Darkstryder Campaign: Endgame adventure supplement 17.00
RPG0051 Darkstryder Supplement: Kathol Rift adventure supplement ...18.00
RPG0052 Death in the Undercity adventure supplement........12.00
RPG0032 Death Star Technical Companion background book..............18.00
RPG0053 Domain of Evil adventure supplement.........................12.00
RPG0085 Droids..16.00
RPG0054 Flashpoint: Brak Sector adventure supplement........13.00
RPG0033 Galladinium's Fantastic Technology background book........18.00
RPG0006 Gamemasters Handbook, 2nd edition............................24.00
RPG0005 Gamemasters Kit...18.00
RPG0004 Gamemasters Screen 8.00
RPG0077 Gamemasters Screen for Second Edition....................8.00
RPG0080 Gamemasters Screen handbook 24.00
RPG0056 Goroth adventure supplement 12.00
RPG0057 Graveyard of Alderaan adventure supplement 12.00
RPG0009 Han Solo and the Corporate Sector Sourcebook........17.00
RPG0010 Heir to the Empire Sourcebook......................................17.00
RPG0084 Hideouts and Strongholds 18.00
RPG0104 Imperial Double-Cross 18.00
RPG0011 Imperial Sourcebook 17.00
RPG0074 Instant Adventures adventure supplement................14.00
RPG0075 Introductory game rulebook 24.00
RPG0058 Isis Coordinates adventure supplement 12.00
RPG0012 Last Command Sourcebook..17.00
RPG0059 Live Action Adventures adventure supplement........20.00

RPG0017   RPG0018   RPG0019 alt. printings   RPG0021   RPG0022   RPG0024   RPG0089   RPG0090   RPG0091

RPG0092   RPG0093   RPG0094   RPG0095   RPG0096   RPG0097   RPG0098   RPG0099   RPG0100   RPG0101

RPG0102   RPG0103   RPG0043   RPG0088   RPG0003   RPG0045   RPG0046   RPG0047   RPG0076   RPG0029

RPG0030   RPG0031   RPG0007   RPG0008   RPG0049   RPG0050   RPG0032   RPG0085   RPG0006   RPG0005

RPG0060 Mission to Lianna adventure supplement 12.00
RPG0013 Movie Trilogy Sourcebook..17.00
RPG0061 No Disintegrations adventure supplement 20.00
RPG0073 Operation: Elrod background book 12.00
RPG0062 Otherspace adventure supplement 12.00
RPG0063 Otherspace II: Invasion adventure supplement 12.00
RPG0034 Pirates and Privateers background book 18.00
RPG0064 Planet of the Mists adventure supplement 12.00
RPG0035 Planets of the Galaxy Vol. I background book 18.00
RPG0036 Planets of the Galaxy Vol. II background book 18.00
RPG0037 Planets of the Galaxy Vol. III background book 18.00
RPG0038 Platt's Starport Guide background book 25.00
RPG0014 Rebel Alliance Sourcebook..17.00
RPG0065 Riders of the Maelstrom adventure supplement..............12.00
RPG0066 Scavenger Hunt adventure supplement 12.00
RPG0086 Secrets of the Sisar Run 14.00
RPG0039 Shadows of the Empire Planet Guide background book........18.00
RPG0016 Shadows of the Empire Sourcebook 25.00
RPG0040 Star Wars Planet Collection background book..................25.00
RPG0015 Star Wars Sourcebook..17.00
RPG0001 Star Wars: The Role Playing Game primary rules book 22.00
RPG0078 Star Wars: The Role Playing Game primary rules book, 2nd edition 20.00
RPG0002 Star Wars: The Role Playing Game rules companion book.......18.00
RPG0067 Starfall adventure supplement...12.00
RPG0068 Strike Force: Shantipole adventure supplement 12.00
RPG0069 Supernova adventure supplement 13.00
RPG0105 Tapanu Sector - Instant Adventures 18.00
RPG0070 Tatooine Manhunt adventure supplement 12.00
RPG0042 The Abduction adventure supplement...............................14.00
RPG0055 The Game Chambers of Questal adventure supplement.......12.00
RPG0079 The Politics of Contraband adventure supplement 12.00
RPG0083 The Truce at Bakura sourcebook 15.00
RPG0071 Twin Stars of Kira adventure supplement 13.00
RPG0041 Wanted by Cracken background book 18.00
RPG0087 Wretched Hives of Scum and Villainy...............................17.00

Wizards of the Coast
RPG0081 Star Wars Roleplaying Game...35.00
RPG0082 Character Record Sheets 10.00

ROLE PLAYING GAME, TPM

Wizards of the Coast
RPH0003 Character Record Sheets...10.00

RPH0001   RPH0002   RPH0003

RPH0004 Core Rulebook..35.00
RPH0006 Living Force Campaign Pack..20.00
RPH0005 Secrets of Tatooine Campaign Pack..................................20.00
RPH0002 Star Wars: Episode I Adventure Game................................15.00
RPH0001 The Secrets of Naboo Campaign Pack................................20.00

ROLE PLAYING MINIATURES

Guide Books

RPM0004   RPM0005

RPM0004 Star Wars Miniatures Battles 18.00
RPM0005 Star Wars Miniatures Battles Companion 15.00

Miniatures Blister Packed

RPM0084   RPM0028   RPM0051   RPM0031   RPM0079

RPM0020 Aliens of the Galaxy...8.00
RPM0084 Aliens of the Galaxy #2..8.00
RPM0086 Aliens of the Galaxy #3..8.00
RPM0021 AT-AT...12.00
RPM0088 AT-PT...9.00

RPG0004   RPG0077   RPG0056   RPG0009   RPG0010   RPG0084   RPG0011   RPG0074   RPG0075   RPG0059

RPG0073   RPG0062   RPG0035   RPG0036   RPG0037   RPG0014 alt. printings   RPG0066   RPG0086   RPG0068

RPG0015 alt. printings   RPG0001   RPG0078   RPG0069   RPG0070   RPG0055   RPG0079   RPG0083   RPG0087

Role Playing Miniatures

RPM0022 Bantha and Rider...8.00
RPM0023 Bounty Hunters #1..8.00
RPM0024 Bounty Hunters #2..8.00
RPM0025 Bounty Hunters #3..8.00
RPM0027 Darkstryder #1...12.00
RPM0028 Darkstryder #2...12.00
RPM0029 Darkstryder #3...12.00
RPM0083 Darth Vader, Leia, and Luke 8.00
RPM0026 Denizens of Cloud City 8.00
RPM0030 Denizens of Tatooine 8.00
RPM0031 Droids...8.00
RPM0032 Emperor...8.00
RPM0033 Encounter on Hoth.....................................12.00
RPM0034 Ewoks...8.00
RPM0035 Gamorrean Guards.....................................12.00
RPM0036 Heir to the Empire Villains 8.00
RPM0037 Heroes #1: Luke, C-3PO, R2-D2...............8.00
RPM0038 Heroes #2: Chewbacca, Han, Leia 8.00
RPM0039 Hoth Rebels...8.00
RPM0040 Imperial Army Troopers #1........................8.00
RPM0041 Imperial Army Troopers #2........................8.00
RPM0042 Imperial Crew with Heavy Blaster 8.00
RPM0043 Imperial Navy Troopers #1........................8.00
RPM0044 Imperial Navy Troopers #2........................8.00
RPM0045 Imperial Officers..8.00
RPM0046 Imperial Speederbikes..............................12.00
RPM0047 Imperial Troop Pack 18.00
RPM0049 Jabba the Hutt..12.00
RPM0048 Jabba's Servants...10.00
RPM0050 Jedi Knights...8.00
RPM0051 Landspeeder..10.00
RPM0052 Mon Calamari..8.00
RPM0053 Mos Eisley Cantina.....................................11.00
RPM0087 Mos Eisley Cantina Aliens #1....................8.00
RPM0085 Mos Eisley Cantina Aliens #2....................8.00
RPM0054 Mos Eisley Space Station..........................10.00
RPM0055 Nogri...8.00
RPM0056 Pilots and Gunners......................................8.00
RPM0057 Pirates..9.00
RPM0058 Rebel Commanders #1...............................8.00
RPM0059 Rebel Commanders #2...............................8.00
RPM0081 Rebel Commandos #1..................................8.00
RPM0082 Rebel Commandos #2..................................8.00
RPM0060 Rebel Operatives..8.00
RPM0061 Rebel Speeder Bikes...................................10.00
RPM0062 Rebel Troop Pack..18.00
RPM0063 Rebel Troopers #1..8.00
RPM0064 Rebel Troopers #2..8.00
RPM0065 Rebel Troopers #3..8.00
RPM0066 Rebel Troopers #4..8.00
RPM0067 Sandtroopers..8.00
RPM0068 Scout Troopers...8.00
RPM0069 Skywalkers...8.00
RPM0070 Snowspeeder..10.00
RPM0072 Snowtroopers..8.00
RPM0071 Storm Skimmers..10.00
RPM0073 Stormtroopers #1...8.00
RPM0074 Stormtroopers #2...8.00
RPM0075 Stormtroopers #3...8.00
RPM0076 Stormtroopers #4...8.00
RPM0077 Tauntaun and Rider......................................8.00
RPM0078 Users of the Force...8.00
RPM0079 Wookies..8.00
RPM0080 Zero G Troopers..8.00

Miniatures Boxed

RPM0007 RPM0008 RPM0010 RPM0012 RPM0013 RPM0014 RPM0015

RPM0006 A New Hope 15.00
RPM0007 Bounty Hunters 15.00
RPM0008 Empire Strikes Back 15.00
RPM0009 Heroes of the Rebellion 15.00
RPM0010 Imperial Forces..15.00
RPM0011 Imperial Troopers..15.00

RPM0012 Jabba's Palace..15.00
RPM0013 Mos Eisley Cantina.....................................15.00
RPM0014 Rancor Pit..15.00
RPM0015 Rebel Characters...15.00
RPM0016 Rebel Troopers...15.00
RPM0017 Return of the Jedi...15.00
RPM0018 Stormtroopers...15.00
RPM0019 Zero G Assault Troopers............................15.00

Starter Sets

RPM0001 Miniature Battles Starter Set......................35.00
RPM0002 Mos Eisley Starter Set.................................35.00
RPM0003 Vehicle Starter Set.......................................35.00

ROLE PLAYING TOYS

Hasbro

PLS0007 PLS0001

PLS0007 Jedi Braid with holographic Royal Starship and holoprojector..16.00
PLS0001 Jedi Gear 26.00

Kenner

PLS0002 PLS0003

PLS0004

PLS0005 PLS0006

PLS0002 Boba Fett's Armor 34.00
PLS0003 Luke Skywalker's Utility Belt 29.00
PLS0004 Utility Belt: Darth Vader, Canada exclusive..............340.00
PLS0005 Utility Belt: Luke Skywalker, Canada exclusive 365.00
PLS0006 Utility Belt: Princess Leia, Canada exclusive 375.00

ROOM ALERT TOYS

Kenner

YI0001 front and back   YI0002 front and back   YI0003 front and back

YI0001 Boba Fett Room Alert and Laser Target Game 36.00
YI0002 Stormtrooper Room Alert and Laser Target Game 32.00

Tiger Electronics

YI0003 Destroyer Droid Room Alarm...39.00

RUBBER STAMPS

Adam Joseph Industries
R0001 Admiral Ackbar 6.00
R0002 Biker Scout 6.00
R0003 C-3PO 6.00
R0004 Chewbacca 6.00
R0005 Darth Vader 6.00
R0006 Emperor's Royal Guard 6.00
R0007 Gamorrean Guard 6.00
R0008 Kneesaa 3-in-1 .... 8.00
R0009 Millennium Falcon 6.00
R0012 Tie Fighter 6.00
R0013 Wicket 6.00
R0014 Wicket 3-in-1 .... 8.00
R0015 X-Wing Pilot 6.00
R0016 Yoda 6.00

R0001   R0002   R0003   R0004   R0005
R0006   R0007   R0009   R0012   R0013
R0015   R0016   R0014

All Night Media Inc.
R0023 Set of six, clear plastic case with color artwork of stamps 24.00

Disney / MGM
R0024 Star Tours Stamp Set 8.00

Rose Art Industries

R0017   R0018   R0019   R0020   R0021   R0022   R0025

R0017 C-3PO 4.00
R0018 Darth Vader 4.00
R0019 R2-D2 .... 4.00
R0020 Stormtrooper 4.00
R0021 Yoda 6.00
R0022 4 Piece gift set 18.00
R0025 Sticker and Stamper Studio, over 175 pieces 19.00

RUGS

RU0001 C-3PO and R2-D2 area rug 19.00

RU0001   RU0002

RU0002 Podracing, 26"x43" 12.00

RULERS

Butterfly Originals

SUR0001

SUR0001 12" with ROTJ logo and characters on glossy label 10.00
SUR0002 12" with SW logo and ROTJ vehicles and characters 12.00
SUR0003 6" with ROTJ logo and battle scenes 8.00

Helix

SUR0004

SUR0004 12" with stormtroopers pressed on back 18.00

SALT SHAKERS

HOY0001   HOY0002

Sigma
HOY0001 R2-D2 and R5-D4 salt and pepper shakers 185.00
HOY0002 Yoda salt and pepper shakers 195.00

SAND ART

SA0001

Rose Art Industries
SA0001 A New Hope Sand Art 9.00

SANDALS

Clarks
SHC0001 Cosmic Rambler 14.00
SHC0002 Landspeeder 16.00
SHC0003 Solar Racer 12.00
SHC0004 Star Rider 12.00

KidNation
SHC0007 Anakin Skywalker heavy sandals, dark tan 14.00

SHC0008   SHC0005   SHC0010   SHC0012

Sandals

SHC0008 Anakin Skywalker sandals, blue...12.00
SHC0005 Anakin Skywalker, slip-ons 10.00
SHC0009 Darth Maul black sport sandal 12.00
SHC0010 Darth Maul face-bottom sandals...13.00
SHC0011 Darth Maul flip-flops, black 10.00
SHC0012 Darth Maul heavy sandals, black/red 14.00
SHC0006 Droids sandals, blue and silver, elastic back 9.00
SHC0013 Podracing black sport sandal..12.00

SCARVES

Grossman
AS0001 C-3PO 8.00
AS0002 Chewbacca 7.00
AS0003 Darth Vader 7.00
AS0004 R2-D2 ....8.00
AS0005 ROTJ logo 7.00
AS0006 Wicket..7.00

SCHOOL BOXES

SBX0002   SBX0001   SBX0003

Impact, Inc.
SBX0002 "Jedi vs. Sith" Qui-Gonn Jinn, Obi-Wan, Darth Sidious, Darth Maul ..4.00
SBX0001 Jar Jar Binks, sculpted 9.00
SBX0003 Watto, Sebulba, Anakin, and Jar Jar...4.00

SCHOOL KITS

Butterfly Originals

SUS0001

SUS0001 ROTJ School Kit w/Ruler, Pencil, Pencil Bag, Sharpener, and
    Eraser 14.00

Helix
SUS0003 Chewbacca and Han padded front, assorted school supplies,
    large 47.00
SUS0002 Pencil box, pencils, eraser and sharpener 34.00
SUS0004 Star Destroyer padded front, assorted school supplies, small....36.00

Impact, Inc.

SUS0005   SUS0013   SUS0006

SUS0013 Carry-Along School Set, carry case, pencil pouch, 2 pencils, memo
    pad,,pencil sharpener, eraser, glue stick, 12" ruler 8.00
SUS0005 Study Kit, "Jedi vs. Sith" eraser, ruler, pencil sharpener, vinyl zip-
    pered pencil case 9.00
SUS0006 Study Kit, "Tatooine" eraser, ruler, pencil sharpener, vinyl zippered
    pencil case 9.00
SUS0007 Value Pack, "Anakin's Pod" portfolio, theme book, memo pad,
    pencil, zippered pencil case, sharpener, eraser, ruler 14.00
SUS0008 Value Pack, "Jedi vs. Sith" portfolio, theme book, memo pad, pen-
    cil, zippered pencil case, sharpener, eraser, ruler 14.00
SUS0018 Zip Pouch, "Jedi vs. Sith" theme book, memo pad, ruler, pencil,
    sharpener, and sticker sheet 6.00
SUS0017 Zip Pouch, "Tatooine" theme book, memo pad, ruler, pencil,
    sharpener, and sticker sheet 6.00

Q-Stat

SUS0011   SUS0016

SUS0014   SUS0015

SUS0009 Bumper Pack, "Obi-Wan Kenobi" Unlined writing pad, lined
    notepad, crayons, pencil, eraser...12.00
SUS0016 Bumper Pack, "Queen Amidala" Unlined writing pad, lined
    notepad, pencil, eraser 7.00
SUS0010 Fun Pack, Sebulba address book, Anakin writing pad, pencil, eras-
    er 6.00
SUS0011 School Set, "Queen Amidala" writing pad, ruler, pencil sharpener,
    eraser..8.00
SUS0012 Tin Set, "Obi-Wan Kenobi" lined notepad, die-cut eraser, Darth
    Maul pencil sharpener, tin, Star Wars ruler, 2 lightsaber pens 14.00
SUS0015 School set: lightsaber pencil, ruler, Obi-Wan eraser, Darth Maul
    sharpener 7.00
SUS0014 School set: pencil, ruler, eraser, sharpener.....................................5.00

SCISSORS

SUW0001 with close-ups of lenticular images

Butterfly Originals
SUW0001 ROTJ Safety Scissors w/image of Darth Vader/Imperial Shuttle .. 12.00

SCOOTERS

SCT0001

Zap World
SCT0001 Stap Scooter, motorized..950.00

SCRAPBOOKS

SCB0002

HC Ford
SCB0001 Collage of character photos 18.00

Letraset
SCB0002 Collage of character photos 28.00

SCRIPTS

Ballantine
National Public Radio dramatizations.

BKR0001   BKR0008

BKR0002 Star Wars...12.00
BKR0003 Empire Strikes Back................................... 12.00
BKR0001 Return of the Jedi.. 12.00
BKR0008 The Annotated Scripts 25.00
BKR0011 The Empire Strikes Back Notebook, illustrated script 29.00

D.S.P. Publishing, Inc.
BKR0018 SW Trilogy Original Movie Scripts Collector's Edition 40.00

Del Rey

BKR0013   BKR0016   BKR0014   BKR0017   BKR0015   BKR0012

BKR0013 Empire Strikes Back The Illustrated Screenplay 14.00
BKR0016 Empire Strikes Back, Complete Script with Special Edition
    Scenes 22.00
BKR0014 Return of the Jedi The Illustrated Screenplay 14.00
BKR0017 Return of the Jedi, Complete Script with Special Edition
    Scenes 22.00
BKR0015 Star Wars, Complete Script with Special Edition Scenes 22.00
BKR0012 Star Wars, The Illustrated Screenplay 14.00

Lucas Books

BKR0019   BKR0020

BKR0019 Episode I: The Phantom Menace 12.00
BKR0020 Episode I: The Phantom Menace, the Illustrated Screenplay ... 16.00

Premiere
BKR0005 Return of the Jedi...15.00
BKR0004 Return of the Jedi, recalled for typographical errors 75.00
BKR0006 Star Wars...15.00
BKR0007 Star Wars Trilogy, boxed set 50.00
BKR0010 The Empire Strikes Back 15.00
BKR0009 The Empire Strikes Back, recalled for typographical errors 75.00

SEWING CRAFT KITS

CRK0001

Craft Master
CRK0001 Wicket and Friends Sew 'N Show Cards 17.00

SHAMPOO

Grosvenor
TOP0010 Darth Maul figural bottle...12.00

TOP0012 R2-D2 bath and shower foam...12.00

TOP0010   TOB0023   TOP0008   TOP0011   TOP0009
                          front and back   front and back

Minnetonka
TOP0009 Anakin Skywalker bottle with sculpted character cap...............6.00
TOP0011 Anakin Skywalker galactic shampoo.....................................6.00
TOP0008 C-3PO bottle with sculpted character cap 6.00

Omni Cosmetics
Shampoo packaged in figural bottles.

TOP0001   TOP0004   TOP0005   TOP0006   TOP0007

TOP0002 Darth Vader...14.00
TOP0003 Jabba the Hutt...14.00
TOP0004 Luke Skywalker 14.00
TOP0005 R2-D2 ....14.00
TOP0006 Wicket the Ewok 14.00
TOP0007 Yoda 14.00
TOP0001 Battle Scene "refuling station" 8.00

SHEET MUSIC

Fox Fanfare Music
MBS0005 Cantina Band Dan Coates Easy Piano Solo 5.00
MBS0004 Empire Strikes Back Han Solo and the Princess.......................5.00
MBS0003 Empire Strikes Back Medley...5.00
MBS0002 Star Wars Princess Leia's Theme 5.00
MBS0001 SW (Main Title) Dan Coates Piano Solo 5.00
MBS0006 SW (Main Title) Original Piano Solo 5.00
MBS0007 Anakin's Theme, easy piano...5.00
MBS0008 Star Wars Main Theme, easy piano......................................5.00

SHEETS

Bibb Co.
CSH0001 ESB: Boba Fett 22.00
CSH0002 ESB: Boba Fett (J.C. Penney)..22.00
CSH0003 ESB: Darth's Den 20.00
CSH0004 ESB: Ice Planet 16.00
CSH0005 ESB: Lord Vader 20.00
CSH0006 ESB: Lord Vader's Chamber 18.00
CSH0007 ESB: Spectre 16.00
CSH0008 ESB: Yoda..22.00
CSH0009 ROTJ: Jabba the Hutt, Ewoks, etc. 20.00
CSH0010 ROTJ: Logos from all 3 films...16.00
CSH0011 ROTJ: Luke and Darth Vader Duel, AT-ST, etc. 18.00
CSH0012 ROTJ: Star Wars Saga...18.00
CSH0013 SW: Aztec Gold 12.00
CSH0014 SW: Galaxy 10.00
CSH0015 SW: Jedi Knights 12.00
CSH0016 SW: Lord Vader 20.00
CSH0017 SW: Space Fantasy...15.00

SHIRTS

Fan Club
ATS0002 Episode I, denim, long sleeve, 100% cotton 47.00
ATS0001 Episode I, 3-button polo, tan, 60% cotton 44.00

Hanes
ATS0003 20th Anniversary logo on black sweatshirt 28.00

Kids Headquarters
ATS0004 Anakin blue knit shirt, short sleeves.......................................14.00

Shirts

ATS0005 Darth Maul button front red with short black sleeves 14.00
ATS0006 Jedi vs. Sith white with short black sleeves 14.00
ATS0007 Sith Lord black knit shirt, short sleeves 14.00

Pepsi Cola
ATS0008 Episode I, polo..26.00

SHOE LACES

PES0001   PES0002   PES0004   PES0005   PES0006

Stride Rite
PES0007 Ewoks and ROTJ logo with Ewoks, 27" 7.00
PES0001 Ewoks and ROTJ logo with Ewoks, 36" 7.00
PES0008 Return of the Jedi Logo, 27" 5.00
PES0002 Return of the Jedi Logo, 36" 5.00
PES0010 Star War Logo w/Darth Vader helmet, 27" 7.00
PES0004 Star War Logo w/Darth Vader helmet, 36" 7.00
PES0009 Star War Logo, 27" 5.00
PES0003 Star War Logo, 36" 5.00
PES0011 Star Wars Logo with Droids, 27" 8.00
PES0005 Star Wars Logo with Droids, 36" 8.00
PES0012 Star Wars Logo with Spaceships, 27" 8.00
PES0006 Star Wars Logo with Spaceships, 36" 8.00

SHOE LACES TAGS

PEU0001

PEU0001 Stamped Metal w/Logo 16.00

SHOEBAGS

SHO0001   SHO0002   SHO0003

SHO0002 Anakin Skywalker, nylon with drawstring 11.00
SHO0003 Jar Jar Binks, nylon with drawstring 11.00
SHO0001 Queen Amidala, nylon with drawstring 11.00

SHOES

Clarks

SHH0004   SHH0040

SHH0001 C-3PO, any style..28.00
SHH0002 Chewbacca, any style..28.00
SHH0003 Darth Vader Lives, any style 25.00
SHH0004 Darth Vader, any style 28.00
SHH0005 Luke Skywalker, any style...28.00
SHH0006 Princess Leia, any style 28.00
SHH0007 R2-D2, any style 28.00
SHH0040 Reflective, any style...16.00
SHH0008 Stormtrooper, any style...28.00
SHH0009 Tusken Raider, any style 28.00

KidNation

SHH0028   SHH0030

SHH0018 right and left sides

SHH0021 Anakin Skywalker pod racing white x-trainer 17.00
SHH0022 Anakin Skywalker pod racing white, velcro 15.00
SHH0024 Anakin Skywalker water shoes 10.00
SHH0025 Anakin Skywalker water shoes red/blue/black........................10.00
SHH0010 Bespin gantry multi-motion image, black 2-strap velcro, court
    shoes..18.00
SHH0027 Darth Maul athletic black/silver/blue..............................14.00
SHH0028 Darth Maul black hiker with blue trim..............................16.00
SHH0030 Darth Maul black x-trainer with white and silver trim.............17.00
SHH0031 Darth Maul black/silver/blue.......................................14.00
SHH0026 Darth Maul "The Dark Side" athletic, black with white strings....14.00
SHH0011 Darth Vader and his Tie fighter, white/blue/black hightops, vel-
    cro..16.00
SHH0012 Darth Vader repeating pattern, black upper / white under, slip-on
    shoes..10.00
SHH0013 Darth Vader with Imperial insignia hiking boot, black 21.00
SHH0014 Darth Vader with Imperial insignia on toe, black shoes, velcro....15.00
SHH0015 Darth Vader, black shoes, velcro 12.00
SHH0036 EPI logo on black and gray suede court shoe........................14.00
SHH0038 Podracing, white/blue/green..14.00
SHH0039 Star Wars canvas sneakers, black/white 14.00
SHH0017 Stormtrooper, black below trooper, white shoes, velcro...........10.00
SHH0018 Stormtrooper, white shoes, strings.................................12.00
SHH0019 Stormtrooper, white shoes, velcro 11.00

SHOULDER BAGS

Adam Joseph Industries
LH0001 Ewoks 10.00
LH0002 Princess Kneesaa and Wicket..12.00
LH0003 Princess Kneesaa, shaped...12.00
LH0004 Wicket the Ewok 10.00
LH0005 Wicket the Ewok, shaped...12.00

SHOWER CURTAINS

SC0001 front, back, and pattern

Jay Franco and Sons
SC0001 TPM: Space Battle, 70"x72", vinyl 12.00

SIGNS

Norben
7"x9½" self-stick plastic with peel-away backing.
SGN0004 Anakin Skywalker Podracer 4.00

SGN0003   SGN0004   SGN0001

SGN0003 Jedi vs. Sith..4.00

TinSigns International
SGN0001 Poster-D movie artwork, tin........................18.00

Unique
SGN0002 Party Door Sign, 27"x60", Darth Maul, "The Party's Here!" 5.00

SIT-AND-SPINS

Kenner
YK0001 Wicket the Ewok Sit'n Spin 85.00

YK0001

SKATEBOARDS

Brookfield Athletic
SKB0001 Darth Vader and Luke Skywalker
    Duel 45.00

SKB0011

MV Sports
SKB0012 Darth Maul 8"x31"...............................25.00
SKB0011 Jar Jar Binks 8"x28" 25.00

Plan B
SKB0002 Boba Fett 43.00
SKB0005 Boba Fett 30.00
SKB0003 Darth Vader 43.00
SKB0004 Yoda..43.00

Seneca Sports Inc.

SKB0006   SKB0010   SKB0013

SKB0006 C-3PO and R2-D2 5"x22" 14.00
SKB0007 Darth Maul / Sith 8"x31" double-sided decal.....19.00
SKB0013 Darth Vader 24.00
SKB0008 Death Star trench battle (McQuarrie art) 24.00
SKB0009 Podracing / Anakin 8"x31" double-sided decal....19.00
SKB0010 Yoda (McQuarrie art) 24.00

SKATES: ROLLER / IN-LINE

Brookfield Athletic

SKR0001   SKR0002

SKR0001 Darth Vader and Emperor's Royal Guards 85.00
SKR0002 Wicket the Ewok 68.00

Seneca Sports Inc.

SKR0006   SKR0004   SKR0003

SKR0005   SKR0007

SKR0006 Darth Maul in-line skates, gray with red accents 18.00
SKR0007 Imperial Runner Quad Skates, black with Tie-fighter accents ...24.00
SKR0004 R2-D2 in-line youth adjustable skates...............18.00
SKR0003 Rogue Squadron in-line skates, black with red accents 23.00
SKR0005 Anakin Skywalker, podracer accents..................23.00

SKETCHPAD

HC Ford
SBK0001 Collage of character photos.........................14.00

SLAP BANDS

WS0001

Tapper Candies
WS0001 Slap Bands, feature photos of Jedi and Sith, 4-pack.....................4.00

SLEEPING BAGS

Bibb Co.
CSB0001 ESB: Boba Fett (J.C. Penney)........................40.00
CSB0002 ESB: Lord Vader's Chamber 35.00
CSB0003 ESB: Spectre..35.00
CSB0004 ESB: Yoda...45.00
CSB0005 ROTJ: Jabba the Hutt, Ewoks, etc....................35.00
CSB0006 ROTJ: Logos from all 3 films 25.00
CSB0007 ROTJ: Star Wars Adventure 40.00
CSB0008 ROTJ: Star Wars Saga 35.00
CSB0009 SW: Galaxy 35.00

ERO Industries
CSB0013 Anakin Skywalker, podracer..........................22.00
CSB0012 Luke and Darth Vader, TRU exclusive.................20.00
CSB0011 R2-D2 with metallic accents, TPM, 54" long 45.00
CSB0010 Space Battle, TPM...................................22.00

SLIPPERS

Clarks
SHK0004 Star Wars logo......................................12.00

KidNation

SHK0014   SHK0012

SHK0009 Darth Maul with hooded sculpted head on toe of slippers.........8.00
SHK0010 Darth Vader, gray 10.00
SHK0014 Jar Jar Binks with sculpted head on toe of slippers 8.00
SHK0011 Naboo fighter 7.00
SHK0013 Podracing gray, velcro..............................8.00
SHK0012 R2-D2...7.00

Stride Rite
SHK0001 C-3PO and R2-D2.....................................16.00

SHK0003   SHK0005   SHK0008

Slippers

SHK0005 C-3PO and R2-D2 Slipper Socks 8.00
SHK0002 Darth Vader 16.00
SHK0006 Darth Vader Slipper Socks 8.00
SHK0003 Ewoks, any style 12.00
SHK0007 Wicket 6.00
SHK0008 Yoda Slipper Socks 8.00

SNEAKERS

Clarks
SHN0007 "May The Force Be With You" 35.00
SHN0002 C-3PO 35.00
SHN0003 Darth Vader 38.00
SHN0006 Luke Skywalker 38.00
SHN0009 Princess Leia 38.00
SHN0010 R2-D2 ....65.00
SHN0011 Tie Fighter 38.00

Stride Rite
SHN0001 C-3PO and R2-D2 ....50.00
SHN0004 Darth Vader 50.00
SHN0005 Ewoks 46.00
SHN0008 Millennium Falcon 65.00
SHN0012 X-Wing Fighter 65.00

SNOWGLOBES

SG0001

SG0001 Snowspeeder Attacking AT-AT on Hoth 65.00

SOAP

Addis
TOS0012 Baby Ewoks and Wicket 2pk. 23.00
TOS0010 C-3PO and R2-D2 2pk. 23.00
TOS0011 Darth Vader and Luke Skywalker 2pk. 23.00

Cliro
TOS0013 C-3PO liquid in figural bottle 30.00
TOS0016 C-3PO "Soap Model" 18.00
TOS0014 Darth Vader liquid in figural bottle 30.00
TOS0015 R2-D2 liquid in figural bottle 30.00
TOS0017 R2-D2 "Soap Model" 18.00

TOS0016

Minnetonka
Galactic Glycerine Soap, 3.5oz., gift figure inside.

TOS0018   **TOS0022**   **TOS0019**   **TOS0021**

TOS0020   **TOS0023**   **TOS0024**   **TOS0025**

TOS0018 C-3PO 5.00
TOS0022 Chewbacca 5.00
TOS0023 Darth Maul 5.00
TOS0019 Darth Vader 5.00
TOS0024 Jar Jar Binks 5.00
TOS0025 Queen Amidala 5.00
TOS0020 R2-D2 ....5.00
TOS0021 Yoda 5.00

Omni Cosmetics
4oz. soap bars with pressed image of character.

TOS0003   **TOS0004**   **TOS0006 TOS0007**   **TOS0005**
package and soap   package and soap   package and soap

TOS0008   **TOS0009**   **TOS0002**
package and soap   package and soap

TOS0003 C-3PO 6.00
TOS0004 Darth Vader 6.00
TOS0005 Gamorrean Guard 6.00
TOS0006 Luke Skywalker 6.00
TOS0007 Princess Leia 6.00
TOS0008 Wicket the Ewok 6.00
TOS0009 Yoda 6.00
TOS0002 4-pack Leia, Luke, Yoda, and Chewbacca sculpted soap, 1oz.
   ea. 18.00

SOAP DISHES

Jay Franco and Sons

HOQ0002   **HOQ0003**

HOQ0002 Anakin seated in podracer, sculpted 16.00
HOQ0003 Star Wars decal, starfighters 6.00

Sigma

HOQ0001

HOQ0001 Landspeeder soap dish 45.00

SOCKS

British Home Stores
AE0016 Socks and Mug Set 24.00

AE0016

318

Charleston Hosiery

AE0001   AE0002   AE0004   AE0005   AE0007

AE0003 "Darth Vader Lives" Star Wars 18.00
AE0006 Boba Fett Empire Strikes Back 18.00
AE0009 C-3PO and R2-D2 Return of the Jedi 18.00
AE0001 C-3PO Star Wars 18.00
AE0002 Chewbacca Star Wars 18.00
AE0007 Darth Vader Empire Strikes Back 18.00
AE0010 Darth Vader Return of the Jedi 18.00
AE0015 Ewok Return of the Jedi 18.00
AE0011 Gamorrean Guard Return of the Jedi 18.00
AE0012 Jabba the Hutt Return of the Jedi 18.00
AE0017 Princess Kneesaa Return of the Jedi 18.00
AE0014 R2-D2 and Darth Vader Return of the Jedi 18.00
AE0013 R2-D2 and Wicket Return of the Jedi 18.00
AE0025 R2-D2 Empire Strikes Back 18.00
AE0004 R2-D2 Star Wars 18.00
AE0005 Space Battle Star Wars 18.00
AE0027 Stormtrooper Empire Strikes back 18.00
AE0008 Yoda Empire Strikes Back 18.00

Handcraft Mfg. Corp.

AE0018   AE0019   AE0020   AE0021   AE0022   AE0023   AE0024

AE0018 Darth Maul, Jedi duel pose 5.00
AE0021 Darth Maul, lightsaber ignited on white background 5.00
AE0020 Darth Maul, Sith Lord 5.00
AE0019 Darth Maul, Tatooine pose 5.00
AE0022 Jar Jar, face above Star Wars logo 5.00
AE0023 Jar Jar, walking 5.00
AE0024 Story Socks, Battle above Naboo 8.00

Quality Socks

AE0029   AE0031

AE0028 Anakin Skywalker 5.00
AE0029 C-3PO 5.00
AE0030 Darth Maul 5.00
AE0031 R2-D2 ....5.00

SOFTWARE

LucasArts

CS0011 front, CD, and back

CS0006 Star Wars: Behind the Magic for Win95/98 ....35.00
CS0007 Star Wars: Behind the Magic for Win95/98 (French Version) 17.00

Pepsi Cola

CS0011 Essential Guide to Star Wars: Episode I, limited edition 14.00

Simon and Schuster Interactive

CS0008 SW Trilogy Moviebook software on CD-ROM for Macintosh 40.00
CS0009 SW Trilogy Moviebook software on CD-ROM for Windows 40.00

SLC Interactive

CS0010

CS0010 The Art of Drew Struzan multimedia 45.00

Sound Source Interactive

CS0001 Star Wars Audio Clips 35.00
CS0002 Star Wars Audio Clips (special offer) 15.00
CS0003 Star Wars Tyrilogy Entertainment Utility, Limited Edition 25.00
CS0004 Star Wars Visual Clips (Macintosh Only) 45.00
CS0005 Star Wars Visual Clips add-on (special offer) 20.00

SPACE SHOOTERS

Hasbro

TG0004

TG0004 Naboo Fighter target game 20.00

Milton Bradley

TG0001   TG0002   TG0003

TG0003 Battle Belt with 32 foam disks 17.00
TG0002 Imperial (Darth Vader's Tie Fighter) target game 34.00
TG0001 Millennium Falcon target game 34.00

SPONGES

Addis
AR0001 Darth Vader pictured on one side 17.00

SQUAWK BOXES

TSB0004 front and side

Pepsi Cola
TSB0004 C-3PO from TPM, premium 15.00

Tiger Electronics
Authentic sounds plus speed adjustable record/playback.

TSB0001   TSB0002   TSB0003

Squawk Boxes

TSB0001 C-3PO 16.00
TSB0002 Darth Vader 16.00
TSB0003 Millennium Falcon 16.00

STAMP COLLECTING KITS

H.E. Harris and Company
6 Star Wars seals, 10 genuine stamps, 300 hinges.
CLS0003 Ass't 1...45.00
CLS0004 Ass't 2...45.00
CLS0005 Ass't 3 Tatooine Residents 45.00
CLS0006 Ass't 4 Space Ships 45.00
CLS0007 Ass't 5 Cantina Scenes 45.00
CLS0008 Ass't 6 Escape from Death Star 45.00

Kits contain album, 24 Star Wars seals, 35 real stamps, 300 hinges, and magnifier.

CLS0002   CLS0005

CLS0006   CLS0007   CLS0008

CLS0001 SW Postage Stamp Collecting Kit, bagged 30.00
CLS0002 SW Postage Stamp Collecting Kit, boxed 35.00

STAMPS: POSTAGE

Chechenia
PS0020 9-sheet Episode I plus classic trilogy...........6.00

PS0020

Republique Centrafricaine

PS0019

PS0019 3-sheet 600f Star Wars 12.00

Republique Du Mali

PS0021   PS0022   PS0023

PS0023 9-sheet 180f Return of the Jedi 8.00
PS0021 9-sheet 310f Star Wars 8.00
PS0022 9-sheet 320f Empire Strikes Back 8.00

Republique Togolaise
PS0016 1-sheet 2000f Star Wars stamp 11.00

PS0016   PS0017   PS0018

PS0018 9-sheet 190f Return of the Jedi 8.00
PS0017 9-sheet 350f Empire Strikes Back 8.00

SSCA

PS0004 front cover and opened

PS0004 stamp only   PS0005 stamp only   PS0008 stamp only

PS0003 Darth Vader Stamp Wallet, gold 50.00
PS0004 Darth Vader Stamp Wallet, silver 40.00
PS0001 First Day Cover Collection $1.00 stamp on 3 different envelope
    designs with covers 20.00
PS0002 Folder with sheet of nine $1 stamps, and sheet of three triangular $2
    stamps 25.00
PS0005 Stormtrooper Stamp Wallet, gold 50.00
PS0006 Stormtrooper Stamp Wallet, silver 40.00
PS0007 Yoda Stamp Wallet, gold 50.00
PS0008 Yoda Stamp Wallet, silver 40.00

Walsall Security Printers

PS0015   PS0011

PS0013 3-sheet souvenir $2 triangular self-adhesive .999 pure silver foil
    stamps; 3 designs: 1995 video artwork, St. Vincent and Grenadines ...15.00
PS0014 3-sheet souvenir $2 triangular self-adhesive 23 carat gold foil stamps;
    3 designs: 1995 video artwork, St. Vincent and Grenadines 22.00
PS0015 3-sheet souvenir $2 triangular self-adhesive foil stamps; 3 designs:
    1995 video artwork, St. Vincent and Grenadines 5.00
PS0012 6-sheet 35-cent horizontal stamps showing scenes from the movie,
    St. Vincent and Grenadines 3.00
PS0009 9-sheet $1 vertical self-adhesive .999 pure silver foil stamps; 3
    designs: 1995 video artwork, St. Vincent and Grenadines 15.00
PS0010 9-sheet $1 vertical self-adhesive 23 carat gold foil stamps; 3 designs:
    1995 video artwork, St. Vincent and Grenadines 24.00
PS0011 9-sheet $1 vertical self-adhesive foil stamps; 3 designs: 1995 video
    artwork, St. Vincent and Grenadines 7.00

STANDEES

Advanced Graphics
ST0001 Admiral Ackbar 25.00
ST0002 Ben Kenobi 25.00
ST0004 Boba Fett...28.00
ST0006 C-3PO 25.00
ST0009 Chewbacca 25.00
ST0012 Darth Vader w/Lightsaber 25.00
ST0013 Darth Vader w/o Lightsaber 25.00
ST0014 Emperor Palpatine 25.00
ST0015 Emperor's Royal Guard 25.00
ST0016 Han Solo 25.00
ST0017 Han Solo in Carbonite 25.00
ST0018 Han Solo, Stormtrooper Disguise.................25.00
ST0019 Jawa 35.00
ST0020 Luke Skywalker 25.00
ST0021 Princess Leia 25.00
ST0022 Princess Leia, Jabba's Prisoner 25.00
ST0024 R2-D2..25.00
ST0025 Stormtrooper 25.00
ST0026 Tusken Raider 27.00

ST0029 Wicket...25.00
ST0028 Yoda..25.00

Bantam Books
ST0031 C-3PO and Jawas standee promotes Visual Dictionary and Incredible Cross-Sections books.............................45.00

Factors, Etc.
ST0003 Boba Fett..40.00
ST0005 C-3PO...34.00
ST0008 Chewbacca...34.00
ST0010 Darth Vader..34.00
ST0023 R2-D2...34.00

Kellogg
ST0032 Standee promotes C-3PO cereal 65.00

Pizza Hut
ST0030 Darth Vader 6' with lightsaber standee promoting Pepsi during SWSE 18.00

Sales Corp. of America
ST0007 C-3PO and R2-D2...20.00
ST0011 Darth Vader and Emperor's Royal Guard.............20.00
ST0027 Wicket the Ewok...15.00

STANDEES, TPM

20th Century Fox
ST10036 Episode I pre-order standee, approx. 5'............32.00
ST10037 Episode I pre-order standee, countertop 8.00

Advanced Graphics
ST10001 Anakin Skywalker...26.00
ST10002 Anakin Skywalker with talking chip 34.00
ST10003 Battle Droid..29.00
ST10004 C-3PO...26.00
ST10005 C-3PO with talking chip...................................34.00
ST10006 Darth Maul...26.00
ST10007 Darth Maul with talking chip............................34.00
ST10008 Darth Sidious..26.00
ST10009 Darth Sidious with talking chip.........................34.00
ST10010 Jar Jar Binks...26.00
ST10011 Jar Jar Binks with talking chip 34.00
ST10012 Obi-Wan Kenobi...26.00
ST10013 Obi-Wan Kenobi with talking chip....................34.00
ST10014 Queen Amidala...26.00
ST10015 Queen Amidala with talking chip......................34.00
ST10016 Qui-Gon Jinn..26.00
ST10017 Qui-Gon Jinn with talking chip.........................34.00
ST10018 Watto...26.00
ST10019 Watto with talking chip 34.00

DK Publishing
3D paper engineered.
ST10020 Battle Droid..95.00
ST10021 Destroyer Droid...140.00
ST10022 Pit Droid...115.00
ST10023 R2-D2..120.00

Pepsi Cola
ST10028 Darth Maul, Pepsi 27.00
ST10024 Jar Jar Binks, Mountain Dew 27.00
ST10026 Mace Windu, Pepsi 27.00
ST10027 Queen Amidala, Pepsi 27.00
ST10025 Watto, Pepsi 24.00

The Empeiros Group
Table-top standees. Approximately 12" in height.

| ST10029 | ST10030 | ST10031 | ST10032 | ST10033 | ST10034 | ST10035 |

ST10029 Darth Maul 3.00
ST10034 Darth Sidious 3.00

ST10030 Jar Jar Binks...3.00
ST10032 Obi-Wan Kenobi...3.00
ST10031 Queen Amidala...3.00
ST10035 Sebulba...3.00
ST10033 Watto...3.00

STATIONARY

Drawing Board

SUX0002   SUX0003

SUX0001 SW Lap Pack Folder w/Droids on Paper, Plain Envelopes; 10 sheets, 10 envelopes 29.00
SUX0002 SW R2-D2 Die-cut Paper; 18 sheets, 12 envelopes, boxed.........20.00
SUX0003 SW Stationary w/X-Wing on Paper, Battle Envelope; 18 sheets, 12 env, boxed.................................25.00

H.C. Ford
SUX0004 Packaged in shallow window box, several designs 16.00

Letraset
SUX0005 Envelopes, 12-pack, illustrated in front corner, and on rear......12.00

Mead

SUX0006   SUX0007   SUX0008

SUX0006 Boba Fett, C-3PO, Darth Vader, Stormtroopers, and Yoda, 16 envelopes, 15 sheets 8.00
SUX0007 Darth Vader, 16 envelopes, 15 sheets.................7.00
SUX0008 X-Wings, 16 envelopes, 15 sheets......................7.00

STATUES AND BUSTS

Applause

FH0001   FH0039   FH0014   FH0013   FH0005

FH0015   FH0006   FH0024   FH0049

FH0032   FH0033   FH0034   FH0038   FH0025

FH0001 Bounty Hunters, limited to 5,000................................70.00
FH0039 Clash Of The Jedi diarama 42.00
FH0032 Darth Maul..28.00
FH0049 Darth Maul Jedi duel, limited to 20,000 Suncoast exclusive 25.00
FH0002 Darth Vader in Meditation Chamber (FAO Schwarz exclusive), limited to 5,000 ....65.00

Statues and Busts

FH0035 Duel of Fates 46.00
FH0003 Emperor, Darth Vader, Prince Xizor, limited to 5,000.....................70.00
FH0014 Han Solo Release from Carbonite, built-in light, limited to 2,500..145.00
FH0004 Jabba the Hutt with Slave Leia, limited to 5,000 ....70.00
FH0013 Leia's Rescue statuette, Luke, Leia, Han, Chewbacca, limited to 5,000...45.00
FH0005 Luke in Bacta tank, limited to 1,500 ....140.00
FH0033 Obi-Wan Kenobi...25.00
FH0038 Queen Amidala..25.00
FH0034 Qui-Gon Jinn...25.00
FH0025 Qui-Gon Jinn and Obi-Wan Kenobi, lights up............125.00
FH0015 Rancor statueuette, limited to 5,000 ....45.00
FH0006 Sandtrooper and Dewback, limited to 5,000 ....70.00
FH0024 Wampa Attack, limited to 3,000.......................75.00

Attakus
Each cast limited to 1,500 pieces.

FH0045   FH0043   FH0044   FH0066   FH0041

FH0040   FH0042   FH0067   FH0068

FH0040 Boba Fett...275.00
FH0066 C-3PO 365.00
FH0041 Darth Maul...270.00
FH0067 Darth Vader...365.00
FH0069 Emperor Palpatine 365.00
FH0070 Emperor's Royal Guard 365.00
FH0042 Han Solo in Carbonite....................................235.00
FH0071 Luke Skywalker..365.00
FH0045 Princess Leia...270.00
FH0043 R2-D2..215.00
FH0068 Stormtrooper 365.00
FH0044 Yoda..230.00

Bowen Designs Inc.

FH0046   FH0047

FH0017 Boba Fett 13½" bronze, limited to 50............3,400.00
FH0046 Chewbacca, 19½" bronze, ltd. to 50 ....3,000.00
FH0047 Darth Vader, 14½" bronze, ltd. to 100 ....3,000.00
FH0023 Rancor, 15" bronze, limited to 50...............3,000.00

Cinemacast

FH0012   FH0050   FH0020

FH0012 Darth Vader, limited to 10,000......................195.00
FH0050 Luke and Leia, movie poster pose....................195.00
FH0020 Luke and Leia, movie poster pose, pewter............250.00

Illusive Originals
FH0007 Admiral Ackbar, bust maquette, limited to 10,000 ....95.00
FH0008 Boba Fett bust maquette, limited to 10,000.............325.00
FH0009 Chewbacca maquette, limited to 7,500 ....236.00
FH0010 Jabba the Hutt maquette, limited to 5,000 ....275.00

FH0008   FH0009   FH0010   FH0011

FH0016 Rancor maquette, limited to 9,500 ....540.00
FH0011 Yoda maquette, limited to 9,500 ....475.00

Kellogg
Plastic statue with mini scroll.

FH0051 FH0052 FH0053 FH0054 FH0055 FH0058 FH0060

FH0057 Anakin Skywalker...4.00
FH0052 Boss Nass..4.00
FH0059 C-3PO 4.00
FH0054 Darth Maul...4.00
FH0060 Darth Sidious..4.00
FH0053 Jar Jar Binks..4.00
FH0056 Obi-Wan Kenobi...4.00
FH0051 Queen Amidala..4.00
FH0055 Qui-Gon Jinn...4.00
FH0058 R2-D2..4.00

Legends in 3-Dimensions

FH0021   FH0027   FH0028

FH0028 Boba Fett bust, limited to 4000 ....210.00
FH0026 Emperor Palpatine bust, limited 150.00
FH0021 Gamorrean Guard, limited to 3,000...................195.00
FH0027 Greedo bust, limited 160.00

Pepsi Cola

FH0064   FH0065

FH0063 Anakin Skywalker, life sized 2,300.00
FH0064 Darth Maul, life sized 2,300.00
FH0019 Ewok, limited to 3,500 ....735.00
FH0065 Jar Jar Binks, life sized.........................2,300.00

Reds, Inc.

FH0036

FH0036 Darth Vader 3', pre-painted 830.00

Royal Tara
Limited to 1,000 pieces, with C.O.A.
FH0061 Luke Skywalker, autographed C.O.A. 350.00
FH0062 Obi-Wan Kenobi with Bohemian crystal lightsaber....500.00

FH0061   FH0062

FH0022 Boba Fett, fiberglass, life-sized 4,500.00
FH0048 Watto life-sized 510.00
FH0037 Yoda life-sized, some given away to promote EP1 video release at Blockbuster...510.00

STEINS

MST0010 sides, front, and box

Avon
MST0010 SW:SE Luke vs. Vader with hinged pewter lid 65.00

Dram Tree

MST0008 MST0009 MST0007

MST0008 Boba Fett, with hinged lid, topped with pewter Boba Fett figure, limited to 3000 pieces...85.00
MST0007 Darth Vader, with hinged lid, topped with pewter Darth Vader figure, limited to 1,977 pieces...115.00
MST0003 Empire Strikes Back, Luke carrying Yoda ceramic relief stein....25.00
MST0005 Return of the Jedi, Jabba's Palace ceramic relief stein...........25.00
MST0001 Star Wars, Millennium Falcon cockpit ceramic relief stein.........25.00
MST0009 Yoda solid pewter with lid, limited to 3,000 pieces.....................85.00

Metallic Impressions
Steins include hinged pewter lid.

MST0004 right and left sides

MST0002 Star Wars 35.00
MST0004 Empire Strikes Back 35.00
MST0006 Return of the Jedi...35.00

STENCILS

SSC0001   SSC0005

SSC0001 C-3PO 8.00
SSC0002 Darth Vader's Tie Fighter 8.00
SSC0003 Death Star 8.00
SSC0004 Landspeeder 8.00
SSC0005 Millennium Falcon 8.00
SSC0006 R2-D2 ....8.00
SSC0007 Star Destroyer 8.00
SSC0008 Tie Fighter 8.00
SSC0009 X-Wing 8.00

SSC0010 Y-Wing 8.00

STICKERS

3D Arts
6"x6" holographic stickers.
SV0337 C-3PO and R2-D2 ....4.00
SV0338 Darth Vader 4.00
SV0339 Millennium Falcon 4.00
SV0340 X-Wing Fighter 4.00

A.H. Prismatic
Holographic stickers.
SV0045 9 Stickers; Uncut Sheet...24.00
SV0046 AT-AT 2.00
SV0047 B-Wing 2.00
SV0048 Darth Vader 2.00
SV0049 Darth Vader's Tie Fighter 2.00
SV0050 Imperial Cruiser 2.00
SV0051 Millennium Falcon 2.00
SV0052 Millennium Falcon w/SW logo...2.00
SV0053 Tie Interceptor...2.00
SV0054 X-Wing Fighter 2.00

Butterfly Originals
Puffed stickers.
SV0358 ROTJ Bib Fortuna, Jabba the Hutt, Lando as Guard, Gamorrean, Leia as Boushh 8.00
SV0016 ROTJ Darth Vader, Luke, Star Destroyer, Tie Fighter, Emperor, Stormtrooper, Millennium Falcon 8.00
SV0028 ROTJ Princess Leia, Han Solo, Lando Calrissian, Rancor, Wicket, Imperial Shuttle 8.00
SV0030 ROTJ R2-D2, Jabba the Hutt, Salacious Crumb, C-3PO, Chewbacca, Yoda 8.00

Disney / MGM
SV0331 "Battle Station", Millennium Falcon...3.00
SV0056 "Commander Rebel Alliance", Luke Skywalker 3.00
SV0057 "Headquarters - X-Wing Fighting Sqaudron" 3.00
SV0058 "Imperial Lord - Darth Vader" 3.00
SV0059 "Moon of Endor", Ewok village 3.00
SV0055 C-3PO, R2-D2, and MGM logos 3.00
SV0060 Star Tours logo, glow-in-the-dark 4.00

SV0047 SV0048 SV0054 SV0358 SV0403

SV0039 SV0038 SV0041 SV0043

SV0025 SV0033 SV0034

SV0334 SV0384 SV0019 SV0380 SV0002

Stickers

Drawing Board

SV0004 ESB Heroes, Perk-up 6.00
SV0005 ESB Heroes, Puffed 8.00
SV0006 ESB Villains, Perk-up 6.00
SV0007 ESB Villains, Puffed 8.00
SV0403 EWOKS 7 individual stickers 6.00
SV0039 EWOKS 8 individual stickers 8.00
SV0038 EWOKS 8 individual stickers; 4 Princess Kneesa, 4 Wicket..............8.00
SV0040 EWOKS 9 individual Scenes, Perk-up 6.00
SV0009 ROTJ Admiral Ackbar, prismatic 3.00
SV0010 ROTJ AT-ST, prismatic 3.00
SV0011 ROTJ Bib Fortuna, Lando, C-3PO, Jabba, Darth Vader, Royal Guard, R2-D2, Princess Leia, Max Rebo Band, Perk-up 8.00
SV0012 ROTJ Biker Scout, Paploo, Wicket, Klaatu, Chewbacca, Gamorrean Guard, Han, Luke, Yoda, Perk-up 8.00
SV0013 ROTJ Boba Fett, prismatic 4.00
SV0014 ROTJ B-Wing, prismatic 4.00
SV0015 ROTJ C-3PO, prismatic large 9.00
SV0043 ROTJ Chewbacca, Darth Vader, R2-D2, C-3PO, Luke, Yoda, X-Wing, Cloud Card, Boba Fett, Han Solo 6.00
SV0017 ROTJ Darth Vader, prismatic large 8.00
SV0018 ROTJ Death Star, prismatic 3.00
SV0020 ROTJ Emperor's Royal Guard, prismatic large 8.00
SV0021 ROTJ Ewoks, prismatic 4.00
SV0022 ROTJ Han Solo, prismatic 3.00
SV0023 ROTJ Jabba the Hutt, prismatic 3.00
SV0024 ROTJ Jabba the Hutt, prismatic large 8.00
SV0025 ROTJ Luke, R2-D2, Chewbacca, Leia, Paploo, X-Wing, Emperor, C-3PO, Wicket, Ackbar, Millennium Falcon, perk-up 8.00
SV0026 ROTJ Millennium Falcon and X-Wing, prismatic large 10.00
SV0027 ROTJ Millennium Falcon, prismatic 4.00
SV0029 ROTJ Princess Leia, prismatic large 8.00
SV0031 ROTJ R2-D2, prismatic large 9.00
SV0032 ROTJ Shuttle Tyderium, prismatic large 8.00
SV0033 ROTJ Shuttle, Death Star, B-Wing, Falcon, Logo, Speeder Bike, X-Wing, Tie Fighter, AT-ST, Perk-up 8.00
SV0034 ROTJ Stormtrooper, Gamorrean Guard, Boba Fett, Slave I, Bib Fortuna, Tie Fighter, Jabba, Royal Guard, Vader, AT-ST, Puffed..............8.00
SV0035 ROTJ Stormtrooper, prismatic 3.00
SV0041 ROTJ Wicket the Ewok, 8 individual scenes, Perk-up 6.00
SV0036 ROTJ Wicket, prismatic large 8.00
SV0037 ROTJ Yoda, prismatic large 8.00

Glow Zone

SV0002 Six EPI Glo Stickers: Anakin, Qui-Gon, C-3PO, R2-D2, Jar Jar, Queen Amidala 6.00
SV0380 Six EPI Glo Stickers: Darth Maul, Obi-Wan, Trade Federation Fighter, Naboo Fighter, Sebulba, Anakin 6.00

Hallmark

SV0334 Kids Stickers: Luke, Leia, Han, Vader, Logo, Yoda, C-3PO, R2-D2, Chewbacca, Ben. 4 Sheets 3.00

Heartline

SV0384 Episode I, 9 stickers, 4 sheets 4.00

Hi-C

SV0019 ROTJ double sticker sheet, folded. Hi-C premium..........................7.00

Kenner

SV0061 Fantastic Sticker Maker Star Wars refill kit, forty photos and machine tape refill 12.00

Panini

SV0063 .s01 Boba Fett and C-3PO.......................................1.35
SV0064 .s02 Han Solo (twice)...1.35
SV0065 .s03 Emperor and Stormtrooper...............................1.35
SV0066 .s04 Luke and R2...1.35
SV0067 .s05 Luke and Wicket...1.35
SV0068 .s06 Jawas and Leia...1.35
SV0069 .s07 Boba Fett and Darth Vader................................1.35
SV0070 .s08 Slave Leia, Leia, and saber light 1.35
SV0071 .s09 Chewbacca, Tusken Raider, and light 1.35
SV0072 .s10 Yoda and Darth 1.35
SV0073 .s11 Stormtrooper and Royal Guard 1.35
SV0074 .s12 Hammerhead 1.35
SV0075 .s13 Cantina Aliens 1.35
SV0076 .s14 Devaronian and Wolfman..................................1.35
SV0077 .s15 Greedo and Walrusman faces...........................1.35
SV0078 .s16 Falcon...1.35
SV0079 .s17 AT-AT and Explosion..1.35

SV0080 .s18 Landspeeder and saber light..............................1.35
SV0081 .s19 AT-ST and saber lights.......................................1.35
SV0082 .s20 Explosion and saber lights..................................1.35
SV0083 .s21 Saber blade and Explosion.................................1.35
SV0084 .s22 Explosion and saber light...................................1.35
SV0085 .s23 Saber and Explosion..1.35
SV0086 .s24 Explosion and saber light...................................1.35
SV0087 .s25 Star Destroyer..1.35
SV0088 .s26 Vader's Tie...1.35
SV0089 .s27 B-Wing...1.35
SV0090 .s28 X-Wing...1.35
SV0091 .s29 Desert skiff and saber light.................................1.35
SV0092 .s30 Snowspeeder...1.35
SV0093 .s31 Tie Bomber...1.35
SV0094 .s32 Tie and laser shots...1.35
SV0095 .s33 Shuttle and saber light.......................................1.35
SV0096 .s34 A-Wing...1.35
SV0097 .s35 Y-Wing...1.35
SV0098 .s36 Sandcrawler..1.35
SV0099 001 Darth Vader...0.65
SV0100 002 The Emperor..0.65
SV0101 003 Jabba the Hutt...0.65
SV0102 004 Boba Fett..0.65
SV0103 005 Into the belly of the Star Destroyer.....................0.65
SV0104 006 Leia gives R2 a message.....................................0.65
SV0105 007 Darth confronts Leia..0.65
SV0106 008 Top 1/2 sandcrawler..0.65
SV0107 009 Bottom 1/2 sandcrawler.......................................0.65
SV0108 010 Luke attacked by Tusken Raider..........................0.65
SV0109 011 Viewing the message from Leia............................0.65
SV0110 012 Practicing with the new lightsaber.......................0.65
SV0111 014 C-3PO and Luke...0.65
SV0112 015 Darth interrogates Leia..0.65
SV0113 016 Landspeeder enters Mos Eisley...........................0.65
SV0114 018 Cantina alien...0.65
SV0115 019 New Mos Eisley scene...0.65
SV0116 020 Cantina Band...0.65
SV0117 021 1/2 Cantina alien...0.65
SV0118 023 1/2 Millennium Falcon...0.65
SV0119 025 Falcon leaving Mos Eisley...................................0.65
SV0120 026 1/2 scene Chewbacca...0.65
SV0121 027 1/2 scene Luke..0.65
SV0122 029 Leia and Darth...0.65
SV0123 030 Obi-Wan Kenobi...0.65
SV0124 031 R2 and C-3PO..0.65
SV0125 032 Luke and Leia prepare to swing...........................0.65
SV0126 033 Leia with blaster..0.65
SV0127 034 Obi-Wan..0.65
SV0128 035 1/2 scene Darth duel...0.65
SV0129 036 1/2 scene Obi-Wan duel.......................................0.65
SV0130 037 Chewbacca and Han..0.65
SV0131 038 Han at Falcon's guns...0.65
SV0132 039 Approaching Death Star (falcon)..........................0.65
SV0133 040 X-Wings..0.65
SV0134 041 Ties in Death Star chasm.....................................0.65
SV0135 042 Death Star laser...0.65
SV0136 043 Leia and rebel observe the battle.........................0.65
SV0137 044 C-3PO and R2 spiffed up......................................0.65
SV0138 045 Awards Ceremony..0.65
SV0139 046 Luke on Tauntaun...0.65
SV0140 047 Hanging in a Wampa's Lair...................................0.65
SV0141 048 Han finds Luke...0.65
SV0142 049 Luke with Binoculars on Hoth..............................0.65
SV0143 050 R2 and C-3PO in Hoth tunnel...............................0.65
SV0144 051 Han on Tauntaun..0.65
SV0145 052 Luke in Bacta tank...0.65
SV0146 053 Leia...0.65
SV0147 054 Chewbacca..0.65
SV0148 055 Probot...0.65
SV0149 056 Leia behind battle screen.....................................0.65
SV0150 057 Han with blaster on Hoth......................................0.65
SV0151 059 Hoth rebels prepare for battle..............................0.65
SV0152 060 Hoth battle in the trenches..................................0.65
SV0153 061 AT-AT..0.65
SV0154 062 Luke in his snowspeeder.....................................0.65
SV0155 063 1/3 snowspeeder battle scene..............................0.65
SV0156 064 1/3 AT-ATs in battle scene...................................0.65
SV0157 065 1/3 AT-ATs in battle scene...................................0.65
SV0158 066 1/2 AT-AT crashes...0.65
SV0159 067 1/2 AT-AT crashes...0.65
SV0160 068 C-3PO in front of famous danger door...................0.65

SV0161 069 Snowtroopers set up 0.65	SV0215 127 Desert skiff 0.65
SV0162 070 Darth 0.65	SV0216 128 Luke battles on skiff 0.65
SV0163 072 Luke on Dagobah 0.65	SV0217 129 Taking aim at the skiff 0.65
SV0164 073 Yoda 0.65	SV0218 130 Leia frees herself 0.65
SV0165 074 R2 observes Yoda's hut 0.65	SV0219 131 Boba Fett 0.65
SV0166 075 Luke and Yoda 0.65	SV0220 132 Han above the Sarlacc 0.65
SV0167 076 Yoda and Luke in his hut 0.65	SV0221 133 Rebel gathering 0.65
SV0168 078 Millennium cockpit 0.65	SV0222 134 Shuttle cockpit 0.65
SV0169 079 Front view cockpit 0.65	SV0223 136 Leia meets Wicket 0.65
SV0170 080 Into the asteroid field 0.65	SV0224 137 1/2 scene Endor battle 0.65
SV0171 081 Above the asteroid 0.65	SV0225 138 1/2 scene Endor battle 0.65
SV0172 083 Bounty hunters 0.65	SV0226 139 Darth 0.65
SV0173 084 1/2 Falcon at Cloud City 0.65	SV0227 140 Royal Guard 0.65
SV0174 086 Leia in Cloud City 0.65	SV0228 143 Darth 0.65
SV0175 087 Walking in Cloud City corridor 0.65	SV0229 144 Falcon and Shuttle in docking bay 0.65
SV0176 088 Lando and Cloud City workers 0.65	SV0230 146 Darth and Luke before throne 0.65
SV0177 089 Lobot and Stormtroopers 0.65	SV0231 147 1/3 scene Darth 0.65
SV0178 090 Chewbacca and bits of C-3PO 0.65	SV0232 148 1/3 scene sabers 0.65
SV0179 091 Han fires at Darth 0.65	SV0233 149 1/3 scene Luke 0.65
SV0180 092 Darth Vader 0.65	SV0234 150 1/2 Death Star 0.65
SV0181 093 1/2 frozen Han 0.65	SV0235 151 1/2 Death Star 0.65
SV0182 094 1/2 frozen Han 0.65	SV0236 152 1/2 scene Darth 0.65
SV0183 095 Probot 0.65	SV0237 153 1/2 scene Luke 0.65
SV0184 096 IG-88 ....0.65	SV0238 154 1/2 scene Luke 0.65
SV0185 097 Medical droid 0.65	SV0239 155 1/2 scene Emperor 0.65
SV0186 098 Lobot 0.65	SV0240 156 Nien and Lando in cockpit 0.65
SV0187 099 Darth, Boba and Lando 0.65	SV0241 A Singer at Jabba's palace 0.75
SV0188 100 "It's a trap!" 0.65	SV0242 B Bib Fortuna 0.75
SV0189 101 Luke in reactor tunnel 0.65	SV0243 C Tusken Raider 0.75
SV0190 102 Luke before window 0.65	SV0244 D Mon Calamari 0.75
SV0191 103 1/3 scene Darth 0.65	SV0245 E Salacious Crumb 0.75
SV0192 104 1/3 scene Lightsabers 0.65	SV0246 F Ewok 0.75
SV0193 105 1/3 scene Luke 0.65	SV0247 G Gamorrean Guard 0.75
SV0194 106 Medical frigate 0.65	SV0248 H Yak Face 0.75
SV0195 107 Cloud car 0.65	SV0249 I Wicket 0.75
SV0196 108 Rebel blockade runner 0.65	SV0250 J Cantina Alien 0.75
SV0197 109 Slave I 0.65	SV0251 K Band Member (Jabba's palace) 0.75
SV0198 110 Falcon 0.65	SV0252 L Max Rebo 0.75
SV0199 111 Sail Barge 0.65	SV0253 M Jawas 0.75
SV0200 112 Mon Cal ship 0.65	SV0254 N Bantha 0.75
SV0201 113 Speeder bike 0.65	SV0255 O Hammerhead 0.75
SV0202 114 R2 and C-3PO at Jabba's door 0.65	SV0256 P No Description Available 0.75
SV0203 115 Boushh 0.65	SV0257 Q Rancor 0.75
SV0204 116 Bib and Boushh 0.65	SV0258 R Cantina band 0.75
SV0205 117 Frozen Han 0.65	SV0259 S No Description Available 0.75
SV0206 118 Boushh before a frozen Han 0.65	SV0260 T Ronto in Mos Eisley 0.75
SV0207 119 Unfreezing 0.65	SV0261 U Cantina alien 0.75
SV0208 120 Lando as Skiff Guard captures Leia 0.65	SV0262 V Yoda 0.75
SV0209 121 Jabba gives Leia a "kiss" 0.65	SV0263 W Nien Nunb 0.75
SV0210 122 Leia before Jabba on throne 0.65	SV0264 X Garindan 0.75
SV0211 123 Luke before Jabba 0.65	
SV0212 124 1/2 scene Rancor's claw 0.65	**Panini / Skybox**
SV0213 125 1/2 scene Rancor 0.65	SV0265 01 Stormtroopers (SE) 0.25
SV0214 126 Sail Barge 0.65	SV0266 02 1/2 - C-3PO 0.25

SV0265	SV0266	SV0267	SV0268	SV0269	SV0270	SV0271	SV0272	SV0273	SV0274	SV0275	SV0276
SV0277	SV0278	SV0279	SV0280	SV0281	SV0282	SV0283	SV0284	SV0285	SV0286	SV0287	SV0288
SV0289	SV0290	SV0291	SV0292	SV0293	SV0294	SV0295	SV0296	SV0297	SV0298	SV0299	SV0300

Stickers

SV0301 SV0302 SV0303 SV0304 SV0305 SV0306 SV0307 SV0308 SV0309 SV0310 SV0311 SV0312

SV0313 SV0314 SV0315 SV0316 SV0317 SV0318 SV0319 SV0320 SV0321 SV0322 SV0323 SV0324

SV0325 SV0326 SV0327 SV0328 SV0329

SV0267 03 1/2 - R2 .... 0.25
SV0268 04 1/2 - Luke with Saber 0.25
SV0269 05 1/2 - Obi-Wan Watching 0.25
SV0270 06 Luke and Obi-Wan 0.25
SV0271 07 Entering Mos Eisley 0.25
SV0272 08 Leia and Darth 0.25
SV0273 09 Firing in the Detention Block 0.25
SV0274 10 Cantina Aliens 0.25
SV0275 11 Blue Cantina Aliens 0.25
SV0276 12 Chewbacca at the Bar 0.25
SV0277 13 Falcon 0.25
SV0278 14 Leia and Darth 0.25
SV0279 15 Falcon Cockpit 0.25
SV0280 16 Falcon Interior 0.25
SV0281 17 Han, Chewbacca, Obi-Wan and Luke Meet 0.25
SV0282 18 1/2 - Obi-Wan Releasing Tractor Beam 0.25
SV0283 19 1/2 - Obi-Wan Releasing Tractor Beam 0.25
SV0284 20 Obi-Wan 0.25
SV0285 21 Darth and Obi-Wan Duel 0.25
SV0286 22 Han and Chewbacca 0.25
SV0287 23 Han 0.25
SV0288 24 Leia Watches the Battle 0.25
SV0289 25 C-3PO 0.25
SV0290 26 Death Star Beam 0.25
SV0291 27 Death Star Gunner 0.25
SV0292 28 R2 and C-3PO 0.25
SV0293 29 Awards Ceremony 0.25
SV0294 30 Luke in Wampa Lair 0.25
SV0295 31 Into the Tauntaun 0.25
SV0296 32 Bacta 0.25
SV0297 33 Battle on Hoth 0.25
SV0298 34 Droids in Hoth Hallway 0.25
SV0299 35 AT-ATs artwork 0.25
SV0300 36 Darth 0.25
SV0301 37 Falcon Cockpit 0.25
SV0302 38 Falcon in Asteroid Field 0.25
SV0303 39 1/2 - Chewbacca 0.25
SV0304 40 1/2 - Chewbacca 0.25
SV0305 41 X-Wing Approaches Dagobah 0.25
SV0306 42 R2 as Voyeur 0.25
SV0307 43 Luke in the Cave 0.25
SV0308 44 Falcon at Cloud City 0.25
SV0309 45 Leia, Han, Chewbacca and Lando 0.25
SV0310 46 1/2 - Stormtroopers 0.25
SV0311 47 1/2 - Stormtroopers with Lobot 0.25
SV0312 48 Han Fires at Vader 0.25
SV0313 49 1/2 - Vader 0.25
SV0314 50 1/2 - Vader 0.25
SV0315 51 Torturing Han 0.25
SV0316 52 Vader talks to Fett 0.25
SV0317 53 Leia Led Away 0.25
SV0318 54 Luke and Vader Duel 0.25
SV0319 55 Han in Carbonite (and Lando) 0.25
SV0320 56 R2 and C-3PO 0.25
SV0321 57 A Captured Chewbacca 0.25
SV0322 58 Jabba, Leia, and Bib 0.25
SV0323 59 Desert Skiff 0.25
SV0324 60 Luke Battles on Skiff 0.25
SV0325 61 War Room 0.25
SV0326 62 Shuttle Cockpit (fly casual) 0.25
SV0327 63 Endor 0.25
SV0328 64 Wicket and Leia 0.25
SV0329 65 AT-ST fires on Bunker 0.25
SV0330 66 Emperor 0.25
SV0001 SW 66 stickers w/album 18.00

Panini / Topps

SV0008 ROTJ 180 stickers w/album 27.00

Party Express

SV0335 Logo, (2) Tie Interceptors, (2) X-Wings, Millennium Falcon, Deathstar, and Imperial Cruiser 3.00

Pizza Hut

Stickers are 2" diameter.

SV0396

SV0342

SV0398

SV0397

SV0343

SV0399

SV0396 Anakin Skywalker 1.50
SV0342 Darth Maul 1.50
SV0398 Jar Jar Binks 1.50
SV0397 Nute Gunray 1.50
SV0343 Queen Amidala 1.50
SV0399 Ree Yees Senator 1.50

Rose Art Industries

SV0044

SV0332

SV0333

SV0333 Fun With Stickers 7.00
SV0044 Sticker Studio, over 200 stickers 7.00
SV0062 Sticker Value Pack, over 145 stickers 5.00
SV0332 Super Sticker and Tattoo Station with case 11.00

Sandylion

SV0393 06-sticker sheet, Obi-Wan Kenobi 4.00

SV0368 SV0369 SV0370 SV0371 SV0372 SV0373 SV0375 SV0376 SV0377 SV0378 SV0379

SV0346 SV0347 SV0348 SV0349 SV0350 SV0351

SV0352 SV0353 SV0354 SV0355 SV0356 SV0357

SV0375 07-sticker sheet, Darth Maul...4.00
SV0376 08-sticker sheet, Qui-Gon Jinn 4.00
SV0392 09-sticker sheet, Jar Jar Binks 4.00
SV0395 09-sticker sheet, Queen Amidala..4.00
SV0378 10-sticker sheet, Heroes, 2 sheets per pack 8.00
SV0379 10-sticker sheet, Space Battle..4.00
SV0377 11-sticker sheet, Villains, 2 sheets per pack.....................8.00
SV0368 12-sticker sheet, Podracing..4.00
SV0394 21-sticker sheet, Create-A-Sticker Scene, starfghters and explo-
    sions...5.00
SV0369 Collector Series 1 "Space Battle": Starfighter Attack, Royal Starship,
    Naboo Starfighter 3.00
SV0370 Collector Series 2 "Ground Battle": Jar Jar Binks, Battle Droid, Fam-
    baa 3.00
SV0371 Collector Series 3 "Podrace": Anakin Skywalker, Sebulba, Podrace
    Explosion...3.00
SV0372 Collector Series 4 "Jedi": Qui-Gon Jinn, Obi-Wan Kenobi, Jedi vs.
    Sith..3.00
SV0373 Collector Series 5 "Villains": Darth Sidious, Darth Maul, Nute Gun-
    ray 3.00
SV0374 Collector Series 6 "Droids": R2-D2, Destroyer Droid, C-3PO 3.00
SV0341 Episode I Sticker Extravaganza..4.00

Vendpack stickers for Episode I.
SV0346 01: Naboo Space Battle 2.00
SV0347 02: Darth Maul 2.00
SV0348 03: Anakin Skywalker..2.00
SV0349 04: Battle Droid 2.00
SV0350 05: Anakin's Podracer...2.00
SV0351 06: Watto 2.00
SV0352 07: Obi-Wan Kenobi 2.00
SV0353 08: R2-D2...2.00
SV0354 09: Qui-Gon Jinn and Obi-Wan Kenobi..............................2.00
SV0355 10: Queen Amidala...2.00
SV0356 11: Jar Jar Binks 2.00
SV0357 12: Naboo Royal Starship 2.00

Star Wars Insider
SV0345 "See You At Star Wars Celebration." 3"x5" promo..........................2.00

Topps
SV0042 ESB Probot, Chewbacca, Stormtrooper, R2-D2, Yoda,
    C-3PO, Boba Fett, and Large Vader, puffed.....................7.00

Vending Supply
Die-cut stickers with prism background.

SV0042

SV0385 SV0405 SV0406 SV0386 SV0387 SV0388

SV0389 SV0390 SV0359 SV0360 SV0361 SV0362

SV0363 SV0364 SV0365 SV0366 SV0367

SV0385 C-3PO 2.00
SV0405 Darth Vader 2.00
SV0406 Death Star and Shuttle Tyderium...2.00
SV0386 Jabba the Hutt 2.00
SV0387 R2-D2..2.00
SV0388 Wicket the Ewok..2.00
SV0389 X-Wing Fighter / Millennium Falcon 2.00
SV0390 Yoda Jedi Master 2.00

Stickers with prism background.
SV0359 Ben Kenobi 3.00
SV0360 C-3PO 3.00
SV0361 Darth Vader 3.00
SV0362 Emperor's Royal Guard 3.00
SV0363 Luke Skywalker 3.00
SV0364 Princess Leia as Boushh..3.00
SV0365 R2-D2..3.00
SV0366 Wicket 3.00
SV0367 Yoda 3.00

SV0404 SV0344 SV0391 SV0381 SV0382

SV0383 SV0400 SV0401 SV0402

SV0344 "Let's See It In THX", 2" round, Star Wars Celebration '99, promotion-
    al 1.00
SV0382 B-Wing Attack, Max Rebo Band, Emperor vs. Luke, Endor Forest .8.00
SV0404 Puffy Stickers: 7 characters, 2 X-Wings..............................6.00
SV0383 Rancor, Speederbike Chase, AT-ST Attack, Imperial Shuttle 8.00
SV0381 Rebel Fleet, Jabba's Palace, DS II Reactor, Escape from Jabba's
    Sail Barge...8.00
SV0391 ROTJ: Darth Vader, Luke Skywalker, Cruiser, Tie Fighter, Galactic
    Emperor, Stormtrooper, Millennium Falcon............................8.00
SV0401 Series: Empire Strikes Back..4.00
SV0402 Series: Return of the Jedi..4.00
SV0400 Series: Star Wars 4.00

STICKERS: PREMIUMS

Burger King
ESB Super Scene sticker sheets.
STP0001 01A-D Chewbacca 2.00
STP0002 02A-D Carbon Freezing Chamber 2.00
STP0003 03A-D Princess Leia 2.00
STP0004 04A-D Luke and Yoda 2.00
STP0005 05A-D Luke on Tauntaun...2.00
STP0006 06A-D R2-D2 and C-3PO 2.00
STP0007 07A-D Boba Fett and IG-88...2.00
STP0008 08A-D Darth Vader 2.00
STP0009 09A-D Darth Vader and Luke, lightsaber duel 2.00
STP0010 10A-D Luke inside Cloud City..2.00
STP0011 11A-D Darth Vader, Boba Fett, and Lando 2.00
STP0012 Sheet A, complete..6.00
STP0013 Sheet B, complete..6.00
STP0014 Sheet C, complete..6.00
STP0015 Sheet D, complete..6.00

Campina Ijsfabbrieken
STP0016 C-3PO and R2-D2 ....11.00

STP0016 STP0017 STP0018 STP0019 STP0020 STP0021

STP0017 Darth Vader 11.00
STP0018 Darth Vader and Death Star Gunner 11.00
STP0019 Luke and Yoda 11.00
STP0020 Star Destroyer 11.00
STP0021 Stormtrooper 11.00

Chupa Chups

STP0022 01 Luke with Blaster (Cloud City) 1.75
STP0023 02 Darth Vader 1.75
STP0024 03 C-3PO 1.75
STP0025 04 Emperor 1.75
STP0026 05 Yoda 1.75
STP0027 06 Royal Guard 1.75
STP0028 07 Chewbacca 1.75
STP0029 08 Gamorrean 1.75
STP0030 09 Han in Carbonite 1.75
STP0031 10 Luke, Leia, and Han 1.75
STP0032 11 Darth and Leia 1.75
STP0033 12 In the Cockpit of the Falcon 1.75
STP0034 13 Stormtroopers 1.75
STP0035 14 The Falcon 1.75
STP0036 15 Star Destroyer 1.75
STP0037 16 X-Wings 1.75
STP0038 17 Ties in Death Star Trench 1.75
STP0039 18 AT-ATs on Hoth 1.75
STP0040 19 Darth and Luke Duel 1.75
STP0041 20 Destroyer Chasing the Falcon 1.75
STP0042 21 R2 repairs C-3PO 1.75
STP0043 22 Darth (artistic) 1.75
STP0044 23 Jabba and Bib Fortuna 1.75
STP0045 24 Desert Skiff 1.75

General Mills

Stick-on cereal premiums. 4 categories: "character", "creature", "robot", and "scene".

STP0050 STP0052 STP0053 STP0055 STP0060

STP0046 Artoo-Detoo (R2-D2), robot 6.00
STP0047 Attack on Darth Vader's Ship, scene 6.00
STP0048 Ben cuts off the tractor beam, scene 6.00
STP0049 C-3PO and R2-D2, robot 6.00
STP0050 Chewbacca, creature 6.00
STP0051 Cockpit of the Millennium Falcon, scene 6.00
STP0052 Darth Vader, creature 6.00
STP0053 Han Solo, character 6.00
STP0054 Han Solo, Princess Leia and Luke, scene 6.00
STP0055 Jawa, creature 6.00
STP0056 Luke Repairs C-3PO, robot 6.00
STP0057 Luke Skywalker, character 6.00
STP0058 Princess Leia Organa, character 6.00
STP0059 See-Threepio (C-3PO), robot 6.00
STP0060 Stormtroopers, creature 6.00

Kellogg's

Stick'R'Card cereal premiums. Removable sticker on trading card. Image on sticker was different from image on card.

STP0067 STP0069

STP0061 01: Luke Skywalker sticker / Luke Skywalker card 7.00
STP0062 02: Han Solo sticker / Han Solo card 7.00
STP0063 03: R2-D2 sticker / R2-D2 and C-3PO card 7.00
STP0064 04: C-3PO sticker / R2-D2 and C-3PO card 7.00
STP0065 05: C-3PO and R2-D2 sticker / C-3PO and Logray card 7.00
STP0066 06: Yoda sticker / Luke and Yoda card 7.00
STP0067 07: Ewok sticker / R2-D2 and Wicket card 7.00
STP0068 08: Darth Vader sticker / Darth Vader and Boba Fett card 7.00
STP0069 09: Chewbacca sticker / Boushh and Chewbacca card 7.00
STP0070 10: Princess Leia sticker / Princess Leia, C-3PO and Chewbacca card 7.00

Nagatanien

STP0124 STP0125 STP0126 STP0127 STP0128 STP0129 STP0130 STP0131 STP0132 STP0133

STP0134 STP0135 STP0136 STP0137 STP0138 STP0139 STP0140 STP0141 STP0142 STP0143

STP0124 01 Obi-Wan Kenobi 1.25
STP0125 02 Anakin Skywalker 1.25
STP0126 03 Jedi vs. Sith 1.25
STP0127 04 Darth Maul 1.25
STP0128 05 Queen Amidala 1.25
STP0129 06 Jedi vs. Sith 1.25
STP0130 07 Jedi Master 1.25
STP0131 08 Battle Droid and Stap 1.25
STP0132 09 Duel on Tatooine Desert 1.25
STP0133 10 Jar Jar Binks 1.25
STP0134 11 Lightsaber Duel 1.25
STP0135 12 Gungan Army 1.25
STP0136 13 Obi-Wan & Qui-Gon 1.25
STP0137 14 C-3PO 1.25
STP0138 15 AAT (Tank) 1.25
STP0139 16 R2-D2 .... 1.25
STP0140 17 Podrace 1.25
STP0141 18 Battle Droids 1.25
STP0142 19 Yoda 1.25
STP0143 20 Naboo Starfighter 1.25

STP0071 STP0073 STP0075 STP0076 STP0077 STP0078 STP0079 STP0080 STP0081

STP0082 STP0084 STP0085 STP0086 STP0087 STP0088 STP0089 STP0090 STP0091

STP0092 STP0093 STP0094 STP0095 STP0096 STP0097 STP0100 STP0102 STP0104

Russian

STP0071 01 Luke and C-3PO 3.40
STP0072 02 No Description Available 3.40
STP0073 03 Leia and C-3PO 3.40
STP0074 04 No Description Available 3.40
STP0075 05 Luke and Leia 3.40

STP0106

STP0076 06 Luke with droids on Tatooine 3.40
STP0077 07 Falcon pursued by Ties 3.40
STP0078 08 Leia gives R2 the Death Star plans................3.40
STP0079 09 Cockpit of the Millennium Falcon 3.40
STP0080 10 Stormtroopers and C-3PO 3.40
STP0081 11 Rebel ship 3.40
STP0082 12 Darth Vader and Stormtroopers.....................3.40
STP0083 13 No Description Available 3.40
STP0084 14 Emperor and Vader (painting)......................3.40
STP0085 15 Darth Vader 3.40
STP0086 16 Chewbacca 3.40
STP0087 17 Vader and Leia as Jabba's prisoner 3.40
STP0088 18 Poster artwork 3.40
STP0089 19 Han and Chewbacca.................................3.40
STP0090 20 ESB poster artwork 3.40
STP0091 21 Star Destroyer 3.40
STP0092 22 ROTJ poster artwork 3.40
STP0093 23 Yoda 3.40
STP0094 24 AT-ATs..3.40
STP0095 25 Leia 3.40
STP0096 26 Han in Hoth control center 3.40
STP0097 27 Leia and Jabba 3.40
STP0098 28 No Description Available 3.40
STP0099 29 No Description Available 3.40
STP0100 30 Sketch of Death Star construction 3.40
STP0101 31 No Description Available 3.40
STP0102 32 Boba Fett 3.40
STP0103 33 No Description Available 3.40
STP0104 34 Chewbacca 3.40
STP0105 35 No Description Available 3.40
STP0106 36 Slave I 3.40
STP0107 37 Han captured by Ewoks 3.40

Schick

![STP0108 STP0109 STP0110 STP0111 STP0112]

STP0108 Anakin Skywalker 4.00
STP0109 Darth Maul 4.00
STP0110 Jar Jar Binks 4.00
STP0111 Obi-Wan Kenobi 4.00
STP0112 Qui-Gon Jinn 4.00

Texaco (UK)
1½"x1½" square stickers.

![STP0117 STP0118 STP0119 STP0120]

![STP0121 STP0122 STP0123]

STP0117 Anakin Skywalker 1.00
STP0118 Darth Maul 1.00
STP0119 Jar Jar Binks (pose) 1.00
STP0120 Jar Jar Binks 1.00
STP0121 Obi-Wan Kenobi 1.00
STP0122 Queen Amidala 1.00
STP0123 Qui-Gon Jinn 1.00

UFO

STP0113 C-3PO 5.00
STP0114 Chewbacca 5.00
STP0115 Princess Leia 5.00
STP0116 Yoda 5.00

STP0113   STP0114   STP0115   STP0116

STICKERS: ROTJ

Fun Products
OSA0181 3-Pack, any 3 listed below 20.00
OSA0182 6-Pack, any 6 listed below 40.00
OSA0183 Admiral Ackbar, 4½" color plastic 6.00
OSA0184 C-3PO, 4½" color plastic 6.00
OSA0185 Chewbacca, 4½" color plastic 6.00
OSA0186 Darth Vader, 4½" color plastic 6.00
OSA0187 Ewoks, 4½" color plastic 6.00
OSA0188 Gamorrean Guard, 4½" color plastic 6.00
OSA0189 Jabba the Hutt, 4½" color plastic 6.00
OSA0190 Klaatu, 4½" color plastic 6.00
OSA0191 Paploo, 4½" color plastic 6.00
OSA0192 R2-D2 (P3-D2), 4½" color plastic 6.00
OSA0193 Shuttle Tyderium, 4½" color plastic 6.00
OSA0194 Yoda, 4½" color plastic 6.00

Topps
OSA0001 001 1 of 9 for a scene 0.60
OSA0002 002 scene shows a star destroyer 0.60
OSA0003 003 approaching the death star.......................0.60
OSA0004 004 with Tie fighter escort..........................0.60
OSA0005 005 5 of 9 ....0.60
OSA0006 006 6 of 9 ....0.60
OSA0007 007 7 of 9 ....0.60
OSA0008 008 8 of 9 ....0.60
OSA0009 009 9 of 9 ....0.60
OSA0010 010 Luke Skywalker 0.60
OSA0011 011 Darth Vader.....................................0.60
OSA0012 012 1 of 6 for a scene 0.60
OSA0013 013 scene shows ROTJ logo 0.60
OSA0014 014 3 of 6 ....0.60
OSA0015 015 4 of 6 ....0.60
OSA0016 016 5 of 6 ....0.60
OSA0017 017 6 of 6 ....0.60
OSA0018 018 top of Luke 0.60
OSA0019 019 bottom of Luke 0.60
OSA0020 020 Luke Skywalker 0.60
OSA0021 021 Luke in Gun Turret 0.60
OSA0022 022 Darth Reaches Out to Luke 0.60
OSA0023 023 Luke Before the Emperor.........................0.60
OSA0024 024 Han Solo 0.60
OSA0025 025 Top of Han 0.60
OSA0026 026 Bottom of Han 0.60
OSA0027 027 Han Solo 0.60
OSA0028 028 Han Solo 0.60
OSA0029 029 Han on Endor....................................0.60
OSA0030 030 Top of Leia 0.60
OSA0031 031 Bottom of Leia 0.60
OSA0032 032 Leia 0.60
OSA0033 033 Leia on Cloud City 0.60
OSA0034 034 Top of Slave Leia 0.60
OSA0035 035 Bottom of Slave Leia 0.60
OSA0036 036 Lando 0.60
OSA0037 037 Lando and Associates...........................0.60
OSA0038 038 Lando and Leia at Jabba's 0.60
OSA0039 039 1 of 4 for scene 0.60
OSA0040 040 scene shows Lando in skiff gear 0.60
OSA0041 041 3 of 4 ....0.60
OSA0042 042 4 of 4 ....0.60
OSA0043 043 1 of 4 for scene 0.60
OSA0044 044 scene shows Jabba 0.60
OSA0045 045 3 of 4 ....0.60
OSA0046 046 4 of 4 ....0.60
OSA0047 047 Top of Salacious Crumb 0.60
OSA0048 048 Bottom of Salacious Crumb.......................0.60
OSA0049 049 Palace Alien 0.60
OSA0050 050 Greedo's Cousin and Jawa 0.60
OSA0051 051 Gamorrean Guard 0.60
OSA0052 052 Leia and Chewie 0.60

Stickers: ROTJ

OSA0053 053 1 of 4 for scene....................0.60
OSA0054 054 C-3PO....................0.60
OSA0055 055 3 of 4....................0.60
OSA0056 056 4 of 4....................0.60
OSA0057 057 Bib Fortuna....................0.60
OSA0058 058 Band Player....................0.60
OSA0059 059 Max Rebo on Keyboards....................0.60
OSA0060 060 Sy Snootles....................0.60
OSA0061 061 1 of 4 for scene....................0.60
OSA0062 062 sketch of the band (drawing)....................0.60
OSA0063 063 3 of 4....................0.60
OSA0064 064 4 of 4....................0.60
OSA0065 065 Han in Carbonite....................0.60
OSA0066 066 Boushh Approaches Han - left....................0.60
OSA0067 067 Same Scene - right....................0.60
OSA0068 068 Unfreezing....................0.60
OSA0069 069 A Kiss - left....................0.60
OSA0070 070 A Kiss - right....................0.60
OSA0071 071 Jabba and Imprisoned Leia - left....................0.60
OSA0072 072 Jabba and Imprisoned Leia - right....................0.60
OSA0073 073 Luke....................0.60
OSA0074 074 Top of R2 the Waiter....................0.60
OSA0075 075 Bottom of R2 the Waiter....................0.60
OSA0076 076 Leia and Jabba - left....................0.60
OSA0077 077 Leia and Jabba - right....................0.60
OSA0078 078 1 of 3 scene....................0.60
OSA0079 079 scene shows Skiff and Sail Barge....................0.60
OSA0080 080 3 of 3....................0.60
OSA0081 081 Top of Luke....................0.60
OSA0082 082 Bottom of Luke....................0.60
OSA0083 083 1 of 4 for scene....................0.60
OSA0084 084 scene shows Lando and Skiff Guard Battle....................0.60
OSA0085 085 3 of 4....................0.60
OSA0086 086 4 of 4....................0.60
OSA0087 087 1 of 6 for scene....................0.60
OSA0088 088 scene shows Luke in Sail Barge Battle....................0.60
OSA0089 089 3 of 6....................0.60
OSA0090 090 4 of 6....................0.60
OSA0091 091 5 of 6....................0.60
OSA0092 092 6 of 6....................0.60
OSA0093 093 Skiff - left....................0.60
OSA0094 094 Skiff - right....................0.60
OSA0095 095 Leia versus Jabba....................0.60
OSA0096 096 1 of 4 for scene....................0.60
OSA0097 097 scene of Han Rescues Lando....................0.60
OSA0098 098 3 of 4....................0.60
OSA0099 099 4 of 4....................0.60
OSA0100 100 Gamorrean Guard....................0.60
OSA0101 101 Leia Fights - left....................0.60
OSA0102 102 Leia Fights - right....................0.60
OSA0103 103 Yoda - left....................0.60
OSA0104 104 Yoda - right....................0.60
OSA0105 105 Rebel Meeting....................0.60
OSA0106 106 Mon Mothma - top....................0.60
OSA0107 107 Mon Mothma - bottom....................0.60
OSA0108 108 Han Solo....................0.60
OSA0109 109 Han and Lando....................0.60
OSA0110 110 Mon Calamari - left....................0.60
OSA0111 111 Mon Calamari - right....................0.60
OSA0112 112 Mon Calamari - top....................0.60
OSA0113 113 Mon Calamari - bottom....................0.60
OSA0114 114 Fly Casual - left....................0.60
OSA0115 115 Fly Casual - right....................0.60
OSA0116 116 Han Solo....................0.60
OSA0117 117 Droids on Endor....................0.60
OSA0118 118 Biker Scout....................0.60
OSA0119 119 Hurt Leia....................0.60
OSA0120 120 Leia Endor - top....................0.60
OSA0121 121 Leia Endor - bottom....................0.60
OSA0122 122 Leia and Wicket....................0.60
OSA0123 123 Caught in a Net - top....................0.60
OSA0124 124 Caught in a Net - bottom....................0.60
OSA0125 125 Chief Chirpa - left....................0.60
OSA0126 126 Chief Chirpa - right....................0.60
OSA0127 127 1 of 4 for scene....................0.60
OSA0128 128 scene shows Wicket....................0.60
OSA0129 129 3 of 4....................0.60
OSA0130 130 4 of 4....................0.60
OSA0131 131 C-3PO....................0.60
OSA0132 132 1 of 4 for scene....................0.60
OSA0133 133 scene shows Baby Ewok....................0.60

OSA0134 134 3 of 4....................0.60
OSA0135 135 4 of 4....................0.60
OSA0136 136 Wicket and R2....................0.60
OSA0137 137 Roast Han - left....................0.60
OSA0138 138 Roast Han - right....................0.60
OSA0139 139 Leia at Ewok Village....................0.60
OSA0140 140 Quiet C-3PO - top....................0.60
OSA0141 141 Quiet C-3PO - bottom....................0.60
OSA0142 142 Biker Scout - left....................0.60
OSA0143 143 Biker Scout - bottom....................0.60
OSA0144 144 1 of 4 for scene....................0.60
OSA0145 145 Sketch of Biker Scout....................0.60
OSA0146 146 3 of 4....................0.60
OSA0147 147 4 of 4....................0.60
OSA0148 148 Logray....................0.60
OSA0149 149 AT-ST - top....................0.60
OSA0150 150 AT-ST - bottom....................0.60
OSA0151 151 Captured Rebels....................0.60
OSA0152 152 Droids in Battle - left....................0.60
OSA0153 153 Droids in Battle - right....................0.60
OSA0154 154 Battle - left....................0.60
OSA0155 155 Battle - right....................0.60
OSA0156 156 Emperor - top....................0.60
OSA0157 157 Emperor - bottom....................0.60
OSA0158 158 Before the Throne....................0.60
OSA0159 159 Luke and Vader....................0.60
OSA0160 160 Jedi Duel - left....................0.60
OSA0161 161 Jedi Duel - right....................0.60
OSA0162 162 1 of 2 Shuttle Cutaway....................0.60
OSA0163 163 2 of 2 Shuttle Cutaway....................0.60
OSA0164 164 1 of 2 A-Wing Cutaway....................0.60
OSA0165 165 2 of 2 A-Wing Cutaway....................0.60
OSA0166 166 1 of 2 Shuttle Cutaway....................0.60
OSA0167 167 2 of 2 Shuttle Cutaway....................0.60
OSA0168 168 1 of 2 B-Wing Cutaway....................0.60
OSA0169 169 2 of 2 B-Wing Cutaway....................0.60
OSA0170 170 1 of 4 Falcon Cutaway....................0.60
OSA0171 171 2 of 4 Falcon Cutaway....................0.60
OSA0172 172 3 of 4 Falcon Cutaway....................0.60
OSA0173 173 4 of 4 Falcon Cutaway....................0.60
OSA0174 174 1 of 2 B-Wing Cutaway....................0.60
OSA0175 175 2 of 2 B-Wing Cutaway....................0.60
OSA0176 176 Celebration - right....................0.60
OSA0177 177 Celebration - left....................0.60
OSA0178 178 Han and Wedge Shake Hands....................0.60
OSA0179 179 Han and Leia - left....................0.60
OSA0180 180 Han and Leia - right....................0.60

STICKERS: TPM

Crazy Planet

SEI0473 Mega 01 Battle Tanks....................2.00
SEI0474 Mega 02 Anakin's Naboo fighter inside Droid Control Ship....................2.00
SEI0475 Mega 03 Darth Maul and Qui-Gon Duel....................2.00
SEI0476 Mega 04 Anakin wears a Naboo helmet....................2.00
SEI0477 Mega 05 Droid ships in battle....................2.00
SEI0478 Mega 06 Naboo fighters in formation....................2.00
SEI0479 Mega 07 Attacking a Droid fighter....................2.00
SEI0480 Mega 08 Qui-Gon Jinn montage....................2.00
SEI0481 Mega 09 Darth Maul montage....................2.00
SEI0482 Mega 10 Jedi vs. Sith montage....................2.00
SEI0483 Mega 11 Obi-Wan Kenobi montage....................2.00
SEI0484 Mega 12 Coruscant at night....................2.00
SEI0485 Mega 13 Queen Amidala montage....................2.00
SEI0486 Mega 14 Good Guys montage....................2.00
SEI0487 Mega 15 Bad Guys montage....................2.00
SEI0488 Mega 16 Anankin Skywalker....................2.00
SEI0489 Mega 17 Senator Palpatine....................2.00
SEI0490 Mega 18 Queen Amidala....................2.00
SEI0491 Mega 19 The Droid Control Ships weapons fire....................2.00
SEI0492 Mega 20 Darth Maul....................2.00
SEI0493 Mega 21 Pod Racing....................2.00
SEI0494 Mega 22 The Final Duel begins....................2.00
SEI0495 Mega 23 Federation Control Ship from above....................2.00
SEI0496 Mega 24 Federation Control Ship....................2.00
SEI0497 Mega 25 The capital city of Naboo....................2.00
SEI0498 Mega 26 Obi-Wan vs. Droids....................2.00
SEI0499 Mega 27 Landing ships....................2.00
SEI0500 Mega 28 R2-D2 repairs the ship....................2.00
SEI0501 Mega 29 Battle droids prepare to march....................2.00

SEI0502 Mega 30 Droids flee explosion 2.00
SEI0503 Mega 31 Obi-Wan and Qui-Gon 2.00
SEI0504 Mega 32 Qui-Gon beside Amidala 2.00
SEI0256 Mini: Aboard the Ambassador's Ship 1.35
SEI0257 Mini: Battle Droids..........1.35
SEI0267 Mini: C-3PO 1.35
SEI0253 Mini: Coruscant 1.35
SEI0258 Mini: Droid Control Ship 1.35
SEI0264 Mini: Droids Flee Explosion..........1.35
SEI0265 Mini: Droids Vs. Jedi..........1.35
SEI0249 Mini: Gungan Bongo 1.35
SEI0252 Mini: Jabba and Bib Fortuna 1.35
SEI0248 Mini: Jar Jar and Other Gungans..........1.35
SEI0247 Mini: Jedi Dueling With Maul..........1.35
SEI0261 Mini: Jedi Ready for Battle 1.35
SEI0251 Mini: Mace Windu 1.35
SEI0262 Mini: Naboo Fighter 1.35
SEI0259 Mini: Naboo Fighter Pilot 1.35
SEI0263 Mini: Obi-Wan Duels Darth Maul 1.35
SEI0245 Mini: Podracer Scene 1.35
SEI0266 Mini: Quadrinaros..........1.35
SEI0260 Mini: R2-D2 Hauls a Pod..........1.35
SEI0246 Mini: R2-D2 near Anakin's Pod..........1.35
SEI0254 Mini: R2-D2 Races to Repair the Queen's starship 1.35
SEI0250 Mini: Theed Palace 1.35
SEI0255 Mini: Troop Transport Ships 1.35

Merlin Publishing Internat'l Ltd.

SEI0001 001 Cockpit Scene - Approaching Naboo..........0.40
SEI0002 002 Interior - Neimoidian Hangar 0.40
SEI0003 003 The Ambassadors are Welcomed 0.40
SEI0004 004 Looking Out at Naboo 0.40
SEI0005 005 Contacting the Sith Lord 0.40
SEI0006 006 Battle Droids Prepare to Face the Jedi 0.40
SEI0007 007 Battle Ship (refractor) 0.40
SEI0008 008 Lightsabers in the Mist..........0.40
SEI0009 009 Qui-Gon Jinn..........0.40
SEI0010 010 Obi-Wan Kenobi..........0.40
SEI0011 011 Qui-Gon Jinn (metallic edge - small)..........0.40
SEI0012 012 Jedi on the Defense 0.40
SEI0013 013 Obi-Wan Kenobi (holofoil) 0.40
SEI0014 014 City of Theed 0.40
SEI0015 015 Queen Amidala 0.40
SEI0016 016 The Neimoidian Ambassador 0.40
SEI0017 017 Nute Gunray..........0.40
SEI0018 018 The Bridge of the Trade Federation Ship..........0.40
SEI0019 019 Queen Amidala (holofoil) 0.40
SEI0020 020 Nute Gunray (metallic edge - small) 0.40
SEI0021 021 Directing the Jedi Hunt..........0.40
SEI0022 022 Darth Sidious (refractor) 0.40
SEI0023 023 Captain Panaka (metallic edge - large) 0.40
SEI0024 024 Queen Amidala 0.40
SEI0025 025 Landing Craft (refractor)..........0.40
SEI0026 026 The Royal Defenders..........0.40
SEI0027 027 Qui-Gon Jinn (holofoil) 0.40
SEI0028 028 Landing Craft 0.40
SEI0029 029 Troop Transport (refractor) 0.40
SEI0030 030 Qui-Gon Meet Jar Jar..........0.40
SEI0031 031 STAP and Battle Droid (refractor) 0.40
SEI0032 032 Jedi and Jar Jar 0.40
SEI0033 033 Talking with Jar Jar..........0.40
SEI0034 034 Jar Jar Prepares to Dive (metallic edge - large)..........0.40
SEI0035 035 Jar Jar (holofoil)..........0.40
SEI0036 036 Jar Jar..........0.40
SEI0037 037 Obi-Wan Swimming 0.40
SEI0038 038 Jar Jar..........0.40
SEI0039 039 Jar Jar Under Arrest..........0.40
SEI0040 040 Qui-Gon and Obi-Wan (metallic edge - large) 0.40
SEI0041 041 Jar Jar Under Guard 0.40
SEI0042 042 Jar Jar Pleads 0.40
SEI0043 043 Aboard the Gungan Sub 0.40
SEI0044 044 1/2 Sub Scene (metallic edge - large) 0.40
SEI0045 045 1/2 Sub Scene (metallic edge - large) 0.40
SEI0046 046 Opee Sea Monster Attack 0.40
SEI0047 047 Jedi Snack..........0.40
SEI0048 048 Gungan Sub (refractor)..........0.40
SEI0049 049 The Mouth of the Beast 0.40
SEI0050 050 Nute Gunray..........0.40
SEI0051 051 Palace Occupation..........0.40
SEI0052 052 Battle Droid Commander 0.40
SEI0053 053 The Trade Federation Invaders..........0.40
SEI0054 054 Captain Panaka (refractor)..........0.40
SEI0055 055 Neimoidians in the Throne Room 0.40
SEI0056 056 Aboard the Escaping Queen's Transport 0.40
SEI0057 057 Running the Blockade..........0.40
SEI0058 058 Captain Panaka (metallic edge - large) 0.40
SEI0059 059 Qui-Gon and Captain Panaka 0.40
SEI0060 060 Jedi in the Cockpit..........0.40
SEI0061 061 The Queen's Transport..........0.40
SEI0062 062 Qui-Gon (metallic edge - small) 0.40
SEI0063 063 Royal Starship (holofoil) 0.40
SEI0064 064 Obi-Wan (metallic edge - small)..........0.40
SEI0065 065 Darth Sidious 0.40
SEI0066 066 Darth Sidious Hologram..........0.40
SEI0067 067 Jar Jar Meets Padme 0.40
SEI0068 068 Captain Panaka Introduces R2 (metallic edge - small)..........0.40
SEI0069 069 R2-D2 (holofoil) 0.40
SEI0070 070 Qui-Gon and Jar Jar on Tatooine 0.40
SEI0071 071 Padme Wants to Come Too 0.40
SEI0072 072 Discussing the Queen's Request 0.40
SEI0073 073 R2 in Mos Espa 0.40
SEI0074 074 Qui-Gon Surveys Mos Espa 0.40
SEI0075 075 Qui-Gon and Watto..........0.40
SEI0076 076 Watto (holofoil) 0.40
SEI0077 077 Toydarians Only Understand Money 0.40
SEI0078 078 Discussion With a Toydarian..........0.40
SEI0079 079 Jar Jar Finds a Snack 0.40
SEI0080 080 Sebulba Faces Anakin..........0.40
SEI0081 081 Sebulba Confronts Jar Jar (metallic edge - large) 0.40
SEI0082 082 Sandstorm 0.40
SEI0083 083 Hearing Sio Bibble's Message..........0.40
SEI0084 084 Sio Bibble..........0.40
SEI0085 085 Anakin and C-3PO 0.40
SEI0086 086 C-3PO (holofoil)..........0.40
SEI0087 087 C-3PO (metallic edge - large)..........0.40
SEI0088 088 C-3PO Meet R2-D2..........0.40
SEI0089 089 Anakin Skywalker (metallic edge - small) 0.40
SEI0090 090 Dinner With Anakin..........0.40
SEI0091 091 Qui-Gon Contacts the Ship 0.40
SEI0092 092 Qui-Gon and Watto..........0.40
SEI0093 093 Watto..........0.40
SEI0094 094 A Tempting Offer..........0.40
SEI0095 095 Don't Touch Anything! 0.40
SEI0096 096 Jar Jar Balancing Act..........0.40
SEI0097 097 Anakin Skywalker (holofoil) 0.40
SEI0098 098 Watto (metallic edge - large) 0.40
SEI0099 099 R2 and the Pod 0.40
SEI0100 100 Anakin's Pod..........0.40
SEI0101 101 The Droids and Jar Jar With the Pod..........0.40
SEI0102 102 Jar Jar at Work (metallic edge - large) 0.40
SEI0103 103 Jar Jar in the Binding Ray..........0.40
SEI0104 104 Starting the Pod..........0.40
SEI0105 105 Obi-Wan Tests the Blood Sample..........0.40
SEI0106 106 Darth Maul 0.40
SEI0107 107 Sith Infiltrator (metallic edge - large) 0.40
SEI0108 108 Podracing Hangar..........0.40
SEI0109 109 Roll of the Dice 0.40
SEI0110 110 You Won This One... ....0.40
SEI0111 111 Wagering With Watto..........0.40
SEI0112 112 Qui-Gon 0.40
SEI0113 113 Arriving at the Arena 0.40
SEI0114 114 Anakin and Padme 0.40
SEI0115 115 C-3PO (metallic edge - small)..........0.40
SEI0116 116 C-3PO and R2 with the Pod..........0.40
SEI0117 117 Jabba (metallic edge - large) 0.40
SEI0118 118 Ringing the Gong..........0.40
SEI0119 119 Sebulba's Pod (refractor)..........0.40
SEI0120 120 Ben Qaudinaros (metallic edge - large) 0.40
SEI0121 121 Ody Mantel..........0.40
SEI0122 122 Sebulba..........0.40
SEI0123 123 Sebulba Cheats 0.40
SEI0124 124 Pod Racer..........0.40
SEI0125 125 Pit Droids (refractor)..........0.40
SEI0126 126 Sebulba..........0.40
SEI0127 127 Anakin Ready to Race 0.40
SEI0128 128 They're Off! 0.40
SEI0129 129 Watching the Race 0.40
SEI0130 130 Pods Across the Desert..........0.40
SEI0131 131 Side-by-Side..........0.40
SEI0132 132 Anakin in the Lead..........0.40
SEI0133 133 Anakin 0.40
SEI0134 134 Anakin's Pod (refractor) 0.40

Stickers: TPM

Salo

SEI0268 SEI0269 SEI0270 SEI0271 SEI0272 SEI0273 SEI0274 SEI0275 SEI0276 SEI0277 SEI0278

SEI0279 SEI0280 SEI0281 SEI0282 SEI0283 SEI0284 SEI0285 SEI0286 SEI0287 SEI0288 SEI0289

SEI0290 SEI0291 SEI0292 SEI0293 SEI0294 SEI0295 SEI0296 SEI0297 SEI0298 SEI0299 SEI0300

SEI0301	SEI0302	SEI0303	SEI0304	SEI0305	SEI0306	SEI0307	SEI0308	SEI0309	SEI0310	SEI0311
SEI0312	SEI0313	SEI0314	SEI0315	SEI0316	SEI0317	SEI0318	SEI0319	SEI0320	SEI0321	SEI0322
SEI0323	SEI0324	SEI0325	SEI0326	SEI0327	SEI0328	SEI0329	SEI0330	SEI0331	SEI0332	SEI0333
SEI0334	SEI0335	SEI0336	SEI0337	SEI0338	SEI0339	SEI0340	SEI0341	SEI0342	SEI0343	SEI0344
SEI0345	SEI0346	SEI0347	SEI0348	SEI0349	SEI0350	SEI0351	SEI0352	SEI0353	SEI0354	SEI0355
SEI0356	SEI0357	SEI0358	SEI0359	SEI0360	SEI0361	SEI0362	SEI0363	SEI0364	SEI0365	SEI0366

Stickers: TPM

SEI0367	SEI0368	SEI0369	SEI0370	SEI0371	SEI0372	SEI0373	SEI0374	SEI0375	SEI0376	SEI0377
SEI0378	SEI0379	SEI0380	SEI0381	SEI0382	SEI0383	SEI0384	SEI0385	SEI0386	SEI0387	SEI0388
SEI0389	SEI0390	SEI0391	SEI0392	SEI0393	SEI0394	SEI0395	SEI0396	SEI0397	SEI0398	SEI0399
SEI0400	SEI0401	SEI0402	SEI0403	SEI0404	SEI0405	SEI0406	SEI0407	SEI0408	SEI0409	SEI0410
SEI0411	SEI0412	SEI0413	SEI0414	SEI0415	SEI0416	SEI0417	SEI0418	SEI0419	SEI0420	SEI0421
SEI0422	SEI0423	SEI0424	SEI0425	SEI0426	SEI0427	SEI0428	SEI0429	SEI0430	SEI0431	SEI0432

SEI0410 143 Anakin Leaps Into Naboo Fighter Cockpit 0.15
SEI0411 144 Qui-Gon Orders Anakin to Stay Put 0.15
SEI0412 145 Looking Out From the Cockpit 0.15
SEI0413 146 Naboo Fighter Above Naboo 0.15
SEI0414 147 Droid Fighter 0.15
SEI0415 148 Naboo Fighter Streaks Out Of The Atmosphere 0.15
SEI0416 149 Naboo Pilot 0.15
SEI0417 150 Naboo Pilot 0.15
SEI0418 151 Naboo Fighters 0.15
SEI0419 152 The Federation Ship Fires 0.15
SEI0420 153 Battle in Space 0.15
SEI0421 154 Qui-Gon With His Lightsaber 0.15
SEI0422 155 Jedi Duel Against Sith 0.15
SEI0423 156 The Duel Seen From a Distance 0.15
SEI0424 157 Maul 0.15
SEI0425 158 Obi-Wan Kenobi 0.15
SEI0426 159 Obi-Wan Races to Catch Up 0.15
SEI0427 160 Obi-Wan Slides to a Stop 0.15
SEI0428 161 Qui-Gon Waits Patiently 0.15
SEI0429 162 Anakin in the Cockpit 0.15
SEI0430 163 Flying Inside the Federation Hangar 0.15
SEI0431 164 R2-D2 ....0.15
SEI0432 165 Inside the Hangar..0.15
SEI0433 166 Droids Run From Fireball 0.15
SEI0434 167 Destruction of the Hangar 0.15
SEI0435 168 The Control Ship Explodes 0.15
SEI0436 169 Qui-Gon and Maul Duel...0.15
SEI0437 170 Maul Waits for Obi-Wan 0.15
SEI0438 171 Obi-Wan and Maul Duel 0.15
SEI0439 172 Lightsabers Clash 0.15
SEI0440 173 Obi-Wan Hangs On 0.15
SEI0441 174 Obi-Wan Hanging Out 0.15
SEI0442 175 Yoda 0.15
SEI0443 176 Celebration on Naboo 0.15
SEI0444 A Droid Control Ship 0.25
SEI0445 B Obi-Wan Kenobi 0.25
SEI0446 C Queen Amidala 0.25
SEI0447 D Trade Federation Landing Ship...0.25
SEI0448 E Qui-Gon Jinn 0.25
SEI0449 F Droid Invasion Vehicle 0.25
SEI0450 G Droid on STAP 0.25
SEI0451 H Jar Jar 0.25
SEI0452 I No Information Available 0.25
SEI0453 J Royal Starship 0.25
SEI0454 K R2-D2 ....0.25
SEI0455 L Watto 0.25
SEI0456 M Anakin Skywalker 0.25
SEI0457 N C-3PO 0.25
SEI0458 N~ Sebulba's Podracer 0.25
SEI0459 O Pit Droids 0.25
SEI0460 P No Information Available 0.25
SEI0461 Q No Information Available 0.25
SEI0462 R Mace Windu 0.25
SEI0463 S Yoda 0.25
SEI0464 T Trade Federation Tank 0.25
SEI0465 U Destroyer Droid 0.25
SEI0466 V Naboo Fighter 0.25
SEI0467 W Droid Fighter 0.25
SEI0468 X No Information Available 0.25

SEI0469 Y No Information Available..0.25
SEI0470 Z No Information Available 0.25

STICKPINS

JSP0001 C-3PO 14.00
JSP0002 Chewbacca 14.00
JSP0003 Darth Vader 14.00
JSP0004 R2-D2 ....14.00
JSP0005 Stormtrooper...14.00
JSP0006 X-Wing Fighter 14.00

STORAGE CASES: ACTION FIGURE, POTF2

P2C0002   P2C0006   P2C0004

Kenner
P2C0002 Millennium Falcon / Imperial Scan Technician 32.00
P2C0004 Millennium Falcon / Wedge, Corrected 34.00
P2C0005 Millennium Falcon / Wedge, Wrong Uniform 39.00
P2C0001 POTF2 Collector's Case 36.00
P2C0006 Talking C-3PO 29.00

STORAGE CASES: ACTION FIGURE, TPM

P3C0001

Hasbro
P3C0001 R2-D2 with rolling Destroyer Droid figure.....................................25.00

STORAGE CASES: ACTION FIGURE, VINTAGE

Kenner
AVA4001 C-3PO Bust, gold chrome finish, loose................................12.00
AVA4002 C-3PO Bust, gold chrome finish, ROTJ pkg. 40.00
AVA4003 Chewbacca Bandolier Strap, loose.....................................8.00
AVA4004 Chewbacca Bandolier Strap, ROTJ pkg. 18.00
AVA4005 Darth Vader Bust plastic, ESB pkg. 35.00
AVA4017 Darth Vader Bust plastic, ESB pkg. 3 free figures....................145.00
AVA4006 Darth Vader Bust plastic, loose 10.00
AVA4007 Darth Vader Bust plastic, ROTJ pkg. 39.00
AVA4008 Empire Strikes Back vinyl, ESB pkg. 28.00

| SEI0433 | SEI0434 | SEI0435 | SEI0436 | SEI0437 |

| SEI0438 | SEI0439 | SEI0440 | SEI0441 | SEI0442 | SEI0443 | SEI0444 | SEI0445 | SEI0446 | SEI0447 | SEI0448 |

| SEI0449 | SEI0450 | SEI0454 | SEI0455 | SEI0456 | SEI0458 | SEI0464 | SEI0466 | SEI0471 | SEI0471 | SEI0472 |

Storage Cases: Action Figure, Vintage

AVA4015

AVA4009 alternate designs

AVA4012

AVA4004

AVA4002

AVA4011

AVA4006

AVA4009 Empire Strikes Back vinyl, loose 10.00
AVA4010 Laser Rifle, loose 12.00
AVA4011 Laser Rifle, ROTJ pkg. 46.00
AVA4012 Return of the Jedi vinyl, loose 10.00
AVA4013 Return of the Jedi vinyl, ROTJ pkg. 85.00
AVA4015 Star Wars vinyl, loose 15.00
AVA4016 Star Wars vinyl, SW pkg. 35.00

STRAWS

Applause
SSS0001 Jar Jar Binks Sipper 5.00
SSS0002 Pit Droid Sipper 5.00
SSS0008 R2-D2 Sipper 5.00
SSS0003 Watto Sipper 5.00

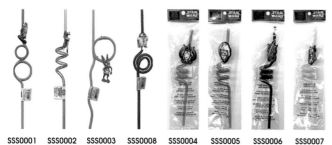

SSS0001   SSS0002   SSS0003   SSS0008   SSS0004   SSS0005   SSS0006   SSS0007

Zak Designs
SSS0005 Anakin Skywalker...6.00
SSS0006 Darth Maul 6.00
SSS0007 Jar Jar Binks...6.00
SSS0004 Queen Amidala 6.00

STRING DISPENSERS

SUY0001 front and back

Sigma
SUY0001 R2-D2 string dispenser with scissors...75.00

SUBWAY TICKETS

SMRT
SWT0007 Empire Strikes Back style A...6.00
SWT0008 Empire Strikes Back style B 6.00

SWT0004 Queen Amidala 5.00
SWT0009 Return of the Jedi 7.00
SWT0003 Sith Lord, Darth Maul 5.00
SWT0005 Star Wars style A 7.00
SWT0006 Star Wars style B 5.00
SWT0002 TPM Heroes 5.00
SWT0001 TPM Villains..5.00

SUCTION CUP TOYS

SCU0001   SCU0003   SCU0004

SCU0001 Ben Kenobi 6.00
SCU0002 Chewbacca 6.00
SCU0003 Darth Vader 6.00
SCU0004 Luke Skywalker as X-Wing Pilot..6.00

SUITCASES

Adam Joseph Industries
LS0001 Darth Vader and Emperor's Royal Guards, any size 75.00
LS0002 Princess Kneesaa and Wicket 45.00

Premier Luggage
LS0011 ESB 2-sided, heroes and villains 55.00

LS0011 right and left sides   **LS0007**

Pyramid
LS0008 Anakin / Podracing pilot carry-on 15.00
LS0003 Boba Fett, wheeled carry-on w/pull-up handle..........................27.00
LS0004 Darth Vader, wheeled carry-on w/pull-up handle 27.00
LS0009 Jedi pilot carry-on 15.00
LS0005 Luke Skywalker, wheeled carry-on w/pull-up handle 27.00
LS0007 Podracing with Anakin and Sebulba, square...............................16.00
LS0010 Sith pilot carry-on 15.00
LS0006 Stormtrooper, wheeled carry-on w/pull-up handle.....................27.00

SUN CATCHER CRAFT KITS

Fundimensions
Makeit and Bakeit kits.

CRS0001   CRS0002   CRS0003   CRS0004

CRS0001 Darth Vader 12.00
CRS0002 Gamorrean Guard 12.00
CRS0003 Jabba the Hutt..12.00
CRS0004 R2-D2 ....12.00

Leewards Creative Crafts
CRS0005 C-3PO...26.00

CRS0007   CRS0011

CRS0006 Darth Vader 26.00
CRS0007 Darth Vader, head 26.00
CRS0008 IG-88 ....26.00
CRS0009 Luke on Tauntaun 26.00
CRS0010 Luke Skywalker 26.00
CRS0011 Millennium Falcon 26.00
CRS0012 Princess Leia 26.00
CRS0013 R2-D2 and Yoda 26.00
CRS0014 Snowspeeder 26.00
CRS0015 Stormtrooper 26.00
CRS0016 X-Wing Fighter 26.00

SUPER PACK

SPP0001   SPP0002

Antioch
SPP0001 Classic trilogy memo board with pen, 2 wallet cards, 1 tasseled bookmark, 1 die-cut bookmark, 1 doorknob hanger.............................11.00
SPP0002 EPI: memo board with pen, 2 wallet cards, 1 tasseled bookmark, 1 die-cut bookmark 11.00

SUSPENDERS

ASP0003

Lee Co.
Striped with character badge.
ASP0001 C-3PO and R2-D2, die cut 18.00
ASP0002 Darth Vader helmet, die-cut 20.00
ASP0003 Yoda, round..15.00

SWIMMING ATTIRE

SWA0001

SWA0001 Darth Maul...8.00

SWITCH PLATES AND COVERS

Kenner
Switcheroos.
HOS0001 C-3PO 26.00
HOS0002 Darth Vader 26.00
HOS0003 R2-D2...26.00

Turn-Ons.
HOS0004 Boba Fett...24.00

HOS0001   HOS0002   HOS0003   HOS0004

TABLE COVERS

Deeko
TC0005 Space Battle design, sold in pkg. of 3 ....21.00

Drawing Board

TC0001   TC0002   TC0003   TC0004

TC0001 C-3PO, R2-D2, and Star Wars logo, 60"x96" 18.00
TC0002 Cloud City and Characters, 60"x96" 16.00
TC0003 Darth Vader and Luke Dueling, 54"x96" 12.00
TC0004 Ewoks flying Gliders, 54"x96" 10.00

Party Express

TC0006   TC0007   TC0008

TC0006 Spaceship art on white background, 54"x90" 8.00
TC0007 Tech design with Jedi and Sith silouette border, 54"x90"...............5.00

Unique
TC0008 Jedi vs. Sith, drawn...6.00

TABLES

FUT0002 table top design

American Toy and Furniture Co.
FUT0001 Ewoks picnic table...125.00
FUT0003 Ewoks table with 2 chairs..135.00
FUT0002 Return of the Jedi table with 2 chairs 135.00

Pipsqueaks
FUT0004 EPI: Pod Racer Table, hardwood 175.00

FUT0004 table and top design

TABLETS

Impact, Inc.
TAB0002 Anakin Skywalker Podracer, 2-pack 4.00
TAB0003 Jedi vs. Sith, 2-pack 4.00
TAB0001 Space Battle, 2-pack............4.00

TAB0001   TAB0002   TAB0003

TAPE DISPENSERS

SUT0002

SUT0001 front and back

Butterfly Originals
SUT0002 Darth Vader ROTJ, with 16 ft. of tape...8.00

Sigma
SUT0001 C-3PO 85.00

TATTOOS

Rose Art Industries

TTO0001 front and back   TTO0002

TTO0001 Fun with Tattoos...9.00

Tapper Candies
TTO0002 SW:EPI Tatoos, pkg. of 16 ....4.00

TAZO

Tazo (Australia)
3D Motion image.
TZC0001 081 Grand Moff Tarkin and Darth Vader...0.75

TZC0021   TZC0022   TZC0023

TZC0024   TZC0025   TZC0026

TZC0002 082 Darth Vader and Princess Leia 0.75
TZC0003 083 Luke Skywalker Practicing with a Seeker 0.75
TZC0004 084 Han Solo and Ben (Obi-Wan) Kenobi 0.75
TZC0005 085 Luke Skywalker and Princess Leia 0.75
TZC0006 086 Stormtrooper 0.75
TZC0007 087 Darth Vader and Ben (Obi-Wan) Kenobi 0.75
TZC0008 088 Tie Fighter 0.75
TZC0009 089 Aboard the Millennium Falcon Chased by a Star Destroyer 0.75
TZC0010 090 Han Solo and Chewbacca...0.75
TZC0011 091 An AT-ST Firing 0.75
TZC0012 092 Emperor Palpatine and Luke Skywalker 0.75
TZC0013 093 Imperial Tie Interceptor Exploding..0.75
TZC0014 094 Rebel Alliance Fighter Pilots 0.75
TZC0015 095 Princess Leia and R2-D2...0.75
TZC0016 096 Jedi Master Yoda and Luke Skywalker.....................................0.75
TZC0017 097 C-3PO and Wicket the Ewok 1.25
TZC0018 098 Lando Calrissian and Luke Skywalker 0.75
TZC0019 099 Han Solo and Luke Skywalker 0.75
TZC0020 100 Wedge Antilles and His X-Wing (Red Two) 0.75

Octagonal shape.
TZC0021 101 Owen Lars and Luke Skywalker 0.75
TZC0022 102 Jawa Firing Weapon 0.75
TZC0023 103 C-3PO and R2D2 ....0.75
TZC0024 104 Tusken Raider With His Gaderffii Stick......................................0.75
TZC0025 105 Luke Skywalker With His Father's Lightsaber 0.75
TZC0026 106 Piloting the Millennium Falcon 0.75
TZC0027 107 Grand Moff Tarkin and Darth Vader 0.75
TZC0028 108 Ben (Obi-Wan) Kenobi 0.75
TZC0029 109 Luke Skywalker 0.75
TZC0030 110 Stormtrooper 0.75
TZC0031 111 Han Solo Firing Quad Cannon 0.75
TZC0032 112 Darth Vader's Tie Fighter and Wingman 0.75
TZC0033 113 Luke Skywalker Riding a Tauntaun 0.75
TZC0034 114 Probe Droid 0.75
TZC0035 115 Chewbacca 0.75
TZC0036 116 Jedi Master Yoda 0.75
TZC0037 117 Lando Calrissian and Han Solo 0.75
TZC0038 118 Captured by Imperial Stormtroopers 0.75
TZC0039 119 Luke Skywalker and Darth Vader in Battle 0.75
TZC0040 120 Millennium Falcon and Star Destroyer 0.75
TZC0041 121 Princess Leia and Bib Fortuna With Jabba 0.75
TZC0042 122 Luke Skywalker 0.75
TZC0043 123 Admiral Ackbar Rebel Commander...0.75
TZC0044 124 Han Solo Captured by Ewoks 0.75
TZC0045 125 Wicket With R2 and C-3PO...0.75

TZC0081   TZC0082   TZC0083

TZC0027   TZC0028   TZC0029   TZC0030   TZC0031   TZC0032   TZC0033   TZC0034

TZC0035   TZC0036   TZC0037   TZC0038   TZC0039   TZC0040   TZC0041   TZC0042

TZC0043   TZC0044   TZC0045   TZC0046   TZC0047   TZC0048   TZC0049   TZC0050

TZC0046 126 Princess Leia 0.75
TZC0047 127 Imperial Scout Trooper Riding a Speeder Bike.....................0.75
TZC0048 128 Ewok Logray - Medicine Man 0.75
TZC0049 129 Princess Leia and Han Solo Held Captive 0.75
TZC0050 130 Darth Vader 0.75

3D image.
TZC0051 131 Sand Trooper on a Dewback 0.75
TZC0052 132 Wampa Ice Creature 0.75
TZC0053 133 Luke Skywalker 0.75
TZC0054 134 Darth Vader and Boba Fett 0.75
TZC0055 135 Han Solo 0.75
TZC0056 136 Jabba the Hutt and Han Solo............................0.75
TZC0057 137 Lyn Me, Greeata, and Rystall 0.75
TZC0058 138 Rancor 0.75
TZC0059 139 Princess Leia and Luke Skywalker.......................0.75
TZC0060 140 B-Wing 0.75

Hologram image.
TZC0061 141 R2-D2 and C-3PO 0.75
TZC0062 142 Princess Leia and C-3PO 0.75
TZC0063 143 Darth Vader's Tie Fighter with Wingman 0.75
TZC0064 144 Darth Vader battles Ben (Obi-Wan) Kenobi 0.75
TZC0065 145 Stormtroopers 0.75
TZC0066 146 The Millennium Falcon 0.75
TZC0067 147 Chewbacca and Han Solo 0.75
TZC0068 148 C-3PO 0.75
TZC0069 149 R2-D2 ....0.75
TZC0070 150 Battle of Hoth 0.75
TZC0071 151 Jedi Master Yoda 0.75
TZC0072 152 Leia, Luke, and R2-D2 ....0.75
TZC0073 153 Chewbacca 0.75
TZC0074 154 Luke Skywalker and Yoda 0.75
TZC0075 155 Luke Skywalker and R2-D2 ....0.75
TZC0076 156 The Millennium Falcon 0.75
TZC0077 157 An Imperial AT-ST in the forest of Endor 0.75
TZC0078 158 Luke Skywalker 0.75
TZC0079 159 Darth Vader and Stormtroopers 0.75
TZC0080 160 Darth Vader 0.75

Connect-a-Tazo.
TZC0081 Shuttle 3.00
TZC0082 Tie Fighter 3.00

TZC0083 X-Wing..3.00

Tazo (China)
TZC0084 01 Scout Trooper...2.25
TZC0085 02 Wicket..2.25
TZC0086 03 Chewbacca, hologram.....................................3.00
TZC0087 04 Luke With New Saber.......................................2.25
TZC0088 05 Luke and Vader Duel, hologram...........................3.00
TZC0089 06 B-Wing, hologram...3.00
TZC0090 07 Vader...2.25
TZC0091 08 Stormtroopers...2.25
TZC0092 09 AT-ST, hologram...3.00
TZC0093 10 R2-D2...2.25
TZC0094 11 Vader Reaching Out to Luke................................2.25
TZC0095 12 Luke, Leia, and R2 Look Out on the Galaxy...............2.25
TZC0096 13 Sandtrooper on Dewback, hologram......................3.00
TZC0097 14 C-3PO and R2 approach Jabba's Palace...................2.25
TZC0098 15 Han About to be Frozen, hologram........................3.00
TZC0099 16 Millennium Falcon, hologram.............................3.00
TZC0100 17 Leia...2.25
TZC0101 18 Falcon in Reactor Core.....................................2.25
TZC0102 19 Luke and Yoda in Training, hologram......................3.00
TZC0103 20 AT-ATs on Hoth..2.25
TZC0104 21 Luke and R2 on Dagobah...................................2.25
TZC0105 22 Luke With Saber in Cave...................................2.25
TZC0106 23 Scout Trooper on Speeder Bike (same image as #1), hologram...3.00
TZC0107 24 Star Destroyers..2.25
TZC0108 25 R2 and C-3PO..2.25
TZC0109 26 Luke in Stormtrooper Gear, hologram.....................3.00
TZC0110 27 Luke in Jabba's Palace......................................2.25
TZC0111 28 R2 and C-3PO on Endor....................................2.25
TZC0112 29 AT-ATs on Hoth (same image as #20), hologram.........3.00
TZC0113 30 Vader Reaching Out to Luke (identical to #11)............2.25
TZC0114 31 Leia and C-3PO..2.25
TZC0115 32 Luke on Tauntaun..2.25
TZC0116 33 Ties in Death Star Trench, hologram.......................3.00
TZC0117 34 Vader...2.25
TZC0118 35 Tusken Raider, hologram....................................3.00
TZC0119 36 Yoda, hologram..3.00
TZC0120 37 Luke and Vader Duel...2.25
TZC0121 38 Obi Wan Kenobi..2.25
TZC0122 39 Luke and Leia on Jabba's Sail Barge, hologram..........3.00
TZC0123 40 R2 and C-3PO Artwork with Star Wars logo...............2.25

| TZC0174 | TZC0175 | TZC0176 | TZC0177 | TZC0178 | TZC0179 | TZC0180 | TZC0181 | TZC0182 | TZC0183 | TZC0184 |

| TZC0185 | TZC0186 | TZC0187 | TZC0188 | TZC0189 | TZC0190 | TZC0191 | TZC0192 | TZC0193 | TZC0194 | TZC0195 |

| TZC0196 | TZC0197 | TZC0198 | TZC0199 | TZC0200 | TZC0201 | TZC0202 | TZC0203 | TZC0204 | TZC0205 | TZC0206 |

| TZC0207 | TZC0208 | TZC0209 | TZC0210 | TZC0211 | TZC0212 | TZC0213 | TZC0214 | TZC0215 | TZC0216 | TZC0217 |

| TZC0218 | TZC0219 | TZC0220 | TZC0221 | TZC0222 | TZC0223 | TZC0199 detail | TZC0224 detail |

Tazo

Tazo (Poland)

TZC0124 01 C-3PO 0.75
TZC0125 02 R2-D2 ....0.75
TZC0126 03 Tusken Raider 0.75
TZC0127 04 Luke Skywalker 0.75
TZC0128 05 Luke, Obi-Wan, and Han 0.75
TZC0129 06 Vader 0.75
TZC0130 07 Tarkin 0.75
TZC0131 08 Luke Skywalker 0.75
TZC0132 09 Stormtroopers 0.75
TZC0133 10 Obi-Wan 0.75
TZC0134 11 Han Solo 0.75
TZC0135 12 Leia and C-3PO 0.75
TZC0136 13 Darth's Tie 0.75
TZC0137 14 Luke Skywalker on a Tauntaun 0.75
TZC0138 15 Han Solo 0.75
TZC0139 16 AT-AT Walkers 0.75
TZC0140 17 Luke and R2-D2 ....0.75
TZC0141 18 Luke Skywalker 0.75
TZC0142 19 Jedi Master Yoda 0.75
TZC0143 20 Yoda and Luke 0.75
TZC0144 21 Chewbacca 0.75
TZC0145 22 Lando Calrissian 0.75
TZC0146 23 Leia and Lando 0.75
TZC0147 24 Frozen Han w/Lando 0.75
TZC0148 25 Darth Vader 0.75
TZC0149 26 Leia, Luke, and R2-D2 ....0.75
TZC0150 27 C-3PO and R2-D2 ....0.75
TZC0151 28 Jabba and Salacious.....................0.75
TZC0152 29 Han Solo and Princess Leia 0.75
TZC0153 30 Princess Leia 0.75
TZC0154 31 Chewbacca and Han Solo 0.75
TZC0155 32 Biker Scout.......................................0.75
TZC0156 33 Wicket the Ewok.............................0.75
TZC0157 34 Luke and Han 0.75
TZC0158 35 Han Solo 0.75
TZC0159 36 Luke and Vader 0.75
TZC0160 37 Emperor Palpatine 0.75
TZC0161 38 Luke and Vader Duel.......................0.75
TZC0162 39 Millennium Falcon 0.75
TZC0163 40 Sandtrooper and Dewback.............0.75
TZC0164 41 Wampa 0.75
TZC0165 42 SE Jabba 0.75
TZC0166 43 Rystall and Greeata 0.75
TZC0167 44 Vader 0.75
TZC0168 45 Han 0.75
TZC0169 46 Luke 0.75
TZC0170 47 Rancor 0.75
TZC0171 48 Luke and Leia 0.75
TZC0172 49 B-Wings 0.75
TZC0173 50 Star Wars SE Logo 0.75

Tazo (UK)

TZC0174 01 C-3PO 0.75
TZC0175 02 R2-D2 ....0.75
TZC0176 03 Tusken Raider 0.75
TZC0177 04 Luke Skywalker 0.75
TZC0178 05 Luke, Obi-Wan, and Han 0.75
TZC0179 06 Vader 0.75
TZC0180 07 Tarkin 0.75
TZC0181 08 Luke Skywalker 0.75
TZC0182 09 Stormtroopers 0.75
TZC0183 10 Obi-Wan 0.75
TZC0184 11 Han Solo 0.75
TZC0185 12 Leia and C-3PO 0.75
TZC0186 13 Darth's Tie 0.75
TZC0187 14 Luke Skywalker on a Tauntaun 0.75
TZC0188 15 Han Solo 0.75
TZC0189 16 AT-AT Walkers 0.75
TZC0190 17 Luke and R2-D2 ....0.75
TZC0191 18 Luke Skywalker 0.75
TZC0192 19 Jedi Master Yoda 0.75
TZC0193 20 Yoda and Luke 0.75
TZC0194 21 Chewbacca 0.75
TZC0195 22 Lando Calrissian 0.75
TZC0196 23 Leia and Lando 0.75
TZC0197 24 Frozen Han w/Lando 0.75
TZC0198 25 Darth Vader 0.75
TZC0199 26 Leia, Luke, and R2-D2 ....0.75
TZC0224 26 Luke, Leia, and R2-D2 ....3.50
TZC0200 27 C3PO and R2-D2 ....0.75

TZC0201 28 Jabba and Salacious.....................0.75
TZC0202 29 Han Solo and Princess Leia 0.75
TZC0203 30 Princess Leia 0.75
TZC0204 31 Chewbacca and Han Solo 0.75
TZC0205 32 Biker Scout.......................................0.75
TZC0225 32 Scout Trooper..................................3.50
TZC0206 33 Wicket the Ewok.............................0.75
TZC0207 34 Luke and Han 0.75
TZC0208 35 Han Solo 0.75
TZC0209 36 Luke and Vader 0.75
TZC0210 37 Emperor Palpatine 0.75
TZC0211 38 Luke and Vader Duel.......................0.75
TZC0212 39 Millennium Falcon 0.75
TZC0213 40 Sandtrooper and Dewback.............0.75
TZC0214 41 Wampa 0.75
TZC0215 42 SE Jabba 0.75
TZC0216 43 Rystall and Greeata 0.75
TZC0217 44 Vader 0.75
TZC0218 45 Han 0.75
TZC0219 46 Luke 0.75
TZC0220 47 Rancor 0.75
TZC0221 48 Luke and Leia 0.75
TZC0222 49 B-Wings 0.75
TZC0223 50 Star Wars SE Logo 0.75

TEAPOTS

HOT0001

Sigma
HOT0001 Luke on Tauntaun.................................245.00

TELEPHONES

American Telecommunications

HOZ0001

HOZ0001 Darth Vader Speakerphone 95.00

Sound Trax

HOZ0003   HOZ0002

HOZ0003 Darth Vader 124.00
HOZ0002 R2-D2...65.00

Telemania
HOZ0004 R2-D2, Episode I Box 65.00

HOZ0004   HOZ0005   HOZ0006

Tiger Electronics
HOZ0005 Darth Maul compact phone 17.00
HOZ0006 Queen Amidala compact phone 17.00

THANK YOU CARDS

Drawing Board
TN0001 R2-D2 Thank You Cards, 8-pack 12.00

Party Express

TN0002 front and back

TN0002 Jar Jar Binks: "Thanks!", 8-pack 4.00

THERMOS

King Seeley-Thermos

THM0004 **THM0005 alternate colors** **THM0006** **THM0007**

THM0005 Empire Strikes Back: Yoda 8.00
THM0007 Ewoks: Princess Kneesaa 11.00
THM0006 Return of the Jedi: Wicket 8.00
THM0004 Star Wars: R2-D2 and C-3PO 8.00

Zak Designs

THM0001 **THM0002** **THM0003** **THM0008**

THM0002 Anakin and Sebulba Sip N' Snack Canteen.................................7.00
THM0003 Anakin and Sebulba Sip N' Snack Canteen w/Podrace cup ..11.00
THM0009 Anakin and Sebulba with cup lid 10.00
THM0001 Anakin Skywalker Sip N' Snack Canteen 7.00
THM0008 Darth Vader pop-up thermos 47.00

TICKET STUBS

TKT0001

Disney / MGM
TKT0001 Star Tours, cast premiere 3.00

TIN CONTAINERS

Chein Industries

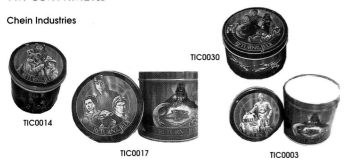

TIC0030
TIC0014
TIC0017
TIC0003

TIC0003 C-3PO and R2-D2 Mini-Tin, 3½" high...............................8.00
TIC0004 C-3PO and R2-D2 Trinket Tin, 1" high..............................4.00
TIC0008 Darth Vader Mini-Tin, 3½" high......................................8.00
TIC0010 Darth Vader Trinket Tin, 1" high.....................................4.00
TIC0013 Ewoks Carry-All rectangular tin with handles and lid...............14.00
TIC0014 Ewoks Mini-Tin, 3½" high..8.00
TIC0015 Ewoks Trinket Tin, 1" high...4.00
TIC0017 Han Solo, Luke Skywalker, and Princess Leia Mini-Tin, 3½" high 8.00
TIC0018 Han Solo, Luke Skywalker, and Princess Leia Trinket Tin, 1" high ...4.00
TIC0019 Jabba the Hutt Mini-Tin, 3½" high...................................8.00
TIC0020 Jabba the Hutt Trinket Tin, 1" high.................................4.00
TIC0025 Max Rebo Band Mini-Tin, 3½" high..................................8.00
TIC0026 Max Rebo Band Trinket Tin, 1" high.................................4.00
TIC0029 ROTJ Carry-All rectangular tin with handles and lid...................17.00
TIC0030 ROTJ Round Cookie Tin with lid..23.00

Metal Box Ltd.

TIC0005 **TIC0011**

TIC0001 AT-AT tin, small 7.00
TIC0002 Boba Fett tin, small 7.00
TIC0005 Chewbacca tin, medium 9.00
TIC0006 Cloud City tin, oval 18.00
TIC0007 Darth Vader and Luke Skywalker Duel tin, small 7.00
TIC0009 Darth Vader tin, medium 9.00
TIC0011 Droids / Probot Space Trunk tin 20.00
TIC0012 Droids / Probot tin, square 20.00
TIC0016 Han Solo tin, medium..9.00
TIC0021 Lando Calrissian tin, small 7.00
TIC0022 Luke on Tauntaun tin, small 7.00
TIC0023 Luke Skywalker Space Trunk tin 20.00
TIC0024 Luke Skywalker tin, medium 9.00
TIC0027 Princess Leia tin, medium 9.00
TIC0028 Probot tin, medium 9.00
TIC0031 Star Destroyer tin, medium 9.00
TIC0032 Yoda tin, medium 9.00
TIC0033 Yoda tin, small 7.00

TISSUE BOXES

Puffs
PAT0001 Bespin scene...16.00
PAT0002 Dagobah scene..16.00
PAT0003 Hoth scene..16.00

TISSUE COVERS

TIS0001

Jay Franco and Sons
TIS0001 Space Battle scene printed on 2 sides 11.00

TOOTHBRUSH HOLDERS

HOW0003 **HOW0004** **HOW0005**

Grosvenor
HOW0005 Darth Maul, electronic 38.00
HOW0003 Droid Fighter and Naboo Fighter, rotating.......................32.00

Toothbrush Holders

HOW0004 Jar Jar Binks, 3D 16.00

Jay Franco and Sons

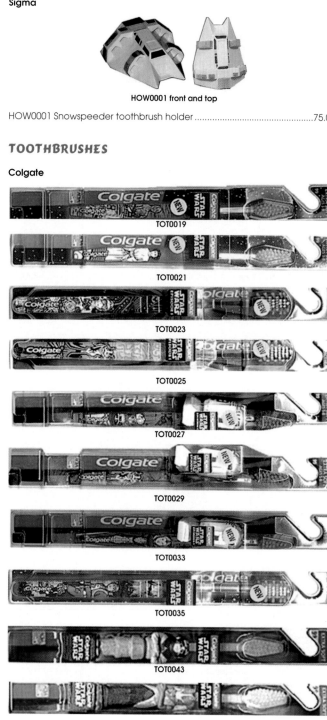

HOW0002 front and back

HOW0002 Anakin / Sebulba 2-sided sculpt 8.00

Sigma

HOW0001 front and top

HOW0001 Snowspeeder toothbrush holder 75.00

TOOTHBRUSHES

Colgate

TOT0019
TOT0021
TOT0023
TOT0025
TOT0027
TOT0029
TOT0033
TOT0035
TOT0043
TOT0045

TOT0020 Darth Vader 6.00
TOT0019 Droids on Tatooine 6.00
TOT0018 Luke Skywalker, X-Wing Pilot 5.00
TOT0035 Luke Skywalker, X-Wing Pilot (Space Battle) 6.00
TOT0021 Princess Leia 7.00
TOT0036 Princess Leia (Rebel Insignia) 7.00
TOT0043 Sculpted, Anakin Skywalker as podracer pilot 8.00
TOT0044 Sculpted, Darth Vader 8.00
TOT0045 Sculpted, Jar Jar Binks 8.00
TOT0046 Sculpted, Yoda 9.00
TOT0038 TPM: Anakin Skywalker 6.00
TOT0026 TPM: Anakin Skywalker w/Free Anakin Holder 9.00
TOT0027 TPM: Anakin Skywalker w/Free R2-D2 Holder 7.00
TOT0023 TPM: C-3PO 6.00

TOT0030   TOT0032   TOT0047

TOT0018

TOT0020

TOT0022

TOT0024

TOT0026

TOT0028

TOT0031

TOT0034

TOT0036

TOT0044

TOT0046

TOT0024 TPM: Darth Maul 6.00
TOT0047 TPM: Darth Maul w/Free Darth Maul Holder and Toothpaste....18.00
TOT0037 TPM: Jar Jar Binks (Naboo) 6.00
TOT0028 TPM: Jar Jar Binks (Naboo) w/Free Jar Jar Holder 9.00
TOT0030 TPM: Jar Jar Binks (Naboo) w/Free Jar Jar Holder and Toothpaste...11.00
TOT0029 TPM: Jar Jar Binks (Naboo) w/Free R2-D2 Holder 7.00
TOT0025 TPM: Jar Jar Binks (Tatooine) 6.00
TOT0042 TPM: "Jedi vs. Sith" w/Free Darth Maul Holder...........................9.00
TOT0040 TPM: Obi-Wan (Jedi vs. Sith) 6.00
TOT0041 TPM: Obi-Wan (Jedi vs. Sith) w/Free Darth Maul Holder 6.00
TOT0034 TPM: Obi-Wan (Jedi vs. Sith) w/Free R2-D2 Holder 8.00
TOT0039 TPM: Queen Amidala (Coruscant) 6.00
TOT0031 TPM: Queen Amidala (Coruscant) w/Free Amidala Holder 9.00
TOT0032 TPM: Queen Amidala (Coruscant) w/Free Amidala Holder and
   Toothpaste 11.00
TOT0033 TPM: Queen Amidala (Coruscant) w/Free R2-D2 Holder 7.00
TOT0022 TPM: Queen Amidala (Travel Gown) 6.00

Kenner

TOT0001   TOT0004

TOT0002 Empire Strikes Back, battery operated 45.00
TOT0003 Return of the Jedi, battery operated 85.00
TOT0001 Star Wars, battery operated 85.00
TOT0004 Wicket the Ewok, battery operated 80.00

Oral-B
Packaged on cardback.

TOT0007   TOT0015

TOT0006

TOT0008

TOT0012

TOT0010

TOT0014

TOT0016

TOT0017

TOT0005 C-3PO and R2-D2 ....5.00
TOT0007 Chewbacca and Han Solo..5.00
TOT0009 Darth Vader 5.00
TOT0011 Ewoks 5.00
TOT0013 Luke Skywalker 5.00
TOT0015 Princess Leia 5.00

Packaged in shrinkwrap.
TOT0006 C-3PO and R2-D2 ....3.00
TOT0008 Chewbacca and Han Solo..3.00
TOT0010 Darth Vader 3.00
TOT0012 Ewoks 3.00
TOT0017 Jedi Masters (mail-in premium)......................................11.00
TOT0014 Luke Skywalker 3.00
TOT0016 Princess Leia 3.00

TOOTHPASTE

Colgate
Galactic bubblemint.
TTP0003 Anakin Skywalker...6.00

TTP0001   TTP0002   TTP0003   TTP0004   TTP0005

TTP0006

TTP0007

TTP0008

TTP0009

TTP0010 front and back

TTP0002 Darth Vader and Deathstar 6.00
TTP0001 Droids on Tatooine 6.00
TTP0004 Jar Jar Binks 6.00
TTP0005 Jedi vs. Sith 6.00

Tartar coltrol with free teen/adult character toothbrush.
TTP0006 Darth Vader 8.00
TTP0007 Princess Leia 8.00
TTP0008 TPM: C-3PO 8.00
TTP0009 TPM: Darth Maul 8.00
TTP0010 TPM: Queen Amidala (Coruscant).....................................8.00

TOTE BAGS

Adam Joseph Industries

LT0011   LT0037

LT0010 Biker Scout, ditty bag 8.00
LT0002 C-3PO and R2-D2 ....12.00
LT0037 C-3PO and R2-D2, barrel bag 17.00
LT0011 C-3PO and R2-D2, ditty bag 8.00
LT0004 Darth Vader with handle 15.00
LT0012 Sail Barge, ditty bag 8.00
LT0008 Wicket the Ewok 10.00
LT0009 Yoda 12.00

Disney / MGM
LT0035 Star Tours, with logo 17.00

Factors, Etc.
LT0003 "Darth Vader Lives" 15.00
LT0006 "May The Force Be With You" 15.00
LT0001 C-3PO and R2-D2 ....15.00
LT0005 Hilderbrandt Art 15.00
LT0007 Star Wars logo 15.00

Pyramid
LT0013 Boba Fett, Dark Side collection, nylon with embossed rubber artwork 20.00

Tote Bags

LT0034

LT0036

LT0017 Boba Fett, Destroyer collection, vinyl with metallic trim and inset art-
work 20.00
LT0021 Boba Fett, Hi-Tech collection, nylon with all-over artwork 20.00
LT0025 Boba Fett, Imperial collection, nylon with rubber patch................20.00
LT0028 Boba Fett, Star Class collection, vinyl with inset artwork 20.00
LT0032 Boba Fett, Zoom collection, vinyl with all-over artwork 20.00
LT0029 C-3PO, Star Class collection, vinyl with inset artwork 20.00
LT0014 Darth Vader, Dark Side collection, nylon with embossed rubber art-
work 20.00
LT0018 Darth Vader, Destroyer collection, vinyl with metallic trim and inset
artwork..20.00
LT0022 Darth Vader, Hi-Tech collection, nylon with all-over artwork........20.00
LT0026 Darth Vader, Imperial collection, nylon with rubber patch..........20.00
LT0030 Darth Vader, Star Class collection, vinyl with inset artwork..........20.00
LT0033 Darth Vader, Zoom collection, vinyl with all-over artwork..........20.00
LT0036 Jedi vs. Sith...6.00
LT0015 Luke Skywalker, Dark Side collection, nylon with embossed rubber
artwork..20.00
LT0019 Luke Skywalker, Destroyer collection, vinyl with metallic trim and inset
artwork..20.00
LT0034 Luke Skywalker, Zoom collection, vinyl with all-over artwork 20.00
LT0016 Stormtrooper, Dark Side collection, nylon with embossed rubber art-
work 20.00
LT0020 Stormtrooper, Destroyer collection, vinyl with metallic trim and inset
artwork..20.00
LT0023 Stormtrooper, Hi-Tech collection, nylon with all-over artwork 20.00
LT0027 Stormtrooper, Imperial collection, nylon with rubber patch.........20.00
LT0031 Stormtrooper, Star Class collection, vinyl with inset artwork 20.00
LT0024 Yoda, Hi-Tech collection, nylon with all-over artwork..................20.00

TOTES, RECORD AND TAPE

Buena Vista Records

PER0001

PER0002

PER0001 Return of the Jedi cassette tote 17.00
PER0002 Star Wars record tote for 45 RPMs 23.00

TOWELS: BATH

Bibb Co.
CTB0001 Boba Fett with Darth Vader and C-3PO, Cloud City, R2-D2, and
Yoda 10.00
CTB0002 Darth Vader, Chewbacca, Han, Leia, Luke, R2-D2, and C-3PO....10.00
CTB0003 Darth Vader, Leia, Luke, R2-D2, and C-3PO 10.00
CTB0004 R2-D2 ....10.00

TOWELS: BEACH

Bibb Co.
CTL0001 Boba Fett, Cloud City, Darth Vader, R2-D2, and C-3PO,
snowspeeders, Yoda 20.00
CTL0002 Boba Fett, Darth Vader, Chewbacca, Han, Leia, Luke, R2-D2, and
C-3PO 20.00

CTL0002

CTL0004

CTL0006

CTL0012

CTL0020

CTL0021

CTL0022

CTL0023

CTL0003 Boba Fett, Darth Vader, Leia, Luke, R2-D2 ....20.00
CTL0006 C-3PO, Chewbacca, Darth Vader, Han, Leia, Luke, and R2-D2....15.00
CTL0004 C-3PO, R2-D2, and planets 25.00
CTL0005 Chewbacca with planets 35.00
CTL0007 Darth Vader with planets 30.00
CTL0008 Darth Vader, Death Star, Jawas, and Stormtroopers 20.00
CTL0009 Darth Vader, Tie Fighters, logo...18.00
CTL0010 Main heros circled by Ewoks, ships, Jabba's palace, and Darth
Vader..16.00
CTL0011 Max Rebo Band, R2-D2 and Wicket, Jabba the Hutt 25.00
CTL0012 ROTJ art, Luke and Darth Vader Duel in front of Darth Vader silhou-
ette 45.00
CTL0013 Wicket the Ewok 15.00
CTL0014 Yoda with Dagobah tree 30.00

Jay Franco and Sons
CTL0022 Anakin Skywalker, Podrace...12.00
CTL0016 Droids on black background, white reverse...............................18.00
CTL0015 Droids on white background, white reverse 18.00
CTL0020 Princess Leia 18.00
CTL0023 Queen Amidala, Coruscant 12.00
CTL0017 Stormtrooper "Freeze you rebel scum" 18.00
CTL0021 TPM movie poster art 12.00
CTL0018 Vader helmet, space battle 18.00
CTL0019 Vader on black background, white reverse.................................18.00

TOWELS: HAND

Bibb Co.
CTH0001 Boba Fett, Darth Vader, and snowspeeders.............................8.00
CTH0002 C-3PO and R2-D2 ....8.00
CTH0003 C-3PO, Leia, Luke, R2-D2 ....8.00
CTH0004 Darth Vader and Dogfight 8.00
CTH0005 R2-D2 ....8.00

Westpoint Stevens

CTH0006

CTH0010

2-piece, washcloth and hand towel.
CTH0006 Classic Starships 11.00
CTH0007 Anakin Skywalker 14.00
CTH0008 Jar Jar Binks 14.00
CTH0009 Queen Amidala 14.00
CTH0010 TPM Starfighters..14.00

3-piece, washcloth, hand, and bath towel.
CTH0011 Anakin Skywalker 17.00

TOY CHESTS

FUU0001

FUU0003 front and side

344

American Toy and Furniture Co.
FUU0003 Ewoks toy chest 125.00
FUU0001 R2-D2 toychest, sculpted details 95.00

Born to Play
FUU0005 Episode I 96.00

FUU0005   FUU0004

Worlds Apart
FUU0004 Pop'n'Fun R2-D2 Pop-Tidy 54.00

TOYS: DIECAST METAL

TYD0001   TYD0005   TYD0008   TYD0010   TYD0013

TYD0003   TYD0006

TYD0011   TYD0014   TYD0035

Kenner
TYD0001 Darth Vader Tie Fighter, large wings 65.00
TYD0002 Darth Vader Tie Fighter, small wings 235.00
TYD0003 Imperial Cruiser 135.00
TYD0004 Imperial Cruiser with Background 325.00
TYD0005 Land Speeder 65.00
TYD0006 Millennium Falcon 125.00
TYD0007 Millennium Falcon with Background 335.00
TYD0008 Slave I 85.00
TYD0009 Snowspeeder 65.00
TYD0010 Tie Fighter 65.00
TYD0035 Tie Fighter, Brown Catalog-Order Box 112.00
TYD0011 Tiebomber 365.00
TYD0012 Twin-Pod Cloud Car 45.00
TYD0013 X-Wing Fighter 75.00
TYD0014 Y-Wing Fighter 95.00
TYD0015 Y-Wing Fighter with Background 375.00

Takara
TYD0017 C-3PO, approx 10" 335.00
TYD0036 Darth Vader, approx 10" 315.00
TYD0016 X-Wing Fighter 85.00

TYD0017   TYD0016 front and back   TYD0036
front and open   front and open

Toltoys
TYD0022 X-Wing Fighter...114.00

TOYS: ELECTRONIC, SPEAKING

TES0013   TES0014   TES0015   TES0016   TES0018

Hasbro
Palm talkers.
TES0013 Boba Fett 15.00
TES0014 C-3PO 15.00
TES0015 Chewbacca 15.00
TES0016 Darth Vader 15.00
TES0017 R2-D2 ....15.00
TES0018 Stormtrooper 15.00

Tiger Electronics
TES0006 Yoda, Interactive..39.00

TES0006 front and back   TES0001   TES0002   TES0003   TES0004   TES0005

TES0008   TES0009   TES0010   TES0012

Tomy
Palm talkers.
TES0001 Battle Droid 45.00
TES0007 Boba Fett 35.00
TES0008 C-3PO 35.00
TES0009 Chewbacca 35.00
TES0002 Darth Maul 45.00
TES0010 Darth Vader 35.00
TES0003 Jar Jar Binks 45.00
TES0004 R2-D2, EPI 45.00
TES0012 Stormtrooper 35.00
TES0005 Yoda 45.00

TOYS: PREMIUMS

Kellogg's
C-3PO's Rebel Rockets.
PCT0021 C-3PO and Darth Vader 35.00
PCT0022 Chewbacca and Stormtrooper 25.00
PCT0023 Luke Skywalker and R2-D2 ....25.00

Kentucky Fried Chicken
PCT0041 Anakin Skywalker's Naboo fighter 3.00
PCT0032 AT-AT with snowtrooper on door 5.00
PCT0033 AT-ST with walking action 5.00
PCT0037 Balancing Tie fighter and X-Wing fighter 4.00
PCT0038 Boss Nass squirter 3.00
PCT0035 Death Star shooter 4.00
PCT0046 Gungan sub squirter 3.00
PCT0039 Jar Jar Binks squirter 3.00
PCT0044 Naboo ground battle 3.00
PCT0043 Opee sea creature chaser 3.00
PCT0047 Planet Naboo 3.00
PCT0042 Queen Amidala's hidden identity 3.00
PCT0036 Sandcrawler with R2 ....4.00
PCT0040 Swimming Jar Jar Binks 3.00

Toys, Premiums

PCT0045 Trade Federation droid fighter 3.00
PCT0034 Vader head spinner.....................................4.00

Pizza Hut
PCT0053 Darth Maul's Sith Infiltrator 3.00
PCT0055 Jar Jar 3.00
PCT0048 Lott Dod walking throne................................3.00
PCT0051 Planet Coruscant 3.00
PCT0050 Queen's ship launcher 3.00
PCT0054 R2-D2 ....3.00
PCT0052 Sith holoprojector 3.00
PCT0049 Yoda Jedi destiny 3.00

Taco Bell
PCT0024 Balancing Boba Fett 3.00
PCT0025 Exploding Death Star 6.00
PCT0026 Floating Cloud City 4.00
PCT0029 Folding Picture Cube, Special Edition scenes 3.00
PCT0027 Illusion Cube 4.00
PCT0028 Millennium Falcon w/zip cord 4.00
PCT0030 R2-D2 3-piece playset 4.00
PCT0031 Yoda figure 5.00

Tambola

PCT0016   PCT0019   PCT0018   PCT0015   PCT0017

PCT0013   PCT0010   PCT0009   PCT0011   PCT0014   PCT0012

PCT0020   PCT0004   PCT0008   PCT0006   PCT0001   PCT0002   PCT0003

PCT0013 AT-AT 4.00
PCT0016 AT-AT Attack, puzzle 6.00
PCT0020 C-3PO 5.00
PCT0004 Chewbacca 5.00
PCT0008 Darth Vader 5.00
PCT0019 Darth Vader on Bespin, puzzle 6.00
PCT0010 Darth Vader's Tie Fighter 4.00

PCT0007   PCT0005

PCT0018 Dogfight Above Death Star II, puzzle 6.00
PCT0006 Han Solo 5.00
PCT0015 Heroes on Hoth, puzzle 6.00
PCT0009 Imperial Shuttle 4.00
PCT0001 Luke Skywalker 5.00
PCT0011 Millennium Falcon 4.00
PCT0002 Princess Leia 5.00
PCT0003 R2-D2 ....5.00
PCT0007 Stormtrooper 5.00
PCT0014 Tie Fighter 4.00
PCT0012 X-Wing Fighter 4.00
PCT0005 Yoda 5.00
PCT0017 Yoda, Puzzle 6.00

TRADING CARDS: TOPPS VINTAGE ESB

Topps
TR20005 Series 1: Box Only (Empty)..............................5.00
TR20001 Series 1: Red, Set of 132...............................80.00
TR20002 Series 1: Red, Set of 132 with 33 Stickers..............97.00
TR20003 Series 1: Red, Unopened Wax Pack, 12 cards, 1 sticker....6.00
TR20004 Series 1: Red, Wax Pack wrapper only....................4.00
TR20006 Series 1: Unopened Box, 36 Wax Packs....................185.00
TR20007 Series 2: Blue, Set of 132..............................80.00
TR20008 Series 2: Blue, Set of 132 with 33 Stickers 97.00

TR20009 Series 2: Blue, Unopened Wax Pack, 12 cards, 1 sticker ...6.00
TR20010 Series 2: Blue, Wax Pack wrapper only...................4.00
TR20011 Series 2: Box Only (Empty).............................5.00
TR20012 Series 2: Unopened Box, 36 Wax Packs...................185.00
TR20017 Series 3: Box Only (Empty).............................5.00
TR20013 Series 3: Green, Set of 132............................80.00
TR20014 Series 3: Green, Set of 132 with 33 Stickers...........97.00
TR20015 Series 3: Green, Unopened Wax Pack, 12 cards, 1 sticker...6.00
TR20016 Series 3: Green, Wax Pack wrapper only.................4.00
TR20018 Series 3: Unopened Box, 36 Wax Packs...................185.00

TRADING CARDS: TOPPS VINTAGE ROTJ

Topps
TR30005 Series 1: Box Only (Empty)..............................5.00
TR30001 Series 1: Red, Set of 132...............................80.00
TR30002 Series 1: Red, Set of 132 with 33 Stickers..............97.00
TR30003 Series 1: Red, Unopened Wax Pack, 10 cards, 1 sticker....6.00
TR30004 Series 1: Red, Wax Pack wrapper only (4 diff.) 4.00
TR30006 Series 1: Unopened Box, 36 Wax Packs....................185.00
TR30007 Series 2: Blue, Set of 88...............................65.00
TR30008 Series 2: Blue, Set of 88 with 22 Stickers..............80.00
TR30009 Series 2: Blue, Unopened Wax Pack, 10 cards, 1 sticker ...5.00
TR30010 Series 2: Blue, Wax Pack wrapper only (4 different) 4.00
TR30011 Series 2: Box Only (Empty)..............................5.00
TR30012 Series 2: Unopened Box, 36 Wax Packs...................165.00

TRADING CARDS: TOPPS VINTAGE SW

Topps
TR10001 Series 1: Blue, Set of 66 ....100.00
TR10002 Series 1: Blue, Set of 66 with 11 Stickers 125.00
TR10003 Series 1: Blue, Unopened Wax Pack, 7 cards, 1 sticker, 1 stick of gum 9.00
TR10004 Series 1: Blue, Wax Pack wrapper only 5.00
TR10006 Series 1: Box Only (Empty)..............................5.00
TR10005 Series 1: Unopened Box, 36 Wax Packs....................350.00
TR10012 Series 2: Box Only (Empty)..............................5.00
TR10007 Series 2: Red, Set of 66 ....90.00
TR10008 Series 2: Red, Set of 66 with 11 Stickers...............125.00
TR10009 Series 2: Red, Unopened Wax Pack, 7 cards, 1 sticker, 1 stick of gum 8.00
TR10010 Series 2: Red, Wax Pack wrapper only 4.00
TR10011 Series 2: Unopened Box, 36 Wax Packs....................300.00
TR10018 Series 3: Box Only (Empty)..............................5.00
TR10017 Series 3: Unopened Box, 36 Wax Packs....................265.00
TR10013 Series 3: Yellow, Set of 66 ....75.00
TR10014 Series 3: Yellow, Set of 66 with 11 Stickers............100.00
TR10015 Series 3: Yellow, Unopened Wax Pack, 7 cards, 1 sticker, 1 stick of gum 7.00
TR10016 Series 3: Yellow, Wax Pack wrapper only 4.00
TR10024 Series 4: Box Only (Empty)..............................5.00
TR10019 Series 4: Green, Set of 66 + Alternate #207 ....115.00
TR10020 Series 4: Green, Set of 66 + Alternate #207 with 11 Stickers 145.00
TR10021 Series 4: Green, Unopened Wax Pack, 7 cards, 1 sticker, 1 stick of gum 7.00
TR10022 Series 4: Green, Wax Pack wrapper only 4.00
TR10023 Series 4: Unopened Box, 36 Wax Packs....................275.00
TR10030 Series 5: Box Only (Empty)..............................5.00
TR10025 Series 5: Orange, Set of 66 ....75.00
TR10026 Series 5: Orange, Set of 66 with 11 Stickers............95.00
TR10027 Series 5: Orange, Unopened Wax Pack, 7 cards, 1 sticker, 1 stick of gum 7.00
TR10028 Series 5: Orange, Wax Pack wrapper only 4.00
TR10029 Series 5: Unopened Box, 36 Wax Packs....................265.00

TRAIN CARS

Lionel
TRC0001 Boxcar, O-scale, reads: "Seasons Greetings 1977 from Lionel", features R2-D2 line drawing. Exclusive Christmas gift to Lionel employees...930.00

TRANSFERS

American Publishing / Presto Magix
CRT0001 Asteroids, bagged 7.00

| CRT0004 | CTR0005 | CRT0012 | CRT0017 | CTR0006 |

| CRT0008 | CTR0014 | CRT0016 | CRT0018 |

| CRT0002 | CRT0010 |

CRT0002 Battle on Endor, boxed 15.00
CRT0004 Beneath Cloud City, bagged 7.00
CRT0003 Cloud City Battle, bagged 7.00
CRT0005 Dagobah Bog Planet, bagged 7.00
CRT0006 Death Star, bagged 7.00
CRT0017 Deck of the Star Destroyer, bagged 7.00
CRT0007 Ewok Hut, bagged 9.00
CRT0008 Ewok Village, bagged..7.00
CRT0009 Ewok Village, boxed 12.00
CRT0010 Ewoks at Home, boxed 12.00
CRT0011 Ewoks at Play, bagged 9.00
CRT0013 Hoth, bagged 7.00
CRT0014 Jabba's Throne Room, bagged 7.00
CRT0015 Jabba's Throne Room, boxed 15.00
CRT0012 Rebel Base, bagged 7.00
CRT0016 Sarlacc Pit, bagged 7.00
CRT0018 Star Wars Activity set, boxed 20.00

Letraset
CRT0019 01 Kidnap of Princess Leia 7.00
CRT0020 02 Sale on Tatooine 7.00
CRT0021 03 Action at Mos Eisley 7.00
CRT0022 04 Escape from Stormtroopers 7.00
CRT0023 05 Flight to Alderaan 7.00
CRT0024 06 Inside the Death Star 7.00
CRT0025 07 Prison Break...7.00
CRT0026 08 Death Star Escape 7.00
CRT0027 09 Rebel Base...7.00
CRT0028 10 Last Battle 7.00
CRT0029 Battle at Mos Eisley, large 16.00
CRT0030 Escape from Death Star, large 16.00
CRT0031 Rebel Attack, large 16.00

Rose Art Industries
CRT0039 Presto Magix Stick 'n Lift 6.00

CRT0039

Thomas Salter

| CRT0040 | CRT0041 | CRT0042 |

CRT0032 Battle on Endor...12.00
CRT0033 Ewok Village 10.00
CRT0034 Ewok Village, boxed 18.00
CRT0035 Ewoks...8.00
CRT0036 Jabba the Hutt...8.00
CRT0037 Jabba's Throne Room 10.00
CRT0038 Sarlacc Pit..11.00
CRT0041 Ewok Village rub down Action Transfers 18.00
CRT0042 POS display complete with ROTJ Action Transfers 215.00
CRT0040 Sarlacc Pit rub down Action Transfers 18.00

TRANSFORMING TOYS

TTY0001 box and contents

Takara
TTY0001 Transforming X-Wing...535.00

TRAVEL KITS

Adam Joseph Industries
TOK0002 Princess Kneesaa personal care bag................................18.00

Omni Cosmetics

| TOK0001 | TOK0003 |

TOK0001 Luke Skywalker Belt Kit; clear vinyl w/belt slots, bubble bath, shampoo, soap, comb, toothbrush 26.00
TOK0003 Princess Leia Beauty Bag; clear vinyl w/straps, shampoo, rinse, cologne, soap, and comb 26.00

Sharper Image
TOK0004 Zippered travel case with logo zipper keys and embossed rebel logo..45.00

TOK0004

Trays

TRAYS

TTT0002

Chein Industries
TIT0001 Ewoks animated scene tray 20.00
TIT0002 ROTJ Logo and collage tray 24.00

Disney / MGM
TIT0003 Star Wars artwork with Star Tours logo 12.00

TRUCKS, TOY

TRK0001

TRK0001 Inter-Transmax 9968 Semi, Star Warrior.........................46.00

T-SHIRTS

American Marketing Enterprises
AT0049 Boba Fett 15.00
AT0059 Bounty Hunters 7.00
AT0060 Chewbacca 7.00
AT0061 Droids and red sky 7.00
AT0062 Emperor 7.00
AT0063 Empire Villains 7.00
AT0064 ESB Vader with crossed lightsabers 7.00
AT0065 Han Solo 7.00
AT0066 Jawa with big wrench 7.00
AT0067 Luke and Leia swinging 7.00
AT0068 Movie Poster 'A' 7.00
AT0069 Rancor 7.00
AT0070 Vader 7.00
AT0071 Yoda 7.00

Barrett Sportswear
AT0045 SW trilogy for Musicland, Sci-Fi Channel and Suncoast Video 35.00

Creative Conventions
AT0001 10th anniversary SW Convention..25.00

Factors, Etc.
AT0013 "Darth Vader Lives"..10.00
AT0031 "May The Force Be With You" 10.00
AT0002 C-3PO 10.00
AT0003 C-3PO and R2-D2 ....10.00
AT0004 C-3PO and R2-D2 on sand 10.00
AT0005 C-3PO, glitter..10.00
AT0006 Chewbacca 10.00
AT0008 Chewbacca, glitter 10.00
AT0009 Darth Vader 10.00
AT0011 Darth Vader and Obi-Wan Kenobi 10.00
AT0012 Darth Vader and X-Wing Fighter 10.00
AT0014 Darth Vader, glitter 10.00
AT0022 Han Solo 10.00
AT0024 Han Solo and Chewbacca 10.00
AT0026 Jawas 10.00
AT0027 Jawas, glitter 10.00
AT0028 Luke Skywalker 10.00
AT0030 Luke Skywalker, glitter 10.00
AT0033 Princess Leia 10.00
AT0034 Princess Leia, glitter 10.00

AT0035 R2-D2 ....10.00
AT0036 R2-D2, glitter 10.00
AT0041 Star Wars logo 10.00
AT0042 Star Wars logo, glitter 10.00
AT0043 Stormtrooper on Dewback 10.00
AT0044 Stormtrooper, glitter 10.00
AT0053 X-Wing and Tie Fighter Dogfight...10.00

Fan Club
AT0057 Episode I, 100% cotton, long sleeve, black with white logo embroidered 24.00
AT0058 Episode I, 100% cotton, short sleeve, black or white with logo
embroidered across chest 24.00

Freeze
AT0078 "Lord Vader" and blueprints of his Tie fighter on black shirt 12.00
AT0079 "Star Wars, May The Force Be With You" silver and black on black
shirt 12.00
AT0072 Boba Fett and Darth Vader on black shirt 12.00
AT0073 Darth Vader and small red plasticized square on black shirt 12.00
AT0074 Darth Vader on gray shirt 12.00
AT0075 Droids and green framing on black shirt 12.00
AT0076 Droids and small blue plasticized square on black shirt 12.00
AT0077 Droids, reflective silver / gold on black...............................12.00

Giant Manufacturing
AT0081 "Abner Yoda" (YODA block letters, Yoda art in oval, "JEDI MASTER")
on dark green shirt 18.00
AT0090 "Darth Star" (crossed sabers Vader and Death Star) on black
shirt 14.00
AT0099 "Sith" Darth Maul on black and red V tie-dye 14.00
AT0108 "Young Vader" two-tone dyed 14.00
AT0080 3-D Jar Jar Binks head 16.00
AT0082 Anakin Skywalker running on half brown, half black shirt...........14.00
AT0083 Darth Maul action pose in green glowing ink on black shirt........14.00
AT0084 Darth Maul and horizontal pattern stripe on white shirt 14.00
AT0085 Darth Maul black spiral tie-dye on red shirt 14.00
AT0086 Darth Maul face and horizontal flames..................................14.00
AT0087 Darth Maul green lettering, tattoo pattern all over 14.00
AT0088 Darth Maul on black and red diagonal tie-dye 14.00
AT0089 Darth Maul "Sith" on green shirt 14.00
AT0091 Darth Vader Anakin Skywalker on dark blue shirt 14.00
AT0092 EPI "Line up"...14.00
AT0093 EPI "The Emperor"...14.00
AT0094 Jar Jar Binks with long tongue on green and blue tie-dye shirt...14.00
AT0095 Pod race scene in large SW logo on red tie-dye shirt 14.00
AT0096 Podracer on blue and brown tie-dye shirt 14.00
AT0097 Queen Amidala on dark blue tie-dye 14.00
AT0098 Queen Amidala on pink and red tie-dye 14.00
AT0100 Sith Lord photo on dark blue shirt 14.00
AT0101 SW orange oval on horizontal double-sided lightsaber 14.00
AT0102 SW yellow oval 14.00
AT0103 TPM "Jedi shadow" tie-dye 14.00
AT0104 TPM lightsaber duel in large SW logo 14.00
AT0105 TPM "New band" on black shirt...14.00
AT0106 TPM space battle in horizontal strip on white shirt 14.00
AT0107 TPM space battle in large SW logo on slate shirt.......................14.00

Hanes
AT0111 "JEDI" in huge lettering with scenes in the letters, on brick red shirt ..18.00
AT0114 "Star Wars" metalized oval logo...18.00
AT0115 "Star Wars", Darth Vader, and lightsaber battle on black shirt...18.00
AT0109 Darth Vader and "Join the Dark Side" 18.00
AT0110 Darth Vader, "The Empire wants you" on blue shirt 18.00
AT0116 Darth Vader's head with glow-in-the-dark "X-ray" features on black
shirt 18.00
AT0112 Rancor on white shirt 18.00
AT0113 Space battle on black shirt...18.00

Hi-C
AT0039 ROTJ: T-Shirt premium from Hi-C...25.00

ILM / Crew
AT0157 "Loose Lips Sink Starships", pre-EPI production crew only, "ILM Dept.
of Defense" 45.00

In Advance
AT0117 ANH style "B" poster art on black shirt 12.00
AT0118 Blue Darth Vader helmet and Luke on black shirt (blue Vader and
crossed lightsabers on back)..12.00
AT0119 C-3PO head fills up orange shirt 14.00

AT0120 Darth Vader and saber and blue window on black shirt.............12.00
AT0121 Darth Vader and saber and blue window on gray shirt (long sleeve, with SW logo on sleeve) 12.00
AT0122 Darth Vader and saber and blue window on white shirt (long sleeve, with SW logo on sleeve) 12.00
AT0123 Darth Vader and star destroyer and "Join the Empire and See the Universe" on black shirt 12.00
AT0124 Darth Vader and "The Galactic Empire Wants You" on gray shirt ...12.00
AT0125 Darth Vader and "The Galactic Empire Wants You" on white shirt .12.00
AT0126 Darth Vader helmet fills up black shirt 14.00
AT0127 Darth Vader, 2 stormtroopers, and blueprint on black shirt (long sleeve, with Imperial emblem on sleeve) 12.00
AT0128 Darth Vader, Death Star II, Falcon on black shirt 12.00
AT0129 Darth Vader, Death Star II, Falcon on black shirt (long sleeve)....12.00
AT0130 Darth Vader, Death Star II, star destroyer, yellow sun on black shirt (long sleeve) 12.00
AT0131 Darth Vader, fighters, and exploding Tie on black shirt (blue Vader and crossed lightsabers on back)...12.00
AT0132 Darth Vader, fighters, and exploding Tie on black shirt (nothing on back) 12.00
AT0133 Darth Vader, star destroyer, and 2 stormtroopers on dark blue shirt.12.00
AT0134 Droids and twin suns on white shirt 12.00
AT0135 Droids in orange glow (yellow SW logo on back) 12.00
AT0136 Fett head fills up brown shirt 15.00
AT0137 Luke and Yoda and ROTJ logo on gray shirt 12.00
AT0138 Stormtrooper head fills up green shirt 14.00
AT0139 Ties and X-wing in trench (XRS logo on back) 12.00
AT0140 Ties shooting an X-wing over the Death Star surface on black shirt .12.00
AT0141 Yoda head fills up black shirt 15.00

JEM Sportswear

AT0149 "SW Darth / Maul" 2-sided black shirt 14.00
AT0150 "SW EPI" Darth Maul eyes on black shirt 14.00
AT0142 Anakin Skywalker on gray shirt..14.00
AT0143 Darth Maul's eyes / "At last." 2-sided black shirt 14.00
AT0144 Droid fighters on tie-dyed dark gray shirt 14.00
AT0145 Jar Jar's head on blue shirt 14.00
AT0146 Jedi vs. Sith on tie-dyed dark gray shirt 14.00
AT0147 Lightsaber battle on black shirt 14.00
AT0148 Naboo space battle on tie-dyed dark blue shirt...........................14.00
AT0151 TPM characters on black shirt..14.00
AT0152 TPM villains on black shirt...14.00

Knitwear, Inc.

AT0156 "EP1 Darth Maul The Dark Side", with rubber oval logo on sleeve...12.00

AT0155 "Sith Lord" all-over print 12.00
AT0153 Black shirt with SW diagonal gray, EP1 red; SW white embroidered on sleeves 15.00
AT0154 Darth Maul "The darkside" 15.00

Liquid Blue

AT0159 Anakin's Podracer...15.00
AT0160 Asteroid Field, 2-sided...15.00
AT0161 Boba Fett...15.00
AT0162 Chewbacca...15.00
AT0163 Darth Maul...15.00
AT0172 Darth Maul Silhouette, 2-sided...15.00
AT0164 Death Star Battle...15.00
AT0194 Death Star II..15.00
AT0165 Droids..15.00
AT0192 Droids on Tatooine...15.00
AT0166 Episode I Teaser...15.00
AT0167 Heroes...15.00
AT0191 Jabba's Palace...15.00
AT0168 Jar Jar Binks..15.00
AT0169 Jedi Council...15.00
AT0170 Jedi Master..15.00
AT0171 Lightsaber Duel, 2-sided..15.00
AT0173 Millennium Falcon...15.00
AT0174 Mos Espa, 2-sided...15.00
AT0175 Planet Hoth, 2-sided..15.00
AT0176 Podracer..15.00
AT0177 Podracer Canyon..15.00
AT0178 Podracer with logo..15.00
AT0179 Queen Amidala..15.00
AT0180 Sand People..15.00
AT0181 Sebulba's Podracer..15.00
AT0182 Slave I...15.00
AT0183 Space Battle, 2-sided...15.00
AT0184 STAP with Battledroid...15.00
AT0185 Star Wars Poster, 2-sided...15.00
AT0193 Star Wars Space Battle, 2-sided..15.00
AT0186 Stormtroopers...15.00
AT0187 Submarine Chase, 2-sided 15.00
AT0188 Tie Fighters...15.00
AT0189 Watto...15.00
AT0190 Yoda..15.00

LucasArts

AT0054 X-Wing polo..35.00

AT0160 front and back — AT0161 — AT0162 — AT0163 — AT0166 — AT0168 — AT0169 — AT0170 — AT0171 front and back

AT0172 front and back — AT0173 — AT0164 front and back — AT0165 — AT0175 front and back — AT0179 — AT0189

AT0180 front and back — AT0181 — AT0174 front and back — AT0178 — AT0183 front and back — AT0184 — AT0182

AT0187 front and back — AT0185 front and back — AT0186 — AT0191 — AT0192 — AT0193 front and back — AT0194 front and back

T-Shirts

Melanie Taylor Kent Ltd.
AT0025 Hollywood Blvd. Artwork 14.00

Patty Marsh Productions
AT0020 Ewoks "Color-Me" 25.00

Taco Bell
AT0055 "Play The Feel The Force Game" 35.00

Uniprints
AT0007 Chewbacca 12.00
AT0010 Darth Vader 12.00
AT0015 ESB: Logo 12.00
AT0016 ESB: Probe Droid 12.00
AT0017 ESB: Tauntaun 12.00
AT0018 ESB: X-Wing Fighter 12.00
AT0019 ESB: Yoda...12.00
AT0021 Ewoks w/ROTJ logo 10.00
AT0023 Han Solo 12.00
AT0029 Luke Skywalker 12.00
AT0032 Millennium Falcon 12.00
AT0037 ROTJ: C-3PO and R2-D2...14.00
AT0038 ROTJ: Stormtrooper and AT-ST Vehicle 14.00
AT0040 Star Wars Cast, main characters 12.00
AT0046 SW: Logo...12.00
AT0047 SW: Tie Fighter 12.00
AT0048 SW: X-Wing Fighter 12.00
AT0050 Wicket on Vine 10.00
AT0051 Wicket the Ewok 10.00
AT0052 Wicket W. Warrick 12.00
AT0056 "All I Need To Know About Life I Learned From Star Wars" 24.00
AT0158 Join the Celebration, SW:SE with release dates 26.00

UMBRELLAS

HOU0003   HOU0004   HOU0005

Adam Joseph Industries
Clear plastic with character art.
HOU0001 C-3PO and R2-D2 ....18.00
HOU0002 Darth Vader and Emperor's Royal Guards.................18.00

Pyramid
Children's umbrella with character figure handle.
HOU0003 Darth Vader, gray and black..12.00
HOU0004 Anakin Skywalker podracing 8.00
HOU0005 Darth Maul Gray, black, and red 8.00

UNDERGARMENTS

AU0023   AU0026   AU0038

Briefly Stated
AU0027 Darth Maul, adult's boxers 12.00
AU0023 Darth Maul, children's boxers 9.00
AU0018 Droids, children's boxers 9.00
AU0019 Hoth Scene, children's boxes 9.00
AU0039 Jar Jar name pattern, adult's boxers 12.00
AU0038 Jar Jar pictured with patch, adult's boxers....................12.00
AU0026 Naboo Space Battle, adult's boxers 12.00
AU0022 Naboo Space Battle, children's boxers 9.00
AU0025 Sebulba, adult's boxers 12.00
AU0024 Sith Lord, adult's boxers 12.00
AU0020 Space Battle, children's boxers 9.00
AU0021 Stormtroopers, children's boxers......................................9.00

Fruit of the Loom

AU0031 front and back   AU0032 front and back   AU0036 front and back

AU0031 Anakin Skywalker pkg., 3 boys briefs................................5.00
AU0032 C-3PO pkg., 3 toddler boys briefs.....................................5.00
AU0040 Darth Maul, 3 toddlers boys boxers 8.00
AU0033 Jar Jar pkg., 3 toddler girls panties...................................5.00
AU0034 Lightsaber green pkg., 5 printed boys briefs......................6.00
AU0035 Lightsaber red pkg., 5 printed boys briefs 6.00
AU0036 Queen Amidala pkg., 3 girls panties..................................5.00
AU0037 R2-D2 shaped box, 5 printed boys briefs.........................15.00

Long Eddies
AU0028 Darth Vader and Luke children's, thermal 10.00

Ralph Marlin and Co.
Boxer shorts.
AU0017 Darth Vader, silk..27.00
AU0001 Spaceships, cotton...23.00

Short Eddies
Children's T-shirt and boxer shorts sets.
AU0029 Darth Vader 14.00
AU0030 Space Battle 14.00

Union Underwear Co.
Underoos.

AU0002   AU0003   AU0004

AU0009   AU0010   AU0011

AU0002 Boba Fett 15.00
AU0003 C-3PO..15.00
AU0004 Chewbacca 15.00
AU0005 Darth Vader 15.00
AU0006 Darth Vader, thermal...20.00
AU0007 Han Solo 15.00
AU0008 Han Solo, thermal..20.00
AU0009 Luke Skywalker..15.00
AU0010 Princess Leia...15.00
AU0011 R2-D2...15.00
AU0012 R2-D2, thermal..20.00
AU0013 Wicket 15.00
AU0014 Wicket, thermal...20.00
AU0015 Yoda..15.00
AU0016 Yoda, thermal 20.00

UTENSILS: EATING

Kellogg's
Cereal premiums, plastic.
SPN0013 Anakin Skywalker 6.00
SPN0012 C-3PO 6.00
SPN0010 Darth Maul...6.00

SPN0009   SPN0010   SPN0011

SPN0012   SPN0013   SPN0014

SPN0014 Jar Jar Binks 6.00
SPN0011 Obi-Wan Kenobi 6.00
SPN0009 Queen Amidala 6.00

Zak Designs

SPN0008   SPN0001   SPN0002   SPN0003   SPN0004   SPN0005   SPN0006   SPN0007

SPN0008 2-Pack Spoon and Fork, Pod Racer scene on handle 6.00
SPN0001 #1 Luke Skywalker 7.00
SPN0002 #2 Princess Leia Organa 7.00
SPN0003 #3 Han Solo 7.00
SPN0004 #4 Chewbacca the Wookie 7.00
SPN0005 #5 See-Threepio 7.00
SPN0006 #6 Artoo-Detoo 7.00
SPN0007 #7 Darth Vader 7.00

VALENTINES: BOXED
Hallmark
VAL0008 32 Metallic Valentines, EPI 5.00

VAL0008 front and back

Paper Magic Group
VAL0010 28 Deluxe Fold and Seal cards with seals, EPI 9.00

VAL0001   VAL0002   VAL0003   VAL0006   VAL0007

VAL0009   VAL0010   VAL0004   VAL0005

VAL0011 30 Stand-Up Valentines, 10 different designs 8.00
VAL0003 30 Holographic with envelopes 7.00
VAL0001 30 Valentines, 10 different designs 5.00
VAL0009 32 Fold and Seal cards with seals, EPI 7.00
VAL0006 32 Holofoil, 10 different designs, 48 seals 7.00
VAL0007 40-Card Kit; 10 different designs, 48 seals, 2 bookmarks, window cling 9.00
VAL0002 40-Card Deluxe Kit: Window Cling, 3D display, 45 seals 9.00
VAL0004 C-3PO and R2-D2, classroom 16.00
VAL0005 ROTJ, classroom 14.00

VASES
Sigma

HOV0001 front and back

HOV0001 Yoda 60.00

VEHICLES, PROPELLER DRIVEN

Estes
Sterling model kit, control line fighter without engine.
MIF0007 X-Wing 28.00
MIF0008 Y-Wing 35.00
MIF0009 Naboo Fighter electronic remote control with display stand 18.00

Estes / Cox

MIF0001   MIF0003   MIF0004

MIF0010   MIF0011

MIF0002 Darth Vader's Tie Fighter kit with Cox engine 50.00
MIF0005 Death Star Battle Station with X-Wing control line fighter kit, radio controller 160.00
MIF0004 Landspeeder radio control vehicle kit with Cox engine 100.00
MIF0010 Naboo Fighter 24.00
MIF0003 Snowspeeder Fighter kit with Cox engine 50.00
MIF0006 Star Wars Combat Set, X-Wing and Tie Fighter with Cox engines .120.00
MIF0011 Trade Federation Droid Fighter 24.00
MIF0001 X-Wing Fighter kit with Cox engine 50.00

VEHICLES, PUNCH-OUT

PRC0001   PRC0002   PRC0004

Vehicles, Punch-Out

General Mills

Cereal premiums.

PRC0004 Landspeeder 11.00
PRC0001 Millennium Falcon 11.00
PRC0003 Tie Fighter 11.00
PRC0002 X-Wing Fighter...11.00

VEHICLES: ACTION FIGURE, POTF2 12"

VA10001

Hasbro

VA10001 Speeder Bike with Scout Trooper.................................85.00

VEHICLES: ACTION FIGURE, POTJ 12"

VA20001

Hasbro

VA20001 Speeder Bike with Luke Skywalker...............................65.00

VEHICLES: ACTION FIGURE, POTF2

P2V0022

P2V0027

Hasbro

P2V0022 Tatooine Skiff w/unique Jedi Knight Luke Skywalker, Target exclu-
  sive 40.00
P2V0027 Y-Wing Fighter w/Y-Wing Pilot, Target exclusive.......................30.00

Kenner

P2V0021 Airspeeder w/Airspeeder Pilot .00...............................15.00
P2V0001 A-Wing Fighter w/A-Wing Fighter Pilot .00..................18.00
P2V0012 Boba Fett's Slave I .00 (purple box) 36.00
P2V0013 Boba Fett's Slave I .01 (green box) 32.00
P2V0026 Cloud Car w/Cloudcar Pilot 24.00
P2V0003 Cruisemissile Trooper .00 ....18.00
P2V0004 Darth Vader's Tie Fighter .00 ....20.00
P2V0005 Dash Rendar's Outrider .00 ....44.00
P2V0006 Imperial AT-AT w/AT-AT Commander and AT-AT Driver .00 ....95.00
P2V0007 Imperial AT-ST .00 ....69.00
P2V0014 Imperial Speeder Bike w/Biker Scout .00 ....15.00
P2V0008 Landspeeder .00 ....16.00
P2V0009 Luke's T-16 Skyhopper .00 ....18.00
P2V0010 Millennium Falcon .00 ....65.00
P2V0011 Rebel Snowspeeder .00 ....47.00
P2V0030 Speeder Bike w/Biker Pilot...12.00
P2V0023 Speeder Bike w/Biker Scout .00 ....25.00
P2V0016 Speeder Bike w/Endor Leia .00 ....26.00
P2V0024 Speeder Bike w/Endor Leia .01 ....15.00
P2V0025 Speeder Bike w/Endor Leia .02 ....20.00
P2V0015 Speeder Bike w/Endor Luke .00 no glove on box photo...........32.00
P2V0017 Speeder Bike w/Endor Luke .01 ....19.00
P2V0018 Swoop w/Swoop Rider .00 ....17.00
P2V0019 Tie Fighter .00 ....22.00
P2V0020 X-Wing Fighter .00 ....39.00
P2V0032 X-Wing Fighter .01 ....46.00
P2V0028 X-Wing Fighter, Power FX 63.00

Kenner (UK)

Vehicles in tri-logo package.

P2V0034 A-Wing Fighter w/A-Wing Fighter Pilot........................23.00
P2V0035 Darth Vader's Tie Fighter 23.00
P2V0033 Imperial AT-ST..69.00
P2V0036 Landspeeder 19.00
P2V0042 Luke's T-16 Skyhopper 22.00
P2V0037 Millennium Falcon 88.00
P2V0038 Rebel Snowspeeder 62.00
P2V0041 Speeder Bike w/Biker Scout 27.00
P2V0040 Speeder Bike w/Endor Leia 23.00
P2V0039 Speeder Bike w/Endor Luke 23.00
P2V0047 Speeder Bike w/Speeder Bike Pilot...............................18.00
P2V0044 Tie Fighter w/free Stormtrooper figure.........................85.00
P2V0043 Tie Fighter...36.00

P1V0003

P1V0002

P2V0001

P1V0001

P1V0004

P2V0003

P2V0004

P2V0005

P2V0006

P2V0019

P2V0020

P2V0012

P2V0032

P2V0028

P2V0016

P2V0008

P2V0009

P2V0010

P2V0013

P2V0011

P2V0014

P2V0015

P2V0017

P2V0018

P2V0007

P2V0030

P2V0023   P2V0026   P2V0021   P2V0034   P2V0035   P2V0033   P2V0036

P2V0042   P2V0038   P2V0046   P2V0041   P2V0040   P2V0039   P2V0044

P2V0047   P2V0043

P2V0046 X-Wing Fighter w/free Luke Skywalker figure 85.00
P2V0045 X-Wing Fighter 42.00

VEHICLES: ACTION FIGURE, POTJ

Hasbro
P1V0001 B-Wing Fighter w/Unique Rebel Pilot 60.00
P1V0004 Hoth Peril Battle Damaged Snowspeeder 40.00
P1V0003 Tie Bomber w/Unique Imperial Pilot 55.00
P1V0002 Tie Interceptor w/Unique Imperial Pilot 40.00

VEHICLES: ACTION FIGURE, TPM

Hasbro
P3S0002 Anakin's Pod Racer with Anakin Skywalker...................................24.00
P3S0011 Armored Scout Tank with Battle Droid .0000, droid in window on box 22.00
P3S0012 Armored Scout Tank with Battle Droid .0100 ....14.00
P3S0004 Flash Speeder...16.00
P3S0015 Gungan Scout Sub with Obi-Wan Kenobi 21.00

P3S0006 Naboo Fighter .01 'Launching Proton Torpedo With Real Sounds', old logo 52.00
P3S0013 Naboo Fighter .0200 'Launching Proton Torpedo', old logo......37.00
P3S0014 Naboo Fighter .0300 'With Real Movie Lights and Sounds', new logo 18.00
P3S0005 Queen Amidala's Starship with Droid 75.00
P3S0007 Sebulba's Pod Racer with Sebulba 24.00
P3S0017 Sith Attack Speeder with Darth Maul 26.00
P3S0008 Sith Speeder with Darth Maul...10.00
P3S0009 STAP and Battledroid, EP1 Box...24.00
P3S0003 Trade Federation Droid Fighters..16.00
P3S0010 Trade Federation Tank 29.00

Hasbro (UK)
Tri-logo packaging.
P3S0021 Anakin's Pod Racer with Anakin Skywalker....................................25.00
P3S0024 Armored Scout Tank with Battle Droid 16.00
P3S0018 Naboo Fighter 18.00
P3S0020 Sebulba's Pod Racer with Sebulba 25.00
P3S0023 Sith Speeder with Darth Maul..10.00
P3S0022 Stap and Battledroid...24.00
P3S0019 Trade Federation Droid Fighters...16.00

Kenner
P3S0001 STAP and Battledroid, Sneak Preview Box 9.00

Kenner (UK)
Tri-logo packaging.
P3S0025 STAP and Battledroid, Sneak Preview Box 11.00

P3S0001   P3S0002   P3S0007   P3S0004   P3S0005

P3S0003   P3S0009   P3S0010   P3S0011   P3S0012

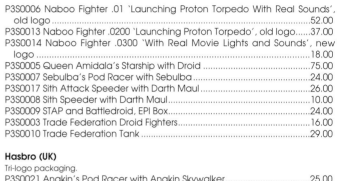

P3S0006   P3S0014   P3S0008   P3S0017   P3S0015

VEHICLES: ACTION FIGURE, TPM MINI

P3U0001   P3U0002

Hasbro
P3U0002 Naboo Fighter, includes 8 mini-figures 64.00
P3U0001 Naboo Fighter, includes Anakin figure 35.00

VEHICLES: ACTION FIGURE, VINTAGE

Glasslite
AVV0107 Tie Fighter...1,125.00
AVV0108 Tie Interceptor 1,430.00

AVV0107   AVV0108

Kenner
AVV0001 All Terrain Attack Transport (AT-AT), ESB 289.00
AVV0002 All Terrain Attack Transport (AT-AT), ROTJ 225.00
AVV0003 All Terrain Attack Transport (AT-AT), loose...................................88.00
AVV0004 Armored Sentinel Transport (AST-5), ROTJ pkg. 22.00
AVV0005 Armored Sentinel Transport (AST-5), loose 5.00
AVV0006 ATL Interceptor, DROIDS packaging 61.00
AVV0007 ATL Interceptor, loose...23.00
AVV0008 A-Wing Fighter, DROIDS packaging 520.00
AVV0009 A-Wing Fighter, loose..175.00
AVV0010 B-Wing Fighter, ROTJ pkg. 130.00
AVV0011 B-Wing Fighter, loose..65.00
AVV0012 Captivator (CAP-2), ESB pkg. 29.00
AVV0013 Captivator (CAP-2), ROTJ pkg. 20.00
AVV0014 Captivator (CAP-2), loose 8.00
AVV0017 Darth Vader's Tie Fighter, SW pkg. 140.00
AVV0106 Darth Vader's Tie Fighter, SW pkg. w/collector series sticker .225.00
AVV0019 Darth Vader's Tie Fighter, loose 55.00
AVV0020 Desert Sail Skiff, ROTJ pkg. 24.00
AVV0100 Desert Sail Skiff, tri-logo pkg. 30.00
AVV0021 Desert Sail Skiff, loose 11.00
AVV0022 Endor Forest Ranger, ROTJ pkg. 38.00
AVV0105 Endor Forest Ranger, tri-logo pkg. 55.00
AVV0023 Endor Forest Ranger, loose 11.00
AVV0026 Ewok Battle Wagon, POTF packaging 160.00
AVV0027 Ewok Battle Wagon, loose 59.00
AVV0030 Imperial Cruiser, ESB pkg. 145.00
AVV0031 Imperial Cruiser, loose 50.00
AVV0034 Imperial Shuttle Pod (ISP-6), ROTJ pkg. 27.00
AVV0035 Imperial Shuttle Pod (ISP-6), loose..8.00

AVV0001	AVV0002	AVV0004	AVV0008	AVV0010

AVV0013	AVV0015	AVV0017	AVV0020	AVV0105

AVV0026	AVV1004	AVV0034	AVV0032	AVV0036	AVV0041

AVV0038	AVV0099	AVV0030

AVV0047	AVV0048	AVV0049	AVV0052	AVV0054

AVV0032 Imperial Shuttle, ROTJ pkg. 365.00
AVV0033 Imperial Shuttle, loose 100.00
AVV0036 Imperial Sniper, POTF packaging........................83.00
AVV0037 Imperial Sniper, loose 30.00
AVV0038 Imperial Troop Transport, SW pkg.....................156.00
AVV0099 Imperial Troop Transport, ESB pkg......................127.00
AVV0039 Imperial Troop Transport, loose 47.00
AVV0040 Interceptor (INT-4), ESB pkg. 29.00
AVV0041 Interceptor (INT-4), ROTJ pkg............................22.00
AVV0042 Interceptor (INT-4), loose 8.00
AVV0045 Landspeeder, Sonic, SW pkg.............................575.00
AVV0046 Landspeeder, Sonic, loose 185.00
AVV0043 Landspeeder, SW pkg. 84.00
AVV0044 Landspeeder, loose 18.00
AVV0047 Millennium Falcon, SW pkg. 375.00
AVV0049 Millennium Falcon, ROTJ pkg............................185.00
AVV0048 Millennium Falcon, ESB pkg..............................255.00
AVV0050 Millennium Falcon, loose 95.00
AVV0051 Mobile Laser Cannon (MLC-3), ESB pkg...............32.00
AVV0052 Mobile Laser Cannon (MLC-3), ROTJ pkg.............28.00
AVV0053 Mobile Laser Cannon (MLC-3), loose 8.00
AVV0054 Multi-Terrain Vehicle (MTV-7), ESB pkg. 32.00
AVV0055 Multi-Terrain Vehicle (MTV-7), ROTJ pkg. 28.00
AVV0056 Multi-Terrain Vehicle (MTV-7), loose.....................8.00
AVV0057 One-Man Sand Skimmer, POTF packaging 95.00
AVV0102 One-Man Sand Skimmer, tri-logo pkg. 135.00
AVV0058 One-Man Sand Skimmer, loose 37.00
AVV0059 Personnel Deployment Transport (PDT-8), ESB.......30.00
AVV0060 Personnel Deployment Transport (PDT-8), ROTJ.......22.00
AVV0061 Personnel Deployment Transport (PDT-8), loose 8.00
AVV0062 Rebel Armored Snowspeeder, ESB pkg.................110.00
AVV0063 Rebel Armored Snowspeeder, loose......................47.00
AVV0064 Rebel Transport, ESB pkg..................................140.00
AVV0065 Rebel Transport, loose 45.00
AVV0066 Sandcrawler, Radio Controlled, SW pkg.................665.00
AVV0101 Sandcrawler, Radio Controlled, ESB pkg...............495.00
AVV0067 Sandcrawler, Radio Controlled, loose 175.00

AVV0068 Scout Walker (AT-ST), ESB pkg............................95.00
AVV0069 Scout Walker (AT-ST), ROTJ pkg..........................79.00
AVV0070 Scout Walker (AT-ST), loose................................35.00
AVV0071 Security Scout, POTF packaging...........................85.00
AVV0072 Security Scout, loose...26.00
AVV0073 Side Gunner, DROIDS packaging...........................86.00
AVV0074 Side Gunner, loose..25.00
AVV0075 Slave I, ESB pkg..185.00
AVV0076 Slave I, loose..58.00
AVV0077 Speeder Bike, ROTJ pkg.....................................42.00
AVV0078 Speeder Bike, loose..14.00
AVV0079 Tatooine Skiff, POTF packaging..........................580.00
AVV0080 Tatooine Skiff, loose..245.00
AVV0084 Tie Fighter w/Battle Damage, ESB pkg..................165.00
AVV0085 Tie Fighter w/Battle Damage, ROTJ pkg.................135.00
AVV0086 Tie Fighter w/Battle Damage, loose 45.00
AVV0081 Tie Fighter, SW pkg..200.00
AVV0104 Tie Fighter, SW pkg. w/free figures inside 385.00
AVV0082 Tie Fighter, ESB pkg...205.00
AVV0083 Tie Fighter, loose...74.00
AVV0087 Tie Interceptor, ROTJ pkg..................................139.00
AVV0088 Tie Interceptor, loose..55.00
AVV0089 Twin-Pod Cloud Car, ESB pkg.............................98.00
AVV0090 Twin-Pod Cloud Car, loose.................................46.00
AVV0094 X-Wing Fighter w/Battle Damage, ESB pkg............155.00
AVV0095 X-Wing Fighter w/Battle Damage, ROTJ pkg...........115.00
AVV0096 X-Wing Fighter w/Battle Damage, loose.................40.00
AVV0091 X-Wing Fighter, SW pkg....................................165.00
AVV0092 X-Wing Fighter, ESB pkg...................................240.00
AVV0093 X-Wing Fighter, loose..62.00
AVV0097 Y-Wing Fighter, ROTJ pkg..................................165.00
AVV0098 Y-Wing Fighter, loose..60.00

Lili Ledy
AVV0115 B-Wing Fighter, ROTJ pkg. 355.00
AVV0110 Cannon Laser Mobile (CLM-3), ROTJ pkg..............207.00
AVV0109 Captivator (CAP-2), ROTJ pkg. 165.00

AVV0055   AVV0102   AVV0059   AVV0062   AVV0068   AVV0071

AVV0064   AVV0073   AVV0075   AVV0077

AVV0079   AVV0081   AVV0104   AVV0082   AVV0085

AVV0087   AVV0089   AVV0091   AVV0092   AVV0094   AVV0095

Vehicles: Action Figure, Vintage

AVV0117 Darth Vader's Tie Fighter, ROTJ pkg. 225.00
AVV0113 Imperial Shuttle, ROTJ pkg. 750.00
AVV0111 Interceptor (INT-4), ROTJ pkg. 175.00
AVV0112 Millennium Falcon, ROTJ pkg. 575.00
AVV0116 Rebel Armored Snowspeeder, ROTJ pkg. 185.00
AVV0118 Speederbike, ROTJ pkg. 135.00
AVV0114 Y-Wing Fighter, ROTJ pkg. 290.00

Palitoy
AVV0103 X-Wing Fighter, SW pkg. 235.00

VENDING MACHINES

VM0001

Pepsi Cola
VM0001 Episode I Pod Racing 1,130.00

VIDEO CASSETTES

20th Century Fox

VV0027   VV0036   VV0055   VV0056   VV0057

VV0047   VV0050   VV0052   VV0054

VV0027 Droids: The Pirates and the Prince 8.00
VV0062 Empire Strikes Back, Beta format 14.00
VV0036 Ewoks: The Haunted Village 11.00
VV0057 Hardware Wars, parody 12.00
VV0053 Return of the Jedi: 2000 THX SE 12.00
VV0054 Return of the Jedi: 2000 THX SE, letterbox 15.00
VV0061 Star Wars, Beta format 16.00
VV0049 Star Wars: 2000 THX SE 14.00
VV0050 Star Wars: 2000 THX SE, letterbox 18.00
VV0051 The Empire Strikes Back: 2000 THX SE 12.00
VV0052 The Empire Strikes Back: 2000 THX SE, letterbox 15.00
VV0055 The Phantom Menace 30.00
VV0056 The Phantom Menace, Widescreen Video Collector's Edition ..40.00
VV0047 Trilogy Boxed Set: 2000 THX SE, letterbox with EP2 footage 65.00
VV0048 Trilogy Boxed Set: 2000 THX SE, with EP2 footage 45.00

CBS / Fox Video
VV0020 Classic Creatures: ROTJ 20.00
VV0065 Droids 1 ....19.00
VV0066 Droids 2: The Pirate and the Prince 19.00
VV0067 Droids 3: Uncharted Space 19.00

VV0020   VV0041   VV0022   VV0022   VV0012

VV0013   VV0014   VV0015   VV0001   VV0003

VV0059   VV0004   VV0006   VV0007   VV0060

VV0008   VV0010   VV0033   VV0016   VV0018

VV0021 ESB Special Effects..15.00
VV0041 Ewoks 1: Morag's Revenge 19.00
VV0063 Ewoks 2: The Gupins 19.00
VV0064 Ewoks 3: Wicket the Hero 19.00
VV0022 From Star Wars to Jedi: The Making of a Saga 25.00
VV0023 Making of Star Wars / ESB Special Effects 20.00
VV0011 Making of Star Wars, Corn Pops special offer 35.00
VV0012 Return of the Jedi 23.00
VV0013 Return of the Jedi: 1996 THX 16.00
VV0014 Return of the Jedi: 1997 Special Edition.....................18.00
VV0015 Return of the Jedi: 1997 S.E., letterbox 20.00
VV0003 Star Wars...20.00
VV0059 Star Wars, Hi-Fi 22.00
VV0002 Star Wars: 1982 First "for-sale" version 65.00
VV0001 Star Wars: 1982 w/Video Rental Library case............250.00
VV0004 Star Wars: 1996 THX 16.00
VV0005 Star Wars: 1997 Special Edition 18.00
VV0006 Star Wars: 1997 Special Edition, letterbox 20.00
VV0007 The Empire Strikes Back..25.00
VV0060 The Empire Strikes Back, Hi-Fi 28.00
VV0008 The Empire Strikes Back: 1996 THX..........................16.00
VV0009 The Empire Strikes Back: 1997 Special Edition 18.00
VV0010 The Empire Strikes Back: 1997 Special Edition, letterbox 23.00
VV0033 The Making of Star Wars 12.00
VV0016 Trilogy Boxed Set: 1996 THX...................................65.00
VV0037 Trilogy Boxed Set: 1996 THX, letterbox 115.00
VV0017 Trilogy Boxed Set: 1997 Special Edition 65.00
VV0018 Trilogy Boxed Set: 1997 Special Edition, letterbox.......85.00
VV0019 Trilogy Boxed Set: Special Collectors Edition, book, certificate, gift box 125.00

Fan Made

VV0058   VV0045   VV0034   VV0046   VV0044   VV0043

VV0058 Carrot Wars 14.00
VV0045 Millennium's End, The Fandom Menace 16.00
VV0034 Star Wars Holiday Special, 1978 TV Broadcast, fan recorded....7.00
VV0046 Star Wars, The Dark Redemption 14.00
VV0044 Star Wars, The Lost Audition Films............................25.00
VV0043 Star Warz - A New Pope, Episode 7 ....12.00
VV0035 Troops: Cops/Star Wars Parody.................................0.00

J2 Communications
VV0026 Droids: The Lost Prince / The New King 12.00
VV0028 Droids: The White Witch / Escape into Terror..............12.00
VV0030 Ewoks: Cries of the Trees / The Tree of Light 12.00
VV0029 Ewoks: Special double length cartoon 12.00
VV0031 Ewoks: The Haunted Village / Blue Harvest 12.00

VV0026   VV0029   VV0031

VV0068 Ewoks: The Tree of Light 12.00

MGM / UA

VV0024   VV0025

VV0025 Ewoks-The Battle for Endor 25.00
VV0024 The Ewok Adventure 25.00

Passport Video

VV0038   VV0039   VV0040   VV0042

VV0038 "Stars of SW: Interviews with the Cast" unauthorized video........16.00
VV0039 Bart Wars: The Simpsons Strike Back 27.00
VV0032 Ewoks - Caravan of Courage 50.00
VV0040 George Lucas in Love..35.00
VV0042 Star Wars Definitive Collection (PAL only)....................185.00

VIDEO DISCS

Videovan Entertainment

VD0006   VD0012   VD0001   VD0008   VD0009

VD0007 front and back   VD0010   VD0011

VD0006 Episode I: The Phantom Menace VCD 49.00
VD0012 Trilogy Boxed Set: 2000 THX SE, with EP2 footage 49.00
VD0001 Star Wars, CED 65.00
VD0002 The Empire Strikes Back, CED 65.00
VD0004 Making of Star Wars / ESB Special Effects, CED 75.00
VD0003 Return of the Jedi, CED 2 disk set 95.00
VD0009 Empire Strikes Back SE video disc 24.00
VD0011 Episode I video disc 17.00
VD0007 Episode I: The Phantom Menace laser disc 155.00
VD0010 Return of the Jedi SE video disc 24.00
VD0008 Star Wars SE video disc 24.00

VIDEO GAMES

Acorn
NH0068 Star Wars for Acorn...19.00

Broderbund
NH0017 Star Wars for PC 45.00

NH0068   NH0017   NH0028   NH0031

Capcom USA
NH0028 Star Wars for Gameboy 25.00
NH0031 The Empire Strikes Back for Gameboy 25.00

Hasbro
NH0042 Millennium Falcon CD-ROM Playset................................50.00
NH0019 Star Wars Monopoly for PC 15.00
NH0020 Star Wars Monopoly, deluxe edition for PC......................25.00

JVC

HN0026   NH0030   NH0032

NH0026 Star Wars for Nintendo 35.00
NH0032 Super Return of the Jedi for Super Nintendo 50.00
NH0027 Super Star Wars for Nintendo 45.00
NH0030 Super The Empire Strikes Back for Super Nintendo 45.00
NH0029 The Empire Strikes Back for Nintendo 35.00

Lucas Learning

NH0070   NH0074   NH0075   NH0053   NH0052

HN0072   NH0073   NH0056   NH0071

NH0070 Anakin's Speedway, Build and Drive 12.00
NH0074 Droidworks, Science and Technology 12.00
NH0075 Early Learning, Activity Center 12.00
NH0053 Gungan Frontier, Ecology and Nature 12.00
NH0052 Gungan Frontier, EPI...18.00
NH0072 Jabba's Game Galaxy, Math...12.00
NH0073 Pit Droids, Logic and Reasoning 12.00
NH0056 Pit Droids: 300+ Puzzles to Drive You Nuts! For Windows and Macln-
    tosh 30.00
NH0071 Yoda's Challenge, Activity Center 12.00

LucasArts
NH0006 B-Wing for PC 35.00
NH0045 Dark Forces for Macintosh 28.00
NH0007 Dark Forces for PC 25.00
NH0034 Dark Forces for Playstation 54.00
NH0008 Dark Forces II: Jedi Knight for PC 35.00
NH0040 Droidworks, EPI...45.00
NH0050 Episode I Racer for Gameboy 42.00
NH0049 Episode I Racer for Nintendo 64 ....35.00
NH0009 Imperial Pursuit for PC 35.00
NH0078 Jar Jar's Adventure 12.00
NH0010 Jedi Knight: Mysteries of the Sith for PC 65.00
NH0058 Jedi Power Battles for Playstation 54.00
NH0048 Jedi Power Battles for Playstation, gold premium pkg. 66.00
NH0011 LucasArts Archives Vol. II: Star Wars Collection for PC................47.00

Video Games

NH0045

NH0034

NH0008

NH0040

NH0050

NH0009

NH0010

NH0058

NH0048

NH0011

NH0062

NH0046

NH0038

NH0015

NH0039

NH0043

NH0033

NH0067

NH0059

NH0021

NH0062 Masters of Teras Kasi for Playstation 29.00
NH0080 Mysteries of the Sith expanded missions for Dark Forces II 14.00
NH0013 Rebel Assault for PC 25.00
NH0035 Rebel Assault for Sega 20.00
NH0046 Rebel Assault II for Macintosh 39.00
NH0014 Rebel Assault II for PC 35.00
NH0038 Rebel Assault II for Playstation...45.00
NH0015 Rebellion for PC 35.00
NH0039 Rogue Squadron for Nintendo 64 ....55.00
NH0051 Rogue Squadron for PC 35.00
NH0033 Shadows of the Empire for Nintendo 65.00
NH0043 Shadows of the Empire for PC 25.00
NH0076 Starfighter for Playstation 2..54.00
NH0079 Super Bombad Racing for Playstation 2 ....50.00
NH0067 Super Star Wars for Super Famicom 65.00
NH0059 Super The Empire Strikes Back for Super Famicom.........................67.00
NH0077 SW Demolition for Playstation 54.00
NH0021 Tie Fighter for PC 50.00
NH0041 X-Wing Flight School for PC 28.00
NH0023 X-Wing vs. Tie Fighter for PC 35.00
NH0057 Yoda Stories for Gameboy Color 26.00
NH0024 Yoda Stories for PC 15.00

Lucasfilm Games
NH0012 Night Shift (parody) for Commodore 64..45.00
NH0069 Night Shift (parody) for PC 34.00
NH0063 X-Wing collector's edition for PC 39.00
NH0022 X-Wing for PC 35.00

Nintendo
NH0047 Nintendo 64 with EPI Pod Racer cartridge and strategy guide .120.00
NH0044 Star Wars for Famicom 55.00
NH0065 Super Return of the Jedi for Gameboy 17.00

Parker Bros.
NH0004 Return of the Jedi: Death Star Battle, Atari 2600 / Sears..............15.00
NH0002 Star Wars: Jedi Arena, Atari 2600 / Sears 15.00

NH0004

NH0002

NH0060

NH0005

NH0003

NH0001 Star Wars: The Arcade Game, Atari 2600 / Sears 15.00
NH0060 Star Wars: The Arcade Game, Atari 5200 ....17.00
NH0005 Star Wars: The Arcade Game, Colecovision.....................................17.00
NH0025 Star Wars: The Empire Strikes Back, for Intellivision 15.00
NH0003 The Empire Strikes Back, Atari 2600 / Sears 15.00

Parody Interactive
NH0016 Star Warped (parody) for PC 10.00

Sega
NH0037 Star Wars: The Arcade Game for Sega 20.00
NH0064 SW Chess for Sega, CD-ROM 17.00

Sega / US Gold
NH0036 Star Wars for Game Gear 25.00

Software Toolworks

NH0055   NH0066   NH0061

NH0055 SW Chess software for IBM-compatible computers, CD-ROM....21.00
NH0054 SW Chess software for IBM-compatible computers, floppy disks14.00
NH0066 Empire Strikes Back for Commodore 64, cassette.......................32.00
NH0061 Star Wars for Namcot..82.00

VIDEO STORAGE CASES

20th Century Fox
VDC0001 SW:EPI plastic case with lenticular cover, TRU
exclusive for pre-ordering video................................8.00

VDC0001

VITAMINS

Natural Balance
PAV0001 60-tablet vitamin bottle and box 16.00
PAV0002 3-tablet vitamin promotional sample 9.00

358

PAV0001 unused box and bottle   PAV0002

VOICE CHANGER

Tiger Electronics
VC0001 Darth Vader authentic sounds plus alters
   voice to sound like Darth Vader's.............25.00

VC0001

WALKIE-TALKIES

Micro Games of America
WT0001 Darth Vader and Stormtrooper helmets
   designed to be clipped to belt.................24.00

WT0001

Tiger Electronics
WT0004 Darth Vader voice changer walkie-talkie, transmit in regular voice
   or altered 28.00
WT0002 Imperial symbol over speaker with belt clips 18.00
WT0005 Jedi Comlink walkie talkies...10.00
WT0003 Rebel Alliance long-range, headset with sound effects function..26.00

WT0005   WT0003   WT0006 box and radio

Titan
WT0006 Executive, shows R2-D2 and C-3PO on Morse Code pad...........85.00

WALL DECORATIONS

Priss Prints

WDC0001   WDC0002

WDC0002 Border Stick-Ups, Podrace 5.00
WDC0003 Border Stick-Ups, Space Battle..5.00
WDC0004 Jumbo Stick-Ups Podrace 10.00
WDC0001 Jumbo Stick-Ups Podrace and Space Battle..........................14.00
WDC0005 Jumbo Stick-Ups Space Battle 10.00

WALLET CARDS

Antioch
IDC0001 Bounty Hunter 3.00
IDC0002 Chewbacca 3.00

IDC0001   IDC0002   IDC0003   IDC0004

IDC0005   IDC0006   IDC0007   IDC0008

IDC0009   IDC0010   IDC0011   IDC0012

IDC0003 Imperial AT-AT...3.00
IDC0004 Imperial Tie Fighter 3.00
IDC0012 Jedi 3.00
IDC0005 Millennium Falcon 3.00
IDC0008 Naboo Bravo Squadron 3.00
IDC0010 Pit Droid 3.00
IDC0006 Rebel Alliance 3.00
IDC0011 Tatooine Pod Racer License 3.00
IDC0009 Trade Federation Starfighter 3.00
IDC0007 X-Wing Starfighter...3.00

WALLETS

PEX0001   PEX0003   PEX0007   PEX0009

PEX0011   PEX0013   PEX0016

Adam Joseph Industries
PEX0001 Darth Vader nylon coin holder...8.00
PEX0002 Darth Vader nylon pocket pal..8.00
PEX0003 Darth Vader nylon wallet..8.00
PEX0004 Darth Vader vinyl billfold..12.00
PEX0005 Darth Vader vinyl wallet...12.00
PEX0007 Droids nylon coin holder..8.00
PEX0008 Droids nylon pocket pal 5.00
PEX0009 Droids nylon wallet..10.00
PEX0010 Droids vinyl billfold..12.00
PEX0011 Droids vinyl wallet...12.00
PEX0006 Princess Kneesaa...16.00
PEX0012 Wicket the Ewok vinyl wallet...14.00
PEX0013 Yoda nylon coin holder...8.00
PEX0014 Yoda nylon pocket pal..5.00
PEX0015 Yoda nylon wallet...10.00
PEX0016 Yoda vinyl billfold...12.00
PEX0017 Yoda vinyl wallet..12.00

Disney / MGM
PEX0018 Star Tours logo...11.00

World Wide Licenses Ltd.

PEX0020   PEX0021   PEX0019

PEX0020 Jedi vs. Sith 7.00
PEX0021 Pod Racing 7.00
PEX0019 Queen Amidala..9.00

WALLPAPER

Imperial Chemicals
Wallpaper, alternating scenes.
WP0001 SW: Vymura ready pasted wall vinyl, 21"x11 yard roll..................38.00

Wallpaper

WP0001   WP0002   WP0003   WP0004

WP0002 ESB: Falcon cockpit, Bespin, Vader Fett and Lando, Luke on Dagobah, asteroid battle, Hoth battle, Probot......................34.00
WP0003 ROTJ: Jabba and guards, Chewbacca and droids, Ewoks and speederbike, Darth Vader and guards, 3 heroes 34.00

Border trim.
WP0005 EWOKS, Wicket swings from the vine while Kneesaa and friends sit below 19.00
WP0004 ROTJ, alternating ovals with: heroes, R2-D2, Chewbacca and C-3PO, Darth Vader, Ewoks, Rebo band 25.00

WARM-UP SUITS

Sales Corp. of America
AW0001 Boys: hooded w/shorts, Admiral Ackbar 10.00
AW0002 Boys: hooded w/shorts, Darth Vader 10.00
AW0003 Boys: hooded w/shorts, Darth Vader and Royal Guards 14.00
AW0004 Boys: hooded w/shorts, Luke and Darth Vader dueling............10.00
AW0005 Boys: hooded w/shorts, ROTJ logo 10.00
AW0006 Boys: with pants, Admiral Ackbar 10.00
AW0007 Boys: with pants, Darth Vader..................................10.00
AW0008 Boys: with pants, Darth Vader and Royal Guards 12.00
AW0009 Boys: with pants, Luke and Darth Vader dueling 10.00
AW0010 Boys: with pants, Paploo 10.00
AW0011 Boys: with pants, ROTJ logo 8.00
AW0012 Girls: Max Rebo Band...10.00
AW0013 Girls: Wicket..10.00
AW0014 Girls: Wicket and Paploo 10.00
AW0015 Girls: Wicket and R2-D2 ....10.00
AW0016 Toddlers: Baby Ewoks 10.00
AW0017 Toddlers: fleece hooded, Wicket and Paploo 10.00
AW0018 Toddlers: fleece hooded, Wicket and R2-D2 ....10.00
AW0019 Toddlers: Wicket and Baby Ewoks 10.00
AW0020 Toddlers: Wicket and Paploo 10.00
AW0021 Toddlers: Wicket and R2-D2 ....10.00

WASH CLOTHS

CWC0008   CWC0009   CWC0010

Bibb Co.
CWC0001 Boba Fett and Darth Vader 8.00
CWC0002 C-3PO and R2-D2 ....8.00
CWC0003 Darth Vader 8.00
CWC0004 Hoth (Ice planet) 8.00
CWC0005 R2-D2...8.00
CWC0006 X-Wing fighter 8.00
CWC0007 Yoda 8.00
CWC0008 Darth Maul 4.00
CWC0009 Jar Jar Binks 4.00
CWC0010 Queen Amidala...4.00

WASTE BASKETS

Chein Industries
TIW0001 Ewoks 14.00
TIW0002 ROTJ collage 16.00

Jay Franco and Sons
TIW0003 Naboo Space Battle, plastic 8.00

TIW0002 front and back   TIW0003

WATCHES

TAW0019   TAW0020   TAW0021

3D Arts
Black rubber band, hologram on face.
TAW0064 Boba Fett 45.00
TAW0019 Darth Vader 40.00
TAW0020 X-Wing Fighter 40.00
TAW0021 Yoda 45.00

A.H. Prismatic

TAW0012

TAW0012 Darth Vader hologram on face, "Star Wars" and "Darth Vader" on band 45.00

Avon

TAW0036

TAW0036 Obi-Wan Kenobi with blue lightsaber second hand 16.00

Bradley Time

TAW0005   TAW0003   TAW0008

TAW0009   TAW0007   TAW0016   TAW0014   TAW0010

TAW0003 C-3PO and R2-D2 in desert, SW logo, blue vinyl strap, silver casing, child size 95.00
TAW0002 C-3PO and R2-D2 in desert, SW logo, gold casing, adult size 115.00
TAW0004 C-3PO, R2-D2, and logo on black face 85.00
TAW0005 C-3PO, R2-D2, and logo on black face; numbers on inner silver ring 115.00
TAW0007 Darth Vader with lightsaber and Star Wars logo on face........78.00
TAW0008 Darth Vader with lightsaber and Star Wars logo on face, planets on inner time ring 85.00
TAW0016 Ewoks 50.00
TAW0015 Jabba the Hutt 60.00
TAW0009 Radio watch with headphones, ROTJ 85.00
TAW0010 Radio watch with headphones, SW 95.00
TAW0017 Wicket with planets and stars on face 55.00
TAW0013 Yoda, gray watch face 65.00
TAW0014 Yoda, white watch face 80.00

TAW0023   TAW0024

TAW0046   TAW0059   TAW0051   TAW0049   TAW0050

Fantasma

TAW0022 Battle of the Force, limited to 7,500 ....65.00
TAW0023 Darth Vader black coin dial, limited to 7,500 ....85.00
TAW0024 Millennium Falcon with flip-up face, brass case, limited to 10,000...75.00

Fossil

TAW0033   TAW0018   TAW0034   TAW0035   TAW0027

TAW0029 Boba Fett Collectors Watch, gold edition, limited to 1,000 ....125.00
TAW0028 Boba Fett Collectors Watch, silver edition, limited to 10,000....86.00
TAW0033 Boba Fett, brass finished face, brown strap, with matching storage box, limited to 10,000..67.00
TAW0018 C-3PO and R2-D2, limited to 500, includes sculpted R2-D2 case...215.00
TAW0034 C-3PO, gold finished face, brown strap, with matching storage box, limited to 10,000..55.00
TAW0048 Darth Vader and his Tie, 23k gold plated, with Vader head storage box, limited to 1,000..120.00
TAW0030 Darth Vader and his Tie, silver color all over, with Vader head storage box, limited to 15,000..95.00
TAW0031 Darth Vader and Imperial insignia, 23k gold case, black strap, with matching storage box, limited to 1,000 ....125.00
TAW0035 Darth Vader, silver finish face, black strap, with matching storage box, limited to 10,000..55.00
TAW0027 SW logo, Rebel insignia, and Imperial insignia, with Death Star storage box, limited to 10,000..95.00

Hope Industries

TAW0032   TAW0055

TAW0054   TAW0056 front and back

TAW0032 Return of the Jedi, quartz analog, gold tone buckle 24.00
TAW0054 Return of the Jedi, quartz analog, gold tone buckle, gold plastic Death Star case 32.00
TAW0055 Star Wars: A New Hope, quartz analog, gold tone buckle 26.00
TAW0025 Star Wars: A New Hope, quartz analog, gold tone buckle, gold tone buckle, gold plastic Death Star case 32.00
TAW0026 The Empire Strikes Back, quartz analog, chrome tone buckle.24.00
TAW0056 The Empire Strikes Back, quartz analog, chrome tone buckle, gold tone buckle, gold plastic Death Star case 32.00

Nelsonic

TAW0045   TAW0052   TAW0040   TAW0044   TAW0039

TAW0041 Anakin Skywalker podracer watch with collectors storage tin .16.00
TAW0045 C-3PO Skeletal Case character watch.......................................30.00
TAW0037 Darth Maul Holographic Character Watch 34.00
TAW0052 Darth Maul laser dial character watch with collectors storage tin 17.00
TAW0040 Darth Maul lightsaber character watch with collectors storage tin 16.00
TAW0044 Darth Maul sculpted case character watch 25.00
TAW0039 Darth Maul sculpted case character watch with collectors storage tin 18.00
TAW0047 Darth Maul Sith Probe Droid sound and lights effects pocket watch 16.00
TAW0046 Jar Jar Binks Rotating Tongue Character Watch.......................24.00
TAW0060 Jar Jar Binks Rotating Tongue Character Watch with collectors storage tin 17.00
TAW0059 Jar Jar Binks water-filled analog watch with collectors storage tin 28.00
TAW0042 Podracer watch with built-in compass with collectors storage tin 24.00
TAW0051 Queen Amidala laser dial character watch with collectors storage tin 17.00
TAW0049 Qui-Gon Jinn laser dial character watch with collectors storage tin 17.00
TAW0043 Space Battle pocket watch 18.00
TAW0050 Space Battle rotating starfighter disk watch with collectors storage tin 19.00

Pepsi Cola

TAW0053

TAW0053 "Feel the Force - Back on the big screen" 18.00

World Wide Licenses Ltd.

TAW0062   TAW0061   TAW0063   TAW0061 – 63 storage tin

TAW0038   TAW0058   TAW0057

TAW0062 Darth Maul communicator, diecast with diecast band, includes storage tin 35.00
TAW0061 Droid Fighter, diecast with leather band, includes storage tin 40.00
TAW0063 Qui-Gon Jinn, hologram face, diecast with diecast band, includes storage tin 45.00
TAW0001 Biker Scout quartz stopwatch..75.00
TAW0006 Clock and calculator ruler..45.00
TAW0038 Episode I college...9.00
TAW0058 Lightsabers, black face on silver 45.00
TAW0057 Queen Amidala clip-on 19.00
TAW0011 Wicket Whistle Time watch 17.00

WATCHES: DIGITAL

TAD0002   TAD0004   TAD0016   TAD0043   TAD0005

Bradley Time

TAD0002 Black face with SW logo on top and C-3PO and R2-D2 on bottom 76.00

TAD0004 Blue face plate with C-3PO and R2-D2 on top and SW logo on bottom of faceplate..65.00

TAD0015 C-3PO and R2-D2 with ROTJ logo.........................36.00

TAD0013 Changing-image round face, Darth Vader/Star Wars logo ...110.00

TAD0043 Darth Vader under time window with Star Wars logo above it...55.00

TAD0016 Ewoks with ROTJ logo 44.00

TAD0017 Jabba the Hutt with ROTJ logo 47.00

TAD0005 Oval face, Droids logo on top, C-3PO on right, and R2-D2 on bottom..35.00

TAD0006 Oval starfield faceplate with C-3PO on left and R2-D2 on right..58.00

TAD0007 Oval starfield faceplate with C-3PO on left and R2-D2 on right, musical..135.00

TAD0009 Round starfield faceplate with C-3PO on left and R2-D2 on right, musical..97.00

TAD0044 Round starfield faceplate with R2-D2 on left and C-3PO on right, blue vinyl strap..46.00

TAD0010 Square blue face with X-Wing, Logo, Tie Fighter on top, C-3PO and R2-D2 on bottom, musical....................................125.00

TAD0014 White face with Darth Vader standing behind time windows, SW logo in foreground 64.00

TAD0012 Wide oval face with X-Wings on top, C-3PO on left and R2-D2 on right 76.00

TAD0018 Yoda with ROTJ logo 45.00

Disney / MGM

TAD0093

TAD0093 Star Tours, Disneyland..24.00

Duracell

TAD0040

TAD0040 Digital Darth Vader SE art, promotional packaged with batteries ...28.00

Hope Industries

TAD0083 2-Pack Darth Maul flip top and Battle Droid flip top with collectors storage tin 26.00

TAD0081 3-Pack Sculpted Collection: Anakin, Jar Jar, Darth Maul with lightsaber case 16.00

TAD0091 4-Pack diecast Battle Droid, Darth Maul, Pit Droid, R2-D2, boxed with magnet seal 65.00

TAD0107 Anakin Skywalker Collector Watch with lighsaber case, box pkg. 9.00

TAD0053 Anakin Skywalker Collector Watch with lighsaber case, bubble pkg. 8.00

TAD0075 Anakin Skywalker, flip top 7.00

TAD0087 Battle Droid diecast watch with tin collector case, boxed, brass finish 18.00

TAD0057 Battle Droid diecast watch with tin collector case, boxed, steel...16.00

TAD0061 Battle Droid diecast watch, plastic pkg. 10.00

TAD0045 Boba Fett 7.00

TAD0081   TAD0055   TAD0053   TAD0054   TAD0056   TAD0083

TAD0045   TAD0046   TAD0047   TAD0049   TAD0025   TAD0026   TAD0028   TAD0029   TAD0031   TAD0032

TAD0019   TAD0042   TAD0027   TAD0030   TAD0075   TAD0078   TAD0077   TAD0076   TAD0079   TAD0074

TAD0091   TAD0087   TAD0088   TAD0089   TAD0090

TAD0042 Boba Fett Collector Timepiece with Death Star watch case ...10.00
TAD0025 Boba Fett Collector Timepiece with Millennium Falcon watch case 8.00
TAD0046 C-3PO..7.00
TAD0026 C-3PO Collector Timepiece with Millennium Falcon watch case.8.00
TAD0108 C-3PO Collector Watch with lightsaber case, box pkg. 9.00
TAD0054 C-3PO Collector Watch with lightsaber case, bubble pkg.........8.00
TAD0078 C-3PO, flip top..7.00
TAD0109 Darth Maul collector watch with Lightsaber Case, box pkg. 9.00
TAD0055 Darth Maul collector watch with Lightsaber Case, bubble pkg......8.00
TAD0088 Darth Maul diecast watch with tin collector case, boxed, brass finish 18.00
TAD0058 Darth Maul diecast watch with tin collector case, boxed, steel..14.00
TAD0062 Darth Maul diecast watch, plastic pkg. 10.00
TAD0077 Darth Maul, flip top...7.00
TAD0047 Darth Vader...7.00
TAD0027 Darth Vader Collector Timepiece with Death Star watch case .10.00
TAD0028 Darth Vader Collector Timepiece with Millennium Falcon watch case 8.00
TAD0021 Imperial Forces Collector Timepiece 4-Piece Giftset, 3 watches plus Death Star Collector Case..24.00
TAD0019 Imperial Forces Collector Timepiece Giftset, Darth Vader and Boba Fett with Death Star Collector Case...........................18.00
TAD0020 Imperial Forces Collector Timepiece Giftset, Darth Vader and Stormtrooper with Death Star Collector Case.......................18.00
TAD0110 Jar Jar Binks Collector Watch with Lightsaber Case, box pkg. 9.00
TAD0056 Jar Jar Binks Collector Watch with Lightsaber Case, bubble pkg. .8.00
TAD0076 Jar Jar Binks, flip top...7.00
TAD0079 Obi-Wan Kenobi, flip top 7.00
TAD0089 Pit Droid diecast watch with tin collector case, boxed, brass finish 18.00
TAD0059 Pit Droid diecast watch with collector case, boxed, steel...15.00
TAD0063 Pit Droid diecast watch, plastic pkg. 12.00
TAD0074 Queen Amidala, flip top 7.00
TAD0048 R2-D2 ....7.00
TAD0029 R2-D2 Collector Timepiece with Millennium Falcon watch case.8.00
TAD0090 R2-D2 diecast watch with tin collector case, boxed, brass finish ..18.00
TAD0060 R2-D2 diecast watch with tin collector case, boxed, steel 15.00
TAD0064 R2-D2 diecast watch, plastic pkg.....................................10.00
TAD0024 Rebel Alliance Collector Timepiece 4-Piece Giftset, 3 watches plus Millennium Falcon Collector Case.........................24.00
TAD0022 Rebel Alliance Collector Timepiece Giftset, C-3PO and R2-D2 with Millennium Falcon Collector Case.............................18.00
TAD0023 Rebel Alliance Collector Timepiece Giftset, C-3PO and Yoda with Millennium Falcon Collector Case.............................18.00
TAD0049 Stormtrooper 7.00
TAD0030 Stormtrooper Collector Timepiece with Death Star watch case..10.00
TAD0031 Stormtrooper Collector Timepiece with Millennium Falcon watch case 8.00
TAD0050 Yoda...7.00
TAD0032 Yoda Collector Timepiece with Millennium Falcon watch case 8.00
TAD0033 Yoda Collector Timepiece with Millennium Falcon watch case, alternate coloring 9.00

It's About Time

TAD0070   **TAD0067**   **TAD0072**   **TAD0073**   **TAD0068**

TAD0102   **TAD0069**   **TAD0100**   **TAD0071**   **TAD0095**

TAD0070 Anakin Skywalker, flip top 8.00
TAD0067 Battle Droid on Stap 8.00
TAD0072 Darth Maul flip top, black band 8.00
TAD0073 Darth Maul flip top, red band 8.00
TAD0095 Destroyer droid transforming watch / clock 17.00
TAD0068 Jar Jar Binks sticking out tongue 8.00
TAD0102 Jar Jar Binks Talking watch 19.00
TAD0069 Obi-Wan on battleship..8.00

TAD0100 Queen Amidala Interchangeable watch, flip-top......................16.00
TAD0071 Queen Amidala, flip top...8.00

Nelsonic

TAD0101   **TAD0082**   **TAD0096**

TAD0101 Darth Maul talking watch w/tin collector case 28.00
TAD0082 Jar Jar Binks talking watch w/tin collector case.......................28.00
TAD0096 Podracer turbine...14.00

Playworks

TAD0035   **TAD0092**   **TAD0036**   **TAD0041**   **TAD0037**   **TAD0038**

TAD0034 Boba Fett 7.00
TAD0035 C-3PO 7.00
TAD0092 Darth Vader face with Tie Fighters on wristband..............7.00
TAD0036 Darth Vader...7.00
TAD0041 Millennium Falcon..11.00
TAD0037 R2-D2 ....7.00
TAD0038 Stormtrooper 7.00
TAD0039 Yoda..7.00

Texas Instruments

TAD0001 Black and silver face plate with Darth Vader and X-Wings on top, Star Wars logo on bottom 95.00
TAD0003 Blue face plate with C-3PO and R2-D2; includes 10 decals for watch face 95.00
TAD0008 Red faceplate with C-3PO and R2-D2 on top, Darth Vader and X-Wings on bottom...95.00
TAD0011 SW logo black on silver, black vinyl band with R2-D2 and Darth Vader...125.00

Toy Options

Silver metal flip-top design.

TAD0114   **TAD0052**

TAD0114 Darth Vader..36.00
TAD0052 Stormtrooper 36.00

Watchit

TAD0097   **TAD0098**   **TAD0111**   **TAD0113**

TAD0097 Darth Maul, flip-top 7.00
TAD0066 Darth Vader Musical Watch, flip-top.................................11.00
TAD0115 Droid Fighter Novelty LCD watch....................................14.00
TAD0098 Queen Amidala interchangeable watch, flip-top.............16.00
TAD0111 Queen Amidala, flip-top..9.00
TAD0113 R2-D2 Light and Sound watch 16.00
TAD0116 Sith Communicator Novelty LCD watch..........................12.00

Watches: Digital

WatchWorks

TAD0085 TAD0104 TAD0084 TAD0105 TAD0094 TAD0106

TAD0085 Battle Droid...6.00
TAD0104 Destroyer droid transforming watch / clock 14.00
TAD0084 Droid Fighter flip-up, sculpted 8.00
TAD0105 Jar Jar Binks Talking watch 19.00
TAD0094 Obi-Wan Kenobi 8.00
TAD0106 Sith Communicator 15.00

World Wide Licenses Ltd.

TAD0099 front and back

TAD0099 Darth Maul sound and FX 29.00
TAD0065 R2-D2 watch face with alarm, timer, stopwatch, and date indicator. Limited to 5,000.....................................195.00

WATER GUNS

Kenner

WG0007 Water Blaster BlasTech DL-44 (Han's
pistol) battery-operated 16.00

WG0007

Larami

WG0001 Battle Droid Rifle power soaker 5.00
WG0002 Battle Droid Rifle super soaker 18.00
WG0003 Battle Mauser power soaker 5.00
WG0004 Naboo Pistol power soaker..5.00
WG0005 Naboo Pistol super soaker..12.00
WG0006 Queen Amidala Pistol super soaker...............................8.00
WG0008 Droid rifle on hanger card 6.00

WG0005 WG0006

WG0002

WG0001 WG0003 WG0004

WG0008

WATERBOTTLES

Disney / MGM
SB0001 Star Tours logo 5.00

SB0002

Pepsi Cola
SB0002 SW:SE Logo with C-3PO...8.00

WATERCOLOR PAINT SETS

Craft House
WPS0005 Star Wars watercolor by number..................................8.00

Fundimensions
WPS0002 Ewok 18.00
WPS0004 Ewok Glider 18.00
WPS0003 Ewok Village...18.00

Kenner

WPS0001

WPS0001 Dip Dots water color paint set, book of 16 Star Wars scenes ...51.00

WEAPON TOYS

TYW0027 TYW0025

TYW0023 TYW0034

Hasbro
TYW0026 Lightsaber, Darth Maul's .0000 (design flaw could cause injury)..65.00
TYW0027 Lightsaber, Darth Maul's .0200.....................................28.00
TYW0034 Lightsaber, Obi-Wan's (blue) 18.00
TYW0023 Lightsaber, Qui-Gon's (green) 24.00
TYW0041 Naboo and Droid Fighter Laser Battle 24.00
TYW0024 Naboo Foam-Firing Blaster 18.00
TYW0025 Tatooine Blaster Pistol, Electronic 16.00

Kenner
TYW0001 3-Position laser rifle 165.00
TYW0002 Biker Scout laser pistol 75.00
TYW0003 Blaster rifle...23.00
TYW0028 Chewbacca's Bowcaster 17.00

TYW0001 TYW0002

TYW0004   TYW0028

TYW0039   TYW0040

TYW0009   TYW0010   TYW0007

TYW0044   TYW0015

TYW0012

TYW0040 Electronic Blaster Rifle, POTF2 green pkg. 19.00
TYW0039 Electronic Blaster Rifle, POTF2 orange pkg. 26.00
TYW0004 Electronic laser rifle, ESB...175.00
TYW0005 Electronic laser rifle, ROTJ..435.00
TYW0009 Heavy blaster, camoflage 14.00
TYW0010 Heavy blaster, orange 12.00
TYW0015 Lightsaber, SW...175.00
TYW0006 Laser Pistol, ESB..99.00
TYW0007 Laser Pistol, ROTJ...85.00
TYW0008 Laser Pistol, SW..125.00
TYW0044 Lightsaber, SW Kenobi / Vader pkg. 235.00
TYW0014 Lightsaber, ROTJ, any color...45.00
TYW0012 Lightsaber, Droids...165.00
TYW0016 Lightsaber, "The Force", any color..................................50.00
TYW0011 Lightsaber, Darth Vader's...22.00
TYW0013 Lightsaber, Luke Skywalker's 20.00

Kenner (UK)
TYW0046 Heavy blaster, orange 12.00

Larami
Electronic micro light and sound.

TYW0036   TYW0037   TYW0038

TYW0036 Battle Droid Rifle 7.00
TYW0037 Battle Mauser 7.00
TYW0038 Naboo Pistol..7.00

Maruka
TYW0033 Lightsaber on Darth Vader header card, includes battery 77.00

TYW0033   TYW0035

Redondo
TYW0035 Galaxia laser gun 79.00

Rubies
Lightsabers, extend to 36 inches.

TYW0019   TYW0021

TYW0022 Blue...6.00
TYW0021 Green..6.00
TYW0020 Red..6.00
TYW0019 White...6.00
TYW0029 Darth Maul's lightsaber (red, double-bladed) 12.00
TYW0030 Obi-Wan's lightsaber (blue) 8.00
TYW0031 Qui-gon's lightsaber (green)...8.00

Tiger Electronics
Laser tag sets.

TYW0017   TYW0032

TYW0032 Naboo Assault 34.00
TYW0017 Star Wars..45.00

Toltoys
TYW0045 Laser Pistol, SW 140.00

TYW0043   TYW0042

Weina
TYW0043 SW Laser Space Pistol..9.00
TYW0042 Galaxi Spacial diecast metal cap gun 14.00

WINDOW CLINGS

Blockbuster Video
WC0010 Win Yoda April 9-14, 2-piece window cling video promotion ...24.00

Fan Club
WC0001 Star Wars cling 8.00

Kentucky Fried Chicken
WC0006 Jar Jar Binks face rectangle, TPM promotion 19.00
WC0007 Queen Amidala full-figure 2-piece door cling, TPM promotion..24.00
WC0008 Queen Amidala portrait rectangle, TPM promotion 18.00
WC0009 Qui-Gon Jinn full-figure 2-piece door cling, TPM promotion......24.00

Liquid Blue
WC0017 Anakin Skywalker in podrace goggles 4.00
WC0018 Darth Maul with 2-sided saber.....................................4.00
WC0019 Jedi vs. Sith...4.00
WC0020 Naboo space battle..4.00

Norben
WC0005 Anakin Skywalker Static Cling Decoration..................3.00
WC0002 Darth Maul Static Cling Decoration..............................3.00

Window Clings

WC0003 Jedi vs. Sith Static Cling Decoration 3.00
WC0004 Space Battle Static Cling Decoration...3.00

Pizza Hut
WC0012 "Don't Leave Coruscant Without Them." (toys, large rectangle)..10.00
WC0013 "Don't Leave Coruscant Without Them." (toys, small rectangle)..8.00
WC0011 "Welcome to Coruscant" 2-sided door cling.............................8.00
WC0014 Darth Maul life-size 2-piece door sticker 35.00
WC0015 Mace Windu and Yoda 22.00
WC0016 Qui-Gon Jinn and pink alien from Jedi Council 17.00

WIND-UP TOYS

TW0002 front and back

Kenner
TW0002 Wind-up walking R2-D2...172.00

Osaka
Tin Age collection.

TW0004   TW0005   TW0030 open   TW0029   TW0031

TW0031 Boba Fett 165.00
TW0005 C-3PO..165.00
TW0029 Darth Vader 165.00
TW0030 R2-D2..165.00
TW0004 Stormtrooper 165.00

Takara
TW0003 Wind-up walking R2-D2...235.00

WIND-UP TOYS: DEFORMED

TWD0001 Anakin Skywalker, hands down 6.00
TWD0002 Anakin Skywalker, hands up..9.00

TWD024   TWD013   TWD022   TWD006   TWD008

TWD026   TWD027   TWD014   TWD002   TWD001

TWD007   TWD005   TWD004   TWD009   TWD010

TWD011   TWD012   TWD015   TWD016   TWD017

TWD019   TWD020   TWD021   TWD023   TWD025

TWD0003 Anakin Skywalker, slave 21.00
TWD0004 Battle Droid, silver..8.00
TWD0005 Battle Droid, tan...7.00
TWD0006 C-3PO...15.00
TWD0007 C-3PO, TPM...9.00
TWD0008 Chewbacca...15.00
TWD0009 Darth Maul empty handed 8.00
TWD0010 Darth Maul empty handed, gold 9.00
TWD0011 Darth Maul with saber 11.00
TWD0012 Darth Maul with saber and hooded cloak 9.00
TWD0013 Darth Vader..15.00
TWD0014 Emperor Palpatine..23.00
TWD0015 Jar Jar Binks...9.00
TWD0016 Mace Windu...9.00
TWD0017 Obi-Wan Kenobi 9.00
TWD0018 OOM-9...9.00
TWD0019 Queen Amidala, hands down 9.00
TWD0020 Queen Amidala, hands up..7.00
TWD0021 Qui-Gon Jinn 9.00
TWD0022 R2-D2...15.00
TWD0023 Sebulba 9.00
TWD0024 Stormtrooper...15.00
TWD0025 Watto...9.00
TWD0026 Yoda..15.00
TWD0027 Yoda (Brown) 25.00

WONDER WORLD

WW0001

Kenner
WW0001 Wonder World, create your own battle scenes in 3D 17.00

WRIST RESTS

American Covers
WR0002 Jedi vs. Sith..12.00
WR0003 Podrace...12.00
WR0001 Scenes from ESB 14.00

WR0001

WR0002

WR0003

WRITING PADS

Drawing Board
PPW0001 Darth Vader, Death Star, and Tie Fighters, 25 sheets 18.00

PPW0002   PPW0003   PPW0004

PPW0005   PPW0007   PPW0008 PPW0009

Stuart Hall
PPW0002 Doodle Pad: Max Rebo Band 6.00
PPW0003 Learn to Letter and Write, Boba Fett 12.00
PPW0004 Learn to Letter and Write, Darth Vader and Stormtroopers 12.00
PPW0005 Learn to Letter and Write, Luke Skywalker 12.00
PPW0006 Learn to Letter and Write, Yoda..12.00
PPW0007 Learn to Letter: Ewok Hang-gliding 5.00
PPW0008 Pencil Tablet: R2-D2 and Wicket the Ewok 10.00
PPW0009 Scribble Pad: C-3PO and R2-D2 outside Jabba's Palace 8.00

YO-YOS

Spectra Star
Sculpted character on sides.
YM0001 Darth Vader..6.00

YM0001   YM0002

YM0002 Stormtrooper...6.00

Tapper Candies
YM0006 Lightsaber paper yo-yos, pkg. of 4 ....4.00

YM0004   YM0005

Tiger Electronics
Electronic with sound FX and flashing lights.

YM0003

YM0004 Destroyer Droid...5.00
YM0005 Trade Federation Battle Ship 6.00

Worlds Apart
YM0003 X-Wings and Tie Fighters...14.00

EPISODE II & ANNIVERSARY MERCHANDISE – WE'RE WAITING!

Unlike the Episode I Star Wars revival in 1999 which flooded the market with low budget goods, EPII and the Silver Anniversary show promise of quality and diversity.

Internet sites follow the production of new releases from the planning stages to the finished product, giving dedicated collectors teasers and gems to hold onto until they can get the finished toy into their possession.

Hoth Peril Battle-Damaged Snow Speeder ended up simply Luke Skywalker's Snowspeeder.

Hasbro has mixed a series of re-release vehicles like the Snowspeeder and a 2-pack with an AT-ST and a Speederbike with a line of never before produced vehicles. The most anticipated ship, perhaps of all time, is the Tie Bomber.

Finishing up the run of the green backer cards associated with the Power of the Jedi series, Hasbro put out four Episode II sneak preview figures: Clone Trooper, Jango Fett, R3-T7, and Zam Wessel.

The sneak preview figures released on March 16 had a new design, an enlarged bubble to allow plenty of room for the figures to be action posed and to clearly display their accessories. The force files from the POTJ series were gone, replaced by a movie photo of that particular character.

The first official look at the new toy product lines being offered was at the 2002 Toy Fair in New York. Visitors to the fair were given a special, limited edition Darth Vader figure.

A new figure line which included characters from each movie was announced, and the Star Wars Saga figures were premiered.

The POTJ Vader/Kenobi logo was replaced by two hands firmly grasping a lightsaber, an icon which would be easily associated with any of the movies.

The enlarged bubbles are still present in the new Saga series, and the pack-ins (35mm film frames, punch-out play scenes, force files, etc.) have been replaced with accessories, adding both play value and flexibility for display. This new attitude toward the figures was appreciated both by the collectors and also by those who bought the toys with intentions of playing with them.

Action figure 2-packs were the first of the silver anniversary toys to be released in the United States. The concept/beta packaging the 2-packs were originally displayed in was a black-and-white vintage type package style which was well received by eager collectors watching the development over the Internet. However, when the figures were actually released, they were in the current green Power of the Jedi logo styled packaging, and collectors bought them with much less enthusiasm.

If any super collector from the vintage years were to be asked to name one toy company they were disappointed in for not participating in the Star Wars phenomenon, the majority would have named Lego. Fortunately, Lego has recently (1997/98) joined the Star Wars license community and has made up for lost time. Episode II finds them still going strong.

A series of Episode II puzzles, both 50-piece mini and 150-piece full-sized, are available for super collectors with too much time on their hands, or parents who want to keep their children preoccupied with scenes and characters from the latest episode.

Tiger Electronics, a manufacturer of electronic entertainment products, is continuing their Star Wars line with hand held games, room alarm/laser target games, keychains, and electronic figures.

Lego is also expanding from the building brick sets to include Star Wars in their Writing System Connect & Build Pens. A set of six mini characters from Attack of the Clones christened the line.

Classic board game enthusiasts will recognize the titles of several games revisited for the Star Wars Saga. Monopoly, Battle Ship, Life, and Stratego all have been given a new look and feel.

The action-packed scenes from Attack of the Clones has fueled the talents of the toy industry. Imaginations can be supplemented by role playing toys, such as the Jango Fett Action Set and electronic lightsabers.

Anakin's lightsaber and Count Dooku's lightsaber allow children, fans, and collectors to recreate the climactic scene and perhaps ultimately explore the path to the Dark Side of the Force.

Twenty-five years after the introduction of the Star Wars universe, dedicated fans are still following the storyline, which is currently at a point 25 years after the destruction of the second Death Star. The last two novels released before EPII were of the New Jedi Order series; book 11, *Rebel Dream*, and book 12, *Rebel Stand*.

For board game players who are looking for something new, the Milton Bradley label has developed new titles including Epic Duels and Jedi Unleashed.

For the ultimate in "spoilers," *The Art of Star Wars, Attack of the Clones* was released nearly a full month ahead of the theatrical release. The hardcover book, which is full of concept art, also contains the final edit of the screenplay.

Dark Horse Comics also released a tribute to the silver anniversary by re-releasing a series of trade paperbacks revisiting the original comic book series done by Marvel Comics in the 1970s and 80s. The series is titled simply, "A Long Time Ago."

Trading card collectors weren't disappointed. Topps produced an initial set of 100 cards. All of the cards are printed on a heavy card stock, then mirror glossed and foil stamped in silver. The set contains 100 cards, divided into three categories.

Twenty character cards highlight characters in Episode II. Each character card features two images, the primary front image, and one on the back of the card.

Sixty-nine cards follow the storyline of the film. Each storyline card also contains two images.

Rounding out the set are nine behind-the-scenes cards, a title card, and a checklist card.

Pictured here are six additional "preview" cards.

Not all merchandise is designed to be collectibles, which is part of the challenge and fun of super collecting. Preschool toys were part of the Kenner line-up in the early 1980s (see Ewok Preschool Toys category) but haven't made a showing since.

Playskool, one of the largest producers of preschool toys, has entered the Star Wars arena with a line of action adventure sets.

The first four released, Duel with Darth Maul, Fast Through the Forest, The Stompin' Wampa, and X-Wing Adventure were instant favorites with collectors ages 3 and up! (Especially "and up"!)

The cartoon-like features capture the true personality of each character, creature, and vehicle, giving parents and children toys they could collect and play with together.

The 2002 Star Wars revival has reached groups outside of the stereotypical collectible producers. The Japan division of Fernandes has made a series of 20 guitar picks, with four collectible checklist cards.

Not stopping there, Fernandes also manufactured two different series of guitars and a whole line of accessories including guitar cases, fretboard knobs, and straps.

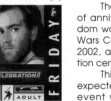

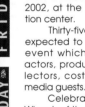

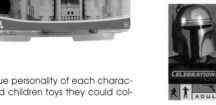

The introduction to the realm of anniversary and Episode II fandom was best exhibited at the Star Wars Celebration II, held May 3-5, 2002, at the Indianapolis convention center.

Thirty-five thousand fans were expected to attend the three-day event which included Star Wars actors, production specialists, collectors, costumers, authors, and media guests.

Celebration II was put on by Wizards of the Coast who own the official Star Wars fan club, have the license for The Star Wars Roleplaying Game, and had just received licensing to produce the new Star Wars Trading Card Game.

Celebration II was the largest Star Wars exclusive gathering ever in the world.

The Star Wars Silver Anniversary is destined not only to keep the diehard collectors happy, but also to remind millions of people around the globe of all the positive memories the movie inspires.

STAR WARS TRADING CARDS...
AFFORDABLE, EXTENSIVE, AND FUN TO COLLECT
by Cathy Kendrick

For the super collector who wants to have it all, there are currently over 200 different Star Wars trading card sets to complete. Such a challenge would keep any person or club busy trading for many, many years.

Each of the over 200 sets of Star Wars trading cards come with their own unique style.

Star Wars trading cards are relatively inexpensive. A typical action figure often retails for as much as $8.99. Many complete sets of common Star Wars trading cards can be found for $5 to $15.

Chase cards seldom cost more than $10 each and can be found for less, especially if obtained through trading. There are some cards though that cost more. Most of those are promotional cards, chase cards, or autograph cards which are not cards the average collector must have to complete their set.

Even vintage cards can be purchased on a budget. With trading cards, patience is more important than money for the collector.

The level of completeness of a card collection is something that every card collector determines for themselves. Most collectors are happy to

Star Wars Chrome Archives by Topps. Pictured above, P1 promo card, card #1, chrome insert card C1, and special insert sticker D1.

have the common cards in a set. Some collectors also like to have the chase cards, and super collectors like to try to find all of the promotional cards, wrapper styles, and even ad sheets before they feel their collection is complete. Collectors can decide if they will collect only the U.S. sets, or if they will also collect sets issued internationally. The possibilities for defining a collection are almost endless where trading cards are concerned.

Cards pictured above represent sets issued in the United States, Japan, Greece, and Chile.

No matter how broad the definition of the card collection, keeping and enjoying the cards is a lot easier than with any other Star Wars collectible. A couple of bookcases in a low humidity room can house an extensive card collection. Card sets can be sorted and stored in protective binder sheets, ready to be pulled out and looked at any time. Cards are a hands-on collectible meant to be enjoyed and looked at, not kept mint in box. It's easy to keep cards in good condition while still being able to enjoy them.

By the very nature of the way trading cards are sold, most collectors will end up with duplicate cards to swap or sell. Because cards have a relatively low dollar value and don't drastically increase in value over time, most collectors learn to appreciate a card for its ability to fill a hole in their collection, and not for its worth at a swap meet. This gives the trading card community a more relaxed pace then many other collecting communities.

Even at 25 years of age, this card from the second series commands a book value of $1.25 in mint condition.

There are very few concerns about scalpers in a trading card community. Anyone can a set ridiculously high price on a card if they want, but they aren't likely to find anyone willing to pay it. Collectors quickly learn that most cards are incredibly common, and only a very few are truly rare. Even rare cards tend to exist in numbers of 1,000 or more, making it possible for the true super collectors to obtain them.

Because trading cards are inexpensive and easy to care for, they are a great hobby for kids. Most adult collectors had Star Wars cards as kids and remember the fun of finding the cards of their favorite characters or reading the trivia on cardbacks. The same is still true of Star Wars cards available today. The cards are a bit fancier. They're designed on heavier card stock in order to hold up better over time and have glossy finishes and foil stamps on them. Overall, the cards of today aren't so very different from those we collected as kids. They still capture the magic of the movie and the characters into a form we can hold in our hands, share, and enjoy.

If you don't already have Star Wars cards as part of your collection, consider them. Chances are you'll enjoy the fun of locating and trading cards, and completing sets of your own selection.

Note: Cathy Kendrick operates a collector-friendly trading card site at: http://www.starwarscards.net where she encourages collectors of all ages to come together in the online community to discuss and trade cards. New collectors and those interested in Star Wars trading cards are encouraged to explore her site and share her knowledge.

MICROMACHINE GENEALOGY
by Joe Lynch

When Star Wars MicroMachines were first introduced in 1993, only three sets of three vehicles were released. The sets were titled "Star Wars," "Empire Strikes Back," and "Return of the Jedi." They each had a silver holofoil logo of series title.

1993 holofoil logo

1994 standard logo

In 1994 Galoob re-released the first three sets and added three more. This now made two sets for each of the three movies. The holofoil logo was replaced with a standard Star Wars logo on all six cards.

Later in 1994 the cards were redesigned for nine sets of vehicles numbered I-IX. The new cards had a large image of a different Star Wars vehicle on each of the nine sets. The 18 vehicles that already existed were included in these nine sets along with nine new vehicles. The first four figure sets were also released. They came on cards with Star Wars characters in the background.

In 1995-1996 the previous 13 sets were released plus two more vehicle sets and three more figure sets were added. These cards all had an image of an X-Wing Fighter on the left side of the cards.

1996-1997 saw the cards changed again with two more vehicle sets, four more figure sets, and all previous sets being released on the new card styles. These cards all had a large Star Wars logo in the center with an all space background. There were then 13 vehicle sets and 11 figure sets available.

Final change came in 1997-1998. Two more vehicle sets and four more figure sets were added to the line, making 15 vehicle and 15 figure sets. The last card style had a gray striped background with an image of the Millennium Falcon on the vehicle sets and an image of a Stormtrooper on the figure sets.

Galoob produced three Star Wars Shadows of the Empire sets in 1996. All three sets initially included an "Exclusive Micro Comic," but the promotion was short-lived.

In 1997 Galoob released MicroMachines from three of the Star Wars novels. Three more sets were produced later and were available only through the Galoob website. The "Dark Apprentice," "Dark Force Rising," and "The Courtship of Princess Leia" sets are the hardest of all the Micro Machines sets to find.

Galoob had seven sets of X-Ray vehicles, the last three of which were not released in the U.S. There was also a boxed set of 10 X-Ray Fleet ships, which was released initially as a J.C. Penney's exclusive, entitled "Trilogy Gift Set."

Nine sets of Mini Heads were released. Each set contains three Mini Heads. The first four sets were the only ones released in the U.S. Some of the Mini Heads, which weren't released in the U.S., were available as a promotion through Pizza Hut in 1998. Another one, C-3PO, was available through a mail in offer at Wal-Mart.

372

VINTAGE CARDBACKS...
NAMED AND DEFINED AT LAST!

SW12:1
Artwork of first 12 figures and the X-Wing, Tie Fighter and Landspeeder vehicles, plus a visual demonstration on how to work the double telescoping lightsaber. The collector's action stand is offered for $2.00 plus 2 proof of purchase seals.

SW12:2
Between the mail-in address and expiration date, a new paragraph reads, "Collector's Action Stand FREE with proofs-of-purchase from 12 STAR WARS Action Figures."

SW12:3
Another paragraph is added to the directions for operating Luke's saber. It reads: "Pull saber out by tip or push saber out using slide lever."

SW20:1
The bottom third of the card shows new playsets and toys. The prototype forms of the Patrol Dewback and the Droid Factory are shown.

SW20:2
The prototype Creature Cantina and Patrol Dewback photos have been replaced with photos of the production toys.

SW20:3
Free Boba Fett figure ad showing a graphic of the rocket being fired is the top two-thirds of the card.

SW20:4
A black sticker with rounded corners covers the firing rocket graphic.

SW20:5
A black sticker with squared corners covers the firing rocket graphic.

SW20:5.1
A round red sticker extends the offer to 3/31/80.

SW20:6
The black sticker is covered by a yellow sticker with rounded corners, explaining Boba Fett.

SW20:6.1
A round red sticker extends the offer to 12/31/80.

SW20:7
The black sticker is no longer used under the yellow sticker.

SW20:8
The yellow sticker is updated to have squared corners.

SW20:8.1
A round red sticker extends the offer to 3/31/80.

SW20:8.2
A square red sticker extends the offer to 12/31/80.

SW20:9
A sticker showing an ad for the "Secret Star Wars Action Figure" covers the top two-thirds of the card.

SW21:1
Boba Fett is moved to be among the rest of the figure photos. Prototype versions of the Patrol Dewback and Droid Factory are shown.

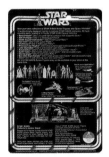

SW12:1

SW20:1

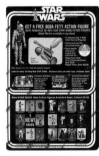

SW20:3

SW20:5

SW20:5.1

SW20:6

SW20:6.1

SW20:8.1

SW20:9

SW21:1

SW21:2

SW21:3

SW21:4

SW32:1

ESB21:1

ESB31:1

ESB31:2

ESB32:1

ESB32:2

ESB41:1

ESB41:2

SW21:2
Prototype Patrol Dewback and Droid Factory have been replaced with photos of the production toys.

SW21:3
A sticker is placed over the bottom two-thirds of the card, advertising "Secret Star Wars Action Figure."

SW21:4
A round red sticker extends offer to 12/31/80 and announces secret figure is Bossk.

SW32:1
Cardback SW12:3 is reused with a sticker over the bottom third of the card, showing 20 more figures.

ESB21:1
Twenty-one original SW figures. The bottom half of the card promotes a "Secret Star Wars Action Figure."

ESB21:1.1
A rectangular red sticker extends offer to 12/30/80.

ESB31:1
Advertisements for Snowspeeder, Millennium Falcon, and Imperial Troop Transport.

ESB31:2
Advertisements for Hoth Ice Planet Action Playset, Star Destroyer Action Playset, and Darth Vader Collector's Case.

ESB32:1
Yoda added. Advertisements for Snowspeeder, Millennium Falcon, and Imperial Attack Base.

ESB32:2
Advertisements for Hoth Ice Planet Action Playset, Star Destroyer Action Playset, and Darth Vader Collector's Case.

ESB41:1
Action Figure Survival Kit ad is the bottom third of the card.

ESB41:2
Advertisements for Dagobah Playset, Darth Vader Collector Case, Imperial Tie Fighter, Millennium Falcon, Twin-Pod Cloud Car, and Slave 1.

ESB41:3
Advertisements for Snowspeeder, Mini Rigs, Tauntaun, Turret-Probot Playset, AT-AT, and Imperial Attack Base.

ESB41:4
ESB41:2 redesigned. Pictures of individual figures replaced with a group photo.

ESB41:5
ESB41:3 redesigned. Pictures of individual figures replaced with a group photo.

ESB45:1
Display Arena is the bottom third of the card.

ESB45:1.1
A rectangular red sticker extends Display Arena offer to July 31, 1982.

ESB47:1
Free 4-LOM action figure ad is the bottom third of the card.

ESB48:1
Advertisements for Scout Walker, Tauntaun (open belly), Wampa, Mini-Rigs, and Rebel Transport.

ESB48:2
Sticker over the bottom half of the card advertises mail-away Admiral Ackbar figure.

ESB48:3
Admiral Ackbar offer is printed.

ROTJ48:1
Nien Nunb figure mail-away ad is bottom third of the card.

ROTJ65:1
Images of Logray and Chief Chirpa are blacked out. Proof of purchase is blue.

ROTJ65:2
Logray and Chief Chirpa are no longer blacked out. Proof of purchase is green.

ROTJ65:3
Free Emperor action figure ad is the bottom third of the card.

ROTJ65:4
Sticker for free Anakin Skywalker is the bottom third of the card.

ROTJ77:1
Advertisements for Rebo Band, Ewok Combat Glider, Ewok Assault Catapult, and Rancor Monster.

ROTJ77:2
Sticker for free Anakin Skywalker is the bottom third of the card.

ROTJ79:1
Advertisements for Rebo Band, Ewok Combat Glider, Ewok Assault Catapult, and Rancor Monster.

ROTJ79:2
Sticker for free Anakin Skywalker is the bottom third of the card.

ROTJ79:3
Anakin Skywalker ad is printed.

POTF
Special Star Wars Coins - Collect All 62 is the bottom third of the card.

Droids
Twelve characters shown and named on top two-thirds of card. Advertisements for ATL Interceptor, Sidecar Gunner, and Lightsaber.

Ewoks
Six characters shown and named on top two-thirds of card. Advertisements for Battle Wagon, Ewok Village, Combat Glider, and Assault Catapult.

ESB41:3

ESB41:4

ESB41:5

ESB45:1

ESB47:1

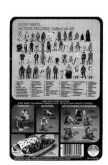
ESB48:1

ESB48:2

ESB48:3

ROTJ48:1

ROTJ65:1

ROTJ65:2

ROTJ65:3

ROTJ65:4

ROTJ77:1

ROTJ77:2

ROTJ79:1

ROTJ79:2

ROTJ79:3

POTF

DROIDS

EWOKS

INDEX

Index

Index

INFORMATION RESOURCES

ACKNOWLEDGMENTS TO CONTRIBUTORS

A majority of the information in this book did not come from picking up books, reading magazines, or surfing the Net. Toy shows, conventions, retail stores, and collector groups were all hot spots to encounter new friends while searching for Star Wars collectibles. The number of people I met who shared their collections and their knowledge with me would easily overflow this page. Those named below are only a small sampling of individuals who have helped complete my own understanding of the Star Wars merchandise universe. A special and personal thanks goes out to all who assisted, especially the following outstanding individuals:

Boryla, James. Lakeside, California. Collector, http://www.swseller.com

Brown, Neil. Wilson, North Carolina. Collector

Eilers, William. Catawissa, Missouri. Collector

Ezell, James. Klamath Falls, Oregon. Collector, Group: SWKennertoys

Flukinger, Jack. Bedford, Texas. Collector

Graham, Brian. Dubuque, Iowa. Collector

Jenson, Neal. Radcliff, Kentucky. Collector, Group: StarWarsMadroom

Lynch, Joe. Boston, Massachusetts. Collector

Marlow, J.D. New York, New York. Collector

Parcesepe, Vinnie. Meriden, Conneticut. Collector, Group: StarWarsMadroom

Roberts, Dave. Battle Ground, Washington. DNS Toys
Collector, http://www.dnstoys.com

Saunders, Buddy. Fort Worth, Texas. Lone Star Comics
http://mycomicshop.com

Stevens, Ben. Plano, Texas. Atomic Entertainment Sci-Fi Expo

Wilkshire, Stuart. Melbourne, Victoria. Australia. Collector, Group: StarWarsMadroom

And most of all...my wife Tamara, and children Kay, Patricia, and Lawrence, who keep Star Wars fresh and fun for me.

EVENTS

Atomic Entertainment, Science Fiction Exposition
http://www.scifiexpo.com

Norwescon
http://www.norwescon.org

BOOKS

Beckett Hot Toys Staff. *A Movie Fan's Extreme Guide to Collectibles From A Galaxy Far, Far Away.* Dallas, Texas: Beckett Publications, 1999.

Cornwell, Sue and Mike Kott. *The Official Price Guide Star Trek and Star Wars Collectibles.* Third Edition. New York: House of Collectibles, Random House, 1991.

Cornwell, Sue and Mike Kott. *House of Collectibles Price Guide to Star Wars Collectibles.* Fourth Edition. New York: House of Collectibles, The Ballantine Publishing Group, 1997.

McCallum, James T. *Irwin Toys: The Canadian Star Wars Connection.* London: CG Publishing, Ltd., 2000.

Sansweet, Stephen J. and T.N. Tumbausch. *Tomart's Price Guide to Worldwide Star Wars Collectibles.* Second Edition. Dayton, Ohio: Tomart Publications, 1997.

Snyder, Jeffrey B. *Collecting Star Wars Toys 1977-Present.* Pennsylvania: Schiffer Publishing, Ltd., 1999

Wells, Stuart W. *The Galaxy Greatest Star Wars Collectibles Price Guide 1999 Edition.* Norfolk, Virginia: Antique Trader Books, 1999.

INTERNET SITES

Decipher, Inc.
http://www.decipher.com

Guyote, M. D. *Toyforce*
http://www.twinsuntimes.com/toyforce

Kendrick, C. *Star Wars Trading Cards.*
http://www.starwarscards.net

Lopez, G. *The Star Wars Collector's Archive*
http://www.toysrgus.com

Thurn, M. *The Star Wars Collector's Bible*
http://www.sandcrawler.com/SWB

COLLECTOR BOOKS
Informing Today's Collector

DOLLS, FIGURES & TEDDY BEARS

2079	**Barbie** Doll Fashion, Volume I, Eames	$24.95
3957	**Barbie** Exclusives, Rana	$18.95
5672	The **Barbie** Doll Years, 4th Edition, Olds	$19.95
3810	**Chatty Cathy** Dolls, Lewis	$15.95
4559	Collectible **Action Figures**, 2nd Ed., Manos	$17.95
2211	Collector's Ency. of **Madame Alexander Dolls**, 1965 – 1990, Smith	$24.95
4863	Collector's Encyclopedia of **Vogue Dolls**, Stover/Izen	$29.95
1799	**Effanbee Dolls**, Smith	$19.95
5611	**Madame Alexander** Store Exclusives & Limited Editions, Crowsey	$24.95
5689	**Nippon Dolls** & Playthings, Van Patten/Lau	$29.95
5253	Story of **Barbie**, 2nd Ed., Westenhouser	$24.95
1513	**Teddy Bears & Steiff** Animals, Mandel	$9.95
1817	**Teddy Bears & Steiff** Animals, 2nd Series, Mandel	$19.95
2084	**Teddy Bears, Annalee's & Steiff** Animals, 3rd Series, Mandel	$19.95
1808	Wonder of **Barbie**, Manos	$9.95
1430	World of **Barbie** Dolls, Manos	$9.95
4880	World of **Raggedy Ann** Collectibles, Avery	$24.95

TOYS, MARBLES & CHRISTMAS COLLECTIBLES

2333	Antique & Collectible **Marbles**, 3rd Ed., Grist	$9.95
5353	**Breyer Animal** Collector's Guide, I.D. and Values, 2nd ed., Browell	$19.95
4976	**Christmas Ornaments**, Lights & Decorations, Johnson	$24.95
4737	**Christmas Ornaments**, Lights & Decorations, Vol. II, Johnson	$24.95
4739	**Christmas Ornaments**, Lights & Decorations, Vol. III, Johnson	$24.95
2338	Collector's Encyclopedia of **Disneyana**, Longest, Stern	$24.95
5038	Collector's Guide to **Diecast Toys** & Scale Models, 2nd Ed., Johnson	$19.95
5681	Collector's Guide to **Lunchboxes**, White	$19.95
4566	Collector's Guide to **Tootsietoys**, 2nd Ed, Richter	$19.95
5360	**Fisher-Price Toys**, Cassity	$19.95
4945	**G-Men and FBI Toys**, Whitworth	$18.95
5593	Grist's Big Book of **Marbles**, 2nd Ed.	$24.95
3970	Grist's Machine-Made & Contemporary **Marbles**, 2nd Ed.	$9.95
5267	**Matchbox Toys**, 3rd Ed., 1947 to 1998, Johnson	$19.95
5830	**McDonald's** Collectibles, Henriques/DuVall	$24.95
5673	Modern **Candy Containers** & Novelties, Brush/Miller	$19.95
1540	Modern **Toys** 1930–1980, Baker	$19.95
3888	**Motorcycle Toys**, Antique & Contemporary, Gentry/Downs	$18.95
5693	Schroeder's Collectible **Toys**, Antique to Modern Price Guide, 7th Ed	$17.95

JEWELRY, HATPINS, WATCHES & PURSES

1712	Antique & Collectible **Thimbles** & Accessories, Mathis	$19.95
1748	Antique **Purses**, Revised Second Ed., Holiner	$19.95
1278	Art Nouveau & Art Deco **Jewelry**, Baker	$9.95
4850	Collectible **Costume Jewelry**, Simonds	$24.95
5675	Collectible **Silver Jewelry**, Rezazadeh	$24.95
3722	Collector's Ency. of **Compacts**, Carryalls & Face Powder Boxes, Mueller	$24.95
4940	**Costume Jewelry**, A Practical Handbook & Value Guide, Rezazadeh	$24.95
1716	Fifty Years of Collectible Fashion **Jewelry**, 1925-1975, Baker	$19.95
1424	**Hatpins** & Hatpin Holders, Baker	$9.95
5695	Ladies' **Vintage Accessories**, Bruton	$24.95
1181	100 Years of Collectible **Jewelry**, 1850 – 1950, Baker	$9.95
5696	Vintage & Vogue Ladies' **Compacts**, 2nd Edition, Gerson	$29.95

FURNITURE

1457	American **Oak** Furniture, McNerney	$9.95
3716	American **Oak** Furniture, Book II, McNerney	$12.95
1118	Antique **Oak** Furniture, Hill	$7.95
2132	Collector's Encyclopedia of **American** Furniture, Vol. I, Swedberg	$24.95
2271	Collector's Encyclopedia of **American** Furniture, Vol. II, Swedberg	$24.95
3720	Collector's Encyclopedia of **American** Furniture, Vol. III, Swedberg	$24.95
5359	Early **American** Furniture, Obbard	$12.95
1755	Furniture of the **Depression Era**, Swedberg	$19.95
3906	**Heywood-Wakefield** Modern Furniture, Rouland	$18.95
1885	**Victorian** Furniture, Our American Heritage, McNerney	$9.95
3829	**Victorian** Furniture, Our American Heritage, Book II, McNerney	$9.95

INDIANS, GUNS, KNIVES, TOOLS, PRIMITIVES

1868	Antique **Tools**, Our American Heritage, McNerney	$9.95
1426	**Arrowheads** & Projectile Points, Hothem	$7.95
5616	Big Book of **Pocket Knives**, Stewart	$19.95
2279	**Indian Artifacts** of the Midwest, Hothem	$14.95
5685	**Indian Artifacts** of the Midwest, Book IV, Hothem	$19.95
5687	Modern **Guns**, Identification & Values, 13th Ed., Quertermous	$14.95

2164	**Primitives**, Our American Heritage, McNerney	$9.95
1759	**Primitives**, Our American Heritage, Series II, McNerney	$14.95
4730	Standard **Knife** Collector's Guide, 3rd Ed., Ritchie & Stewart	$12.95

PAPER COLLECTIBLES & BOOKS

4633	**Big Little Books**, A Collector's Reference & Value Guide, Jacobs	$18.95
4710	Collector's Guide to **Children's Books**, 1850 to 1950, Jones	$18.95
5596	Collector's Guide to **Children's Books**, 1950 to 1975, Jones	$19.95
1441	Collector's Guide to **Post Cards**, Wood	$9.95
2081	Guide to Collecting **Cookbooks**, Allen	$14.95
2080	Price Guide to **Cookbooks** & Recipe Leaflets, Dickinson	$9.95
3973	**Sheet Music** Reference & Price Guide, 2nd Ed., Pafik & Guiheen	$19.95
4654	**Victorian Trade Cards**, Historical Reference & Value Guide, Cheadle	$19.95
4733	**Whitman Juvenile Books**, Brown	$17.95

OTHER COLLECTIBLES

2269	Antique **Brass & Copper** Collectibles, Gaston	$16.95
1880	Antique **Iron**, McNerney	$9.95
3872	Antique **Tins**, Dodge	$24.95
5607	Antiquing and Collecting on the **Internet**, Parry	$12.95
1128	**Bottle** Pricing Guide, 3rd Ed., Cleveland	$7.95
3718	Collectible **Aluminum**, Grist	$16.95
4560	Collectible **Cats**, An Identification & Value Guide, Book II, Fyke	$19.95
5676	Collectible **Souvenir Spoons**, Book II, Bednersh	$29.95
5666	Collector's Encyclopedia of **Granite Ware**, Book II, Greguire	$29.95
4857	Collector's Guide to **Art Deco**, 2nd Ed., Gaston	$17.95
5608	Collector's Guide to Buying, Selling, & Trading on the **Internet**, 2nd Ed., Hix	$12.95
4887	Collector's Guide to **Creek Chub Lures** & Collectibles, Smith	$24.95
3966	Collector's Guide to **Inkwells**, Identification & Values, Badders	$18.95
3881	Collector's Guide to **Novelty Radios**, Bunis/Breed	$18.95
5621	Collector's Guide to **Online Auctions**, Hix	$12.95
4652	Collector's Guide to **Transistor Radios**, 2nd Ed., Bunis	$16.95
4864	Collector's Guide to **Wallace Nutting Pictures**, Ivankovich	$18.95
1629	**Doorstops**, Identification & Values, Bertoia	$9.95
5683	**Fishing Lure Collectibles**, 2nd Ed., Murphy/Edmisten	$29.95
5259	**Flea Market Trader**, 12th Ed., Huxford	$9.95
3819	**General Store** Collectibles, Wilson	$24.95
2216	**Kitchen Antiques**, 1790–1940, McNerney	$14.95
5686	**Lighting Fixtures** of the Depression Era, Book I, Thomas	$24.95
4950	The **Lone Ranger**, Collector's Reference & Value Guide, Felbinger	$18.95
5603	19th Century **Fishing Lures**, Carter	$29.95
2026	**Railroad** Collectibles, 4th Ed., Baker	$14.95
5619	**Roy Rogers and Dale Evans** Toys & Memorabilia, Coyle	$24.95
1632	**Salt & Pepper Shakers**, Guarnaccia	$9.95
5091	**Salt & Pepper Shakers** II, Guarnaccia	$18.95
3443	**Salt & Pepper Shakers** IV, Guarnaccia	$18.95
5007	**Silverplated Flatware**, Revised 4th Edition, Hagan	$18.95
3892	**Toy & Miniature Sewing Machines**, Thomas	$18.95
5144	Value Guide to **Advertising Memorabilia**, 2nd Ed., Summers	$19.95
3977	Value Guide to **Gas Station Memorabilia**, Summers	$24.95
4877	Vintage **Bar Ware**, Visakay	$24.95
4935	The W.F. Cody **Buffalo Bill** Collector's Guide with Values, Wojtowicz	$24.95
5281	**Wanted to Buy**, 7th Edition	$9.95

GLASSWARE & POTTERY

4929	**American Art Pottery**, 1880 – 1950, Sigafoose	$24.95
5358	Collector's Encyclopedia of **Depression Glass**, 14th Ed., Florence	$19.95
5748	Collector's Encyclopedia of **Fiesta**, 9th Ed., Huxford	$24.95
4946	Collector's Encyclopedia of **Howard Pierce Porcelain**, Dommel	$24.95
5609	Collector's Encyclopedia of **Limoges Porcelain**, 3rd Ed., Gaston	$29.95
1358	Collector's Encyclopedia of **McCoy Pottery**, Huxford	$19.95
5677	Collector's Encyclopedia of **Niloak**, 2nd Edition, Gifford	$29.95
5678	Collector's Encyclopedia of **Nippon Porcelain**, 6th Series, Van Patten	$29.95
5618	Collector's Encyclopedia of **Rosemeade Pottery**, Dommel	$24.95
5680	Collector's Guide to **Feather Edge Ware**, McAllister	$19.95
2339	Collector's Guide to **Shawnee Pottery**, Vanderbilt	$19.95
1523	Colors in **Cambridge Glass**, National Cambridge Society	$19.95
4714	**Czechoslovakian Glass** and Collectibles, Book II, Barta	$16.95
5528	Early American **Pattern Glass**, Metz	$17.95
5257	**Fenton Art Glass** Patterns, 1939 – 1980, Whitmyer	$29.95
5261	**Fostoria Tableware**, 1924 – 1943, Long/Seate	$24.95
5691	**Post86 Fiesta**, Identification & Value Guide, Racheter	$19.95
5617	Standard Encyclopedia of **Pressed Glass**, 2nd Ed., Edwards/Carwile	$29.95

This is only a partial listing of the books on collectibles that are available from Collector Books. All books are well illustrated and contain current values. Most of our books are available from your local bookseller, antique dealer, or public library. If you are unable to locate certain titles in your area, you may order by mail from COLLECTOR BOOKS, P.O. Box 3009, Paducah, KY 42002-3009. Customers with Visa, MasterCard, or Discover may phone in orders from 7:00–5:00 CST, Monday–Friday, Toll Free 1-800-626-5420, or online at www.collectorbooks.com. Add $3.00 for postage for the first book ordered and 50¢ for each additional book. Include item number, title, and price when ordering. Allow 14 to 21 days for delivery.

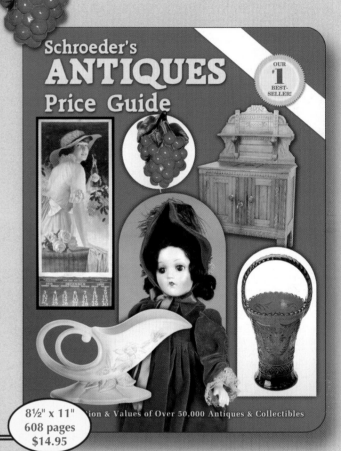